LANDSCAPE DESIGN AND CONSTRUCTION

Richard Skiba

AFTER MIDNIGHT
PUBLISHING

Copyright © 2024 by Richard Skiba

All rights reserved.

No portion of this book may be reproduced in any form without written permission from the publisher or author, except as permitted by copyright law.

This publication is designed to provide accurate and authoritative information in regard to the subject matter covered. While the publisher and author have used their best efforts in preparing this book, they make no representations or warranties with respect to the accuracy or completeness of the contents of this book and specifically disclaim any implied warranties of merchantability or fitness for a particular purpose. No warranty may be created or extended by sales representatives or written sales materials. The advice and strategies contained herein may not be suitable for your situation. You should consult with a professional when appropriate. Neither the publisher nor the author shall be liable for any loss of profit or any other commercial damages, including but not limited to special, incidental, consequential, personal, or other damages.

Skiba, Richard (author)

Landscape Design and Construction

ISBN 978-1-7636112-0-7 (paperback) 978-1-7636112-1-4 (eBook)

Non-fiction

CONTENTS

1. Introduction — 1
2. Types of Landscapes and Gardens — 14
3. Landscape Design — 62
4. Landscaping Work Health and Safety — 90
5. Setting Out the Site for Construction Works — 146
6. Installing Drainage Systems — 210
7. Constructing Brick and Block Structures and Features — 231
8. Constructing Stone Structures and Features — 263
9. Paving Projects — 307
10. Constructing Landscape Features Using Concrete — 317
11. Implementing a Retaining Wall Project — 341
12. Plants and Plant Culture — 354
13. Recognising Plants — 389
14. Implementing a Plant Establishment Program — 461
15. Implementing Soil Improvements for Garden and Turf areas — 482
16. Erecting Timber Structures and Features — 503
17. Implementing a Landscape Lighting System — 567
18. Implementing a Landscape Maintenance Program — 577
19. Sustainable Landscaping — 605

References — 614

Index — 620

Chapter One
Introduction

Landscaping and landscape construction are closely related fields that involve designing, planning, and implementing outdoor spaces to enhance their aesthetic appeal, functionality, and environmental sustainability. Landscaping encompasses the modification of visible features in outdoor areas, including gardens, yards, parks, and commercial properties, with the aim of achieving desired aesthetic and functional outcomes. This involves tasks such as planting trees, shrubs, flowers, and other vegetation, as well as installing hardscape elements like pathways, patios, decks, and water features. Additionally, landscaping entails soil management, grading, drainage, and irrigation to establish a balanced and harmonious outdoor environment.

On the other hand, landscape construction focuses on the physical implementation of landscape designs. It involves various tasks such as excavation, site preparation, installation of hardscape elements such as retaining walls, pergolas, and outdoor kitchens, as well as planting trees and shrubs, laying sod or seeding for lawns, and constructing drainage and irrigation systems. Landscape construction demands expertise in multiple trades including carpentry, masonry, horticulture, and irrigation systems installation.

Key aspects of landscaping and landscape construction include design, plant selection, hardscape installation, environmental considerations, and maintenance. The design process entails creating a plan for the outdoor space considering factors such as site characteristics, client preferences, budget, and environmental concerns, often using software tools, sketches, and blueprints. Plant selection is critical for achieving desired aesthetic effects and ensuring long-term sustainability, taking into account factors like climate, soil conditions, and maintenance requirements. Hardscape installation involves the proper construction of elements like pathways, walls, and outdoor structures to provide structure and functionality, requiring skilled construction techniques for durability and safety.

Figure 1: Using stepping stones to create a south Florida landscape walkway. Iconlandscapesolutions, CC BY-SA 4.0, via Wikimedia Commons.

Furthermore, environmental considerations are essential, with sustainable landscaping practices aiming to minimize environmental impact and promote ecosystem health. This may involve using native plants, implementing water-efficient irrigation systems, and adopting organic gardening practices. Regular maintenance is also crucial to keep landscaped areas looking their best and to ensure the health and longevity of plants and hardscape features, involving tasks such as pruning, weeding, fertilizing, mulching, and repairing or replacing damaged elements.

In summary, landscaping and landscape construction are multidisciplinary fields that blend art, science, and craftsmanship to create beautiful, functional, and sustainable outdoor spaces for residential, commercial, and public use.

Figure 2: Sculptural sunbeds in the North Harbour, Lysekil, Sweden. W.carter, CC BY-SA 4.0, via Wikimedia Commons.

Landscaping and landscape construction require a combination of technical skills, creative abilities, and knowledge of various disciplines. Here are some key skills and knowledge areas essential for success in these fields:

- **Design Skills**: Ability to conceptualize and create landscape designs that meet client needs and aesthetic preferences. This includes proficiency in design software, sketching, and understanding principles of design such as balance, proportion, and focal points.

- **Plant Knowledge**: Understanding of plant species, their characteristics, growth habits, and maintenance requirements. Knowledge of horticulture principles, soil types, climate considerations, and plant compatibility is crucial for successful plant selection and landscaping.

- **Construction Techniques**: Proficiency in construction methods and techniques for installing hardscape elements such as pathways, walls, decks, and outdoor structures. This includes knowledge of materials, tools, and safety procedures, as well as skills in carpentry, masonry, and other construction trades.

- **Irrigation and Drainage Systems**: Understanding of irrigation and drainage principles, including the design, installation, and maintenance of irrigation systems to ensure proper water distribution and drainage to prevent waterlogging and erosion.

- **Environmental Awareness**: Awareness of environmental factors and sustainable landscaping practices aimed at minimizing environmental impact and promoting ecosystem health. This includes knowledge of native plants, water conservation techniques, organic gardening practices, and methods for reducing chemical use.

- **Project Management**: Ability to plan, organize, and manage landscaping projects effectively, including budgeting, scheduling, and coordination of resources and personnel. Project management skills are essential for ensuring projects are completed on time, within budget, and to client specifications.

- **Communication and Client Relations**: Strong communication skills are necessary for effectively communicating with clients, understanding their needs and preferences, and conveying design concepts and project progress. Building rapport with clients and providing excellent customer service is essential for client satisfaction and repeat business.

- **Problem-Solving Skills**: Ability to identify challenges and obstacles that may arise during landscaping projects and develop creative solutions to address them. Problem-solving skills are valuable for overcoming site constraints, environmental issues, and unexpected complications.

- **Physical Fitness**: Landscaping and landscape construction often involve physical labour, including lifting heavy objects, digging, and working outdoors in various weather conditions. Good physical fitness and stamina are important for performing these tasks safely and efficiently.

- **Continuous Learning**: Given the evolving nature of landscaping practices, staying updated on industry trends, new technologies, and best practices is essential. Continuous learning through workshops, seminars, certifications, and professional development opportunities helps landscapers and landscape contractors stay competitive and enhance their skills and knowledge base.

A combination of technical expertise, creativity, environmental awareness, and effective communication and management skills is essential for success in landscaping and landscape construction. Good landscape design and construction entail several key elements to create functional, aesthetically pleasing, and sustainable outdoor spaces. Here are some essential aspects:

- **Understanding Client Needs**: A successful landscape project begins with a thorough understanding of the client's needs, preferences, and budget. Designers and contractors should engage in effective communication with clients to identify their goals, lifestyle requirements, aesthetic preferences, and any specific features they desire.

- **Site Analysis**: Conducting a comprehensive site analysis is crucial to assess the existing conditions, including topography, soil quality, drainage patterns, sun exposure, existing vegetation, and any architectural features. This information informs the design process and helps identify opportunities and constraints.

- **Functional Design**: Good landscape design prioritizes functionality and usability to ensure that outdoor spaces meet the needs of the users. Designers consider factors such as circulation patterns, outdoor activities, seating areas, entertainment spaces, and practical requirements like storage, utilities, and access to amenities.

- **Aesthetic Appeal**: Aesthetics play a significant role in landscape design, with emphasis on creating visually pleasing and harmonious outdoor environments. Designers use principles of design such as balance, proportion, rhythm, and focal points to create cohesive compositions that complement the surrounding architecture and natural landscape.

- **Plant Selection and Placement**: Careful selection and placement of plants are essential for creating diverse, attractive, and sustainable landscapes. Designers consider factors such as climate, soil conditions, sun exposure, and maintenance requirements when choosing plants to ensure they thrive and contribute to the overall design scheme.

- **Hardscape Elements**: Incorporating hardscape elements such as pathways, patios, decks, walls, and outdoor structures adds structure, functionality, and visual interest to outdoor spaces. Good landscape design integrates hardscape features seamlessly with the surrounding landscape, using materials that complement the architecture and natural environment.

- **Sustainability**: Sustainable landscape practices aim to minimize environmental impact, conserve resources, and promote ecosystem health. This may include using native plants, incorporating water-efficient irrigation systems, reducing chemical use, implementing permeable paving materials to reduce runoff, and maximizing energy efficiency.

- **Attention to Detail**: Attention to detail is crucial in landscape construction to ensure quality craftsmanship and attention to finishing touches. This includes precision in installation techniques, proper grading and drainage, careful selection and placement of materials, and meticulous attention to aesthetic details.

- **Maintenance Considerations**: Good landscape design considers long-term maintenance requirements to ensure that outdoor spaces remain healthy, vibrant, and attractive over time. Designers and contractors may recommend low-maintenance plantings, efficient irrigation systems, and easy-to-maintain hardscape materials to simplify upkeep for clients.

- **Client Education and Collaboration**: Effective communication and collaboration with clients are essential throughout the design and construction process. Providing guidance on maintenance practices, plant care, and seasonal changes helps clients feel confident in caring for their landscapes and ensures the longevity of the project.

Good landscape design and construction involve a holistic approach that integrates functionality, aesthetics, sustainability, and client needs to create outdoor spaces that are beautiful, enjoyable, and enduring.

To ensure the success of a landscape project, it is crucial to have a deep understanding of the client's needs, preferences, and budget. Effective communication between designers, contractors, and clients plays a pivotal role in identifying the client's goals, lifestyle requirements, aesthetic inclinations, and specific features they desire [1]. Engaging in discussions about preferences with clients is most effective when accompanied by a detailed description of available options [1]. Research indicates that accommodating client preferences in landscape architecture leads to positive outcomes, as demonstrated by a meta-analysis that compared design outcomes between clients whose preferences were considered and those whose were not [2]. Furthermore, a study on the impact of accommodating client preferences in landscape architecture provides practical recommendations for working with client preferences [3].

In the realm of landscape architecture, understanding client preferences is essential for designing spaces that resonate with individuals. Studies have shown that designing landscapes based on people's preferences is necessary for creating appealing environments [4]. Integrating 3D landscape pattern analysis with people's landscape preferences can enhance urban landscape configurations, providing valuable insights for landscape planners and decision-makers [5]. Moreover, the evaluation and comparison of sustainability performance and visual preference of residential landscape elements suggest that it is possible to design landscapes that are both sustainable and visually appealing [6].

Conducting a thorough site analysis is a crucial initial step in landscape design to comprehend the existing conditions and limitations of a site. This analysis encompasses evaluating factors like topography, soil quality, drainage patterns, sun exposure, existing vegetation, and architectural features. By scrutinizing these elements, landscape designers can pinpoint opportunities for improvement and potential challenges that must be tackled during the design process.

An important aspect of site analysis involves utilizing historical and iconographical sources to interpret the cultural value of spatial planning components [7]. This method enables a deeper understanding of the site's historical significance, influencing design decisions that honour and enhance the site's heritage.

Furthermore, integrating 3D landscape pattern analysis with people's landscape preferences can optimize urban landscape configurations [8]. By considering both the physical landscape attributes and the preferences of the individuals interacting with the space, designers can craft more harmonious and functional landscapes.

Moreover, leveraging advanced technology such as artificial intelligence and digital space technology can offer a scientific analysis and prediction of site factors like topography, climate conditions, and spatial layout [9]. This objective data can serve as a dependable foundation for landscape design decisions.

Figure 3: Bath, Parade Gardens. Landscape design. Natalia Semenova, CC BY 3.0, via Wikimedia Commons.

Additionally, conducting landscape efficiency assessments based on a structural equation model can aid in evaluating the effectiveness of urban features like subway station entrances [10]. This type of assessment takes into account intricate correlations between variables to enhance the design of urban elements.

Functional design in landscape architecture is a critical aspect that aims to ensure outdoor spaces are not only visually appealing but also highly functional and practical for users. Designers consider various factors such as circulation patterns, outdoor activities, seating areas, entertainment spaces, as well as practical requirements like storage, utilities, and access to amenities [11]. When designing landscape spaces, it is crucial to integrate information about users, including age and needs, with considerations of the size, shape, and function of the space being designed [11]. Additionally, collaboration with stakeholders and communities has become an essential part of landscape architecture practice in recent years [12].

The incorporation of modern technologies such as big data and parametric design has transformed landscape architecture, enabling greater adaptability and consideration of ecological and scientific factors [13]. The utilization of remote sensing technology and spatial information technology has further improved the design process in landscape architecture by integrating various disciplines and elements within the landscape space [14]. Furthermore, fostering landscape architecture design students' pro-environmental awareness through project-based learning has been demonstrated to be effective in cultivating a comprehensive understanding of the profession [15].

Figure 4: Landscape design, Parque del Retiro. La Citta Vita, CC BY-SA 2.0, via Wikimedia Commons.

Aesthetic appeal is a fundamental aspect of landscape design, focusing on creating visually pleasing and harmonious outdoor spaces. Designers utilize key design principles such as balance, proportion, rhythm, and focal points to develop cohesive compositions that enhance the surrounding architecture and natural environment. Research has shown that the contour of architectural structures significantly influences aesthetic judgments and decisions [16]. Moreover, studies have indicated that the default-mode network in the brain represents aesthetic appeal across various visual domains, including landscapes and cultural artifacts like architecture and artwork [17].

Balance is fundamental in landscape design, striving for equilibrium and visual stability through the distribution of elements within the space. Whether symmetrical or asymmetrical, balance creates a sense of order and harmony that resonates with viewers. Proportion, meanwhile, governs the relative sizes and scales of features within the landscape, ensuring that each element relates harmoniously to the whole. By maintaining appropriate proportions, designers create a sense of coherence and proportionality that enhances the overall aesthetic appeal.

Rhythm introduces a sense of movement and flow within the landscape, guiding the eye along pathways and through spaces with a deliberate cadence. Through the repetition of patterns, textures, or forms, designers establish a rhythm that animates the landscape and engages the observer. Additionally, focal points serve as visual anchors within the composition, drawing attention and providing points of interest that enrich the overall experience.

Ultimately, the goal of prioritizing aesthetic appeal in landscape design is to create outdoor environments that not only please the eye but also evoke a sense of harmony, tranquillity, and connection with nature. By adhering to principles of design and carefully orchestrating the arrangement of elements, designers craft landscapes that resonate with viewers and enhance the beauty of the surrounding architecture and natural landscape.

Figure 5: New York Plantings Garden Designers and Landscape contracting has completed this landscape design project in NYC. This is an image of this project in spring time. Nyplanting, CC BY-SA 4.0, via Wikimedia Commons.

Plant selection and placement are critical components of landscape design as they contribute to the diversity, attractiveness, and sustainability of outdoor spaces. Designers must carefully consider various factors such as climate, soil conditions, sun exposure, and maintenance requirements when choosing plants to ensure their successful integration into the overall design scheme.

Plant landscaping in urban areas is crucial for enhancing urban green spaces. To achieve visually appealing and sustainable outdoor spaces, it is essential to consider various factors such as plant morphology, colour composition, species diversity, and naturalness [18]. Integrating user information with considerations of size, shape, and function when designing landscape spaces is recommended to develop well-suited designs that align with environmental conditions and user preferences [18]. Additionally, incorporating seasonal diversity in plant selection is vital for enhancing the visual appeal of landscapes throughout the year [18].

Urban parks are significant components of urban green spaces and are essential for urban biodiversity due to their large plant area, rich plant species, complex community structure, and diverse biological functions [19]. They serve as the ecological heart of the city, contributing to mitigating urban ecological degradation, preserving native species, and maintaining ecological balance, thus supporting urban sustainability [20]. Furthermore, urban green spaces, including parks, provide habitat for various wildlife species, contributing to biodiversity conservation in urban areas [21].

The selection and placement of plants in landscape design require a comprehensive understanding of environmental factors, aesthetic considerations, and user needs to create visually appealing, functional, and sustainable outdoor spaces [18]. Studies have shown that urban green spaces support a wide array of species and play a crucial role in long-term sustainability [22]. Moreover, the conservation of plant diversity in urban ecosystems is essential for urban biodiversity protection and the healthy development of urban ecosystem functions [23].

Incorporating hardscape elements such as pathways, patios, decks, walls, and outdoor structures into landscape design is essential for adding structure, functionality, and visual interest to outdoor spaces. Good landscape design seamlessly integrates hardscape features with the surrounding environment, using materials that complement both the architecture and natural surroundings [24]. Hardscape elements, which include sidewalks, paving, fences, walls, pergolas, stairs, lighting elements, seating elements, signs, banners, umbrellas, trash cans, sculptural elements, gates, and others, play a crucial role in defining the layout and aesthetics of outdoor areas [25].

The term "hardscape" captures the essence of man-made elements within outdoor spaces and highlights their significance in creating a harmonious blend between human-made structures and the natural environment [26]. These elements are categorized into two main groups: softscape, which comprises natural elements like trees, brush, and grass, and hardscape, which includes human-made items such as furniture, chairs, rocks, and other structural components [27]. The integration of hardscape elements with softscape features, water elements, and rocks contributes to the overall appeal and functionality of outdoor landscapes [28].

Successful outdoor space designs incorporate key elements such as adequate seating, access to sunlight, shelter from the wind, and the inclusion of water elements and vegetation [29]. Design details, materials, vegetation, and the variety of spaces can be tailored to suit specific demographics and site-specific needs, enhancing the overall user experience and functionality of outdoor areas [30]. Furthermore, the stress-reducing effects of connecting with green spaces have been well-documented, emphasizing the importance of incorporating natural and hardscape elements in outdoor environments [31].

Sustainable landscape practices are essential for minimizing environmental impact, conserving resources, and promoting ecosystem health. These practices involve strategies such as using native plants, implementing water-efficient irrigation systems, reducing chemical usage, incorporating permeable paving materials to reduce runoff, and maximizing energy efficiency. The adoption of sustainable landscape practices is crucial given the increasing populations, consumption rates, and technological advancements that strain the environment [32].

Nature-based solutions are significant for climate change mitigation and adaptation in urban areas. Encouraging the adoption of sustainable residential landscapes and practices can help minimize environmental consequences while maintaining essential lifestyle qualities [33, 34]. Sustainable drainage systems (SuDS) are effective for stormwater management, water pollution prevention, and flood control due to their environmentally friendly and cost-effective approaches [35].

Integrating technologies and alternative sources of water and energy is crucial for promoting the sustainability of urban landscapes [36]. Additionally, the use of waste materials as alternative aggregates in construction practices enhances eco-sustainability in the civil and construction sectors [37]. Furthermore, the importance of permeable and pervious pavements in reducing urban stormwater runoff and improving water quality is increasingly recognized [38].

Figure 6: Large bioswayle (raingarden) integrates stormwater runoff treatment with planting feature for neighborhood. Architect-sea, CC BY-SA 3.0, via Wikimedia Commons.

Attention to detail in landscape construction is a critical aspect that ensures the delivery of high-quality work with a focus on finishing touches and craftsmanship. This meticulous approach involves precise installation techniques, proper grading and drainage, thoughtful selection and placement of materials, and a keen eye for aesthetic details [39]. The aesthetic quality of a landscape is not only influenced by its physical features but also by the perceptual processes they evoke in viewers [40]. Studies have shown that human perceptions and attitudes play a significant role in landscape management, emphasizing the importance of considering cultural ecosystem services and aesthetic values in landscape design [41].

Furthermore, the selection and distribution of colours in urban and suburban green spaces have been found to significantly impact visual aesthetics quality, highlighting the importance of design proportion and colour distribution in enhancing the attractiveness of landscapes [42]. Expert-based evaluations have been conducted to analyse landscape aesthetics, shedding light on the impact of scenic beauty on human well-being and exploring public perceptions of landscape beauty [43]. Additionally, the cognitive schema of contemporary urban landscapes has been explored, emphasizing the integration of various perspectives to understand the aesthetic essence of urban environments [44].

Precision in installation techniques is paramount in landscape construction to ensure that all elements are installed correctly and securely. Whether it's laying pavers for a pathway, constructing a retaining wall, or installing outdoor structures, precise measurements and proper techniques are crucial to the structural integrity and longevity of the features. Skilled craftsmanship and attention to detail during the installation process help to minimize errors and ensure that the finished product meets the highest standards of quality.

Proper grading and drainage are fundamental aspects of landscape construction that require careful attention to detail. Grading ensures that the land is properly sloped to direct water away from structures and prevent waterlogging or erosion. Effective drainage systems, including drains, swales, and French drains, are meticulously installed to manage stormwater runoff and protect the integrity of the landscape. Attention to detail in grading and drainage is essential for ensuring the functionality and longevity of the outdoor space.

The selection and placement of materials play a significant role in the aesthetic appeal and durability of the landscape. From choosing the right type of stone for a retaining wall to selecting the perfect plants for a garden bed, every material decision requires careful consideration. Factors such as durability, compatibility with the environment, and visual harmony with the surrounding landscape must be taken into account. Meticulous attention to detail in material selection ensures that the landscape not only looks beautiful but also stands the test of time.

Aesthetic details are the finishing touches that elevate the landscape from functional to exceptional. Whether it's meticulously placing decorative stones in a garden bed, carefully arranging plants to create a naturalistic composition, or adding decorative elements such as sculptures or lighting fixtures, attention to aesthetic details adds depth, character, and visual interest to the outdoor space. These small but significant details contribute to the overall beauty and ambiance of the landscape, enhancing the enjoyment and satisfaction of those who experience it.

Maintenance considerations are essential aspects of good landscape design, emphasizing the importance of planning for the long-term care and upkeep of outdoor spaces. By integrating maintenance considerations into the design process, designers and contractors ensure that landscapes remain healthy, vibrant, and attractive over time, minimizing the need for extensive and costly maintenance efforts. This proactive approach not only benefits clients by reducing the time and resources required for upkeep but also contributes to the overall sustainability and longevity of the landscape.

One key aspect of maintenance considerations is the selection of plantings that require minimal upkeep. Designers and contractors may recommend low-maintenance plant species that are well-suited to the local climate and soil conditions. These plants typically have minimal water and nutrient requirements and are resistant to pests and diseases, making them easier to care for and less prone to issues that require frequent attention. By incorporating low-maintenance plantings into the landscape design, designers can help clients achieve beautiful and sustainable outdoor spaces with minimal effort.

Efficient irrigation systems are another important consideration in landscape maintenance. Designers may recommend the installation of irrigation systems that deliver water precisely and efficiently to plants, minimizing water waste and reducing the need for manual watering. Automated irrigation systems with programmable timers and sensors can adjust watering schedules based on weather conditions, further optimizing water usage and ensuring that plants receive the right amount of water at the right time. By implementing efficient irrigation systems, designers and contractors help clients conserve water and reduce the time and effort required for irrigation maintenance.

In addition to plantings and irrigation systems, hardscape materials also play a role in maintenance considerations. Designers may recommend the use of durable and easy-to-maintain materials for hardscape features such as pathways, patios, and retaining walls. Materials such as concrete, stone, and composite decking are often preferred for their durability, resistance to wear and tear, and ease of cleaning. By selecting hardscape materials that require minimal maintenance, designers can help clients minimize the time and effort required for upkeep while ensuring that outdoor spaces remain attractive and functional for years to come.

Client education and collaboration are foundational principles in landscape design and construction, emphasizing the importance of open communication and active involvement from the client throughout the entire process. Effective communication begins with the initial consultation, where designers and clients discuss the client's vision, preferences, and objectives for the project. By actively listening to the client's needs and desires, designers can gain valuable insights that inform the design and construction process, ensuring that the final outcome reflects the client's vision and meets their expectations.

Throughout the design and construction process, ongoing collaboration between designers and clients is essential for making informed decisions and addressing any concerns or preferences that may arise. Designers may present design concepts and proposals to clients, seeking feedback and input to refine and finalize the design. By involving clients in the decision-making process, designers empower them to take ownership of the project and feel invested in the outcome, fostering a sense of partnership and collaboration.

One key aspect of client education is providing guidance on maintenance practices, plant care, and seasonal changes. Designers may offer recommendations and resources to help clients understand how to properly care for their landscapes, including watering schedules, pruning techniques, and fertilization requirements. By equipping clients with the knowledge and skills they need to maintain their landscapes effectively, designers empower them to take an active role in caring for their outdoor spaces, ensuring their longevity and vitality over time.

In addition to maintenance guidance, designers may also educate clients about seasonal changes and how they can affect their landscapes. This may include information on how different plants respond to seasonal variations in temperature, light, and moisture, as well as tips for preparing the landscape for seasonal transitions. By educating clients about seasonal changes, designers help them anticipate and respond to the evolving needs of their landscapes, fostering a deeper appreciation and understanding of the natural rhythms and cycles of the outdoor environment.

Chapter Two

Types of Landscapes and Gardens

Different types of landscapes and gardens exist to meet a variety of needs, preferences, and environmental conditions. This includes:

- **Cultural and Historical Influences**: Landscapes and gardens often reflect the cultural and historical context in which they are created. For example, traditional Japanese gardens are designed to embody Zen principles of simplicity and harmony with nature, while formal French gardens are characterized by their geometric layouts and ornate features.

- **Climate and Geography**: Environmental factors such as climate, soil type, and topography play a significant role in determining the type of landscape or garden that is suitable for a particular area. Desert landscapes, for instance, require drought-tolerant plants and water-conserving design principles, while tropical gardens thrive in warm, humid climates.

- **Personal Preferences and Lifestyle**: Individuals have different preferences when it comes to the aesthetics and functions of their outdoor spaces. Some may prefer formal, manicured gardens with structured layouts and geometric shapes, while others may prefer informal, naturalistic landscapes that mimic the wilderness.

- **Functional Requirements**: Landscapes and gardens can serve a variety of functions, ranging from aesthetic enjoyment to food production, wildlife habitat, and recreational activities. For example, a vegetable garden is designed primarily for growing edible crops, while a wildlife garden is created to attract and support native fauna.

- **Health and Well-being**: Gardens can have therapeutic benefits for physical and mental health. Healing gardens, for instance, are designed to provide a peaceful and restorative environment for patients in healthcare facilities, while sensory gardens stimulate the senses and promote relaxation and mindfulness.

- **Urban Planning and Development**: In urban areas, landscapes and gardens play a crucial role in enhancing the quality of life for residents. Urban parks, green spaces, and community gardens provide opportunities for recreation, social interaction, and connection with nature in densely populated environments.

Overall, the diversity of landscapes and gardens reflects the complex interplay of cultural, environmental, and individual factors shaping our relationship with the outdoor world. By understanding the various types of landscapes and gardens, we can better appreciate the beauty and significance of these spaces in our lives. Some of these are described following, keeping in mind that this is not an exhaustive overview and there are many different types and approaches to consider. These are just a few examples of the many types of gardens that exist, each offering its own unique beauty, functionality, and purpose.

Accessible Gardens

Accessible gardens are transformative spaces designed to remove barriers and ensure that individuals of all ages and abilities can participate in gardening activities. These gardens are particularly beneficial for senior gardeners and those with limited mobility, providing them with the opportunity to engage in therapeutic and rewarding outdoor activities. One of the key features of accessible gardens is the implementation of pathways that are wide enough to accommodate wheelchairs and are often paved or made of crushed stone. Additionally, ramps with railings are commonly integrated into the design to facilitate easy movement throughout the garden, ensuring inclusivity and accessibility for all individuals.

Accessible gardens are specially designed outdoor spaces that are created to be inclusive and accommodating for individuals of all ages and abilities, including those with physical disabilities, mobility challenges, or other limitations. These gardens are structured to eliminate barriers that might prevent people from fully engaging in gardening activities, providing a welcoming environment where everyone can participate and enjoy the benefits of gardening.

Key features of accessible gardens typically include:

- **Pathways:** Accessible gardens often feature wide, level pathways that are designed to accommodate wheelchairs, walkers, and other mobility aids. These pathways are typically paved with materials such as concrete, asphalt, or compacted gravel to ensure smooth and stable surfaces for easy navigation.

- **Ramps and Handrails:** In addition to pathways, accessible gardens may incorporate ramps with handrails to provide access to raised areas or different levels of the garden. Ramps offer an alternative to stairs and make it easier for individuals with mobility issues to move around the garden independently.

- **Raised Beds:** Raised garden beds are a central feature of accessible gardens, allowing individuals to garden at waist height without having to bend or kneel. These beds are often constructed from materials such as wood, stone, or recycled plastic and can be customized to suit the needs and preferences of the gardener. Raised beds provide easy access for wheelchair users and those with limited mobility, making gardening more accessible and enjoyable.

- **Seating Areas:** Accessible gardens may include seating areas or benches strategically placed throughout the space to provide opportunities for rest and relaxation. These seating areas offer a comfortable place for individuals to take breaks, socialize with others, or simply enjoy the beauty of the garden.

- **Adaptive Tools and Equipment:** To further enhance accessibility, accessible gardens may be equipped with adaptive tools and equipment designed specifically for individuals with disabilities or physical limitations. These tools can include ergonomic garden tools, raised planting tables, and other assistive devices that make gardening tasks easier and more manageable.

Raised beds are a hallmark of accessible gardens, offering numerous benefits for gardeners with mobility challenges. These beds are elevated from the ground, making them easily accessible to individuals in wheelchairs or those who have difficulty bending or kneeling. Raised beds can be constructed using a variety of materials, including bricks, concrete blocks, recycled plastic, or wood, and can be customized to suit the specific needs and preferences of the gardener. For those who may not have the skills or resources to build raised beds from scratch, simple-to-use kits are readily available, offering a convenient and accessible solution.

Figure 7: The walkway addresses a steep slope with a universal design approach at Brisbane Botanic Gardens, Mount Coot-tha. John Robert McPherson, CC BY-SA 4.0, via Wikimedia Commons.

When creating a raised garden bed, it's important to consider the dimensions and depth of the bed to ensure optimal growing conditions. Most raised beds are typically three to four feet wide, but can vary in depth depending on the specific requirements of the plants being grown. It's essential to fill the raised bed with a custom soil mix that provides adequate nutrients and drainage for healthy plant growth. For individuals who require even greater accessibility, table gardens are an excellent option, placing the soil level at tabletop height to accommodate individuals who may need to garden from a seated position. These gardens are ideal for growing drought-tolerant plants with short roots or can be constructed deeper at one end to accommodate a chair underneath the work surface [45].

Figure 8: Accessible community garden. Gerry Thomasen from Nanaimo, Canada, CC BY 2.0, via Wikimedia Commons.

In addition to raised beds, accessible gardens often include features such as seating areas and shade canopies to create comfortable and inviting spaces for relaxation and enjoyment. These elements enhance the overall accessibility and usability of the garden, ensuring that individuals of all abilities can fully participate in and benefit from the gardening experience. By removing physical barriers and providing accessible amenities, accessible gardens foster inclusivity, empowerment, and a sense of community among gardeners of diverse backgrounds and abilities.

Bog Gardens

Soggy areas within a yard can often present a challenge for gardeners, but with the right selection of plants, they can be transformed into vibrant and thriving bog gardens. Unlike stagnant water bodies, bogs in nature are characterized by consistently wet soil conditions without standing water. Bog gardens offer an opportunity to capitalize on such wet, sunny areas within a landscape, whether they be natural depressions, ditches, or areas prone to water runoff.

A bog garden is a specialized type of wetland garden that is designed to mimic the unique environmental conditions found in natural bog habitats. Bogs are characterized by their acidic, nutrient-poor soils and high water content, which create a distinct ecosystem that supports a variety of specialized plant species.

In a bog garden, these conditions are replicated to create a habitat suitable for plants that thrive in wet, acidic environments. Typically, bog gardens are constructed in low-lying areas or depressions in the landscape where water naturally collects, such as alongside streams or in poorly draining soil.

Key features of a bog garden may include:

- **Waterlogged Soil:** Bog gardens are characterized by permanently waterlogged or saturated soil conditions, which are created by allowing water to pool or collecting rainwater in the garden area. The waterlogged soil helps to mimic the bog environment and creates the ideal conditions for bog plants to thrive.

- **Acidic Soil:** Bogs are known for their acidic soils, which are low in nutrients and have a pH level below 7. In a bog garden, the soil is often amended or supplemented with acidic materials such as peat moss, sphagnum moss, or pine needles to create the acidic conditions preferred by bog plants.

- **Specialized Plant Species:** Bog gardens are planted with a diverse selection of plants that are adapted to wet, acidic environments. These may include bog-loving species such as pitcher plants, sundews, Venus flytraps, bog orchids, sphagnum mosses, and various species of ferns and grasses. These plants have specialized adaptations that allow them to thrive in the unique conditions of a bog habitat.

- **Careful Water Management:** While bog gardens require consistently moist soil conditions, it's important to ensure that water does not become stagnant or create breeding grounds for mosquitoes and other pests. Proper water management techniques, such as installing drainage systems or incorporating water features like streams or fountains, can help to maintain healthy water levels while preventing waterlogging.

- **Naturalistic Design:** Bog gardens are often designed to mimic the appearance of natural bog habitats, with winding pathways, irregularly shaped planting beds, and naturalistic features such as rocks, logs, and driftwood. This creates a visually appealing and immersive environment that evokes the beauty and tranquillity of a natural bog.

Building a bog garden doesn't necessarily require an excessively wet yard; it can also be established in relatively dry areas, making it a versatile option for various landscapes. In fact, it can even be an excellent way to utilize rainwater collected in a rain barrel. One approach to creating a bog garden involves lining a shallow hole with perforated rubber material to allow for proper drainage while retaining moisture in the soil. This ensures that the bog garden maintains the necessary damp conditions for optimal plant growth.

Figure 9: The Bog Garden, Forde Abbey. The Bog Garden, Forde Abbey by Oliver Dixon, CC BY-SA 2.0, via Wikimedia Commons.

The key to a successful bog garden lies in selecting the right plants that are well-suited to wet soil conditions and can thrive in sunny environments. Tall flowering plants like red hibiscus, yellow cannas, and blue flag irises can provide vertical interest and add a splash of colour to the garden. Meanwhile, shorter plants such as carnivorous pitcher plants and sundews can be used to fill in the foreground and add texture to the landscape.

It's essential to consider the sunlight requirements of bog garden plants, as most of them typically need six to eight hours of sun each day to flourish. During dry spells, supplemental watering may be necessary to ensure that the soil remains consistently moist. Additionally, proper positioning of plants is crucial for maximizing sunlight exposure, with shorter plants ideally placed on the south side of taller ones to prevent shading and ensure optimal growth conditions.

Figure 10: Bog garden, Woburn Abbey. Bog garden, Woburn Abbey by Philip Halling, CC BY-SA 2.0, via Wikimedia Commons.

By carefully selecting and arranging a diverse array of bog-loving plants, gardeners can create a visually striking and ecologically diverse landscape feature that thrives in wet, sunny conditions. Bog gardens not only add beauty and interest to the yard but also provide valuable habitat for a variety of wildlife, making them a valuable addition to any landscape.

Cut Flower Garden

A cut flower garden, also known as a cutting garden, is a dedicated area within a landscape or garden that is specifically designed and cultivated for the purpose of growing flowers to be cut and used in floral arrangements, bouquets, and other decorative displays. Unlike traditional flower gardens, where flowers are primarily grown for their ornamental value in the landscape, cut flower gardens prioritize the production of blooms that can be harvested and enjoyed indoors.

Key features of a cut flower garden typically include:

- **Selection of Flower Varieties:** Cut flower gardens are planted with a diverse selection of flowering plants chosen for their suitability for cutting and their ability to produce long-lasting blooms. Popular choices for cut flower gardens include traditional favourites such as roses, peonies, dahlias, zinnias, sunflowers, and lilies, as well as a variety of annuals, perennials, and bulbs that offer a range of colours, shapes, and textures.

- **Succession Planting:** To ensure a continuous supply of fresh blooms throughout the growing season, cut flower gardens often employ succession planting techniques. This involves planting multiple batches of flowers at staggered intervals to ensure a steady harvest of flowers from early spring to late fall. By staggering planting times, gardeners can extend the flowering season and maintain a consistent supply of blooms for cutting.

- **Optimal Growing Conditions:** Cut flower gardens require well-drained soil, ample sunlight, and regular watering to thrive. Gardeners may amend the soil with organic matter such as compost or aged manure to improve soil fertility and structure. Adequate spacing between plants is also important to promote air circulation and reduce the risk of disease. Additionally, providing support structures such as stakes or trellises can help to keep tall or heavy-flowered plants upright and prevent them from flopping over.

- **Harvesting Techniques:** Flowers are typically harvested from cut flower gardens when they are at their peak of freshness and beauty. For most flowers, this means cutting them early in the morning or late in the evening when they are well-hydrated and temperatures are cooler. Using clean, sharp pruners or scissors, gardeners carefully cut the stems at an angle and immediately place them in a bucket of water to prevent wilting. Proper harvesting techniques help to prolong the vase life of cut flowers and ensure that they look their best when arranged in bouquets or floral displays.

- **Seasonal Planning:** Cut flower gardens are often planned with consideration for the seasons, with different flowers chosen for planting based on their bloom times and suitability for each season. Early spring may feature bulbs such as tulips and daffodils, while summer may bring an abundance of annuals such as cosmos, zinnias, and snapdragons. In the fall, dahlias, asters, and chrysanthemums may take centre stage, providing a final burst of colour before winter sets in.

Overall, cut flower gardens offer a rewarding and enjoyable way to bring the beauty of the garden indoors. By cultivating a diverse selection of flowers and employing proper planting, care, and harvesting techniques, gardeners can enjoy a continuous supply of fresh blooms to adorn their homes and share with others throughout the growing season.

The beauty of gardening extends beyond the boundaries of the outdoor landscape, as it offers the opportunity to bring the vibrant colours and delightful fragrances of blooming flowers indoors. Harnessing the joys of gardening within the comfort of your home allows for a seamless transition from outdoor to indoor relaxation, enveloping your living space in the sights and scents of nature's bounty. While roses are often the first flowers that come to mind when considering cut flowers, there exists a diverse array of plant species that hold up admirably when brought indoors, offering an abundance of options to adorn your home with freshly cut blooms.

Among the warm-season flowering plants that excel both in the landscape and in a vase, salvias emerge as versatile contenders. Renowned for their attractiveness to butterflies and hummingbirds, salvias also serve as delightful additions to cut flower gardens, boasting an extensive selection of annual and perennial species in a myriad of colours and sizes. With their ability to thrive without succumbing to serious pests, salvias present an appealing choice for gardeners seeking enduring floral beauty.

Zinnias, with their charmingly vibrant blooms in hues of red, pink, yellow, and purple, represent another beloved favourite in Florida gardens [45]. These heat-loving annuals, available in a variety of forms ranging from single-layered petals to multi-layered varieties resembling dahlias, add a cheerful burst of colour to both the landscape and indoor floral arrangements. Despite their inability to bloom in blue, zinnias' versatility and resilience make them indispensable assets to any cut flower garden.

For those seeking dramatic flair, the iconic sunflower emerges as an undeniable choice. With its towering stature and colossal, cheerful blooms spanning up to 12 inches across, the sunflower commands attention with its vibrant shades ranging from cream to maroon. Available in a range of cultivars, including pollenless varieties suitable for cut flowers, sunflowers offer a captivating focal point in both garden landscapes and indoor floral displays.

Figure 11: Sunflower 'ProCut Plum' on July 24, 2017 in Santa Rosa, Ca. Don McCulley, CC BY-SA 4.0, via Wikimedia Commons.

Celosia, distinguished by its distinctive cockscomb and plume flower types, presents an intriguing option for adding texture and visual interest to floral arrangements. With its velvety, brain-like cockscomb flowers and light, fluffy plume flowers in an array of captivating shades, celosia makes a striking addition to cut flower gardens, providing an eye-catching element to indoor floral compositions.

Gerbera daisies, with their bold, long-lasting flowers available in an array of vibrant hues, offer a burst of colour and cheerfulness to any floral arrangement. With their enduring popularity and availability in several forms and shades, including yellow, white, pink, lavender, red, and orange, gerbera daisies add a touch of whimsy and charm to both indoor and outdoor spaces.

The bird of paradise, with its striking tropical allure and distinctive orange and blue bracts, captivates with its resemblance to a bird in flight. While gardeners may hesitate to cut these unique flowers due to their limited production, the long-lasting blooms of the bird of paradise add a touch of exotic elegance to indoor floral displays, infusing spaces with a tropical ambiance.

Figure 12: Bird of paradise, Kensington, Sydney. Sardaka, CC BY-SA 4.0, via Wikimedia Commons.

Caladiums, though not flowering plants, boast stunning foliage that complements floral arrangements beautifully. With their unique patterns and vibrant colours, caladium leaves make a striking addition to indoor bouquets, offering an alternative to traditional cut flowers. Available in a variety of colour combinations and leaf shapes, caladiums lend a touch of sophistication and visual interest to floral compositions, showcasing the versatility of foliage in indoor decor.

In addition to the aforementioned plant species, a myriad of other cutting options exist, including annuals such as snapdragons and coleus, as well as perennials like agapanthus, pentas, and gingers. With their enduring appeal and suitability for both indoor and outdoor use, these long-lived cut flowers and foliage plants provide endless possibilities for creating captivating floral arrangements that bring the beauty of the garden into your home.

Foodscaping

Foodscaping, also known as edible landscaping or garden-to-table landscaping, is a practice that combines the principles of traditional landscaping with the cultivation of edible plants. Instead of focusing solely on ornamental plants, foodscaping integrates fruits, vegetables, herbs, and edible flowers into the landscape design, creating a multifunctional and sustainable outdoor space. The concept of foodscaping aims to make food production more accessible, efficient, and aesthetically pleasing, while also promoting self-sufficiency and healthy living.

The essence of foodscaping lies in its ability to merge the beauty of landscapes with the functionality of food production. By engaging in foodscaping, individuals not only enhance the visual appeal of their surroundings but also contribute to ecological sustainability by reducing reliance on the industrial food system [46]. This practice aligns with the growing trend of seeking aesthetically pleasing yet ecologically beneficial landscapes, as studies have shown that people tend to prefer natural or near-natural landscapes that are both visually appealing and ecologically sound [47].

In a foodscaped garden, edible plants are strategically incorporated into various elements of the landscape, including flower beds, borders, hedges, and containers. Fruit trees may be planted as focal points or used to provide shade, while vegetable patches and herb gardens can be integrated seamlessly into existing flower beds or dedicated growing areas. Edible flowers, such as nasturtiums and calendula, add colour and flavour to the landscape while attracting pollinators.

One of the key principles of foodscaping is the concept of "growing where you live," which emphasizes the use of locally adapted and climate-appropriate edible plants. By selecting varieties that thrive in their specific growing conditions, foodscapers can minimize the need for chemical inputs, water, and maintenance while maximizing yield and flavour. Companion planting, the practice of growing complementary plants together to enhance growth and deter pests, is also commonly employed in foodscaping to promote biodiversity and natural pest control.

Foodscaping offers numerous benefits beyond just providing fresh, homegrown produce. By incorporating edible plants into the landscape, homeowners can reduce their ecological footprint, lower grocery bills, and increase food security. Foodscaped gardens also serve as educational tools, helping to reconnect people with the origins of their food and encouraging healthier eating habits. Additionally, the beauty and diversity of a foodscaped garden can enhance property value and curb appeal, making it an attractive option for homeowners and communities alike.

Figure 13: Edible garden design at Pixie Hollow Garden, Epcot, Disney world Florida, featuring purple and green kale, as well as chard varieties. Myrna Litt, CC BY 2.0, via Wikimedia Commons.

Foodscaping represents a holistic approach to gardening that seeks to harmonize the aesthetic, ecological, and practical aspects of landscaping with the satisfaction of growing and enjoying your own food. Whether it's a small herb garden on a balcony or a sprawling backyard orchard, foodscaping offers endless opportunities for creativity, sustainability, and culinary delight.

In foodscaping, the selection of suitable plants is essential for a successful garden. Emphasizing the principle of "right plant, right place," it's crucial to choose edible plants that thrive in the existing environmental conditions of your landscape. Opt for perennials, low-maintenance varieties, and herbs that can self-sow, saving both time and resources. Considering water usage is also vital, with a preference for drought-tolerant edibles, especially in regions where water availability is a concern. Grouping plants based on their water needs into hydrozones can streamline irrigation efforts, promoting efficient water use and reducing costs. However, it's essential to avoid using reclaimed water on edibles due to potential contamination risks.

When planning a foodscape in the front yard, it's prudent to check with homeowner associations for any regulations. Additionally, precautions should be taken to prevent tampering from neighbourhood pets or children, particularly if the front yard is unfenced. Prioritizing cleanliness by washing harvested edibles before consumption ensures safety and minimizes potential health risks.

A well-thought-out design is integral to a functional and aesthetically pleasing foodscape. Before planting, developing a design that considers the garden's appearance throughout the year is crucial, as it likely includes a mix of annuals and perennials. Establishing a design style or theme guides plant selection, whether opting for a formal layout with straight lines or a more organic, naturalistic approach. Incorporating a variety of textures, sizes, and colours creates visual interest, while adhering to a cohesive colour scheme promotes harmony within the foodscape.

Implementing design elements such as ornamentals alongside edibles ensures visual appeal year-round, especially during periods when edibles may not be in peak condition. Structures like trellises and arbours provide support for climbing plants while adding architectural interest. Utilizing planters and raised beds not only contributes to a tidy appearance but also simplifies maintenance. Neat edges delineate planting areas and can be achieved using various materials, including recycled options for sustainability. Well-designed pathways facilitate access to plants and connect different areas of the garden, enhancing both functionality and aesthetics.

Maintaining a foodscape involves several practices to ensure optimal plant health and productivity. Following recommended fertilization guidelines specific to each crop ensures proper nutrient levels without risking overapplication. Soil amendments such as compost enrich soil quality, improve nutrient availability, and enhance water retention capacity, contributing to overall plant vitality. Regular soil testing helps monitor soil health and informs necessary adjustments to fertilizer and amendment applications.

Mulching serves multiple purposes in a foodscape, including weed suppression, moisture retention, and temperature moderation. Different mulch types are suitable for various plantings, with considerations for crop sensitivity and overall garden aesthetics. Incorporating pollinator-friendly plants attracts beneficial insects, contributing to pest management and overall garden biodiversity. Employing integrated pest management strategies prioritizes least-toxic pest control methods and minimizes reliance on chemical pesticides, promoting ecological balance within the foodscape. Additionally, communicating with professional landscaping services about the presence of edibles ensures the application of appropriate practices and products, safeguarding both plant health and food safety.

Fragrance Gardens

A fragrance garden is a specialized type of garden designed to engage the sense of smell, providing visitors with a delightful olfactory experience. Unlike traditional gardens that primarily focus on visual aesthetics, fragrance gardens prioritize aromatic plants that emit pleasant scents. These gardens are carefully curated to showcase a diverse selection of fragrant flowers, herbs, and shrubs, creating an immersive sensory experience.

Creating a fragrance garden is an artful endeavour that taps into the power of scent to enrich the outdoor experience. From the delicate floral notes of roses to the invigorating aroma of herbs, fragrant plants can evoke a range of emotions and memories. With careful planning and selection, a fragrance garden can be a sensory oasis that delights visitors throughout the year.

The plants chosen for a fragrance garden are selected based on their ability to produce captivating scents that range from sweet and floral to spicy and herbal. Common selections include roses, lavender, jasmine, lilac, honeysuckle, and gardenia, among others. Each plant contributes its unique fragrance to the overall ambiance of the garden, creating layers of scent that evolve throughout the seasons.

In addition to flowers, fragrance gardens often incorporate aromatic foliage and herbs, such as mint, basil, thyme, and rosemary. These plants not only add variety to the garden but also offer the opportunity for visitors to interact with the plants by brushing against them or crushing their leaves to release their fragrance.

The layout and design of a fragrance garden are carefully considered to enhance the olfactory experience. Paths and walkways are strategically positioned to guide visitors through the garden, allowing them to meander among the plants and enjoy the different scents. Seating areas may be strategically placed to encourage relaxation and contemplation, allowing visitors to fully immerse themselves in the fragrant surroundings.

Fragrance gardens are often designed to be enjoyed year-round, with plants selected to bloom at different times throughout the seasons. Spring may bring the sweet scent of lilacs and hyacinths, while summer may be filled with the heady aroma of roses and jasmine. In autumn, fragrant herbs like sage and lavender may take centre stage, followed by the spicy scent of evergreen shrubs in winter.

Fragrance gardens offer a multisensory experience that celebrates the beauty and diversity of plant scents. Whether visitors are seeking relaxation, inspiration, or simply a moment of sensory delight, fragrance gardens provide a tranquil oasis where the sense of smell takes centre stage.

Figure 14: Fragrance garden. Milan Suvajac, CC BY-SA 4.0, via Wikimedia Commons.

In South Florida as an example, the ylang-ylang (Cananga odorata) is a tropical tree known for its exotic fragrance. This plant produces clusters of yellow flowers with a rich, sweet scent, making it a popular choice in perfumery and aromatherapy. The allure and versatility of ylang-ylang are exemplified by its inclusion in the iconic Chanel No. 5 perfume, showcasing its significance in the fragrance industry (Jourjine et al., 2022). Ylang-ylang essential oil, extracted from the flowers of Cananga odorata, is widely utilized in perfumes, cosmetics, and traditional medicine due to its aromatic qualities (Kuspradini et al., 2019). The essential oil of ylang-ylang is a key raw material in the fragrance industry, highlighting its economic importance and widespread use (Benini et al., 2012).

Figure 15: Cananga odorata. Prenn, CC BY-SA 3.0, via Wikimedia Commons.

The timing of scent release varies among plants, adding complexity to the olfactory experience. Some plants, like angel's trumpet, star jasmine, and water lilies, unveil their fragrance under the cover of night, enticing nocturnal visitors with their alluring scents. This nocturnal bloom adds a touch of mystery to the garden, inviting exploration after dark.

Seasonal changes also play a role in the fragrance garden's dynamic scent profile. In winter, sweet alyssum (Lobularia maritima) and pink bud jasmine (Jasminum polyanthum) take centre stage with their delicate blooms and intoxicating fragrances. These winter bloomers infuse the garden with warmth and vitality during the cooler months, offering a welcome respite from the winter chill.

The fragrance garden isn't limited to flowers alone; edible plants also contribute their unique scents to the landscape. The aroma of ripe tomatoes, citrus blossoms, and fresh herbs like basil and rosemary can awaken the senses and tantalize the taste buds. Incorporating these edible plants into the fragrance garden adds another layer of sensory richness, blurring the lines between the culinary and horticultural realms.

Ultimately, a fragrance garden is a celebration of nature's olfactory bounty, showcasing the diversity and beauty of fragrant plants from around the world. By selecting a variety of plants with different blooming times, scent intensities, and fragrance profiles, gardeners can create a harmonious tapestry of scents that delights the senses year-round. Whether enjoyed during a leisurely stroll or a quiet moment of reflection, the fragrance garden offers a sensory escape that nourishes the soul.

Butterfly Gardens

A butterfly garden is a carefully planned and cultivated space designed to attract and support butterflies throughout their life cycle. These gardens are typically filled with nectar-rich flowers, host plants for butterfly larvae (caterpillars), and other features that provide food, shelter, and breeding opportunities for butterflies.

The primary goal of a butterfly garden is to create a habitat that attracts a diverse range of butterfly species, thereby enhancing biodiversity and promoting conservation efforts. By providing the essential resources that butterflies need to thrive, such as food sources and breeding sites, butterfly gardens play a crucial role in supporting these important pollinators.

Key elements of a butterfly garden include:

- Nectar-rich flowers: Planting a variety of flowering plants that produce abundant nectar is essential for attracting adult butterflies. These flowers should bloom at different times throughout the growing season to ensure a continuous food supply for butterflies.

- Host plants: Butterfly larvae, or caterpillars, have specific dietary requirements and can only feed on certain plant species. Including host plants for various butterfly species in the garden is critical for supporting the entire life cycle of butterflies, from egg to adult. For example, milkweed is a host plant for monarch butterflies, while parsley and dill are host plants for swallowtail butterflies.

- Sunlight and warmth: Butterflies are ectothermic, meaning they rely on external sources of heat to regulate their body temperature. Providing sunny, sheltered areas in the garden where butterflies can bask and warm their wings is essential for their health and vitality.

- Shelter and resting spots: Butterflies need sheltered areas where they can rest, roost, and seek refuge from predators and adverse weather conditions. Features such as shrubs, trees, and rock piles provide suitable shelter for butterflies in the garden.

- Water source: Providing a shallow water source, such as a butterfly puddling area or a small birdbath with stones for perching, allows butterflies to drink water and obtain essential minerals and nutrients.

By incorporating these elements into their design, butterfly gardens can attract a diverse array of butterfly species, including both native and migratory butterflies. These gardens not only provide a beautiful and tranquil space for humans to enjoy but also contribute to the conservation of butterflies and other pollinators in their natural habitats.

Figure 16: Butterfly Garden at Norfolk Botanical Garden, Norfolk, Virginia. PumpkinSky, CC BY-SA 4.0, via Wikimedia Commons.

Creating a successful butterfly garden requires careful consideration of the needs of both adult butterflies and their caterpillars. Adult butterflies primarily feed on nectar from flowering plants, while their caterpillars have more specific dietary requirements and typically feed on certain host plants. Therefore, a well-rounded butterfly garden should include a variety of nectar sources for adults and appropriate host plants for caterpillars. Additionally, providing shelter, water sources, and suitable garden design are essential components of a thriving butterfly habitat.

The major components of a successful butterfly garden include adult nectar sources, larval host plants, shelter, and a water source. Adult nectar sources attract and nourish adult butterflies, while larval host plants serve as food sources for developing caterpillars. Shelter, such as vegetation that provides protection from extreme temperatures and predators, is crucial for butterflies' survival. A water source, such as a fountain or shallow dish, provides butterflies with access to water for drinking and thermoregulation.

Figure 17: Monarch butterfly (Danaus plexippus) in Brooklyn Botanic Garden. Rhododendrites, CC BY-SA 4.0, via Wikimedia Commons.

When designing a butterfly garden, it's important to consider several factors to maximize its effectiveness and appeal to a diverse range of butterfly species. Incorporating a wide assortment of flowers with different colours, shapes, and blooming times ensures that nectar is always available and attracts a variety of butterflies. Native plants should be prioritized whenever possible, as they are adapted to the local environment and provide essential resources for native butterfly species.

Creating horizontal and vertical heterogeneity by choosing plants with different heights and growth habits enhances the garden's appeal to a greater diversity of butterfly species. Planting in groupings, providing a mix of flower shapes, and including both shade and full sun plants further increase the garden's attractiveness to butterflies. Additionally, selecting appropriate plants for each location based on their water, light, and soil requirements ensures optimal growth and performance.

Garden maintenance plays a crucial role in supporting butterfly populations and conserving their habitats. Carefully selecting plants that are suitable for the landscape and avoiding pesticide application whenever possible are important practices to protect butterflies and other beneficial insects. Fertilizing, watering, and identifying butterfly species in the garden contribute to its overall health and success.

The benefits of butterfly gardening extend beyond mere enjoyment and aesthetic appeal. These gardens provide valuable habitat and resources for butterflies and other wildlife, contributing to ecosystem conservation efforts. Using native plants, attracting natural enemies of garden pests, and promoting plant diversity are additional practical benefits of butterfly gardening.

Furthermore, keeping detailed records of butterfly species encountered in the garden can contribute to scientific research and conservation efforts. Lastly, the therapeutic benefits of spending time in a butterfly garden, coupled with the aromatic scents of fragrant herbs, provide a soothing retreat from everyday life.

Figure 18: Butterfly Garden at Garden Hill Park, Bedok, Singapore. Wzhkevin, CC BY-SA 4.0, via Wikimedia Commons.

Hydroponic Vegetable Garden

A hydroponic vegetable garden is a method of growing vegetables without soil, using a nutrient-rich water solution instead. In this system, plants are typically grown in a controlled environment, such as a greenhouse or indoor space, where environmental factors like temperature, humidity, and light can be closely monitored and regulated. Hydroponic gardening has gained popularity due to its efficiency, scalability, and ability to produce high-quality vegetables with minimal space and resources.

In a hydroponic vegetable garden, plants are placed in a growing medium such as perlite, vermiculite, coconut coir, or rockwool, which provides support to the roots while allowing them to come into contact with the nutrient solution. The nutrient solution, which contains essential minerals and nutrients required for plant growth, is continuously circulated or periodically replenished to ensure that plants receive the necessary nutrients for healthy growth.

Figure 19: Hydroponics with leafy vegetables. Ryan Somma, CC BY-SA 2.0, via Wikimedia Commons.

There are several different types of hydroponic systems used in vegetable gardening, each with its own advantages and disadvantages. Some common types include:

1. Deep Water Culture (DWC): In DWC systems, plants are suspended in a nutrient solution with their roots submerged in the water. Oxygen is provided to the roots through the use of air stones or oxygen pumps. DWC systems are relatively simple and low-cost, making them suitable for beginners.

2. Nutrient Film Technique (NFT): NFT systems involve continuously flowing a thin film of nutrient solution over the roots of the plants, which are held in channels or tubes. This system provides a steady supply of nutrients and oxygen to the roots and is commonly used for growing leafy greens and herbs.

3. Ebb and Flow (Flood and Drain): Ebb and flow systems periodically flood the growing medium with nutrient solution and then allow it to drain away. This cycle ensures that the roots receive both water and oxygen, promoting healthy growth. Ebb and flow systems are versatile and can be used to grow a wide range of vegetables.

4. Aeroponics: Aeroponic systems mist the roots of the plants with a nutrient solution, allowing them to absorb nutrients and oxygen directly from the air. This system is highly efficient and can produce faster growth rates and higher yields compared to other hydroponic systems.

Hydroponic vegetable gardening offers several advantages over traditional soil-based gardening. It allows for precise control over environmental conditions, such as pH levels, nutrient concentrations, and water availability, which can optimize plant growth and productivity. Additionally, hydroponic systems typically require less water and space compared to traditional gardening methods, making them ideal for urban or indoor gardening settings where space is limited.

Furthermore, hydroponic gardening can be practiced year-round, regardless of external weather conditions, allowing for continuous vegetable production and harvest. This makes it particularly attractive for commercial growers looking to maximize crop yields and profits.

Hydroponic vegetable gardening offers a sustainable and efficient way to grow fresh, nutritious vegetables using minimal resources, making it an increasingly popular choice for both home gardeners and commercial growers alike.

Mediterranean Gardens

A Mediterranean garden is a type of garden inspired by the landscapes and climates found in regions surrounding the Mediterranean Sea, such as Southern Europe, North Africa, and parts of the Middle East. These gardens are characterized by their lush greenery, vibrant colours, aromatic plants, and emphasis on outdoor living spaces.

Figure 20: The Mediterranean Garden at Kew Gardens. Swphotouk, CC BY 4.0, via Wikimedia Commons.

Key features of Mediterranean gardens include:

- **Climate-Adapted Plants**: Mediterranean gardens typically feature plants that are well-suited to the warm, dry summers and mild, wet winters of Mediterranean climates. These plants are often drought-tolerant and able to thrive in poor, rocky soils. Common plants include olive trees, citrus trees, lavender, rosemary, sage, thyme, cypress trees, bougainvillea, and various succulents.

- **Hardscape Elements**: Mediterranean gardens often incorporate hardscape elements such as stone or terracotta pathways, walls, and terraces. These elements not only add visual interest but also help to retain moisture in the soil and create microclimates that support the growth of heat-loving plants.

- **Water Features**: While water is often scarce in Mediterranean climates, water features such as fountains, reflecting pools, and ornamental ponds are common in Mediterranean gardens. These features provide a cooling effect and create a sense of tranquillity in the garden.

- **Outdoor Living Spaces**: Mediterranean gardens are designed to be extensions of the home, with outdoor living spaces such as patios, courtyards, and pergolas for dining, entertaining, and relaxing. These spaces are often shaded by pergolas or covered with climbing vines to provide relief from the sun.

- **Colourful Plantings**: Mediterranean gardens are known for their vibrant colours, with plants chosen for their ability to bloom profusely and provide year-round interest. Warm, earthy tones such as reds, oranges, yellows, and purples are commonly used to create a sense of warmth and vitality in the garden.

- **Fragrance**: Aromatic plants play a significant role in Mediterranean gardens, adding to the sensory experience with their pleasant scents. Fragrant herbs like lavender, rosemary, and thyme are often planted near pathways or seating areas where their scent can be enjoyed.

- **Terraced Landscapes**: In hilly or sloped areas, Mediterranean gardens may feature terraced landscapes to create flat planting areas and prevent soil erosion. Terraces are often planted with a mix of flowering shrubs, herbs, and groundcovers to create a lush, layered effect.

Overall, Mediterranean gardens are designed to evoke the beauty and serenity of the Mediterranean landscape, offering a tranquil retreat where homeowners can relax, entertain, and connect with nature. Whether large or small, these gardens celebrate the rich cultural and botanical heritage of the Mediterranean region while providing a sustainable and low-maintenance landscape design option.

Figure 21: Mediterranean, United States Botanic Garden, Washington, D.C. Bohemian Baltimore, CC BY-SA 4.0, via Wikimedia Commons.

Moonlight Gardens

A moonlight garden, also known as a night garden or a white garden, is meticulously designed to be appreciated primarily after sunset. Its purpose is to highlight the allure of plants and features that are most captivating or fragrant in the evening, whether illuminated by the moon's soft glow or artificial lighting. These gardens aim to create a serene and enchanting atmosphere, often characterized by a monochromatic or limited colour scheme dominated by white, silver, and pale hues that reflect and enhance the moonlight.

Key components of a moonlight garden include a selection of white and silver plants, such as roses, moonflowers, lilies, hydrangeas, Artemisia, and variegated hostas. These plants stand out in low light conditions and emit a luminous effect when bathed in moonlight. Fragrance also plays a vital role, with flowers like jasmine, night-blooming cereus, gardenias, tuberose, and nicotiana releasing their scents most intensely at night to attract nocturnal pollinators like moths and bats.

Reflective surfaces, such as white gravel pathways, polished stones, or light-coloured paving stones, are often incorporated to enhance the moonlight effect. These surfaces help to bounce and amplify the available light, contributing to the ethereal ambiance of the garden. Additionally, night-blooming plants like evening primrose, night-blooming jasmine, and four o'clock flowers add an element of surprise and enchantment to the garden with their evening blooms.

Figure 22: Moonlight Garden, Edison and Ford Winter Estates, Fort Myers, Florida, USA, designed by Ellen Biddle Shipman for Mina Miller Edison. No machine-readable author provided. Cornellrockey04 assumed (based on copyright claims)., CC BY-SA 2.5, via Wikimedia Commons.

Texture and form are also carefully considered in moonlight gardens, with plants chosen for their contrasting leaf shapes, sizes, and textures to create visual interest and depth. Sensory elements are incorporated to engage multiple senses, including sight, smell, and touch. Rustling ornamental grasses, soft foliage, and the soothing sound of water features like fountains or bubbling streams contribute to the sensory experience.

While moonlight is the primary source of illumination, strategic lighting design can further enhance the garden's beauty and functionality after dark. Soft, ambient lighting such as string lights, lanterns, or strategically placed uplights can highlight focal points, pathways, and architectural features without overpowering the natural beauty of the moonlit landscape.

Overall, moonlight gardens provide a tranquil and enchanting retreat where visitors can unwind, reconnect with nature, and experience the magic of the nighttime garden. Whether enjoyed for quiet contemplation, romantic strolls, or social gatherings, these gardens evoke a sense of mystery and wonder under the silvery glow of the moon.

Shimmering silver foliage adds a touch of elegance and visual contrast to any landscape, especially in nighttime gardens where it glimmers under the moonlight. Dusty miller, scientifically known as Senecio cineraria, is a cool-season annual in Florida celebrated for its silvery, fern-like leaves. These plants thrive in the cooler months, their foliage providing a stunning backdrop that shines in the soft glow of the moon. Texas sage (Leucophyllum frutescens), a native shrub with delicate silver to gray-green leaves, is another excellent choice for Florida gardens. Not only are these shrubs drought and heat tolerant, but they also boast foliage that exudes a subtle silvery sheen, enhancing the nocturnal allure of the garden.

Wondrous white flowers further enhance the enchanting ambiance of moonlit gardens. Gardenias, though not low-maintenance, are cherished by dedicated gardeners for their exquisite blooms and intoxicating fragrance. With everblooming varieties, gardenias can grace Florida landscapes with their fragrant blossoms year-round. Fringetree, with its delicate white flowers that cover the tree in spring, adds a touch of ethereal beauty to nighttime gardens. Native varieties like Chionanthus virginicus and pygmy fringetrees bloom before new leaves emerge in spring, while Chinese fringetrees bloom at the end of the spring growth flush. Flowering dogwood (Cornus florida), a popular native tree in eastern U.S., offers stunning white blooms in spring, adding charm and elegance to moonlit landscapes.

Spider lilies, such as Hymenocallis latifolia, produce exquisite white flowers in summer and fall that are not only fragrant but also long-lasting and delicate. These flowers, particularly captivating when illuminated at night, contribute to the enchanting allure of moonlight gardens. Stokes' aster varieties, including 'Alba' and 'Silver Moon', boast white blooms that shine brilliantly in the moonlight, making them a versatile and captivating addition to any nighttime garden. For those preferring annuals, white varieties of petunias, alyssum, snaps, impatiens, and vinca offer a plethora of options to brighten up moonlit landscapes with their stunning blooms.

Figure 23: Angel's trumpet, Coleton Fishacre. Derek Harper, CC BY 4.0, via Wikimedia Commons.

Fragrant flowers further elevate the sensory experience in moonlight gardens. Angel's trumpet, with its large, trumpet-shaped flowers emitting a sweet fragrance, is a showstopper in nighttime gardens. Star jasmine, known for its shining white flowers and intoxicating fragrance, perfumes the air with its sweet scent, adding to the magical ambiance of moonlit landscapes. Water lilies, with their exquisite flowers available in both day and night-blooming varieties, contribute to the sensory delight of moonlight gardens, offering beauty and fragrance under the enchanting glow of the moon.

Sensory Gardens

A sensory garden is meticulously crafted outdoor space, purposefully designed to engage the senses through a rich tapestry of plants, textures, fragrances, colours, and sounds. Unlike conventional gardens that predominantly emphasize visual aesthetics, sensory gardens aim to stimulate all five senses—sight, smell, touch, taste, and hearing—providing visitors with a multi-dimensional experience. These gardens are thoughtfully created to be accessible to individuals of all ages and abilities, including those with disabilities or sensory challenges, fostering an inclusive environment where everyone can partake in the sensory journey.

Figure 24: Sensory Garden at the Ohio Library for the Blind and Physically Disabled attached to the Cleveland Public Library Memorial-Nottingham Branch Library, Cleveland, Ohio. Hamaxides, CC BY-SA 4.0, via Wikimedia Commons.

Central to the concept of a sensory garden are several key elements carefully integrated into the design:

- Firstly, the selection of plants with diverse textures is paramount. Sensory gardens showcase a myriad of foliage with varying shapes, sizes, and textures, ranging from velvety leaves to rough bark and delicate flowers. Visitors are encouraged to touch and interact with the foliage, immersing themselves in the tactile sensations it offers.

- Furthermore, fragrance assumes a pivotal role in sensory gardens, with aromatic plants strategically positioned to release their scents as visitors traverse the space. Fragrant blooms like roses, lavender, and jasmine, alongside herbs such as mint, rosemary, and basil, enchant the olfactory senses, contributing to an inviting and immersive atmosphere.

- Colourful blooms serve to captivate the sense of sight, with vibrant flowers in an array of hues adding visual interest and splendour to the garden. From radiant reds and oranges to soothing blues and purples, the kaleidoscope of colours creates a visually stunning display that enchants and uplifts visitors.

- Incorporating edible plants offers visitors the opportunity to engage their sense of taste, allowing them to sample fresh herbs, fruits, and vegetables grown within the garden. Herbs like thyme, sage, and parsley, as well as fruits like strawberries and blueberries, tantalize the taste buds, inviting exploration and culinary delight.

- The presence of water features, such as fountains, ponds, or waterfalls, introduces a soothing auditory element to the garden, fostering tranquillity and mindfulness. The gentle sound of trickling water permeates the atmosphere, enhancing the overall sensory experience and promoting a sense of calm.

- Comfortable seating areas dispersed throughout the garden encourage visitors to pause and immerse themselves fully in the sensory delights of the space. Whether nestled among fragrant flowers or overlooking a serene pond, these seating areas provide opportunities for reflection, contemplation, and relaxation.

- Thoughtfully designed pathways ensure that the garden is accessible to all visitors, including those with mobility aids, such as wheelchairs or walkers. Smooth, level pathways with handrails and non-slip surfaces facilitate comfortable and safe navigation, catering to individuals with diverse physical abilities.

Figure 25: Clarence Park Sensory Garden. Clarence Park Sensory Garden by Ian Capper, CC BY-SA 2.0, via Wikimedia Commons.

Sensory gardens offer a rich and immersive experience that celebrates the beauty and diversity of the natural world while promoting relaxation, well-being, and a deeper connection with nature. Through a harmonious interplay of sights, sounds, textures, and fragrances, these gardens engage the senses in a symphony of sensory delights, inviting visitors to embark on a transformative journey of exploration and discovery.

Sensory gardens serve a multitude of purposes, ranging from educational to therapeutic, and they provide spaces for socialization and relaxation. These gardens can be tailored to specific user groups, such as children or individuals with visual impairments, with features like raised beds and wide pathways to ensure accessibility for all. They are designed to engage the senses, promoting interaction with plants and fostering a deeper connection with nature. Interpretive signs and easy access to plants are essential components, with a focus on selecting people-friendly plants and minimizing the use of pesticides to create safe and inviting environments [45].

Touch gardens, a hallmark of sensory gardening, offer visitors the opportunity to explore the garden through tactile experiences [45]. By incorporating plants with contrasting textures, such as soft and fuzzy or rough and spiky, these gardens appeal to the sense of touch. Visitors can run their fingers over the velvety petals of a rose or feel the smooth bark of a crape myrtle. Plants like the Southern magnolia provide diverse textures within a single specimen, with slick, leathery leaves on top and fuzzy, soft undersides. Touch gardens are particularly enjoyable for children and individuals with visual impairments, although precautions should be taken to avoid spiny plants in high-traffic areas.

Incorporating sound into a sensory garden enhances the overall experience, expanding the senses and immersing visitors in the auditory delights of nature. Seating areas within the garden allow visitors to pause and listen to the soothing sounds of wind rustling through leaves, bamboo stems knocking together, or grasses gently swaying. Natural elements like fallen leaves crunching underfoot and the chatter of squirrels add to the sensory richness of the garden [45]. Additionally, features such as waterfalls, fountains, wind chimes, and outdoor speakers playing soft music can further enhance the auditory experience, creating a tranquil and immersive atmosphere.

Fragrance gardens offer yet another dimension to sensory gardening, tapping into the power of scent to evoke emotions and memories. By carefully selecting fragrant plants, gardeners can create a delightful olfactory experience for visitors. Plants like tea olive, gardenia, and pine emit captivating scents that enrich the garden atmosphere. Some plants release their fragrance in response to sunlight, while others, like night-blooming jasmine, moon vine, and angel's trumpet, unveil their fragrant blooms only after dusk. Edible plants such as herbs and citrus add another layer to fragrance gardens, infusing the air with their aromatic oils and inviting visitors to savour the scent of nature's bounty [45].

Coastal Gardens

A coastal garden is a type of garden specifically designed and cultivated in coastal regions, taking into account the unique environmental conditions and challenges present in these areas. Coastal gardens are typically located near the ocean or other bodies of water, and they must contend with factors such as salt spray, strong winds, sandy soils, and intense sunlight. Despite these challenges, coastal gardens offer a unique opportunity to create stunning landscapes that complement the natural beauty of the coastline.

Figure 26: Coastal Georgia Botanical Gardens, Savannah, Chatham County, Georgia. Michael Rivera, CC BY-SA 4.0, via Wikimedia Commons.

Key features of coastal gardens include:

- Salt-Tolerant Plants: Coastal gardens often feature plants that are adapted to thrive in salty conditions. These plants have mechanisms to prevent salt accumulation in their tissues and can withstand exposure to salt spray from ocean breezes. Examples of salt-tolerant plants include sea oats, beach sunflower, dune grasses, and various species of succulents.

- Wind-Resistant Plants: Given the strong winds common in coastal areas, coastal gardens often include plants with sturdy stems and flexible foliage that can withstand gusts without being damaged. Wind-resistant plants may have small or narrow leaves, or they may be low-growing and compact to minimize wind resistance. Examples include coastal shrubs like wax myrtle, coastal rosemary, and seaside goldenrod.

- Drought-Tolerant Plants: Coastal gardens may experience periods of drought, particularly in regions with low rainfall or sandy soils that drain quickly. Therefore, selecting drought-tolerant plants is essential for conserving water and maintaining a resilient garden. Drought-tolerant plants often have adaptations such as deep root systems, succulent leaves, or waxy coatings to reduce water loss. Examples include lavender, yarrow, agave, and prickly pear cactus.

- Native Plants: Using native plants in coastal gardens is beneficial for several reasons. Native plants are well adapted to the local climate and soil conditions, making them more resilient and requiring less maintenance. Additionally, native plants support local wildlife and ecosystems, providing food and habitat for birds, butterflies, and other native species. Examples of native coastal plants vary depending on the specific region but may include seaside goldenrod, beach morning glory, and coastal dune sunflower.

- Coastal-Friendly Hardscaping: In addition to plants, coastal gardens may incorporate hardscaping elements such as pathways, seating areas, and garden structures that are designed to withstand coastal conditions. Materials like weather-resistant wood, marine-grade stainless steel, and natural stone are commonly used for coastal-friendly hardscaping to ensure durability and longevity in the harsh coastal environment.

Overall, coastal gardens offer a unique opportunity to create beautiful and resilient landscapes that embrace the coastal lifestyle. By selecting the right plants and materials and carefully considering the local environmental conditions, gardeners can create thriving coastal gardens that enhance the natural beauty of the shoreline and provide enjoyment for years to come.

Figure 27: An American Daylily Society Display Garden, Coastal Georgia Botanical Gardens, Savannah, Chatham County, Georgia. Michael Rivera, CC BY-SA 4.0, via Wikimedia Commons.

Contemporary Minimal Garden

A contemporary minimal garden is a modern and streamlined outdoor space characterized by simplicity, clean lines, and a focus on functionality. This style of garden design embraces the principles of minimalism, emphasizing simplicity, restraint, and the use of space as essential elements of beauty. Contemporary minimal gardens often feature geometric shapes, monochromatic colour schemes, and carefully curated plant selections to create a sense of calm, order, and serenity.

Key features of contemporary minimal gardens include:

- Clean Lines and Geometric Shapes: Contemporary minimal gardens typically incorporate straight lines, sharp angles, and geometric forms to create a sense of order and structure. This design approach often extends to pathways, plant beds, and hardscape elements such as walls, fences, and seating areas.

- Simplified Planting Palettes: Rather than overwhelming the space with a wide variety of plants, contemporary minimal gardens often showcase a limited selection of carefully chosen species. Plants with clean, architectural forms and foliage in shades of green, white, or gray are favoured, contributing to the garden's sleek and sophisticated aesthetic.

- Functional Outdoor Spaces: Contemporary minimal gardens are designed with functionality in mind, providing practical and versatile outdoor living areas for relaxation, dining, and entertainment. These spaces may include minimalist furniture, sleek outdoor kitchens, fire pits, and water features, arranged in a way that maximizes usability while maintaining visual harmony.

- Strategic Use of Materials: The choice of materials plays a crucial role in contemporary minimal garden design, with an emphasis on natural, durable, and low-maintenance materials. Common materials used in contemporary minimal gardens include concrete, stone, wood, metal, and glass, often presented in their raw or unadorned state to emphasize their inherent beauty and texture.

- Negative Space and Balance: Contemporary minimal gardens often incorporate negative space, or empty areas, as an essential design element to create balance and visual interest. By carefully considering the placement of plants, hardscape features, and open areas, designers can achieve a harmonious and well-proportioned composition that feels calm and uncluttered.

- Lighting and Ambiance: Lighting is an essential aspect of contemporary minimal garden design, used to enhance the garden's atmosphere and extend its usability into the evening hours. Integrated LED lighting fixtures, strategically placed along pathways, under planters, and around architectural features, can create dramatic effects and highlight key elements of the garden's design.

Overall, contemporary minimal gardens offer a sophisticated and understated approach to outdoor living, emphasizing simplicity, functionality, and timeless elegance. By embracing minimalist principles and carefully selecting materials and plants, designers can create modern and tranquil outdoor spaces that provide a welcome retreat from the complexities of urban life.

Cottage Gardens

A cottage garden, originating in England, boasts an informal and romantic design, characterized by its abundant plantings and rustic aesthetic. It conjures the cozy ambiance of traditional English countryside cottages, adorned with a rich tapestry of flowers, herbs, and other plants arranged in a relaxed and naturalistic manner.

This style of garden is marked by several key features. Firstly, its layout is informal, often featuring winding pathways, meandering borders, and irregularly shaped beds. Unlike formal gardens with rigid geometric patterns, cottage gardens embrace a more casual arrangement, echoing the spontaneity of nature.

One of the hallmarks of cottage gardens is their dense and lush plantings. They overflow with a profusion of flowers, foliage, and herbs, encompassing a mix of annuals, perennials, shrubs, and climbers. This eclectic combination creates a riot of colour and texture throughout the seasons, contributing to the garden's charm.

Common plants found in cottage gardens include old-fashioned favourites like roses, peonies, lavender, delphiniums, and hollyhocks, along with herbs such as thyme, sage, rosemary, and lavender. These plants not only provide ornamental value but also serve practical purposes in cooking and aromatherapy.

Cottage gardens are typically bordered by low hedges, picket fences, or rustic wooden trellises, which define the garden space without creating a sense of enclosure. These boundaries seamlessly blend with the surrounding landscape, facilitating a soft and natural transition between the garden and its surroundings.

Figure 28: The Cottage Garden. Akaroa. Bernard Spragg, NZ, Public Domain, via Flikr.

To enhance the rustic charm of the garden, cottage gardeners often incorporate whimsical accessories such as vintage garden tools, antique containers, weathered wooden benches, and decorative ornaments like birdhouses and garden sculptures. These elements infuse the garden with personality and character, evoking a sense of nostalgia and romanticism.

In terms of colour palette, cottage gardens often feature a soft and harmonious range of pastel shades and gentle hues, including pinks, blues, purples, whites, and soft yellows. This creates a romantic and dreamy ambiance reminiscent of the English countryside landscape.

Overall, cottage gardens offer a charming and idyllic retreat where gardeners can indulge their love of flowers, connect with nature, and create a timeless haven of beauty and tranquillity. Whether nestled in a suburban backyard or sprawling across a rural countryside estate, cottage gardens epitomize the timeless allure of English cottage living, inspiring gardeners worldwide with their romantic and nostalgic appeal.

Hamptons Gardens

A Hamptons garden embodies a style of garden design inspired by the luxurious coastal communities of the Hamptons on Long Island, New York. These gardens are renowned for their sophisticated yet relaxed aesthetic, mirroring the laid-back luxury and coastal allure of the Hamptons lifestyle. Several defining features characterize Hamptons gardens:

Firstly, they often draw inspiration from the nearby coastline, integrating elements such as beach grasses, sand dunes, and driftwood into their design. Coastal plants like hydrangeas, beach roses, and sea oats are commonly incorporated to evoke the ambiance of the seaside.

Moreover, Hamptons gardens strike a harmonious balance between casual and sophisticated elements, blending formal design aspects with naturalistic features. This blend creates an inviting and comfortable atmosphere that is both refined and approachable.

The colour palette of Hamptons gardens tends to be soft and neutral, with shades of white, cream, gray, and pale blue dominating the landscape. These subtle hues evoke a sense of serenity and tranquillity, harmonizing with the coastal surroundings.

Classic garden plants such as roses, hydrangeas, boxwood, lavender, and peonies are staples of Hamptons garden design. These timeless favourites contribute to the elegance and charm of the garden, adding colour, fragrance, and texture.

While Hamptons gardens embrace a relaxed and informal vibe, they often incorporate elements of formal garden design, such as symmetrical layouts, clipped hedges, and geometric patterns. These structured features provide a sense of order and balance, creating visual interest and focal points within the garden.

Given the mild climate and emphasis on outdoor living in the Hamptons, gardens often feature well-appointed outdoor living areas such as patios, pergolas, and seating areas. These spaces are designed for relaxation, entertaining, and enjoying the natural beauty of the garden.

Hamptons gardens are renowned for their meticulous attention to detail, with careful consideration given to every aspect of the design, from plant selection to hardscape materials to decorative accents. This meticulous approach ensures that every element contributes to the overall beauty and charm of the garden.

Hamptons gardens exude timeless sophistication and coastal elegance, providing a serene and inviting retreat for homeowners and visitors alike. Whether nestled within a seaside estate or tucked away in a suburban neighbourhood, these gardens capture the essence of the Hamptons lifestyle and offer a tranquil escape from the hustle and bustle of everyday life.

Drought Tolerant Garden

A drought-tolerant garden, also known as a xeriscape or water-wise garden, is a type of garden designed to thrive with minimal water requirements. These gardens are specifically planned and cultivated to withstand periods of drought or limited water availability, making them ideal for regions prone to dry conditions or water restrictions. The primary goal of a drought-tolerant garden is to conserve water while still creating an attractive and sustainable landscape.

Figure 29: This demonstration garden, located in front of Avondale City Hall (Arizona), shows just how beautiful and functional a water-efficient landscape can be. The garden features examples of drought tolerant trees, shrubs, and ground covers. Plants used: Ocotillo, Red bird of paradise, Agave attenuata, Purple lantana. USEPA Environmental-Protection-Agency, Public domain, via Wikimedia Commons.

Key features of drought-tolerant gardens include:
- **Water-Efficient Plants**: Drought-tolerant gardens typically consist of plants that have evolved to survive in arid or semi-arid environments with little water. These plants are selected for their ability to thrive in low-water conditions, often requiring less irrigation than traditional garden plants. Examples of drought-tolerant plants include succulents,

cacti, ornamental grasses, Mediterranean herbs, and native wildflowers.

- **Water-Saving Techniques**: Drought-tolerant gardens utilize various water-saving techniques to minimize water usage and maximize efficiency. These techniques may include mulching, which helps retain soil moisture and suppresses weed growth; drip irrigation systems, which deliver water directly to the root zones of plants to minimize evaporation; and soil amendment with organic matter to improve water retention and drainage.

- **Xeriscaping Principles**: Xeriscaping is a landscaping approach that emphasizes water conservation and sustainability. Drought-tolerant gardens often incorporate xeriscaping principles such as proper plant selection, efficient irrigation, soil improvement, and minimal turf areas. By following these principles, gardeners can create landscapes that are both environmentally friendly and visually appealing.

- **Native and Adapted Plants**: Native plants are well-suited to local climate conditions and soil types, making them naturally drought-tolerant. Drought-tolerant gardens often include a mix of native plants and non-native species that are well-adapted to the local environment. By selecting plants that are adapted to the region's natural conditions, gardeners can reduce the need for supplemental irrigation and maintenance.

- **Low-Maintenance Design**: Drought-tolerant gardens are often designed to be low-maintenance, requiring minimal watering, pruning, and fertilizing once established. By choosing plants that are well-suited to the local climate and soil conditions, gardeners can create landscapes that are resilient and self-sustaining, requiring less time and effort to maintain.

Drought-tolerant gardens offer an environmentally conscious and sustainable landscaping solution for regions facing water scarcity or conservation concerns. By utilizing water-efficient plants, techniques, and design principles, gardeners can create beautiful and resilient landscapes that thrive with minimal water input, conserving water resources and promoting environmental stewardship.

Japanese-inspired Gardens

A Japanese garden is a meticulously designed outdoor space that reflects the aesthetic principles and philosophies of traditional Japanese culture. These gardens, influenced by Zen Buddhism and Shinto traditions, are carefully crafted to create harmonious compositions that evoke a sense of tranquillity, simplicity, and serenity. Key elements of Japanese gardens include:

- **Natural Elements**: Japanese gardens incorporate natural elements such as rocks, stones, water, and plants to create landscapes that mimic the beauty of the natural world. Rocks are often arranged in carefully composed formations to represent mountains, islands, or other natural features, while water features like ponds, streams, and waterfalls provide a sense of movement and vitality.

- **Balance and Symmetry**: Balance and symmetry are fundamental principles in Japanese garden design, with elements arranged in a harmonious and orderly manner to create a sense of equilibrium and tranquillity. Symmetrical layouts, mirrored reflections, and carefully placed focal points contribute to the overall sense of balance and harmony.

- **Minimalism and Simplicity**: Japanese gardens emphasize simplicity and restraint, with an emphasis on creating beauty through understated elegance and minimalistic design. Uncluttered spaces, clean lines, and a limited colour palette help to create a sense of calm and serenity, allowing visitors to focus on the beauty of the natural elements.

- **Seasonal Beauty**: Japanese gardens change with the seasons, with each season offering its own unique beauty and charm. Spring brings the delicate blossoms of cherry trees and azaleas, while summer is characterized by lush foliage and the vibrant greens of moss and ferns. Autumn brings fiery hues of red, orange, and gold as the leaves change colour, while winter reveals the graceful forms of bare branches and the tranquillity of snow-covered landscapes.

- **Symbolism and Meaning**: Many elements in Japanese gardens are imbued with symbolic meaning, drawing on Buddhist and Shinto traditions. For example, stones may represent islands or mountains, while water symbolizes purity and renewal. Bridges, lanterns, and gates are often used as metaphors for spiritual transition and enlightenment, inviting visitors on a journey of contemplation and self-reflection.

Figure 30: Japanese style stone cistern fountain at the Japanese Garden at Norfolk Botanical Garden, Norfolk, Virginia. PumpkinSky, CC BY-SA 4.0, via Wikimedia Commons.

Japanese gardens offer a tranquil retreat from the chaos of everyday life, providing a place for quiet contemplation, meditation, and connection with nature. Whether nestled within a temple complex, public park, or private residence, these gardens continue to inspire and captivate visitors with their timeless beauty and profound sense of harmony.

Figure 31: A Japanese garden created between 1906 and 1910 by Tasse Eida is a feature of the Irish National Stud, County Kildare, Ireland. David Stanley from Nanaimo, Canada, CC BY 2.0, via Wikimedia Commons.

Low-maintenance Garden

A low-maintenance garden is carefully crafted to reduce the time, energy, and resources needed for maintenance while still providing an attractive and functional outdoor space. These gardens are especially favoured by busy homeowners, those with limited gardening experience, or individuals who simply prefer to spend less time on upkeep.

A low maintenance garden is designed to require minimal upkeep and care while still offering an aesthetically pleasing and functional outdoor space. These gardens thrive with little intervention, making them ideal for individuals seeking to enjoy a garden without extensive maintenance [48-53].

Key features of low maintenance gardens include the use of diverse vegetation that can thrive in various conditions and spaces, the predominance of perennials, ornamentals, and low-maintenance species, and the incorporation of efficient garden management practices that reduce the need for constant attention [48, 51, 52]. For example, rain gardens are highlighted as economically feasible due to their low maintenance costs once established, making them an attractive option for sustainable landscaping [50]. Key features of low-maintenance gardens include:

- Carefully Selected Plants: These gardens typically showcase plants that thrive in the local climate and soil conditions, requiring minimal watering, fertilizing, and pruning. Drought-tolerant species, native plants, and slow-growing varieties are often chosen for their resilience and ease of care.

- Perennial Plants: Low-maintenance gardens often prioritize perennial plants, which return year after year with minimal replanting and upkeep compared to annuals. Once established, perennials typically demand less watering and attention, making them ideal for busy gardeners.

- Mulching and Weed Control: To combat weed growth, retain soil moisture, and minimize watering needs, low-maintenance gardens frequently utilize organic mulches like wood chips, shredded leaves, or compost. Additionally, weed barriers or landscape fabric may be employed to further reduce weed proliferation and maintenance efforts.

- Reduced Lawn Area: Lawns demand regular mowing, watering, and fertilizing, making them high-maintenance features. In low-maintenance gardens, lawns are often minimized or replaced with alternative ground covers such as gravel, mulch, or drought-tolerant plants to lessen maintenance requirements.

- Efficient Irrigation Systems: Installing drip irrigation or soaker hoses can significantly decrease water waste and the need for manual watering. These systems deliver water directly to plant roots, ensuring efficient water usage and reducing watering time and effort.

- Strategic Design and Planning: Low-maintenance gardens are designed with efficiency and practicality in mind. Plant placement, layout, and hardscape features are carefully considered to minimize pruning, trimming, and other maintenance tasks. Well-defined planting areas, clear pathways, and easy access to garden beds are common design elements.

In addition to the practical benefits, low maintenance gardens can also have positive environmental impacts. The stability of the bacterial composition in these gardens can contribute to improved soil suppressiveness, which is beneficial for overall soil health [51]. Furthermore, the creation and maintenance of gardens, even low maintenance ones, can foster a sense of community and resilience among individuals, highlighting the social benefits of such outdoor spaces [54].

Figure 32: Low maintenance garden Michael Young Centre, Purbeck Road. Sebastian Ballard, CC BY-SA 2.0, via Wikimedia Commons.

Low-maintenance gardens offer a sustainable and practical approach to landscaping, allowing homeowners to enjoy a beautiful outdoor space with minimal effort and upkeep. By selecting suitable plants, implementing efficient irrigation systems, and incorporating thoughtful design principles, these gardens can provide years of enjoyment with minimal maintenance requirements.

Topiary Garden

A topiary garden is a type of garden that features meticulously trimmed plants, typically shrubs and trees, into intricate shapes and designs. These designs can range from simple geometric forms to elaborate sculptures, animals, or architectural elements. The art of topiary has ancient origins and has been practiced in various cultures throughout history, but it became particularly popular in European gardens during the Renaissance period.

Figure 33: Topiary, Rufford Old Hall garden. David Hawgood, CC BY-SA 2.0, via Wikimedia Commons.

Key features of a topiary garden include:
- Trimmed Plants: The defining feature of a topiary garden is the use of trimmed plants to create sculptural forms. Common plants used for topiary include boxwood, yew, privet, and holly, as they respond well to shaping and pruning.

- Sculptural Designs: Topiary designs can vary widely, from traditional geometric shapes like spheres, cones, and spirals to more whimsical forms such as animals, birds, and even human figures. The designs are often inspired by natural forms or architectural motifs.

- Formal Layout: Topiary gardens often have a formal layout with well-defined paths, symmetrical planting beds, and carefully manicured hedges. The geometric precision of the design provides a sense of order and structure to the garden.

- Focal Points: Topiary specimens are often used as focal points or centrepieces within the garden, drawing the eye and adding visual interest. They can be positioned at key junctions along pathways, in formal parterres, or as accents within larger garden designs.

- Maintenance: Maintaining a topiary garden requires regular pruning and shaping to keep the plants looking neat and well-defined. Skilled gardeners or topiary artists may use specialized tools such as shears, clippers, and topiary frames to achieve the desired shapes and forms.

Figure 34: Residential topiary London Ontario. WayneRay, Public domain, via Wikimedia Commons.

Topiary gardens are admired for their artistry, precision, and ability to create striking visual effects in the landscape. Whether formal or whimsical, these gardens showcase the skill and creativity of the gardener while providing a unique and memorable experience for visitors.

Figure 35: Shrubs and topiaries in Leonardslee Rock Garden, West Sussex, England. Leimenide, CC BY 2.0, via Wikimedia Commons.

Modern Garden

A modern garden, also known as a contemporary garden, is a type of garden design that reflects the aesthetic and lifestyle preferences of the present era. Unlike traditional or historical garden styles, which may be rooted in specific cultural or architectural traditions, modern gardens embrace innovation, minimalism, and functionality. Key features of modern gardens include:

1. Clean Lines and Minimalist Design: Modern gardens often feature clean, straight lines and simple geometric shapes, creating a sense of order and clarity in the design. Minimalist elements such as sleek planters, smooth surfaces, and uncluttered spaces contribute to the contemporary aesthetic.

2. Integration of Indoor and Outdoor Spaces: Modern gardens blur the boundaries between indoor and outdoor living areas, creating seamless transitions between the two. Outdoor rooms, patio seating areas, and open-air kitchens are common features of modern garden designs, allowing homeowners to enjoy the benefits of outdoor living year-round.

3. Sustainable Practices: Sustainability and eco-friendliness are important considerations in modern garden design. Features such as native plantings, drought-tolerant landscaping, rainwater harvesting systems, and energy-efficient lighting are often incorporated into modern gardens to minimize environmental impact and conserve resources.

4. Innovative Materials and Technology: Modern gardens make use of innovative materials and technology to create functional and visually striking outdoor spaces. Materials such as corten steel, concrete, glass, and composite decking are commonly used for pathways, decking, and hardscape elements. Smart irrigation systems, outdoor lighting controls, and automated garden features may also be integrated into modern garden designs for added convenience and efficiency.

5. Emphasis on Outdoor Living and Entertaining: Modern gardens are designed for outdoor living and entertaining, with features such as fire pits, built-in seating, outdoor kitchens, and dining areas. These spaces are often arranged to facilitate socializing, relaxation, and recreation, allowing homeowners to fully enjoy their outdoor environment.

6. Plant Selection: In modern gardens, plant selection tends to be carefully curated to complement the overall design aesthetic. Architectural plants with bold forms, striking foliage, and interesting textures are favoured, while traditional cottage garden flowers may be less common. Grasses, succulents, ornamental trees, and low-maintenance perennials are popular choices for modern garden plantings.

Figure 36: Modern garden. CC0, via Rawpixel.

Modern gardens reflect a contemporary approach to outdoor design, embracing innovation, functionality, and sustainability while creating stylish and inviting outdoor spaces for relaxation, entertainment, and enjoyment.

Figure 37: Modern formal garden, Dallas, Texas. Jean Beaufort, CC0, via Wikimedia Commons.

Selecting a Garden Type

Landscapers play a pivotal role in helping clients select the most suitable garden type for their outdoor spaces. This process involves a comprehensive understanding of the client's preferences, needs, and the unique characteristics of their property. Here's a detailed overview of how landscapers can guide clients through selecting a garden type:

- **Initial Consultation and Assessment**: The process typically begins with an initial consultation between the landscaper and the client. During this meeting, the landscaper will gather information about the client's preferences, lifestyle, and vision for their outdoor space. They'll discuss the intended use of the garden, whether it's for relaxation, entertaining, gardening, or a combination of purposes. Additionally, the landscaper will assess the site conditions, including sunlight exposure, soil type, drainage, existing vegetation, and any architectural features that may influence the design.

- **Understanding Client Preferences**: Landscapers work closely with clients to understand their aesthetic preferences and desired garden style. Clients may express a preference for formal gardens with structured layouts and geometric patterns, informal cottage gardens with a relaxed, rustic charm, contemporary gardens with clean lines and minimalist design, or other styles such as tropical, desert, or Japanese-inspired gardens. By understanding the client's preferences, landscapers can tailor the design to reflect their individual taste and personality.

- **Site Analysis and Environmental Considerations**: Landscapers conduct a thorough site analysis to determine the environmental conditions and microclimates within the property. They consider factors such as sunlight exposure, wind patterns, temperature variations, soil pH, and moisture levels. This information helps landscapers select plants that are well-suited to the site conditions and ensure the long-term success of the garden. For example, a garden in a coastal area may require salt-tolerant plants, while a garden in a hot, arid climate may benefit from drought-resistant species.

- **Assessment of Maintenance Requirements**: Landscapers assess the client's preferences and lifestyle to determine the level of maintenance they're willing to commit to the garden. Some clients may prefer low-maintenance gardens that require minimal upkeep, while others may enjoy spending time tending to their plants and landscapes. Landscapers offer guidance on selecting plants and design elements that align with the client's maintenance preferences, ensuring that the garden remains beautiful and manageable over time.

- **Exploration of Garden Themes and Features**: Based on the client's preferences and site conditions, landscapers explore various garden themes, features, and design elements that can enhance the outdoor space. They may recommend incorporating elements such as water features, seating areas, pathways, lighting, and hardscape materials to create a cohesive and inviting garden design. Landscapers also consider the overall layout, flow, and focal points within the garden to optimize functionality and visual appeal.

- **Presentation of Design Concepts**: Once the initial assessment and exploration phase is complete, landscapers present design concepts and recommendations to the client. This may include conceptual drawings, mood boards, plant palettes, and 3D renderings to help the client visualize the proposed garden design. Landscapers explain the rationale behind their recommendations, highlighting how each element contributes to the overall vision and goals of the project.

- **Collaborative Refinement and Finalization**: The client and landscaper collaborate to refine the design concepts based on feedback and preferences. Landscapers make adjustments and modifications as needed to ensure that the final garden design meets the client's expectations and requirements. This collaborative process allows clients to actively participate in shaping their outdoor space and ensures that the garden reflects their personal style and vision.

- **Implementation and Installation**: Once the garden design is finalized, landscapers oversee the implementation and installation process. This may involve site preparation, soil amendment, plant selection and procurement, hardscape construction, and installation of irrigation systems and lighting. Landscapers coordinate with contractors, suppliers, and other professionals to ensure that the project is executed efficiently and according to the design specifications.

- **Post-Installation Care and Maintenance**: After the garden is installed, landscapers provide guidance on post-installation care and maintenance to help clients preserve the beauty and health of their outdoor space. This may include instructions on watering, fertilizing, pruning, and seasonal maintenance tasks. Landscapers may offer ongoing maintenance services or provide clients with a maintenance plan tailored to their specific needs and preferences.

Overall, landscapers play a crucial role in helping clients select the right garden type by assessing their preferences, understanding site conditions, exploring design options, and guiding them through the design and installation process. By collaborating closely with clients and drawing on their expertise in landscape design and horticulture, landscapers create beautiful and functional outdoor spaces that enhance the client's quality of life and connect them with nature.

Chapter Three
Landscape Design

When embarking on the journey of landscape design, it's crucial to consider a myriad of factors that will influence the outcome of your project. Whether you're aiming for a complete overhaul or just a few adjustments, having a well-thought-out plan in place is key to success. While it may be tempting to dive right into plant selection at the local nursery, taking the time to develop a plan beforehand will ensure that your choices align with your needs and thrive in your landscape. This proactive approach not only saves you time and resources but also sets the stage for creating a beautiful, cohesive, and flourishing outdoor environment.

Understanding your yard is paramount in the planning process. Consider factors such as your regional climate, topography, and soil type, all of which play a significant role in determining the suitability of plants for your landscape. By utilizing resources like the USDA Plant Hardiness Zone Map, in the USA, and recognizing the microclimates within your yard, such as full sun, partial shade, or deep shade areas, you can make informed decisions when selecting plants that will thrive in your specific environment. Additionally, paying attention to how water drains in your landscape will help inform the design to promote proper water movement away from your home and towards other areas of your yard.

Moreover, it's essential to consider who will be using your yard and how they will use it. Whether it's children playing, pets roaming, or outdoor entertaining, different users have different needs that should be addressed in the design. Creating distinct spaces for various activities using strategic plantings and hardscapes allows for versatility and functionality in your landscape. Furthermore, understanding your maintenance style and budget is crucial. Realistically assessing how much time and money you can dedicate to maintaining your landscape will help ensure its success and longevity.

Themes can also serve as guiding principles in landscape design, unifying your outdoor space and influencing plant and material selections. Whether you're drawn to geometric shapes, naturalistic elements, or specific colour palettes, a cohesive theme can create a unified and visually appealing landscape. Additionally, structuring your plantings and highlighting important points help to create visual interest and draw attention to key features within your landscape. Paying attention to details such as plant forms, colours, textures, and scents can further enhance the overall experience of your garden.

Looking towards the future is also important when planning your landscape. Consider how your plants will grow over time, their maintenance needs, and how they will interact with other elements in your landscape. By choosing resource-efficient plants and environmentally sound hardscapes, you can help protect and preserve your natural resources. Incorporating rainwater catchment systems and reusing construction materials are just a few examples of how you can minimize your environmental impact while creating a sustainable and beautiful landscape for years to come.

Basic Principles of Landscape Design

When crafting a landscape layout, it's essential to consider the six basic principles of garden design to achieve optimal results. These principles are divided into two categories: those that influence the overall feel of the landscape (proportion, transition, and unity) and those that control the movement of the viewer's eye (rhythm, balance, and focalization). Each principle is instrumental in creating a cohesive and visually appealing outdoor environment [55].

Proportion is the first principle to consider, focusing on ensuring that the size of individual components or groups of components in the landscape harmonize with the landscape as a whole. This means that elements such as plants or structures should be proportionate to the overall scale of the landscape to maintain visual balance and harmony.

Transition is closely related to proportion and involves creating gradual changes between different elements in the landscape. Abrupt transitions can disrupt the flow of the landscape design, while smooth transitions create a sense of continuity and cohesion. For example, tall trees can serve as a transitional element between a house and a stone wall, preventing a stark contrast in height that would disrupt the visual harmony.

Unity is achieved when all elements in the landscape complement each other and contribute to a cohesive overall design. This can be achieved through thoughtful placement of landscape plants that share similar forms or by repeating specific forms throughout the design. When viewers sense that every element in the landscape has been chosen with a unified theme in mind, unity is achieved.

Rhythm involves the patterned repetition of a motif, such as landscaping plants or hardscape elements. By creating repetitive patterns, such as planting the same type of shrub in a row or hedge, designers can guide the viewer's gaze in a specific direction and create a sense of order and flow in the landscape.

Balance refers to the visual weight and consistency of attractions in the yard. Achieving balance involves distributing elements evenly throughout the landscape and ensuring that no single feature dominates the space. For example, placing large trees on both sides of a house can help balance the visual weight of the yard.

Focalization is the final principle and involves directing the viewer's perspective to a specific focal point without causing visual jarring. This can be accomplished through balanced and consistent arrangements of elements that draw the viewer's eye naturally toward the focal point, creating a harmonious and visually engaging landscape design.

Figure 38: Landscaping is the art and practice of designing and arranging outdoor spaces to enhance their aesthetic appeal, functionality, and environmental sustainability. Peterclosek, CC BY 4.0, via Wikimedia Commons.

In landscape design, incorporating the five basic elements—colour, form, texture, line, and scale—is essential for creating visually appealing and harmonious outdoor spaces. Each element contributes to the overall aesthetic and functionality of the landscape, guiding the viewer's experience and enhancing the visual impact of the design [55].

Colour is often considered the most crucial element in landscape design, as it can greatly influence the mood and atmosphere of the outdoor space. By strategically combining flowers and foliage of warm and cool colours, designers can create contrast or opt for a unified look. Utilizing a colour wheel helps in determining complementary or harmonious colour schemes that enhance the overall appeal of the landscape.

Form refers to the shape and structure of plants, including their branching patterns and overall silhouette. Trees, for example, come in various shapes, from columnar to globular, and their forms can be further manipulated through pruning. Considering the form of individual plant components, such as leaf shapes, ensures a diverse and visually interesting landscape.

Texture primarily pertains to the visual quality of plant surfaces and foliage. Leaf size and surface characteristics determine a plant's texture, with some plants having coarse textures while others are more delicate. Incorporating plants with varying textures adds depth and dimension to the landscape, preventing monotony and enhancing visual interest.

Line in landscape design refers to the arrangement of borders and plant groupings to direct the viewer's eye movement. Whether it's horizontal or vertical, the flow of lines created by plantings influences how viewers perceive and navigate the space.

Straight rows of trees, for instance, can delineate boundaries and guide the viewer's gaze, creating structure and visual rhythm within the landscape.

Scale is the size relationship between landscape components, ensuring that elements harmonize with their surroundings. Shrubs, trees, and other features should be scaled appropriately to the overall size of the landscape and architectural elements. Maintaining proper scale prevents elements from appearing disproportionate or out of place, contributing to a cohesive and well-balanced design.

Line

In landscape design, line is a fundamental element that is defined by the boundary between two different materials, the contour or shape of an object, or a prolonged linear feature [56]. These lines serve as a potent tool for designers, enabling them to generate a myriad of shapes and structures while guiding the movement of both the observer's eye and body within the landscape. Landscape designers strategically employ lines to establish patterns, delineate spaces, sculpt forms, regulate movement, assert dominance, and foster a unified theme throughout the landscape. These lines manifest in various ways, such as the juncture of disparate materials on the ground plane, the silhouette of an object against its backdrop, or the linear arrangement of materials like fences or walls.

Distinct characteristics of lines influence how individuals perceive and interact with the landscape on both emotional and physical levels. Straight lines, for instance, exude a sense of rigidity and authority, evoking a formal ambiance typically associated with symmetrical designs and leading the observer's gaze directly to a focal point. Diagonal lines, a subset of straight lines, impart intentional directionality to the composition. Conversely, curved lines imbue a sense of informality and naturalness, invoking a relaxed atmosphere reminiscent of asymmetrical balance found in natural settings. They guide the eye at a leisurely pace and introduce an element of intrigue by concealing views beyond their gentle curves.

Vertical lines, by elevating the observer's perspective, create an illusion of spaciousness within a confined area, emphasizing features and infusing the space with a dynamic sense of energy or motion. These lines are exemplified by towering plant material such as trees or tall structures like arbours or poles. On the other hand, horizontal lines traverse the ground plane, imparting a sense of expansiveness and tranquillity. Low horizontal lines, in particular, evoke feelings of calmness and repose, serving to either segment a space or unify its disparate elements. They are commonly formed by low garden walls, pathways, or short hedges [56].

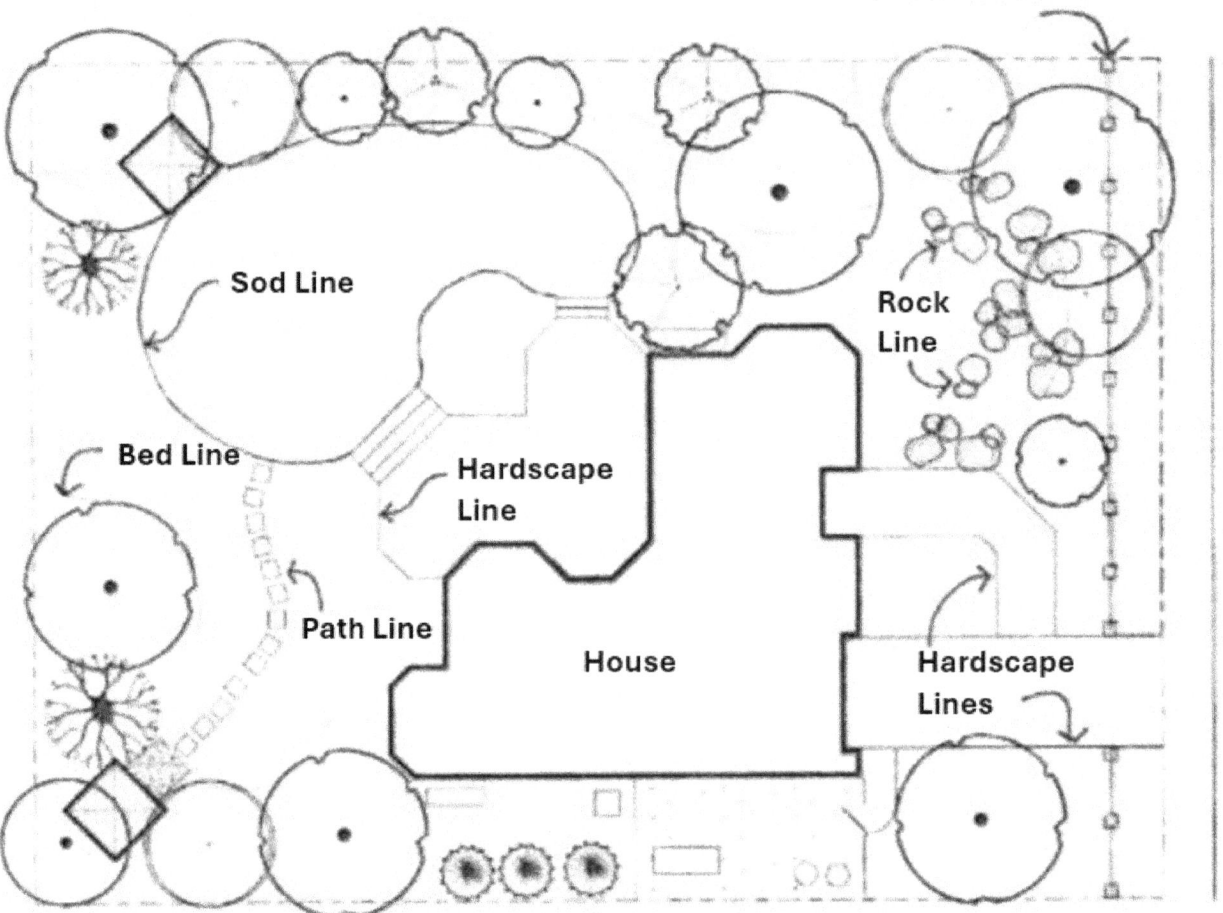

Figure 39: Lines in landscape design [56].

Lines play a crucial role in delineating forms within the landscape, both on paper and in reality. In plan view, lines demarcate the boundaries of plant beds and hardscape areas, facilitating the organization of space and guiding the placement of elements. Vertical forms of built features and plant material contribute to the creation of lines, further defining the contours of the landscape. Three primary line types—bedlines, hardscape lines, and plant lines—work in concert to shape the overall form and structure of the landscape. Bedlines, for instance, connect plant beds to surrounding surfaces, seamlessly integrating greenery with built elements. Hardscape lines delineate the edges of constructed elements, while long, narrow materials like fences or walls serve as linear features that define space and create visual interest [56].

Form

Shape in landscape design refers to the delineation of space through an outline, while form encompasses the three-dimensional bulk of that shape. Both elements are integral to both hardscape structures and plantings, significantly influencing the visual appeal and spatial organization of the garden. Indeed, the form often dictates the overall style of the garden and plays a pivotal role in establishing its character and ambiance. Whether manifested in the structural layout, plant beds, or decorative embellishments, the form theme of the garden is invariably shaped by the form of its constituent elements [56].

Formal garden designs often embrace geometric shapes such as circles, squares, and polygons, imparting a sense of order and symmetry to the landscape. Circles, whether complete or fragmented into segments, are particularly compelling as they naturally draw the eye towards the centre, thus serving as focal points or facilitating visual connections between different garden elements. Squares, with their clean lines and right angles, are frequently employed for various features like stepping stones, paving materials, and structural elements owing to their ease of construction and versatility. Meanwhile, polygons, characterized by their multiple straight sides, offer opportunities for creating intricate shapes and patterns, though their complexity necessitates careful integration into the overall design.

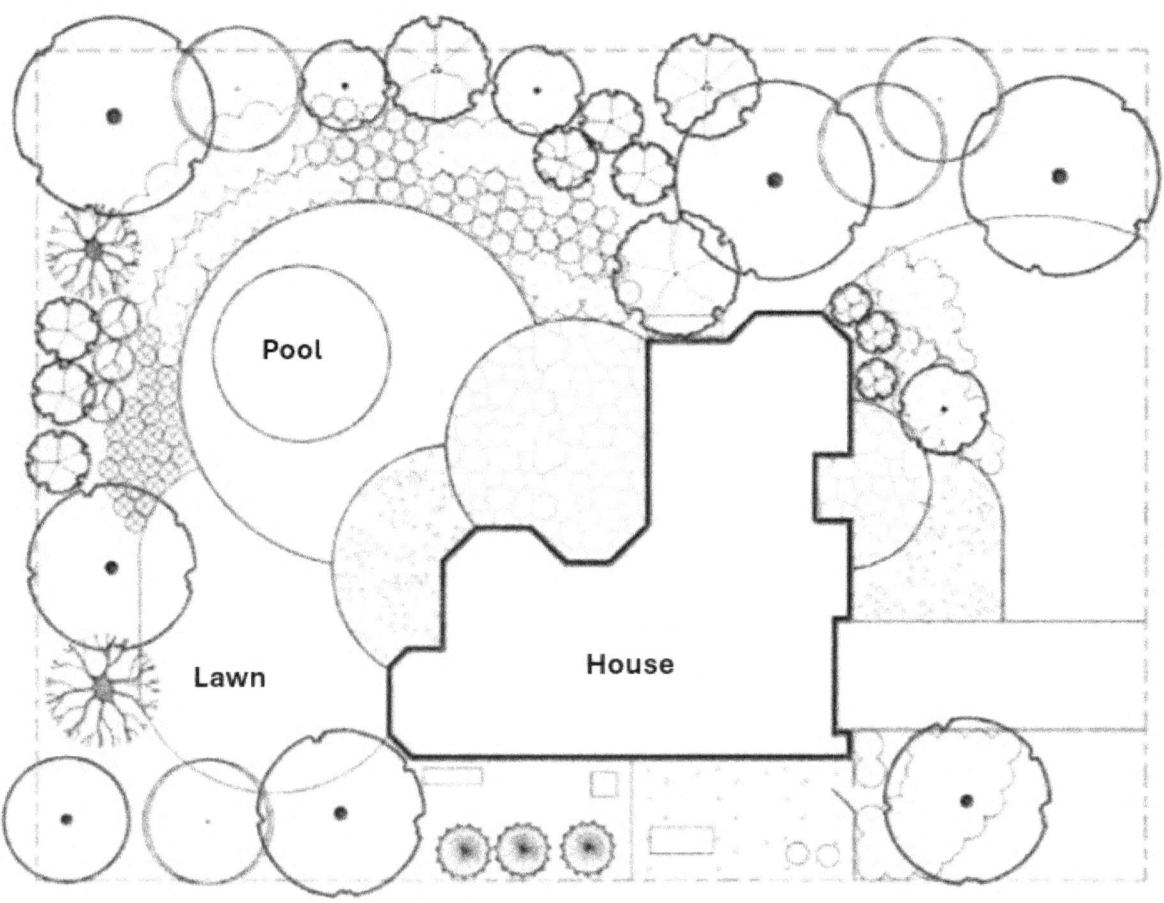

Figure 40: Circular forms in hardscape and lawn panels [56].

Conversely, informal garden styles gravitate towards naturalistic forms that mimic the organic contours found in nature. Meandering lines, reminiscent of winding rivers or streams, impart a sense of fluidity and movement to pathways and garden borders, enticing exploration and discovery. Organic edges, mirroring the irregular shapes of foliage and rocks, add an element of rugged charm to garden features like rockeries and dry creek beds, infusing the landscape with a touch of wild beauty.

Fragmented edges, resembling scattered stones or pavers, contribute to the gradual blending of hardscape elements with the surrounding environment, fostering a seamless transition between built and natural elements.

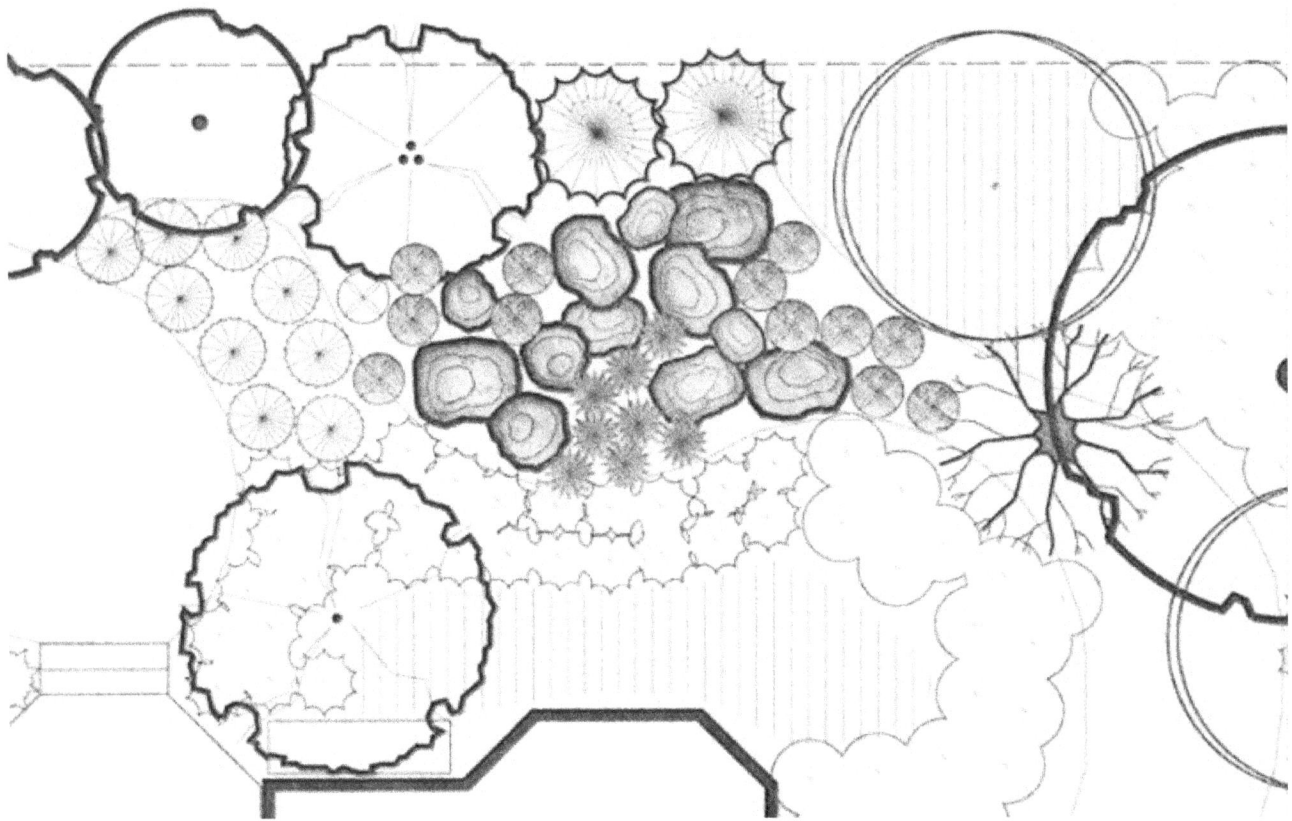

Figure 41: Organic edges: irregular edge of rock garden [56].

The forms of plants are equally significant in shaping the overall composition of the garden. Plants not only possess distinct forms themselves but also influence the creation of voids or negative spaces between them. Tree forms, ranging from round and columnar to oval and weeping, are selected based on both aesthetic appeal and functional requirements, whether to provide shade, serve as a screen, or serve as a focal point.

LANDSCAPE DESIGN AND CONSTRUCTION

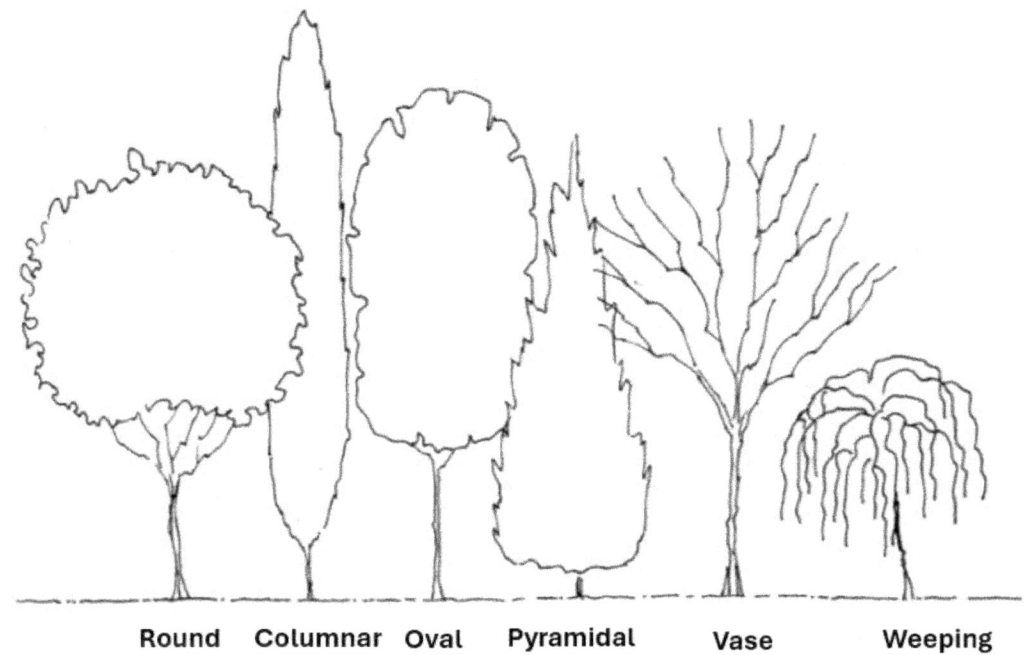

Figure 42: Tree forms [56].

Shrub forms, encompassing upright, spreading, cascading, and irregular shapes, are chosen based on their intended use as mass plantings or specimen specimens. Similarly, groundcover forms, including matting, spreading, clumping, and short spikes, are typically employed en masse to create visually cohesive ground covers.

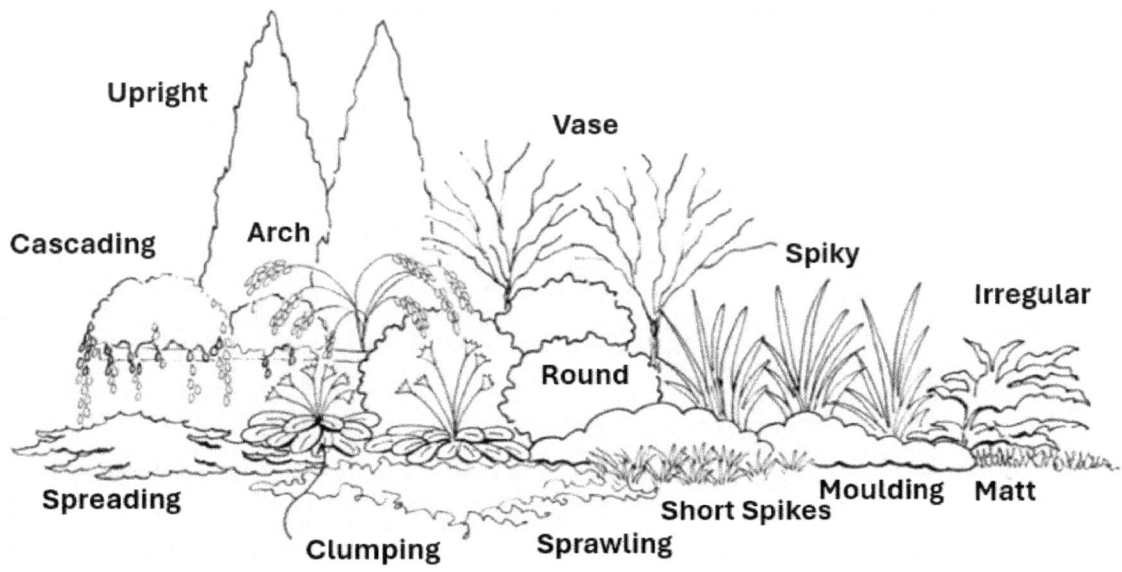

Figure 43: Shrub and groundcover forms [56].

The properties of form extend beyond mere aesthetics, as they play a crucial role in organizing space and establishing unity within the landscape. Form recognition is deeply ingrained in human perception, allowing individuals to identify features based solely on their outline or silhouette. This familiarity enables the eye to perceive a form even when only a portion of it is visible, thereby facilitating the creation of patterns—a fundamental organizational structure in landscape design. Moreover, form serves as a primary determinant of garden style, with geometric forms evoking a formal ambiance characteristic of established garden styles, while organic forms impart a more relaxed, naturalistic vibe. Ultimately, achieving harmony and coherence in garden design necessitates careful consideration of form compatibility, ensuring that all elements contribute to a unified and visually pleasing composition.

Texture

Texture in landscape design encompasses both tactile and visual aspects, referring to the perceived coarseness or fineness of the surface of plants or hardscape materials. It serves as a crucial tool for introducing variety, interest, and contrast into the garden, enriching the sensory experience and contributing to the overall aesthetic appeal. Texture is evident in various elements of the landscape, including the foliage, flowers, bark, and branching patterns of plants, as well as the surface characteristics of hardscape features such as buildings, patios, walls, and walkways.

The texture of a plant is largely determined by the size and shape of its leaves, with coarse, medium, and fine textures being the primary classifications. Coarse-textured plants are characterized by large leaves, irregular edges, deep veins, and bold forms, which impart a dominant presence in the landscape and attract attention through their stark light and shadow contrasts. Examples of coarse-textured plants include philodendrons, agaves, hollies, and hydrangeas, while rough-cut stone and unfinished wood with raised grain exemplify coarse-textured hardscape materials.

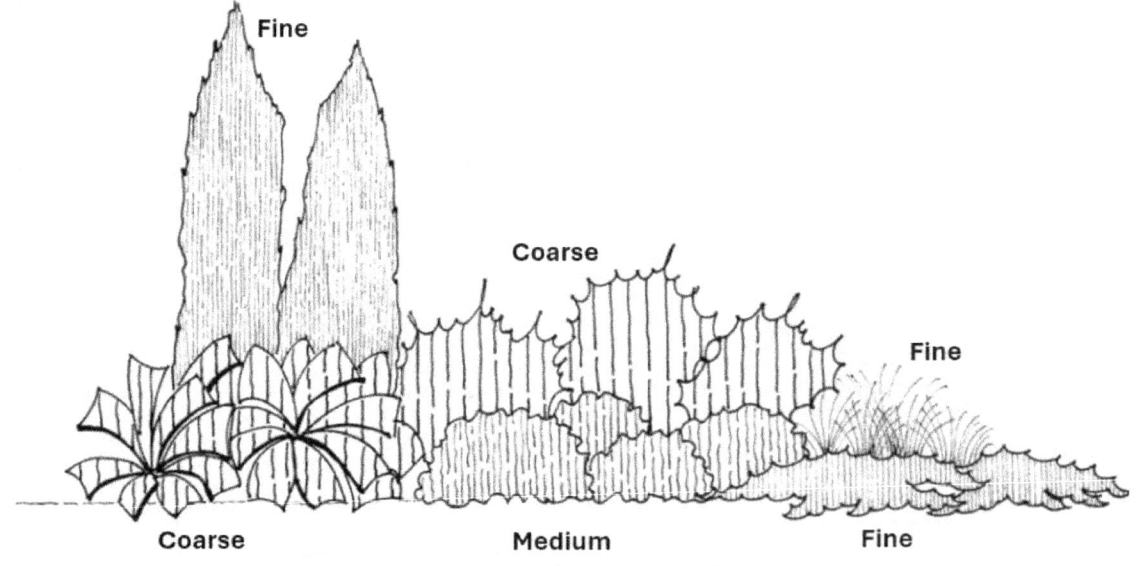

Figure 44: Plant texture [56].

In contrast, fine-textured plants exhibit small foliage, delicate stems, and intricate branching patterns, creating a sense of lightness and airiness in the garden. They are often described as wispy or delicate and are effective at softening harsh lines and adding a sense of depth to the landscape. Grasses, ferns, Japanese maples, and many vines exemplify fine-textured plants, while smooth stone and glass ornaments represent fine-textured hardscape materials.

Medium-textured plants, which constitute the majority, strike a balance between coarse and fine textures, featuring medium-sized leaves and branches with simple shapes and smooth edges. They serve as a backdrop to unify the overall composition, linking the more dominant coarse-textured elements with the finer textures. Examples of medium-textured plants include agapanthus, camellia, pittosporum, and viburnum, while standard flagstone pavers and broom-brushed concrete represent medium-textured hardscape materials.

The properties of texture extend beyond visual aesthetics, influencing the perception of distance and scale within the landscape. To create a sense of expansiveness, designers strategically arrange plants so that fine textures are positioned along the outer perimeter, while coarse textures are placed closer to the viewer, effectively exaggerating the depth of the space. Conversely, to create a more intimate setting, coarse textures are deployed along the outer edges, with fine textures arranged in proximity to the viewer, thereby minimizing perceived distance and enclosing the space.

Furthermore, the perceived texture of plants can vary depending on viewing distance and colour intensity. Plants that appear coarse up close may appear fine textured from a distance, while bold colours enhance texture contrast, making it appear coarser, whereas muted colours have a flattening effect. Designers often utilize texture studies on paper to inform plant arrangement decisions, employing different line weights and spacing to represent fine, medium, and coarse textures and ensuring visual harmony and cohesion within the landscape composition.

Colour

Colour plays a pivotal role in landscape design, injecting interest, vibrancy, and visual appeal into the outdoor space. It is perhaps the most striking element in the landscape, often capturing the attention of homeowners and visitors alike. However, it's important to note that colour is also transient, with its impact typically lasting only for brief periods throughout the year, especially in the case of flowering plants. To effectively harness the power of colour in landscaping, designers often rely on colour theory, which utilizes the colour wheel to create harmonious and visually pleasing colour schemes [56].

The colour wheel comprises three primary colours—red, blue, and yellow—along with their corresponding secondary and tertiary colours. Secondary colours are formed by mixing two primary colours, while tertiary colours result from combining a primary and secondary colour adjacent to each other on the wheel. By understanding the relationships between colours, designers can strategically employ various colour schemes to achieve specific aesthetic effects in the landscape.

One such scheme is the monochromatic scheme, which involves using variations of a single colour, besides green, which dominates the foliage. This approach relies on subtle light and dark variations within the chosen colour to add depth and interest to the garden. For instance, a white garden featuring white flowers, variegated foliage, and garden ornaments exemplifies a monochromatic scheme [56].

Analogous schemes, also known as harmonious schemes, consist of three to five colours that are adjacent to each other on the colour wheel. These colours share common properties, typically including two primary colours mixed to form a secondary colour, as well as two tertiary colours. Analogous schemes create a sense of cohesion and unity in the landscape, fostering a harmonious visual experience.

In contrast, complementary schemes utilize colours that are opposite each other on the colour wheel, resulting in high-contrast pairings. Examples of complementary colours include violet and yellow, red and green, and blue and orange. These schemes often evoke a dynamic and visually striking effect, with complementary colours frequently occurring in natural elements such as flowers.

Colour is not limited to plant material but also extends to hardscape features such as buildings, rocks, pavers, and furniture. While green foliage remains the dominant colour in the landscape, other colours, particularly those with high contrast to green, capture attention more readily. Bright colours are often found in man-made materials such as painted furniture, ceramic containers, and glass ornaments, while natural materials like stone and wood tend to exhibit muted, earthy tones.

Beyond aesthetics, colour influences emotions, spatial perception, and visual balance in the landscape. Warm colours like red and orange exude energy and excitement, while cool colours such as blue and green evoke a sense of calm and tranquillity. Moreover, colour intensity and saturation can vary depending on factors like light quality and time of day, with brighter, more intense colours appearing more saturated in direct sunlight.

When selecting a colour scheme, designers consider factors like the intended use of the space, seasonal variations, and the interplay of light and shadow. Because colour is ephemeral, it should complement more enduring elements like texture and form, which provide structure and visual interest year-round. Designers often develop colour studies on plans to visualize proposed colour schemes and ensure their coherence and effectiveness in enhancing the overall landscape composition [56].

Visual Weight

Visual weight is a fundamental concept in landscape design that pertains to the perceived importance or prominence of various elements within a composition. It revolves around the idea that certain features carry more significance based on their mass and level of contrast, thereby drawing greater attention from observers. Conversely, other elements may possess less visual weight and recede into the background, serving to create balance and cohesion in the overall design [56].

The notion of visual weight does not imply that background features are inconsequential; on the contrary, they play a crucial role in establishing visual continuity and unity within the composition. By linking together elements of high visual weight, background features contribute to a harmonious aesthetic and provide a sense of visual respite for the eye. In essence, they serve as the backdrop against which more prominent elements stand out.

Compositions where every feature possesses high visual weight can appear cluttered and chaotic, as the eye is constantly drawn to competing focal points. Therefore, achieving a balanced distribution of visual weight is essential for creating visually pleasing landscapes. Elements that typically contribute to high visual weight include plants with upright or unusual forms, large size, bright colours, bold texture, and diagonal lines. These characteristics command attention and dominate the visual field.

Conversely, elements with low visual weight tend to blend into the background and are perceived as less prominent. They are characterized by low horizontal lines, prostrate or low-growing forms, fine texture, and subdued or dull colours. While they may not immediately capture the viewer's attention, these elements play a vital role in providing visual relief and establishing a sense of depth and dimensionality within the composition [56].

By strategically balancing elements of high and low visual weight, landscape designers can create compositions that are visually engaging, harmonious, and well-integrated. This involves careful consideration of the characteristics and placement of each element to ensure a pleasing hierarchy of visual importance throughout the landscape. Ultimately, an understanding of visual weight allows designers to orchestrate compositions that captivate the viewer's gaze while maintaining a sense of balance and cohesion.

Proportion

Psychological comfort in a landscape is often attained through order and repetition. Humans tend to feel more at ease in environments that exhibit a sense of organization and predictability [56]. Landscapes characterized by orderly patterns and repetitive elements are easier to comprehend and navigate, instilling a sense of calmness and security in users. Furthermore, a harmonious and unified landscape design can evoke a sense of pleasure and satisfaction, further enhancing psychological comfort.

Physical comfort, on the other hand, is influenced by proportions that are compatible with human scale. Proportion refers to the relative size of objects in relation to one another and can be assessed in terms of both absolute and relative scales. Absolute proportion considers the scale or size of individual objects, while relative proportion assesses the size of objects in relation to human dimensions. In landscape design, it is essential to consider the proportions of plant material, garden structures, and hardscape features relative to human scale to ensure usability and comfort.

In plants, proportion can be achieved by selecting plant sizes that harmonize with human proportions and the surrounding environment. A balanced composition can be achieved when plants, the surrounding landscape, and built structures are proportionally aligned. Similarly, hardscape features such as benches, pathways, and arbours should be designed with human comfort in mind, ensuring ease of use and functionality [56].

Additionally, the spatial layout and organization of design elements contribute to the overall order and balance of a landscape. Order is often achieved through balance, which can be symmetrical, asymmetrical, or perspective-based. Symmetrical balance involves the placement of identical objects on either side of a central axis and is commonly associated with formal designs. Asymmetrical balance, on the other hand, relies on the equal distribution of visual weight without mirroring forms. Perspective balance considers the relative visual weight of objects in the foreground, midground, and background to create a harmonious composition.

Mass collection, another aspect of order, involves grouping similar features together and arranging them around a central focal point or space. By clustering elements based on similarities, such as plant types or architectural features, designers can create visually cohesive and organized landscapes that promote both physical and psychological comfort for users [56].

Repetition

Repetition in landscape design involves the deliberate reuse of elements or features to establish patterns or sequences within the outdoor environment. By repeating lines, forms, colours, and textures, designers create a sense of rhythm that enhances the visual coherence of the landscape. However, the judicious application of repetition is essential, as excessive repetition can lead to monotony, while insufficient repetition may result in visual clutter and confusion [56].

At its simplest, repetition entails the consistent use of identical objects arranged in a line or pattern. For instance, a row of evenly spaced trees or a series of identical paving stones exemplifies straightforward repetition. Yet, repetition can be rendered more dynamic by incorporating alternation. Alternation introduces minor variations within the sequence, injecting subtle visual interest. For example, a sequence of square forms may include occasional circular elements, breaking the uniformity while maintaining an organized pattern. Inversion, another form of alternation, involves altering selected elements to possess characteristics opposite those of the original elements. This technique adds complexity and intrigue to the repetitive scheme. For instance, a row of vase-shaped plants interspersed with pyramidal plants creates an ordered yet visually engaging sequence.

Moreover, repetition can be enriched through gradation, which entails a gradual change in certain attributes of a feature. By varying characteristics such as size or colour along a repeated sequence, designers introduce a sense of progression and dynamism. For instance, a row of square forms may gradually transition from small to large, or from one colour hue to another, creating a visually compelling gradient effect.

It's important to note that repetition doesn't always manifest as a discernible pattern; sometimes, it simply involves the consistent use of the same colour, texture, or form throughout the landscape [56]. This repetition contributes to visual unity and cohesion across the outdoor space.

In the realm of plants and hardscape, repetition plays a significant role in shaping the overall design. Repeated use of the same plant species throughout a landscape exemplifies simple repetition, establishing visual continuity and coherence. For instance, a garden predominantly featuring various types of grasses showcases subtle yet effective plant repetition. Gradation can be achieved by introducing gradual changes in plant height, size, or texture, creating nuanced transitions within the landscape [56].

Similarly, hardscape materials can be repetitively deployed to foster unity and coherence. By employing consistent materials such as stone or wood throughout the yard, designers establish a sense of continuity and cohesion. However, subtle variations in size, texture, or colour within the repeated hardscape elements can add visual interest and depth to the design. Repetition and pattern are particularly evident in hardscape elements, as manufactured materials allow for precise duplication and consistent patterning, enhancing the overall aesthetic appeal of the landscape.

Unity

Unity in landscape design is the culmination of efforts to harmoniously link various elements and features, resulting in a cohesive and consistent composition. Often synonymous with harmony, unity embodies the notion that every aspect of the landscape fits together seamlessly, creating a sense of visual coherence and completeness. In contrast, landscapes characterized by disjointed arrangements of plants and unrelated ornaments lack unity and appear chaotic. Achieving unity involves leveraging principles such as dominance, interconnection, unity of three, and simplicity to organize colours, textures, and forms [56].

Dominance, or emphasis, plays a crucial role in establishing unity by directing attention to specific elements within the landscape. Focal points, characterized by their ability to captivate and hold attention, serve as prominent features that guide the viewer's gaze and movement throughout the space. These focal points are often created through deliberate contrasts in size, colour, form, or texture. Specimen plants, distinguished by their unique attributes, serve as effective focal points, drawing attention to key areas such as entrances or pathways. Similarly, garden ornaments with distinct forms and colours provide visual contrast against the surrounding foliage, enhancing the overall sense of emphasis and unity.

Interconnection underscores the physical linkage between various features within the landscape. By ensuring that elements touch or visually interact with one another in a seamless manner, designers create a cohesive and integrated environment. Hardscape elements, such as pathways or built structures, play a pivotal role in facilitating interconnection by organizing spatial arrangements and delineating boundaries. Continuation of lines, whether in the form of pathways or defined edges of plant beds, further reinforces unity by establishing visual connections between disparate elements [56].

The principle of unity of three emphasizes the effectiveness of grouping features in threes or other odd-numbered configurations. Such groupings foster a sense of balance and harmony, as odd numbers allow for staggered variations in height and size, adding visual interest to the composition. Odd-numbered groupings are perceived as cohesive wholes, offering a more unified aesthetic compared to even-numbered arrangements, which can appear visually divided or disjointed.

Simplicity, as a guiding principle, advocates for the reduction or elimination of nonessential elements to maintain clarity and purpose in the design. Designers often achieve simplicity by judiciously removing superfluous features while preserving the overall integrity of the composition. By prioritizing essential elements and decluttering the landscape, simplicity promotes a cohesive and uncluttered aesthetic, reinforcing the overarching sense of unity and harmony [56].

Applying the Principles of Design

To effectively apply the principles of landscape design, one must adopt a multidisciplinary approach that integrates various aspects such as aesthetics, ecology, functionality, and cultural elements. Landscape design aims to create environments that are visually appealing, ecologically sustainable, and practical for human use [57]. Modern landscape design methods have evolved to encompass concepts like landscape architecture, space design, cultural elements, and ecological considerations [58]. These methods emphasize creating landscapes that harmonize with nature, provide recreational opportunities, and support sustainable development [59].

One crucial aspect of landscape design is the integration of ecological principles. Designing multifunctional landscapes involves understanding the site, analysing its structure and function, planning with an ecosystem approach, highlighting ecological functions, and monitoring these functions over time [60]. Sustainable landscape design further emphasizes the importance of creating designs that minimize damage, restore landscapes, and meet community needs while following natural ecological principles [61]. Additionally, incorporating traditional culture into landscape design can lead to diversified and culturally rich landscapes that resonate with local communities [62].

Moreover, landscape design should consider climate impacts to ensure that the design responds appropriately to different climatic conditions [63]. By applying engineering principles to landscaping, such as in the design of constructed wetlands, landscapes can not only be aesthetically pleasing but also contribute to environmental and economic benefits [64]. Furthermore, the use of technology, such as virtual reality and digital media, can enhance the intelligence and beauty of landscape designs [13].

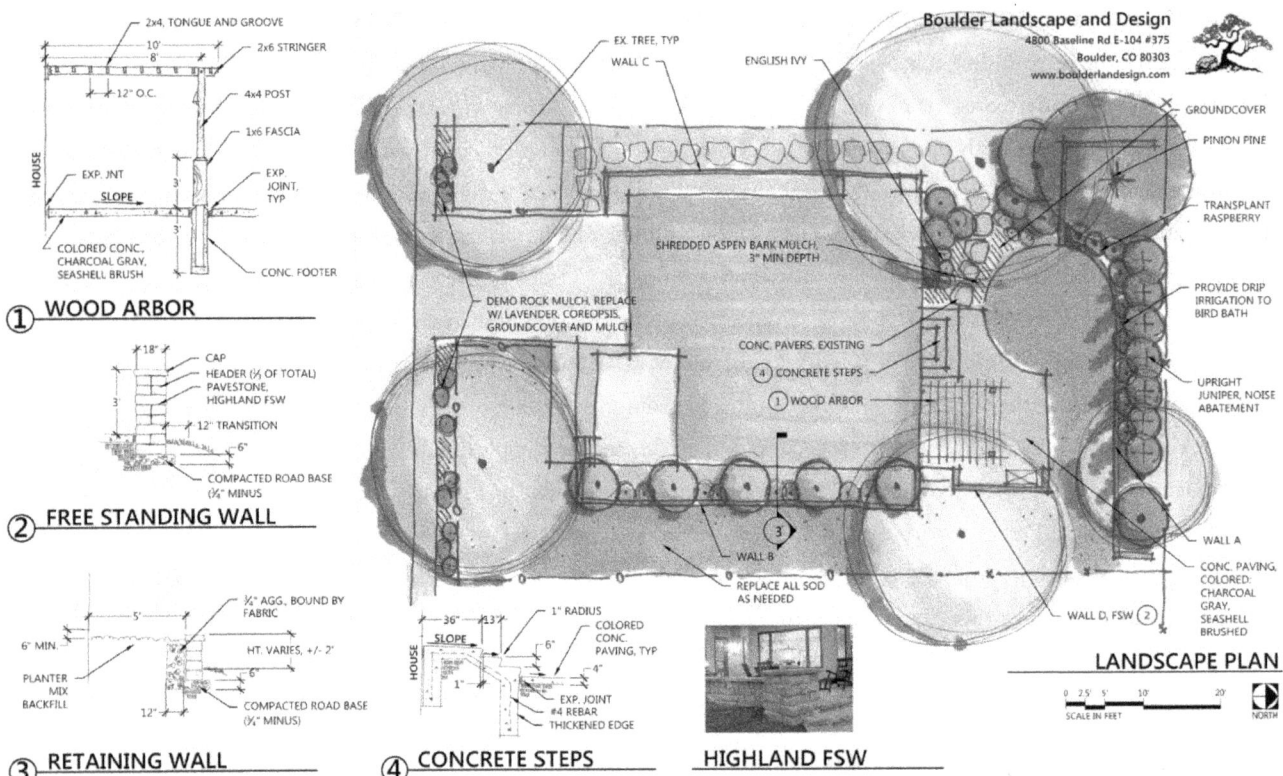

Figure 45: Applying design principles. Girolimon Residence- Landscape Plan providing a graphic representation of the proposed improvements at the residence. Work included retaining walls, coloured concrete patio, low-voltage lighting, planting, cedar pergola and pondless water feature. Jay@MorphoLA, CC BY 2.0, via Flickr.

When designing a landscape for a client, a landscape designer can apply the principles and elements of design in the following ways:

- **Studying Existing Designs:**

    ○ Examine landscapes that appeal to the client and analyse how design elements have been applied.

    ○ Look for features such as colour, texture, form, line, balance, rhythm, dominance, and unity in existing landscapes.

    ○ Observe local landscapes to understand the prevailing style and social context, which will inform the design choices for the client's property.

- **Personal Style and Sense of Place:**

    ○ Identify the client's personal style by discussing landscapes that evoke positive emotions and resonate with them emotionally.

    ○ Consider the regional context and how the surrounding landscapes influence design choices to ensure the design fits the client's sense of place.

- Visit local botanical gardens, demonstration gardens, and nurseries to gather inspiration and select plants that are well-suited to the local climate and ecosystem.

- **Drawing Inspiration:**

  - Look for inspiration in magazines, books, and online resources, adapting elements that resonate with the client's preferences and the site's unique characteristics.

  - Consider practical factors such as maintenance requirements, sunlight exposure, soil type, and available space when selecting plants and hardscape materials.

- **Assessing Site Conditions:**

  - Carefully assess the site conditions, including the architectural style of the client's house, lot size and shape, and existing features such as trees, slopes, and structures.

  - Determine how the proposed design will complement the architectural style of the client's home and enhance the overall aesthetic of the property.

  - Pay attention to the shape of spaces between the house and property lines, as these areas will influence the layout and form of design features.

- **Site Inventory and Analysis:**

  - Conduct a thorough site inventory and analysis to identify opportunities and constraints, considering factors such as topography, drainage patterns, existing vegetation, and utility lines.

  - View each site condition as an opportunity to enhance the design creatively, addressing constraints in ways that add value to the overall landscape.

  - Consider how each element of the design can integrate harmoniously with the site's natural features and enhance the overall quality of the outdoor living space.

By carefully considering these factors and applying the principles of design, a landscape designer can create a tailored landscape that reflects the client's personal style, integrates seamlessly with the surrounding environment, and enhances the overall beauty and functionality of the property.

In designing a landscape for a client, a landscape designer employs a set of design principles to strategically locate features and define outdoor rooms. First, they consider various factors such as the architectural style of the house, the layout of yard spaces, and site opportunities to determine logical locations for features. This involves placing heavily used elements like outdoor dining or seating areas near backdoor entrances for convenience and comfort, while discretely positioning others like dog runs and vegetable gardens on the side of the house to maintain aesthetics and privacy. Similarly, play or recreation areas are often situated within view of kitchen or family rooms to allow for easy supervision.

The concept of creating outdoor rooms is integral to landscape design, involving the spatial division of the yard into distinct functional areas. These areas are delineated using different materials, changes in elevation, distinct forms, or features like low garden walls or small trees to create implied boundaries. By employing elements and principles of design, such as colour, texture, and form, designers define these spaces, add visual interest, and ensure a cohesive overall landscape design.

Differentiating spaces within the landscape is crucial for creating visual interest and hierarchy. Designers utilize colour, texture, and scale to make each area unique and distinct, while also establishing a hierarchy of spaces based on their importance. Attention is drawn to key features through the use of high visual weight, ensuring that each space has the necessary square footage to fulfill its intended function.

Connecting spaces within the landscape is achieved through various techniques, including the use of lines such as pathways, or focal points that guide the viewer's gaze. Repetition of elements creates visual continuity throughout the landscape, while careful consideration of the direction of physical movement ensures efficient circulation within the space.

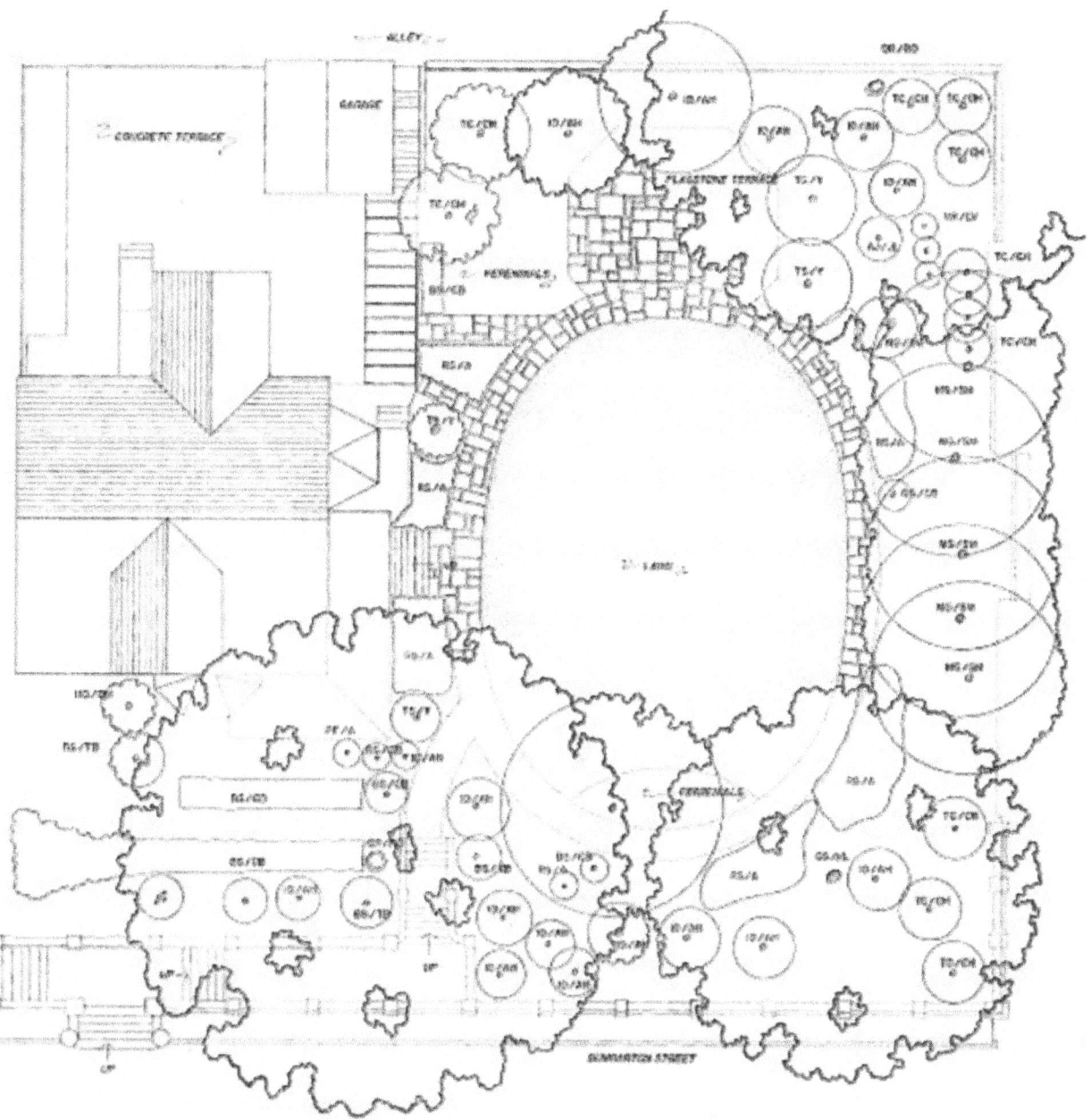

Figure 46: Combining the principles of design to develop a landscape Plan. Historic American Buildings Survey, CC0, via LOC's Public Domain Archive.

Ultimately, the goal of the landscape designer is to achieve unity and functionality across the entire landscape. By employing all elements and principles of design, they ensure that each feature and outdoor room contributes to a harmonious and usable outdoor living space that meets the client's needs and enhances the aesthetic appeal of the property.

Before embarking on any landscape project, it's crucial to thoroughly assess and understand what you have to work with. This includes identifying aspects of your landscape that are either permanent fixtures or elements you don't intend to change, such as driveways or large trees. Additionally, it's essential to keep budget constraints in mind throughout the planning process [65].

Start by taking a notebook and objectively evaluating your space by walking around the perimeter of your property, as if you were a stranger. This site analysis serves as your roadmap for change.

Identify the assets of your property by making lists for both the house and the yard. Look beyond overgrown shrubs or vines to uncover hidden treasures, such as attractive stairs, brick patios, or lovely views. Focus on details like steps, paving patterns, views, and door locations. Similarly, recognize any liabilities in your yard, such as unattractive neighbouring properties or under-landscaped areas around appealing house features.

Understanding your environment is crucial. Note the topography, including slopes, sunlight exposure, and shade patterns. Consider how these factors impact the usability and comfort of different areas throughout the year. For example, southern or southeastern-facing areas may provide warmth in winter but be too hot in summer.

Once you have a clear understanding of your space, you can decide what features to add. Consider steps, paths, structures like pergolas or arbours, walls, decks, patios, and various other elements like lighting, ponds, or play areas.

Creating a comprehensive map of your property is a fundamental step in landscape planning. Start by drawing a bird's-eye view to scale on graph paper. Begin with the largest items on your property, such as the house, and then fill in the surrounding features. It's important to include various elements in your map [65]:

- **The House**: This serves as a focal point and often dictates the layout and design of the landscape.

- **Exposure**: Note which direction the house faces (north, south, east, or west) as this will impact sunlight exposure and planting choices.

- **Boundaries**: Clearly mark the boundaries of your property, and make note of your neighbours' landscape styles to ensure harmony.

- **Outdoor Spaces**: Include existing outdoor areas like decks, patios, or seating areas.

- **Features**: Identify any existing or planned features such as pergolas, fire pits, or water features.

- **Existing Plants**: Mark the locations of any trees, shrubs, or other plants that you want to keep or remove.

- **Utilities**: Note the locations of dryer vents, air conditioning units, heat pumps, or any other utility features that may impact design decisions.

- **Service Areas**: Identify spaces dedicated to practical purposes, such as dog kennels, storage buildings, or trash cans.

- **Views**: Determine which views you want to preserve or enhance and which you may want to hide or screen.

- **Privacy Issues**: Take into account any privacy concerns, such as neighbouring properties or street visibility.

- **Downspouts and Drains**: Mark the locations of downspouts and drainage systems to ensure proper water management.

- **Grades, Slopes, and Drainage**: Note any changes in elevation, slopes, or areas prone to drainage issues.

- **Existing Irrigation Systems**: If you have an irrigation system in place, mark its components on the map.

By mapping out these elements, you gain a comprehensive understanding of your property's layout and features. This information serves as a valuable foundation for developing a cohesive and functional landscape design that aligns with your vision and practical considerations.

Create a base map for your landscape planning by adding sketches to your notes. Include existing features that won't change, such as property lines, trees, walkways, and patios. Label the locations of doors, windows, utilities, and other services. This visual representation helps you explore possibilities and avoid costly mistakes.

Finalize your landscape planning design concept by drawing bubble diagrams on your base map to represent how you intend to use different parts of your yard. These bubbles should include ideas for screening, pathways, flowerbeds, seating areas, and plantings. Don't worry about cost at this stage; focus on brainstorming and refining your vision.

Once you've placed your bubbles, create a clean, final drawing that incorporates all your decisions. This design concept will guide each phase of your landscape planning projects, ensuring cohesion and well-thought-out results. Refer to it regularly to stay on track and achieve your landscaping goals.

Keep in mind that when planning your landscape, it's essential to have a clear vision of what you want and need from your outdoor space. This involves considering your priorities, lifestyle, and future plans to create a cohesive and functional design. Here's a breakdown of the points to consider [65]:

- **Style and Inspiration**:

  - Just as you have a decorating style for your home, use a consistent style outdoors to maintain cohesiveness.

  - Take inspiration from the exterior of your house. Match landscaping choices to complement the architectural style of your home.

  - Consider the neighbourhood's aesthetic to ensure your landscape fits in with the surrounding homes.

- **Theme and Personality**:

  - Determine if you want your landscape to have a theme or reflect your personality, whether formal or informal, public or private.

  - Consider the needs of individuals in your household, such as special access requirements for easier mobility.

- **View and Maintenance**:

  - Evaluate the view from inside your house to ensure your landscape enhances indoor-outdoor connectivity.

  - Determine the level of maintenance you're willing to commit to and choose plants and features accordingly.

- **Design Process**:

  - Use tracing paper to sketch your ideas over the property map to visualize how the landscape will look.

- Involve the whole family in the design process to gather diverse perspectives and ideas.

Once you have a plan in place, consider the following elements to bring your landscape design to life:

- **Plants**:
  - Decide on the shape of planting beds, opting for clean lines or natural curves.
  - Choose plant colours and textures that complement each other and consider mature plant size to prevent obstruction.
  - Arrange plants in odd numbers for aesthetic appeal and balance.
  - Use plants to soften corners of the house but keep larger plants a few feet away from the foundation to prevent damage.

- **Privacy**:
  - Consider planting trees, hedges, or installing fences for privacy, choosing styles that suit your preferences.

- **Elevation**:
  - Utilize slopes for planting or incorporate small retaining walls to define different areas of interest.

- **Pathways**:
  - Plan pathways to navigate different areas of the yard, choosing materials that suit the desired aesthetic and level of formality.

- **Water Features**:
  - Add tranquillity to your landscape with water features such as ponds or fountains, which can also help mask noise.

- **Lighting**:
  - Illuminate your landscape with strategically placed lights, highlighting trees, pathways, and other features for nighttime enjoyment and safety.

By considering these elements and incorporating them into your landscape design, you can create an outdoor space that meets your needs, reflects your style, and enhances the beauty and functionality of your property.

Landscape Planning and Design Tools

Several tools are available for landscape design, catering to various needs and preferences. Here's an overview of some commonly used tools:

- **Computer-Aided Design (CAD) Software**:
  - CAD software allows designers to create detailed and precise landscape designs using computer programs.

- It offers features like drawing tools, customizable templates, 3D modelling, and rendering capabilities.
- Popular CAD software for landscape design includes AutoCAD, SketchUp, and Vectorworks.

- **Landscape Design Software**:
  - Dedicated landscape design software provides specialized tools and templates tailored specifically for designing outdoor spaces.
  - These programs often include libraries of plants, trees, shrubs, hardscape materials, and outdoor furniture.
  - Examples of landscape design software include Land F/X, PRO Landscape, and DynaScape.

- **Online Design Tools**:
  - Various online platforms offer web-based landscape design tools that allow users to create designs directly in their web browsers.
  - These tools are often user-friendly and accessible, requiring no software installation.
  - Websites like iScape, Garden Planner, and Marshalls Paving Planner provide online design tools for landscaping.

- **Sketching and Drawing Tools**:
  - Traditional sketching and drawing tools, such as pencils, pens, markers, and sketch pads, are essential for creating initial design concepts and rough sketches.
  - These tools allow designers to quickly capture ideas and concepts before translating them into digital or detailed plans.

- **Photography and Visualization Tools**:
  - Photography plays a crucial role in landscape design by capturing existing site conditions and providing reference points for design decisions.
  - Visualization tools, including photo editing software and collage makers, help designers overlay proposed changes onto existing photographs for visual representation.

- **Measuring Tools**:
  - Accurate measurements are essential for creating scale drawings and plans. Tools like measuring tapes, laser distance metres, and surveying equipment help designers gather precise dimensions of the site.

- **Plant Databases and Reference Materials**:
  - Plant databases, field guides, and botanical reference materials assist designers in selecting appropriate plant species

based on factors like climate, soil conditions, and aesthetic preferences.

- Websites, books, and online resources provide valuable information on plant characteristics, growing requirements, and landscaping techniques.

- **Garden Planning Apps**:
    - Mobile apps designed for garden planning and landscaping offer features like plant identification, garden layout planning, and maintenance reminders.
    - Apps like Gardenize, Garden Planner, and My Garden provide tools for organizing, planning, and managing garden projects on smartphones and tablets.

Landscape planning tools encompass a range of resources and techniques designed to assist in the creation of outdoor spaces. Understanding how to effectively use these tools is essential for landscape designers to conceptualize, plan, and execute their projects successfully.

One fundamental tool in landscape planning is computer-aided design (CAD) software. CAD programs offer a comprehensive platform for creating detailed and precise landscape designs. Users can leverage drawing tools, customizable templates, and 3D modelling features to visualize their ideas. CAD software allows designers to experiment with various layouts, hardscape elements, and plant selections, facilitating the exploration of different design possibilities. By mastering CAD tools, designers can efficiently translate conceptual sketches into professional-grade plans, enhancing communication with clients and collaborators.

In addition to CAD software, dedicated landscape design software provides specialized functionalities tailored specifically for outdoor design projects. These programs often include extensive libraries of plants, trees, shrubs, and hardscape materials, enabling designers to quickly populate their designs with realistic elements. Landscape design software offers intuitive interfaces and user-friendly tools, making it accessible to both professionals and hobbyists. By utilizing these software solutions, designers can streamline the design process, optimize workflow efficiency, and produce high-quality landscape plans that meet their clients' requirements.

For those seeking a more accessible and user-friendly approach, online design tools offer convenient options for landscape planning. These web-based platforms provide intuitive interfaces that allow users to create designs directly in their web browsers. With features like drag-and-drop functionality, pre-designed templates, and interactive design elements, online design tools cater to individuals with varying levels of expertise. Whether sketching out initial concepts or refining detailed plans, these tools offer flexibility and convenience, enabling designers to collaborate with clients remotely and share design ideas effortlessly.

In addition to digital tools, traditional sketching and drawing techniques remain indispensable in landscape planning. Pencils, pens, markers, and sketch pads provide a tactile and intuitive means of capturing design concepts and exploring creative ideas. Sketching allows designers to quickly iterate on different layout options, experiment with proportions, and communicate design intent effectively. By combining traditional and digital tools, designers can leverage the strengths of each approach to develop well-rounded and visually compelling landscape designs.

Ultimately, effective landscape planning requires a combination of technical proficiency, creativity, and attention to detail. By mastering landscape planning tools and techniques, designers can unleash their creativity, transform ideas into reality, and create outdoor spaces that inspire and delight. Whether utilizing CAD software, specialized design programs, online tools, or traditional sketching methods, each tool plays a vital role in the design process, empowering designers to bring their vision to life and create landscapes that fulfill their clients' needs and aspirations.

Plant Selection

Selecting the appropriate plants and placing them correctly is a critical aspect of landscape design and management. The principle of "the right plant in the right place" encapsulates the importance of choosing plants that are well-suited to their specific environment, which can help prevent common landscape issues and minimize maintenance requirements. This principle is rooted in both art and science, requiring an understanding of plant characteristics, environmental conditions, functional needs, and aesthetic preferences [66].

Functionality, aesthetics, and environmental requirements are key considerations when selecting plants for a landscape. Functionally, it's important to determine what purpose the plant will serve. For example, is it intended to provide shade, privacy, or erosion control? Aesthetically, considerations include the plant's size, shape, colour, texture, and overall appearance. Environmental factors such as sunlight exposure, soil type, moisture levels, and climate conditions are also crucial in determining which plants will thrive in a given location [66].

Conducting a thorough site inventory and analysis is essential for guiding plant selection. This process involves assessing the environmental conditions of the site, including sun and shade patterns, soil characteristics, drainage, wind exposure, and existing architectural features. Additionally, understanding the functional needs and aesthetic preferences of the client or users of the space is integral to creating a successful planting design.

The site inventory provides a comprehensive overview of the site's conditions, while the analysis helps determine which plants are best suited to meet those conditions. This analysis considers factors such as the plant's tolerance to specific environmental stressors, its ability to fulfill functional requirements, and its compatibility with the desired aesthetic goals.

Ultimately, a successful planting design is often a balance between the practical considerations of plant suitability and the artistic expression of the designer. By carefully considering the functional, aesthetic, and environmental aspects of plant selection and placement, landscape designers can create landscapes that are both visually pleasing and ecologically sustainable [66].

Plants play multifaceted roles in landscaping, serving functions such as enhancing human comfort, providing visual screens, controlling erosion, and mitigating noise and odour. When selecting plants for these purposes, it's crucial to consider their functional characteristics, including size, shape, foliage density, texture, root mass, and growth rate. These attributes determine the plants' ability to fulfill specific functional roles and thrive in the site's growing conditions.

Climate Control: Plants can significantly impact the microclimate to enhance human comfort by influencing humidity, air temperature, and airflow. Trees, for example, create shade through solar radiation reflection and cool the air through transpiration. They can also act as windbreaks, blocking cold air or channelling cooling breezes.

Visual Control: Plants are strategically placed to screen undesirable views, direct views towards focal points, or create privacy. They can shield buildings from unsightly elements like roads or parking lots and create outdoor gathering spaces by enclosing areas with vegetation overhead. Additionally, plants can reduce glare and reflected light, enhancing visual comfort.

Physical Control: Plants serve as barriers to control the movement of people or animals. Tall, dense plants act as physical barriers, while shorter, wider plantings create implied barriers. Plants are chosen based on their wear resistance, especially in areas where pedestrian traffic is expected.

Erosion and Water Control: Plants play a crucial role in preventing erosion by breaking the impact of raindrops, slowing water flow, and trapping soil with their roots. They also help retain stormwater on-site, filtering and cleaning it before it enters larger water bodies. Plant buffers along waterfronts can mitigate the flow of pollutants into water bodies.

Noise and Odor Control: Properly selected and located plants can mitigate sounds and odours by blocking prevailing winds carrying odours or noise from their source.

In addition to their functional roles, plants contribute to the aesthetic appeal of a landscape. Factors such as colour, texture, form, and size influence the visual impact of plants and their compatibility with the surrounding environment [66].

Colour: Plants add visual interest through their colours, but colour perception can vary based on light conditions. Warm, bright colours are suitable for shaded areas, while all colours work well in sunny locations. Colour theory guides the selection of colour schemes for mixed plantings.

Texture: Plants exhibit a wide range of textures, from soft to coarse. Texture influences contrast and interest in the landscape and should be chosen based on the intended use of the space.

Form: The growth habit of plants, or their form, is a prominent visual characteristic. The selection of plant forms should align with functional requirements and the spatial characteristics of the site.

Size: Plant size, both at maturity and in relation to surrounding elements, is critical for proper landscape planning. Failure to consider mature plant size can lead to overcrowding or inadequate screening. Proximity to structures must also be considered to avoid potential damage.

Soil Characteristics: Soil composition significantly impacts plant health and growth. Factors such as pH, salinity, fertility, and moisture content must be considered when selecting plants. It's crucial to choose plant species that can thrive in the existing soil conditions to minimize the need for artificial irrigation or drainage [66].

Light Level: The amount of sunlight a site receives affects plant growth and performance. Factors like building orientation and surrounding vegetation influence light availability. Plants adapted to shade or full sunlight should be selected based on the site's light conditions to ensure optimal growth.

Water Quality: Water quality, including salinity and alkalinity levels, affects plant health. Irrigation water with high salinity can damage plants, while alkaline water can alter soil pH and nutrient availability. Careful plant selection is necessary to mitigate the negative effects of water quality on plant growth.

Temperature Ranges: Temperature fluctuations, both daytime and nighttime, impact plant growth and metabolism. Plants should be selected based on their temperature tolerance to ensure they can thrive in the site's climate conditions.

Wind Tolerance: Wind exposure can affect plant selection, especially in areas prone to storms or frequent winds. Plants should be chosen based on their ability to withstand wind stress to prevent damage and ensure long-term viability.

Disease and Pest Interactions: Plant selection should consider prevalent diseases and pests in the area. Choosing disease-resistant plant varieties helps minimize the risk of plant damage and reduces the need for chemical interventions.

Air Pollution: High levels of air pollution can adversely affect plant health. Selecting plants tolerant of pollutants like ozone and sulphur oxides ensures their resilience in polluted environments.

Maintenance and Cultural Practices: Consider the maintenance requirements of plant materials when selecting them for specific areas. Low-maintenance plants are ideal for areas with limited accessibility, while plants requiring frequent care should be placed in easily accessible areas.

Life Span: Plants have varying life spans, and their life cycle should be considered in landscape planning. Incorporating a mix of long-lived and short-lived plants allows for planned changes in the landscape over time, ensuring its dynamic and evolving nature.

As such, choosing the "right plant for the right place" is a fundamental principle in landscaping that ensures the optimal health and vitality of plants while minimizing maintenance requirements. Ignoring this principle can lead to various issues, including increased maintenance efforts, poor plant growth, and even plant death.

To apply this concept effectively, careful planning and site evaluation are necessary. This includes:

- **Understanding Site Conditions**: Before selecting plants, it's crucial to assess the environmental conditions of the site where they will be planted. Factors such as light availability (full sun to deep shade), water availability and quality, exposure to wind and temperature extremes, soil type, drainage, compaction, hardiness zone, competition from existing vegetation, and any above or below-ground obstructions should be considered.

- **Selecting Suitable Plants**: Different plants have varying tolerances to site conditions. Therefore, it's essential to choose plants that match the specific growing conditions of the site. This includes considering factors like a plant's ability to tolerate sunlight, soil moisture levels, wind exposure, and soil type.

- **Insect and Disease Resistance**: When selecting plants, it's wise to choose species that are resistant to common pests and diseases in your area. This helps reduce the need for pesticide application and minimizes the risk of plant damage or loss due to pests and diseases.

- **Aesthetic Considerations**: While environmental suitability is paramount, aesthetic factors also play a role in plant selection. Considerations such as growth habit, bloom colour and season, foliage colour and texture, winter interest (e.g., bark or fruit), benefits to wildlife, fall colour, and longevity should be taken into account.

- **Plant Size and Spacing**: Understanding the mature size of selected plants is essential to prevent overcrowding and ensure they fit within the allotted space without outgrowing it. Proper spacing allows plants to grow to their full potential without competing excessively with neighbouring plants.

- **Low-Maintenance Landscaping**: While no landscape is entirely maintenance-free, selecting low-maintenance plants and grouping them according to their water, fertilizer, and maintenance needs can significantly reduce the amount of upkeep required.

- **Plant Lists**: Provided lists categorize plants based on their characteristics and suitability for different site conditions, including shade tolerance, soil moisture, and other factors. These lists serve as valuable resources for landscapers and gardeners seeking appropriate plant choices for specific environments.

Overall, by adhering to the principles of selecting the right plants for the right place, landscapers can create sustainable and visually appealing landscapes that thrive with minimal intervention. Careful selection and placement of plants contribute significantly to the overall aesthetic and functionality of the garden space. This includes [67]:

- **Trees and Perspective**: Trees play a crucial role in garden design by providing scale, depth, and visual interest. They can nestle the house and garden into the site, offering a sense of being in nature. Additionally, trees offer shade, screen unwanted sights, and serve as habitat for birds.

- **Screening and Privacy**: Plants are used to screen undesirable elements such as fences, sheds, or service areas for both privacy and aesthetic reasons. Careful selection of long-lived plants that grow to an appropriate height is essential. Climbing plants should be used cautiously due to maintenance issues and the potential to invade neighbouring properties.

- **Open Space and Light**: Ground-covering plants are employed to create a sense of space in the garden. They allow through-views into garden beds, soften hard structures like paths and paved areas, and prevent the garden from feeling enclosed.

- **Vistas**: Vistas are designed views down pathways or through garden beds that evoke a sense of wonder and pleasure. They are framed by tall shrubs or trees and can offer glimpses of distant views or focus on internal garden features.

- **Peace and Excitement**: Gardens can evoke different emotional responses based on their design. While flowering plants can bring excitement, other gardens, like rainforest gardens, rely more on shades of green and varied textures for visual interest. Seasonal colour, texture, form, and growth habits of plants are key considerations.

- **Unity for Harmony**: Well-designed gardens have unity and harmony achieved through repetition of plant forms, foliage size, texture, or colour. Repeating visual cues throughout the garden creates flow and rhythm.

- **Balance for Harmony**: Balance in garden design refers to the arrangement of plants in space to create aesthetic harmony. It involves both symmetrical and asymmetrical arrangements to achieve visual balance.

- **Allure**: Gardens can be designed to reveal their beauty gradually, enticing visitors to explore further. Paths with obscured views and deliberate layout choices can create a sense of anticipation and allure.

- **Inside Views**: The design of the garden should integrate with the indoor space, offering pleasant views from windows and fostering a connection with nature even while indoors.

- **Safe and Secure**: Plants can contribute to a sense of safety by stabilizing embankments, providing perspective, and creating physical barriers around paths or vulnerable areas.

Plants are integral to garden design, serving various functions such as providing scale, privacy, visual interest, emotional responses, and a sense of harmony and security. Careful selection and placement of plants contribute significantly to the overall aesthetic and functionality of the garden space.

Choosing and using plants effectively in garden design involves careful consideration of various factors to ensure a successful and harmonious outdoor space. The following tips offer guidance in this regard [67].

Firstly, selecting plants suitable for the existing conditions in your garden is paramount. Understanding seasonal moisture levels, sunlight exposure, wind patterns, and other environmental factors helps match plants to their ideal growing conditions. It's essential to work with the natural characteristics of your garden rather than attempting to alter them artificially.

Additionally, prioritizing hardy plants that can thrive in your garden's specific conditions contributes to long-term success. While experimenting with less reliable plants can add excitement, focusing on hardy species ensures a resilient and flourishing garden.

When selecting plants from nurseries, prioritize strong and healthy specimens over simply choosing the largest ones. Healthy plants are more likely to establish well and contribute to the overall vitality of the garden.

Consideration of a plant's growth habit is also crucial. Beyond overall dimensions, understanding how a plant grows, whether it has a solid form or a soft, weeping shape, influences the overall feel and aesthetic of the garden.

To create visual cohesion, relate different plants with similar foliage types to simplify the garden's look. Incorporating contrasting foliage types and colours adds interest and accentuates the overall design.

Clumping plants, despite not having showy flowers, can serve as valuable accent plants due to their distinct visual elements. While flowers can add seasonal colour, they should be considered last when selecting plants, given their temporary nature.

A diverse range of plants not only adds interest and seasonal colour but also supports wildlife by providing habitats and food sources for insects, birds, and other animals. Ground-covering and small plants play a significant role in filling gaps, adding texture, and suppressing weed growth, acting as living mulch.

Chapter Four
Landscaping Work Health and Safety

Construction site safety is an essential aspect of any project, ensuring the well-being of workers and minimizing the risk of accidents and injuries. Historically, worker safety was not always a priority for employers, and working conditions were often hazardous, with long hours and dangerous environments. Stories of children working in mines and factories during the 18th and 19th centuries highlight the grim realities of the past, where workplace accidents and fatalities were sadly considered a normal part of the job.

Over time, there has been significant progress in improving conditions and work methods, driven by stricter legislation and increased awareness among both workers and management. This shift has led to a dramatic decrease in workplace injuries and fatalities compared to the past. However, even with these improvements, any workplace fatality is still considered unacceptable.

While individuals at the beginning of their careers may not have direct responsibility for workplace safety, it is essential for everyone to be aware of the laws and regulations in place to protect workers. Safety is a collective responsibility, and every worker plays a role in ensuring a safe work environment. Understanding and adhering to safety protocols not only protect individuals but also contribute to a culture of safety where everyone can return home safely at the end of the day.

Health and safety in the landscaping industry is crucial for protecting workers from potential hazards and ensuring a safe working environment. Landscaping work involves a variety of tasks, including planting, pruning, mowing, and using heavy machinery, which can pose risks if proper safety measures are not in place. Here are some key aspects of health and safety in the landscaping industry:

- **Risk Assessment**: Before beginning any landscaping project, it's essential to conduct a thorough risk assessment to identify potential hazards. This includes assessing risks related to machinery, tools, chemicals, uneven terrain, and weather conditions.

- **Training and Education**: Proper training is essential for all workers involved in landscaping activities. This includes training on how to safely operate machinery and equipment, as well as education on recognizing and mitigating hazards. Workers should also receive training on emergency procedures and first aid.

- **Personal Protective Equipment (PPE)**: Workers should be provided with appropriate personal protective equipment, including gloves, safety goggles, hard hats, ear protection, and high-visibility clothing. The use of PPE can help prevent injuries from flying debris, loud machinery, and other hazards.

- **Safe Equipment Use**: Machinery and equipment used in landscaping, such as lawnmowers, chainsaws, and hedge trimmers, should be properly maintained and inspected regularly to ensure they are in safe working condition. Workers should also be trained on how to use equipment safely and follow manufacturer guidelines.

- **Chemical Safety**: Landscaping often involves the use of chemicals such as fertilizers, pesticides, and herbicides. Workers should be trained on how to handle and apply chemicals safely, including proper storage, mixing, and application techniques. They should also be aware of the potential health risks associated with exposure to chemicals and how to mitigate them.

- **Manual Handling**: Lifting and carrying heavy objects, such as bags of mulch or potted plants, can lead to musculoskeletal injuries if not done correctly. Workers should be trained on proper lifting techniques and provided with equipment such as wheelbarrows or lifting aids to reduce the risk of injury.

- **Weather Conditions**: Landscaping work often takes place outdoors, exposing workers to various weather conditions. Extreme heat, cold, rain, or high winds can pose health risks, such as heatstroke, hypothermia, or slips and falls. Employers should have policies in place for working in adverse weather conditions and provide appropriate protective measures, such as shade structures or hydration stations.

- **Emergency Preparedness**: Employers should have procedures in place for responding to emergencies, such as accidents, injuries, or severe weather events. This includes ensuring access to first aid supplies, establishing communication protocols, and having evacuation plans in place for severe weather or other emergencies.

By implementing these measures, landscaping companies can create a safer work environment for their employees and reduce the risk of accidents and injuries. Additionally, promoting a culture of safety where workers are encouraged to report hazards and follow safety protocols can further enhance workplace safety in the landscaping industry.

Work Health and Safety Legislation

Health and safety legislation applicable to landscaping varies from country to country, but there are common themes and standards that many jurisdictions follow. Here's an overview of health and safety legislation related to landscaping in several regions around the world:

- **United States**:

    - In the United States, the Occupational Safety and Health Administration (OSHA) sets and enforces standards to ensure safe and healthy working conditions for workers across various industries, including landscaping.

    - OSHA regulations relevant to landscaping cover areas such as hazard communication, personal protective equipment (PPE), machinery and equipment safety, and fall protection.

- States may also have their own occupational safety and health agencies with additional regulations that landscaping companies must comply with.

- **United Kingdom**:
    - In the UK, health and safety legislation is primarily governed by the Health and Safety at Work etc. Act 1974, which places a general duty on employers to ensure the health, safety, and welfare of their employees.
    - The Control of Substances Hazardous to Health (COSHH) Regulations require employers to control exposure to hazardous substances, including chemicals used in landscaping.
    - The Provision and Use of Work Equipment Regulations (PUWER) set requirements for the safe use of machinery and equipment, such as lawnmowers and chainsaws.
    - The Work at Height Regulations require employers to assess and control the risks of working at height, which may apply to tasks such as tree pruning or hedge trimming.

- **Australia**:
    - In Australia, workplace health and safety legislation varies by state and territory but generally follows similar principles. Work health and safety (WHS) laws aim to protect the health and safety of workers and others affected by work activities.
    - Each state and territory has its own regulatory authority responsible for enforcing WHS laws. For example, WorkSafe Victoria in Victoria and SafeWork NSW in New South Wales.
    - WHS regulations relevant to landscaping may include requirements for risk assessment, safe work practices, personal protective equipment, and handling hazardous substances.

- **Canada**:
    - In Canada, occupational health and safety (OHS) legislation is primarily regulated at the provincial and territorial levels, with each jurisdiction having its own OHS laws and regulatory agencies.
    - OHS regulations in Canada cover a wide range of topics, including workplace hazard identification and control, training and education, PPE, and machinery safety.
    - Employers in the landscaping industry must comply with relevant OHS regulations specific to their province or territory.

- **European Union**:
    - In the European Union (EU), health and safety legislation is governed by EU directives that member states are required to transpose into national laws.

- The Framework Directive 89/391/EEC sets out general principles for workplace health and safety, including risk assessment, prevention measures, and worker participation.

- Specific directives may apply to areas such as manual handling, machinery safety, and the use of hazardous substances, all of which are relevant to landscaping activities.

Overall, health and safety legislation applicable to landscaping aims to protect workers from workplace hazards and ensure that employers take appropriate measures to create safe working environments. Compliance with these regulations is essential for landscaping companies to prevent accidents and injuries and promote worker well-being.

Legislation, comprising laws established by federal or state parliaments, forms the backbone of legal frameworks governing workplace health and safety. Acts passed by parliaments provide the foundation of the law, outlining the general duties, responsibilities, and penalties concerning health and safety in various industries. These Acts empower specific individuals or agencies to create regulations, which serve as detailed guidelines stipulating minimum requirements and protocols related to the Acts.

In the United States, the Occupational Safety and Health Administration (OSHA) plays a pivotal role in setting and enforcing standards to ensure safe and healthy working conditions across industries, including landscaping. OSHA regulations relevant to landscaping encompass areas such as hazard communication, personal protective equipment (PPE), machinery and equipment safety, and fall protection. Additionally, individual states may have their own occupational safety and health agencies with supplementary regulations that landscaping companies must adhere to.

In the United Kingdom, health and safety legislation is primarily governed by the Health and Safety at Work etc. Act 1974. This Act imposes a general duty on employers to ensure the health, safety, and welfare of their employees. Regulations such as the Control of Substances Hazardous to Health (COSHH) Regulations and the Provision and Use of Work Equipment Regulations (PUWER) provide detailed requirements for controlling exposure to hazardous substances and ensuring the safe use of machinery and equipment, respectively. The Work at Height Regulations further mandate risk assessment and control measures for tasks involving elevated work.

Similarly, in Australia, workplace health and safety legislation varies by state and territory but generally follows similar principles. Work health and safety (WHS) laws aim to safeguard the health and safety of workers and others affected by work activities. Each state and territory has its own regulatory authority responsible for enforcing WHS laws, such as WorkSafe Victoria and SafeWork NSW. WHS regulations pertinent to landscaping may encompass risk assessment, safe work practices, PPE requirements, and handling of hazardous substances, among other aspects.

The role of regulatory bodies, such as WorkSafe authorities, is crucial in overseeing compliance with WHS laws and promoting safe work environments. Inspectors are employed to enforce the Act, resolve workplace issues, provide guidance to employers and employees, and investigate workplace accidents. These inspectors possess extensive powers, including the authority to conduct workplace inspections, issue improvement notices, and prohibit unsafe work practices or conditions until rectified.

Additionally, workplace policies and procedures, including duty of care obligations, further contribute to maintaining safety standards in the landscaping industry. Employers are legally obligated to provide a safe work environment, while employees have responsibilities to ensure their own safety and report hazards or incidents promptly. Compliance with legislative requirements, supported by codes of practice, guidance material, and Australian Standards, enhances safety outcomes and mitigates risks in landscaping operations.

United States

In the United States, ensuring safe and healthy working conditions for employees is a paramount concern, and this responsibility falls under the purview of the Occupational Safety and Health Administration (OSHA). As the primary federal agency tasked with setting and enforcing workplace safety standards, OSHA plays a crucial role in safeguarding workers across a wide range of industries, including landscaping [68].

OSHA regulations relevant to the landscaping sector are comprehensive and address various aspects of workplace safety. One of the key areas covered by these regulations is hazard communication, which requires employers to inform workers about potential workplace hazards through labels, safety data sheets, and employee training programs. This ensures that landscaping workers are aware of the risks associated with their tasks and equipped with the knowledge to mitigate them effectively.

Additionally, OSHA regulations pertaining to landscaping encompass the use of personal protective equipment (PPE). These standards mandate the provision and proper use of PPE such as gloves, eye protection, and respiratory protection, depending on the nature of the work being performed. By requiring employers to furnish adequate PPE and ensure its correct utilization, OSHA aims to minimize the risk of injuries and illnesses among landscaping workers.

Furthermore, machinery and equipment safety constitute another crucial aspect of OSHA regulations in the landscaping industry. These standards dictate the safe operation and maintenance of landscaping equipment, such as lawnmowers, chainsaws, and trimmers, to prevent accidents and injuries. Employers are required to implement measures such as equipment inspections, operator training, and machine guarding to mitigate hazards associated with machinery use.

Moreover, fall protection is a significant focus area within OSHA regulations for landscaping. Given the elevated nature of certain tasks, such as tree trimming or roof maintenance, employers must implement fall protection measures to prevent falls from heights. This may involve the use of guardrails, safety harnesses, and other fall arrest systems to protect workers working at elevated positions.

It's important to note that while OSHA sets federal standards, individual states may have their own occupational safety and health agencies with additional regulations specific to the landscaping industry. These state-level agencies may enforce OSHA standards or promulgate additional requirements to address unique regional concerns or hazards. Therefore, landscaping companies must ensure compliance with both federal OSHA regulations and any applicable state-specific requirements to maintain safe working environments for their employees.

United Kingdom

In the United Kingdom, the Health and Safety at Work etc. Act 1974 serves as the cornerstone legislation for ensuring workplace health and safety [69]. This Act places a general duty on employers to safeguard the health, safety, and welfare of their employees while at work. It mandates that employers assess and manage risks, provide necessary information, instruction, training, and supervision to employees, and maintain a safe working environment. This overarching legislation forms the basis for more specific regulations and guidelines that address various aspects of workplace safety, including those relevant to the landscaping industry.

One crucial regulation for the landscaping sector in the UK is the Control of Substances Hazardous to Health (COSHH) Regulations [70]. These regulations require employers to control exposure to hazardous substances, such as pesticides, herbicides, and fertilizers commonly used in landscaping activities. Employers must conduct risk assessments, implement control measures to minimize exposure, provide appropriate personal protective equipment (PPE), and ensure adequate training for employees handling hazardous substances.

Moreover, the Provision and Use of Work Equipment Regulations (PUWER) are essential for ensuring the safe use of machinery and equipment in the landscaping industry [71]. PUWER sets requirements for the inspection, maintenance, and safe operation of work equipment like lawnmowers and chainsaws. Employers must ensure that equipment is suitable for its intended use, properly maintained, and used by competent individuals who have received adequate training.

Additionally, the Work at Height Regulations are particularly relevant to tasks like tree pruning or hedge trimming in the landscaping sector [72]. These regulations necessitate that employers assess and control the risks associated with working at height, including falls from ladders or elevated platforms. Employers must take measures to prevent falls by using appropriate access equipment, providing fall protection systems, and ensuring that workers are trained in safe work practices for tasks performed at height.

Adhering to health and safety legislation in the UK, including the Health and Safety at Work Act, COSHH, PUWER, and the Work at Height Regulations, is crucial for fostering a safety culture in the landscaping industry. Compliance with these regulations enables employers to mitigate risks, protect the health and well-being of their employees, and maintain safe working environments conducive to productivity and professionalism in the landscaping sector.

Australia

In Australia, workplace health and safety legislation is designed to ensure the health and safety of workers and others affected by work activities. While the overarching principles remain consistent across the country, specific regulations may vary between different states and territories. These regulations are typically governed by work health and safety (WHS) laws, which outline the responsibilities of employers, employees, and other parties to maintain safe work environments.

Each state and territory in Australia has its own regulatory authority responsible for enforcing WHS laws and promoting workplace safety. For instance, WorkSafe Victoria oversees workplace safety in Victoria, while SafeWork NSW fulfills this role in New South Wales. These regulatory bodies provide guidance, conduct inspections, and enforce compliance with WHS regulations to prevent workplace accidents and injuries.

In the landscaping industry, WHS regulations cover a range of areas to mitigate risks and ensure safe work practices. These regulations may include requirements for conducting risk assessments to identify potential hazards associated with landscaping activities. Employers are expected to implement measures to control and minimize these risks, such as providing appropriate training, supervision, and personal protective equipment (PPE) to workers.

Furthermore, WHS regulations may address specific concerns related to landscaping work, such as the handling of hazardous substances commonly used in landscaping activities. Employers must adhere to guidelines for the safe storage, handling, and disposal of chemicals and other hazardous materials to protect the health and well-being of workers and the environment.

Additionally, WHS regulations may outline requirements for safe work practices, including operating machinery and equipment safely, ensuring proper maintenance and inspection of tools and vehicles, and implementing measures to prevent falls and other accidents. By complying with these regulations, employers can create safer work environments, reduce the risk of injuries, and promote the health and well-being of workers in the landscaping industry.

Acts of Parliament form the foundation of the law. Most workers are safeguarded by a Work Health and Safety Act (WHS) which outlines the duties, responsibilities, and penalties for various individuals regarding health and safety in the workplace.

Supporting the Act are the Work Health and Safety (WHS) Regulations. These regulations are a detailed list of dos and don'ts intended to cover most health and safety issues relevant to workplaces. Although they span hundreds of pages, they cannot encompass all potential hazards that may be encountered at work. However, they do address many issues particularly pertinent to construction sites, including first aid, personal protective equipment (PPE) and clothing, workplace facilities, evacuation procedures, ladders, warning signs, electricity, noise control, manual handling, and prevention of falls. It's crucial to remember that the absence of a specific mention in the Regulations does not imply unrestricted freedom.

Each state and territory in Australia has a regulatory body responsible for administering its WHS Act. One of the regulator's roles is to ensure that all parties adhere to the Act and regulations, thereby maintaining safe and healthy workplaces. To assist in this task, the regulator employs inspectors who enforce the Act, help resolve workplace issues, provide advice to employers and employees on improving workplace health and safety performance, and investigate workplace accidents. These inspectors possess significant powers under the Act, including the right to inspect workplaces, enter and inspect at any reasonable time, examine workplace elements, and interview individuals. They can issue improvement notices and prohibition notices to address breaches, specifying deadlines for rectification and requiring prominent display of the notices at the relevant part of the workplace. The regulator's role is to oversee compliance with WHS laws, not to manage workplace health and safety.

State and federal agencies periodically publish codes of practice to provide practical advice and guidance on managing WHS hazards and risks in relation to legislation. These codes describe the preferred methods for managing hazards and risks to achieve the required standards of health, safety, and welfare. While a code of practice does not have the same legal force as Acts or Regulations and cannot be the basis for prosecution, it may be used as evidence in court cases involving non-compliance with Regulations.

Regulators offer guidance notes that provide detailed information on the requirements of the Regulations, standards, and codes of practice. Although this material is not part of the law, it is highly useful for understanding and complying with WHS requirements.

Australian Standards® are nationally recognized documents setting quality requirements for products and services to ensure safety, reliability, and consistency of performance. Some regulatory requirements are covered by these standards, which are referenced in the Regulations to keep the document manageable. Australian Standards® are not provided by state, territory, or Commonwealth regulators but must be purchased. Topics covered by these standards include safety helmets, scaffolding setups, electrical installations on building sites, and safety sign colours.

Companies develop policies and procedures to inform workers about how work should be conducted and the standards for work, equipment, and materials. These documents ensure compliance with laws and regulations and meet company requirements. WHS policies outline the company's approach to health and safety issues, while procedures provide step-by-step guides for creating and maintaining a safe working environment. They may include information on responsible individuals, resources for safe practices, training availability, tool and equipment operating procedures, emergency procedures, and workplace safety assessments.

Duty of care is the legal obligation for all employers and employees to take reasonable care to avoid harming others in the workplace. The WHS Acts and Regulations outline duty of care requirements and associated penalties. Employers are expected to provide a hazard-free workplace as far as practicable, considering known hazards, available solutions, their suitability, cost, potential harm, and the likelihood of occurrence. If an accident occurs and the case goes to court, the judge will evaluate the employer's efforts to ensure workplace safety. Employers must also provide instructions, supervision, free PPE, maintain safe workplaces, and ensure safe use of plant and materials. Penalties for breaching these laws can be severe, including fines and imprisonment for causing death or serious harm through negligence.

Employees also have legal duties and responsibilities, such as taking reasonable care to ensure their own health and safety and avoiding actions or omissions that could harm others. They must report workplace hazards they cannot fix, inform employers about any accidents or incidents, and use any PPE supplied by the employer. An employee causing death or serious harm can be fined.

Canada

In Canada, the landscape of occupational health and safety (OHS) legislation is diverse, primarily regulated at the provincial and territorial levels [73]. Each province and territory in Canada possesses its own set of OHS laws and regulatory agencies, reflecting the decentralized nature of the Canadian legal system. Consequently, the specifics of OHS regulations may vary significantly from one jurisdiction to another, tailored to address the unique needs and priorities of each region.

OHS regulations in Canada encompass a broad spectrum of topics aimed at ensuring safe and healthy working environments across industries, including the landscaping sector. These regulations often address crucial aspects such as workplace hazard identification and control, employee training and education, the provision of personal protective equipment (PPE), and machinery safety protocols. By delineating clear guidelines and requirements, OHS regulations seek to mitigate risks, prevent accidents, and safeguard the well-being of workers.

In the landscaping industry, employers are mandated to adhere to the OHS regulations pertinent to their respective province or territory. This entails understanding and implementing the specific requirements outlined in the relevant legislation to maintain compliance and uphold safety standards within their operations. Given the localized nature of OHS regulations, landscaping companies operating across different provinces or territories must navigate and ensure compliance with the distinct legislative frameworks applicable to each jurisdiction.

Compliance with OHS regulations is essential for fostering a culture of safety and minimizing workplace hazards in the landscaping industry. By prioritizing worker safety and adhering to regulatory requirements, employers can create safer work environments, reduce the likelihood of accidents or injuries, and enhance overall occupational health outcomes. Additionally, ongoing awareness, training, and collaboration with regulatory agencies play pivotal roles in promoting continuous improvement and best practices in OHS management within the Canadian landscaping sector.

European Union

In the European Union (EU), the landscape of health and safety legislation is shaped by a framework of directives that member states are obligated to implement into their national laws. This regulatory framework seeks to harmonize standards and practices across EU member states, ensuring a consistent approach to workplace health and safety while respecting the diverse socio-economic contexts and industrial landscapes of each country. At the heart of this framework is the Framework Directive 89/391/EEC, which lays down fundamental principles for safeguarding the health and safety of workers across all sectors, including landscaping.

The Framework Directive 89/391/EEC serves as a cornerstone of EU health and safety legislation, delineating overarching principles and obligations that member states must uphold to protect the well-being of workers. These principles encompass various aspects of workplace health and safety management, including the requirement for employers to conduct risk assessments, implement preventive measures to mitigate hazards, and actively involve workers in health and safety decision-making processes. By establishing a comprehensive framework for occupational health and safety, the directive aims to foster a culture of prevention and risk management within workplaces, thereby reducing the incidence of work-related accidents and illnesses.

In addition to the overarching Framework Directive, specific directives within the EU's regulatory framework address various occupational health and safety issues that are pertinent to landscaping activities. These directives may cover areas such as manual handling, machinery safety, and the use of hazardous substances, all of which have direct implications for workers engaged in landscaping tasks. For instance, directives related to manual handling aim to prevent musculoskeletal injuries by providing guidelines for safe lifting and carrying techniques, while directives on machinery safety establish requirements for the safe operation and maintenance of equipment commonly used in landscaping, such as lawnmowers and chainsaws. Similarly, directives addressing the use of hazardous substances seek to minimize exposure to potentially harmful chemicals encountered in landscaping operations, promoting the adoption of safe handling practices and risk mitigation measures.

By transposing EU directives into national legislation, member states play a vital role in ensuring the effective implementation and enforcement of health and safety standards within their territories. National authorities are responsible for translating EU directives into actionable measures, monitoring compliance with regulatory requirements, and providing support and guidance to employers and workers. Through robust enforcement mechanisms and regulatory oversight, member states strive to uphold the principles enshrined in EU health and safety directives, safeguarding the well-being of workers and promoting a culture of safety and prevention in the landscaping industry and beyond.

Hazard Identification and Reporting

Hazard reporting plays a crucial role in business operations by enabling organizations to identify and mitigate risks within the workplace. Workplace accidents can have severe consequences, ranging from serious injuries to fatalities among employees or visitors. Such incidents can not only result in financial penalties but also tarnish the reputation of the business and even lead to legal repercussions, including imprisonment for those responsible [74].

Despite the perception of keeping up with legislation and relevant publications as an additional burden, there are numerous benefits associated with staying informed. Firstly, it enables individuals to make informed decisions and proactively identify threats and issues, providing a competitive advantage, particularly for those involved in shaping organizational strategies. Additionally, staying abreast of legislative changes and relevant publications fosters the development of expertise in one's field and health and safety matters, garnering trust and respect from peers and superiors alike, which is invaluable from a leadership standpoint.

Remaining updated with legislative changes and industry publications is essential for being aware of any necessary adjustments. To facilitate this, individuals must identify reliable sources of information [74]. Traditional sources such as mentorship within the organization, participation in trade organizations, attendance at trade shows and conferences, and face-to-face networking events provide valuable insights and networking opportunities. On the other hand, online platforms like Twitter/X, LinkedIn, Google Alerts, and forums offer convenient avenues for accessing real-time updates, connecting with industry leaders, and engaging in discussions pertinent to one's area of expertise.

Twitter/X serves as a platform to connect with industry leaders and organizations and stay abreast of relevant news and trends. By searching relevant keywords, individuals can identify knowledgeable professionals within their industry and initiate dialogues to stay informed. Similarly, LinkedIn offers opportunities to connect with colleagues, join industry-specific groups, and receive updates from individuals and organizations. Google Alerts, meanwhile, notifies users when resources featuring specific keywords are indexed by Google's search engine, providing a convenient way to access industry news without the need for extensive web searches. Additionally, membership sites and discussion forums provide tailored insider information and opportunities for networking and skill development, particularly in technology-related fields like IT. Seeking recommendations from colleagues or leveraging existing online connections can help individuals identify the most suitable forums for their needs [74].

Participative agreements pertain to the method by which management engages with and involves employees in matters concerning health and safety. It's imperative to acknowledge that organizations have a legal duty to consult with employees regarding health and safety matters. Establishing and maintaining participative agreements offer numerous advantages:

- Enhanced Understanding: Both employers and employees gain a deeper comprehension of health and safety issues within the workplace.

- Employee Empowerment: Employees increase their knowledge of health and safety practices, contributing to a safer work environment.

- Increased Ownership: Encouraging employee participation fosters a sense of ownership and responsibility for health and safety initiatives.

- Cooperative Resolution: Engaging employees in decision-making ensures a collaborative approach to resolving health and safety concerns.

- Process Improvement: Participative agreements provide avenues for reviewing processes, addressing issues, and generating suggestions for enhancement.

Some organizations implement safety incentive programs to incentivize staff members to prioritize safety and report any WHS-related findings. Companies that emphasize safety initiatives gain a competitive advantage in creating and maintaining safe workplaces.

When discussing consultative mechanisms for managing health and safety risks, it's essential to consider who should be involved in the process. Generally, there are three primary groups:

- Experts: These individuals serve as consultants and possess expertise in health and safety matters. They often work within the Human Resources department, overseeing safety protocols and documentation.

- Supervisors: Front-line supervisors play a crucial role in coordinating and implementing health and safety policies and procedures within their respective workgroups.

- Workers: Employees function as the eyes and ears of the organization, identifying hazards and potential risks in their workstations.

While not everyone can be an expert in health and safety, most organizations have designated personnel responsible for overseeing safety protocols. These individuals not only track safety metrics but also serve as consultants for front-line supervisors and employees, offering guidance on safety matters.

Front-line supervisors are directly involved in ensuring compliance with health and safety policies and procedures. They coordinate with their teams to integrate safety protocols into daily work activities, fostering a culture of safety within the organization.

Employees, as the frontline workforce, play a pivotal role in identifying and mitigating workplace hazards. They possess firsthand knowledge of potential risks and are in a prime position to address them promptly. Effective communication among these groups is crucial for sharing information and addressing safety concerns collectively.

Encouraging open communication and dialogue about safety risks promotes a proactive approach to mitigating hazards. Supervisors should educate their teams on the importance of reporting hazards and provide mechanisms for doing so. Additionally, involving the company's safety coordinator as a consultant fosters a collaborative approach to workplace safety, where employees perceive safety initiatives as protective measures rather than interruptions to their workflow.

Reporting incidents and hazards in the workplace is fundamentally centred on fostering a safe working environment. Rather than assigning blame or singling out individuals or environments, it revolves around cultivating a culture where safety is paramount. This culture not only promotes physical safety but also nurtures an atmosphere where employees feel secure and valued. In this paradigm, both employees and supervisors play integral roles in identifying and addressing potential risks to ensure workplace safety.

Emphasizing the importance of reporting even minor hazards is crucial in this context. By promptly reporting any hazards, regardless of their perceived severity, the likelihood of recurrence can be minimized or ideally eradicated altogether. This proactive approach serves to prevent minor issues from escalating into more serious risks, thereby safeguarding the well-being of employees and preserving the integrity of the work environment.

Moreover, the reporting of hazards facilitates the collection of valuable data, contributing to a deeper understanding of risk patterns within the workplace. This data-driven insight enables organizations to pinpoint areas of vulnerability and devise more effective strategies for risk management in the future. By systematically documenting and analysing reported hazards, organizations can identify trends, root causes, and emerging threats, thereby empowering them to implement targeted interventions and preventive measures to enhance workplace safety comprehensively.

Types of Hazards

In the realm of workplace safety, understanding the diverse array of hazards is paramount to ensuring the well-being of employees and the integrity of the work environment. There are six main types of hazards that can potentially exist in a workplace, each presenting unique risks and challenges:

1. **Chemical Hazards**: These encompass any hazardous substances that have the potential to cause harm or illness to individuals exposed to them. Chemical hazards can include toxic gases, corrosive liquids, flammable materials, and other harmful substances commonly found in industrial or laboratory settings. Proper handling, storage, and disposal procedures are essential for mitigating the risks associated with chemical hazards.

2. **Biological Hazards**: This category encompasses exposure to biological agents such as viruses, bacteria, fungi, and other microorganisms that have the potential to cause illness or infection in humans. Biological hazards can arise in various occupational settings, including healthcare facilities, laboratories, agricultural environments, and waste management facilities. Effective infection control measures, including vaccination, personal protective equipment (PPE), and sanitation protocols, are crucial for minimizing the risk of exposure to biological hazards.

3. **Ergonomic Hazards**: Ergonomic hazards refer to physical factors in the workplace environment that can contribute to musculoskeletal disorders, repetitive strain injuries, and other ergonomic-related health issues. These hazards may include poor workstation design, improper lifting techniques, prolonged sitting or standing, and repetitive motions. Implementing ergonomic workstation assessments, ergonomic training programs, and ergonomic equipment can help

mitigate the risks associated with ergonomic hazards and promote employee health and comfort.

4. **Physical Hazards**: Physical hazards encompass environmental factors that pose a threat to the health and safety of individuals in the workplace. These hazards can include exposure to extreme temperatures, loud noise levels, ionizing radiation, mechanical hazards (e.g., moving machinery), and ergonomic hazards. Implementing engineering controls, such as ventilation systems, noise barriers, and machine guards, can help minimize the risk of injury or illness associated with physical hazards.

5. **Safety Conditions Hazards**: Safety conditions hazards are those that create unsafe working conditions and increase the risk of accidents or injuries in the workplace. Examples of safety conditions hazards include slippery floors, inadequate lighting, unsecured equipment or machinery, electrical hazards, and insufficient safety signage. Conducting regular safety inspections, implementing proper housekeeping protocols, and providing adequate training on hazard recognition and control are essential for preventing accidents and injuries related to safety conditions hazards.

6. **Physiological Hazards**: These hazards encompass any form of physical or emotional stressors that can adversely affect an individual's mental or emotional well-being. Examples of physiological hazards include workplace bullying, harassment, discrimination, and exposure to traumatic events or situations. Creating a supportive work environment, promoting open communication, and implementing policies and procedures to address and prevent workplace harassment or discrimination are crucial for safeguarding employees' psychological health and well-being.

By identifying and addressing these various types of hazards, employers can create a safer and healthier work environment for their employees while complying with relevant occupational health and safety regulations. Regular risk assessments, employee training programs, and ongoing monitoring and evaluation efforts are essential components of an effective hazard management strategy.

Figure 47: Typical landscaping work environment. Guardrail and paving work. Washington State Dept of Transportation, CC BY 2.0, via Flickr.

Hazard Identification

In ensuring workplace safety, employers play a critical role in identifying and addressing potential hazards that may exist in the work environment. Recognizing the presence of hazards is essential for maintaining a safe and healthy workplace, and this process often involves consultation with workers to gather their insights and perspectives on potential threats to their health and safety.

Consulting workers allows employers to tap into the frontline experiences and observations of employees who are directly involved in the day-to-day operations of the workplace. Employees are often in the best position to identify hazards and risks because they have firsthand knowledge of the tasks they perform, the equipment they use, and the conditions they encounter in their work environment.

Employees should feel empowered to contribute to the hazard identification process by reporting any potential health and safety concerns they observe or encounter during their work activities. This open communication between employees and supervisors is crucial for creating a proactive approach to hazard identification and mitigation.

In the horticulture environment, where workers may be exposed to a variety of unique hazards, conducting thorough OHS (Occupational Health and Safety) risk analysis is essential. This analysis typically involves three main steps: hazard identification, workplace assessment, and risk control.

Hazard identification entails identifying any potential sources of harm or danger in the workplace. In the horticulture industry, hazards can encompass a wide range of factors, including machinery, chemicals, noise, electrical hazards, poor work design, inadequate management systems and procedures, and even human behaviour.

Once hazards are identified, they must be assessed to determine their potential to cause harm or damage. This assessment involves evaluating the severity of the hazard and the likelihood of it causing harm to workers or property. By assessing hazards, employers can prioritize their efforts and focus on addressing the most significant risks first.

After assessing hazards, employers must implement effective risk control measures to eliminate or minimize the identified risks. This may involve implementing engineering controls, administrative controls, or providing personal protective equipment (PPE) to mitigate the risks associated with identified hazards.

The process of identifying hazards in the workplace and implementing appropriate risk control measures is essential for safeguarding the health and safety of workers in the horticulture industry. By involving workers in the hazard identification process and taking proactive steps to address risks, employers can create a safer work environment for everyone involved.

Recognizing and promptly reporting hazards in the workplace is paramount for maintaining a safe and healthy work environment. Regardless of the size or severity of the hazard, immediate reporting is essential to mitigate risks and prevent potential accidents or injuries. When a hazard is identified, employees have a responsibility to report it promptly to the appropriate personnel within the organization. This could involve notifying a supervisor, management team, or directly contacting the safety department, depending on the established protocols within the business.

The urgency of reporting hazards stems from the understanding that even seemingly minor hazards can escalate into significant risks if left unaddressed. By reporting hazards promptly, employees contribute to the proactive identification and resolution of potential dangers, helping to ensure the safety and well-being of everyone in the workplace. Additionally, prompt reporting minimizes the likelihood of incidents occurring and prevents hazards from escalating into more serious threats.

Every business is obligated to have workplace hazard reporting procedures in place to facilitate the timely identification and resolution of hazards. These procedures typically outline the steps employees should take when they encounter a hazard, including whom to report it to and how to document the details of the hazard. Following these established procedures is crucial for maintaining a consistent approach to hazard reporting across the organization and ensuring that hazards are addressed efficiently and effectively.

The process of reporting hazards serves as a fundamental component of the organization's overall risk management strategy. It enables employers to proactively identify areas of concern, assess potential risks, and implement appropriate control measures to mitigate those risks. By fostering a culture of hazard reporting and accountability, businesses can create an environment where employees feel empowered to contribute to workplace safety and actively participate in risk management efforts.

Numerous large construction sites employ a systematic approach to identify and document workplace hazards. Various methods are utilized for this purpose, including the examination of injury and accident records, the implementation of workplace checklists, the completion of incident/accident report forms, the appointment of dedicated safety officers, the establishment of WHS committees, and the selection of safety representatives. While these methods are effective in identifying potential hazards in larger construction settings, they may not always yield the same results on smaller to medium-sized building sites due to several reasons.

Firstly, smaller sites may not have a permanent supervisor present at all times to maintain records and oversee safety protocols. Additionally, the workforce on such sites often comprises subcontractors who may only be present for short durations, making it challenging to ensure consistent hazard identification and reporting. Moreover, the subcontracting system may foster a mentality among workers where they view themselves more as individual entities or "small businesses" rather than integral members of a cohesive team.

Despite efforts by businesses to prioritize employee safety, it remains imperative for individuals to remain vigilant and proactive in identifying hazards. Workplace accidents typically stem from a combination of unsafe acts and conditions, highlighting the shared responsibility for safety among all personnel. Unsafe acts encompass a range of behaviours, such as improper lifting techniques, tampering with safety devices on machinery, operating equipment without proper training, disregarding basic safety principles (e.g., using electrical tools in wet conditions), neglecting to use personal protective equipment (PPE) when necessary, engaging in horseplay, or working under the influence of drugs or alcohol.

Conversely, unsafe conditions within the workplace may arise due to inadequate guards or barriers, poor housekeeping practices leading to cluttered or untidy workspaces, poorly maintained machinery or equipment, insufficient safety signage, or the absence of appropriate safety equipment like scaffolding. In light of these factors, maintaining a heightened awareness of potential hazards and adhering to safety protocols is essential for mitigating risks and ensuring a safe working environment for all individuals involved in construction activities.

Identifying hazards in landscape construction is crucial for ensuring the safety of workers and others on the job site. To identify hazards in landscape construction:

- **Conduct Site Surveys and Inspections:** Begin by thoroughly surveying the construction site and inspecting the areas where landscape work will take place. This includes examining the terrain, vegetation, existing structures, and any potential hazards such as uneven ground, debris, or overhead power lines.

- **Review Plans and Specifications:** Study the landscape construction plans and specifications to understand the scope of work and identify any potential hazards indicated in the design. Pay attention to elements such as excavation areas, grading plans, planting layouts, and irrigation systems.

- **Assess Environmental Factors:** Consider environmental factors that may pose hazards during construction, such as extreme weather conditions (e.g., heat, cold, rain), natural obstacles (e.g., trees, rocks), and proximity to water bodies or steep slopes.

- **Identify Equipment and Machinery Hazards:** Evaluate the equipment and machinery that will be used in landscape construction, including power tools, heavy machinery (e.g., excavators, bulldozers), and vehicles (e.g., trucks, tractors). Check for potential hazards such as mechanical failures, improper operation, and inadequate safety guards.

- **Evaluate Material Hazards:** Assess the materials and substances involved in landscape construction, including soil, fertilizers, pesticides, and construction materials (e.g., timber, concrete). Identify potential hazards such as chemical exposure, allergic reactions, and fire hazards.

- **Consider Work Processes and Practices:** Analyse the work processes and practices involved in landscape construction, such as excavation, trenching, tree removal, and planting. Identify hazards related to manual handling, falls from heights, slips and trips, and working in confined spaces.

- **Review Safety Data Sheets (SDS):** Consult Safety Data Sheets (SDS) for any hazardous substances or chemicals used in landscape construction. SDS provide detailed information on the hazards, safe handling procedures, and emergency response measures for each chemical.

- **Involve Workers in Hazard Identification:** Encourage workers to actively participate in identifying hazards by soliciting their input and observations. They may have firsthand knowledge of potential hazards and risks based on their experience and familiarity with the job site.

- **Document Hazards and Risk Assessments:** Maintain records of identified hazards and conduct risk assessments to evaluate the likelihood and severity of potential accidents or injuries. Documenting hazards allows for proper mitigation measures to be implemented and helps track the effectiveness of control measures over time.

- **Regular Monitoring and Review:** Continuously monitor the job site for new hazards that may arise during construction and conduct regular reviews of hazard identification processes. Stay vigilant for changes in site conditions, work activities, and environmental factors that may impact safety.

Controlling Hazards and Managing Risks

Assessing risk involves evaluating the likelihood or probability that a hazard will cause harm to individuals. For instance, consider household chemicals like bleach, which pose a low risk when stored correctly. However, if a bottle of bleach is left unattended in a drink bottle on a coffee table, the risk increases due to the potential for accidental ingestion or exposure. When determining the level of risk posed by a hazard in the workplace, several questions should be considered: Is the risk acceptable? What is the likelihood of an accident occurring due to the hazard? Is control necessary?

Controlling hazards and managing risks often require intervention by supervisors or designated personnel. While some hazards can be immediately addressed by individuals, many need to be reported to supervisors for proper handling. Supervisors are responsible for directing these reports to the appropriate authorities, and if a hazard persists, they may implement permanent controls to mitigate risks and ensure safety.

Control measures aim to reduce the risks associated with hazards to an acceptable level. Ideally, hazards should be eliminated entirely to minimize risks. The hierarchy of control is a framework used to prioritize control measures, listing options from the most to the least preferable. This hierarchy assists in decision-making by outlining the most effective approaches for hazard management.

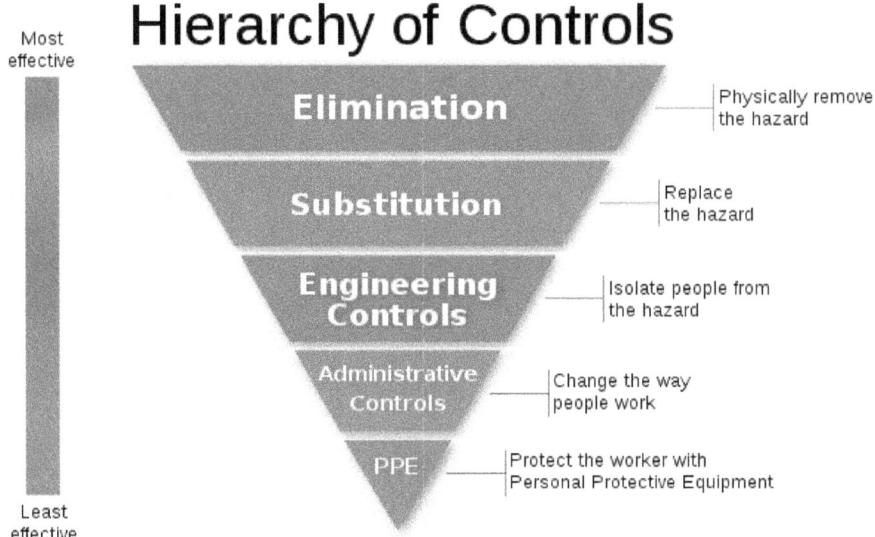

Figure 48: NIOSH's "Hierarchy of Controls infographic". Original version: NIOSHVector version: Michael Pittman, CC0, via Wikimedia Commons.

Control measures are crucial in reducing the risks associated with hazards to an acceptable level. Ideally, hazards should be completely eliminated to minimize risks. The hierarchy of control provides a structured approach to prioritize control measures, ranging from the most to the least preferable options. This hierarchy aids decision-making by delineating the most effective strategies for managing hazards [75, 76].

Proactive hazard identification and elimination are highlighted as safer and more cost-effective compared to reactive hazard management [76]. This approach aligns with the concept of eliminating hazards at the source, which is a fundamental principle in the hierarchy of control. By addressing hazards at their root cause, the risks can be significantly reduced [76, 77].

Controlling hazards and managing risks in landscape construction is essential for ensuring the safety of workers and minimizing the potential for accidents or injuries. Here's a detailed guide on how to control hazards and manage risks effectively:

- **Hierarchy of Control:** Adhere to the hierarchy of control measures, which prioritizes methods for controlling hazards from most effective to least effective. The hierarchy typically includes:

  - Elimination: Completely removing the hazard from the workplace, if feasible. For example, using alternative landscaping techniques that eliminate the need for hazardous chemicals.

  - Substitution: Replacing the hazard with a safer alternative. This could involve using less toxic materials or equipment with built-in safety features.

  - Engineering controls: Implementing physical changes to the work environment or equipment to minimize the risk. Examples include installing guardrails around excavation sites or using noise-reducing equipment.

  - Administrative controls: Implementing policies, procedures, and training programs to reduce exposure to hazards. This may involve scheduling work to minimize exposure to extreme weather conditions or providing training on safe work practices.

- Personal protective equipment (PPE): Providing workers with appropriate PPE, such as gloves, safety glasses, and respiratory protection, to protect against identified hazards. PPE should be used as a last resort when other control measures are not feasible.

- **Risk Assessment:** Conduct comprehensive risk assessments to identify potential hazards, assess their likelihood and severity, and prioritize control measures. Consider factors such as the nature of the work, environmental conditions, equipment and machinery used, and the experience level of workers.

- **Safe Work Practices:** Establish and enforce safe work practices and procedures that address specific hazards encountered in landscape construction. Provide thorough training to workers on the proper use of equipment, handling of materials, and implementation of safety protocols.

- **Regular Inspections:** Conduct regular inspections of the job site to identify new hazards or changes in existing hazards. Inspections should cover all areas of the workplace, including excavation sites, machinery, tools, and storage areas.

- **Equipment Maintenance:** Implement a regular maintenance schedule for equipment and machinery to ensure they are in safe working condition. Inspect tools and equipment before each use, and promptly repair or replace any damaged or malfunctioning items.

- **Emergency Preparedness:** Develop and implement emergency response plans to address potential hazards and accidents in landscape construction. Provide training to workers on emergency procedures, evacuation routes, and first aid protocols.

- **Communication and Training:** Foster open communication between workers, supervisors, and management regarding hazards, risks, and safety concerns. Provide ongoing training and education on hazard recognition, risk management, and safe work practices.

- **Documentation and Record-Keeping:** Maintain accurate records of hazard assessments, risk control measures, safety inspections, training sessions, and incident reports. Documentation helps track compliance with safety regulations and facilitates continuous improvement in safety performance.

- **Worker Involvement:** Encourage active participation and involvement of workers in hazard identification, risk assessment, and safety decision-making processes. Workers often have valuable insights and firsthand knowledge of job site hazards that can contribute to effective risk management.

- **Continuous Improvement:** Regularly review and evaluate the effectiveness of hazard controls and risk management strategies. Identify areas for improvement and implement corrective actions to enhance workplace safety over time.

Contributing to WHS, Hazard, Accident or Incident Reports

Responsibilities regarding incident reporting and recording accidents and injuries are paramount for effective hazard control and accident prevention in any workplace. Employers are mandated to maintain comprehensive records of all work-related injuries, illnesses, and dangerous occurrences. Such dangerous events might encompass various scenarios, including the collapse, overturning, or malfunction of high-risk machinery or equipment, excavation failures, structural collapses, equipment malfunctions, hazardous substance leaks, falls from heights, boiler or pressure vessel damages, and uncontrolled explosions or fires.

Furthermore, the term "serious bodily injury" is defined as any injury resulting in death, loss of a body part or organ, or an absence from employment for more than four days. Similarly, "work-caused illness" refers to illnesses contracted due to work, workplace activities, or exposure to specified high-risk machinery or equipment.

When delivering a speech or presentation, it's crucial to maintain authenticity and speak about topics within your expertise. Avoid pretending to be an expert in areas beyond your knowledge. Preparation is key; develop thorough notes that you can easily reference during your speech. Be ready to address counterarguments and support your points with factual evidence and concrete examples, steering clear of hearsay and exaggeration.

Variation in delivery speed is natural and can be used to emphasize key points. Embrace moments of silence, as they can enhance the impact of your speech. Accept that feeling nervous before speaking is normal and indicates a genuine investment in the topic. Maintain eye contact with your audience to establish a connection, and if necessary, focus on supportive faces to regain confidence.

Rehearsal is essential for improving public speaking skills and building confidence over time. Just as one learns to ride a bike through practice, speaking proficiency improves with repeated exposure. The more you speak, the more comfortable and adept you'll become at delivering engaging presentations.

Contributing to Workplace Health and Safety (WHS/OHS) involves various proactive measures aimed at fostering a safer working environment. Here's a breakdown of ways individuals can contribute:

- Understanding Health and Safety Consultation and Communication: It's essential to grasp how communication regarding health and safety should be conducted in the workplace. This includes understanding the protocols for consultation and effectively communicating safety information to colleagues.

- Improving Communication Skills: Enhancing communication abilities enables individuals to articulate safety concerns clearly and effectively convey relevant information to colleagues and supervisors.

- Understanding Safety Rules: Familiarizing oneself with the safety regulations and protocols specific to their workplace is crucial for ensuring compliance and identifying potential hazards.

- Making Suggestions for Safety: Encouraging an environment where employees feel empowered to suggest safety improvements fosters a culture of continuous improvement in workplace safety.

- Participating in Health and Safety Activities: Actively engaging in Health and Safety meetings, emergency drills, safety training sessions, and completing safety checklists demonstrates a commitment to workplace safety.

- When communicating health and safety information, several factors should be considered:

- Purpose and Outcome: Clarify the purpose of the communication and the desired outcome to ensure the message is effectively conveyed.

- Audience Information Requirements: Tailor the communication to meet the information needs of the audience, considering their existing knowledge and what additional information they require.

- Format and Diversity Considerations: Choose the most suitable format for communication, considering factors such as language barriers, literacy levels, and visual aids.

- Accessibility: Ensure that health and safety information is accessible to all workers, including those with disabilities or special requirements, by utilizing various communication methods.

- Timeliness: Provide health and safety information when workers are most receptive, ensuring prompt communication in urgent situations and utilizing standard reporting procedures for less urgent matters.

- Health and Safety consultation and communication yield numerous benefits for the workplace:

- Increased Awareness: Promotes awareness of WHS/OHS requirements and the importance of workplace safety among employees.

- Enhanced Knowledge and Skills: Empowers employees to fulfill their Duty of Care obligations by equipping them with the necessary knowledge and skills.

- Improved Decision-Making: Facilitates informed decision-making regarding health and safety matters, leading to better workplace practices and standards.

- Enhanced Relationships: Fosters better working relationships among colleagues and between management and employees through open communication and collaboration.

- Boosted Morale and Satisfaction: Contributes to increased morale and job satisfaction among employees by prioritizing their safety and well-being.

Effective consultation and communication in Health and Safety contribute to creating a safer, healthier, and more productive work environment for everyone involved.

Hazardous Substances

Hazardous materials or substances pose a risk of harm if they enter the body through ingestion, absorption, or inhalation. To prevent this, personal protective equipment (PPE) is often employed, acting as a barrier against such substances. These materials can be categorized into three main groups: solids, liquids, and gases. Solid hazardous materials include powders and dusts, while liquids and gases can encompass various chemicals commonly found in workplaces.

Chemicals used in the workplace, known as hazardous substances, can present significant health risks. These substances can range from everyday chemicals like cleaning liquids to more specialized compounds like those used in industrial processes. The level of danger posed by a hazardous substance depends on its type, the route of entry into the body, and the amount that enters.

Hazardous substances can enter the body through inhalation, swallowing, or skin contact. Exposure to these substances can result in immediate effects such as dizziness, nausea, or burns, or lead to long-term health issues like dermatitis or cancer.

To mitigate risks associated with hazardous substances, it's crucial to identify the hazards they pose. This can be achieved by reading labels and Material Safety Data Sheets (MSDS) provided by manufacturers or suppliers. Efforts should be made to eliminate the use of hazardous substances where possible. If elimination isn't feasible, substitution with less harmful alternatives should be considered. Engineering controls like ventilation systems can also be implemented to reduce exposure.

Additionally, personal protective equipment such as gloves, coats, masks, and safety glasses serve as secondary measures to minimize exposure to hazardous substances. These protective measures should be utilized in conjunction with other control measures to ensure comprehensive risk management in the workplace.

Specific Substances

Chemical hazards can be classified into several categories based on their properties and potential risks to human health and the environment. These classifications help in identifying and managing chemical hazards effectively. Here are the main classes of chemical hazards:

1. **Flammable and Combustible Materials**: These chemicals have the potential to ignite and burn, posing fire hazards. Examples include gasoline, solvents, and some gases like hydrogen.

2. **Toxic Chemicals**: Toxic chemicals can cause harm or even death when inhaled, ingested, or absorbed through the skin. They may damage organs, disrupt bodily functions, or cause long-term health issues. Examples include heavy metals like lead and mercury, pesticides, and certain industrial chemicals.

3. **Corrosive Chemicals**: Corrosive substances can cause severe damage to skin, eyes, and other materials upon contact. They often have high acidity or alkalinity and can corrode metals and other surfaces. Examples include strong acids like sulfuric acid and bases like sodium hydroxide.

4. **Reactive Chemicals**: Reactive chemicals are unstable and can undergo violent reactions when exposed to heat, pressure, or incompatible substances. They may release toxic gases, explode, or cause fires. Examples include peroxides, oxidizers, and reactive metals like sodium and potassium.

5. **Carcinogens**: Carcinogenic chemicals have the potential to cause cancer in humans or animals after prolonged exposure. They may damage DNA or disrupt cellular processes, leading to the development of cancerous tumors. Examples include asbestos, benzene, and formaldehyde.

6. **Mutagens**: Mutagenic chemicals can induce changes in DNA, increasing the risk of genetic mutations and hereditary disorders in exposed individuals or their offspring. They may lead to birth defects or other genetic abnormalities. Examples include certain pesticides, radiation, and some pharmaceuticals.

7. **Teratogens**: Teratogenic chemicals can interfere with fetal development during pregnancy, causing birth defects or reproductive harm. Exposure to these substances during critical stages of pregnancy can result in abnormalities in the unborn child. Examples include alcohol, certain medications, and some industrial chemicals.

8. **Allergens**: Allergenic chemicals can trigger allergic reactions in sensitive individuals upon exposure. These reactions may range from mild irritation to severe respiratory distress or anaphylaxis. Examples include latex, certain dyes, and

some food additives.

Understanding these classes of chemical hazards is essential for assessing risks, implementing safety measures, and preventing accidents or exposures in various settings, including workplaces, laboratories, and households. Proper handling, storage, and disposal practices are necessary to minimize the potential harm associated with chemical hazards.

Silica Dust: Silica, a primary component of sand, is present in materials like bricks, mortar, and concrete. When these materials are manipulated, such as through cutting, drilling, or grinding, silica dust is generated, releasing tiny particles into the air. Inhalation of these particles can lead to lung diseases like silicosis. It's crucial to employ safety measures like proper ventilation and respiratory protection when working with materials containing silica dust.

Treated Timber: Timber preservation treatments, particularly those containing chromium, copper, and arsenic (CCA), pose health hazards. Exposure to these chemicals can cause nausea, skin irritation, and eye irritation. Precautions such as wearing gloves, avoiding contact with open wounds, and thorough handwashing after handling treated timber are essential. Additionally, burning treated timber as firewood or for barbecues should be avoided due to the toxic gases released.

Figure 49: Retaining wall pressure treated lumber, supported by vertical I-beams. Tomwsulcer, CC0, via Wikimedia Commons.

Glass Fibres: Glass fibres, commonly used in insulation, can cause skin, eye, and respiratory irritation. Protective gear like gloves, masks, and eye protection should be worn when working with glass fibre insulation. Avoiding exposure to glass fibres is recommended for individuals not involved in tasks involving their manipulation.

Cement and Lime: Fine powders like cement and lime, used in mortar and concrete, can cause dermatitis upon inhalation. Safety precautions such as wearing gloves and avoiding dust inhalation are necessary when working with these materials. Individuals not engaged in tasks involving cement or lime should also avoid inhaling dust.

Asbestos: Asbestos, once widely used in construction materials, poses severe health risks if disturbed. Inhalation of asbestos fibres can lead to fatal diseases like asbestosis, lung cancer, and mesothelioma. Identification and handling of asbestos-containing materials (ACM) should be performed by trained professionals following specific safety protocols. Individuals not trained in asbestos removal should steer clear of areas where ACM is present.

Liquids: Hazardous substances in liquid form, including fuels and cleaning chemicals, can pose risks through ingestion, skin contact, or inhalation of fine mists. Proper handling, storage, and disposal procedures should be followed to minimize exposure to liquid hazards in the workplace.

Vermin Treatment: Liquid vermin treatments are commonly used on building sites to control pests like termites. These chemicals, while effective for pest control, can be harmful to humans. Exposure to these chemicals can lead to symptoms such as nausea and headaches if inhaled, and skin contamination if touched. When working with vermin treatments, individuals should avoid direct contact with the chemicals or treated soil. Protective gloves should be worn if contact is unavoidable, and thorough handwashing should follow. Those not directly involved in tasks using vermin treatments should steer clear of the treated area due to the lingering presence of chemicals.

Petrol and Diesel: Petrol and diesel fuels, although in liquid form, emit hazardous gases that are highly flammable. Care must be taken during refuelling to prevent ignition, as vapours can cause explosions. Inhalation of these vapours can lead to nausea, headaches, and asphyxiation in poorly ventilated areas. Individuals working with petrol or diesel should avoid skin contact and inhalation of fumes, and smoking should be prohibited during refuelling. Avoiding enclosed spaces during fuel handling is essential, and thorough washing is recommended if skin contact occurs.

Solvents: Solvents like turpentine, kerosene, acetone, and methylated spirits, commonly used for thinning and cleaning in construction, emit toxic fumes and are harmful upon skin contact. Safety precautions such as wearing gloves, eye protection, and face masks are necessary when working with solvents. Smoking around solvents and using them in enclosed spaces should be avoided. Individuals not involved in solvent-related tasks should also steer clear of the area and refrain from smoking.

Hydrochloric Acid: Hydrochloric acid, used for cleaning brickwork, is highly corrosive and can cause skin irritation and eye damage. Diluted forms can still irritate upon contact. Safety measures like wearing protective clothing, gloves, eyewear, and face protection are crucial when handling hydrochloric acid. Splashes should be avoided, and containers should be kept in well-ventilated areas. Those not involved in tasks using hydrochloric acid should avoid the area to prevent exposure.

Sodium Hypochlorite: Found in bleaching and sanitising liquids, sodium hypochlorite is corrosive to eyes, skin, and the stomach and can irritate the lungs. Safety measures such as avoiding skin contact and inhaling fumes are essential when using cleaning products containing sodium hypochlorite. Smoking around these chemicals and handling them in enclosed spaces should be avoided. Individuals not involved in cleaning tasks should stay away from the area to prevent exposure.

Gases: Hazardous gases like carbon monoxide and industrial gases can pose significant health risks. Carbon monoxide, produced by internal combustion engines, can lead to nausea, asphyxiation, and even death upon inhalation. Industrial gases like acetylene and LPG are flammable and explosive, causing nausea and asphyxia if inhaled. Proper ventilation and avoidance of prolonged exposure are crucial when working with or near these gases. Individuals not involved in tasks producing these gases should also avoid the area and ensure proper ventilation in their surroundings.

Producers and importers of dangerous substances are mandated by law to provide cautionary labels and Safety Data Sheets (SDS) alongside their products. These documents offer guidance on the proper handling procedures for safety.

"Dangerous goods" refer to materials or items possessing hazardous properties that, if not appropriately managed, pose a potential threat to human health and safety, infrastructure, and/or the transportation vehicles used to convey them.

The transportation of dangerous goods is subject to strict control and regulation, enforced through various regulatory frameworks operating at both national and international levels. Key regulatory guidelines governing the transportation of dangerous goods include the United Nations Recommendations on the Transport of Dangerous Goods, the Technical Instructions of the International Civil Aviation Organization (ICAO), the Dangerous Goods Regulations of the International Air Transport Association (IATA), and the International Maritime Dangerous Goods Code of the International Maritime Organization (IMO). These regulatory regimes establish standards for the handling, packaging, labelling, and transportation of dangerous goods.

These regulatory frameworks employ comprehensive classification systems to categorize hazards and provide a standardized taxonomy of dangerous goods.

Figure 50: US DOT hazardous material placard for oxidizer 5.1. en:User:Cburnett, CC BY-SA 3.0, via Wikimedia Commons.

The nine classifications of dangerous goods categorize substances and articles based on their inherent hazards, providing a standardized system for their handling, packaging, labelling, and transportation. Here's an overview of each classification:

- **Class 1: Explosives**: This class includes substances and articles that can cause an explosion or release of energy. Explosives are further divided into divisions based on their characteristics, such as sensitivity to heat, shock, or friction.

- **Class 2: Gases**: Gases are substances that can exist in a gaseous state at normal temperatures and pressures. This class includes flammable gases, non-flammable gases, and toxic gases. Examples include propane, oxygen, and chlorine.

- **Class 3: Flammable Liquids**: Flammable liquids are substances that can easily ignite and burn at relatively low temperatures. This class includes fuels, solvents, and certain chemicals like gasoline, alcohol, and acetone.

- **Class 4: Flammable Solids**: Flammable solids are substances that can ignite and burn when exposed to heat or friction. This class includes materials like matches, certain metals, and self-reactive substances.

- **Class 5: Oxidizing Substances and Organic Peroxides**: Oxidizing substances are chemicals that can promote combustion by releasing oxygen. Organic peroxides are chemicals that can undergo exothermic decomposition, leading to fire or explosion. Examples include hydrogen peroxide and potassium permanganate.

- **Class 6: Toxic and Infectious Substances**: Toxic substances are chemicals that can cause harm to human health when inhaled, ingested, or absorbed through the skin. Infectious substances are materials containing pathogens that can cause disease in humans or animals. Examples include pesticides, certain drugs, and infectious cultures.

- **Class 7: Radioactive Materials**: Radioactive materials are substances that emit radiation and can pose a risk to human health and the environment. This class includes uranium, plutonium, and medical isotopes used in nuclear medicine.

- **Class 8: Corrosive Substances**: Corrosive substances are chemicals that can cause severe damage to living tissue or materials they come into contact with through chemical reaction. Examples include acids, alkalis, and certain cleaning agents.

- **Class 9: Miscellaneous Dangerous Goods**: This class includes substances and articles that present a danger during transportation but do not fit into the other eight classes. Examples include environmentally hazardous substances, magnetized materials, and lithium batteries.

Electrical Safety

Electrical safety in landscaping construction is paramount to prevent accidents, injuries, and fatalities caused by electric shocks, fires, or other hazards associated with electricity. Here's an overview of key aspects of electrical safety in landscaping construction:

- **Risk Assessment**: Before beginning any landscaping project involving electrical work, it's crucial to conduct a thorough risk assessment. Identify potential electrical hazards in the work area, such as overhead power lines, buried cables, or electrical equipment.

- **Training and Qualifications**: Ensure that all personnel involved in landscaping construction projects have received adequate training and are qualified to perform electrical work safely. This includes understanding electrical systems, recognizing hazards, and knowing how to use protective equipment.

- **Use of Ground Fault Circuit Interrupters (GFCIs)**: GFCIs are devices designed to quickly shut off power in the event of a ground fault, which can occur when electrical current leaks from a circuit. GFCIs should be used for all outdoor electrical outlets and power tools to protect against electric shocks.

- **Proper Wiring and Installation**: All electrical wiring and installations should comply with relevant electrical codes and standards. This includes using weatherproof wiring, properly grounding electrical systems, and installing conduits or protective barriers where necessary to prevent damage.

- **Overhead Power Lines**: When working near overhead power lines, maintain a safe distance as specified by local regulations. Use non-conductive ladders and tools, and consider contacting the utility company to de-energize or insulate the power lines if necessary.

- **Equipment Maintenance**: Regularly inspect and maintain electrical equipment and tools to ensure they are in good working condition. Replace damaged cords or equipment immediately, and perform routine checks for signs of wear, overheating, or other potential hazards.

- **Safe Work Practices**: Implement safe work practices to minimize the risk of electrical accidents. This includes de-energizing electrical circuits before performing maintenance or repairs, using lockout/tagout procedures when necessary, and never working on live electrical systems unless absolutely necessary and with proper safety precautions.

- **Personal Protective Equipment (PPE)**: Provide appropriate PPE, such as insulated gloves, goggles, and footwear, to workers who may be exposed to electrical hazards. Ensure that PPE is used correctly and regularly inspected for defects.

- **Emergency Preparedness**: Develop and communicate emergency procedures for dealing with electrical accidents or incidents. Ensure that workers know how to respond to electrical shocks, fires, or other emergencies, and provide first aid training as necessary.

By implementing these measures and promoting a culture of safety awareness, landscaping construction companies can effectively mitigate electrical hazards and ensure the well-being of their workers and the public.

Note: Ground Fault Circuit Interrupters (GFCIs) and Residual Current Devices (RCDs) are similar devices designed to protect against electrical shocks caused by ground faults, but they have some technical differences.

- **Functionality**: Both GFCIs and RCDs monitor the flow of electrical current in a circuit. When they detect a deviation in the current flow, such as leakage to ground, they quickly interrupt the circuit to prevent electric shocks. However, they may operate slightly differently based on the specific design and application.

- **Naming**: The terminology used to refer to these devices can vary depending on the region. In North America, devices that protect against ground faults are commonly known as GFCIs. In other parts of the world, including Europe and Australia, they are often called Residual Current Devices (RCDs).

- **Trip Current Levels**: One key difference between GFCIs and RCDs is the trip current level. GFCIs typically trip at lower current levels, usually around 5 milliamperes (mA), whereas RCDs may have trip currents ranging from 10 mA to 30 mA or higher, depending on the application and regulatory requirements.

- **Applications**: GFCIs are commonly used to protect individual outlets or circuits in residential, commercial, and industrial settings. They are often integrated into electrical outlets, circuit breakers, or extension cords. RCDs, on the other hand, may provide broader protection for entire circuits or groups of circuits in electrical distribution panels or switchboards.

- **Sensitivity**: RCDs may offer additional sensitivity settings to accommodate different electrical environments and applications. This allows them to be adjusted to provide the optimal balance between protection against electrical faults and minimizing nuisance tripping.

While GFCIs and RCDs serve similar purposes and provide important safety benefits, the terminology, trip current levels, and specific applications may differ based on regional standards and regulations. It's essential to understand the specific requirements and guidelines applicable to your location when selecting and installing these protective devices.

Portable Appliance Testing (PAT) and Tagging

Portable Appliance Testing (PAT) and tagging is a process used to ensure the electrical safety of portable appliances in various environments, including workplaces, schools, and public spaces. The process involves visually inspecting and electrically testing appliances to identify any faults or defects that could pose a risk of electric shock, fire, or other hazards. Here's a detailed explanation of the process:

- **Visual Inspection**: The first step in the testing and tagging process is a visual inspection of the appliance. A qualified technician examines the appliance for any visible signs of damage, wear, or deterioration. This includes checking the power cord, plug, casing, switches, and other components for cracks, fraying, exposed wires, or other abnormalities.

- **Electrical Testing**: After the visual inspection, the appliance undergoes electrical testing using specialized equipment. This testing typically involves measuring the insulation resistance, earth continuity, and leakage current of the appliance to ensure it meets safety standards. The specific tests performed may vary depending on the type of appliance and regulatory requirements.

- **Testing Procedures**: The testing equipment used for PAT may include insulation resistance testers, earth bond testers, and leakage current testers. These devices apply test voltages and currents to the appliance to assess its electrical integrity. The technician interprets the test results to determine whether the appliance passes or fails the test.

- **Tagging**: Once an appliance has been tested and deemed safe, it is labeled or tagged with a visual indicator to signify its compliance. This typically involves attaching a durable tag or label to the appliance that indicates the date of the test, the name of the tester, and the next scheduled test date. This tagging system helps keep track of when appliances were last tested and when they are due for retesting.

- **Documentation**: A record of the testing and tagging process is maintained for each appliance. This documentation includes details such as the appliance identification number, test results, date of testing, and any remedial actions taken. Keeping accurate records ensures compliance with regulatory requirements and provides a history of appliance safety maintenance.

- **Regular Inspection and Maintenance**: Testing and tagging is not a one-time process; it requires regular inspection and maintenance to ensure ongoing safety. The frequency of testing depends on various factors, including the type of appliance, its environment of use, and regulatory requirements. Some appliances may need testing every few months, while others may require annual testing.

Portable Appliance Testing and tagging are essential practices for maintaining electrical safety in workplaces and other settings. By identifying and addressing potential hazards in portable appliances, testing and tagging help prevent electrical accidents and ensure the safety of personnel and property.

Manual Handling

Manual handling refers to the physical activities involved in moving, carrying, lifting, lowering, pushing, or pulling objects or loads. In the construction industry, where equipment and materials are often large, heavy, and cumbersome, manual handling is a common task. Unfortunately, manual handling injuries account for more lost time than any other type of injury in this industry.

Some hazards associated with manual handling include excessive bending, twisting, or reaching; sudden or jerky movements; exposure to vibration from tools or surfaces; tasks requiring excessive force; maintaining fixed postures for extended periods; repetitive motions; and lifting heavy loads.

These tasks can lead to a variety of injuries, including sprains, strains, back injuries, hernias, and soft tissue damage. In fact, manual handling injuries are responsible for over half of the total cost of workers' compensation claims and the number of days lost from work.

Employers are legally responsible for preventing work-related injuries caused by manual handling tasks. Legislation requires them to identify hazardous tasks, assess associated risks, and implement controls to eliminate or reduce the risk of injury to workers.

Some typical manual handling risks include tasks involving excessive bending, twisting, or reaching; tasks requiring sudden or jerky movements; exposure to vibration; tasks requiring excessive force; maintaining fixed postures for extended periods; repetitive motions; and lifting heavy loads.

While it's not always possible to avoid manual lifting and carrying, there are some guidelines workers can follow to minimize the risk of injury. These include bending the knees and keeping the back straight when lifting, using proper lifting techniques, avoiding twisting the body while carrying loads, and asking for help when handling heavy items. Additionally, employers should provide training on safe lifting practices and ensure that mechanical lifting aids are available when needed.

The guidelines for lifting and carrying objects aim to minimize the risk of injury and strain on the body, especially in situations where heavy or awkwardly shaped items need to be moved. Here's a detailed explanation of each aspect:

- **Plan the lift**: Before lifting anything, it's important to plan the movement carefully. This involves knowing the destination of the object, ensuring the pathway is clear and safe, and assessing whether the load is manageable without straining. It's also advisable to warm up before lifting and to consider using mechanical devices or seeking assistance for heavy loads.

- **Maintain the body's natural curves**: To maintain balance and control, position your feet properly with one foot beside the load and the other slightly to the rear. When bending to lift, always bend your knees and keep your back straight. Lifting with a bent back can lead to serious spine injuries. Use your leg muscles to lift by straightening your legs, ensuring a good grip on the object with your hands.

- **Moving during the lift**: Lift the load smoothly and steadily, avoiding jerky movements. Keep the load close to your body to minimize strain, and avoid twisting while lifting or carrying, as this can put excessive pressure on the spine. Always face the direction of movement to maintain control.

- **After the lift**: Take short breaks between lifting heavy items to give your muscles time to rest. After lifting, gently stretch your spine, legs, and arms to relieve any tension and prevent stiffness.

- **Safe carrying methods**: When carrying heavy objects, it's essential to maintain proper posture and technique to avoid strain. Avoid twisting your body while carrying and instead change direction by moving your feet. Maintain clear vision to prevent tripping or bumping into obstacles. If possible, slide the load rather than lifting it entirely, as this can reduce strain. When placing the load on a surface, such as a bench, do so by placing it on the edge and sliding it forward to avoid excessive lifting. Following these guidelines can help minimize the risk of injury and ensure safe lifting and carrying practices.

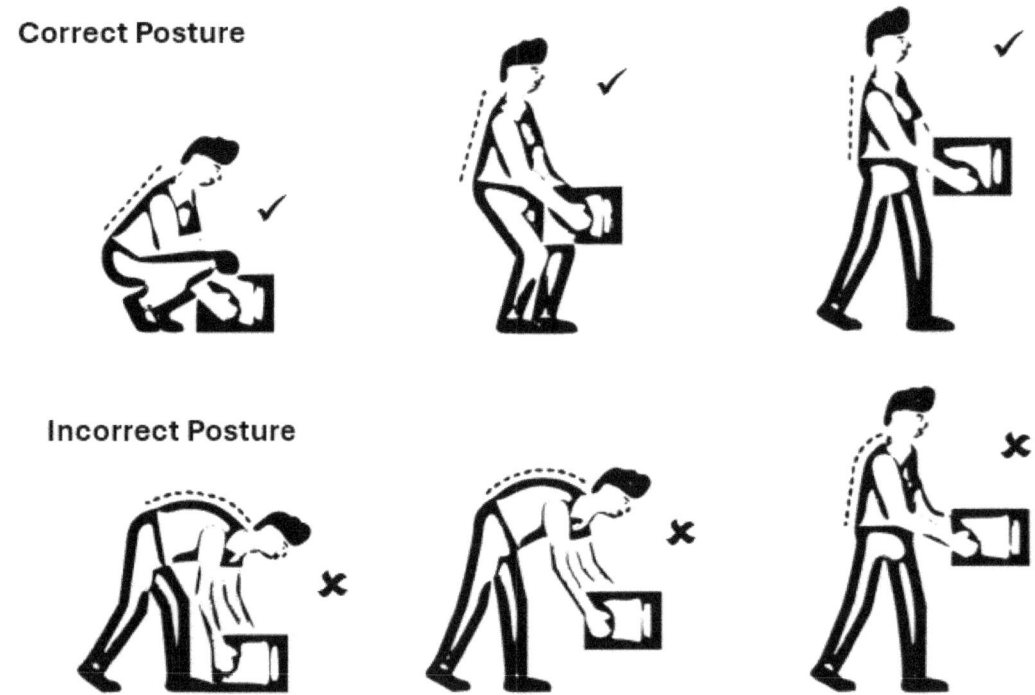

Figure 51: Correct and incorrect lifting techniques.

Slips, Trips and Falls

Slips, trips, and falls pose significant risks in the workplace, not only from working at heights but also from various other hazards like tripping over cords, slipping on wet surfaces, or stumbling on uneven ground. While these hazards may seem commonplace, they can lead to severe injuries if not properly managed. Here's a detailed explanation of some practices to control and reduce the risk of slip, trip, or fall hazards:

- **Maintain tidy work areas**: Keep workspaces organized and free from clutter to prevent obstructions in passages or aisle ways. This reduces the likelihood of tripping over objects left lying around.

- **Promptly clean up spills**: Spills should be cleaned up immediately to prevent slippery surfaces, reducing the risk of slips and falls.

- **Proper disposal of rubbish**: Dispose of rubbish in designated areas to prevent it from becoming a tripping hazard in workspaces.

- **Correct storage of equipment**: Ensure equipment is stored in appropriate locations to avoid creating obstacles in walkways or passages.

- **Secure drawers, cords, and hand tools**: Avoid leaving drawers open or cords strewn across walkways to prevent tripping hazards. Hand tools should be stored properly when not in use.

- **Mark and rope off hazardous areas**: Excavation works, trenches, holes, pits, or lift wells should be clearly marked and roped off to prevent accidental falls.

- **Address uneven surfaces**: Report and fix uneven or worn surfaces or mats to minimize the risk of tripping.

- **Store equipment awaiting maintenance properly**: Equipment awaiting maintenance should be stored away from aisles and passages to prevent obstruction.

- **Avoid unsafe practices**: Refrain from using chairs, stools, or crates as makeshift ladders to reach high shelves or machinery, as this can lead to falls.

- **Wear suitable footwear**: Use appropriate footwear suitable for the type of work being performed, providing adequate grip and support to minimize the risk of slips and falls.

Signs and Symbols

Safety signs and symbols play a crucial role in ensuring workplace safety by effectively communicating hazards and providing guidance on necessary precautions. These can include:

- **Purpose of Safety Signs and Symbols**: Safety signs and symbols are essential tools used to convey important information about hazards, prohibitions, mandatory actions, and emergency procedures in the workplace. Their primary purpose is to alert individuals to potential dangers and guide them on how to respond appropriately to ensure their safety and the safety of others.

- **Standardization and International Symbols**: Safety signs and symbols are standardized internationally to ensure consistency and clarity across different workplaces and regions. These standardized symbols are easily recognizable and understood by workers regardless of language barriers. For example, symbols indicating the need for eye protection or the location of emergency showers are universally understood, allowing workers to quickly identify and respond to potential hazards.

- **Emergency Shower Signs**: Emergency shower signs typically feature a symbol of a person standing under a shower with water flowing over them. This symbol indicates the location of emergency showers, which are essential safety equipment used to decontaminate individuals exposed to hazardous substances. These signs are usually placed near areas where hazardous chemicals are handled or stored, ensuring quick access to emergency showers in case of accidental exposure.

- **Chemical Storage Area Signs**: Signs indicating chemical storage areas often feature symbols representing hazardous materials, such as a skull and crossbones or a flame icon, along with text indicating the type of chemicals stored and any associated hazards. These signs serve as visual warnings to remind workers of the potential dangers posed by the chemicals stored in the area. They also help prevent accidental exposure and guide individuals on the necessary precautions to take when working near or accessing these areas.

- **Placement and Compliance**: Safety signs should be strategically placed in visible locations where everyone in the workplace can easily see them. The directions provided by safety signs are mandatory, meaning that individuals must comply with the instructions indicated on the signs at all times. Compliance with safety signs is crucial for maintaining a safe work environment and preventing accidents or injuries.

Safety signs and symbols, including those indicating emergency showers and chemical storage areas, are essential tools for promoting workplace safety. By familiarizing themselves with these signs and complying with their instructions, workers can effectively identify hazards, take necessary precautions, and respond appropriately in emergency situations, ultimately reducing the risk of accidents and injuries.

Barricades

Using barricades effectively in landscaping involves strategic placement and clear communication to ensure safety and organization in the work area. Here's a detailed guide on how to effectively use barricades in landscaping:

- **Identify Hazardous Areas**: Before setting up barricades, assess the landscaping site to identify hazardous zones such as areas with heavy equipment, ongoing construction, uneven terrain, or potential falling debris.

- **Plan Barricade Placement**: Determine where barricades are needed to cordon off hazardous areas, mark boundaries, or guide pedestrian and vehicle traffic. Consider factors like visibility, accessibility, and the size of the work area.

- **Select Appropriate Barricades**: Choose barricades suitable for the specific landscaping project. Options include:

    - Plastic or metal barricades: Lightweight and portable, ideal for marking boundaries or restricting access.

    - Traffic cones: Easily visible and useful for directing traffic or marking off smaller areas.

- Temporary fencing: Provides a sturdy barrier for larger work zones or areas requiring increased security.

- Reflective tape or flags: Enhances visibility, especially in low-light conditions or during nighttime work.

- **Establish Clear Signage**: Attach signage to barricades to convey important messages or warnings to workers and passersby. Signage may include:

  - Caution signs: Warn of potential hazards such as slippery surfaces, falling objects, or construction work.

  - Directional signs: Provide guidance on alternative routes or safe passage around the work area.

  - Safety instructions: Remind workers and visitors to wear protective gear, maintain a safe distance, or follow specific protocols.

- **Secure Barricades Properly**: Ensure barricades are securely anchored to prevent displacement by wind, vibrations, or accidental contact. Use stakes, sandbags, or weights to stabilize barricades, especially in outdoor environments with variable weather conditions.

- **Maintain Visibility**: Keep barricades clearly visible by using bright colors, reflective materials, or lighting, particularly if work continues after dark. Regularly inspect barricades for damage or obstruction and promptly address any issues to maintain visibility and effectiveness.

- **Monitor and Adjust Placement**: Continuously monitor the landscaping site and adjust barricade placement as needed based on changing conditions, project progress, or safety requirements. Periodically review barricade effectiveness and make adjustments to optimize safety and efficiency.

- **Communicate and Educate**: Ensure all workers and personnel are aware of barricade locations, meanings, and safety protocols. Conduct regular safety briefings and training sessions to reinforce proper barricade usage and emphasize the importance of adhering to safety measures.

Asbestos

Asbestos, a naturally occurring mineral composed of long, thin fibres, has been extensively mined and used in various industries due to its desirable properties such as fire resistance and durability. However, exposure to asbestos fibres can lead to severe health risks, including lung cancer, asbestosis, and mesothelioma. Here's a detailed explanation of asbestos, its types, associated risks, and precautions:

- **Definition and Types**: Asbestos is classified into two main groups:

  - **Serpentine**: Accounts for approximately 95% of all asbestos found in commercial buildings and households. Commonly used in construction materials like asbestos-cement sheeting, gaskets, roof shingles, and wall claddings.

- **Amphibole**: Primarily utilized in thermal insulation products and ceiling tiles.

- **Health Risks**: Inhalation of asbestos fibres or dust can lead to severe health conditions, including lung cancer, asbestosis (scarring of the lungs), and mesothelioma (cancer of the lining of the lungs). The risk of these diseases is particularly high among individuals exposed to friable asbestos, which can be easily broken into microscopic fibres and inhaled.

- **Regulations and Removal**: While the manufacture of asbestos-based products is now prohibited, the legacy of existing asbestos-containing materials requires careful management during removal or demolition. Friable asbestos, which can be reduced to powder when squeezed, requires a Class A license for removal if the amount exceeds 10 square metres. Non-friable asbestos, which does not become powdery under pressure, requires a Class B license for removal.

- **Safe Removal Practices**: Specialist contractors involved in asbestos removal must adhere to stringent standards to minimize health risks, including:

    - Conducting air quality reports in the immediate area.
    - Providing full protective clothing and respirators to all staff.
    - Neatly stacking and wrapping removed asbestos in plastic sheeting.
    - Disposing of asbestos at licensed disposal areas.
    - Monitoring air quality during removal and upon completion.

- **Precautions and Safety Measures**: When working with asbestos cement products or removing fibro sheeting, the following precautions should be observed:

    - Minimize dust generation by using non-powered hand tools and wetting down materials.
    - Work in open, ventilated areas and use appropriate respirators.
    - Avoid using high-pressure jets and power tools for sanding or cutting asbestos-containing materials.
    - Dispose of asbestos waste properly and in accordance with state regulations.

Figure 52: Roof made of corrugated asbestos. Harald Weber, CC BY-SA 3.0, via Wikimedia Commons.

Asbestos poses significant health risks, and proper precautions must be taken to ensure safe handling and removal. Adhering to regulatory guidelines and implementing stringent safety measures are essential for protecting workers and the environment from the hazards associated with asbestos exposure.

Personal Protective Equipment (PPE)

In an ideal scenario, the necessity for Personal Protective Equipment (PPE) would be non-existent as all risks would be either completely eradicated or significantly minimized. However, in the hierarchy of risk control measures, PPE is positioned as the last resort, indicating its status as the least preferred method for risk reduction. Nevertheless, there are instances where controlling risks through alternative means is unfeasible, leading to the indispensable need for PPE in various work environments.

PPE serves as a vital safeguard against occupational hazards in many workplaces. It's crucial to acknowledge that while appropriate PPE can be worn, it doesn't entirely eradicate the underlying hazards. Hence, the selection, fitting, cleaning, and maintenance of PPE are paramount, with close monitoring of its usage to ensure effective mitigation of associated dangers. If PPE fails to be effective, it provides little to no protection against hazards.

PPE becomes essential when it's impractical to eliminate or diminish hazards using alternative methods. Additionally, it proves valuable in emergency situations, clean-up operations, or during maintenance procedures. Although PPE doesn't eliminate workplace hazards, it offers protection to workers against these hazards, provided it's correctly fitted, maintained, and cleaned. Workers are mandated to adhere to all instructions and wear PPE once adequately trained in its use and upkeep.

Different types of PPE cater to specific risks and must be utilized accordingly:

- **Eye Protection**: Safety glasses made of appropriate materials and with correct fitting are necessary to shield against flying objects or harmful UV radiation, especially during welding tasks.

- **Ear Protection**: Given that noise levels on construction sites can exceed legal limits, employers are obligated to provide workers with suitable hearing protection like earplugs or earmuffs.

- **Respiratory Protection**: When working with hazardous chemicals, respiratory equipment is indispensable to prevent inhalation of toxic fumes.

- **Hand Protection**: Gloves designed for specific tasks are essential to protect against chemical burns, cuts, and facilitate safe handling of objects.

- **Foot Protection**: Safety boots with steel caps and adequate tread are vital to safeguard against foot injuries on worksites.

- **Head Protection**: Helmets must be worn in designated areas, with additional features like chin straps or face shields based on the nature of work.

Proper use, maintenance, and storage of PPE are imperative:

- PPE should be cleaned regularly, inspected for damage, and replaced if found ineffective.

- Equipment has a defined lifespan, and worn-out PPE should be promptly replaced.

- After use, PPE should be stored in a clean, accessible location, preferably following the manufacturer's recommendations.

By ensuring correct usage and maintenance of PPE, workers can effectively minimize risks and protect themselves against potential hazards in the workplace.

Working at Heights

Working at heights poses significant risks to workers, making it crucial to implement comprehensive safety measures to prevent accidents and injuries. This includes:

- **Identification of Risks:** Before any work begins, it's essential to thoroughly identify all potential hazards associated with working at heights. This includes assessing risks related to portable and fixed ladders, roofs, scaffolding, mezzanine floors, platforms, and elevated walkways.

- **Risk Assessment and Control:** Once identified, risks must be assessed and controlled before work commences. This involves implementing measures to mitigate the likelihood of accidents, such as utilizing fall injury prevention systems like elevating work platforms.

- **Fall Injury Prevention Systems:** Employers should provide and enforce the use of appropriate fall injury prevention systems, such as elevating work platforms (e.g., scissor lifts, cherry pickers), to ensure worker safety while working at heights.

- **Safe Access and Protection:** Ensuring safe access to elevated work areas and implementing adequate protection from falls are critical. This may involve installing guardrails, safety nets, or personal fall arrest systems to minimize the risk of accidents.

- **Proper Equipment Usage and Maintenance:** Workers must use the right equipment for the job and ensure it is correctly assembled and maintained. This includes regular inspections to identify any defects or issues that could compromise safety.

- **Good Housekeeping:** Maintaining a tidy and clutter-free work area is essential for preventing accidents. Clearing obstacles and debris from workspaces helps minimize trip hazards and enhances overall safety.

- **Regulatory Compliance:** Employers are legally obligated to identify all potential fall hazards exceeding 2 metres and implement measures to control these risks. This may involve conducting risk assessments, implementing safety protocols, and providing appropriate training to workers.

- **Risk Reduction Measures:** If eliminating the risk of a fall hazard is not feasible, employers must implement measures to reduce the risk. This could include performing work on solid ground, using passive fall prevention devices like temporary work platforms or scaffolds, or utilizing elevating work platforms.

- **Assessment of Lower Height Risks:** Even tasks involving heights below 2 metres can pose significant risks of injury. Therefore, it's recommended to assess all work at heights for potential fall hazards and implement appropriate controls to minimize risks.

Ladder Control

Ensuring proper ladder control is crucial for the safety of workers who use ladders in various settings. Let's break down the detailed instructions provided:

- **Choosing the Correct Ladder:** Selecting the right ladder for the task at hand is essential. Factors to consider include the height needed, weight capacity, and the type of work being performed.

- **Avoiding Metal Ladders Near Electricity:** Metal ladders should not be used near electricity or power lines to prevent the risk of electrical shock or electrocution.

- **Checking for Maintenance:** Before use, inspect the ladder to ensure it is well maintained. Look for any signs of damage, such as cracked or damaged rungs, and address any issues promptly.

- **Cordoning Off the Area:** If there are pedestrians or traffic nearby, it's important to cordon off the area to prevent accidents or collisions while the ladder is in use.

- **Securing the Head and Base:** Secure both the head and base of the ladder to ensure stability during use. Alternatively, have someone hold the base of the ladder to prevent it from slipping.

- **Locking the Spreaders:** If using a step ladder, lock the spreaders into position to prevent accidental collapse while climbing.

- **Suitable Footwear:** Wear appropriate footwear for climbing the ladder to ensure good grip and stability.

- **Using Both Hands:** Maintain a firm grip on the ladder by using both hands while climbing. Tools can be passed up or carried in a tool belt to keep hands free.

- **Ensuring Proper Extension:** Ensure that the stiles (side rails) of the ladder extend at least 900 mm (about 3 feet) above the stepping-off point to provide a secure handhold when transitioning off the ladder.

- **Compliance with Standards:** Ladders must adhere to relevant Australian Standards, whether used in an office or on a construction site. Homemade or makeshift ladders may not meet safety standards and should be avoided.

- **Condition of Ladders:** Ladders must be in good condition, with no broken or loose rungs, splintered edges, or splits. Damaged ladders pose significant safety hazards and should be repaired or replaced promptly.

- **Proper Slope and Placement:** The slope of the ladder should fall within the range of 1 in 4 to 1 in 6 for optimal stability and safety. Additionally, the base of the ladder should be positioned at least one metre from the wall, and the top should extend 900 mm above the landing point. Ladders should sit on firm, stable ground, and the top should be secured to prevent sideways movement.

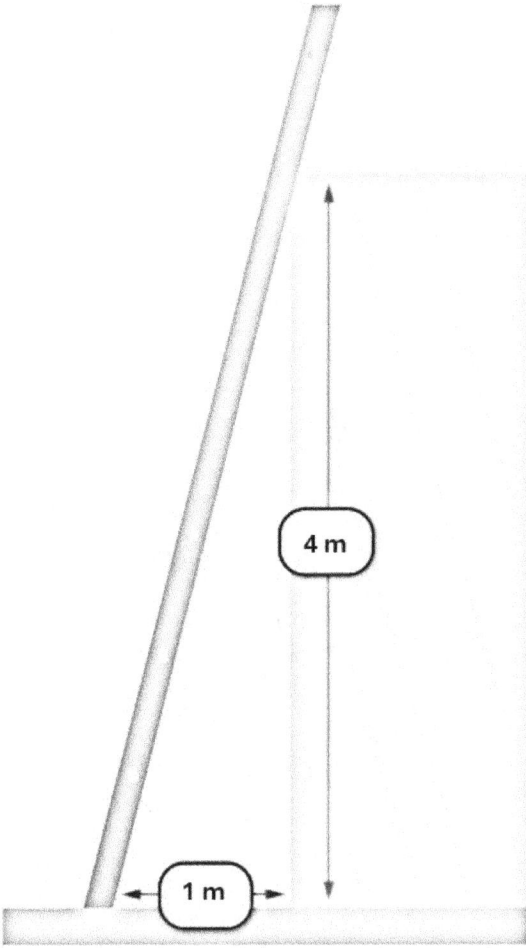

Figure 53: Correct ladder slope.

Working in Confined Spaces

Working in confined spaces presents significant health and safety risks for employees, often due to a lack of identification or underestimation of hazards. Tragically, confined space accidents can result in multiple fatalities, particularly when unplanned rescue attempts are made by unprepared individuals. Therefore, only appropriately trained and qualified personnel should undertake work in confined spaces. A confined space is defined as any volume with limited or restricted means of entry and exit, making it physically challenging to enter or exit. These spaces may lack adequate ventilation, contain contaminated or oxygen-deficient atmospheres, and are typically not intended for regular occupation but may be entered by personnel.

Identifying hazards and planning accordingly for work in confined spaces is crucial to ensuring successful outcomes and preventing disasters. Planning involves conducting a detailed risk assessment of the intended work, which includes identifying associated hazards, assessing the risk of harm from these hazards, and implementing suitable controls to eliminate or reduce the risk. Hazards commonly associated with working in confined spaces include gases or fumes emitted by stored materials or chemicals, the risk of being trapped by fluids entering the space, accidental leaks or spills contaminating the atmosphere and creating slipping or tripping hazards, and the potential for workers to be trapped or crushed by moving machinery.

Figure 54: Example confined space. Jenny Cestnik, CC BY-ND 2.0, via Flickr.

Other hazards include suffocation or engulfment by solids, oxygen depletion due to machinery use or exhaust gases, chemical reactions leading to explosions or contaminated atmospheres, extremes of temperature causing heat exhaustion or hypothermia, noise impairing communication with those outside the confined space, and manual handling injuries from working in cramped or awkward positions. Proper risk assessment and control measures are essential to mitigate these hazards and ensure the safety of workers in confined spaces. By adequately identifying risks and implementing appropriate safety protocols, employers can minimize the likelihood of accidents and protect the well-being of their employees.

Working in culverts, is an example of working in a confined space and presents a range of hazards that can pose significant risks to workers' health and safety. Culverts are typically enclosed drainage structures found beneath roads, railways, or embankments, designed to channel water flow. Here are some of the hazards related to working in culverts:

- **Limited Entry and Exit Points:** Culverts often have restricted means of entry and exit, making it challenging for workers to enter and exit quickly in case of emergencies. This limited access can increase the risk of entrapment or being unable to escape if hazards arise.

- **Confined Space Conditions:** Culverts are confined spaces by nature, with restricted ventilation and limited space for movement. Working in such confined environments can lead to feelings of claustrophobia, discomfort, and difficulty manoeuvring, increasing the risk of accidents.

- **Poor Visibility:** The enclosed nature of culverts can result in poor lighting conditions, limited visibility, and shadows, making it challenging for workers to see potential hazards and obstacles. This can increase the risk of slips, trips, and falls.

- **Atmospheric Hazards:** Culverts may contain hazardous atmospheres due to the accumulation of gases, such as methane or hydrogen sulphide, or the presence of toxic substances. Without proper ventilation or monitoring, workers may be exposed to dangerous concentrations of these gases, leading to asphyxiation or chemical poisoning.

- **Water Hazards:** Culverts may contain water, which can pose drowning hazards, particularly during heavy rainfall or when working in flooded conditions. Rapidly rising water levels can trap workers inside culverts, leading to drowning or injury.

- **Structural Instability:** Older culverts or those subjected to heavy loads may exhibit structural weaknesses, such as corrosion, cracks, or collapses. Working in such unstable conditions increases the risk of structural failure, entrapment, or being struck by falling debris.

- **Biological Hazards:** Culverts may harbor biological hazards, such as mold, bacteria, or pests, due to the damp and enclosed environment. Exposure to these hazards can lead to respiratory problems, allergic reactions, or the spread of infectious diseases.

- **Traffic Hazards:** Culverts located beneath roads or railways pose risks from passing vehicles or trains. Workers may be at risk of being struck by moving vehicles or equipment while entering or exiting culverts, especially if proper traffic control measures are not in place.

- **Manual Handling Risks:** Working in culverts often involves manual handling tasks, such as lifting or carrying equipment and materials in confined spaces. Improper lifting techniques or cramped working conditions can increase the risk of musculoskeletal injuries.

- **Communication Challenges:** Communication can be difficult in culverts due to limited visibility, noise from flowing water, and the confined space. This can hinder coordination between workers and increase the risk of accidents or delays in responding to emergencies.

To mitigate these hazards, thorough risk assessments should be conducted before commencing work in culverts, and appropriate safety measures should be implemented, including proper training, ventilation, monitoring, personal protective equipment (PPE), and emergency procedures. Regular inspections and maintenance of culverts are also essential to ensure structural integrity and minimize risks to workers.

Figure 55: Example of a culvert. Andrew Abbott, CC BY-SA 2.0, via Wikimedia Commons.

Excavations

During the initial phases of a construction endeavour, it's common to find earthmoving equipment present on the site, with trenches being excavated. In residential construction, the scope of work is typically minor. However, in larger-scale projects, multiple machines may operate simultaneously, and trenches could extend several metres deep.

Figure 56: Example of a typical site excavation. Khaosaming, CC BY-SA 3.0, via Wikimedia Commons.

Working around excavations requires careful planning, proper equipment, and adherence to safety protocols to mitigate the risks associated with potential hazards. Here's a detailed guide on how to safely work around excavations:

- **Risk Assessment:** Before commencing work, conduct a thorough risk assessment of the excavation site. Identify potential hazards such as cave-ins, falling objects, hazardous atmospheres, and utility conflicts.

- **Training and Qualifications:** Ensure that all personnel involved in the excavation work are adequately trained and qualified. This includes training in excavation safety, the proper use of equipment, emergency procedures, and the recognition of hazards.

- **Protective Systems:** Implement appropriate protective systems to prevent cave-ins and protect workers inside the excavation. This may include sloping, benching, shoring, or trench shielding systems based on the soil type and depth of the excavation.

- **Excavation Design:** Design the excavation with safety in mind, considering factors such as the stability of the soil, groundwater levels, and the presence of nearby structures or utilities. Ensure that the excavation is properly sloped or supported to prevent collapse.

- **Access and Egress:** Provide safe access and egress points for workers entering and exiting the excavation. Use ladders, ramps, or stairways with secure footholds and handholds to facilitate safe entry and exit.

- **Barriers and Signage:** Erect barriers and signage around the excavation site to prevent unauthorized access and alert workers and pedestrians to the potential hazards. Use barricades, fencing, and warning signs to mark the boundaries of the excavation area.

- **Utility Locating:** Before digging, contact the appropriate authorities to locate and mark the underground utilities in the vicinity of the excavation site. Take precautions to avoid damaging utility lines, which can pose serious safety risks.

- **Personal Protective Equipment (PPE):** Ensure that all workers wear appropriate PPE, including hard hats, high-visibility clothing, safety glasses, gloves, and steel-toed boots. Additional PPE such as respiratory protection may be required if working in confined spaces or areas with hazardous atmospheres.

- **Monitoring and Testing:** Regularly monitor and test the atmosphere inside the excavation for hazardous gases or low oxygen levels. Use gas detectors and atmospheric testing equipment to ensure that the air quality is safe for workers.

- **Emergency Procedures:** Establish clear emergency procedures and rescue plans in case of accidents or emergencies. Ensure that all workers are familiar with these procedures and know how to respond effectively to incidents such as cave-ins, injuries, or hazardous material spills.

- **Supervision and Communication:** Assign a competent person to supervise the excavation work and communicate safety instructions to workers. Maintain open lines of communication between workers, supervisors, and other personnel involved in the project.

- **Regular Inspections:** Conduct regular inspections of the excavation site and protective systems to identify any signs of instability, damage, or hazards. Address any issues promptly to ensure ongoing safety.

Underground Services

Underground services encompass a wide array of essential infrastructure, including electric, telephone, and broadband cables, as well as water, sewer, stormwater, and gas pipes. These critical utilities are vital for maintaining modern living standards, providing power, communication, and sanitation services to communities. However, damage to these underground services can have severe consequences, posing potential hazards to both public safety and infrastructure integrity while also causing significant disruption and financial costs. Therefore, it is imperative to carefully consider the presence of underground services before undertaking any excavation activities.

One of the primary challenges associated with underground services is their hidden nature, as they are typically concealed beneath the ground. Existing services are often located beneath road verges and sites where buildings have previously stood, making them susceptible to accidental damage during construction or excavation work. While drawings or records may sometimes be available, indicating the approximate location of these services, their accuracy and completeness can vary significantly.

In cases where precise information about the location of underground services is not available or is uncertain, excavation must proceed with extreme caution and meticulousness. Hand excavation techniques may be necessary to minimize the risk of accidental damage to buried utilities. This approach allows workers to carefully uncover and identify underground services without the use of mechanical equipment, reducing the likelihood of unintended disruptions or hazardous incidents.

The importance of proper planning and precautionary measures cannot be overstated when dealing with underground services. Failure to accurately identify and protect these utilities before excavation can lead to severe consequences, including service outages, environmental damage, injuries, and costly repair or replacement efforts. Therefore, thorough assessment and coordination with relevant utility providers are essential to ensure the safety, integrity, and efficiency of construction projects while minimizing risks to both workers and the surrounding community.

General Housekeeping

Good housekeeping and maintenance form the cornerstone of industrial safety and health practices. While closely related, they serve distinct functions in ensuring workplace safety and efficiency. Maintenance encompasses the upkeep of buildings, machinery, equipment, and facilities to ensure they remain in safe, efficient working order. This includes regular inspections, repairs, and servicing to prevent malfunctions and hazards. Additionally, maintenance involves the upkeep of sanitary facilities and the cleaning and painting of surfaces to maintain a safe and hygienic working environment.

On the other hand, good housekeeping involves the day-to-day cleanliness, tidiness, and organization of the workplace. It encompasses maintaining orderliness in all areas of the facility, from production floors to office spaces. Good housekeeping is closely intertwined with maintenance, as proper upkeep of machinery and equipment is essential for maintaining cleanliness and orderliness. For example, a poorly maintained floor may be difficult to keep clean, or leaks from ill-maintained equipment can lead to slippery surfaces.

Defective maintenance can contribute to accidents, such as falls due to broken floors or faulty equipment guarding, scalds from leaking pipes, and other incidents resulting from inadequate upkeep. Similarly, poor housekeeping practices can lead to a wide range of accidents, including slips and falls on slippery or obstructed floors, collisions with obstructions left in walkways, and injuries from protruding nails or poorly stacked materials.

Internal transport risks are heightened in cluttered environments where passageways are not kept clear, and materials are poorly stacked. Fires can also be sparked by the accumulation of combustible waste or excessive quantities of flammable materials. Moreover, health risks from dangerous dusts and chemicals are exacerbated in unclean environments, emphasizing the importance of regular cleaning and waste removal.

Effective housekeeping requires proactive management and planning. Management should establish clear guidelines and allocate resources to maintain cleanliness and orderliness throughout the facility. This includes proper layout planning to facilitate easy observation of order and cleanliness, clearly marking aisles, walkways, and exits, and providing designated storage areas for raw materials, finished products, tools, and accessories.

Furthermore, adequate waste disposal receptacles should be strategically placed, and floors and workbenches should be constructed of suitable materials that are easy to clean and maintain. Non-slip surfaces and polishing methods can help prevent slips and falls, while screening and physical barriers can prevent spills and debris from accumulating on surrounding floors.

Each industry faces unique housekeeping challenges, from large-scale manufacturing plants to small workshops. Construction sites, in particular, present significant difficulties due to the dynamic nature of the environment. Rigorous supervision and employee cooperation are essential to maintain cleanliness and orderliness, thus reducing the risk of accidents and injuries on site.

Equipment Inspection

Performing a pre-start check before using any workplace system or equipment is a fundamental safety practice aimed at ensuring that the equipment is in optimal working condition and safe to use. This preventive measure is crucial for identifying potential hazards or defects that could pose risks to the user's safety or result in equipment malfunction. The pre-start check involves a systematic examination of various components and features of the equipment to verify its safe operating condition.

One aspect of the pre-start check involves inspecting electrical and power outlets on the wall to ensure they are functioning properly and free from damage or defects. This includes checking for loose connections, exposed wires, or signs of overheating, which could indicate potential electrical hazards. Additionally, it is essential to verify whether the equipment has a current electrical safety tag attached to it, indicating that it has been tested and deemed safe for use. This tag serves as a visual indicator of the equipment's compliance with safety standards and regulations.

Furthermore, the pre-start check involves inspecting plugs and power cords to ensure they are in good repair and free from damage, fraying, or wear and tear. Damaged plugs or cords can pose serious electrical hazards, such as electric shock or fire, making it imperative to address any issues promptly before using the equipment. Regular inspection and maintenance of plugs and cords help prevent accidents and ensure the safe operation of electrical equipment.

It is essential to follow the manufacturer's instructions and guidelines when performing a pre-start check, as they provide valuable insights into specific inspection procedures and safety precautions for the equipment. Manufacturers typically outline recommended inspection points, maintenance procedures, and safety considerations to help users ensure the equipment's safe and effective operation. Adhering to these instructions helps maintain compliance with safety standards and minimize the risk of accidents or equipment failure.

If any tools or equipment are found to require maintenance or replacement during the pre-start check, it is crucial to report these issues to a supervisor immediately. Attempting to repair or modify equipment without proper training or authorization can pose significant safety risks and may void warranties or compromise equipment integrity. It is essential to prioritize safety and avoid using unsafe equipment to prevent accidents, injuries, or damage to property. By conducting thorough pre-start checks and promptly addressing any issues, workers can help maintain a safe working environment and mitigate risks associated with equipment operation.

Equipment Maintenance

Regular inspection and maintenance of plant and equipment are essential practices to ensure their safe and efficient operation in the workplace. Different types of equipment require varying levels of inspection and servicing, according to the manufacturer's instructions and industry standards. Maintenance tasks may include periodic servicing of machinery engines, such as oil changes and filter replacements, testing warning alarms, such as fire alarms, and replacing worn parts to prevent malfunctions or failures. Additionally, ensuring that overload and cut-out switches are functional and inspecting and tagging electrical equipment are critical maintenance activities to prevent electrical hazards.

Maintenance tasks vary in frequency, with some requiring more frequent attention than others based on the equipment's usage and operating conditions. For example, equipment equipped with trip switches, such as residual-current devices (RCDs), should have their test button pressed at the start of each day's work to verify their proper functioning. Similarly, petrol and diesel motors should undergo daily checks for fuel, oil, and water levels to maintain optimal performance and prevent mechanical issues.

Many organizations implement procedures to track and manage equipment maintenance effectively. This may include maintaining a service logbook for each machine, documenting maintenance activities, inspections, and servicing performed. Additionally, organizations may use checklists for routine inspections to ensure that all necessary maintenance tasks are completed systematically and consistently. Incident forms may be used to record equipment breakdowns, malfunctions, or safety incidents, providing valuable data for identifying recurring issues and implementing preventive measures.

Adhering to manufacturer's instructions and industry best practices is crucial for maintaining the safety and reliability of plant and equipment. Neglecting maintenance tasks or failing to follow proper procedures can result in equipment malfunction, breakdowns, and safety hazards, potentially leading to accidents, injuries, or damage to property. By implementing a proactive maintenance program and ensuring regular inspections and servicing according to manufacturer's guidelines, organizations can minimize downtime, prolong equipment lifespan, and create a safer working environment for employees. Effective maintenance practices contribute to improved productivity, reduced costs, and enhanced overall operational efficiency in the workplace.

Emergency Plans

An emergency plan serves as a crucial framework for guiding individuals' actions and responses in the event of unforeseen incidents or emergencies within a workplace. It comprises a set of written instructions detailing the procedures to be followed by workers and other personnel to ensure an effective and coordinated response to emergencies. Essential components of an emergency plan include delineating emergency procedures, evacuation protocols, communication channels, medical treatment provisions, and arrangements for notifying emergency service organizations promptly. Furthermore, the plan must outline the frequency of testing emergency procedures and provide comprehensive information, training, and instruction to relevant personnel regarding their implementation.

Various types of emergencies may occur in workplaces, ranging from fires and explosions to medical emergencies, hazardous chemical incidents, bomb threats, armed confrontations, and natural disasters. Hence, emergency plans should encompass a comprehensive range of potential scenarios to ensure preparedness for any eventuality. These plans should be based on a practical assessment of workplace hazards and the possible consequences of emergencies arising from such hazards. Additionally, external hazards, such as neighbouring chemical storage facilities, should also be considered when formulating emergency plans to mitigate risks effectively.

The level of detail in emergency plans should be tailored to the specific workplace's needs and characteristics. While they do not necessarily have to be lengthy or complex, they must be easy to understand and practical for implementation. Factors to be considered when developing emergency plans include the nature of work activities, workplace hazards, the size and location of the facility, and the composition of the workforce. Special considerations may be required for workers who travel for work, work alone, or operate in remote locations to ensure their safety during emergencies.

An emergency plan typically includes practical information and resources for workers, such as emergency contact details for key personnel, contact information for local emergency services, alert mechanisms, evacuation procedures, and the location of emergency equipment. It may also outline processes for advising neighbouring businesses about emergencies and post-incident follow-up procedures, such as notifying regulatory authorities or organizing trauma counselling. Furthermore, emergency plans must incorporate procedures for testing their effectiveness, including the frequency of testing and documentation requirements.

Higher-risk workplaces, such as those with confined spaces, fall arrest harness systems, hazardous chemical storage, or demolition sites, may require additional information and procedures in their emergency plans to address specific risks adequately. It is essential to consult relevant regulations and codes of practice to ensure compliance with applicable requirements. Emergency plans, or summaries thereof, should be readily accessible to workers and prominently displayed in the workplace, such as on notice boards, to facilitate quick reference during emergencies.

Adequate training in emergency procedures is paramount to ensure workers can respond effectively during emergencies. Training may include practicing evacuations, identifying assembly points, familiarizing with emergency equipment, and understanding first aid arrangements. Training requirements should be determined based on factors such as worker roles, induction processes for new workers, refresher training for existing workers, and specific training for individuals with formal emergency response roles, such as fire wardens or first aid officers. Regular review and revision of emergency plans are necessary to ensure they remain current, effective, and aligned with any changes in the workplace, staffing, activities, or regulatory requirements. Periodic reviews may be triggered by changes to the workplace layout, staff composition, introduction of new activities, or after conducting tests of the emergency plan's effectiveness.

Emergency Procedures

Emergency procedures are essential protocols designed to guide individuals' actions and responses during emergency situations in the workplace. These procedures are disseminated to employees through various means, such as signs, pamphlets, toolbox meetings, formal training sessions, and demonstrations or drills. It is crucial for individuals to familiarize themselves with these procedures and understand their roles and responsibilities in emergency situations. In a real emergency, there may not be time to read or review emergency signage and procedures, underscoring the importance of thorough preparation and understanding beforehand.

Employees have a responsibility to understand, practice, and follow workplace emergency procedures. This includes identifying who to report to in an emergency, possessing basic firefighting and first aid skills, and understanding evacuation protocols. In situations requiring specialist expertise and training, individuals without the necessary training should prioritize evacuation, allowing trained personnel to address the emergency safely. While larger organizations typically have predefined procedures for various emergencies, smaller organizations may have less complex procedures. Nevertheless, basic emergency information is relevant across all workplaces.

Fire safety is a critical aspect of emergency preparedness, as fires can result in serious injuries, loss of life, and significant damage to property and production facilities. Most workplace fires are preventable and may be caused by factors such as open flames, faulty electrical equipment, improper chemical use or storage, and smoking. Pre-planning is essential for fire prevention, involving the identification of fire risks and the implementation of preventive measures. Strategies for fire prevention include good housekeeping, safe handling of chemicals, regular equipment inspection and testing, and strict control of tasks involving 'hot work.'

Employees play a vital role in fire prevention by maintaining clean work areas, ensuring the safety of electrical wiring and appliances, correctly disposing of flammable materials, and adhering to safe work procedures. Smoking in designated non-smoking areas should be strictly prohibited due to the associated fire and explosion risks. Fire protection measures, such as fire extinguishers, smoke detectors, and sprinkler systems, should be provided and easily accessible. Employees should be aware of the location of fire fighting equipment and evacuation routes, as well as designated assembly areas.

In workplaces where combustible and flammable materials are present, such as construction sites, the risk of fires is heightened. Potential fuels include sawdust, timber, petrol, gas, solvents, and chemicals, while ignition sources may arise from faulty machinery, welding activities, or smoking. To prevent fires, maintaining good housekeeping and keeping ignition sources away from flammable materials are paramount. This involves regular cleaning of the workplace and ensuring activities that may cause sparks or flames are conducted safely away from fuel storage areas. By implementing preventive measures and adhering to fire safety protocols, workplaces can minimize the risk of fires and ensure the safety of employees and property.

Fire Fighting Equipment

Fires are categorized into classes depending on the materials or substances involved. But what exactly are the classifications of fires? In the United States, there are five fundamental classes of fire, each described below. It's worth noting that in other countries, such as those in Europe and Australia, the names and characteristics of these classes vary. For instance, in the United States, the National Fire Protection Association (NFPA) assigns names to fire classes, while in Europe, they adhere to the European Standard Classification of Fires.

Fire extinguishers and hose reels are vital equipment commonly found on-site for fighting fires. Fire extinguishers are color-coded and labelled based on their contents, and it's crucial to match the correct extinguisher to the type or class of fire to effectively combat it. Using the wrong extinguisher can be ineffective or even dangerous. Fire classes categorize fires according to the type of material burning, ranging from Class A to Class F, covering solids, liquids, gases, combustible metals, electrical currents, and cooking oils and fats commonly found in industrial kitchens.

In Australia, Class A fires involve ordinary combustible solids such as wood, paper, cloth, plastics, rubber, and coal. Class B fires include flammable and combustible liquids like petrol, oil, paint, thinners, kerosene, and alcohol. Class C fires involve flammable gases such as LPG, butane, acetylene, hydrogen, and natural gas. Class D fires encompass combustible metals like magnesium, aluminium, sodium, or potassium. Class E fires involve electrical equipment like computers, switchboards, and power boards. Finally, Class F fires involve cooking oils and fats typically found in industrial kitchens.

Figure 57: CO2 extinguisher, in case of fire. Newtown grafitti from Sydney, Australia, CC BY 2.0, via Wikimedia Commons.

In the United States, there are five types of fires denoted as: A, B, C, D, and K. Let's delve into the distinct characteristics of each type of fire, including their fuel sources, associated hazards, and prevalent methods employed to combat them.

- **Class A Fire:** Class A fires are the most prevalent and typically arise from common combustible materials like wood, paper, fabric, rubber, and plastic. These fires feature relatively low ignition temperatures and extinguish once the fuel or oxygen is depleted. For instance, a garbage fire exemplifies a Class A fire. Generally, if ash remains after the fire, it likely indicates a Class A Fire. Water and foam agents are commonly utilized to extinguish Class A fires.

- **Class B Fire:** Class B fires occur when flammable liquids or gases, such as alcohol, kerosene, paint, gasoline, methane, oil-based coolants, or propane ignite. They are frequently encountered in industrial settings but may also arise in residential or commercial environments. Class B fires possess a low flashpoint, burn easily at any temperature, and spread rapidly, emitting thick black smoke. Water is ineffective against Class B fires. Instead, Carbon Dioxide (CO_2) or dry chemical agents are preferred extinguishing agents.

- **Class C Fire:** Class C fires involve live electrical currents or electrical equipment as the fuel source. This category encompasses electric tools, appliances, motors, and transformers. They are prevalent in industrial settings dealing with energy or electrically-powered equipment, although occurrences in commercial or residential environments due to faulty wiring are not uncommon. Electrical fires cannot be fought with water—in fact, it can make it worse. Non-conductive chemical agents, including clean agents, are suitable for extinguishing Class C fires.

- **Class D Fire:** Class D fires pertain to fires fuelled by combustible metals such as aluminium, lithium, magnesium, potassium, titanium, and zirconium. These metals are commonly found in laboratories and manufacturing settings, posing significant hazards in these industries. Water usage can cause certain combustible metals to explode, making dry powder agents the preferred choice to absorb heat and smother flames by obstructing the fire's oxygen supply.

- **Class K Fire:** Finally, Class K fires refer to cooking fires resulting from the combustion of cooking liquids like grease, oil, vegetable fat, or animal fat. Although technically a type of liquid fire, they are distinguished as a separate class due to their unique culinary context. Class K fires are rampant in the food service and restaurant sector but can occur in any kitchen environment.

To use a fire extinguisher, one must pull out the pin, squeeze the handle while aiming the hose at the fire, and use a sweeping action to spray the substance across the fire from front to back and side to side. Hose reels, which use water, are designed for Class A fires only, involving materials like paper, wood, and cardboard. They should never be used on fires involving fats or electrical equipment.

Figure 58: Fire extinguisher guide. Challiyan, CC BY-SA 4.0, via Wikimedia Commons.

To use a hose reel, the water should be turned on at the reel before unrolling the hose, and then the water should be turned on at the nozzle.

Fire blankets are valuable for smothering small fires associated with cooking stoves or high-risk electrical appliances. To use a fire blanket, one must pull the tabs downwards to remove the blanket, shake it open while holding onto the tags, hold the blanket in front of the body to form a heat shield, and if an appliance is on fire, place the blanket over the fire and turn off the source of the flame. If a person's clothes are on fire, wrap the blanket around them and roll them on the ground to extinguish the flames. These procedures ensure the safe and effective use of fire fighting equipment, helping to mitigate the risks associated with fires in the workplace.

Health and Safety Checklist for Landscape Construction Workers

Pre-Work Preparation

- **Site Assessment**

    - Conduct a risk assessment of the site.

    - Identify and mark potential hazards (e.g., underground utilities, overhead power lines).

- **Training and Certification**

    - Ensure all workers have relevant training (e.g., machinery operation, first aid).

    - Verify that certifications and licenses are up to date.

- **Personal Protective Equipment (PPE)**

    - Helmets

    - Safety glasses or face shields

    - Hearing protection

    - Gloves

    - High-visibility vests

    - Steel-toe boots

    - Respirators (if required)

- **Emergency Preparedness**

    - First aid kits accessible and fully stocked.

    - Emergency contact numbers clearly posted.

    - Emergency procedures reviewed and understood by all workers.

Daily Safety Procedures

- **Morning Briefing**

    - Review daily tasks and potential hazards.

    - Assign roles and responsibilities.

    - Conduct a toolbox talk on specific safety topics.

- **Site Inspection**

- Check for new hazards or changes in conditions.
- Ensure all equipment and tools are in good working order.
- Verify that safety measures (e.g., barriers, signs) are in place.

Machinery and Equipment
- **Operation**
  - Only trained and authorized personnel to operate machinery.
  - Perform pre-operation checks (e.g., fluid levels, brakes, lights).
- **Maintenance**
  - Regularly scheduled maintenance performed.
  - Document and report any malfunctions or defects immediately.
- **Usage**
  - Follow manufacturer's guidelines for use.
  - Ensure proper guarding and safety features are in place.

Manual Handling
- **Lifting Techniques**
  - Use proper lifting techniques to avoid back injuries.
  - Use mechanical aids or seek assistance for heavy loads.
- **Ergonomics**
  - Rotate tasks to avoid repetitive strain injuries.
  - Ensure proper posture and movements.

Chemical Safety
- **Handling and Storage**
  - Store chemicals in labelled, secure containers.
  - Use appropriate PPE when handling chemicals.
  - Follow Material Safety Data Sheets (MSDS) for each chemical.

- **Spill Response**
  - Have spill kits readily available.
  - Train workers on spill response procedures.

Environmental Conditions
- **Weather**
  - Monitor weather conditions regularly.
  - Adjust work schedules for extreme weather (e.g., heat, cold, rain).

- **Sun Protection**
  - Provide sunscreen and encourage its use.
  - Ensure access to shaded areas for breaks.

- **Hydration**
  - Supply ample drinking water.
  - Encourage regular hydration breaks.

Excavation and Trenching
- **Safety Measures**
  - Ensure trenches over 1.2 metres (4 feet) have protective systems (e.g., shoring, trench boxes).
  - Inspect trenches daily and after any weather events.

- **Access and Egress**
  - Provide safe entry and exit points from trenches.
  - Ensure ladders or ramps are within 25 feet of all workers.

Working at Heights
- **Fall Protection**
  - Use guardrails, safety nets, or personal fall arrest systems.
  - Ensure all fall protection equipment is inspected and maintained.

- **Ladders and Scaffolding**

- Use ladders and scaffolding that meet safety standards.
- Inspect for defects before use.

Electrical Safety

- **Lockout/Tagout Procedures**
  - Follow proper lockout/tagout procedures for equipment.
  - Ensure electrical panels are properly marked and accessible.
- **Overhead Power Lines**
  - Maintain a safe distance from overhead power lines.
  - Use non-conductive tools and equipment near power lines.

Wildlife and Plants

- **Insect and Animal Hazards**
  - Identify and avoid areas with known wildlife hazards.
  - Provide training on dealing with insect stings and bites.
- **Toxic Plants**
  - Identify and avoid contact with toxic plants (e.g., poison ivy).
  - Provide training on recognizing and handling toxic plants.

Communication

- **Two-Way Communication**
  - Provide radios or mobile phones for communication.
  - Ensure all workers know the communication protocols.
- **Signage**
  - Post clear and visible safety signs around the site.
  - Use warning signs to highlight specific hazards.

Post-Work Procedures

- **Cleanup**
  - Ensure all tools and equipment are properly stored.

- Remove any debris or potential hazards from the site.

- **Inspection and Reporting**

    - Conduct a final inspection of the site.

    - Report any incidents or near-misses immediately.

- **Review**

    - Hold a debriefing session to review the day's work and safety performance.

    - Discuss any issues and plan improvements for the next day.

Record Keeping
- **Documentation**

    - Keep records of all training, inspections, and incidents.

    - Maintain up-to-date safety checklists and logs.

This comprehensive checklist is designed to cover the essential health and safety aspects for landscape construction workers, ensuring a safe and efficient work environment.

Chapter Five

Setting Out the Site for Construction Works

Site Preparation

Site preparation is a crucial phase in the construction process, encompassing tasks such as clearing the site and preparing essential services. However, it's often overlooked in the initial construction cost estimate due to the unpredictability of what lies beneath the surface. Before any demolition of existing structures can commence, various preparatory steps must be taken. This includes disconnecting all services like power, water, and gas, as well as sealing stormwater and sewer drains. Additionally, measures must be put in place to protect adjoining properties, and the site itself must be securely fenced or barricaded to prevent public access during demolition.

Recent legislation mandates that materials from demolition should be retained for reuse, resale, or recycling wherever possible. Compliance with safety regulations is essential, particularly when asbestos or asbestos-containing materials are involved in the demolition process. Establishing services such as water, electricity, stormwater, sewerage, and gas is another critical aspect of site preparation. Council regulations often stipulate the need for a temporary electrical sub-station and toilet facilities before construction can commence. Permission from relevant authorities may be necessary if existing services need to be extended or if there are insufficient services on-site.

Security measures are paramount during construction, requiring the erection of hoarding or site fencing to safeguard the site throughout the construction period. Sediment control is also vital, especially on sloping blocks, where techniques like swaling, hay bales, and sedimentation fencing may be employed to prevent soil erosion into roads, drains, and waterways. Once these preparatory tasks are complete, the set-out of the dwelling begins. This involves pegging out the dwelling footprint based on design drawings, typically carried out by the builder in collaboration with a surveyor. String lines are used to outline the perimeter of construction, with careful attention paid to any variations in wall alignment, ensuring accurate positioning of the building on the site. Overall, thorough site preparation is essential for laying the foundation of a successful construction project while ensuring compliance with regulatory requirements and environmental considerations.

Setting Out

Setting out and pegging out in landscaping refer to the process of marking the boundaries, layout, and key features of a landscaping project on the ground before actual construction begins. This crucial step ensures that the design plan is accurately translated onto the site and provides a guide for the installation of various landscape elements.

The process typically begins with reviewing the landscape design plans, which outline the desired layout, dimensions, and features of the project. These plans serve as a blueprint for the setting out and pegging out process.

Next, surveying equipment such as measuring tapes, string lines, levels, and pegs are used to mark the boundaries and key points of the landscape design on the ground. This involves accurately measuring distances, angles, and elevations to ensure precise alignment and positioning of landscape elements such as pathways, planting beds, structures, and water features.

Pegs or stakes are driven into the ground at specific locations to mark key reference points, corners, and edges of various landscape features. String lines are then attached to these pegs to establish straight lines and define the layout of pathways, walls, and other linear elements.

During the setting out process, attention is also given to factors such as site topography, drainage patterns, and existing features that may influence the placement of landscape elements. Adjustments may be made to the design plan as needed to accommodate site conditions and ensure practicality and functionality.

Overall, setting out and pegging out are essential steps in the landscaping process, providing a visual guide for construction crews and ensuring that the final result aligns with the intended design vision. Accurate and meticulous execution of this phase is crucial for the successful implementation of a landscaping project, delivering a result that meets both aesthetic and functional requirements.

Setting Out, Pegging Out for a Slab on the Ground

Before beginning any construction project, there are several critical checks and preparatory steps that need to be undertaken to ensure a smooth and successful start. Firstly, it's essential to confirm that all relevant permits and approvals for the construction have been obtained, adhering to local regulations and building codes. This ensures legal compliance and avoids potential delays or complications later on.

Having an accurate block plan with the lengths and angles of all boundaries marked is crucial for verifying property lines and boundaries. Using this plan, every fence line should be checked meticulously to ensure alignment with the property boundaries. Utilizing a long tape measure or other measuring tools may be necessary for this task, ensuring precise measurements.

In cases where construction is planned along boundary lines, it's prudent to hire a certified surveyor to verify the accuracy of existing boundary markers or fences. This extra precaution can prevent costly mistakes or disputes later on, as demonstrated by instances where discrepancies between actual boundaries and perceived boundaries were uncovered.

Once initial checks are completed, preliminary site works can commence. This typically involves clearing the site of any obstacles, such as trees or vegetation, that may interfere with construction activities. While preserving trees is desirable, those too close to the new building may need to be removed to facilitate construction processes effectively.

Following site clearance, the process of setting out the construction site begins. This entails marking key reference points and lines on the ground, typically indicated on construction drawings or plans. Steel pegs or other suitable markers are used to delineate the corners and boundaries of the proposed construction area accurately.

In addition to marking out the perimeter of the construction site, there may be requirements to strip the area of topsoil and deleterious materials before commencing construction. This ensures a stable foundation for the construction and removes any organic matter that could compromise structural integrity.

Once the initial layout is established, further checks for accuracy and squareness are conducted, ensuring that the construction aligns with the intended design. This may involve adjusting pegs or markers as needed to achieve precise alignment and symmetry.

String lines may be employed between pegs to delineate specific areas such as trenches or pier holes, providing visual guidance for excavation work. Depending on the size and complexity of the project, excavation work may commence at this stage, preparing the site for subsequent construction activities.

Profiles play a crucial role in construction projects, providing a visual and physical reference for various aspects of the build. Typically, profiles consist of pegs, stakes, or pickets driven into the ground at strategic locations across the construction site. These vertical elements are often accompanied by crosspieces of timber attached to them, forming a framework that outlines specific dimensions, levels, and alignments.

Despite their temporary nature, profiles are indispensable tools in construction, serving as guides for builders and contractors during different stages of the project. While they may not always appear aesthetically pleasing, with a hodgepodge of materials and components, their functionality outweighs their appearance. Profiles are designed to convey critical information and facilitate accurate construction, even in the case of relatively simple projects like a house extension.

One of the primary functions of profiles is to establish precise levels and alignments throughout the construction site. By driving pegs or stakes into the ground at predetermined positions and heights, builders can create a framework that reflects the desired elevations of various structural elements, such as foundations, walls, and floors. This ensures that the construction progresses according to the intended specifications and maintains uniformity and stability.

In addition to providing vertical reference points, profiles also convey important horizontal information. Crosspieces of timber attached to the pegs or stakes may indicate the boundaries of specific areas, such as the footprint of a building or the layout of utilities. Builders rely on these horizontal markers to ensure accurate positioning and spacing of structural components and to avoid encroachment or misalignment.

Furthermore, profiles serve as a visual aid for communicating design details and construction requirements to the construction team. Even on a simple house extension, profiles can convey critical information such as setback distances, wall heights, and slope gradients. This ensures that all stakeholders involved in the project, from architects and engineers to contractors and labourers, have a clear understanding of the project scope and objectives.

Despite their utilitarian appearance, profiles are instrumental in maintaining construction accuracy and efficiency. They provide a tangible framework for translating design intent into physical reality, guiding the construction process from start to finish. Whether it's establishing levels, defining boundaries, or communicating design specifications, profiles play a vital role in ensuring the successful execution of construction projects, regardless of their complexity.

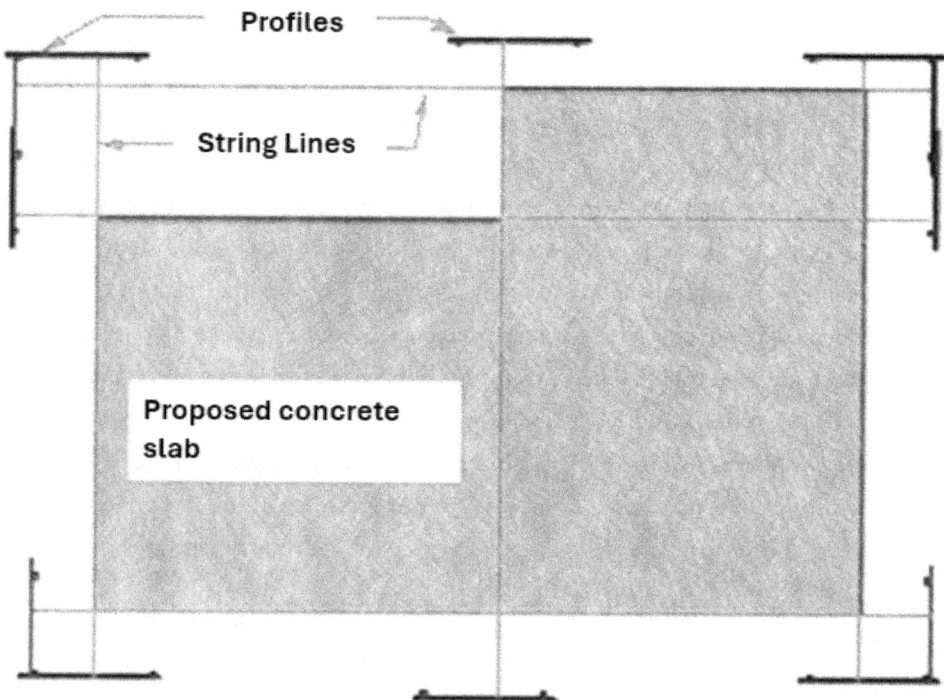

Figure 59: Setting out - A plan of a concrete slab showing the profile positions.

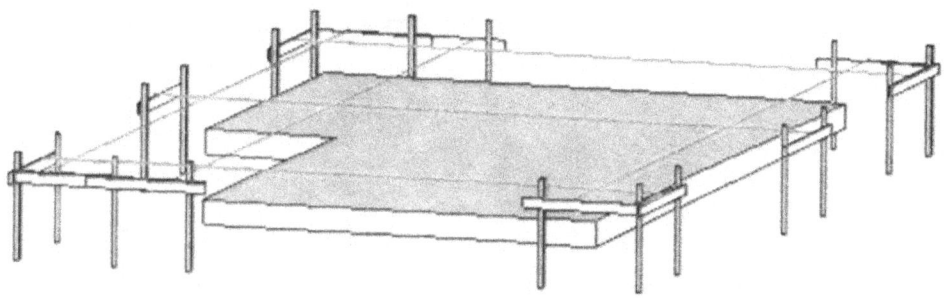

Figure 60: Setting out - A 3D view showing the use of profiles on the above slab.

Profiles serve as crucial tools in construction projects, acting as a bridge between the original pegs in the ground and a semi-permanent yet accurate reference for essential measurements, sizes, and offsets at various stages of the job. While the initial pegs provide a starting point, profiles are instrumental in translating these basic markers into tangible frameworks that guide the construction process with precision. Despite their temporary nature, profiles offer a level of permanence during critical stages of construction, ensuring that key dimensions and alignments are maintained accurately.

In the context of a concrete slab construction, profiles play a pivotal role in setting the stage for subsequent activities. Before the excavator begins its work, profiles are utilized to mark essential details on the construction site. This includes indicating the precise positions of all foundations for external and internal walls, facilitating the accurate placement of plumbing fixtures such as sewerage pipes and floor wastes, and identifying locations for underground power supply and entry points. By clearly delineating these elements on the profiles, construction teams can ensure that each subsequent trade or activity is executed with precision and efficiency.

The first trade to utilize the profiles is typically the excavator, whose task involves digging trenches and preparing the site for foundation work. To accommodate the excavator's equipment and operations, it is essential to maintain a reasonable clearance between the work area and the profiles themselves. This ensures that the machinery can manoeuvre effectively without compromising the accuracy or integrity of the profiles. Additionally, profiles may be marked with the overall dimensions of the concrete slab or other relevant parameters, providing a comprehensive guide for subsequent construction activities.

Profiles can take various forms, depending on the specific requirements of the construction project. While some profiles may consist of stakes or pegs driven into the ground, others may involve boards attached to existing boundary fences or other stable structures. The key criterion for selecting a profile is its ability to serve as a reliable reference point, capable of withstanding the rigors of the construction environment without being easily displaced or compromised. Ultimately, the goal of profiles is to provide construction teams with a clear and accurate framework for executing each stage of the project, from excavation to final finishing, ensuring that the completed structure meets the desired specifications and standards.

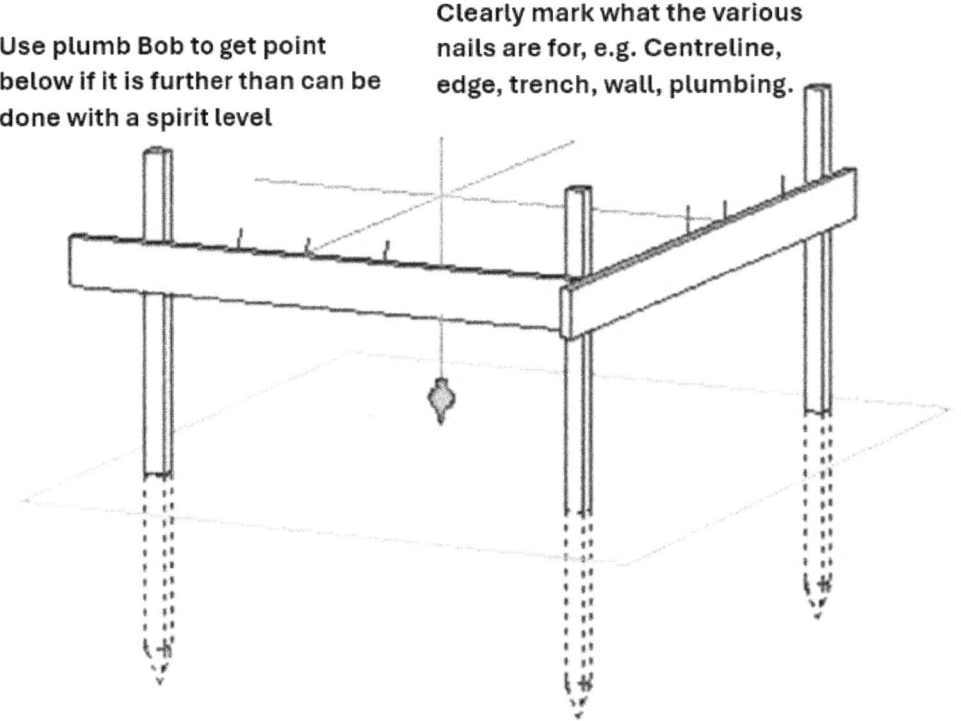

Figure 61: Setting out - A hurdle or profile used for setting out.

In construction projects, achieving precise alignment and levelness is essential for ensuring the structural integrity and aesthetic appeal of the final product. Traditionally, spirit levels have been the go-to tool for tradespeople to ensure their work is plumb and level. Whether it's a plumber setting a floor waste or a carpenter fixing perimeter formwork, the spirit level provides a reliable method for measuring vertical and horizontal alignments accurately. However, in certain situations, such as sloping ground or cramped excavations where using a level may be challenging, alternative methods like the plumb bob come into play.

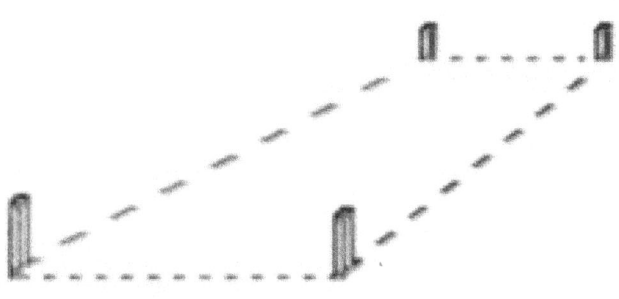

Figure 62: Peg the corners of the construction.

The plumb bob, a simple yet effective tool, offers a solution for achieving vertical alignment when traditional methods are impractical. Particularly in basement construction scenarios or areas with limited space, where manoeuvring a spirit level may be cumbersome, the plumb bob proves invaluable. By suspending a weighted line from a fixed point, such as a profile line or stake, tradespeople can establish a true vertical reference with ease. Adjusting the length of the plumb line using a tie wire hook allows for precise positioning, offering a practical alternative to conventional levelling methods.

Building profiles serve as critical components in the construction process, providing a framework for establishing the building line, also known as the perimeter of the structure. Ensuring the accuracy and squareness of the building profile is essential for laying the foundation and framing the structure correctly. Typically, the process begins by pegging the four outside corners of the building, marking the intended footprint on the construction site.

To verify that the pegs form a precise rectangle and that the building lines are square and parallel, specific checks are conducted. Tradespeople examine the alignment of the pegs along two intersecting lines, AA-CC and BB-DD, ensuring they are parallel to each other. Additionally, they measure the distances between various pairs of pegs to confirm uniformity, ensuring that the building profile is symmetrical and properly aligned. Checking the diagonals of the rectangle for equal lengths further confirms the squareness of the building lines, providing assurance that the structure will be constructed with precision and accuracy.

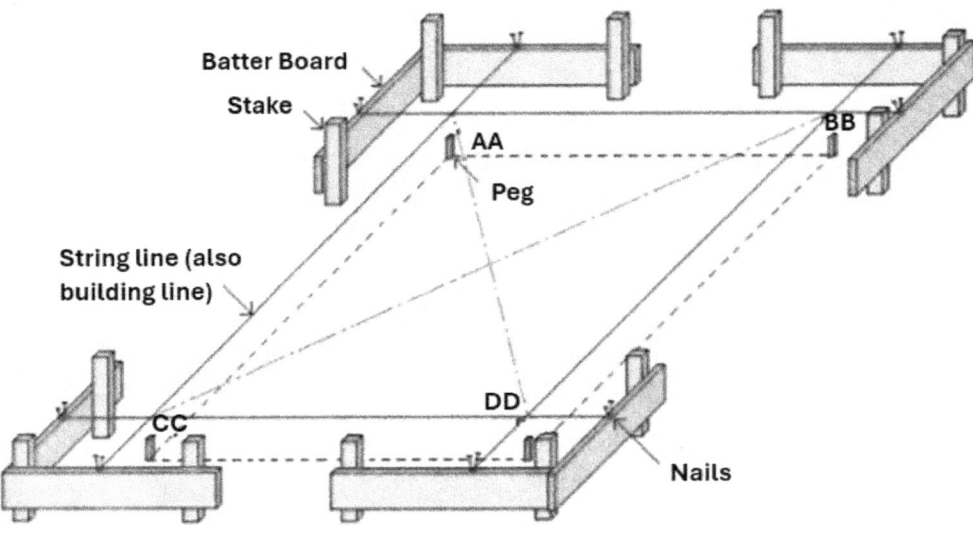

Figure 63: Squaring pegs.

Setting up the groundwork for a construction project involves several precise steps to ensure accuracy and alignment. One crucial aspect is establishing the building line, which serves as a reference point for subsequent construction activities. The process typically begins with hammering in stakes and marking their height. These stakes, usually around twelve in number, are positioned strategically, with three at each corner of the intended structure. It's essential to ensure that the stakes are firmly secured into the ground, especially in sloping terrain where adjustments may be necessary to maintain consistency.

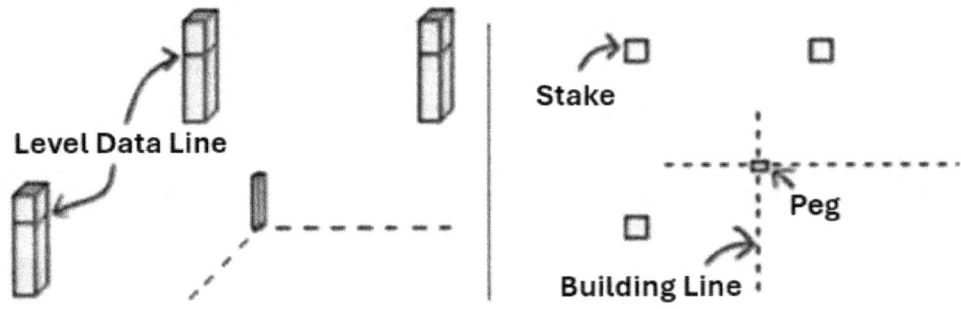

Figure 64: Hammer in the stakes and mark the height.

The height of the stakes is marked, typically around 150 millimetres (6 inches) above ground level, providing a reference point for subsequent measurements. This reference height is crucial for maintaining uniformity throughout the construction process. The batter boards, usually made of timber, are then fixed to the stakes, ensuring that the top of the batter board aligns with the level line marked on the stakes. These batter boards provide a stable framework for running the string lines, which define the building line and perimeter of the project.

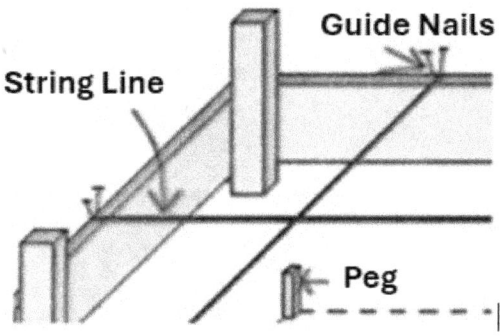

Figure 65: String Line.

Running a taut string line between the batter boards establishes the approximate building line, but more precise measurements are required to ensure accuracy. The parallels and diagonals of the building line are meticulously checked to confirm squareness and alignment. This involves verifying that the distances between various points along the string line are equal, indicating parallelism, and measuring the diagonals to ensure symmetry. Any necessary adjustments are made to correct discrepancies and achieve a level, square building line.

Once the building lines are parallel, and the diagonals are equal, the structure's foundation is established. The height of the string line serves as a reference datum for determining specific building heights relative to the ground level. For instance, if the string line is set at 200 millimetres (8 inches) above ground level, and the foundations are to be 150 millimetres (6 inches) above ground, then the foundations will be 50 millimetres (2 inches) below the string line.

Lastly, if the profiles used for setting out the building line are elevated from the ground to allow for sway movement, they may need additional bracing to ensure stability during construction activities. This ensures that the profiles remain in position and accurately reflect the intended building dimensions throughout the construction process, contributing to the overall quality and precision of the project.

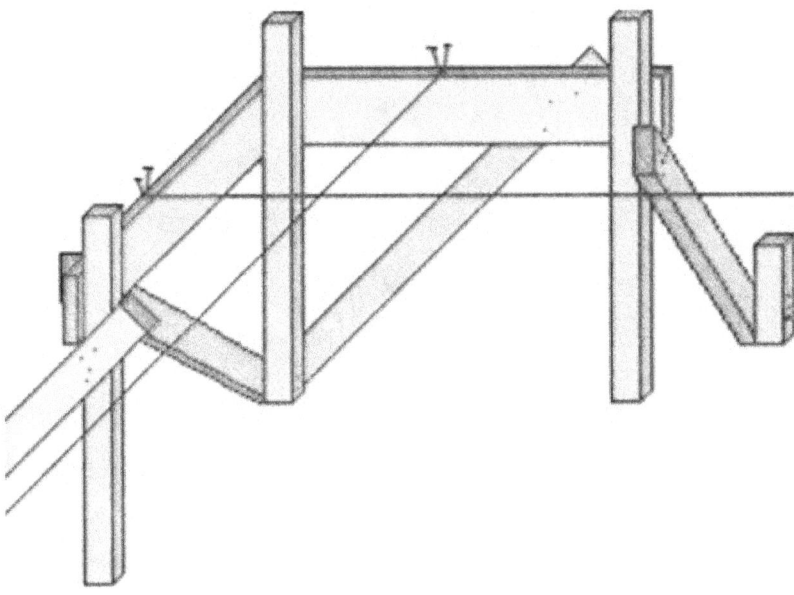

Figure 66: Bracing profiles.

Ensuring accuracy and precision in construction projects is paramount to avoid costly mistakes and ensure the structural integrity of the building. One of the critical aspects of setting out is achieving squareness, especially for rectangular structures. Failure to do so can lead to a cascade of issues throughout the construction process, affecting various trades and resulting in inconsistencies that are difficult to rectify later on. For example, if the floor plan is not square, it can cause problems for roofers and create significant challenges for floor tilers when installing tiles of varying widths along the walls.

Rectangles offer specific attributes that simplify the process of setting out building work. Firstly, each of the four angles in a rectangle measures 90 degrees, commonly referred to as being square. This characteristic provides a straightforward method for establishing the sides of the structure. By setting up a baseline side and then positioning a second line at a right angle to the first, two sides of the rectangle can be accurately determined.

Moreover, the opposite sides of a rectangle are parallel, meaning they are equidistant from each other. This parallelism facilitates the precise measurement of the remaining sides of the structure. By measuring the correct length from both ends of one side, the same distance can be marked from the corresponding ends of the opposite side, effectively fixing the third and fourth sides of the rectangle.

Additionally, the diagonals of a rectangle are equal in length, providing a reliable method for verifying the accuracy of the set-out. By measuring the distance between opposite corners, builders can confirm that the structure is indeed square. This diagonal measurement serves as a robust check against any discrepancies that may have occurred during the initial stages of setting out.

However, it's essential to note that the reliability of diagonal measurements may vary depending on the angle of the rectangle. Diagonals are most effective for checking squareness when the rectangle has a reasonably balanced shape. In cases where the rectangle is elongated and narrow, the angle of the diagonals becomes flatter, diminishing their reliability as a means of verification. Therefore, while diagonals offer a valuable tool for ensuring squareness, builders must consider the geometry of the structure when employing this method.

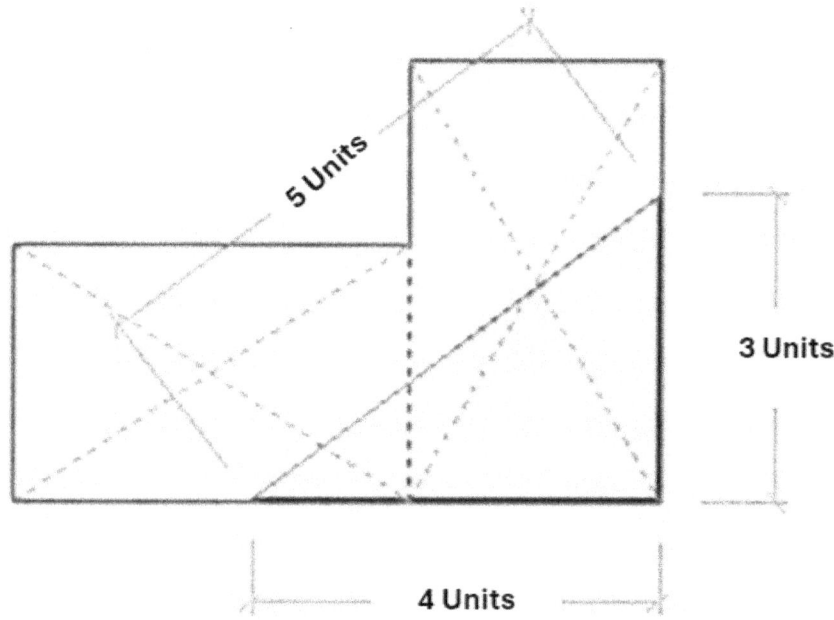

Figure 67: Setting out - Using a 3,4,5 triangle.

Setting out the plan for a house slab involves several crucial steps to ensure accuracy and alignment. One fundamental consideration is determining the most significant side of the slab, from which the rest of the structure will be squared and parallel. This primary side serves as a reference point for subsequent measurements and alignments, laying the foundation for the entire layout.

To establish squareness, the plan is divided into rectangles, and the diagonals of these rectangles are checked for equality. This process helps confirm that the structure is geometrically sound and that right angles are accurately maintained throughout. Additionally, a three-four-five triangle, a concept attributed to the ancient Greek philosopher Pythagoras, is commonly employed by builders for verifying squareness. This triangle, with sides measuring 3, 4, and 5 units, embodies Pythagoras' theorem, which states that in a right-angled triangle, the square of the length of the hypotenuse (the side opposite the right angle) equals the sum of the squares of the other two sides.

The principles of Pythagoras' theorem can be applied using simple calculations, allowing builders to determine the length of diagonal sides based on the measurements of other sides. The ratio of 3, 4, and 5 units in the triangle signifies a 90-degree angle opposite the longest side, serving as a reliable indicator of squareness. Importantly, this ratio-based approach emphasizes that the specific units used (whether miles, centimetres, or metres) are immaterial, as long as the ratio remains consistent.

In practice, builders can apply this concept by selecting a convenient unit of measurement and positioning nails or markers at specific distances along the formwork. For example, using a unit of 2 metres, nails may be placed at 8 metres and 6 metres along two adjacent edges of the formwork. By measuring the distance between these nails and comparing it to the expected value, builders can verify the accuracy of their layout. Any discrepancies can be corrected by adjusting the position of the string line or markers accordingly, ensuring that the set-out remains precise and aligned with the intended design.

Regular checks and adjustments during the setting out process are essential to catch and rectify any errors early on, preventing costly rework or structural issues later in the construction process. By diligently applying geometric principles and practical techniques like the three-four-five triangle, builders can achieve accurate and reliable results in their construction projects.

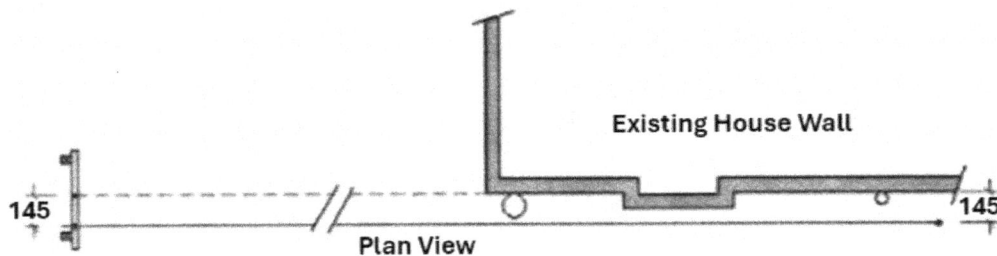

Figure 68: Offset line around obstacles.

Setting out on-site is a crucial step in construction, laying the foundation for the entire project. The process begins by establishing a reference stringline, often starting with the front of the house, as it serves as a key point of alignment. Pegs are then measured forward from this line, typically 2 metres, to mark the first side of the building "envelope." This initial setup provides the framework for subsequent measurements and alignments.

To create the first vertical line, such as the left-most edge of the house, a peg is knocked in at the top envelope line where the edge will be. A string is attached and extended to the opposite side of the envelope, incorporating the 3, 4, 5 rule to ensure squareness. By measuring specific distances along the horizontal and vertical lines, the position of the vertical line is accurately determined, ensuring proper alignment with the rest of the structure.

Subsequent measurements and alignments are carried out using similar methods, gradually outlining the perimeter of the building envelope. The 3, 4, 5 rule is repeatedly applied to maintain squareness and alignment at each stage of the process. Throughout this process, attention to detail is crucial, as even minor deviations can have significant consequences later in the construction process.

Once the perimeter of the envelope is established, attention turns to ensuring levelness across the site. Laser levels or other leveling tools are used to measure the height at each corner of the envelope, ensuring consistency and accuracy. This step is essential for establishing a level and square foundation for the construction process.

With the perimeter established and levelled, the next step involves setting up hurdles or pegs along the outer edge of the house. These serve as reference points for stringlines, guiding the placement of structural elements. Careful consideration is given to ensure that all measurements are accurate and consistent, minimizing the potential for errors during construction.

After all the hurdles or pegs are set up, a critical step is to check for exact squareness. This involves measuring the diagonals of the rectangle formed by the perimeter lines and adjusting the position of nails or pegs as needed to ensure squareness. This meticulous process ensures that the final structure is properly aligned and square, laying the foundation for a successful construction project.

Finally, as the process nears completion, thorough checks and verifications are conducted to ensure the accuracy of all measurements and alignments. Double and triple-checking ensures that no errors are overlooked, guaranteeing a smooth and precise construction process from start to finish.

Reading Construction Plans

Reading construction plans is a fundamental skill for anyone involved in the building industry, from architects and engineers to contractors and tradespeople. To read construction plans:

- **Understand the Plan Layout**: Construction plans typically consist of multiple sheets or pages, each containing different types of information such as floor plans, elevations, sections, details, schedules, and notes. Familiarize yourself with the layout of the plan set to understand where to find specific information.

- **Title Block and Index**: The title block usually appears on the first page of the plan set and contains essential information such as the project title, address, architect/engineer's name, project number, and date. The index provides an overview of all the sheets included in the plan set and helps you locate specific drawings quickly.

- **Scale:** Pay attention to the scale of the drawings, usually provided in a scale bar or noted in the title block. The scale indicates the relationship between the size of objects on the drawing and their actual size in the built environment. Common scales include 1/4" = 1'-0" (quarter-inch scale) for floor plans and 1/8" = 1'-0" (eighth-inch scale) for larger site plans.

- **Floor Plans**: Floor plans depict the layout of each level of the building, including walls, doors, windows, rooms, and major fixtures. Walls are represented by solid lines, while doors and windows are shown with specific symbols. Pay attention to dimensions, labels, and annotations, which provide critical information about room sizes, clearances, and other spatial relationships.

- **Elevations**: Elevations are orthographic projections that show the exterior views of the building from different angles, such as front, rear, sides, and roof. They illustrate the architectural features, materials, and overall appearance of the building. Elevation drawings include annotations for heights, finishes, and other details.

- **Sections**: Sections are vertical cutaway views that reveal the interior structure of the building, such as walls, floors, ceilings, and roof assemblies. They provide insights into the building's construction and help visualize how different components fit together. Sections often include dimensions, annotations, and material callouts.

- **Details**: Details are enlarged views of specific building components or assemblies, such as wall sections, foundation details, and connections. They provide close-up information about construction methods, materials, and dimensions. Pay close attention to notes and symbols used in detail drawings to understand construction requirements accurately.

- **Schedules and Legends**: Construction plans often include schedules for doors, windows, finishes, and other components, providing comprehensive lists of quantities, sizes, and specifications. Legends or keynotes explain the symbols, abbreviations, and other graphic elements used throughout the plan set, ensuring clarity and consistency in communication.

- **Notes and Specifications**: Notes are textual annotations that convey important information, instructions, or clarifications about specific aspects of the project. Specifications complement the drawings by providing detailed written descriptions of materials, construction methods, and quality standards. Refer to notes and specifications to understand project requirements thoroughly.

- **Review Revisions**: Construction plans may undergo revisions or updates during the design and construction process. Always check for revision clouds, revision dates, and revision notes to ensure that you are working with the latest version of the drawings. Pay attention to any changes or revisions, and update your records accordingly.

Location Plans

A location plan, or plot plan, is a detailed drawing that provides an overview of a specific area of land, such as a property, site, or landscape. It typically includes various elements such as buildings, structures, property boundaries, existing vegetation, utilities, access points, and other relevant features. Landscapers use location plans as essential tools for designing, planning, and executing landscaping projects. Here's how location plans are used by landscapers:

- **Site Analysis**: Location plans serve as the starting point for site analysis by providing landscapers with a comprehensive overview of the existing conditions and constraints of the site. They can assess factors such as the site's topography, soil composition, drainage patterns, sun/shade exposure, existing vegetation, and surrounding environment. This information helps landscapers understand the site's opportunities and limitations, guiding their design decisions.

- **Design Development**: Landscapers use location plans as a basis for developing their design concepts and proposals. By overlaying their design ideas onto the location plan, they can visualize how various elements such as garden beds, pathways, hardscapes, water features, and plantings will fit within the site's context. Location plans help landscapers determine the optimal placement and arrangement of design elements to create functional and aesthetically pleasing outdoor spaces.

- **Spatial Planning**: Location plans help landscapers allocate space efficiently and organize different functional areas within the landscape. They can designate zones for various purposes, such as entertaining, dining, gardening, recreation, and relaxation. Landscapers consider factors such as traffic flow, accessibility, privacy, and views when laying out the spatial arrangement of elements on the location plan.

- **Coordination with Clients and Stakeholders**: Location plans serve as visual communication tools for landscapers to present their design concepts to clients, property owners, developers, and other stakeholders. Landscapers use location plans to illustrate their vision for the project, discuss design ideas, address concerns, and solicit feedback from stakeholders. Clear and accurate location plans help facilitate productive discussions and ensure that everyone involved in the project shares a common understanding of the proposed landscaping design.

- **Construction Documentation**: Landscapers use location plans to generate detailed construction drawings and documentation for implementing the landscaping project on-site. They may develop additional drawings such as planting plans, irrigation plans, lighting plans, grading plans, and material specifications based on the information provided in the location plan. These documents serve as a guide for contractors and installers during the construction phase, ensuring that the design intent is realized accurately.

- **Permitting and Approvals**: Location plans are often required as part of the permitting process for landscaping projects, especially for larger-scale or commercial projects. Landscapers submit location plans to local authorities and regulatory agencies to obtain necessary permits and approvals for site development, landscaping, grading, drainage, and other activities. The plans demonstrate compliance with zoning regulations, building codes, environmental regulations, and other applicable requirements.

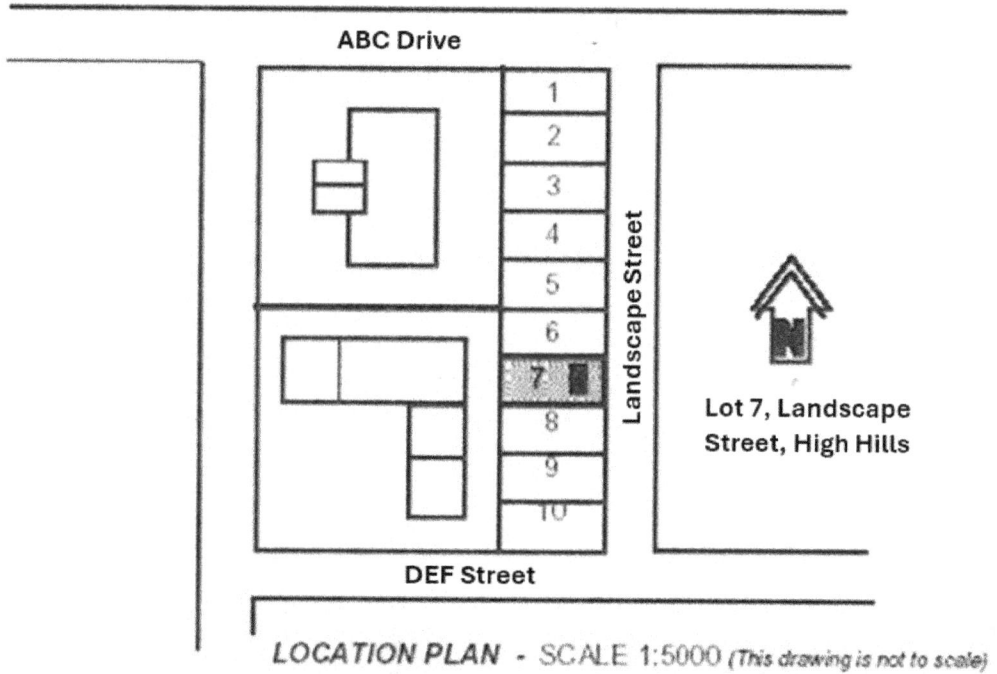

Figure 69: Example location plan.

Location plans play a crucial role in the landscape design and planning process by providing essential information, facilitating communication, guiding decision-making, and ensuring successful project implementation. They enable landscapers to create outdoor spaces that meet the functional, aesthetic, and environmental needs of their clients while respecting the site's unique characteristics and context.

Site Plans

Site plans are crucial documents in the construction and development process, providing a detailed and comprehensive overview of how a building or structure will be situated within its surrounding environment. Essentially, a site plan offers an overhead view of the construction site, illustrating the precise location of the building in relation to the boundaries of the lot or parcel of land. This visualization helps stakeholders, including architects, engineers, contractors, and regulatory authorities, understand the spatial context and layout of the proposed development.

One of the primary functions of a site plan is to outline the key features and elements that will affect the construction and design of the building. This includes identifying the location of utility services such as water, sewer, electricity, and gas lines. Knowing the placement of these utilities is essential for coordinating with utility providers, ensuring proper connections, and avoiding conflicts during excavation and construction activities.

Additionally, site plans delineate the positions of retaining walls, which are structures designed to hold back soil or other materials and prevent erosion or landslides. By indicating the location and dimensions of retaining walls on the plan, designers and engineers can effectively address grading and drainage issues, optimize site utilization, and enhance stability and safety.

Setback requirements, which dictate the minimum distance between the building and property lines, are also a critical aspect of site planning. Site plans specify setback distances for front, rear, and side yards in accordance with local zoning regulations and building codes. Compliance with setback requirements ensures that the building is appropriately positioned within the lot, maintains adequate separation from neighbouring structures, and preserves privacy and open space.

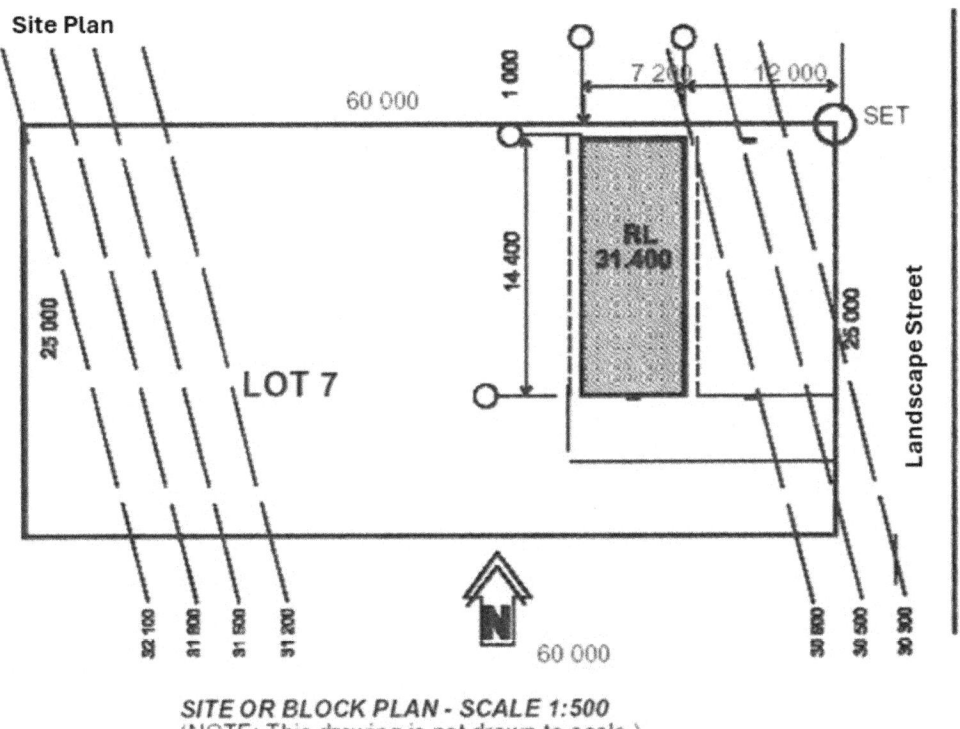

Figure 70: Sample site plan.

Easements, which grant rights of access or use to another party, are typically indicated on site plans to inform stakeholders about any encumbrances or restrictions on the property. This could include utility easements for power lines or pipelines, as well as access easements for shared driveways or pedestrian pathways. Understanding the location and extent of easements helps developers and designers avoid conflicts and plan around these designated areas.

Furthermore, site plans may include details about fences, driveways, and walkways to facilitate circulation and access on the property. Fences demarcate property boundaries, provide security and privacy, and enhance aesthetic appeal, while driveways and walkways ensure safe and convenient vehicular and pedestrian movement throughout the site. By integrating these elements into the site plan, designers can optimize traffic flow, improve connectivity, and enhance the overall functionality of the development.

In some cases, site plans may also incorporate topographical data, such as contour lines or elevation points, to depict the slope and terrain characteristics of the site. This information is invaluable for assessing site drainage, grading, and earthwork requirements, as well as for informing design decisions related to building placement, foundation design, and landscaping. Understanding the topography allows designers to adapt the building design to the natural features of the site and minimize the need for costly earthmoving or site modifications.

Site plans serve as essential tools for coordinating and communicating the site layout and design intent to all stakeholders involved in the construction process. By accurately depicting the location of utilities, structures, setbacks, easements, and other site elements, site plans help ensure compliance with regulations, optimize site utilization, mitigate risks, and facilitate the successful execution of construction projects.

When examining construction plans, there are several key features that individuals should pay close attention to in order to fully understand the proposed project and its implications. One crucial aspect is the establishment of a datum, which serves as a reference point of known or assumed height to which all other site levels will be referenced. The datum provides a consistent baseline for understanding elevation changes and ensuring accurate measurements throughout the site.

Additionally, it's essential to review the information provided on the plan page itself, including the page number, client's name, project address, scales used, and the name and reference numbers of the draftsperson. These details help identify the specific plan and provide essential context for its interpretation. Furthermore, noting the date the plans were drawn is important for understanding the currency and relevance of the information presented.

Certain features of the site may need to be preserved or accounted for in the construction process, such as trees, rocks, or existing structures. These elements are typically marked on the plans to ensure they are protected or integrated into the design as necessary. Preservation of existing features can have both practical and regulatory implications, influencing site layout, grading, and landscaping decisions.

Contours, which depict the fall of the land, are another critical component of construction plans, providing valuable information about the site's topography and elevation changes. Contours are often related to the datum and spaced at regular intervals, such as 500mm horizontally. By analysing contour lines, stakeholders can assess drainage patterns, identify high and low points on the site, and plan for earthwork and grading requirements.

Reduced levels (RL), indicated on the plans, specify the elevation of various features in relation to the datum. For example, RL 100.000 might denote the finished floor level, ceiling height, eave height, or roof apex. Understanding these elevation references is essential for accurately positioning building elements and ensuring proper alignment with the surrounding terrain.

The distance between the building's outer walls or footprint and the property boundaries is another crucial consideration, especially in terms of compliance with local regulations and neighbourly relations. Most councils have specific codes or specifications regarding setback requirements, which dictate the minimum distances between structures and property lines. This information, including the front building line, is typically depicted on the plans for reference.

Finally, construction plans often include details related to site infrastructure and amenities, such as driveways, stormwater drainage systems, paths, easements, and rights of way. These elements are essential for ensuring proper access, circulation, and utility service provision within the development. Reviewing these features on the plans helps stakeholders understand how the site will be organized and how various systems will be integrated into the overall design.

Elevation Plans

Elevations in construction plans provide a non-perspective view of the house, offering detailed information about its exterior appearance and architectural features. Unlike perspective drawings, elevations are drawn to scale, allowing precise measurements to be taken for various aspects of the structure. Typically, plans include front, rear, and both side elevations, providing comprehensive views of the entire exterior.

One of the primary purposes of elevations is to specify ridge heights, which represent the highest points of the roofline. Understanding ridge heights is crucial for ensuring proper proportion and balance in the design, as well as determining the overall scale of the building. By depicting ridge heights on elevations, architects and builders can accurately visualize the height and profile of the structure.

In addition to ridge heights, elevations also indicate the positioning of the final fall of the land, which refers to the slope or grade of the terrain surrounding the building. This information helps to ensure proper drainage and grading around the foundation, preventing issues such as water accumulation or erosion. By incorporating the final fall of the land into the elevations, designers can plan for appropriate site preparation and landscaping measures.

Exterior finishes play a significant role in defining the aesthetic appearance of a house, and elevations provide detailed information about the materials and textures used on the exterior surfaces. From siding and brickwork to stucco and stone veneer, elevations specify the types of finishes applied to different areas of the building facade. This level of detail is essential for achieving the desired architectural style and visual appeal.

Roof pitches are another critical aspect depicted on elevations, indicating the angle or slope of the roof surfaces. Roof pitch influences not only the overall appearance of the house but also factors such as water runoff, snow load resistance, and attic space. By specifying roof pitches on elevations, designers and builders can ensure structural integrity and aesthetic coherence in the roof design.

Fence locations and other exterior details are also commonly included on elevations to provide comprehensive guidance for site development and landscaping. Fence locations delineate property boundaries and privacy enclosures, while other details such as window placements, door configurations, and architectural embellishments contribute to the overall character and personality of the house.

Elevations serve as essential tools for communicating the exterior architectural styling and design intent of a building. By accurately depicting ridge heights, land falls, exterior finishes, roof pitches, fence locations, and other details, elevations enable architects, builders, and other stakeholders to visualize and understand the exterior appearance of the structure in detail, ensuring a cohesive and well-executed design outcome.

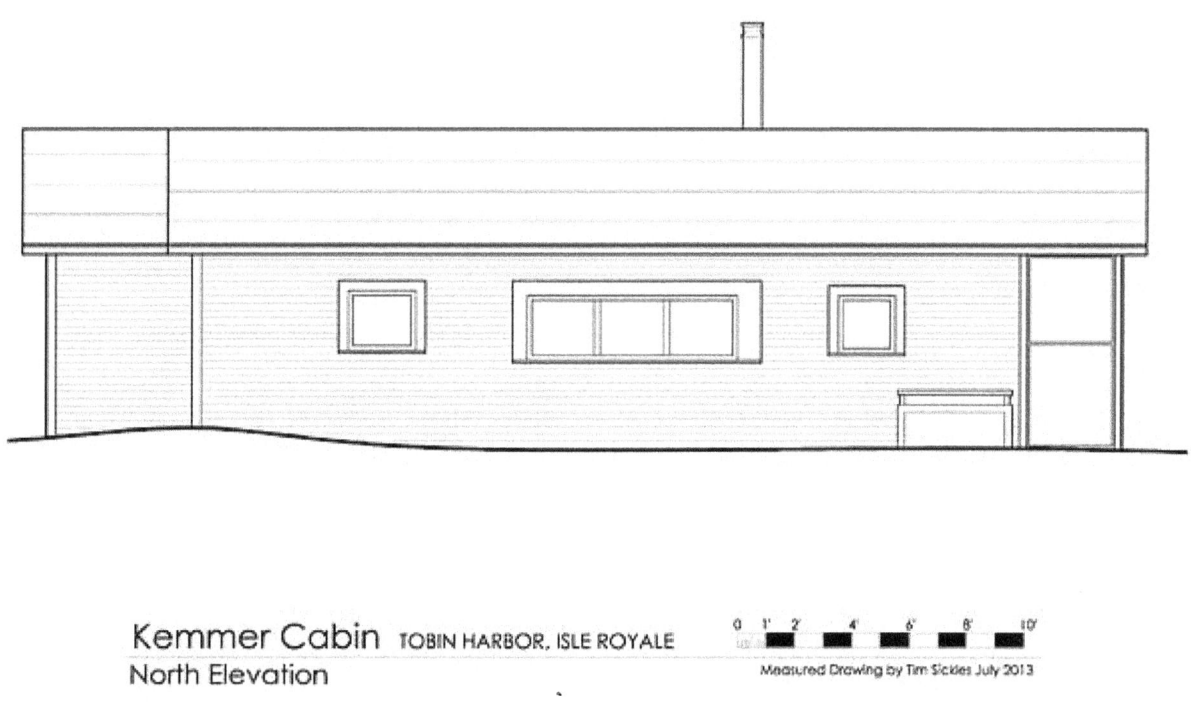

Figure 71: Sample elevation diagram - Kemmer Cabin - North Elevation. National Parks Gallery, public domain, via Picryl.

Landscapers use elevation plans as crucial reference documents to understand the vertical dimensions and visual aspects of a landscape design. These plans provide non-perspective views of the landscape from various angles, offering detailed information about the terrain, hardscape elements, and plantings. Here's how landscapers utilize elevation plans:

- **Understanding Terrain Features**: Elevation plans depict the existing topography of the site, including changes in elevation, slopes, and contours. Landscapers use this information to design grading and drainage solutions, ensuring proper water flow and erosion control. By analyzing the terrain features on elevation plans, landscapers can plan the placement of retaining walls, terraces, and other structural elements to maximize functionality and aesthetic appeal.

- **Visualizing Vertical Structures**: Elevation plans illustrate vertical structures such as walls, fences, pergolas, and other architectural elements within the landscape. Landscapers use these drawings to determine the height, scale, and placement of these features relative to the surrounding environment. By incorporating vertical structures into the elevation plan, landscapers can create visually striking and harmonious outdoor spaces that complement the overall design concept.

- **Specifying Planting Heights and Arrangements**: Elevation plans indicate the heights and arrangements of plants, trees, and shrubs within the landscape. Landscapers use this information to design cohesive planting schemes that enhance the vertical dimension of the space and create visual interest. By considering factors such as mature plant heights, growth habits, and seasonal variations, landscapers can create balanced and attractive compositions that contribute to the overall aesthetic of the landscape.

- **Planning Grading and Earthworks**: Elevation plans help landscapers plan grading and earthworks to sculpt the land according to the desired contours and elevations. Landscapers use elevation lines and contour intervals to determine the best locations for grading changes, earth berms, and swales to manage water runoff and create visual interest. By analysing elevation plans, landscapers can optimize the flow of water across the site while minimizing soil erosion and drainage issues.

- **Designing Outdoor Living Spaces**: Elevation plans often include features such as patios, decks, outdoor kitchens, and seating areas. Landscapers use these drawings to visualize the layout and configuration of these outdoor living spaces, taking into account factors such as accessibility, views, and sun exposure. By incorporating outdoor living elements into the elevation plan, landscapers can create functional and inviting environments that cater to the needs and preferences of the client.

Elevation plans serve as valuable tools for landscapers to translate design concepts into tangible landscapes. By providing detailed information about terrain features, vertical structures, planting arrangements, grading, and outdoor amenities, elevation plans enable landscapers to create visually stunning and functional outdoor spaces that meet the needs and aspirations of their clients.

Construction lines, Perpendiculars and Arcs

Setting out in paving and landscape projects is a fundamental process that involves the precise establishment of lines, levels, curves, arcs, and the positioning of various features relative to a reference point, often a house or another building. This process is crucial for ensuring accuracy, consistency, and alignment throughout the project, ultimately contributing to the overall success and functionality of the design.

One of the primary objectives of setting out is to translate the design concept from paper or digital plans into the physical environment accurately. Landscapers and paving professionals use geometry principles and specialized tools to mark key points, lines, and dimensions on the site, laying the foundation for construction and installation activities.

At the outset of a project, careful consideration is given to the selection of a suitable reference point, typically a fixed structure such as a house or building. This reference point serves as the starting point for all measurements and alignments, providing a stable and consistent basis for the entire setting out process.

Lines and levels are established to define the boundaries, pathways, and features of the landscape or paved area. Straight lines are marked using measuring tapes, strings, or laser levels, ensuring that edges are crisp, straight, and aligned with the overall design intent. Levels are determined to establish the gradient, slope, or elevation changes necessary for proper drainage and functionality.

Curves and arcs add visual interest and flow to the landscape design, softening rigid lines and creating dynamic movement within the space. Landscapers use geometric principles and specialized techniques to accurately mark and construct curves, ensuring smooth transitions and aesthetically pleasing results.

In addition to defining the layout of hardscape elements such as paving, walls, and structures, setting out also involves positioning other landscape features such as plantings, lighting, and irrigation components. These elements are carefully placed relative to the established lines and levels, taking into account factors such as access, sunlight, and aesthetic considerations.

Throughout the setting out process, precision and attention to detail are paramount. Landscapers meticulously measure and mark key points, frequently checking alignments, angles, and dimensions to ensure accuracy and consistency. Any discrepancies or errors are promptly corrected to maintain the integrity of the design and prevent future issues during construction.

Overall, setting out is a critical phase in paving and landscape projects, laying the groundwork for successful implementation and execution. By applying geometry principles, utilizing specialized tools, and adhering to meticulous standards, landscapers can transform design concepts into beautifully crafted outdoor spaces that meet the functional, aesthetic, and environmental needs of their clients.

Geometry plays a foundational role in paving and street masonry, providing the framework for understanding and executing various design elements with precision and accuracy. While the terminology may seem daunting at first, much of it revolves around basic geometric principles, particularly those related to circles and right-angled triangles. By grasping these fundamental concepts, professionals in the field can effectively translate design specifications into tangible structures and layouts.

Kerbs serve as a prime example for illustrating geometric principles in paving and street masonry. These elements often represent the physical manifestation of geometric relationships envisioned by designers, specifiers, or architects. Whether it's the curvature of a radius or the alignment of straight lines, kerbs encapsulate the geometric intricacies inherent in many paving projects. Similarly, other elements of hardscaping, such as retaining walls, pathways, and plazas, are governed by the same geometric principles.

Understanding geometric terms and relationships is essential for professionals working in paving, street masonry, and hardscaping. From calculating angles to determining distances, geometric concepts inform every aspect of project planning and execution. For instance, when preparing a flagstone fan radius, meticulous attention to geometric detail is required to ensure the desired curvature and alignment of the paving materials.

On a practical level, geometric principles help pave the way for precise layout and construction techniques. Professionals rely on geometric measurements, calculations, and diagrams to establish accurate lines, angles, and dimensions in the field. Whether it's laying out patterns for paving stones or aligning kerbs along a curved path, a solid grasp of geometry ensures that the finished product meets design specifications and quality standards.

Some commonly encountered geometric terms in paving and street masonry include radius, diameter, circumference, chord, tangent, and right angle, among others. These terms describe various aspects of circles, angles, and lines, providing a shared language for communication and collaboration among project stakeholders. By defining and understanding these terms, professionals can effectively navigate the intricacies of geometric design and implementation in paving projects.

Geometry serves as the backbone of paving and street masonry, guiding the layout, construction, and execution of various design elements. By mastering fundamental geometric principles and terminology, professionals can tackle complex projects with confidence and precision, ensuring that the final result reflects the vision and intent of the design.

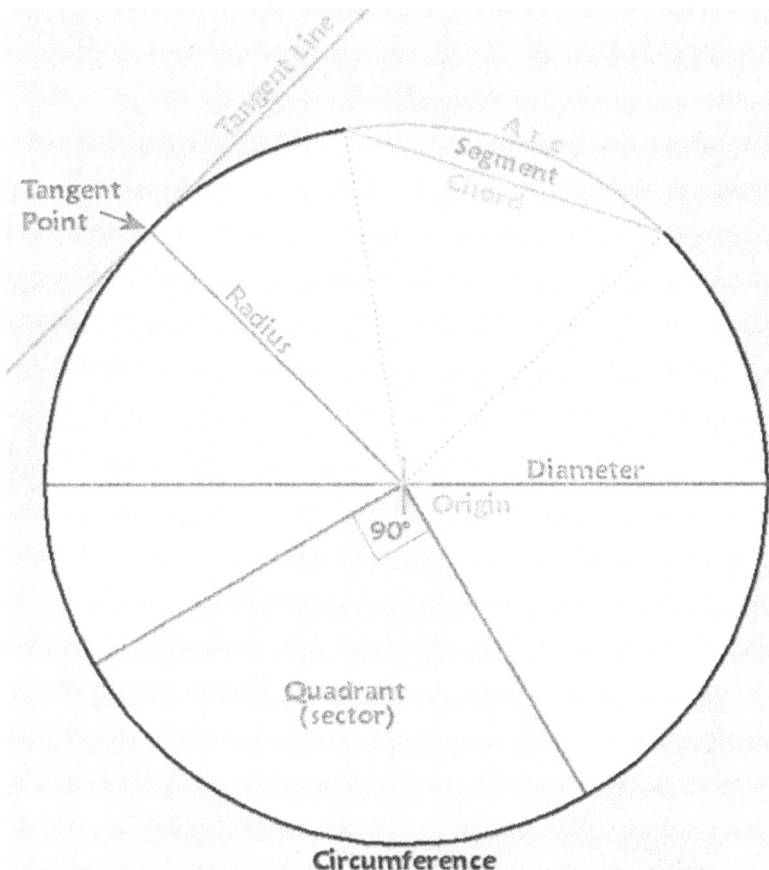

Figure 72: Circle and Arc Terms.

In paving and street masonry, understanding circle and arc definitions is crucial for accurately designing and implementing various elements of a project. These definitions provide the vocabulary necessary for communicating and executing geometric concepts related to curves, circles, and circular segments.

The origin serves as the centre point of a circle, from which all measurements are taken. It is the point from which a radius is swung, and all points on the circle's circumference are equidistant from the origin. The radius, perhaps the most commonly used term in street masonry, refers to the distance from the centre of a circle to any point on its outer edge (circumference). This measurement is essential for determining the size and curvature of kerblines and other design elements.

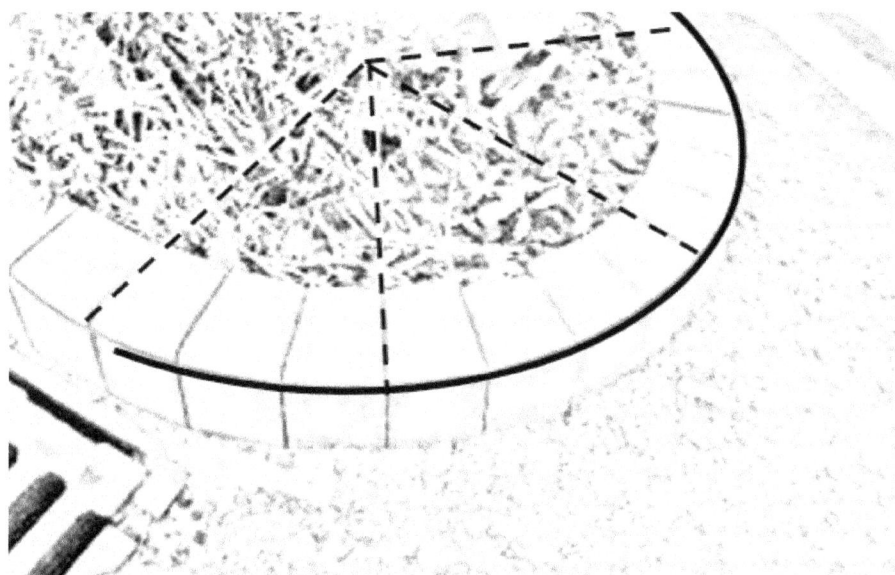

Figure 73: The kerbline follows the circumference of a circle and each kerb unit is the same distance from the origin, shown as radial lines (dotted).

Diameter, on the other hand, represents the span across a full circle, from one side to the other, passing through the origin. It is always equal to twice the length of the radius and is typically used to define the overall size and shape of circular elements in a paving or masonry project.

Figure 74: The 'step' running across this feature kerb circle is a diameter, as it touches both sides of the circle and passes through the origin (lighting column).

Tangent lines or constructions meet or "kiss" a circle or arc at only one point, known as the tangent point. This term is often used to describe transitions from straight lines to curves in kerblines or other features.

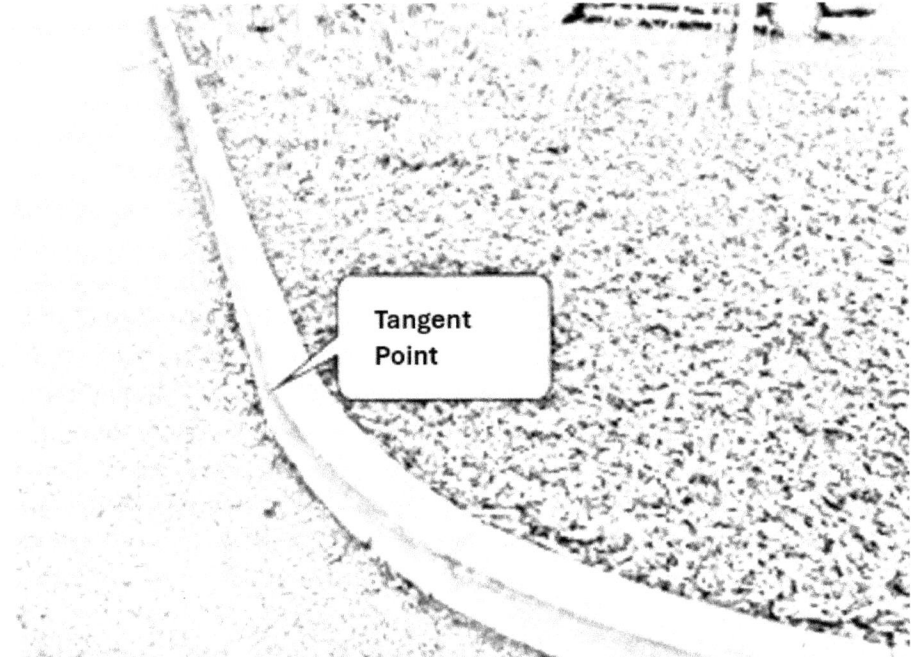

Figure 75: Tangent point on a curve.

An arc is any part of the circumference of a circle, ranging from short and shallow bends to almost complete circles. Arcs are fundamental to creating curves and bends in paving and street masonry, providing the flexibility to design various shapes and layouts. Quadrants, which represent one-quarter of a full circle, are a special type of arc or sector. They are commonly used in paving for creating single-piece quarter-circle kerbs or other curved elements.

Figure 76: An s-curve formed by linking an internal and external arc by a short length of straight.

Chords, unlike tangents, touch the circumference of a circle or arc at two points. While a chord passing through the origin becomes a diameter, any other line touching the circle at two points is considered a chord. Chords play a crucial role in determining the radius of an arc from a single kerb or section of arc, making them valuable tools in geometric calculations.

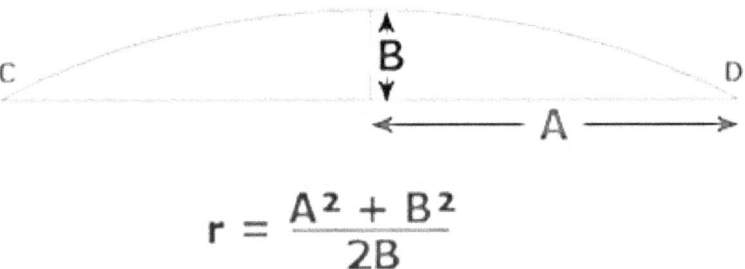

Figure 77: Chord components.

To determine the radius (r) of an arc, follow these steps:
- Begin by creating a chord, labelled C - D, and measure its length.

- Next, divide the length of the chord by 2 and designate the result as "A."

- Measure the perpendicular distance from the arc to the midpoint of the chord, denoting it as "B."

- Then, calculate the sum of the squares of A and B. Finally, divide the result by 2B, which is twice the measured perpendicular distance.

Finally, segments represent the area of a circle bounded by an arc and a chord. While not as widely used in paving and street masonry, segments are included for completeness and provide additional context for understanding circular geometry. Overall, these definitions form the foundation for accurately conceptualizing, designing, and constructing circular elements in paving and street masonry projects.

Circle and Arc Equations

Calculating circumference

The circumference of a circle is calculated using Pi (Π) which can be as a fraction, 22/7, or as a decimal number, roughly 3.142

C = 2 x Π x r

Where C = circumference

Π = 3.142

r = radius of the circle

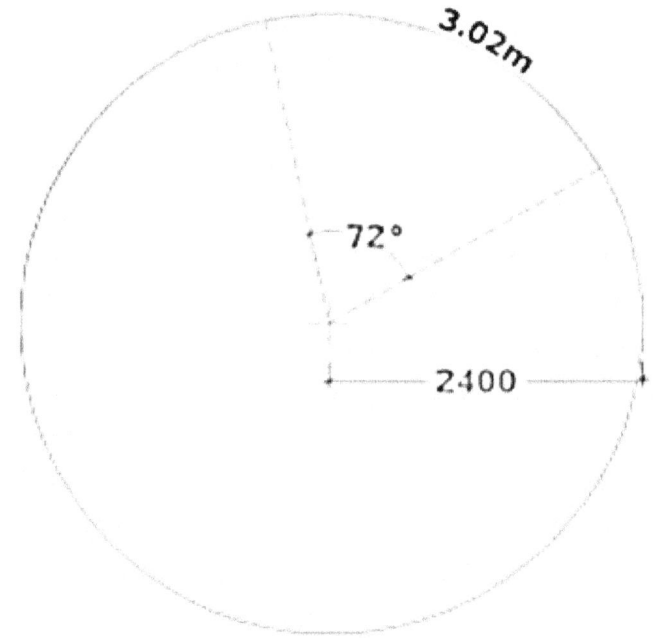

Figure 78: 2.4m circle.

So: a circle with a measured radius of, say, 2.4m has a circumference of…

2 x 3.142 x 2.4 = 15.08m

For the length of an arc, the calculated circumference is simply multiplied by the ratio of the angle of the arc over 360°…

arc = 2 x Π x r x (∠ ÷ 360)

Where C = circumference

$\Pi = 3.142$

r = radius of the circle

∠ = angle of arc

So: in our 2.4m radius circle described above, an arc of 72° has a circumference of...

2 x 3.142 x 2.4 x (72 ÷ 360)

15.08 x 0.2 = 3.02m

Calculating area

Generally speaking, the ability to calculate the area of a circle or arc is more useful to the typical paving contractor than circumference, and once again, the calculation depends on that magic figure, Π

$A = \Pi \times r^2$

Where A = Area

$\Pi = 3.142$

r = radius of the circle

So: the now-familiar circle with a measured radius of 2.4m has an area of...

3.142 x (2.4 x 2.4)

3.142 x 5.76 = 18.1m²

For the area under an arc (more correctly known as a 'sector'), the calculated whole circle area is simply multiplied by the ratio of the angle of the arc over 360°...

$A = \Pi \times r^2 : (∠ ÷ 360)$

Where A = Area of sector

$\Pi = 3.142$

r = radius of the circle

∠ = angle of arc

So: in our 2.4m radius circle described above, an arc of 72° has a sector with an area of...

3.142 x (2.4 x 2.4) x (72 ÷ 360)

3.142 x 5.76 x 0.2 = 3.62m²

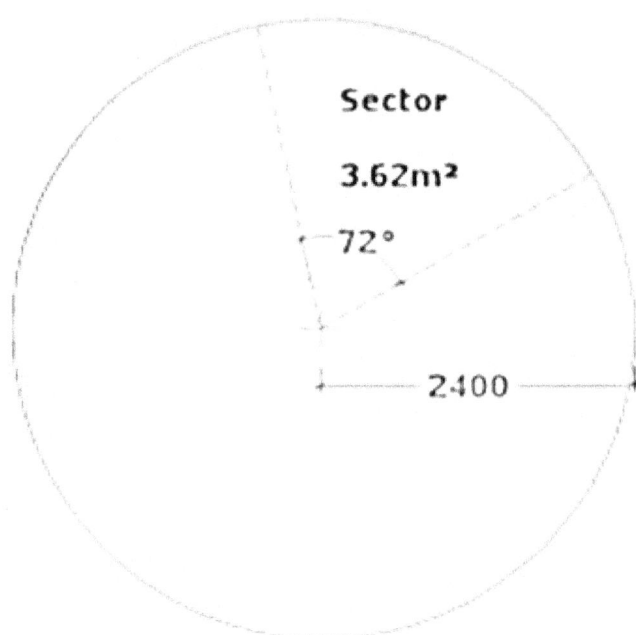

Figure 79: Sector area.

On larger landscaping projects, a variety of advanced tools like automatic levels, theodolites, laser levels, and even GPS systems are employed to assist in the setting-out process. These tools offer high precision and efficiency, making them indispensable for complex projects with intricate designs and specific requirements. However, even with these sophisticated instruments, there remains a fundamental need for basic setting-out skills that can be achieved with simpler tools.

The core tools required for basic setting-out tasks include a string line, an accurate spirit level, a tape measure, marker pegs (preferably 12mm steel road pins), and occasionally, a calculator. These tools are readily available and provide sufficient accuracy for many landscaping projects, particularly those of smaller or medium scale. Despite the availability of more advanced equipment, these basic tools are essential for ensuring accurate measurements and alignments in the field.

The string line serves as a fundamental tool for establishing straight lines and guiding the layout of various landscape elements such as pathways, retaining walls, and planting beds. Paired with marker pegs, it helps define boundaries, edges, and contours with precision. The accuracy of the string line relies on the proper tensioning and alignment, which can be achieved with careful attention to detail.

An accurate spirit level is indispensable for ensuring that surfaces, structures, and features are correctly levelled and aligned. It is used to establish horizontal planes, determine gradients, and ensure uniformity across the landscape. Whether setting the elevation of a patio, verifying the slope of a drainage channel, or aligning a fence, the spirit level plays a crucial role in achieving desired outcomes.

A tape measure is essential for taking precise measurements of distances, dimensions, and clearances on the site. It enables landscapers to accurately mark out areas, determine setback requirements, and establish spacing between elements such as plants, fixtures, or paving stones. By providing accurate measurements, the tape measure facilitates the proper layout and positioning of landscape features.

Marker pegs, particularly sturdy ones like 12mm steel road pins, are used to physically mark key points, lines, or reference levels on the site. They serve as anchor points for the string line, indicate boundaries or corners, and provide visual cues for excavation, construction, or installation activities. Marker pegs help maintain consistency and alignment throughout the project, acting as a tangible guide for the execution of the design plan.

Occasionally, a calculator may be needed for performing calculations related to dimensions, areas, volumes, or gradients. While basic arithmetic is often sufficient for many setting-out tasks, a calculator can be useful for more complex calculations or when dealing with large quantities of measurements. It ensures accuracy in determining quantities of materials, estimating costs, or verifying design specifications.

While advanced tools offer significant benefits in terms of precision and efficiency, basic setting-out skills remain essential for landscaping projects. By utilizing simple tools such as string lines, spirit levels, tape measures, marker pegs, and calculators, landscapers can achieve accurate layouts, alignments, and measurements on the site, laying the foundation for successful project execution.

Setting out a driveway involves a combination of careful planning, precise measurements, and adherence to design specifications. In the case study provided, the objective is to create a block paved driveway with specific dimensions and layout features. The driveway is intended to be 7 metres wide, aligning with the left-hand edge of the front door, with additional curves on both the right and left sides to accommodate the garage and a pathway respectively.

One of the key considerations in setting out the driveway is alignment with existing features of the property, such as the front door and the garage. Aligning the driveway with the left-hand edge of the front door ensures visual cohesion and practical access to the house. Similarly, incorporating curves on both sides allows for seamless integration with the garage and the pathway, enhancing the overall aesthetic appeal and functionality of the driveway.

In addition to aesthetic considerations, practical aspects such as drainage must also be taken into account during the setting-out process. The plan mentions existing surface water gullies positioned at the front corners of the property, which serve to collect water runoff from downspouts. Ensuring proper alignment and grading of the driveway to facilitate drainage towards these gullies is essential for preventing water accumulation and potential flooding issues.

Furthermore, understanding the topography of the site is crucial for effective setting out. In this case study, the site is described as generally flat, with minimal fall from the paving level at the front of the house to the threshold with the public footpath. This information informs decisions regarding the gradient and levelling of the driveway to ensure proper water runoff and accessibility while maximizing the use of available space.

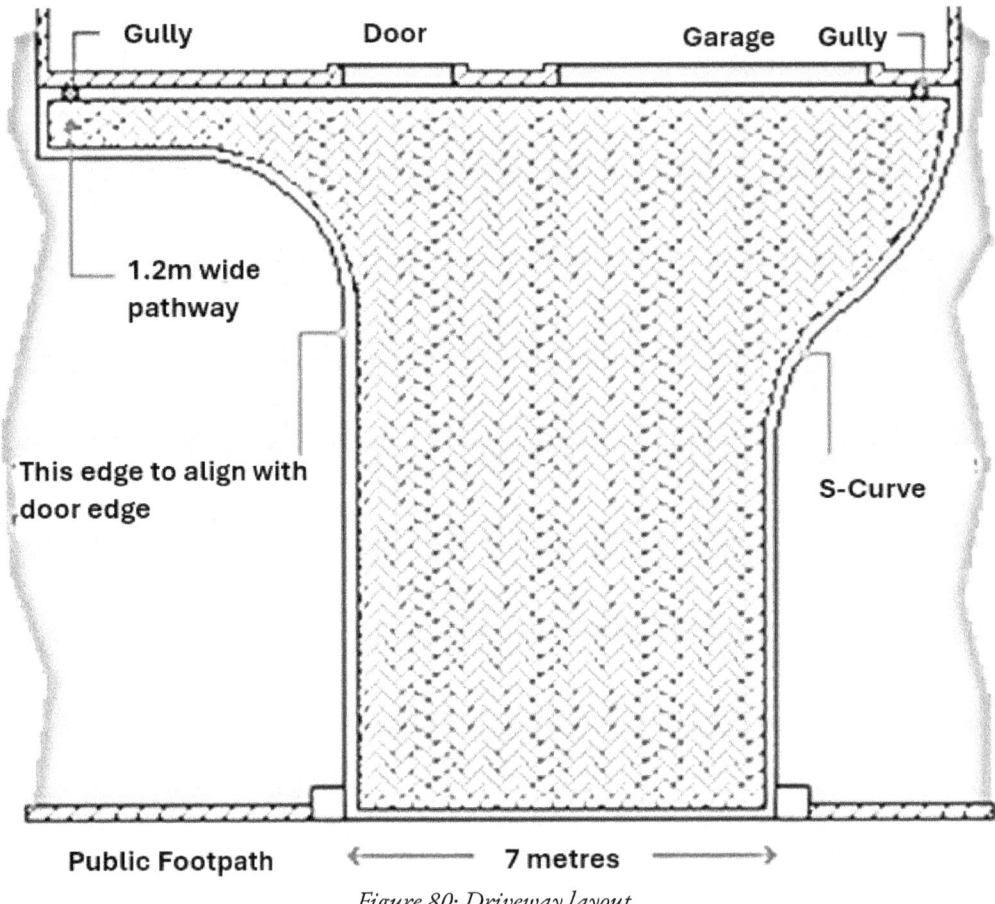

Figure 80: Driveway layout.

To achieve the desired layout and dimensions, various setting-out techniques and tools may be employed. String lines, marker pegs, and measuring devices are likely used to establish reference points, mark boundaries, and determine alignments. Careful attention to detail is necessary to ensure accuracy in measurements and consistency in the layout, particularly when dealing with curves and transitions between different sections of the driveway.

Overall, setting out a driveway involves a systematic approach that integrates design requirements, practical considerations, and site-specific conditions. By carefully planning and executing the setting-out process, landscapers can create driveways that not only enhance the visual appeal of the property but also provide functionality, durability, and efficient drainage solutions.

Setting Up a Straight String Line

Setting out a perpendicular line is a fundamental aspect of construction, crucial for ensuring accuracy and precision in building work. A perpendicular line is one that forms a perfect right angle, measuring exactly 90 degrees, in relation to a base line. This perpendicularity is essential for maintaining alignment and proper geometry in various construction projects. To achieve this, builders rely on fundamental principles such as the 3-4-5 triangle, derived from Pythagoras' theorem.

According to Pythagoras' theorem, a triangle with side lengths in the ratio of 3:4:5 will always form a right-angled triangle. This principle holds true regardless of the specific measurements, whether in metres, feet, or any other unit, as long as the ratio is maintained. However, while this theorem provides a reliable method for establishing right angles, accuracy can become compromised with longer side lengths. As a result, builders typically aim to use triangles with a maximum hypotenuse length of around 15 metres to maintain precision.

In practical construction applications, setting out a perpendicular line involves applying the principles of the 3-4-5 triangle to establish right angles. Referring to the construction plan for the driveway in the provided case study, the left-hand edge of the driveway (line A-B) is identified as a critical reference line. This line must be perpendicular to the front of the house and aligned with the left-hand edge of the doorway for proper alignment and symmetry.

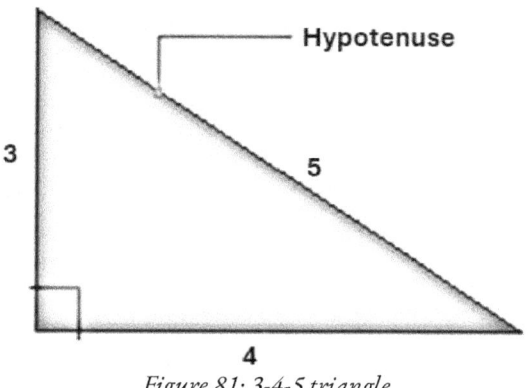

Figure 81: 3-4-5 triangle.

To establish this perpendicular line, builders utilize the 3-4-5 triangle method. This involves measuring three units along one side of the triangle, four units along another side, and ensuring that the diagonal connecting the endpoints measures five units. By adhering to this ratio, builders can confidently create a right angle, ensuring that the driveway edge is precisely perpendicular to the front of the house. This meticulous approach to setting out ensures accuracy and consistency in the construction process, laying the foundation for a well-executed project.

In the practical application of construction knowledge, the construction plan for the driveway reveals that the driveway's shape comprises a combination of rectangles and arcs. Among the various lines delineating the driveway's layout, one of paramount importance is the left-hand edge of the driveway, denoted as line A-B and highlighted in red on the drawing. This line serves as a crucial reference point, as it must be perpendicular to the front of the house and aligned with the left-hand edge of the doorway. Achieving this perpendicularity is pivotal for maintaining proper alignment and symmetry in the driveway's design.

To establish the perpendicular line (A-B) accurately, builders employ the 3-4-5 triangle method, a geometric principle derived from Pythagoras' theorem. The construction plan specifies that the distance from the left-hand edge of the front doorway (point A) to the right-hand corner of the property (point C) measures 7 metres plus an additional 3 metres, totalling 10 metres. However, due to the typical scale at which landscape plans are drawn (often 1:100 or greater) and the associated margin of error of approximately ±75mm, precision in measurements becomes paramount to ensure the creation of a true right angle at 90 degrees.

To mitigate potential errors and ensure accuracy, a meticulous approach is adopted. A measurement is made along the front of the house, and a distance of 8 metres is marked with crayon or chalk at point D, positioned just in front of the garage door. This marked point serves as a critical reference for setting out the perpendicular line (A-B) accurately. By adhering to precise measurements and employing the 3-4-5 triangle method, builders can confidently establish a true right angle, laying the foundation for a well-aligned and visually pleasing driveway layout.

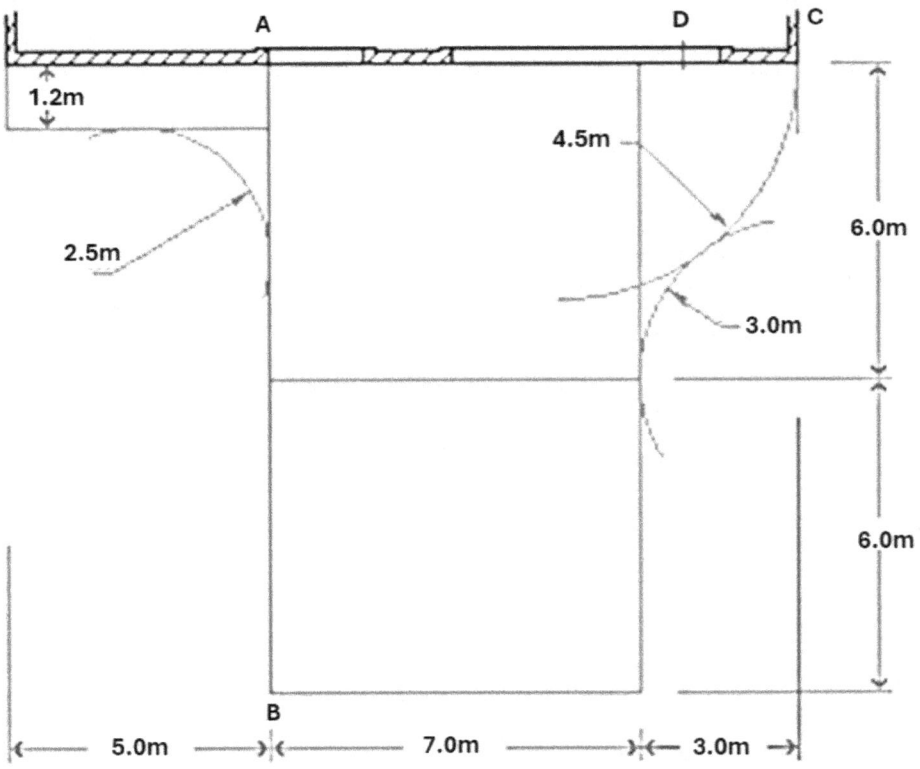

Figure 82: Construction Plan for driveway.

In the process of setting out a perpendicular line using the 3-4-5 triangle method, the length of the base line A-C is a crucial determinant. In this scenario, 8 metres has been selected as the length of the base line because it is a multiple of 4, which is the largest side of the 3-4-5 triangle other than the hypotenuse. The base line is considered true and serves as the longest available edge, with the '4' side consistently aligned along it. This strategic choice ensures stability and accuracy in establishing the perpendicular line, laying a reliable foundation for subsequent construction activities.

With the base line A-C securely in place, attention turns to marking out two arcs from fixed points A and D. These arcs can be delineated using various methods, such as scratches on the ground, sand lines, spray paint, or crayon. From Point A, a 6-metre arc is marked out, representing the '3' side of the 3-4-5 triangle. Conversely, from Point D, a 10-metre arc is marked out, representing the '5' side, which corresponds to the hypotenuse of the triangle. The intersection of these two arcs, denoted as Point E, signifies the apex of the 3-4-5 triangle.

Alternatively, if two tape measures are available, they can be utilized instead of marking arcs. The tapes are anchored securely at points A and D, and then extended towards Point E. By aligning the 6-metre mark on the tape from A with the 10-metre mark on the tape from D, the exact location of Point E is determined. A steel pin is then driven into the ground at this point to serve as a marker for subsequent construction activities. This method offers an efficient and precise alternative to arc marking, facilitating accurate setting out of the perpendicular line with minimal margin for error.

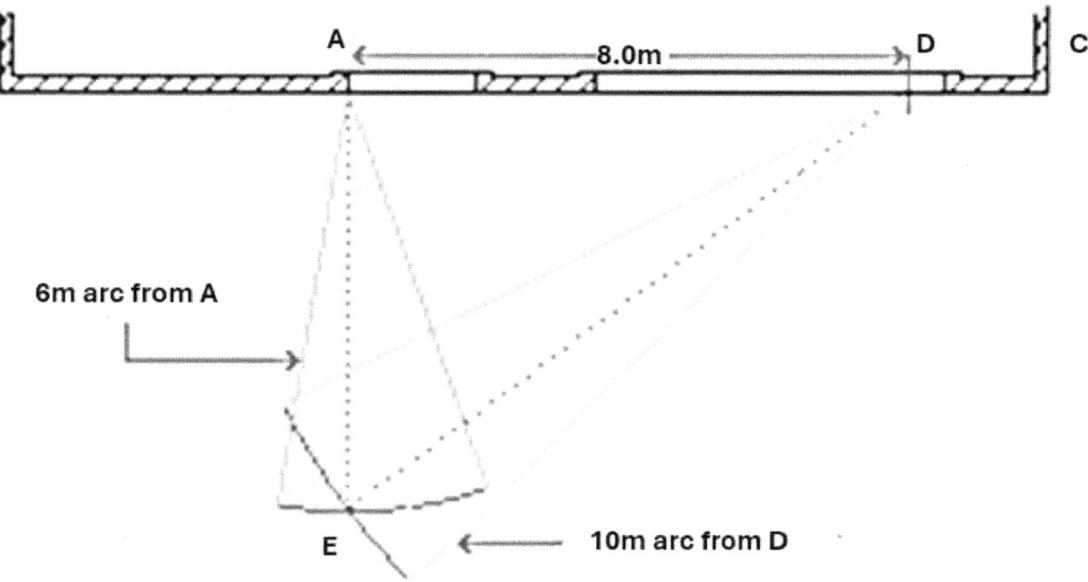

Figure 83: Setting out a perpendicular line using the 3-4-5 triangle method.

Upon drawing a line from point A to point E, a perpendicular line is established relative to the front of the property, aligning precisely with the left-hand edge of the doorway as required. At point E, a stake or steel pin is then firmly embedded into the ground to mark this pivotal position. Subsequently, a string line is securely fastened to point A and pulled taut, extending past the marker pin at E and continuing all the way to the threshold of the driveway. The integrity of the perpendicular line is maintained as long as the string line grazes the marker pin at E. This process effectively extends the perpendicular line created from the 3-4-5 triangle, facilitating the determination of point B.

With the string line securely in place, point B can now be established and marked with another steel pin. This pivotal point finalizes the accurate positioning of the perpendicular line, ensuring alignment with the desired specifications outlined in the construction plan. However, to validate the accuracy of the perpendicular, further measurements are necessary, particularly focusing on the hypotenuse B-D.

To assess the accuracy of the perpendicular, the hypotenuse B-D is measured. Given that the distance from point A to point D (A-D) is 8 metres, and the distance from point A to point B (A-B) is 12 metres, Pythagoras' theorem is employed to calculate the length of the hypotenuse. According to the theorem, the hypotenuse B-D is equal to the square root of the sum of the squares of the other two sides. Thus, the calculation for B-D involves taking the square root of the sum of the squares of 8 and 12, resulting in approximately 14.42 metres.

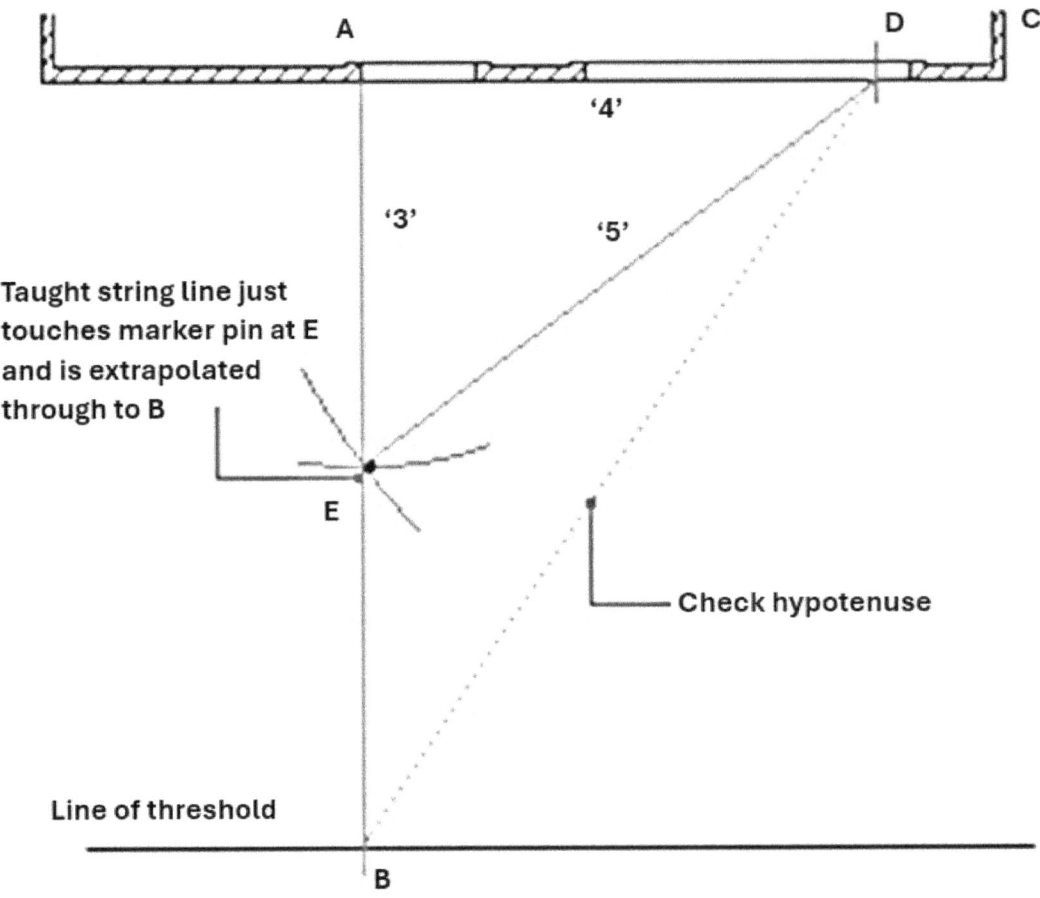

Figure 84: Checking accuracy.

Following the calculation, the actual distance from point B to point D is measured and compared against the calculated value to assess the accuracy of the perpendicular line. Ideally, the measured distance should fall within a specific tolerance range, typically between 14.40 metres and 14.45 metres, ensuring precise alignment with the intended specifications. If the measured distance deviates beyond this acceptable range, corrective measures may be required, including rechecking the perpendicular or setting out an alternative 3-4-5 triangle from the base line to rectify any discrepancies.

Setting Out Arcs and Curves

Setting out arcs and curves involves identifying and establishing key points that define the curvature of the desired shape. These points include the start tangent point, end tangent point, and the origin of the arc. A tangent point denotes where the arc intersects or touches a straight line or another arc. In the context of the construction plan for the driveway, points C, F, and H serve as tangent points.

In the specified construction plan, two arcs are utilized on the right-hand side of the driveway to create an 'S' curve. The 4.5-metre arc originates at point G and intersects the building at point C, forming a tangent. Similarly, the 3-metre arc originates at point I, with a tangent point at H, where it meets the line extending towards the public footpath. At the intersection of these arcs, point F serves as a common tangent point, shared by both arcs.

It's essential to recognize that these arcs are relatively straightforward, characterized by their orthogonality, meaning their origins and major tangent points coincide with other construction lines that are 'square' or true perpendiculars. However, situations may arise where the origin of an arc is inaccessible, such as being within the building or obscured by obstacles like trees. In such cases, accurate setting out of arcs can be achieved through the use of chords, which are straight lines connecting two known points on an arc, or 'inverse arcs,' a method addressed in dealing with obstructed arcs.

To establish the 4.5-metre arc, a measurement is taken along the face of the building, and the origin is marked at 4.5 metres from point C, denoted as point G. Subsequently, the tape measure is anchored at point G, and the arc is scribed by swinging it around from point C towards point H, marking the arc's trajectory using spray paint or a similar marking tool.

Establishing the 3-metre arc requires a slightly more intricate process. Its origin, point I, lies on a perpendicular from the building, aligned with corner C, and is located 6 metres from the base line. Utilizing the method described earlier for constructing perpendiculars, the exact position of the origin, point I, is determined, and the tape measure is anchored at this point. The resulting arc is then scribed in a similar manner to the 4.5-metre arc. If executed accurately, the two arcs will intersect at point F, representing the common tangent point.

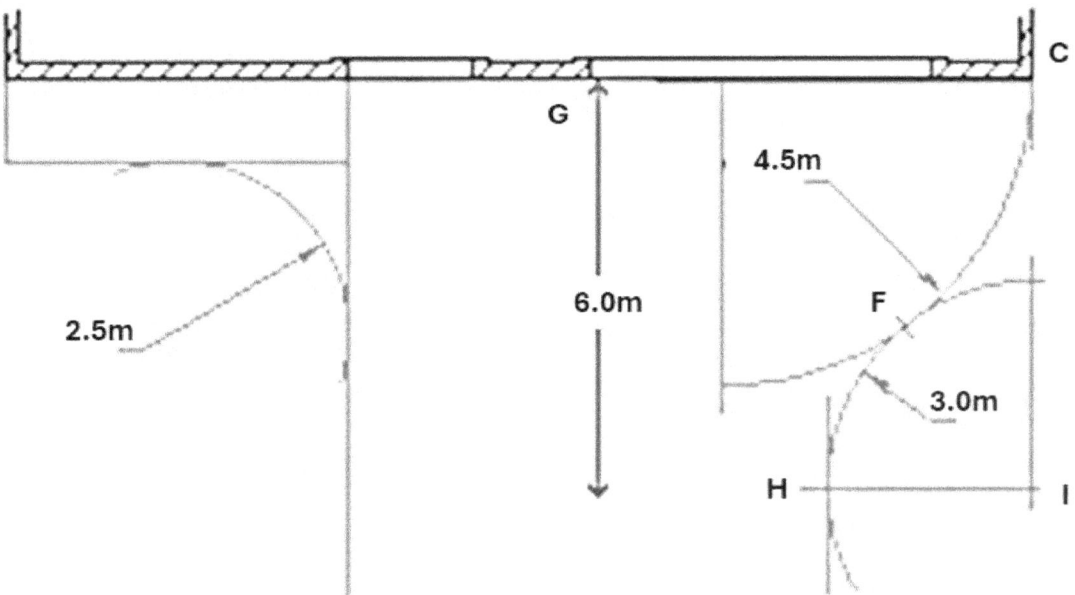

Figure 85: Tangent points.

The two arcs discussed are relatively straightforward because they are orthogonal, meaning their origins and major tangent points align with other construction lines that are 'square' or true perpendiculars to the base line of the front of the house. However, in some cases, the origin of an arc may be inaccessible, such as if it lies within the building itself or is obstructed by trees. In such instances, accurate setting out of arcs can be achieved through the use of chords, which are straight lines connecting two known points on an arc, or 'inverse arcs,' which are explained in more detail on the Setting Out Obstructed Arcs page.

To establish the 4.5-metre arc, a measurement is taken along the face of the building, and the origin is marked at 4.5 metres from point C, denoted as point G. The tape measure is then anchored at point G, and the arc is scribed by swinging it around from point C towards point H, marking the arc's trajectory using spray paint or a similar marking tool.

Establishing the 3-metre arc is a bit more complex. Its origin, point I, is located on a perpendicular from the building, aligned with the corner, C, and is positioned 6 metres from the base line. Perpendiculars are constructed to pinpoint the exact position of its origin, I, and the tape is then anchored at this point. The resulting arc is scribed in a similar manner to the 4.5-metre arc. If executed accurately, the two arcs will intersect at point F, which serves as the common tangent point.

After setting out the arcs, marker pins are driven into the ground at regular intervals along the arcs. The separation between marker pins depends on the radius of the arc, with larger arcs allowing for greater separation between pins. For arcs with radii of less than 5 metres, marker pins are typically spaced at 600-900mm intervals. Once in position, a taut string line is fastened to the pins to create a guide for the laying of the arcs.

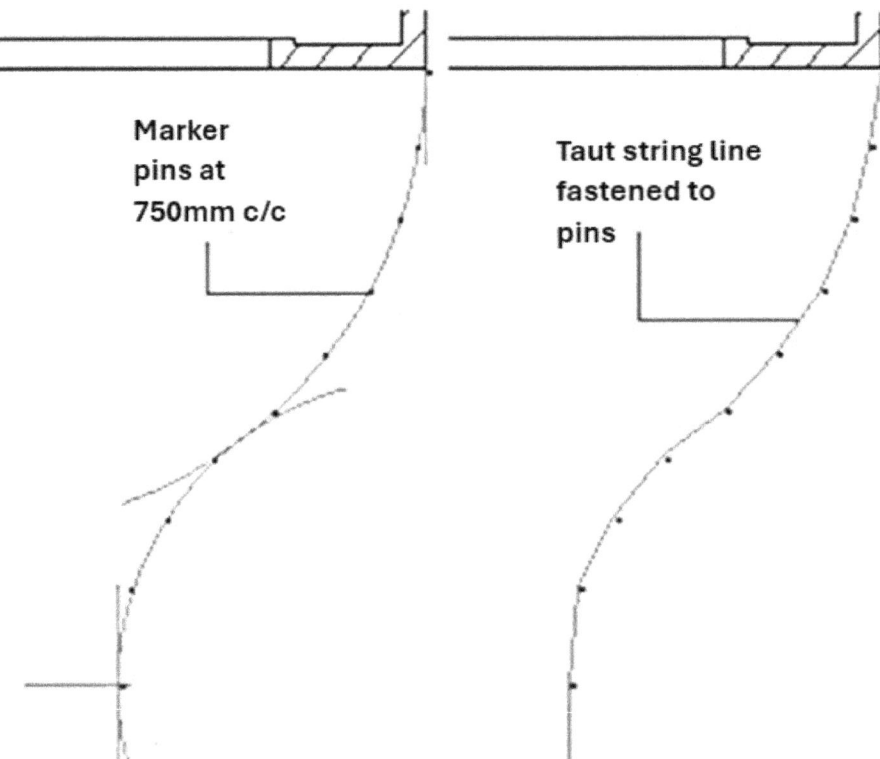

Figure 86: Methods for setting out the driveway.

While setting out the driveway with marker pins and a taut string line provides a guide to the shape of the driveway, establishing levels is essential to ensure proper drainage. The height of the taut string line above ground level is adjusted at the marker pins to guide both line and level accurately. It's crucial that the pins are driven into the ground deep enough to be secure and are absolutely plumb, meaning vertical, to prevent errors in layout caused by adjustments to the string line level. A cross-sectional view illustrates how a leaning pin can result in the displacement of the line position when the line level is adjusted.

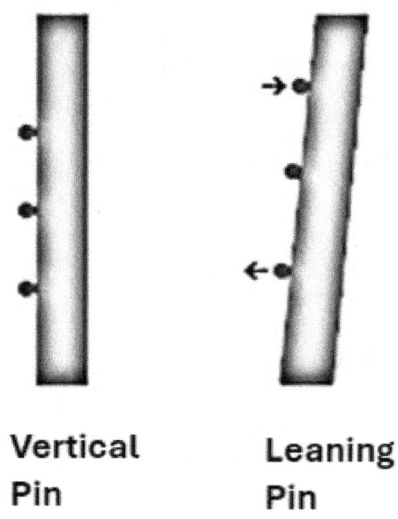
Figure 87: Pin cross-sectional view.

Automatic and Laser Levels

Automatic (or 'dumpy') levels and laser levels are invaluable tools for builders and skilled paving contractors when it comes to setting site levels accurately. These instruments operate on the same fundamental principle, which involves setting up the equipment to define a horizontal plane at a known height around 360°. This plane enables precise measurements to be taken to establish point levels across the construction site. While both types of levels serve the same purpose, laser levels have become increasingly popular due to their affordability and widespread availability in recent years.

Figure 88: Optical level on tripod. Clicgauche at fr.wikipedia, CC BY-SA 1.0, via Wikimedia Commons.

Setting up these levelling devices typically involves mounting them on a stable platform. While they could theoretically be placed on any stable surface like a bale of blocks, it's advisable to use a tripod. A tripod offers several advantages, including stability and adjustability, allowing the instrument to be positioned precisely where it's needed. Moreover, tripods can be elevated to ensure that the level is out of the way of ongoing work while still providing visibility to all points where levels need to be established.

The ability to establish accurate point levels across the construction site is crucial for various tasks, such as determining the slope of the terrain, setting the height of foundations or structures, and ensuring proper drainage. Automatic and laser levels streamline these processes by providing a reliable reference point from which measurements can be taken. This precision is especially important in projects where even slight discrepancies in elevation can lead to significant issues during construction or after completion.

While automatic levels use a telescopic sight to align with a levelling staff held at different points on the site, laser levels emit a beam of light that indicates the desired elevation. Laser levels offer additional features such as self-leveling capabilities and the ability to project a horizontal or vertical line over long distances, making them versatile tools for various applications in construction and paving projects.

The use of automatic and laser levels has revolutionized the process of setting site levels in construction and paving projects. These instruments provide builders and contractors with the accuracy and efficiency needed to ensure that structures are built on level ground and that drainage systems function correctly. By employing tripod-mounted levels, professionals can streamline the levelling process while maintaining precision and accuracy throughout the project.

Automatic levels and laser levels are indispensable tools in construction and paving projects, each offering unique features and benefits. While both types of levels serve the same purpose of establishing accurate horizontal planes, they differ in their operational mechanisms and methods of measurement.

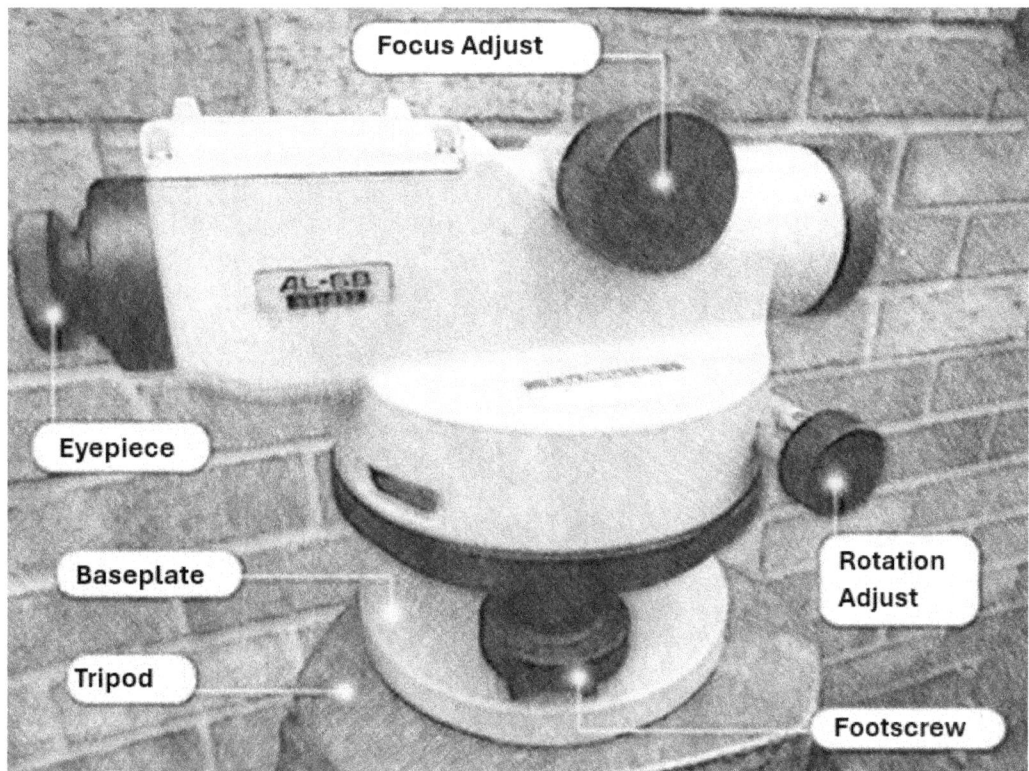

Figure 89: Automatic level components.

Automatic levels rely on line of sight, albeit enhanced through a telescope, to establish horizontal planes. These levels utilize a graduated staff to measure the difference between the level plane and the point to be established. In contrast, laser levels emit a barely visible beam that is detected by a receiver. This beam provides a precise reference point for determining elevations across the construction site.

Typically, both automatic and laser levels are mounted on tripods for stability and accuracy. Automatic levels often feature adjustable screw-feet, allowing them to be precisely aligned to true horizontal. On the other hand, the better-quality laser levels are equipped with self-leveling mechanisms, which automatically adjust the internal components to ensure a horizontal plane, eliminating the need for manual adjustments.

To ensure accuracy, automatic levels commonly incorporate a circular bubble tube, which serves as a visual indicator of horizontality. The foot-screws of the level are adjusted until the bubble is centred within the tube, indicating that the instrument is properly aligned. While this method provides adequate accuracy for most site groundworks, landscaping, and paving jobs, there are more precise levels available for exacting work where precision is paramount.

The accuracy of automatic and laser levels varies depending on the model and manufacturer. Generally, automatic levels are considered accurate to within 10 minutes, which translates to one-sixth of a degree. This level of accuracy is suitable for the majority of construction and paving tasks. However, for projects requiring exceptional precision, such as high-precision surveying or specialized engineering work, more accurate and costly levels may be necessary.

Laser levels are innovative tools that revolutionize the process of establishing horizontal planes in construction and paving projects. Unlike traditional automatic levels that rely on line of sight, laser levels utilize advanced technology to project a laser beam over a significant distance, typically ranging from 100 to 300 metres, as a perfectly horizontal reference line. This laser beam is emitted from within a protective housing and directed by a spinning floating mirror, ensuring accuracy and consistency across the site.

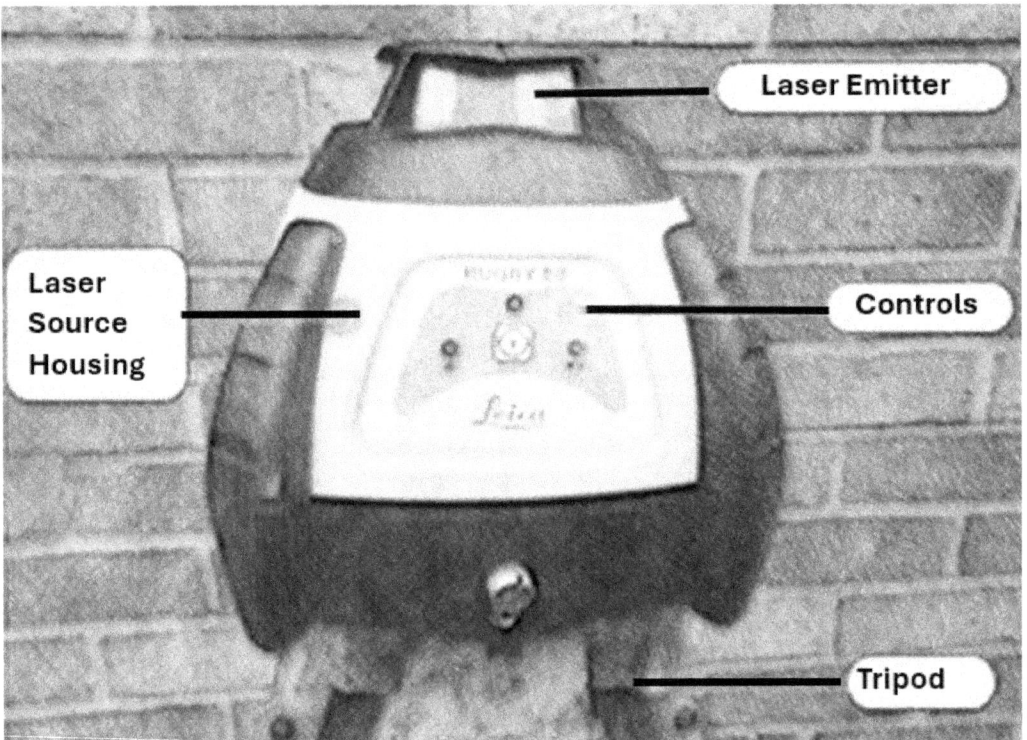

Figure 90: Key features of a laser level.

The laser beam generated by a laser level is nearly invisible to the human eye, although specialized glasses can enhance its visibility. However, the visibility of the laser beam is not critical to its operation. Instead of relying on visual cues, laser levels are equipped with special detectors that are attached to standard graduated staffs. These detectors serve as a means of precisely determining the height of the laser beam above ground level.

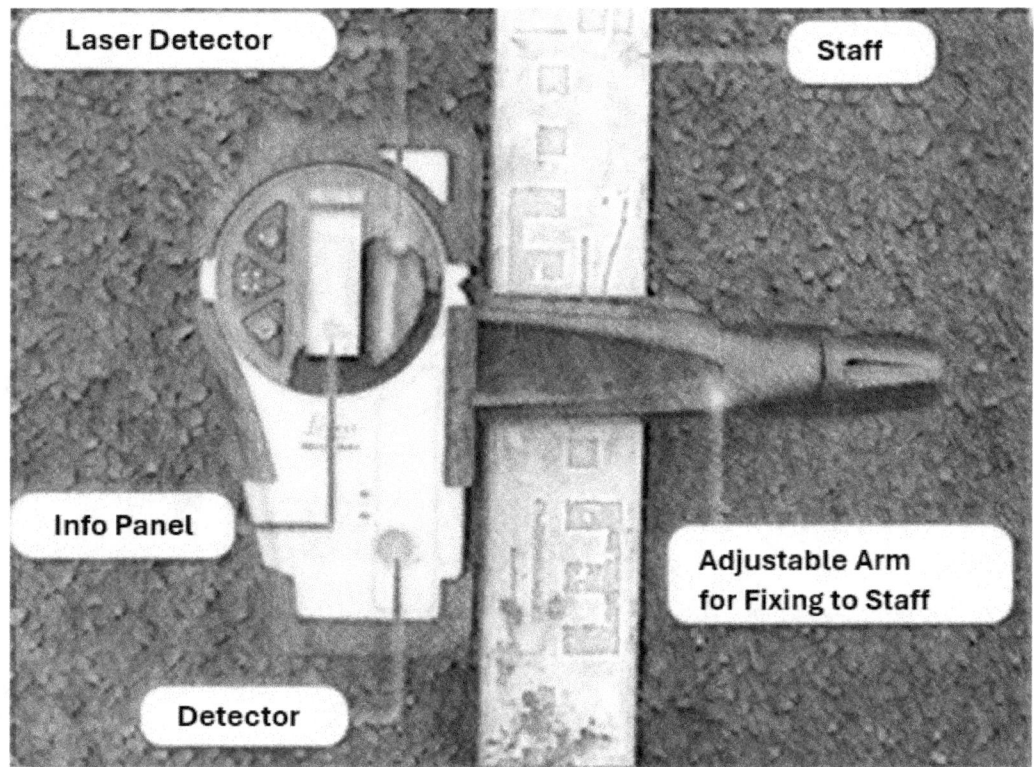

Figure 91: Laser Receiver attached to graduated staff.

During the setup process, the detector is moved up and down the staff until it reaches the exact height of the laser beam. As the detector approaches the height of the laser beam, it emits a series of beeps that progressively increase in frequency. This auditory feedback helps the user identify when the detector is nearing the correct height. Once the detector aligns precisely with the laser beam, the beeping transitions into a continuous tone, indicating that the detector is at the exact level to detect the laser.

By using this sophisticated detection system, laser levels offer unparalleled precision and ease of use in establishing horizontal planes on construction sites. The audible feedback provided by the detector ensures that users can accurately determine the height of the laser beam without relying on visual cues, making laser levels suitable for use in various lighting conditions and environments. Overall, laser levels represent a significant advancement in levelling technology, allowing construction professionals to achieve precise and reliable results in their projects.

Setting-up a Station

When setting up a levelling unit, it's crucial to choose a position that provides an unobstructed view of all the points that need to be levelled, or as many as possible given the conditions of the site. This strategic positioning ensures that the levelling process can proceed smoothly and accurately. The area where the levelling unit is placed is commonly referred to as a "station."

Each station where the levelling unit is set up can be marked for future reference using various methods such as timber pegs, steel pins, brass tags, or paint marks, depending on the site's requirements and conditions. These markers serve as reference points, allowing for the easy relocation of the levelling unit if necessary and ensuring consistency and accuracy in subsequent measurements and levelling tasks.

Figure 92: Setting up a station. Pokarwr, CC BY-SA 4.0, via Wikimedia Commons.

Marking stations in this manner also facilitates the verification of levels and angles at a later date if any discrepancies or inconsistencies are discovered during the construction or inspection process. By having clearly defined stations and reference markers in place, construction professionals can conduct thorough checks and assessments to ensure that the levelling work meets the required standards and specifications. This practice enhances quality control and helps prevent errors or deviations from occurring in the construction project.

Staffs, Benchmarks and Datums

Establishing a surveying station marks the initial step in determining the relative height of the viewing or laser plane. At this stage, it's essential to identify a point with a known level, typically referred to as a "Benchmark" (BM). Benchmarks can originate from various sources such as survey maps or official records, providing a height measurement in metres Above Ordnance Datum (AOD), commonly regarded as sea level. These benchmarks serve as reference points for establishing levels elsewhere on the site and are often termed Temporary Benchmarks (TBM) when used for levelling purposes.

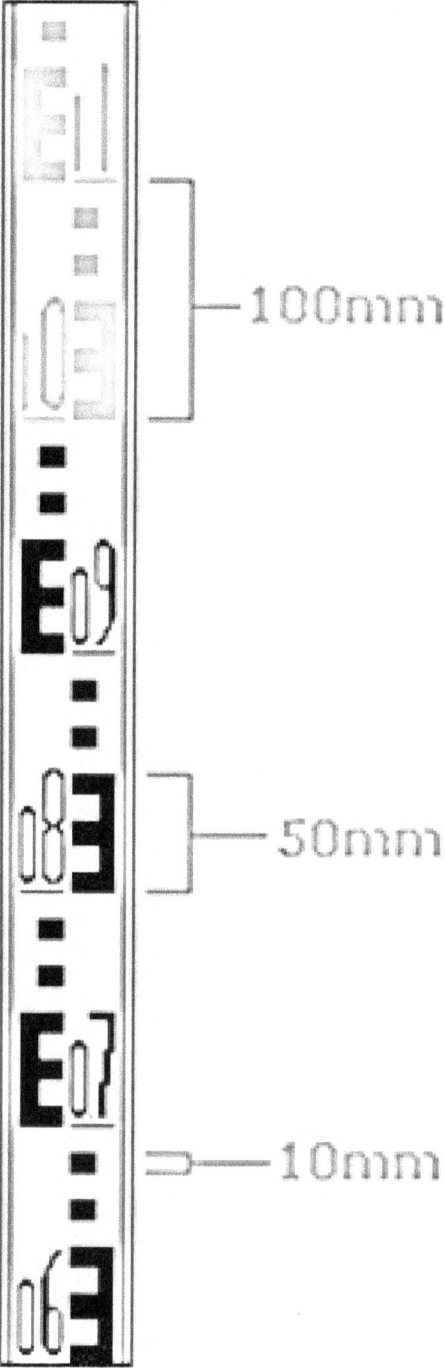

Figure 93: Graduations on staff.

For smaller-scale projects, the absolute height AOD may hold less significance compared to the relative spot heights concerning a specific reference point. In residential paving projects, this reference point is typically the floor level (FL) of the property. Alternatively, other fixed points with known height relationships to the works can serve as the benchmark. For instance, the FL of a garage might be adopted as the BM since the paving must align with the garage floor threshold, allowing all other levels to be derived from this point.

To determine the height at the Benchmark or TBM, a graduated staff is held vertically, and a measurement is taken. With an automatic level, the surveyor directs the telescope at the staff, adjusting the focus until the scale on the staff becomes clearly visible. The measurement is then read off from the cross-hairs of the eyepiece and recorded. Alternatively, with a laser level, the visible laser line intersects with a receiver attached to the staff, and the measurement is read and recorded accordingly. Most automatic levels feature a magnification of approximately x10, enhancing the visibility of the staff. This magnification enables surveyors to read measurements with reasonable accuracy, often within ±2mm, even at distances of around 20 metres.

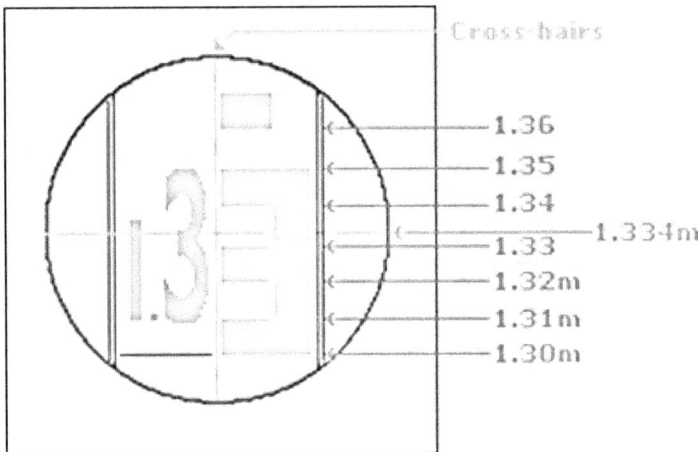

Figure 94: View through automatic level : Measurement reads 1.3 from the scale, with the cross-hairs clear of the 3rd section of the 'E', so the measurement becomes 1.33, and finally the horizontal cross-hair is approximately 4/10 of the way through the white section, so the actual measurement is 1.334m.

Once the initial reading is recorded, the next phase involves transferring this level to other critical points across the project site and making necessary adjustments in alignment with the plans. This process ensures that the levelling work aligns accurately with the intended design specifications, contributing to the overall quality and precision of the construction project.

Absolute Levels

Absolute levels refer to spot heights recorded during a site survey or depicted on a plan, representing the true elevation above Ordnance Datum (AOD), commonly known as "sea level." These measurements provide precise vertical positioning and are crucial for projects requiring utmost accuracy, such as the construction of critical infrastructure like nuclear power stations. In such high-stakes projects, even minor discrepancies in elevation can have significant implications, necessitating the use of absolute levels to ensure the integrity and safety of the structure.

However, the importance of absolute levels varies depending on the nature and scale of the construction project. For endeavours like building a driveway or residential landscaping, where the consequences of minor elevation variations are less critical, relative levels may be more suitable. Relative levels are measured in relation to a specific reference point, such as the existing ground level or a designated benchmark within the project site. While they offer sufficient precision for many residential and small-scale projects, they do not provide the same level of accuracy as absolute levels.

The decision to use absolute or relative levels depends on several factors, including the project's purpose, complexity, and regulatory requirements. Projects with stringent safety standards, environmental considerations, or those subject to regulatory oversight often necessitate the use of absolute levels to ensure compliance and mitigate risks. In contrast, simpler projects where precise elevation measurements are less critical may opt for relative levels, which offer adequate accuracy while minimizing costs and complexity.

While absolute levels offer unparalleled accuracy and reliability in determining vertical elevation, they are typically reserved for projects where precision is paramount, such as large-scale infrastructure developments or projects with strict regulatory requirements. For smaller-scale endeavours like driveway construction or landscaping projects, relative levels may suffice, providing sufficient accuracy at a lower cost and complexity. Ultimately, the choice between absolute and relative levels depends on the specific needs and constraints of each individual project.

Spot Heights

Spot heights play a crucial role in construction and landscaping projects, representing the elevation of specific points on a site. These heights, typically marked on plans, provide essential information for determining the height or level of various features across the project area. For instance, a spot height might indicate the elevation of the top face of a kerbline at a particular tangent point, allowing engineers and contractors to assess the slope or gradient between different sections of the site. By comparing spot heights at different locations, one can calculate the amount of elevation change, such as the degree of fall along a kerbline over a certain distance.

In large-scale commercial projects, absolute levels are often utilized to ensure consistency and accuracy across the site. Absolute levels establish every point on the site relative to a single universal reference point, typically referred to as the height Above Ordnance Datum (AOD), equivalent to sea level. This approach ensures that all measurements and designs are based on a standardized reference, facilitating coordination and collaboration among various contractors and tradespeople involved in the project. The use of absolute levels helps maintain uniformity and precision throughout the construction process, from groundwork to finishing touches.

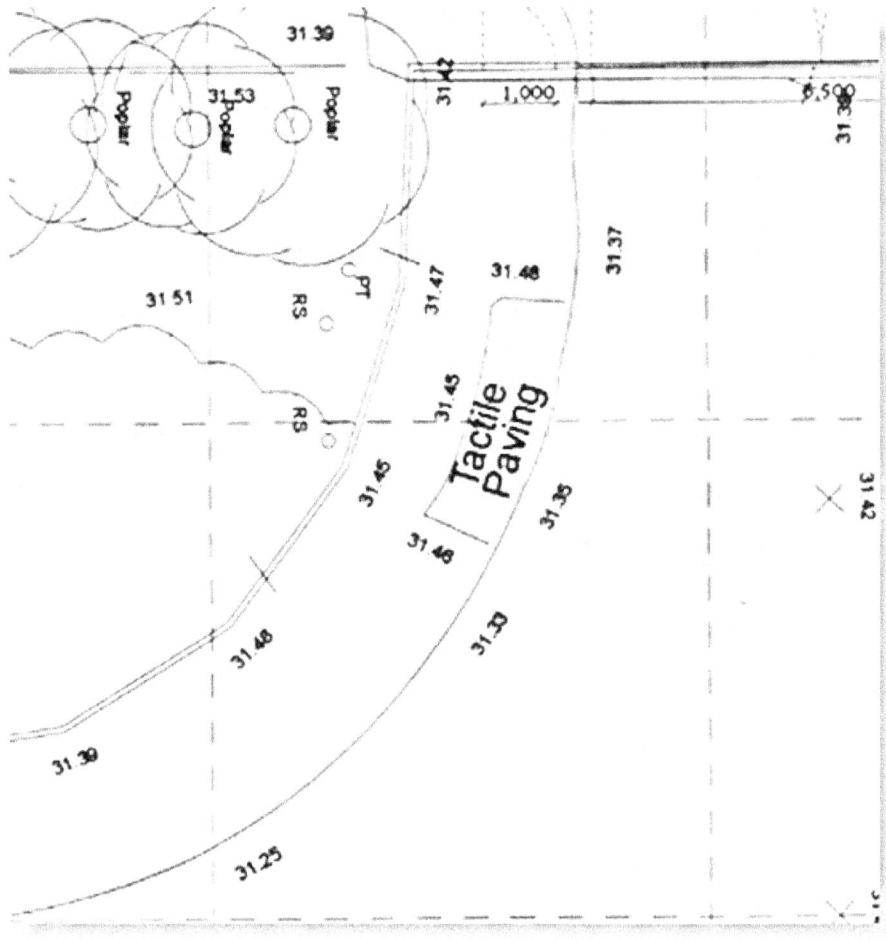

Figure 95: Spot heights.

To establish absolute levels, a Master Benchmark (MBM) is identified within or near the project site. The MBM serves as a known point with a specified height AOD, often marked with visible indicators like plaques or engravings. Surveyors and engineers use the height of the MBM as a reference to calculate the elevation of other points on the site. By taking readings with levelling equipment at the MBM, they can determine the line of collimation—the imaginary line of sight through an automatic level or laser level. This line of collimation provides the basis for establishing consistent elevation measurements across the project area.

When determining the elevation at a specific point on the site, such as point A, engineers use calculations based on the known height AOD of the MBM. By subtracting or adding the desired elevation change from the height of the MBM, they determine the target elevation for the point of interest. Once the target elevation is established, an operative holds a levelling staff at the designated point and adjusts its height until it intersects with the line of collimation at the desired elevation. This process ensures that the point is accurately levelled according to the project specifications. Finally, the marked or adjusted point is verified for accuracy using the levelling equipment, providing assurance that the elevation has been correctly established.

Relative Levels

Relative levels are a pragmatic approach to elevation determination, particularly suited for smaller-scale projects like home renovations, driveway installations, and patio constructions. Unlike absolute levels, which reference elevations to a universal benchmark such as sea level, relative levels focus on the height differentials between various points within the project site. This method simplifies the levelling process by establishing a token level, or "datum," from which all other elevations are derived.

In relative levelling, a fixed point on the project site is designated as the datum and assigned a nominal value, often set at 100.000 metres. This value serves as a reference point for all subsequent elevation measurements. By choosing a positive value for the datum, calculations become more straightforward, eliminating the need to deal with negative elevation values, which can complicate the arithmetic.

To illustrate the application of relative levels, let's consider the driveway project previously discussed in the Setting Out section. In the Calculating Falls sub-section, elevation requirements for key points along the driveway were established based on factors such as drainage and design considerations. These predetermined elevation values serve as the basis for setting out the levels across the site.

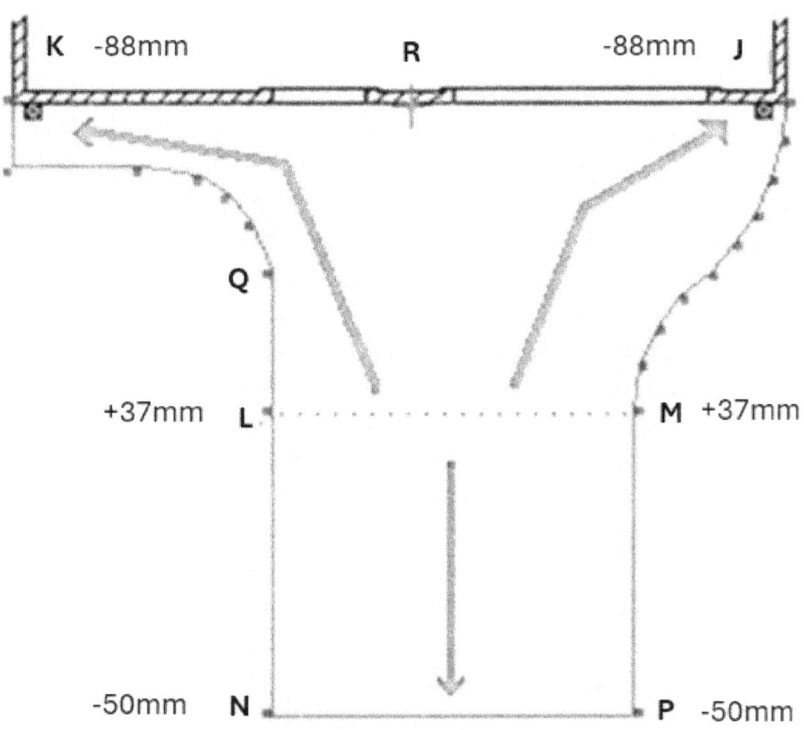

Figure 96: Driveway falls.

In the driveway project example, the datum is established at a designated point, denoted as point R, with an assigned value of 100.000 metres. This value signifies the baseline elevation from which all other points on the site will be measured. Using the predetermined elevation values derived from the calculations in the Calculating Falls sub-section, engineers and contractors can accurately determine the relative elevations of various features and components within the project area.

By referencing the datum and applying the calculated elevation differentials, workers can effectively set out levels for the driveway, ensuring proper drainage, alignment, and aesthetic appeal. The use of relative levels simplifies the leveling process, making it more accessible and manageable for smaller-scale projects where absolute elevation values may be less critical than the relationships between different points on the site.

In the process of setting out levels for a project, particularly in construction and landscaping, it's common to encounter elevation values that are provided with respect to a specific reference point or datum. These values, typically expressed with plus or minus symbols, need to be converted into values that are relative to the established datum point. This conversion is often referred to as determining "Reduced Levels" (RL). The RL values indicate the elevation of various points on the site relative to the chosen datum.

For example, if a point (let's say point K) is given an elevation of -88mm relative to the datum point R, the RL value for point K can be calculated by subtracting the given value from the elevation of the datum point. In this case, if the elevation of point R is 100.000 metres, then the RL for point K would be 99.912 metres. This arithmetic process is repeated for all key points on the site to establish their respective RL values.

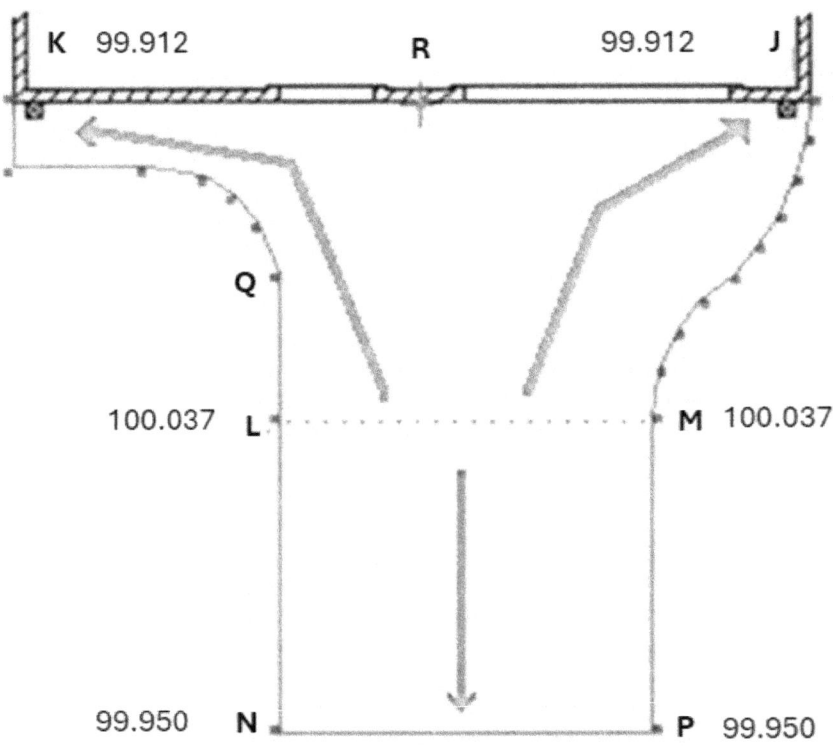

Figure 97: Driveway relative values.

After determining the RL values for all relevant points, the next step is to establish the "height of collimation," which essentially refers to the elevation of the line of sight or instrument used for levelling purposes. This is typically done by taking a reading from a staff held vertically at the datum point. For instance, if the reading taken from the staff at point R is 1.334 metres, then the height of the instrument (or height of collimation) is determined to be 101.334 metres.

With the RL values and the height of collimation established, the process continues by calculating the required staff readings at each point to achieve the desired elevation. This involves simple mathematical calculations to adjust the staff readings based on the difference between the RL value for each point and the height of collimation. Once these adjusted readings are determined for all points, the levelling process can proceed.

There are various methods for transferring levels to the different points on the site. One common approach is to use the calculated staff readings to set the appropriate elevations at each point simultaneously. Alternatively, the datum level could be transferred to each relevant point, and then adjustments made up or down from the datum mark to reach the desired elevation at each point. Ultimately, the choice of method depends on factors such as project requirements, site conditions, and the preference of the surveyor or engineer overseeing the levelling process.

Working Lines and Levels

Setting line levels involves ensuring that the string line, which serves as a guide for establishing the correct elevation of the ground surface, is positioned accurately at each marker pin along the project area. Once the pins are securely in place and the string line is stretched between them, the next step is to adjust the string line to the desired level at each pin. This adjustment is crucial for ensuring that the final surface gradient meets the project specifications and drainage requirements.

To adjust the string line to the correct level at each pin, a technique involving half-hitch knots is commonly employed. By pulling the string line on each side of the pin towards the pin itself, the tension on the half-hitch knot is reduced, allowing it to be moved up or down the pin as necessary. This adjustment process allows for precise control over the elevation of the string line at each point along the project area.

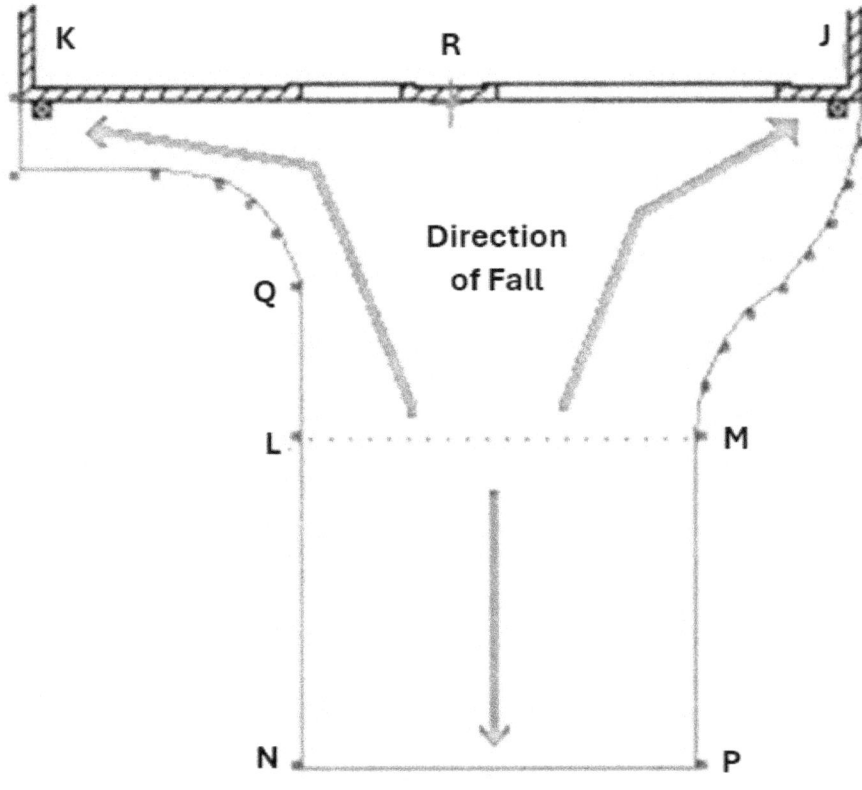

Figure 98: Direction of fall.

In planning the drainage for the driveway project, certain considerations must be taken into account. The drawing provided illustrates that the part of the driveway closest to the house is designed to be drained towards specific gullies located at points J and K. Conversely, the lower section of the driveway is intended to be drained towards the public footpath. This necessitates the establishment of an imaginary "change of fall" line between points L and M, indicating the transition in slope direction.

Furthermore, the drawing reveals that the driveway needs to slope in two directions along the front of the house, with a high point identified at point R and sloping towards the gullies at points J and K. However, it's essential to ensure that the elevation of point R, being adjacent to the brickwork of the property, does not exceed a certain height below the damp proof course (dpc). For instance, if the dpc specifies that the point R cannot be any higher than 150mm below the dpc, this constraint must be taken into consideration when setting the elevation at point R during the levelling process.

Calculating Falls

Calculating falls is a critical aspect of planning any construction project, particularly when it comes to ensuring proper drainage. In the context of a driveway project, determining the appropriate gradient or slope is essential for directing surface water runoff away from the paved surface to prevent pooling or flooding. This calculation involves considering various factors such as the distance between drainage points, the desired gradient, and the type of pavement material being used.

In the scenario described, the distance between the gullies at points J and K and the midpoint R is approximately 7 metres each. To achieve effective drainage, a minimum gradient of 1:80 is required for block pavements, ensuring that water flows away efficiently. It's important to note that different pavement materials may necessitate varying degrees of slope; for instance, hand-laid tarmac surfaces typically require a steeper gradient, often around 1:60, to facilitate adequate drainage.

To calculate the fall or drop in elevation between the midpoint R and the gullies at J and K, the distance of 7 metres is multiplied by the gradient factor of 1/80. This calculation yields a fall of approximately 0.0875 metres or 88 millimetres. Consequently, the levels at the gullies must be adjusted to be 88 millimetres lower than the level at point R. Given that point R has been established as 150 millimetres below the damp proof course (dpc), the levels at J and K need to be set at (150 + 88) = 238 millimetres below the dpc, assuming the dpc is level.

With the required level established for the gullies, the next step involves marking this level onto the brickwork at the respective points and adjusting the gully levels accordingly. This ensures that the drainage system is properly aligned with the desired gradient, allowing for efficient water runoff and minimizing the risk of water accumulation on the driveway surface. By accurately calculating falls and adjusting levels accordingly, builders can ensure the effective performance and longevity of the paved area, enhancing both functionality and aesthetics.

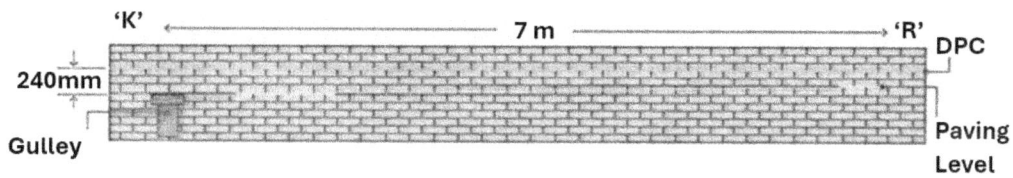

Figure 99: Cross-sectional view through K and R showing fall to gully.

With R, J, and K established, the focus shifts to determining the high points along the break line L-M on the driveway. This break line serves as a crucial transition between the sections of the driveway that slope towards different drainage points. By accurately setting the levels along L-M, builders ensure proper water flow management and prevent potential pooling or flooding issues.

To calculate the required elevation at the midpoint of line L-M, the distance from this midpoint to the furthest gully, K, is measured, approximately 10 metres. Utilizing the standard 1:80 fall, the elevation at the midpoint of L-M needs to be determined. Multiplying the distance of 10 metres by the gradient factor of 1/80 yields a rise of approximately 0.125 metres or 125 millimetres above the level of the gully at K.

Given that the gully at K is established as 88 millimetres below point R, the levels at points L and M need to be adjusted accordingly. Subtracting the elevation of the gully at K from the required elevation at the midpoint of L-M (125 millimetres), we find that points L and M need to be set 37 millimetres higher than point R.

Additionally, it's essential to consider the threshold level at points N and P, which is 50 millimetres lower than point R. This information allows for further calculation of the fall from points L and M to points N and P. Combining the rise from points L and M to point R (37 millimetres) with the drop from point R to points N and P (50 millimetres), we determine that there is a total fall of (37 + 50) = 87 millimetres over a distance of 6 metres between L-M and N-P.

This calculated fall translates to a gradient of (87 ÷ 6000) = 1:67, which falls comfortably within the required minimum gradient of 1:80 for effective drainage. By meticulously determining these critical levels along the break line L-M and ensuring that they align with the specified gradients, builders can optimize the drainage performance of the driveway, mitigating the risk of water-related issues and ensuring long-term durability and functionality.

Level Transfer

Level transfer is a crucial step in construction projects, ensuring that consistent elevation is maintained across various points of the site. This process involves moving the established level from one reference point to another accurately. While more sophisticated methods exist, such as using boning rods and automatic levels for precise measurements, simpler techniques using everyday tools can also be effective.

One common method of level transfer involves the use of a straight-edged timber and a reliable spirit level. This approach is practical and accessible, requiring tools that are readily available on most construction sites. However, it's essential to use a spirit level of adequate length to ensure accuracy. Typically, a spirit level measuring at least 1200mm in length is recommended to achieve precise results. This length ensures that the level can effectively span the distance between reference points while maintaining accuracy.

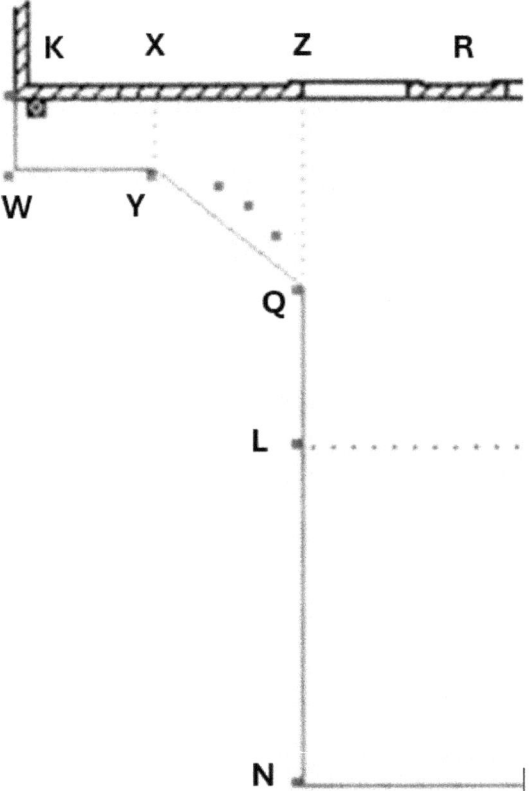

Figure 100: Levels for key points on layout.

Small boat levels, despite their compact size, are generally not suitable for this type of work due to their limited precision. Using a longer spirit level minimizes the risk of inaccuracies during the level transfer process. The straight-edged timber, usually 3 to 4 metres in length, serves as a guide for transferring the level across the site.

However, in situations where the distance between reference points exceeds the length of the straight-edged timber, additional steps are required. To bridge this gap, a temporary intermediate level is set up. This intermediate level serves as a midpoint between the reference point (Point R) and the target points (Points L and M). By carefully aligning the intermediate level with the reference point and adjusting it as necessary, builders can ensure accurate level transfer over longer distances.

While the process may seem straightforward, attention to detail is crucial to achieving precise results. Any inaccuracies during level transfer can lead to significant discrepancies in the final construction, potentially affecting the functionality and aesthetics of the project. Therefore, construction teams must adhere to proper techniques and use reliable tools to ensure consistent and accurate level transfer across the site.

Level transfer using physical objects like bricks and a straight-edge is a practical technique commonly employed on construction sites, particularly for smaller projects. This method involves setting a brick at the desired elevation at a reference point, in this case, Point R, ensuring its surface aligns precisely with the intended paving level, which is determined to be 150mm below the damp proof course (dpc). Another brick is then positioned between Point R and the target point, Point L, also on a sand bed.

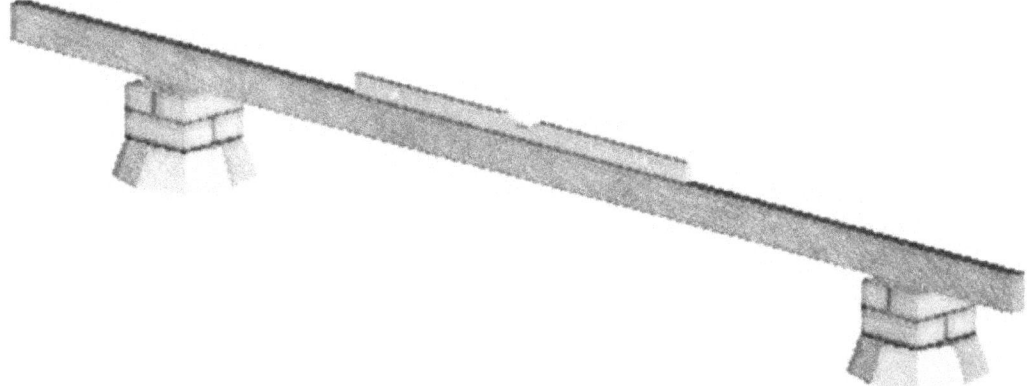

Figure 101: Using a straight edge and a spirit level to transfer levels from one point to another.

Once both bricks are in place, a straight-edge is laid across them to create a bridge between the two points. A spirit level is then used to check the alignment of the straight-edge, ensuring that it remains perfectly horizontal. The intermediate brick positioned between Points R and L is adjusted accordingly, either tapped down or built up, until the spirit level indicates that it is exactly level with the brick at Point R.

While this method provides a straightforward way to transfer levels between points, it is generally recommended for use on smaller projects due to its limitations. One key consideration is the potential for errors to accumulate when transferring levels over multiple stages. To minimize inaccuracies, it's advisable to limit the number of stages in level transfer to two, helping to maintain acceptable levels of precision.

By employing this intermediate level transfer technique, construction teams can establish the paving level at points L and M, complementing the levels previously determined at points J, K, and R. Additionally, the existing footpath provides reference points at N and P, facilitating seamless integration with the surrounding environment. With these critical levels now established, attention can be turned to setting the remaining levels on the intermediate pins around the curves, ensuring consistency and accuracy throughout the project.

Setting Levels to Curves

Setting levels along the S-curve of the driveway involves a systematic approach that ensures precision and uniformity. The process begins by establishing a temporary line between two known points, C and M, which provides a reference for transferring levels to the intermediate pins. This temporary line, typically created using a taut string, is positioned to pass near one of the marker pins at 'S', allowing for easy level transfer to the adjacent pins.

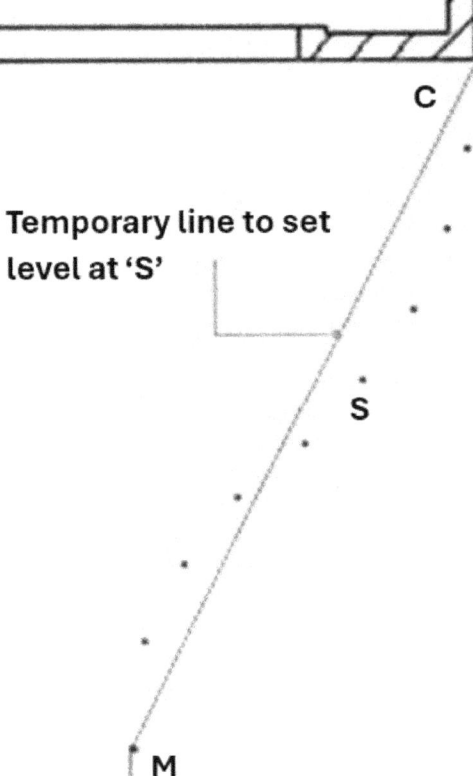

Figure 102: Temporary line to set level at 'S'.

With the temporary line in place, the next step involves using a spirit level to transfer the level from this line to the nearest marker pin, ensuring accuracy at each point along the curve. The line is then looped around the pin at 'S' using a half hitch, securing it in position for further level transfer to adjacent pins at points T and U. This process of level transfer is repeated systematically, with the string line half-hitched around each successive pin, allowing for consistent levelling across the entire curve.

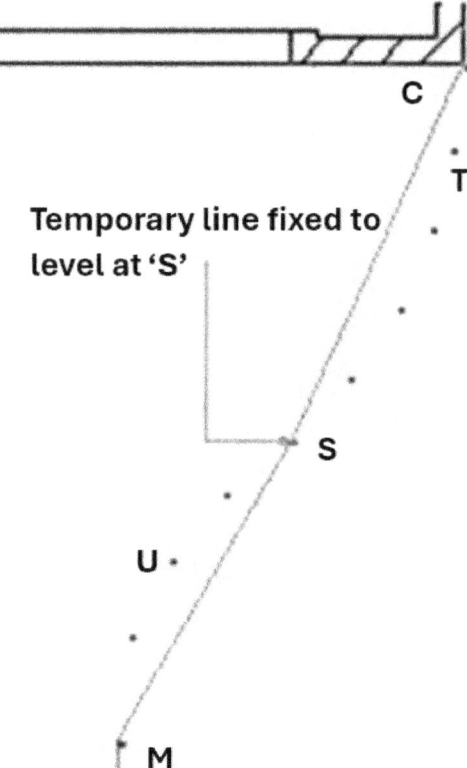

Figure 103: Temporary line fixed to level at 'S'.

As the string line is adjusted and secured at each pin, meticulous attention is paid to maintaining a smooth, continuous level profile. This requires careful observation by lying flat on the ground and aligning one's eye level with the string line, ensuring that there are no noticeable high or low points as the line traverses from point C to M. Minor adjustments may be necessary at each pin to achieve a seamless and uniform level along the curve.

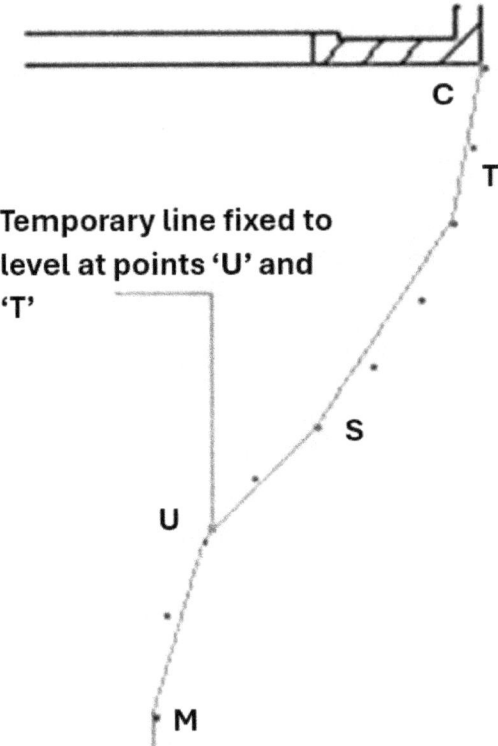

Figure 104: Temporary line fixed to level at points 'U' and 'T'.

Once the levels are accurately established on each pin through repeated level transfers, the string line can be set up permanently as a guide for paving the driveway. In this setup, the edges of the soldier course, typically laid on a concrete bed, are aligned with the taut string line. The blocks are then tapped down until their tops are flush with the string line, ensuring a consistent and level surface for the entire driveway. This meticulous process ensures both the structural integrity and aesthetic appeal of the finished driveway, reflecting the attention to detail required in construction projects.

Setting Intermediate Levels

Setting intermediate levels along the left-hand curve of the driveway and the access path in front of the house marks the final stage of the setting-out process, ensuring that all areas of the project are accurately prepared for paving. While the principles for setting levels remain consistent with previous sections, careful attention is given to specific points to minimize the need for extensive level transfers and maximize overall accuracy.

Prioritizing certain key points such as Points Q, Y, and W streamlines the level-setting process. Point W, for example, is established by levelling across from the top of the gully at Point K, allowing for a slight slope of approximately 20mm along the 1.2-metre-wide path towards the gully. This slope falls well within the specified 1:80 tolerance, ensuring proper drainage. Consequently, Point W is set to be 20mm higher than Point K to achieve the desired slope.

Similarly, Point Y's level is determined by levelling across from the line established between Points K and R at Point X. However, as there is no gully at Point X, the path should not slope towards the house like the previous point. Therefore, Point Y is set to be 10mm below Point X to maintain the desired level.

Establishing Point Q involves extrapolating the line from Point N to Point L until it intersects the line from Point K to Point R at Point Z. The taut string line should just touch the pin at Point Q, indicating the appropriate level for paving, which can then be marked accordingly.

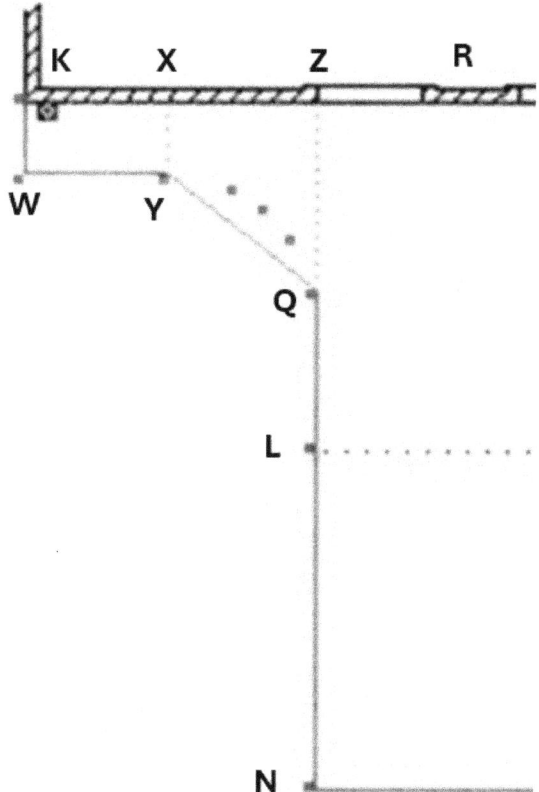

Figure 105: Setting intermediate levels.

With these key points established, the paving level can be transferred systematically using a temporary string line stretched between known Points Q and Y. By half-hitching the string line around each pin along the curve and carefully adjusting the levels as needed, a consistent and accurate paving level is achieved.

Once all levels are confirmed to be correct and the alignment is true through a thorough check, the paving work can commence with confidence. This meticulous approach to setting intermediate levels ensures that the entire driveway project is executed with precision, resulting in a visually appealing and structurally sound finished product.

Boning Rods and Sight-rails

Boning rods and sight-rails serve as fundamental tools for establishing levels in construction, tracing back to ancient civilizations like the Sumerians and Ancient Egyptians. Despite their antiquity, these tools remain integral to contemporary construction practices, although their prevalence has diminished with the advent of affordable laser levels in recent years. The term "boning rod" originates from Old English, referring to a slope or gradient, emphasizing the tool's simplicity and effectiveness over millennia.

The principle behind boning rods is elegantly straightforward: by fixing two known levels, construction workers can easily set any number of intermediate levels along a line of sight. Typically, a set of boning rods comprises three T-shaped staffs, each identical in design. However, in cases where precise measurements are paramount, such as when using fixed sight rails, one staff may be constructed to a specified length to serve as the "traveller" along the rail. While most paving and groundworks contractors possess a set of boning rods for routine tasks, larger projects may necessitate the use of fixed sight rails for establishing numerous levels efficiently.

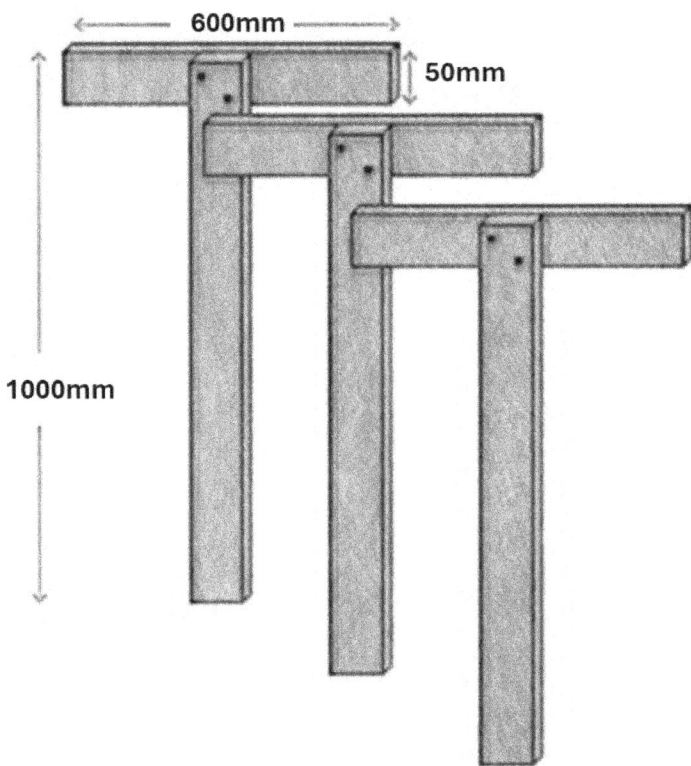

Figure 106: Typical Boning rods.

Traditionally, boning rods are wielded by manually sighting along the line of the rods to determine level positions. This method allows for a high degree of accuracy, particularly in situations where laser levels may be impractical or unavailable. The versatility of boning rods lies in their adaptability to various terrains and conditions, making them invaluable for projects ranging from residential driveways to complex commercial developments.

Despite their simplicity, boning rods require skill and precision to operate effectively. Workers must ensure that the rods are correctly aligned and that sight lines are accurately established to achieve reliable level measurements. Additionally, proper calibration and regular maintenance of the rods are essential to maintain accuracy over time.

While laser levels have largely supplanted boning rods in many construction contexts due to their speed and automation, these traditional tools continue to find utility in scenarios where precision and versatility are paramount. Their enduring legacy underscores the timeless value of simple yet ingenious solutions in the ever-evolving field of construction.

Using a set of three boning rods is a tried and tested method for establishing levels with precision and efficiency in construction projects. The process begins by setting up one of the rods at a predetermined height above a known level. Typically, a stable and temporary platform, often constructed from bricks or broken flagstones, is erected to ensure the top of the platform aligns precisely with the desired level. Once the platform is in place, the boning rod is positioned atop it and secured either by an operative or a brace. Subsequently, another rod is set up at the next designated level point, following the same procedure to ensure accuracy. It's crucial that the cross-pieces of these rods are perfectly horizontal, requiring verification with a spirit level before proceeding.

The third rod in the set, known as the Traveller, plays a pivotal role in the level-setting process. Positioned between the two established rods, the Traveller is held against or on top of a steel pin or timber peg driven into the ground at the desired intermediate level point. An operative stationed at one of the established levels then sights through the Traveller to the backsight rod, providing instructions to the operative holding the Traveller to raise or lower it until it aligns precisely between the foresight and backsight. Once the Traveller reaches the correct level, the operative can mark the pin at its base or adjust the height of a peg to match the required level.

With this method, intermediate levels can be established seamlessly between the two known levels, accommodating deviations from the true line, especially when setting out curves or arcs. The flexibility of boning rods allows for adjustments as needed, such as when establishing a level that is higher or lower than two adjacent points. For instance, if two points are determined to be level with each other, but an intermediate level needs to be 100mm higher to facilitate pavement drainage, this can be achieved by setting the intermediate level and then adding the required height adjustment.

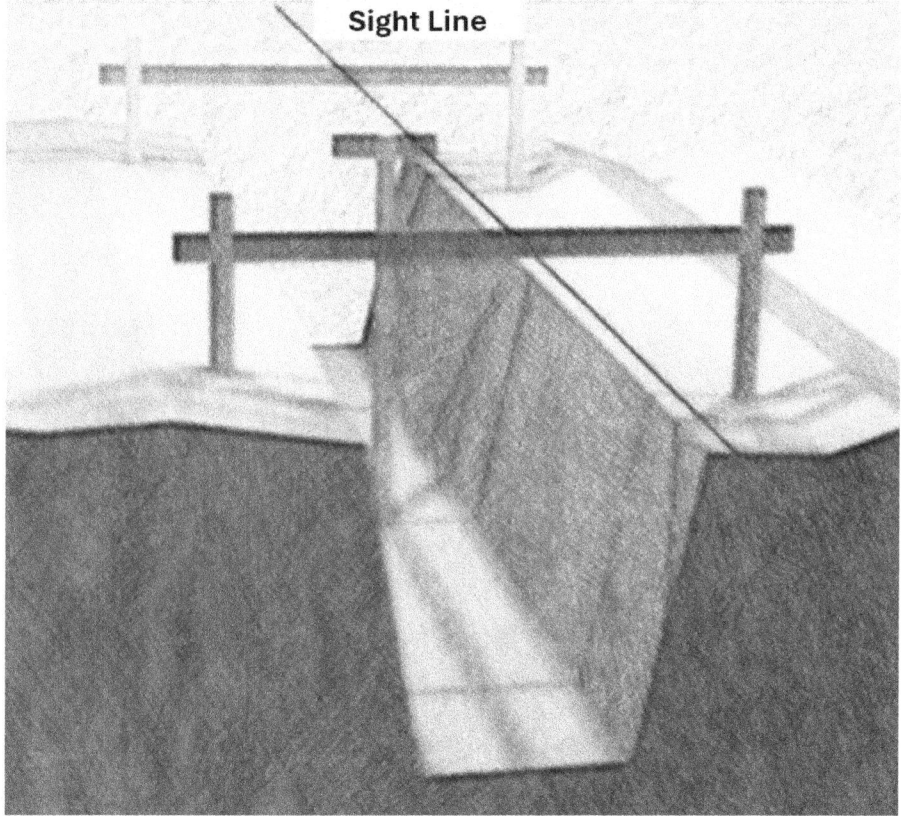

Figure 107: Using three rods.

Boning-in technique finds particular utility in excavations and trenching projects, where precise depth control is paramount. Sight-rails can be set up in advance, and a traveller is constructed to guide excavation depth to the desired reduced level. In drainage projects, sight-rails are typically positioned outside the excavation limits and spaced up to 50 metres apart. A mechanical excavator can then progress along the trench line, while a banksman utilizes the traveller to verify excavation depth at regular intervals, ensuring compliance with project specifications.

Boning rods and sight-rails are invaluable tools in landscaping projects, offering a straightforward and precise method for establishing levels across various terrains and features. They can be used as follows:

- **Planning and Preparation**: Before utilizing boning rods and sight-rails, it's essential to have a clear plan for the landscaping project. This includes identifying key elevation points, such as high and low spots, slopes, and any desired gradients. Additionally, ensure that you have the necessary equipment, including boning rods, sight-rails, steel pins or timber pegs, and a spirit level.

- **Setting Up Sight-rails**: Begin by determining the reference points for your project. These could be existing structures, like a building foundation or a pathway, or predetermined benchmarks. Install sight-rails at these reference points, ensuring they are securely anchored and perfectly level. Sight-rails can be positioned horizontally using a spirit level or laser level.

- **Establishing Intermediate Levels**: With the sight-rails in place, use boning rods to establish intermediate levels between the reference points. One boning rod is set up at each reference point, while the third, known as the Traveller, is positioned between them. Drive steel pins or timber pegs into the ground at locations where intermediate levels are required.

- **Aligning the Traveller**: An operative stationed at one reference point sights through the Traveller to the backsight rod, while another operative adjusts the height of the Traveller until it aligns precisely between the foresight and backsight rods. This ensures that the Traveller is set at the correct level relative to the reference points.

- **Marking Intermediate Levels**: Once the Traveller is aligned, mark the height of the steel pins or timber pegs at the base of the boning rods. These marks indicate the established intermediate levels across the landscape.

- **Repeating the Process**: Continue the process of setting up boning rods and aligning the Traveller at various points throughout the landscaping area. By systematically moving from one reference point to another, you can establish a grid of intermediate levels across the entire site.

- **Adjustments and Fine-tuning**: After all intermediate levels are marked, double-check their accuracy using a spirit level. Make any necessary adjustments to ensure that the landscape features, such as pathways, flower beds, or retaining walls, will drain properly and appear visually pleasing.

- **Execution of Landscaping Tasks**: Once the levels are established and verified, proceed with the execution of landscaping tasks, such as grading, excavation, or installation of hardscape elements. The marked levels serve as a reliable guide for ensuring uniformity and precision in the construction process.

- **Monitoring and Maintenance**: Throughout the landscaping project, periodically check the established levels to ensure they remain accurate, especially after significant earth-moving activities or changes in weather conditions. Adjustments may be required to maintain the desired grades and slopes over time.

By following these steps and leveraging boning rods and sight-rails effectively, landscapers can achieve consistent and professional results in grading, levelling, and shaping outdoor spaces to meet client expectations and project requirements.

Profile Boards

Sight-rails, also known as profile boards in the context of house foundation setting, are essential tools used in construction to ensure precise excavation depths and accurate levelling for various components of a building's foundation. These boards are typically positioned outside the excavation area and are installed in pairs to provide a reference framework for the construction process.

The primary function of sight-rails is to serve as guides for excavation depth. By setting them up outside the excavation limits, contractors establish clear boundaries for digging while ensuring that the desired depth is maintained consistently throughout the site. This helps prevent over-excavation or deviations from the planned foundation dimensions, which could compromise the structural integrity of the building.

In addition to guiding excavation, sight-rails play a crucial role in setting levels for different elements of the foundation. They serve as reference points for determining the top of the concrete foundation, internal floor level, finished ground level, and other critical elevations. By aligning the sight-rails precisely and accurately measuring heights relative to them, builders can ensure that the foundation components are installed at the correct elevations as per the building plans.

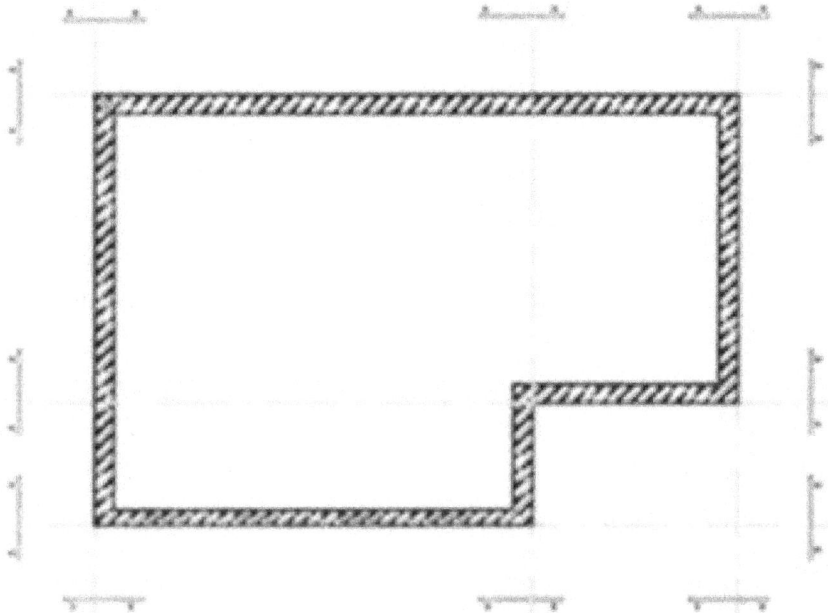

Figure 108: Sight-rails set up to guide excavation of strip footings for a typical house.

The use of sight-rails with a traveller further enhances their functionality during the construction process. The traveller, typically a movable rod or marker, can be adjusted along the sight-rails to check excavation depths at various points across the site. This allows contractors to verify that the excavation is uniform and conforms to the specified depths required for the foundation design. Any discrepancies can be promptly addressed to maintain consistency and quality in the excavation process.

Moreover, sight-rails provide a visual reference for other construction tasks beyond excavation. Once the foundation excavation is complete, they continue to guide the placement of concrete forms, reinforcement, and other structural elements. By aligning subsequent construction activities with the established sight-rails, builders ensure that the foundation is built according to the prescribed specifications and meets structural and safety standards.

Overall, sight-rails serve as indispensable tools in the construction of house foundations, providing both guidance and precision throughout the excavation and foundation installation process. By accurately setting levels and ensuring uniform excavation depths, these profile boards contribute to the structural integrity, stability, and quality of the building's foundation, laying a solid groundwork for the entire construction project.

Profile boards play a crucial role in various stages of construction beyond excavation and foundation setting, serving as essential reference points for subsequent tasks performed by different trades on the construction site. Once installed, these boards provide a stable and reliable framework that guides multiple aspects of the building process, from establishing foundation width to ensuring accurate masonry layout by bricklayers.

For groundworkers, profile boards serve as guides for determining the width of the foundation trenches. By aligning the boards with the intended foundation limits and centrelines marked on the ground, groundworkers can accurately excavate the trenches to the required dimensions. The profile boards provide a visual reference that helps maintain consistency in trench width across the construction site, ensuring uniformity in the foundation layout.

During excavation, groundworkers use a traveller—a movable rod or marker—alongside the profile boards to check the depth of the trenches. The traveller is adjusted along the profile boards to verify that the excavation depth meets the specified requirements. By comparing the depth of the trenches against the predetermined levels indicated by the profile boards, groundworkers can ensure that the foundation trenches are excavated to the correct depth, essential for the stability and structural integrity of the building foundation.

Once the foundation trenches are excavated, bricklayers rely on the profile boards for setting out the masonry accurately. Nails are typically hammered into the top of the profile boards directly along the relevant lines, such as the building line and foundation limits. These nails serve as reference points that guide the positioning of bricks and the layout of the masonry walls. Bricklayers use the nails on the profile boards to ensure that corners are precisely positioned and that the masonry walls are built in alignment with the intended building dimensions.

The building line nails on the profile boards act as visual cues for bricklayers, indicating the exact locations where the masonry walls should be constructed. By following the positions of these nails, bricklayers can maintain consistency and accuracy in the placement of bricks, ensuring that the walls are erected according to the architectural plans and specifications. Additionally, the profile boards help bricklayers maintain straight and plumb walls, contributing to the overall quality and structural integrity of the building.

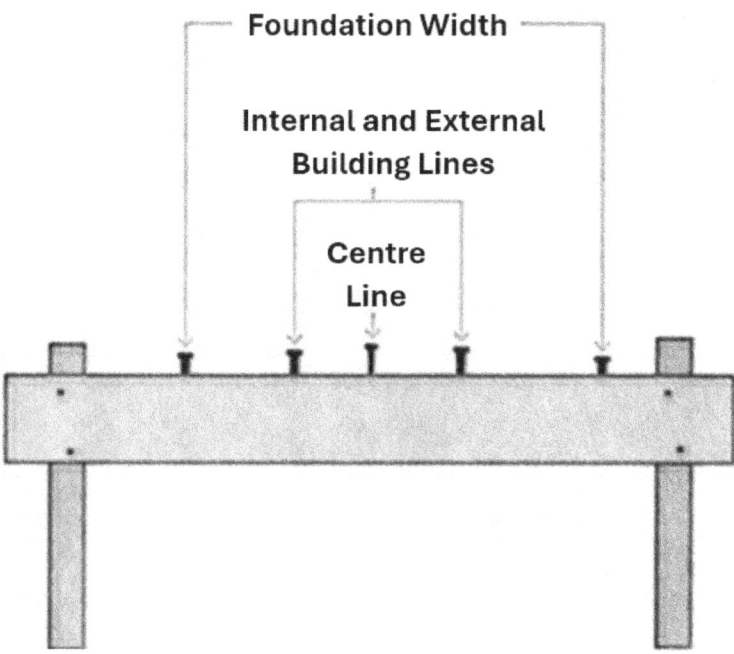

Figure 109: Establishing foundation width.

In summary, profile boards serve as versatile tools that facilitate various construction tasks, from foundation excavation to masonry layout. By providing clear reference points and guiding lines, these boards ensure accuracy, consistency, and precision in construction activities performed by groundworkers, bricklayers, and other trades involved in building construction. Their role in establishing foundation width and guiding masonry layout makes profile boards indispensable assets on construction sites, helping streamline construction processes and maintain high standards of quality and craftsmanship.

In construction and surveying, the traveller—a movable rod or marker—plays a crucial role in transferring levels between sets of sight-rails or profile boards. The traveller's length must be adjusted accordingly to ensure accurate level transfer between different elevation points or reference markers. In a typical scenario where sight-rails or profile boards are installed at intervals along a construction site, the traveller's length needs to be modified when moving between these reference points.

To maintain accuracy in level transfer, a systematic approach is adopted to adjust the traveller's length between sets of sight-rails or profile boards. In this example, let's consider a situation where the sight-rails or profile boards are set up at regular intervals, with each set positioned at a fixed height difference known as a "lift." For simplicity, suppose each lift between successive sets of sight-rails or profile boards is set at 1000mm.

When moving from one set of sight-rails or profile boards to the next, the traveller's length must be increased by the same amount as the lift between these sets. In this case, since the lift is 1000mm, the traveller's length needs to be adjusted upwards by 1000mm to align with the new reference level established by the next set of sight-rails or profile boards. This adjustment ensures that the traveller remains consistent with the elevation changes across the construction site.

The process of adjusting the traveller's length involves extending or retracting the rod or marker to match the specified increment between the sight-rails or profile boards. This adjustment is critical for maintaining the integrity of level transfer operations, as any discrepancy in the traveller's length could result in inaccuracies in the final elevation measurements or setting out.

By adhering to a standardized approach of adjusting the traveller's length between sets of sight-rails or profile boards, construction professionals can ensure the reliability and precision of level transfer operations across the construction site. This systematic adjustment process minimizes errors and discrepancies, enabling accurate alignment of various construction elements and ensuring that the project progresses according to the specified design and elevation requirements.

The adjustment of the traveller's length between sets of sight-rails or profile boards is a fundamental aspect of level transfer operations in construction and surveying. By increasing or decreasing the traveller's length in accordance with the predetermined increments between reference markers, construction professionals can maintain accuracy and consistency in elevation measurements and setting out activities, thereby contributing to the successful execution of construction projects.

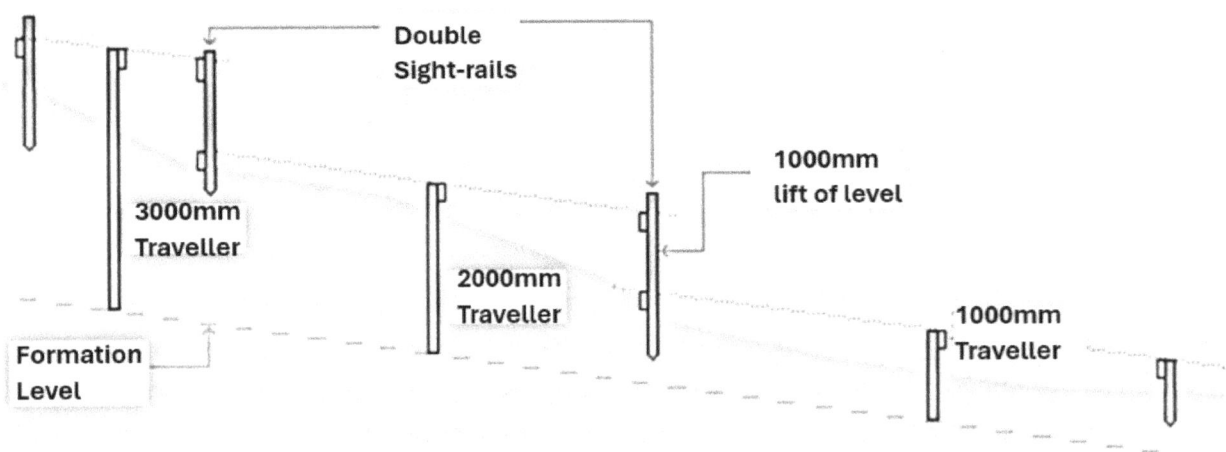

Figure 110: Traveller length adjustment.

Oblique sight-rails serve as essential tools in guiding the construction of embankments or excavations for cuttings, ensuring that the slopes or batters are built or excavated to the correct specifications. These sight-rails are positioned outside the working area but are strategically placed to provide quick confirmation that the work is progressing as required.

The term "oblique" refers to the diagonal or slanting position of these sight-rails, which are set at an angle relative to the direction of the embankment or cutting. By positioning the sight-rails in this manner, they provide a visual reference for maintaining the desired slope angle during construction.

In the context of embankments, oblique sight-rails help ensure that the slopes are built at the appropriate angle to achieve stability and prevent erosion. They guide the construction crew in shaping the embankment to the specified slope gradient, whether it's a gentle incline for landscaping purposes or a steeper slope for infrastructure projects like roads or railways.

Similarly, in excavations for cuttings, oblique sight-rails assist in maintaining the correct angle of the cut slopes, ensuring safety and stability during the excavation process. They help prevent over-excavation or undercutting, which can compromise the integrity of the cutting and pose risks such as slope instability or collapse.

The placement of oblique sight-rails outside the working area allows construction personnel to easily monitor the progress of the embankment or cutting from a distance. By visually inspecting the alignment of the sight-rails with the constructed or excavated slopes, supervisors and engineers can quickly assess whether the work meets the specified requirements.

Oblique sight-rails are particularly useful during the initial stages of construction when establishing the correct slope angles is critical. They provide a visual reference point for operators of earth-moving equipment, guiding them in shaping the terrain to achieve the desired contours and gradients.

Overall, oblique sight-rails play a vital role in ensuring the accuracy, safety, and quality of embankment and cutting construction projects. By providing clear visual guidance on slope angles, these sight-rails help construction crews maintain precise alignment and adherence to project specifications, ultimately contributing to the successful completion of infrastructure projects.

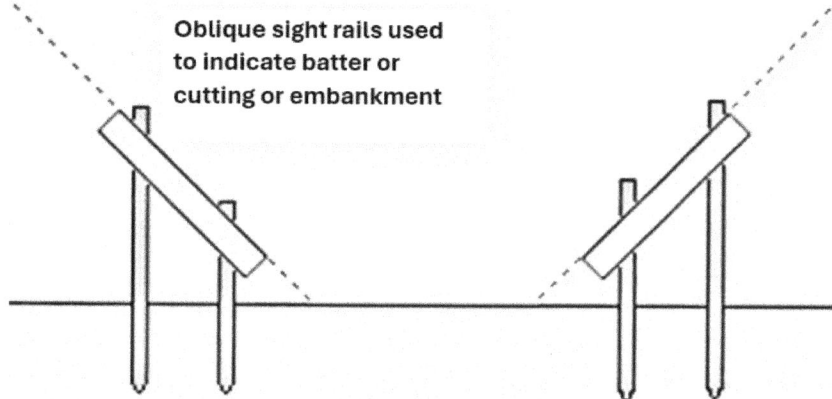

Figure 111: Oblique Sight Rails.

Chapter Six

Installing Drainage Systems

Landscaping drainage systems are crucial components of outdoor spaces designed to manage the flow of water and prevent issues such as erosion, waterlogging, and flooding. These systems are designed to effectively channel excess water away from landscaped areas, ensuring the preservation of the site's integrity and functionality. Drainage systems include:

- **Types of Drainage Systems**:

  - **Surface Drainage**: This system involves the use of surface features such as swales, berms, and grading to direct water flow away from the landscaped area. It relies on gravity to move water downhill and is effective for managing runoff from rainstorms.

  - **Subsurface Drainage**: Subsurface drainage systems utilize pipes, drains, and perforated tubes installed beneath the soil surface to collect and transport water away from the area. These systems are especially useful for addressing groundwater issues and preventing waterlogging in the soil.

- **Components of Landscaping Drainage Systems**:

  - **Catch Basins**: Catch basins are collection points for surface water runoff. They are typically installed at low points in the landscape and connected to underground drainage pipes.

  - **Channel Drains**: Channel drains, also known as trench drains, are linear drains installed flush with the ground surface. They effectively capture and redirect surface water along paved surfaces such as driveways, patios, and walkways.

  - **French Drains**: French drains consist of a perforated pipe surrounded by gravel or rock and wrapped in filter fabric. They are installed underground to collect and redirect excess groundwater away from buildings and landscaped areas.

  - **Dry Wells**: Dry wells are underground chambers filled with gravel or rock that collect and temporarily store excess water from drainage pipes. They allow water to slowly infiltrate into the surrounding soil or be absorbed by vegetation.

- **Swales**: Swales are shallow, vegetated channels designed to slow down and absorb surface water runoff. They help filter out pollutants and promote infiltration while directing water away from sensitive areas.

- **Sump Pumps**: In areas prone to flooding or high groundwater levels, sump pumps may be installed to remove excess water from basements, crawl spaces, or other below-grade areas and discharge it safely away from the property.

- **Design Considerations**:

  - **Site Topography**: The natural slope and contours of the landscape influence the design and layout of drainage systems. Proper grading and channelling are essential for effective water management.

  - **Soil Type**: Soil permeability affects the rate of water infiltration and drainage. Sandy soils drain more quickly than clay soils, which may require additional drainage measures.

  - **Land Use**: The intended use of the landscaped area, whether it's a residential garden, commercial site, or public park, influences the design requirements of the drainage system.

  - **Local Climate**: Rainfall patterns, snowmelt, and seasonal variations in precipitation dictate the capacity and efficiency of drainage systems. Designs should account for extreme weather events and ensure adequate capacity to handle peak flows.

- **Installation and Maintenance**:

  - Proper installation by trained professionals is essential to ensure the effectiveness and longevity of drainage systems.

  - Regular maintenance, including debris removal, cleaning of drains and catch basins, and inspection for signs of damage or clogging, helps prevent system failures and ensures optimal performance.

  - Periodic assessment and adjustment of drainage systems may be necessary to address changes in site conditions, such as soil erosion, vegetation growth, or alterations to the landscape layout.

Landscaping drainage systems play a critical role in managing water runoff and maintaining the health and functionality of outdoor spaces. By carefully considering site characteristics, design requirements, and installation techniques, effective drainage solutions can be implemented to mitigate water-related issues and preserve the integrity of the landscape.

Poor drainage can wreak havoc on an otherwise beautiful lawn, turning it into a soggy mess that's unsuitable for outdoor activities. Fortunately, there are three primary types of landscape drainage systems that can come to the rescue, ensuring your backyard remains dry and enjoyable, even after heavy rainfall. Identifying signs of poor drainage is the first step in determining which system is best suited for your lawn.

One common sign of poor landscape drainage is soil erosion, which occurs when excess water washes away the topsoil, leaving behind bare patches and uneven surfaces. Loose topsoil is another indicator, as waterlogged soil becomes compacted and easily displaced. Additionally, a water-stained foundation or standing water underneath gutter spouts suggests that water is not properly draining away from the home's perimeter. Flooding walkways or driveways after rain showers is yet another symptom of inadequate drainage, posing safety hazards and causing inconvenience.

These telltale signs should prompt homeowners to consider investing in a drainage system to address the underlying issues. Cracked pipes, improper yard slope, insufficient downspouts, and other factors can contribute to poor drainage, exacerbating the problem during periods of heavy rainfall. Instead of enduring muddy shoes, waterlogged lawns, and frequent dog baths, installing a new drainage system can offer a long-term solution to these problems.

By implementing an appropriate drainage system, homeowners can mitigate the effects of poor drainage and restore their lawn to its former glory. Whether it's a French drain, a dry well, or a surface drainage system, each option has its unique advantages and applications. Consulting with a landscaping professional can help determine the most suitable solution based on the specific drainage issues present in your yard. Ultimately, investing in proper drainage infrastructure is essential for maintaining a healthy, vibrant lawn and ensuring a pleasant outdoor living space for years to come.

Sub-Surface Systems

Subsurface drainage systems are vital tools in managing excess water within the soil profile, and their selection depends on various factors such as topography, rainfall patterns, outfall type and location, and soil characteristics. In regions like southern Victoria, where soils are often prone to waterlogging, the assessment of drainage characteristics becomes crucial. Farmers, particularly in dairy farming, often experience waterlogging for extended periods during wet years, highlighting the necessity for effective drainage solutions tailored to their specific soil types.

One of the challenges farmers face is understanding the physical and chemical properties of their soil to ensure the proper installation of drainage systems. Subsurface drainage systems, although costly to install initially, offer significant short and long-term benefits that outweigh their upfront expenses, provided they are adequately maintained. While surface drains are essential for removing excess surface water from paddocks, subsurface drains address waterlogging issues within the soil profile, reducing the load on the underground drainage system and ultimately lowering costs.

The benefits of subsurface drainage systems extend beyond improved pasture utilization and increased growth. They include intangible advantages such as enhanced soil health due to improved soil aeration, better responses to fertilizers, and reduced mineral imbalances. Additionally, subsurface drainage contributes to long-term sustainability by preventing or reducing salinity, enabling earlier fodder conservation, and promoting the retention of desirable pasture species while discouraging the growth of waterlogged condition plants.

Subsurface drainage systems offer relief to farmers by reducing stress associated with managing stock and pastures during wetter months. They facilitate fodder conservation, improve animal production, and enhance overall farm productivity. There are several types of subsurface drainage systems available, including corrugated and PVC slotted subsurface pipes, mole drainage (including mole drains, mole drains over collector pipe systems, and gravel mole drains), interceptor drains, and groundwater pumps. Each type has its advantages and suitability depending on the specific needs and conditions of the farm.

Subsurface Pipes

Subsurface pipes are an effective method for draining heavy, poorly drained soils, particularly clay soils. In the past, this technique was known as "tile drainage" due to the use of short clay pipes. However, clay pipes were expensive and challenging to install, leading to their replacement with slotted PVC or flexible corrugated plastic pipes of various diameters. These modern pipes offer greater flexibility and cost-effectiveness compared to clay pipes.

The installation process for subsurface pipes involves the use of specially designed drainage trenchers equipped with laser guidance equipment. These trenchers dig the trench, lay the slotted pipe, and then place permeable backfill on top of the laid pipe. The backfill material is typically delivered by trucks or trailers equipped with conveyor belts, which feed the material into the trench. The depth and amount of backfill material laid on top of the pipe depend on factors such as soil permeability and the presence of moles in the area.

In soils with high permeability, minimal backfill is required, while in less permeable soils or areas where moles may interfere with the drainage system, the backfill depth may reach near the ground surface. This variation in backfill depth ensures optimal drainage performance in different soil conditions.

Mole drainage is another method used to improve soil drainage, which can be classified into three types: mole drains, mole drains over a collector pipe system, and gravel mole drains. The choice of mole drainage method depends on factors such as soil composition, gradient, and outfall location.

Mole drains are suitable for heavy soils with a high clay content, where clay subsoil near the moling depth prevents the downward movement of groundwater. The success and longevity of mole drains rely on soils maintaining the mole channel formed by the mole plough for many years. However, mole drains are not suitable for soils with clay types that have dispersive or slaking characteristics, nor for permeable soils with high sand or loam content.

Figure 112: Mole plough. CosyCobra, CC BY-SA 4.0, via Wikimedia Commons.

The mole plough is the primary tool used to create mole drains. It consists of a leg or blade to which a torpedo or foot is attached at the bottom. Sometimes, a plug or expander with a slightly larger diameter is attached to the rear of the torpedo to ensure the mole channel is left with the correct shape. This process allows water to flow into the mole channel, improving soil drainage in heavy clay soils.

Mole drains over collector pipe systems represent a drainage solution employed in soils where traditional mole drains may not be feasible due to various factors such as the presence of stones, sandy pockets, uneven surfaces, or excessive distances to the outfall. In such cases, this system offers an alternative approach to effectively manage subsurface water.

In heavy soils where the formation of mole drains alone may not reach the desired outfall point, subsurface pipes are installed at intervals of approximately 60 to 100 meters. These pipes serve as conduits for drainage water over longer distances. To facilitate drainage, washed sand or small-diameter gravel is backfilled into the trench containing the pipes, typically up to near the ground surface during installation.

Subsequently, mole drains are installed either perpendicular or at a close angle to the direction of the subsurface pipes. These mole drains act as secondary drainage channels, allowing excess groundwater to flow into and along them. Eventually, the water drains into the porous backfill material surrounding the subsurface pipes, effectively managing subsurface water and preventing waterlogging in the soil.

This integrated approach combines the benefits of subsurface pipes, which provide a conduit for drainage over longer distances, with the localized drainage capability of mole drains. By leveraging both systems, this approach addresses the challenges posed by soil conditions that may hinder the effectiveness of traditional drainage methods alone.

The use of washed sand or small-diameter gravel in the backfill material ensures efficient water flow within the subsurface pipe trench and enhances drainage performance. Additionally, the installation of mole drains perpendicular or at an angle to the subsurface pipes optimizes the collection and removal of excess groundwater, contributing to improved soil drainage and overall land productivity.

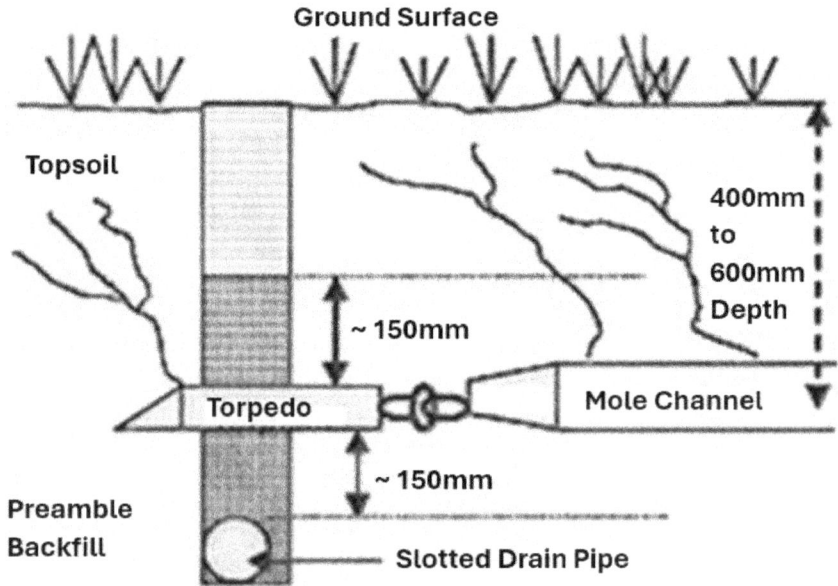

Figure 113: Mole drain over collector pipe system.

Overall, mole drains over collector pipe systems offer a practical solution for managing subsurface water in soils with challenging conditions, providing effective drainage and contributing to the sustainability of agricultural land management practices.

Gravel mole drains represent an alternative drainage solution suitable for soils and conditions where traditional subsurface pipes may not be viable or where mole drains alone have a limited lifespan. This method is particularly well-suited for situations where soils are prone to slaking or where the formation of a stable mole channel is challenging. Unlike conventional mole drains or subsurface pipes, gravel mole drains consist of unlined channels or leg slots filled with small-diameter gravel or washed sand.

The design and implementation of gravel mole drains involve creating channels or slots in the soil profile using specialized machinery designed for this purpose. However, it's worth noting that there are relatively few gravel mole drainage machines available in Australia, which may limit widespread adoption of this technique. Additionally, the cost of installing gravel mole drains tends to be higher compared to other drainage methods due to the considerable amount of backfill material required and the close spacing necessary for optimal drainage performance.

Despite the potential challenges associated with gravel mole drains, they offer a viable solution in certain "difficult to drain" situations. For example, in soils prone to slaking or dispersive characteristics, gravel mole drains can help maintain the integrity of the drainage channel, preventing collapse or deterioration over time. However, given the specialized nature of this drainage method and its associated costs, it's advisable to seek expert advice when considering the use of gravel mole drains, especially in challenging soil conditions.

Gravel mole drains provide an alternative approach to subsurface drainage, offering flexibility in situations where traditional drainage methods may not be feasible or effective. By filling the drainage channels with small-diameter gravel or washed sand, these drains facilitate the efficient removal of excess groundwater from the soil profile, helping to mitigate waterlogging and improve soil conditions for agricultural productivity.

Overall, while gravel mole drains may not be suitable for every drainage scenario, they serve as a valuable tool in the drainage toolkit, particularly in situations where conventional methods are impractical or insufficient. With proper planning, design, and implementation, gravel mole drains can contribute to improved land productivity and sustainability, helping farmers effectively manage excess subsurface water and optimize soil conditions for crop growth.

Interceptor drains serve a crucial role in managing subsurface water flow, particularly at the base of slopes where changes in gradient occur. These drainage systems are strategically installed to intercept and redirect the downhill flow of subsurface water, preventing it from accumulating and causing waterlogging or erosion issues downstream. Typically, interceptor drains are positioned where steeper slopes transition into flatter terrain, as this is where the subsurface water tends to emerge and become more noticeable on the surface.

One of the primary functions of interceptor drains is to address subsurface water movement that originates from higher elevations and slopes. In many cases, the soil composition on slopes is more permeable compared to flatter areas, causing water to percolate through the soil and resurface at the base of the slope. By installing interceptor drains at these critical junctures, water can be intercepted and directed away from vulnerable areas, mitigating the risk of soil erosion, waterlogging, and associated land degradation issues.

Moreover, interceptor drains can also be strategically positioned below springs and spring lines to intercept spring water effectively. Springs often emerge at the base of slopes or in low-lying areas, leading to localized waterlogging and soil saturation. Grazing animals tend to congregate around these areas, exacerbating soil compaction and damage. By installing interceptor drains below springs, excess water can be intercepted and drained away, reducing the extent of soil damage caused by pugging and preserving soil structure and integrity.

The installation of interceptor drains offers several benefits beyond mitigating soil erosion and waterlogging. By effectively managing subsurface water flow, these drainage systems help maintain soil strength and structure, reducing the likelihood of soil compaction and degradation, especially in areas prone to intensive grazing or heavy foot traffic. Additionally, by preventing waterlogging and surface runoff, interceptor drains contribute to improved land productivity and sustainability, supporting healthy vegetation growth and minimizing land degradation risks.

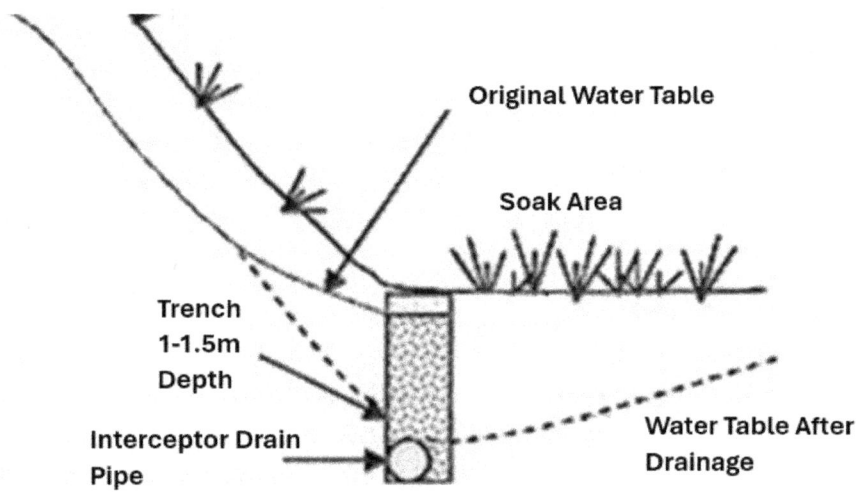

Figure 114: Interceptor drain.

Interceptor drains play a critical role in effective land management, particularly in agricultural and grazing areas where subsurface water movement can pose significant challenges. By strategically installing these drainage systems at key locations, landowners and farmers can better manage water flow, protect soil integrity, and maintain productive and sustainable land use practices.

Soil suitability for subsurface pipe drainage

Soil surveying forms the foundation of any subsurface drainage project, allowing for informed decision-making regarding the drainage system's design and installation. Auguring to a depth of at least one meter provides crucial insights into soil type and permeability, which are essential factors in determining the most suitable drainage solution. Conducting this survey during winter is optimal as it allows for the assessment of soil permeability based on the rate at which water fills the auger hole. Permeability, or hydraulic conductivity, directly influences drain spacing, depth, and ultimately, the project's cost.

The suitability of subsurface pipe drainage hinges on soil permeability, with sandy or loam-based soils generally more conducive to this method. However, even well-structured clay loam soils can be viable candidates for pipe drainage systems.

Design considerations play a crucial role in the effectiveness and efficiency of subsurface drainage systems. Drain depth is influenced by soil characteristics, with permeable soils allowing for deeper placement and wider drain spacing, thus reducing costs. Machines equipped with trenching and pipe-laying capabilities are utilized to achieve depths of up to two meters, with experienced contractors overseeing their operation. In layered soils prone to perched water tables, drains are strategically installed near impeding layers, with backfill materials ensuring effective water removal.

Drain spacing is determined by factors such as soil hydraulic conductivity, crop or pasture requirements, and the desired drainage rate. Soil permeability dictates the speed at which water moves through the soil, allowing for wider drain pipe spacing in more permeable soils. For pasture management, maintaining the water table at least 300 mm below the surface between drains is typically recommended to minimize soil and pasture damage.

Pipe diameter selection depends on the volume of water to be removed per unit area per day, soil gradient, and drain type. In pasture settings, slotted corrugated polythene pipes are commonly used for laterals, while larger PVC pipes serve as main drains to outfalls. Designing the drainage system with future extensions in mind ensures scalability and accommodates increased flow from additional areas.

Gradient plays a critical role in facilitating water flow within the drainage system. Laser-graded trenches are essential for achieving consistent gradients, particularly in low-gradient situations. Proper lateral pipe placement across the slope maximizes water interception and ensures effective drainage throughout the area. Additionally, selecting appropriate backfill materials and ensuring proper pipe installation techniques are crucial for optimizing drainage system performance and longevity.

The costs associated with implementing a drainage system can vary significantly based on several factors. The size of the area to be drained, soil type, suitability for different drainage methods (such as mole drainage), location of outfalls, and availability of suitable backfill materials all influence the overall cost. For example, a drainage system utilizing mole drains over a pipe collector system in soils requiring re-moling every 5 to 7 years may cost between $2000 to $2500 per hectare. However, these costs need to be weighed against potential benefits and payback periods, which can range from 3 to 5 years depending on factors like pasture management and milk prices in an agricultural setting.

Certain considerations must be taken into account during the planning and implementation of a drainage system to ensure its effectiveness and longevity. Inspection pits, also known as sediment traps, should be installed at specific pipe junctions to facilitate the detection and removal of blockages. Properly marking drain locations on a farm plan is crucial for future maintenance and extension projects, as drainage systems may become obscured over time. Drain outlets are essential components that must be well-marked and protected from blockages caused by factors like stock trampling or debris accumulation. Self-closing flaps can prevent vermin from obstructing outlets and ensure continuous water flow.

The quality of drainage water is another important consideration, especially regarding nutrient levels and salt content. Drainage water may contain nutrients like nitrogen and phosphorus, as well as high salt levels in saline areas. Effective management practices, such as avoiding fertilizer application before predicted rainfall, can help minimize nutrient runoff. Well-drained soils are less likely to lose nitrogen through denitrification, while phosphorus leaching can be reduced compared to surface runoff from saturated soils.

Tree roots pose a potential challenge to drainage systems, as fine roots can quickly infiltrate slotted pipes. Using un-slotted pipes in areas prone to tree root intrusion can mitigate this issue. Additionally, proper grazing management of drained paddocks is essential to prevent soil compaction and maintain soil structure. Grazing should be avoided for at least 24 to 48 hours after heavy rainfall to allow the soil to drain and regain strength, reducing the risk of damage from hooves and machinery.

Careful planning, implementation, and management are essential for ensuring the effectiveness, longevity, and cost-effectiveness of drainage systems in agricultural settings. Proper consideration of factors such as costs, maintenance requirements, environmental impacts, and land management practices is crucial for successful drainage system implementation and operation.

Surface drainage

Surface drainage plays a vital role in managing excess water on land, ensuring it is channelled away in a controlled manner either into artificial drainage systems or natural watercourses without causing damage to the environment. While surface drains primarily address excess surface water, they are essential tools in managing wet soils effectively when employed in appropriate locations and for suitable reasons. Surface drainage becomes particularly crucial in dairy farming, where excess surface and subsurface water can lead to various challenges.

Diverse applications of surface drains include draining large quantities of surface water rapidly, intercepting water flowing downhill from upper slopes to lower-lying areas, and capturing runoff from sources like road side drains or neighbouring properties. Additionally, surface drains can serve as collector systems for subsurface drainage setups like mole or tile drains, enhancing their efficiency. Surface drainage systems encompass various types, each tailored to specific needs and conditions.

Open drains, also known as ditches, come in different sizes and depths, ranging from shallow drains formed by hand shovel to larger drains created by excavators or specific drainage machines. These drains must be designed with appropriate slopes or batters to prevent collapse and ensure efficient water flow. Grassed waterways, on the other hand, are shallow channels often integrated into grazing paddocks to manage water runoff and prevent erosion. Careful attention to slope, grass cover, and soil stability is necessary for their effective functioning.

Figure 115: Example of a surface drainage channel. Surface drainage channel by John Haynes, CC BY-SA 2.0, via Wikimedia Commons.

Humps and hollows, a method involving forming parallel convex surfaces separated by shallow depressions, offer an alternative surface drainage approach suitable for areas unsuitable for subsurface drainage. This method involves lateral surface drains discharging into headland drains, ultimately leading water into natural watercourses or open drains. While effective, humps and hollows can present challenges such as hindering machinery activity and potential soil erosion.

Levees or graded banks serve to channel surface runoff away from vulnerable areas, particularly on sloping land, while laser levelling or grading techniques ensure even water flow off flood irrigation bays. These methods require careful planning to account for factors like slope gradient, rainfall intensity, and soil stability to prevent erosion and maximize water management efficiency.

Despite their effectiveness, surface drainage systems have drawbacks, including the need for regular maintenance, potential hazards to animals and machinery, and limitations in addressing subsurface drainage issues. However, when implemented thoughtfully and in conjunction with other drainage methods, surface drainage systems play a crucial role in optimizing land productivity and minimizing water-related challenges in agricultural settings.

Sand Slitting and Sand Grooving (Secondary Drainage)

Sand slitting is a technique employed in land drainage management to facilitate the efficient removal of excess surface water by creating narrow trenches at regular intervals across the primary drainage system. These trenches typically measure between 50mm to 100mm in width and are dug to depths ranging from 250mm to 350mm, spaced approximately 1 to 2 meters apart. The purpose of these slits is to enable surface water to drain more rapidly into the primary drainage system, thereby reducing waterlogging and promoting healthier soil conditions.

Figure 116: Slitting 'E' green, Victoria Park. Robin Stott, CC BY-SA 2.0, via Geograph.

During the installation of sand slits, specialized equipment such as the Mastenbroek sandslitter is utilized. This equipment is specifically designed to trench, remove soil, and backfill the trenches with granular material in a single operation. The sandslitter efficiently creates the narrow trenches required for sand slitting while simultaneously backfilling them with approximately 50mm of granular material. This streamlined process ensures optimal efficiency and accuracy in the installation of sand slits.

Sand grooving represents a revolutionary approach to addressing rootzone drainage issues by combining de-compaction and sandslitting into a single pass. This innovative technique involves the use of machinery equipped with 250mm long blades spaced at 250mm intervals. As the machine operates, it effectively fractures the soil profile, alleviating compaction and improving soil structure. Simultaneously, the trenches created by the blades are backfilled with a free-draining sand, establishing continuous drainage channels within the soil.

The integration of sand grooving into land drainage management practices offers several benefits. Firstly, it addresses soil compaction, a common issue that can impede water infiltration and root growth. By breaking up compacted soil layers, sand grooving enhances soil aeration and water penetration, promoting healthier plant growth. Additionally, the creation of continuous sand drainage channels facilitates the efficient removal of excess water from the rootzone, reducing the risk of waterlogging and associated problems such as root rot and nutrient leaching.

Sand slitting and sand grooving techniques play vital roles in land drainage management, particularly in areas prone to waterlogging or soil compaction. These methods offer efficient solutions for improving soil drainage, promoting healthier plant growth, and maximizing land productivity. By utilizing specialized equipment and innovative approaches, land managers can effectively address drainage issues and create optimal growing conditions for various crops and vegetation.

Culverts

Culverts are commonly used in landscaping to manage the flow of water, particularly in areas where natural watercourses intersect with roads, pathways, or other landscaped areas. They serve several important purposes:

1. **Water Passage**: Culverts provide a conduit for the natural flow of water, such as streams, rivers, or drainage channels, beneath roads, driveways, or pathways. By allowing water to pass underneath, culverts prevent flooding or erosion that could occur if the water were to flow over the surface.

2. **Erosion Control**: Culverts help control erosion by directing water away from vulnerable areas. Without culverts, water runoff from heavy rains or melting snow could erode the soil along roadsides or pathways, leading to instability and potential damage to the landscape.

3. **Infrastructure Protection**: Culverts protect infrastructure such as roads, bridges, and buildings by preventing water accumulation that could undermine their foundations or cause structural damage. By safely diverting water away from these structures, culverts help maintain their integrity and longevity.

4. **Wildlife Passage**: In landscaped areas where natural habitats are preserved or restored, culverts can serve as wildlife crossings, allowing animals to move freely between different habitats without the need to navigate busy roads or other barriers. Properly designed culverts can facilitate the movement of wildlife while minimizing the risk of accidents or disturbances.

5. **Landscaping Integration**: Culverts can be designed to blend seamlessly with the surrounding landscape, incorporating natural materials, vegetation, or aesthetic features to enhance their visual appeal. By integrating culverts into the overall design of the landscape, they become functional elements that contribute to the beauty and functionality of the environment.

Figure 117: Culvert under the Great Northern Greenway. Ian Calderwood, CC BY-SA 2.0, via Wikimedia Commons.

Overall, culverts play a critical role in landscaping by managing the flow of water, controlling erosion, protecting infrastructure, facilitating wildlife movement, and enhancing the overall aesthetic and functionality of landscaped areas. Properly designed and maintained culverts are essential components of sustainable landscape management practices.

Culverts play a crucial role in managing water flow within a landscape, particularly in areas where roads intersect natural watercourses. By providing a closed conduit for water to pass from one side of the road to the other, culverts help maintain stability, prevent flooding, reduce erosion, and preserve water quality. Properly installed and maintained culverts contribute to the overall health and functionality of the landscape while minimizing maintenance issues.

One of the primary benefits of culverts is their ability to dispose of runoff from roadway ditches, thereby preserving the road bed, ditches, and banks. By strategically placing culverts and road ditch turn-outs, water velocity and flow capacity within road ditches can be maintained, reducing the risk of roadway flooding and erosion. Additionally, culverts help distribute roadway runoff over a larger riparian filtering area, improving water quality and preserving the road base by draining water from ditches along the road.

Culverts can be categorized into two functional types: stream crossing culverts and runoff management culverts. Stream crossing culverts are installed where the roadway crosses a stream channel, allowing water to pass downstream. Runoff management culverts, on the other hand, are strategically placed to manage and route roadway runoff along, under, and away from the roadway. These culverts, often called cross-drains, transport upland runoff from road ditches on the upland side of the roadway to the lower side for disposal.

Installation, modification, and improvements of culverts should ideally be done when stream flows are low and rain expectancy is minimal. It's essential to complete the entire installation process before the next rain event to reduce or avoid sedimentation below the installation site. When installing culverts for stream crossings, efforts should be made to maintain the original and natural full bank capacity of the channel to avoid costly bridge and culvert "blow-outs" and minimize sediment deposition into the stream. Aligning and centring the culvert with the existing stream channel and minimizing disturbance to the channel bottom and surrounding landscape are key considerations.

For runoff management culverts, it's ideal to place culverts no more than 150 meters apart along the roadway to control volume and velocity of flow within road ditches. Steeper road slopes may require closer spacing to discharge accumulated runoff. Energy dissipating structures and/or armour should be installed at the outlet to prevent scour and erosion from high exit velocity. Additionally, maintaining adequate road bed cover over all culverts is essential to ensure their stability and longevity. Properly designed and maintained culverts are essential components of sustainable landscape management practices, contributing to water management, erosion control, and overall landscape health.

During culvert installation or replacement, it's essential to take several precautions to minimize environmental impact and ensure the proper functioning of the culvert system. In live streams where water is flowing, various measures such as sandbags, silt fences, or earthen dikes should be used to inhibit flow when possible. If necessary, a pump can be employed to divert water around the excavation or work site, with the discharged water directed to a stable outlet to prevent scour. In cases where live stream flows cannot be impounded, the flow should be diverted to one side of the culvert alignment to facilitate safe installation.

Adequate room must be allowed for the proper excavation of the entire pipe trench and bedding of the culvert. Disturbance to the surrounding soil and vegetation should be minimized to protect the natural environment. Trench side slopes should be excavated on a safe grade to prevent caving, and the bottom of the trench should ideally be at least twice the width of the culvert to be installed and graded to match the designed culvert grade as closely as possible.

Proper installation of the culvert involves starting at the outlet end and laying the culvert up-slope, ensuring each joint is properly bedded as installation proceeds. Special attention should be given to the first section or joint to reduce the potential for scour and erosion from water discharge and to ensure proper alignment. Pipe joints should be wrapped with geotextile filter fabric to prevent soil erosion and ensure a secure seal. Once the culvert is installed, flow should be diverted through it, and backfilling can commence around the culvert. Backfilling should be done evenly and level in maximum 30cm loose lifts, with thorough compaction between successive lifts.

After installation, all disturbed areas should be mulched and vegetated to promote stabilization and prevent erosion. Additional erosion control measures such as silt fences may be necessary to reduce sedimentation until stabilizing vegetation is established. It's crucial to be mindful of potential waterway impacts associated with culvert crossings, including alterations to the natural flow pattern and hydraulic capacity of the stream, increased erosion due to flow concentration, risk of blockage or damage from debris, reduced capacity for aquatic fauna movement, and habitat reduction in the vicinity of the crossing. Proper planning, installation techniques, and post-installation measures are essential to mitigate these potential impacts and ensure the long-term environmental integrity of culvert installations.

Reed Bed System

Reed bed treatment plants offer an eco-friendly and efficient method for treating wastewater, whether from households or commercial properties. They utilize natural processes, primarily through the growth of Common Reed (Phragmites Australis), to effectively break down impurities and contaminants present in sewage. The treatment process involves multiple stages, beginning with primary treatment (such as septic tanks) and culminating in the distribution of treated water underground for absorption into the soil.

The key principle behind reed bed treatment is the oxygenation of the wastewater. Common Reed has the remarkable ability to transfer oxygen from the air through its stem and root system, creating conditions suitable for a high population of microorganisms. As the wastewater moves slowly through the mass of reed roots, these microorganisms facilitate the breakdown of waste and impurities, similar to conventional biological filter bed systems in sewage treatment plants. This process occurs within zones of aerobic, anoxic, and anaerobic conditions, ensuring thorough treatment.

Reed bed sewage treatment systems are versatile and can handle various pollution loadings. However, careful design, implementation, and installation are crucial to maximizing efficiency and ensuring optimal performance. Trained technicians are typically responsible for the construction and maintenance of these systems to achieve the desired treatment outcomes.

Figure 118: Reed Bed Filtration System. Alan Hughes, CC BY-SA 2.0, via Wikimedia Commons.

One of the notable advantages of reed bed systems is their low energy requirements, often requiring minimal or no power. They also have relatively low operating costs and servicing intervals, typically requiring maintenance once a year. Additionally, reeds create a visually appealing green oasis, enhancing the aesthetic value of the surrounding landscape.

These systems are environmentally sustainable, providing an effective means of wastewater treatment without the need for extensive energy consumption or chemical additives. Greywater-only systems further enhance water reuse by treating bath, shower, laundry, and basin wastewater to a high-quality standard suitable for garden irrigation.

Figure 119: Reed bed sewage system. Jim Barton, CC BY-SA 2.0, via Wikimedia Commons.

Vertical reed bed filters, developed over several decades in Europe, offer a cost-effective solution for mineralizing industrial sludges and sewage. These beds reduce sludge volume significantly, thereby lowering handling costs. The design of these beds depends on factors such as dry matter content and volume of applied sludge, with periodic removal of residue every 10-20 years. The reeds play a crucial role in moisture removal from the sludge, aiding in its natural composting process and conversion into water and carbon dioxide. Overall, reed bed treatment plants represent a sustainable and efficient approach to wastewater management, contributing to environmental conservation and water resource sustainability.

The Rootzone Vertical Aerobic Filter represents an innovative approach to wastewater treatment, harnessing the natural processes of wetland vegetation to purify contaminated water. This type of filter, often used as a tertiary treatment device, functions similarly to a slow sand filter but is enhanced with the inclusion of reeds. These reed beds are capable of substantial nutrient reduction, making them an effective solution for treating various types of wastewater.

Horizontal subsurface filters (HSF), which form the basis of Rootzone Filters, have undergone significant development over the past four decades. Originally observed as a natural phenomenon, these filters have evolved into a carefully designed engineering process recognized worldwide for their ability to reduce pollutants to low levels in an environmentally safe manner. They offer a cost-effective solution for treating wastewater from households, industries, and remote areas, providing an efficient means of pollution control.

Rootzone Filters have been deployed across the globe for diverse purposes, including wastewater treatment from industries such as oil exploration, chemical laboratories, mining, and metal plating. They are also utilized in facilities such as hospitals, hotels, motels, schools, and private houses. Each design is tailored to the specific requirements of the project, although standard designs have been developed for common applications like domestic wastewater treatment.

The design of Rootzone Filters aims to optimize conditions for hydraulic and microbial activities, facilitating biological, chemical, and mechanical filtration processes to remove contaminant compounds. These filters integrate natural processes within their design, delivering consistent purification performance even during heavy rainfall events. Unlike conventional treatment plants, Rootzone Filters have negligible energy consumption, as they rely on solar-driven oxygenation through the root system of wetland plants, particularly Phragmites Australis (Common Reed).

Gravel plays a crucial role in Rootzone Filters, providing a substrate for wetland plants to grow and facilitating microbial activity. The plants create aerobic zones within the gravel beds, stimulating microbial activity and bacterial growth, which aids in the breakdown of pollutants suspended in the water. Wetland plants are adapted to thrive in waterlogged soils with low oxygen levels, making them ideal for use in Rootzone Filters. As they decay, these plants serve as a carbon source for microbial activity, further enhancing the filtration process.

Various species of wetland plants are suitable for Rootzone Filters, including those capable of growing in permanent water swamps and freshwater environments. These plants, such as Phragmites australis (Native Reed), Juncus kraussii (Sea Rush), and Lomandra longifolia (Spiny-headed Mat-rush), contribute to the effectiveness of Rootzone Filters by providing habitat for diverse microbial communities and assisting in nutrient uptake and water purification.

The operation of a Reed Bed Treatment Plant involves a sophisticated yet natural process of wastewater treatment. Reeds, growing hydroponically in the effluent, transfer oxygen to their roots, creating an aerobic root zone within an otherwise anaerobic environment. This environment provides favourable conditions for aerobic and anaerobic microorganisms to reduce contaminant levels in water. Nutrients are absorbed by plants and microorganisms, organic matter is stabilized, suspended solids are filtered by gravel and roots, and pathogens are destroyed through natural processes over time. It typically takes about 24 months for reeds to become well established and fully effective in the treatment process.

Effluent enters the reed bed through entry ports equipped with removable lids for monitoring purposes. Large rocks in the inlet area mitigate the risk of clogging. Similarly, effluent exits the reed bed through exit ports with removable lids. Some water is transpired from the reed bed by the reeds themselves, approximately at the same rate as open water evaporation. This transpiration process helps manage the water levels within the system.

Effluent is then pumped out of the reed bed to a sunken sump using a submersible pump. The sump, located at least 2.5 meters away from the reed bed, has a capacity of 500 litres and is constructed with reinforced concrete components to withstand hydrostatic pressures and other loads. A 100 mesh screen filter ensures that only treated effluent is pumped out, while any bleed water from the filter is cycled back to the septic tank. The pump-out cycle is controlled by float switches in the sump, with an alarm system in place to indicate high or low levels.

The pumped effluent is directed to a subsurface irrigation area comprising a woodlot with eucalypts and wattles. Laterals branching from the main irrigation line ensure even distribution of water, with simple jab adaptors and nozzles inserted at regular intervals. Gravel around each jab adaptor prevents blockage, and the entire plot is mulched to prevent access by pests and maximize water use by plants. Water application below the mulch but above ground allows further treatment of effluent as it percolates through biologically active topsoil.

The design of the subsurface irrigation area accounts for the volume of effluent generated and the water absorption capacity of the soil and plants. Safety measures ensure that the disposal area is adequately sized to handle peak loads and provide sufficient absorption capacity. By utilizing native trees and plants known for their water-hungry nature and fast growth rate, the system optimizes nutrient uptake and contributes to the overall sustainability of the treatment process.

Traditional Trench Drains

Traditional trench drains are a tried-and-true solution for managing surface water effectively, offering a range of benefits that make them a popular choice in various settings. One of the defining features of these drainage systems is their design, which typically involves a long and narrow trench or channel made from durable materials like concrete or polymer concrete. This construction allows the drains to efficiently collect and redirect surface water, helping to prevent issues such as flooding, erosion, and property damage.

One of the key advantages of traditional trench drains is their effectiveness in managing surface water. Their linear design enables them to handle large volumes of water efficiently, making them particularly well-suited for areas prone to heavy rainfall or runoff. By collecting water and directing it away from vulnerable areas, trench drains help to safeguard properties and infrastructure against water-related damage.

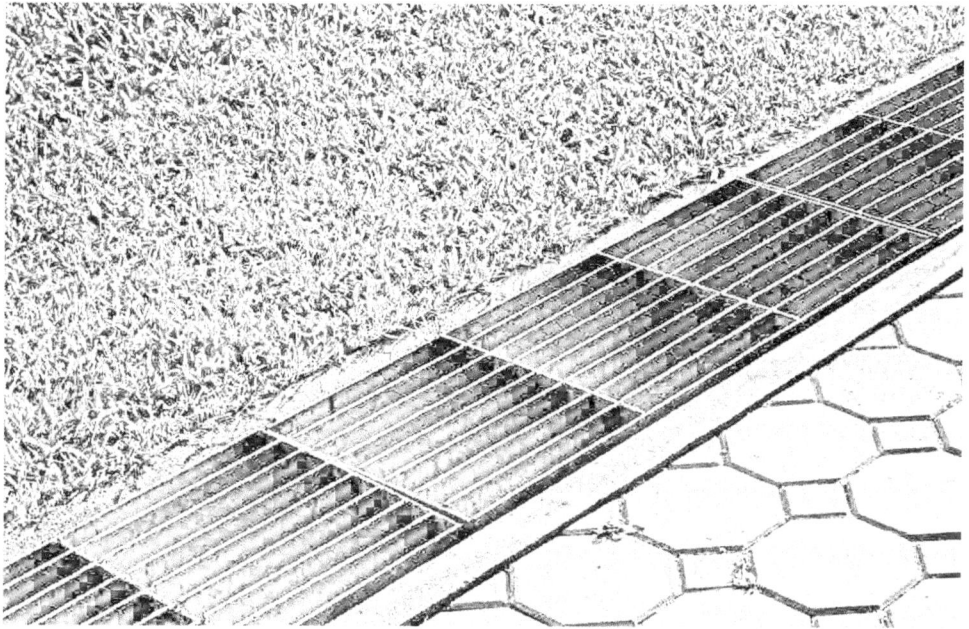

Figure 120: Traditional trench drain.

In addition to their functional benefits, trench drains also offer aesthetic versatility. These drainage systems can be seamlessly integrated into various landscapes, ensuring they blend in with their surroundings without detracting from the overall visual appeal of the property. With a range of designs and materials available, property owners can choose trench drains that complement the architectural style and landscaping features of their space.

Furthermore, traditional trench drains are highly versatile and adaptable, making them suitable for a wide range of applications. Whether installed in residential driveways, commercial parking lots, or industrial facilities, these drainage systems perform reliably in high-traffic areas where effective water management is essential for safety and property preservation.

Another advantage of traditional trench drains is their low maintenance requirements. Routine upkeep typically involves periodic cleaning of the grates to remove debris and ensure unobstructed water flow. This simplicity and ease of maintenance make trench drains a practical choice for property owners seeking an efficient and hassle-free solution for managing surface water.

Traditional trench drains offer a combination of functionality, versatility, and low maintenance that makes them a valuable asset in any property's drainage infrastructure. Whether used to prevent flooding on a residential patio or protect a commercial building from water damage, these drainage systems provide reliable performance and peace of mind for property owners.

Chapter Seven

Constructing Brick and Block Structures and Features

Bricks and Blocks

Brick, renowned for its robustness and longevity, is a staple in the construction industry, often serving as the primary material for exterior walls of houses and buildings. However, its versatility extends far beyond structural applications, finding its way into garden designs and landscaping projects. Homeowners and garden enthusiasts alike have discovered creative ways to incorporate brick into their outdoor spaces, adding both functionality and aesthetic appeal.

One popular use of brick in garden design is as edging and garden markers. By laying bricks along garden beds, pathways, or flower borders, homeowners can create clean, defined lines that separate different areas of the garden. Additionally, individual bricks can be painted or labelled to serve as markers, identifying various herbs, vegetables, or plants, adding both organization and charm to the garden space.

Brick pathways and walls are another common feature in garden landscapes. These pathways not only provide a functional route for navigating the garden but also contribute to the overall aesthetic by adding texture and visual interest. Whether constructed as solid paths covered in bricks or incorporating open spaces and loose stones, brick pathways can enhance the curb appeal of a property while reducing the accumulation of mud in the yard.

Raised beds for plants offer both practical and decorative benefits to gardeners. Constructed using brick walls, these raised beds add depth and dimension to garden layouts while improving drainage and soil aeration. By elevating the planting area, raised beds also make gardening more accessible and can be designed to fit into various landscapes, including flat yards or sloped terrain.

Brick patios and firepits are popular features in outdoor living spaces, providing areas for relaxation, entertainment, and recreation. Builders often use bricks to create intricate patterns or simple platforms for seating and dining areas. The addition of a brick firepit adds warmth and ambiance to outdoor gatherings, extending the usability of the patio into the cooler months and evenings.

Figure 121: Old Mill Brickwork and Slate Patio. R3dus-01, CC BY-SA 4.0, via Wikimedia Commons.

Water features constructed using bricks add a touch of elegance and luxury to garden settings. Whether it's a fountain, pond, or stream, bricks provide a durable and visually appealing material choice that complements the flowing water and aquatic surroundings. The soothing sound of trickling water and the presence of aquatic plants or fish create a tranquil atmosphere, enhancing the overall ambiance of the garden and making it more inviting to visitors.

The versatility of brick makes it an ideal choice for various garden projects, from edging and pathways to raised beds, patios, firepits, and water features. With its durability, aesthetic appeal, and functional benefits, brick adds character and charm to outdoor spaces, transforming ordinary gardens into stunning retreats that homeowners can enjoy for years to come.

Bricks are rectangular blocks made from clay, shale, concrete, or other materials that are dried and fired in a kiln or oven to harden them. They are one of the oldest and most common building materials used in construction worldwide. Bricks are typically laid in courses and bonded together with mortar to form walls, partitions, and other structural elements in buildings.

Standard bricks, also known as common or modular bricks, are prevalent in construction due to their adherence to standardized measurements, making them easy to handle and install. These bricks typically measure around 8.625 inches long, 4.125

inches wide, and 2.625 inches thick (in metric units are approximately 21.91 centimetres long, 10.48 centimetres wide, and 6.67 centimetres thick), with these dimensions being widely recognized in countries like the United States and the United Kingdom [78].

These standardized dimensions allow standard bricks to be easily combined and integrated into various building designs and layouts. They provide consistent sizing, which simplifies construction processes and ensures uniformity in the finished structure. Standard bricks are available in different colours, textures, and finishes to suit different architectural styles and design preferences.

Bricks and blocks are both common building materials used in construction, but they have some key differences:

- **Size and Shape**:
  - Bricks are smaller, rectangular-shaped units typically made of clay or concrete. They are commonly used for constructing walls, pathways, and decorative elements.
  - Blocks, also known as concrete blocks or cinder blocks, are larger and heavier than bricks. They are usually made of concrete and come in various sizes and shapes, such as rectangular, square, or interlocking. Blocks are often used for building walls, foundations, and structural elements in construction.

- **Purpose**:
  - Bricks are primarily used for constructing walls, both exterior and interior, as well as for paving and decorative purposes.
  - Blocks are commonly used for load-bearing walls, retaining walls, foundations, and structural elements in buildings. They are often preferred for larger-scale construction projects due to their size and strength.

- **Material**:
  - Bricks are typically made from clay that is moulded, dried, and fired in a kiln. They can also be made from concrete, which is poured into moulds and cured.
  - Blocks are predominantly made from concrete, which consists of cement, aggregates (such as sand and gravel), and water. Some blocks may also contain additives or reinforcement materials for added strength.

- **Installation**:
  - Bricks are usually laid in rows and bonded together with mortar, a cementitious material that acts as an adhesive.
  - Blocks are stacked on top of each other and typically secured with mortar or adhesive. They may also feature interlocking designs that provide additional stability without the need for mortar.

- **Appearance**:
  - Bricks often have a smoother surface and come in various colours and finishes, such as glazed or textured.
  - Blocks tend to have a more rough and industrial appearance, with visible aggregates and a plain or textured surface.

However, they can also be painted or finished for aesthetic purposes.

Figure 122: Concrete Block Retaining Wall Construction. Retainingwallexperts, CC BY-SA 4.0, via Wikimedia Commons.

While both bricks and blocks serve essential roles in construction, the choice between them depends on factors such as project requirements, structural needs, aesthetics, and budget considerations.

Bricks, one of the oldest building materials known to humanity, have been utilized in construction for thousands of years. Typically composed of clay and water, these ingredients are abundant worldwide, contributing to the widespread use of bricks across various cultures and regions. One of the primary advantages of bricks is their durability, offering resilience against environmental elements while providing insulation against both heat and cold. Their versatility allows for diverse applications in construction, from serving as load-bearing elements in solid cavity walls to providing a decorative veneer cladding on building exteriors.

In terms of appearance and functionality, bricks exhibit considerable diversity. They come in different sizes, shapes, textures, qualities, classes, and levels of durability. Traditional bricks, characterized by their rectangular shape, are often segmented into three sections: the header, stretcher, and arris. However, bricks can also vary significantly in their manufacturing processes. Wire cut bricks, also known as extruded bricks, are formed by pushing clay columns through wire frames, resulting in individual bricks with core holes. In contrast, pressed bricks are made by compacting clay into moulds, often featuring a distinctive depression or "frog" on the top surface. Additionally, bricks are not limited to the standard rectangular shape; specialized varieties such as bullnose bricks and plinth shapes cater to specific architectural needs and design preferences.

Colour is another distinguishing feature of bricks, with variations ranging from cream to red-brown, reflecting regional preferences and architectural styles. In terms of quality, bricks are classified into "Firsts" and "Seconds." Firsts, also known as facing bricks, represent the highest quality and are used prominently on visible surfaces. On the other hand, Seconds may exhibit irregularities in shape, colour, or strength, making them unsuitable for facing applications. Another classification criterion is class, which categorizes bricks based on characteristics such as colour consistency and surface texture. Engineering class, regular class, and character class are the three main categories.

Durability is a critical consideration when selecting bricks for construction projects. Bricks are classified into three categories based on their durability: exposure durability, general-purpose durability, and protected durability. Exposure durability denotes suitability for use in harsh environments, such as coastal areas with high salt content. General-purpose durability indicates suitability for standard outdoor conditions, while protected durability suggests suitability for internal wall applications.

When estimating quantities for a bricklaying project, standard brick sizes and paving brick dimensions are important factors to consider. Standard bricks in Australia typically measure 230mm x 110mm x 76mm, while paving bricks have slightly larger dimensions at 230mm x 115mm. A common method for estimating brick quantities involves calculating the number of bricks required per square meter of wall area, factoring in mortar joints and deducting the area of any openings. This calculation helps ensure accurate material planning and budgeting for brickwork projects of various scales and complexities.

In bricklaying, stretcher, header, and arris are terms used to describe different parts of a brick and their orientation within a wall:

1. Stretcher: A stretcher is the long, narrow face of the brick that is visible when it is laid in the wall with its longest dimension parallel to the surface. When bricks are laid end to end with their stretchers facing outwards, it creates the majority of the visible surface area of the wall. Stretcher courses are the rows of bricks laid in this manner.

2. Header: A header refers to the short end of the brick, perpendicular to the stretcher. When a brick is laid so that its header end is visible from the exterior of the wall, it is called a header course. Header courses are typically used at intervals in a brick wall for structural stability and to create bond patterns.

3. Arris: The arris is the sharp edge or corner formed by the intersection of two adjacent faces of a brick. In bricklaying, the arris can be exposed or concealed depending on the desired aesthetic and structural considerations. Exposed arrises are commonly found in decorative brickwork, where the sharp edges of the bricks are intentionally left visible to accentuate the pattern or texture of the wall. Concealed arrises occur when bricks are laid in such a way that the edges are hidden within the mortar joints, resulting in a smoother surface finish.

Understanding these terms is essential for bricklayers to accurately interpret construction plans, follow specific laying patterns, and achieve the desired visual and structural outcomes in brickwork projects.

Figure 123: Parts of a brick. Back Image: Andrewlister, Public domain, via Wikimedia Commons.

Bricks come in various types, each tailored to specific construction needs and preferences. Here are the main types of bricks:

- **Common Bricks:** Also known as modular or building bricks, common bricks are the most basic type. They are made from clay and are uniform in size and shape. Common bricks are versatile and used for a wide range of construction projects, from residential homes to commercial buildings.

- **Facing Bricks:** Facing bricks, also called face bricks, are designed to be visible and aesthetically pleasing. They often have a smoother texture and come in a variety of colours, finishes, and patterns. Facing bricks are commonly used for the exterior walls of buildings to enhance curb appeal.

- **Engineering Bricks:** Engineering bricks are dense and strong, designed to withstand high pressure and provide structural support. They are often used in areas requiring high durability and resistance to moisture and frost, such as below-grade applications, retaining walls, and pavements.

- **Fire Bricks:** Fire bricks, or refractory bricks, are specially made to withstand high temperatures without deforming or cracking. They are commonly used in fireplaces, furnaces, kilns, and other high-heat environments where regular bricks would fail.

- **Pavers:** Paver bricks are thick and durable, designed for use in outdoor applications such as driveways, walkways, patios, and pool decks. They come in various shapes, sizes, and textures to create different patterns and designs.

- **Perforated Bricks:** Perforated bricks have holes or perforations throughout their structure, which allow for better ventilation and drainage. They are often used in cavity walls and areas where moisture control is important.

- **Special Shaped Bricks:** Special shaped bricks are customized to fit specific architectural requirements. They come in various shapes and sizes, including bullnose bricks (with rounded edges), coping bricks (for capping walls), and angled bricks (for corners and arches).

- **Clinker Bricks:** Clinker bricks are over-fired during the manufacturing process, resulting in a unique appearance with irregular shapes, rough textures, and varied colours. They are often used for decorative accents and to create rustic or vintage aesthetics.

- **Concrete Bricks:** Concrete bricks are made from a mixture of cement, aggregate, and water, providing strength and durability similar to engineering bricks. They are commonly used in load-bearing walls, retaining walls, and other structural applications.

- **Hollow Bricks:** Hollow bricks have hollow cores, which reduce their weight and improve insulation properties. They are used in load-bearing walls, partitions, and infill panels to reduce material costs and improve thermal efficiency.

These are just some of the main types of bricks available, each serving different purposes and offering unique characteristics suited to various construction projects and architectural styles.

Mortar

Mortar is a mixture of binding materials, such as cement, lime, or a combination of both, mixed with sand and water. It is used to bind building blocks or bricks together in masonry construction, providing structural integrity and stability to the overall structure.

- Mortar is a critical component in masonry construction, providing the adhesive bond that holds bricks or other building blocks together to form structures. Understanding the composition of mortar and how its ingredients interact is essential for ensuring the durability, strength, and overall quality of the finished construction project.

- **Sand:** Sand, also known as aggregate, is a fundamental ingredient in mortar. The type of sand used can significantly impact the workability and performance of the mortar. Different regions may have varying types of sand, so it's essential to choose the appropriate sand for the job. Bricklayers typically use sharp, clean pit sand or a blend of bricklayer's loam and pit sand in equal proportions. It's crucial to ensure that the sand is free from any contaminants such as vegetable matter, as these can weaken the mortar.

- **Cement and Lime:** Cement and lime are the matrix components of mortar responsible for binding the sand particles together and causing the mortar to set. Cement is typically made from clay and chalk and provides strength to the mortar mix. Lime, whether in the form of rock lime or hydrated lime, enhances the mortar's workability, adhesion, water retention, and elasticity. It's vital to store the matrix components in a dry environment, as moisture can cause premature setting.

- **Water:** Water acts as a crucial agent in making the other mortar materials workable. The quantity of water used is essential, as too much or too little can significantly impact the mortar's workability, strength, and setting time. Clean, drinking-quality water should always be used in mortar mixes to prevent any contaminants from affecting the mortar's performance.

- **Waterproofer:** Waterproofer is an additive used in mortar mixes to enhance water resistance, particularly in applications where the wall may be exposed to moisture from the soil, such as retaining walls. It's essential to follow the manufacturer's instructions carefully when using waterproofer additives, and it's worth noting that they are not a sole method of waterproofing in some regions.

- **Plasticiser (Water-Retaining Agent):** In hot weather conditions, mortar can dry too quickly, affecting its workability and bonding properties. Plasticisers or water-retaining agents are additives that can be incorporated into the mortar mix to slow down the drying process, allowing for better workability and adhesion. As with other additives, it's crucial to follow the manufacturer's instructions when using plasticisers.

- **Colouring Agents:** Colouring agents are additives used to impart specific hues to the mortar, enhancing its aesthetic appeal. These agents can be in liquid or powder form, with the liquid variety mixed with water and the powder variety mixed with cement. Using a measuring device ensures consistency in colour from batch to batch. As with other additives, it's essential to follow the manufacturer's instructions carefully to achieve the desired colour and performance.

Figure 124: Mortar mix. Stanisław Skowron, Public domain, via Wikimedia Commons.

Here's a general overview of how mortar is mixed:

- **Selecting Materials:** The first step in mixing mortar is selecting the appropriate materials based on the requirements of the construction project. This includes choosing the type of cement (Portland cement, lime, or a blend), the type and gradation of sand, and any additional additives or admixtures required for specific purposes, such as improving workability, enhancing durability, or increasing water resistance.

- **Measuring Ingredients:** Once the materials are selected, the next step is to measure and proportion the ingredients accurately. The proportions of cement, lime, sand, and water can vary depending on factors such as the type of masonry units being used, the desired strength of the mortar, and the environmental conditions at the construction site. Standard mortar mixes typically consist of one part cement or lime to three or four parts sand, although variations are common.

- **Mixing Dry Ingredients:** In a clean, dry container such as a wheelbarrow or mortar mixing box, combine the dry ingredients – cement or lime and sand – thoroughly using a shovel or hoe. It's essential to mix the dry ingredients evenly to ensure uniform distribution of binding materials throughout the mortar mix.

- **Adding Water:** Once the dry ingredients are mixed, gradually add water while continuing to mix. The amount of water required depends on the specific characteristics of the materials and the desired consistency of the mortar. It's crucial to add water slowly and incrementally to avoid over-saturating the mix, which can weaken the mortar's strength and durability.

- **Mixing to Consistency:** Mix the mortar thoroughly until it reaches the desired consistency. The ideal consistency is typically smooth, workable, and able to hold its shape without slumping or sagging excessively when applied. The mortar should be stiff enough to support the weight of the masonry units but soft enough to spread easily and form a strong bond.

- **Testing and Adjusting:** Once mixed, test the mortar by applying a small amount to a masonry unit and checking its adhesion and workability. If necessary, adjust the mix by adding more water or dry ingredients to achieve the desired properties.

- **Storage and Use:** After mixing, use the mortar promptly to prevent it from drying out or setting prematurely. If not using immediately, cover the mortar mix with a damp cloth or plastic sheeting to keep it moist and workable. Unused mortar can be stored in a sealed container or bag for future use, but it may need to be remixed before use to restore its consistency.

Mortar is a versatile building material, and different types of mortar are used based on the specific requirements of the construction project. Here are some of the most common types of mortar and their uses:

- **Type N Mortar:** Type N mortar is a general-purpose mortar commonly used for above-grade, exterior, and interior load-bearing walls. It provides good structural strength and is suitable for most masonry applications, including brick, block, and stone.

- **Type S Mortar:** Type S mortar is similar to Type N mortar but contains a higher proportion of cement, making it stronger and more durable. It is often used in applications where additional strength is required, such as below-grade masonry, retaining walls, and exterior veneers.

- **Type M Mortar:** Type M mortar is the strongest and most durable type of mortar, with a high cement content and minimal lime. It is primarily used in applications where extreme strength is necessary, such as in below-grade masonry, foundations, and load-bearing walls.

- **Type O Mortar:** Type O mortar is a low-strength mortar with a high lime content. It is commonly used for interior, non-load-bearing walls, as well as for repointing and repair work. Type O mortar is more flexible than other types, making it suitable for older or historic masonry structures.

- **Type K Mortar:** Type K mortar is the softest and weakest type of mortar, with a high lime content and minimal cement. It is typically used for restoration work on historic buildings and monuments, as well as for soft or deteriorated masonry substrates where minimal structural stress is expected.

- **Mortar Additives:** In addition to these standard types of mortar, various additives can be incorporated into mortar mixes to enhance specific properties. For example, waterproofing additives can improve the water resistance of mortar, while plasticisers can increase workability and reduce shrinkage. These additives allow for greater flexibility and customization of mortar mixes to suit the needs of different construction projects.

Type S mortar mix is renowned for its robust properties, boasting a compressive strength exceeding 1,800 psi and a high-tensile bond strength, making it well-suited for various projects situated at or below grade [79]. This type of mortar mix is specifically designed to bear substantial loads, including pressure from the structure it supports, as well as external factors like soil pressure, wind forces, and seismic loads.

The composition of Type S mortar mix typically involves a ratio of two parts Portland cement, one part hydrated lime, and nine parts sand, although variations in the mixing ratio can result in strengths ranging from 2,300 to 3,000 psi [79]. This versatility allows for tailored mixes suitable for different project requirements. Type S mortar is commonly chosen for below-grade applications such as masonry foundations, manholes, retaining walls, and sewers, as well as for at-grade projects like brick patios and walkways. Its water-resistant properties, attributed to the lime content, make it particularly suitable for such applications compared to mortar mixes with lower lime ratios.

Type N mortar mix, on the other hand, serves as a versatile, general-purpose option, typically recommended for exterior and above-grade walls exposed to harsh weather conditions and high temperatures. With a medium compressive strength, Type N mortar mix typically comprises one part Portland cement, one part lime, and six parts sand. This mix finds utility in a wide range of applications, including above-grade exterior and interior load-bearing installations, as well as soft stone masonry projects. It is a preferred choice for homeowners due to its versatility and reliability [79].

Conversely, Type O mortar mix exhibits relatively low compressive strength, approximately 350 psi, making it suitable primarily for interior, above-grade, non-load-bearing walls. While it can serve as an alternative to Type N for some interior applications, its exterior use is limited due to its lower structural capacity. However, its consistency and ease of application make it ideal for repointing and repair work on existing structures.

Type M mortar mix boasts the highest amount of Portland cement and is recommended for heavy loads and below-grade applications such as foundations, retaining walls, and driveways. Although it provides a compressive strength of at least 2,500 psi, it may not offer optimal adhesion and sealing properties, rendering it unsuitable for many exposed applications. Type M is particularly favoured for use with natural stone due to its comparable strength [79].

Lastly, Type K mortar mix is seldom used for new construction but finds application in restoration or specialty projects due to its very low compressive strength of approximately 75 psi [79]. This softness makes it suitable for restoring masonry on historic or ancient buildings that require a mix with minimal strength deviation from the existing masonry.

Selecting the right mortar for a landscaping brick project is crucial to ensure the longevity, stability, and aesthetic appeal of the structure. Several factors should be considered when making this decision.

Firstly, the type of bricks being used and the specific requirements of the project play a significant role. Different types of mortar offer varying levels of compressive strength, adhesion, and durability. For instance, if the project involves heavy loads or below-grade applications such as retaining walls or foundations, a mortar with high compressive strength like Type M or Type S would be more suitable. On the other hand, for above-grade walls or general-purpose applications, Type N or Type O mortar may suffice.

Secondly, the environmental conditions to which the structure will be exposed should be taken into account. Factors such as climate, weather patterns, and exposure to moisture can impact the performance of the mortar over time. In areas with harsh weather conditions or high humidity, mortar with enhanced water resistance properties may be preferred to prevent deterioration and ensure long-term structural integrity.

Additionally, the aesthetic requirements of the project should not be overlooked. The colour and texture of the mortar can significantly influence the overall appearance of the brickwork. Some mortars come in a variety of colours or can be custom tinted to match the colour of the bricks, enhancing the visual appeal of the finished structure. Careful consideration should be given to selecting a mortar that complements the colour and style of the bricks to achieve the desired aesthetic effect.

Furthermore, practical considerations such as ease of application and availability of materials should be taken into account. Certain types of mortar may require special mixing procedures or additives, while others may be readily available and easy to work with. Contractors should assess their familiarity with different mortar types and choose one that aligns with their expertise and resources.

Overall, selecting the right mortar for a landscaping brick project involves evaluating various factors including the type of bricks, environmental conditions, aesthetic preferences, and practical considerations. By carefully considering these factors and choosing a mortar that meets the specific requirements of the project, builders can ensure the success and longevity of their brickwork structures.

Other Materials

In a bricklaying project, alongside bricks and mortar, several other materials and equipment are essential for ensuring the success and efficiency of the construction process. The storage and organization of these materials can vary, with equipment either being kept in a designated site shed or stored in the contractor's vehicle, depending on the scale of the project. It falls upon the responsibility of the project manager or site supervisor to ensure that all necessary equipment is readily available and in good condition, minimizing any potential delays for the bricklayers.

Among the equipment required for various tasks throughout the project are vents, reflective foil laminate, clips, wall ties, steel lintels, and reinforcing rods. Vents play a crucial role in subfloor construction, where they are strategically placed to facilitate air circulation. Typically made of galvanized metal or terra cotta, vents are essential for maintaining proper ventilation in timber floors, ensuring the longevity and integrity of the structure.

Reflective foil laminate, also known as reflective insulation paper, is a vital component in brick veneer wall construction. Installed onto timber frames before laying the brick veneer, this insulation paper consists of layers of aluminium foil bonded to high-density craft paper, laminated with a fire-resistant adhesive. Its primary function is to conserve energy by providing thermal insulation, enhancing the energy efficiency of the building.

Clips are small metal fixtures used to secure reflective insulation paper to timber frames effectively. Their compact and efficient design ensures that the paper remains securely in place without tearing or compromising its integrity, contributing to the overall efficiency and quality of the insulation installation process.

Wall ties are indispensable components in brick veneer wall construction, serving to anchor the outer masonry skin to the timber frame. Typically made of metal, various types of wall ties are available to suit different construction requirements. The spacing and type of wall ties may vary depending on regional building codes and regulations, with specific requirements enforced to ensure structural integrity and compliance with safety standards.

Steel lintels are steel beams essential for providing structural support to brickwork above openings such as doorways, windows, garage doors, or fireboxes. Serving as load-bearing elements, steel lintels distribute the weight of the brickwork evenly, preventing sagging or structural failure over time.

Reinforcing rods, often made of steel, are inserted into the hollow cavities of blocks to reinforce the structure and enhance its structural integrity. These rods are then filled with concrete, adding strength and stability to the construction. The size and spacing of reinforcing rods are typically specified in the building's design and specifications, ensuring that the structure meets the required standards for strength and durability.

Working Safely with Cement and Lime

Working safely with cement and lime is crucial due to the highly alkaline nature of these materials, which can cause severe burns and skin irritation upon contact. Similar to acids, alkaline substances like lime and cement require careful handling to prevent accidents and injuries. Therefore, it's essential to adhere to specific safety guidelines when working with these materials. Firstly, always wear gloves and safety goggles while mixing cement and lime to protect your skin and eyes from potential burns and irritation. Additionally, use a trowel or small tool to apply mortar, keeping the handles of tools and the back of trowels clear of mortar to avoid contact with your hands.

In the event of skin contact with cement or lime, it's imperative to wash the affected area immediately and thoroughly with water and dry the skin to minimize the risk of burns or irritation. Furthermore, it's essential to wash your hands well in warm soapy water each time you take a break to remove any traces of cement or lime and prevent skin irritation. Using a barrier cream daily can also help prevent skin dryness and cracking, providing an added layer of protection against exposure to these alkaline materials.

Eye contamination is a significant concern when working with lime, as it is highly caustic and can cause severe damage if it comes into contact with the eyes. If lime gets in your eyes, it's crucial not to rub them, as this can exacerbate the irritation. Instead, immediately wash your eyes with lots of flowing water from a tap or hose for at least 10 minutes until any pain or discomfort subsides. If the pain or discomfort persists, seek medical attention promptly, and notify your supervisor or teacher of the incident. Lime putty, in particular, is extremely caustic and can cause severe burns if splashed into the eyes, necessitating immediate medical attention and thorough eye washing.

Maintaining good housekeeping practices on the worksite is essential for creating a safe and efficient working environment. All workers involved in various trades on-site have a responsibility for maintaining site tidiness, and routine cleanups should be scheduled as part of the workday. A tidy and well-maintained site not only makes the job easier but also reduces the risk of accidents and injuries associated with clutter and debris.

Furthermore, when lifting heavy objects, such as bricks or bags of cement, team lifting practices should be followed to minimize the risk of back injuries and strains. Training must be provided for all workers involved in team lifting, with lifts coordinated by a designated leader. However, it's important to note that while team lifting can help distribute the weight of heavy objects, it should not be considered a long-term control measure for preventing injuries. Alternative solutions should be explored to mitigate the inherent dangers associated with team lifting, prioritizing worker safety and well-being on the construction site.

Concrete mixers are essential tools in construction projects for efficiently blending cement, aggregate, and water to produce concrete. However, the operation of concrete mixers requires careful attention to safety protocols to prevent accidents and ensure the well-being of workers on-site. When using loaded mixers, several precautions must be taken to minimize the risk of mishaps. Firstly, it's crucial to stabilize the mixer properly to prevent it from tipping over during operation, which could lead to serious accidents or injuries. Additionally, all guards must be securely in place to protect operators from moving parts and potential hazards. Overloading the mixer should be avoided to prevent strain on the equipment and ensure optimal mixing performance. Importantly, workers should never insert objects like shovels or trowels into the turning bowl of a mixer, as this could result in entanglement or injury.

Figure 125: Cement Mixer. User:Jacks Rache, Public domain, via Wikimedia Commons.

In the case of electric mixers, specific safety measures must be observed to mitigate the risk of electrical hazards. It is essential to ensure that the mixer is equipped with a residual current device (RCD) to provide protection against electric shock in the event of a fault. Regular inspection of electrical leads is necessary, with checks performed every three months and tagging by a qualified electrician to verify safety and compliance. Workers should also avoid leaving electric leads lying in water to prevent damage and minimize the risk of electrocution. Damaged or wet leads can pose serious safety hazards, and proper maintenance and care are essential to prevent accidents and ensure worker safety.

For petrol-driven mixers, additional precautions must be taken to minimize risks associated with exhaust fumes. It is crucial not to operate petrol-driven mixers in enclosed spaces such as garages or basements, where there is limited ventilation. Using petrol-powered equipment in confined areas can lead to the accumulation of carbon monoxide fumes, which poses a severe risk of carbon monoxide poisoning to workers. Adequate ventilation is necessary when operating petrol-driven mixers to ensure the safe dispersal of exhaust gases and prevent exposure to harmful fumes. By adhering to these safety guidelines and exercising caution when using concrete mixers, construction workers can minimize the risk of accidents and create a safer working environment on-site.

Bricklaying Tools

Ensuring the safe and effective use of tools is paramount in any construction or landscaping project. Regardless of the type or purpose of the tools being used, it's essential to keep them in good repair and safely stored to prevent accidents and injuries. Here are some key points to remember when working with various tools:

- **Keep tools clean**: At the end of each day, it's crucial to wash off any materials or dirt from the tools to maintain their functionality and prolong their lifespan.

- **Maintain tools carefully**: Electrically-driven tools, in particular, require careful maintenance to ensure safety. These tools should be inspected and tagged by an electrician every three months to identify and address any potential issues.

- **Lock tools away**: Especially those that are dangerous should be securely locked away at the end of the day to prevent unauthorized or unsafe use.

Now, let's consider the different categories of tools and their maintenance requirements:

Cutting and Shaping Tools:

- **Bolster**: Used with a lump hammer for cutting masonry and bricks accurately, the bolster should have a straight and clean shaft and blade.

- **Brick Hammer**: This small hammer with a sharp end is used for cutting masonry and bricks roughly.

- **Masonry Saw**: A motor-driven power tool useful for making accurate cuts in masonry and bricks.

- **Lump Hammer or Mash Hammer**: Used with cutting tools like bolsters and chisels, ensuring that the head is securely fixed, and the handle is not splintered or broken.

Applying and Flattening Tools:

- **Raking Tool**: Used to rake out joints, it should have an adjustable pin and be capable of raking to a specific depth.

- **Round Iron Jointer**: Leaves a recessed (concave) joint and is used for facing concrete blocks.

- **Trowel (Large)**: With steel blades and wooden handles, trowels come in various shapes and sizes and are used for spreading mortar or plaster, tapping things into place, and pointing.

- **Trowel (Pointing)**: Used for quality pointing work, pointing trowels come in various sizes.

- **Trowel (Finger)**: A thin, narrow trowel used for smoothing out joints, caulking, and filling mortar joints.

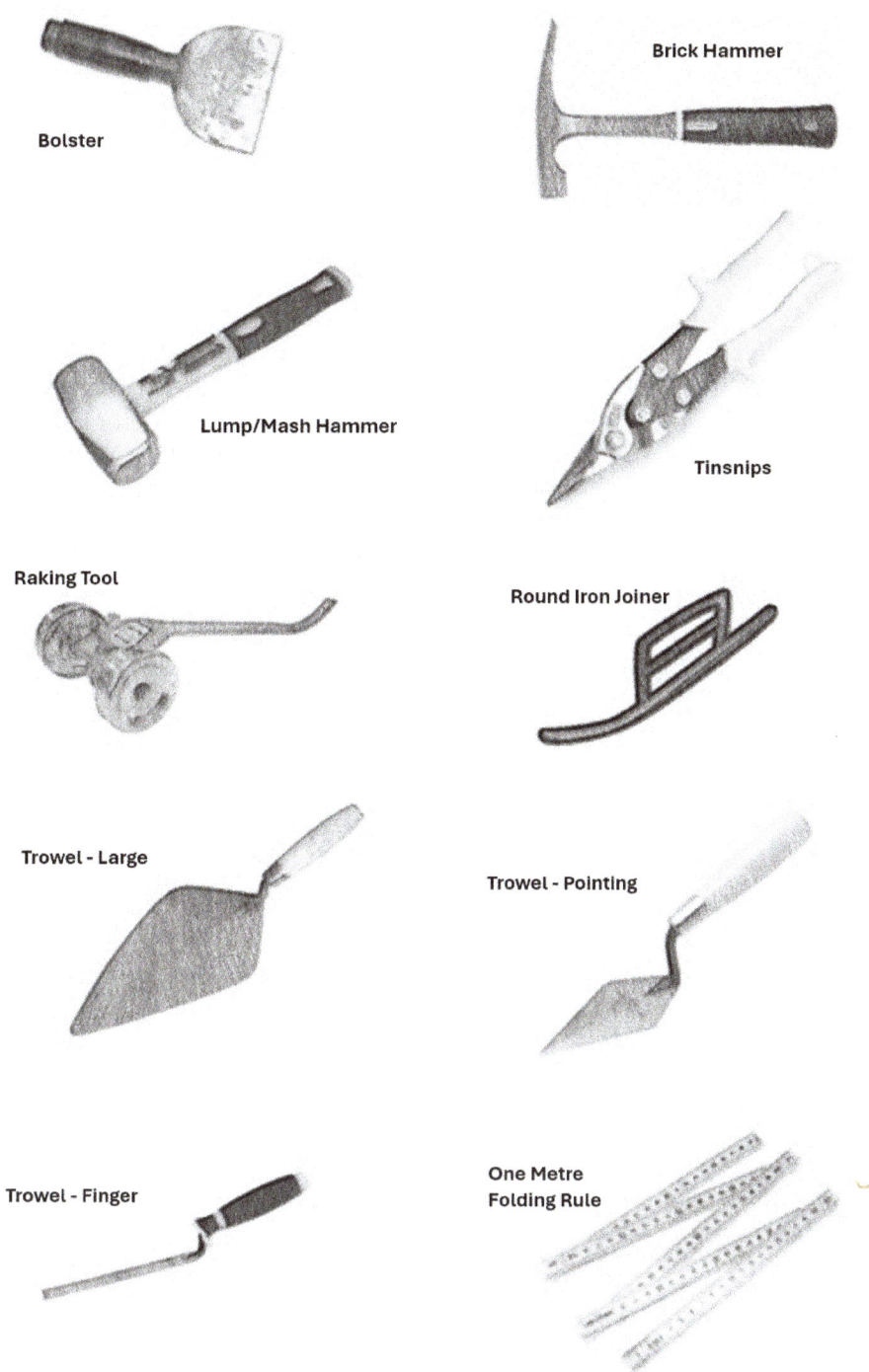

Figure 126: Bricklaying tools.

Measuring, Aligning, and Leveling Tools:

- **One Metre Folding Rule**: Used to measure short distances, it folds to a length of 250 mm.

- **Gauge Rod**: Helps bricklayers work out courses and is marked off in required vertical measurements.

- **Bevel**: Useful for cutting materials at angles other than 90º.

- **Spirit Level**: Checks the level of horizontal or vertical surfaces.

- **Long Straight Edge**: Used with spirit levels to check levels, typically used in building trades for setting out.

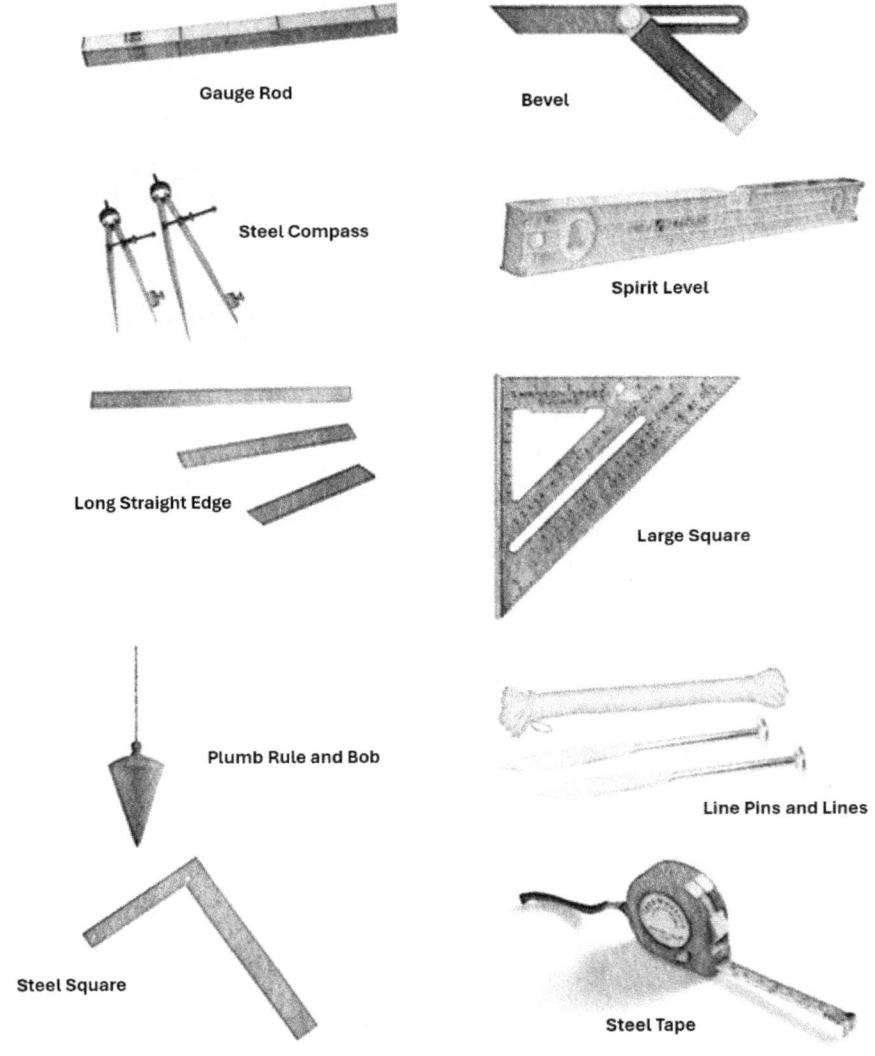

Figure 127: Bricklaying tools.

General Equipment:

- **Concrete Mixer**: Used to mix large amounts of mortar or concrete, available in electric or petrol-driven versions.

- **Extension/Power Leads**: Connect electrically-driven power tools to the power source, regularly inspected for safety.

- **Hoses**: Used for cleaning and connecting to clean water supplies for mixing materials.

- **Wheelbarrow**: Moves heavy materials, removes debris, and mixes smaller quantities of mortar and concrete.

- **Mortar Board**: Used by bricklayers for 'working' already mixed mortar before laying bricks.

Elevating and Holding Tools:
- **Scaffolding**: Allows workers to work at height safely, but scaffolding above four meters must be erected or dismantled by a certified individual.

Hammering and Fixing Tools:
- **Claw Hammer**: Used for gripping and levering nails, hammering nails, and hitting other tools lightly, it's essential for various tasks.

Brick Walls

The construction of walls using bricks and blocks offers various methods, each with distinct advantages in terms of environmental impact, cost-effectiveness, and structural integrity. Understanding these methods is crucial in choosing the most suitable approach for building a home. While it's feasible to incorporate multiple methods within the same structure, it's generally more practical and efficient to focus on one or two methods.

Brick veneer construction is a widely adopted approach where bricks form the external layer of a timber-framed home. This method capitalizes on the durability and low maintenance of bricks while offering little contribution to the building's thermal performance. The bricks are attached to a lightweight frame, and while the veneer itself is non-structural, it must be securely tied to the load-bearing frame to withstand external forces such as wind and earthquakes. Proper design of the backing frame and attention to factors like wall ties' strength and durability are essential for ensuring the veneer's stability and longevity. Additionally, measures such as flashing, damp-proof courses, and weep-holes are employed to prevent moisture infiltration, although veneer walls still have the potential to crack and require careful detailing during construction.

Reverse brick veneer flips the conventional approach by placing the brickwork or blockwork on the inside of the building, tied to a lightweight stud-framed structure. This method leverages the thermal mass properties of bricks, resulting in buildings with reduced energy demands for heating and cooling.

Double brick construction involves two leaves of brick walls separated by a cavity, which helps in reducing thermal transmission and preventing direct moisture transfer from the exterior to the interior of the building. This method offers improved insulation and moisture resistance compared to single brick constructions, with the cavity serving as an additional barrier.

Solid brick or blockwork walls provide excellent load-bearing capacity and substantial thermal mass, offering a unique blend of structural strength, thermal efficiency, and aesthetic appeal. Internal walls made from solid brick or blockwork can either support themselves or carry loads, providing well-positioned thermal mass within the building.

Each of these methods has its merits and considerations, and the choice depends on factors such as climate, budget, building regulations, and aesthetic preferences. By understanding the characteristics and implications of each method, builders can make informed decisions to ensure the optimal performance and longevity of their structures while meeting environmental and economic objectives.

Using a Brick Saw

A brick saw is an essential electrically operated tool in masonry work, facilitating quick and precise cutting of various masonry materials. Two common types of brick saws are the Drop Brick Saw, which features a rotating blade, and Table Brick Saws. Drop Brick Saws involve pulling the rotating saw blade downwards onto the workpiece, usually against a fence or on a slide table. In contrast, Table Brick Saws have a sliding table base that allows the masonry material to be pushed onto the stationary rotating blade.

Figure 128: Brick Saw.

Understanding the hazards associated with brick saw operations is crucial for maintaining safety in the workplace. These hazards range from common risks in concrete and masonry cutting operations to specific dangers related to the use of particular equipment. Kick-back, push-back, or pull-in forces pose significant risks, especially with hand-held or quick-cut saws, potentially causing injuries or dislodging fixed concrete saws. Obstructions or resistance in the material being cut can lead to sudden movements of the saw, as can crooked or off-line cuts, resulting in biting or pinching and subsequent reactions. Pinched cuts and blunt cutting edges further increase the risk of accidents, as do unsafe grip, stance, or stop-start procedures with hand-held saws.

Blade-related hazards, such as worn, misshapen, or damaged blades, pose risks of wobbling, shattering, or fragmenting, potentially causing injuries to operators and others nearby. Inadequate coolant flow, incompatible flanges and blades, incorrectly secured blades, and insufficient guarding are additional concerns that can lead to equipment malfunction or failure. Moreover, environmental factors like hazardous dust, toxic fumes, and uneven or unstable surfaces contribute to the overall risk during brick cutting operations.

Implementing risk control measures is essential for mitigating these hazards and ensuring a safe working environment. Strategies may include substituting hazardous equipment with safer alternatives, modifying equipment designs, isolating equipment, using engineering controls, and providing appropriate personal protective equipment (PPE). PPE selection should consider identified hazards and conform to agreed-upon safety procedures. Regular inspection and maintenance of equipment and PPE are also crucial for preventing accidents and ensuring continued safety in the workplace.

Understanding how diamond blades work is fundamental for safe operation. These blades feature diamond particles as the abrasive agent, which wear down over time, exposing new diamonds for efficient cutting. Safety precautions for both wet and dry cutting operations include following manufacturer's recommendations for blade specifications, inspecting blades for damage, maintaining proper mounting and machine conditions, and wearing appropriate safety equipment at all times.

Adherence to safety guidelines, proper equipment maintenance, and vigilant risk management practices are essential for preventing accidents and ensuring the safety of workers in masonry and concrete cutting operations.

Batching Mortar

Batching the Mortar in a Mixer

Batching mortar in a mixer is a systematic process crucial for ensuring the quality and consistency of the mortar used in construction. This method, commonly employed in concrete mixers, involves several steps to achieve the desired mortar consistency. The first step entails pouring approximately two-thirds of the required water into the mixer, with precise measurement facilitated by using a bucket rather than a shovel, ensuring accuracy. Following this, any specified additives such as water proofer, plasticiser, or liquid colouring are incorporated into the mixture to meet project specifications. Next, about one-third of the sand is added, followed by the cement, lime, and powder colouring if necessary. These components are mixed until a "slurry" consistency is attained. Finally, the remaining sand and any additional water needed are added, and the mixture is blended for at least three minutes to ensure thorough integration.

For specific applications such as paths and driveways, understanding the appropriate mix ratio is essential for achieving optimal results. Typically, for concrete intended for paths and driveways, a mix ratio of 1 part cement to 2 parts sand and 3 parts aggregate is recommended. This ratio ensures the desired strength and durability of the concrete, with approximately 16 bags of Builders Cement required per cubic meter of finished concrete.

Handling cement-based products necessitates adherence to stringent safety measures to mitigate potential health risks associated with their alkaline nature and fine powder form. Personal protective equipment (PPE) requirements include gloves to prevent skin irritation, face masks to prevent dust inhalation, eye protection to safeguard against eye irritation, long pants and sleeves to shield against skin irritation, and safety boots to prevent foot injuries. Additionally, it's essential to wash clothes separately if they come into contact with cement-based products to prevent skin irritation or contamination.

Understanding terms like MPa (megapascal) is crucial in the context of concrete construction, as it denotes the compressive strength of concrete. For instance, a concrete mix designated as 20MPa indicates a compressive strength of 20 megapascals. This knowledge is instrumental in selecting the appropriate concrete mix for specific applications, ensuring structural integrity and performance.

Environmental factors such as ambient temperature can significantly influence the setting time and overall performance of concrete products. Extreme temperatures, either below 10°C or above 35°C, can adversely affect the setting times, necessitating adjustments to the construction schedule to optimize conditions for concrete placement and curing.

Curing freshly laid concrete is a critical step in ensuring its strength, durability, and surface quality. Proper curing involves maintaining adequate moisture levels on the concrete surface for up to seven days, either through mist spraying or covering with black plastic sheets. This process facilitates hydration, reduces dusting, and enhances surface abrasion resistance, contributing to the long-term performance of the concrete.

Differentiating between cement and concrete is fundamental, as they are often used interchangeably but represent distinct materials and processes. Cement serves as an ingredient in concrete, providing the binding agent that holds the aggregate and sand together. Concrete, on the other hand, is a mixture of aggregates, sand, water, and cement, which undergoes a chemical reaction known as hydration to harden into a solid mass.

Using accurate measurement methods during concrete and mortar mixing is paramount to achieving the desired consistency and strength. While a shovel may seem convenient, it's not recommended for measuring as cement tends to lie flat and clump together, leading to inaccuracies. Instead, using a container such as a bucket ensures precise measurement of raw materials, minimizing the risk of overwatering, which can compromise the strength and durability of the final product.

Rapid Set Concrete offers accelerated setting times, with hardening occurring within 15 minutes of water addition, making it ideal for rapid construction projects. However, it requires careful handling, as it can set hard in vessels like buckets or wheelbarrows, rendering them unusable.

For foundational applications, the recommended mix ratio typically involves blending 1 part cement with 3 parts sand and 3 parts aggregate, ensuring the requisite strength and stability for the intended use.

The procedure for laying a concrete surface involves several key steps, including screeding, which entails initial leveling of the placed concrete using a straight edge, followed by allowing bleedwater accumulation to evaporate. Final floating and trowelling are subsequent steps, which further refine the concrete surface to achieve the desired finish and durability.

Batching the Mortar in a Wheelbarrow

Batching mortar manually involves a systematic process to ensure the proper mixing of ingredients for construction purposes. This method is often employed for small-scale projects where a concrete mixer may not be necessary. The process typically consists of several steps to achieve the desired mortar consistency. Firstly, the sand is measured and placed into the mixing container, often a wheelbarrow, serving as the base for the mortar mixture. Next, cement, lime, and any required powder colouring are added to the sand, followed by creating a well or hole in the middle of these dry ingredients for the water and liquid colouring, if needed. Finally, all the ingredients are thoroughly mixed with a shovel until a workable mixture is achieved, ensuring uniform distribution of components.

Safety precautions are paramount when handling cement-based products due to their caustic nature, which can cause skin burns and eye irritation. Protective gear such as gloves and safety glasses should be worn to minimize risks. Additionally, proper mixing techniques are essential to ensure the concrete's strength and integrity. While mixing bags of concrete may seem straightforward, achieving the correct water-to-concrete ratio is crucial for optimal performance. Too little water results in poor cohesion, while excess water weakens the concrete. Beginners often make the mistake of adding too much water, leading to a thin and soupy mixture. Using a measured amount of water added gradually, along with thorough mixing, helps prevent this issue and ensures a proper consistency.

Selecting the appropriate concrete mix for a project is essential for achieving desired results. Bagged concrete mix is commonly used for small-scale tasks due to its convenience and affordability. However, for larger projects requiring significant quantities of concrete, ordering ready-mix concrete from a truck may be more economical and efficient. Different types of concrete mixes are available, including fast-setting and high early strength options, catering to specific project requirements. Understanding the differences between these mixes and their suitability for various applications is crucial for successful project outcomes.

A sturdy wheelbarrow serves as an ideal mixing container for small-scale concrete mixing, offering mobility and ease of use. Mixing techniques involve gradually incorporating the dry mix into the water using a hoe or shovel, ensuring thorough wetting of all particles. The consistency of the mix is assessed visually and tactilely, with the ideal mixture exhibiting a slightly shiny surface when patted with a tool. Careful attention to the mixing process, including water measurement and gradual incorporation of dry mix, helps achieve the desired consistency and strength of the concrete.

Prompt cleanup of equipment and tools is essential to prevent hardened concrete buildup, which can be challenging to remove once it sets. Scrubbing the wheelbarrow and tools with a stiff-bristle brush before the concrete hardens helps facilitate cleanup, while rinsing promptly with water removes residual concrete. Proper disposal of rinse water is important to avoid environmental damage, such as grass damage from the caustic properties of concrete. By adhering to these guidelines, individuals can effectively mix concrete manually for small-scale construction projects while ensuring safety and quality.

Avoiding a Weak Mortar

Ensuring the strength and integrity of mortar is crucial in construction projects to avoid potential hazards and costly rework. Weak mortar not only compromises the stability of structures but also poses safety risks. Understanding the causes of weak mortar and implementing preventive measures is essential for maintaining construction quality and longevity.

Weak mortar can result from various factors, including insufficient mixing time, incorrect additives, and inadequate cement content. Insufficient mixing time prevents proper hydration of cement, resulting in poor bond strength and reduced durability. Similarly, using incorrect additives or not adding enough cement can alter the mortar's composition, leading to weakened structural integrity.

To avoid weak mortar, it's imperative to adhere to job specifications meticulously. Project specifications often provide precise instructions regarding the required mortar mix, including proportions of sand, cement, and lime. Following these specifications ensures consistency and quality in the mortar composition. Additionally, experienced bricklayers should rely on their expertise to select the appropriate mortar mix for specific applications, considering factors such as load-bearing requirements, environmental conditions, and material compatibility.

Accurate measuring is paramount in achieving the desired mortar mix. Using a shovel to gauge mixture proportions is highly inaccurate and can result in inconsistent mixes. Instead, using a bucket allows for precise measurement of sand, cement, and lime, ensuring uniformity and strength in the mortar. Careful attention to detail during the measuring process minimizes the risk of weak mortar due to improper proportions.

Timing also plays a crucial role in mortar mixing. Adequate mixing time is essential for ensuring thorough integration of ingredients and proper hydration of cement. Mixing mortar for at least three minutes in a mixer ensures uniformity and optimal bonding properties. Proper timing prevents the development of weak spots in the mortar and promotes consistent quality throughout the construction process.

Cleaning up excess mortar is essential to maintain the aesthetic appeal and functionality of masonry work. Excess mortar or drops must be removed promptly before they dry and harden, as they can be difficult to remove once set. Mortar that oozes out of joints can be removed using a large trowel or a pointing trowel, while drops on the face of bricks can be brushed off with a soft brush. Care should be taken to wash off any mortar residue on window panes and door frames using a soft brush or cloth to avoid scratching the glass.

Building a Retaining Wall Using Concrete Blocks

To construct a retaining wall, meticulous planning and execution are crucial. The process begins with setting the levels, where the line of the wall and the excavation area are established. Long pegs are driven beyond the wall's ends, and a dumpy is employed to ensure the excavation depth is accurate. Heights for both the footing and the finished wall are marked at various points along the designated area.

Excavation follows, typically performed with an excavator to cut the line of the wall and dig the footing. The surrounding area is levelled, and the waste material is removed using equipment like a bobcat and truck. Alternatively, for smaller projects, manual tools like picks and shovels can suffice, avoiding the need for heavy machinery.

Next, drainage considerations come into play. Drainage pits are positioned at the front, connected with stormwater pipes, while agricultural pipes are placed at the back of the footing. Steel bars are positioned longitudinally and at the base, with starter bars tied at specified intervals.

Concrete is then poured into the trench up to the set height, carefully levelled using a screed, and checked for accuracy with a dumpy. Starter bars are integrated into the concrete, and a timber float finishes the surface. It's essential to ensure proper alignment of the bars at designated intervals.

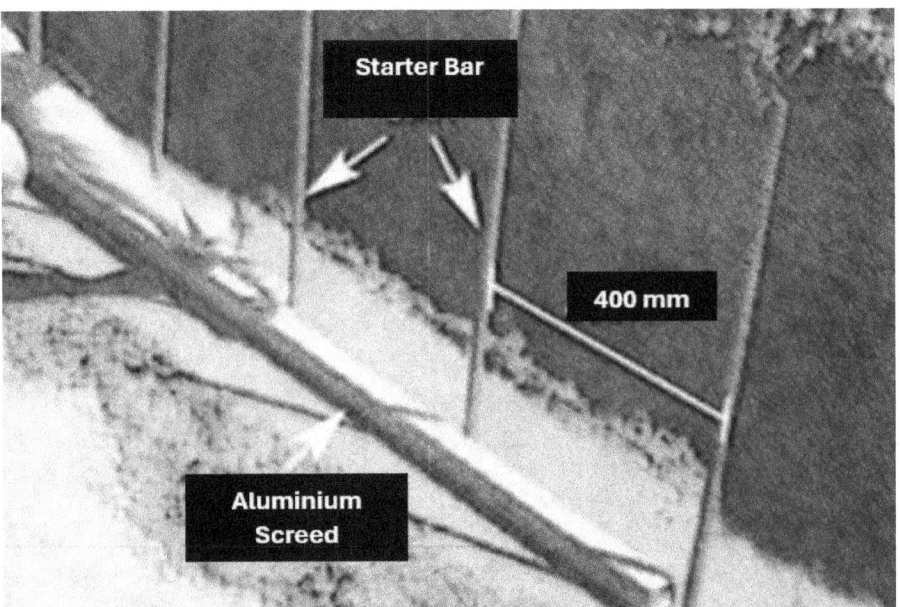

Figure 129: Pour concrete and screed.

Building the ends of the wall involves setting out the first course of blocks, laying them dry on the footing, and ensuring square corners. Mortar is mixed and applied as blocks are laid, particularly focusing on the end or corner blocks. A spirit level ensures blocks are correctly positioned.

Figure 130: Lay the blocks.

Laying lines are established using stringlines to guide each course. Mortar is spread on the footing to bed the blocks, and the base course is laid over starter bars, tapping them level. Weep holes are left open at specified intervals for drainage.

Reinforcing bars are positioned on every second course, overlapping and alternating to enhance stability. Additionally, geo-fabric socked agricultural pipe is rolled out behind the wall to facilitate drainage.

As the wall is built, mortar is spread along the edges of each course, blocks are positioned and tapped into place, and jointing iron is used to finish joints. The wall is then brushed and sponged down for a clean finish.

Finally, the wall is filled and backfilled. Concrete is poured into the core of the blocks and compacted, allowing it to cure for at least seven days. Behind the wall, geo-textile fabric is laid over the soil, and drainage material such as recycled crushed concrete is backfilled to provide further support and drainage.

Bonds

In masonry construction, the concept of "bonds" encompasses three distinct meanings: structural bond, mortar bond, and pattern bond, each playing a crucial role in the stability, aesthetics, and integrity of the finished structure.

Firstly, structural bond pertains to how individual masonry units, such as bricks or tiles, interlock or tie together to form a cohesive and unified structural unit. There are several methods to achieve structural bonding, including overlapping or interlocking the masonry units, embedding metal ties within connecting joints, or using grout to adhere adjacent layers or "wythes" of masonry. These techniques ensure that the masonry components work together effectively to withstand loads and stresses imposed on the structure.

Secondly, mortar bond refers to the adhesion of the joint mortar to the masonry units or to any reinforcing steel present within the masonry assembly. The quality of mortar bond is critical for the overall strength and durability of the masonry structure, as it provides cohesion between the individual units and enhances structural stability. Proper mortar application and curing are essential to achieve a strong and lasting bond between the masonry elements.

Lastly, pattern bond refers to the visual pattern formed by the arrangement of masonry units and mortar joints on the face of a wall. This pattern may result from the structural bond, where the layout of the masonry units creates a distinct pattern, or it may be purely decorative and unrelated to the structural integrity of the wall. Pattern bonds offer opportunities for architectural expression and aesthetic enhancement, allowing designers to create visually appealing facades through various arrangements of bricks, tiles, or stones, as well as different styles of mortar joints.

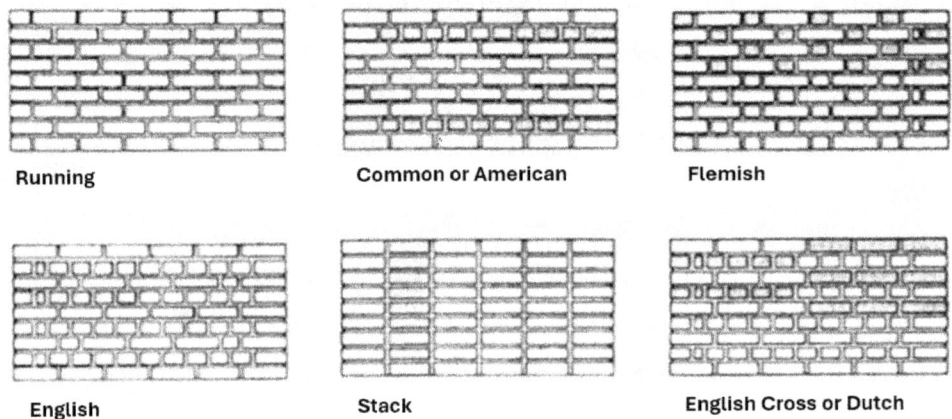

Figure 131: Types of masonry bonds.

Overall, understanding the significance of structural bond, mortar bond, and pattern bond is essential for achieving both structural integrity and aesthetic appeal in masonry construction. By carefully considering and implementing these bonding principles, masons and designers can create durable, visually striking, and architecturally sound masonry structures.

Masonry bonds are essential aspects of construction, determining both the structural integrity and aesthetic appeal of a wall. Among these bonds, the running bond stands out as the simplest pattern, consisting solely of stretchers without headers. Due to the absence of headers, metal ties are typically employed to provide the necessary structural bond. This bond finds extensive use in cavity wall construction, brick veneer walls, and facing tile walls featuring wide stretcher tiles. Its straightforward layout makes it popular for various applications where simplicity and efficiency are paramount.

The common bond, also known as the American bond, is a variation of the running bond with intermittent courses of full-length headers. These headers serve both as structural elements and components of the pattern. Typically, header courses are spaced at regular intervals, often appearing every fifth, sixth, or seventh course, depending on structural requirements. Variations of the common bond, such as the Flemish header course, offer flexibility in design. Proper corner layout is crucial in achieving a visually pleasing and structurally sound common bond, often involving three-quarter closures to maintain alignment.

In the Flemish bond, each course comprises alternating headers and stretchers, with headers in every other course centring over and under the stretchers. This bond pattern ensures strong structural bonding while presenting an aesthetically pleasing alternating pattern. When headers are unnecessary for structural bonding, blind headers may be used. Corner layout options include the Dutch corner and the English corner, each employing specific closure techniques to maintain bond continuity.

The English bond features alternating courses of headers and stretchers, with headers centred over and under the stretchers. However, unlike the Flemish bond, the joints between stretchers in stretcher courses do not align vertically. This bond pattern offers a robust structural bond while presenting a visually distinct arrangement. Blind headers may also be integrated into non-structural courses as needed.

The stack bond, primarily a pattern bond, features vertically aligned joints without overlapping units. Achieving proper alignment requires dimensionally accurate units or meticulous rematching. This bond pattern offers versatility through combinations and modifications of basic patterns. For enhanced stability, rigid steel ties or thick stretcher units may be used, particularly in large wall areas or load-bearing constructions.

The English cross or Dutch bond, a variation of the English bond, aligns the joints between stretchers in stretcher courses vertically. This bond pattern maintains structural integrity while offering a unique visual arrangement. Metal ties are employed when header courses are absent, ensuring proper bonding between exterior wall brick and backing courses.

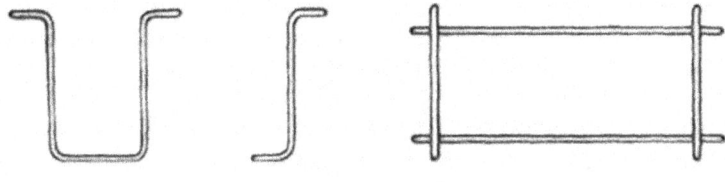

Figure 132: Metal ties.

Mortar Joints and Pointing

Mortar joints play a crucial role in brick masonry construction, providing both structural support and aesthetic coherence to the wall. Unlike the bricks themselves, there's no universally set standard for the thickness of mortar joints. Irregularly shaped bricks may necessitate thicker mortar joints, sometimes up to 1/2 inch, to compensate for their unevenness. However, for optimal strength, mortar joints typically measure 1/4 inch thick. This thickness is preferred when the bricks exhibit regularity in shape, allowing for a more consistent application of mortar.

One method of creating mortar joints is the slushed joint technique, where mortar is deposited onto the head joints and allowed to flow down between the bricks to form the joint. However, this method isn't suitable for producing solid joints due to the inability to compact the mortar against the brick faces effectively. Consequently, it leads to poor bonding. For a robust and durable joint, the mortar must be trowelled in place.

The technique of trowelling mortar joints requires precision and proper grip of the trowel. Holding the trowel firmly with the thumb resting on top of the handle, rather than encircling it, ensures better control and manoeuvrability. When spreading mortar, the trowel is loaded from the outside edge of the mortar board pile. Working from left to right along the wall (if right-handed), the trowel is positioned over the centre line of the previous course, tilted slightly, and moved to the right to evenly spread mortar on each brick.

To maintain the workability of the mortar and ensure a strong bond, it's essential not to spread the mortar for a bed joint too far ahead of laying the bricks. Ideally, mortar should be spread approximately 1 inch thick, with a shallow furrow made to prevent gaps between the mortar and the bedded brick. Excess mortar projecting beyond the wall line is trimmed off with the trowel to achieve a neat finish.

When laying bricks, excess mortar is squeezed out at the head joints and sides, ensuring complete filling of the joint. Proper placement of closure bricks, whether in header or stretcher courses, is crucial for maintaining structural integrity and preventing moisture penetration into the wall. This involves carefully applying mortar to the sides of the brick and ensuring a seamless fit within the existing brickwork.

The process of filling exposed joints with mortar immediately after laying a wall is known as pointing. It's also used to fill holes and correct defective mortar joints, typically done using a pointing trowel. Pointing ensures a uniform appearance and reinforces the integrity of the masonry structure, providing protection against water infiltration and enhancing the overall longevity of the wall.

Finishing mortar joints in brick masonry is essential for both aesthetic appeal and structural integrity. Without proper finishing, shallow cracks can develop between the brick and mortar, compromising the waterproofing and appearance of the wall. It's crucial to finish the joints before the mortar hardens too much. Several types of joint finishes are commonly used, with the most important ones being concave, flush, and weather joints.

Among these finishes, the concave joint is known for its superior weather tightness. After excess mortar is removed with a trowel, a jointer slightly larger than the joint is used to create this finish. Pressure is applied against the tool to press the mortar tightly against the brick on both sides of the joint. The flush joint, on the other hand, is achieved by holding the trowel almost parallel to the wall face while drawing its point along the joint. Meanwhile, the weather joint facilitates water shedding from the wall surface by pushing downward on the mortar with the top edge of the trowel.

Constructing brick arches requires careful planning and execution due to their unique structural characteristics. Arch shapes commonly used include elliptical and circular. Full mortar joints are essential for arch construction, with the joint width typically narrower at the bottom than at the top but not less than 1/4 inch at any point. To ensure stability and proper positioning, temporary wooden supports called templets are used during arch construction. These templets provide both support during construction and the necessary geometry for the arch's proper appearance.

Constructing an arch over a templet involves meticulous layout and positioning to avoid the need for cutting bricks. An odd number of bricks is used so that the key, or middle, brick falls into place at the exact arch centre or crown. The key brick, the last one laid, is critical for maintaining the arch's structural integrity. The number of bricks required for the arch is determined by laying the templet on level ground and arranging a trial number of bricks around the curve. The positions of these bricks are then marked on the templet and used as a guide during brick laying to ensure proper alignment and spacing. By adhering to these principles and techniques, builders can create sturdy, visually appealing brick arches that effectively distribute weight and enhance the overall architectural quality of a structure.

Cleaning Concrete Masonry

Good building practice in the context of block laying emphasizes meticulous care to minimize mortar staining on face concrete masonry. Block layers are tasked with several responsibilities to achieve this, including keeping face blocks clean during laying and tooling, covering unused pallets and unfinished walls during rain to prevent water penetration and efflorescence, and promptly cleaning any mortar dags and smears before they set hard. Removal of mortar stains typically involves a combination of hand tools, pressure cleaning, and, in extreme cases, acid treatments.

Hand cleaning with appropriate tools is the initial step in removing mortar stains. After using a bucket and brush, any remaining mortar dags and smears can be rubbed with a piece of 'like coloured' block or wood to prevent scratching. Careful use of a paint scraper, wide-bladed chisel, or wire brush may also aid in removing mortar buildup, although caution is advised to avoid damaging the masonry surface.

Pressure cleaning is another method employed for stain removal but should only be used after hand cleaning methods have been exhausted. Preliminary steps include removing mortar smears back to a flat surface with hand tools and allowing the mortar to harden for at least seven days. The pressure cleaning process involves testing on an inconspicuous area, using a pressure not exceeding 7MPa and volume not exceeding 20 litres/minute, and ensuring continuous and even cleaning to avoid surface erosion.

In cases where hand cleaning and pressure washing methods fail, acid treatments may be considered as a last resort. Acid treatments, however, are potentially damaging and must be approached with caution. Preliminary trials in inconspicuous areas are essential, and the acid must be applied with care to prevent damage to the masonry finish. Only after exhausting other options should acid treatments be considered, and they must strictly adhere to established procedures.

In addition to mortar stains, other types of stains such as timber (tannin), clay or loam, mosses, molds, lichens, and efflorescence may require specific treatment methods. Efflorescence, in particular, is a common issue on new masonry surfaces and requires a combination of dry brushing, wet brushing, and washing down to remove. Proper storage practices, good laying practice, and site procedures are crucial for minimizing efflorescence and other staining issues.

Safety precautions and warnings are paramount when dealing with chemicals and cleaning methods. Protective clothing, including vapor cartridge breathing masks, should be worn, and chemicals must be handled according to manufacturer recommendations to avoid personal injury and damage to adjacent materials. Diluting acid properly, avoiding mixing unfamiliar chemicals, and disposing of chemical wastes responsibly are essential safety measures to prevent accidents and environmental damage.

Brick Stair and Step Construction

Stairs, an essential architectural feature in buildings, consist of a series of steps comprising treads and risers that facilitate vertical movement between different levels. The terms "Stair" or "Stairway" are preferred over "Staircase," which originally referred to the space where a flight of stairs was built. Stairs come in various types, each with its unique design and functionality.

Figure 133: Stairway in garden at the Biltmore Estate. Dslcards, CC BY-SA 4.0, via Wikimedia Commons.

One common type is the bracketed stair, also known as "Cut and bracketed," characterized by strings shaped like treads and risers, cut out on the top edge, and adorned with ornamental brackets or fretwork underneath. Circular stairs, on the other hand, radiate from a central point, with or without a central well. Closed stairs, often referred to as "Boxed" or "Enclosed" stairs, have side walls or partitions on both sides and are typically closed by a door at one end.

Dogleg stairs, also called "Half-turn stairs," consist of two flights connected by a half landing for a 180° turn. Geometric stairs feature a continuous sweeping or flying design, with no newel posts or landings, often fitting semicircular or elliptical stairwells. Helical stairs, known as "Spiral" or "Winding" stairs, have a circular plan with all treads as winders.

Open newel stairs, open riser stairs, and open string stairs offer varying degrees of openness in design, with different configurations of landings, flights, and newel posts. Quarter turn stairs have two flights at right angles with a quarter-space landing between them, while return flight stairs feature outer strings of each flight vertically aligned.

Spine string stairs, typically made of steel, feature a single central spine (spine string) with welded tread supports, offering a sleek and modern aesthetic. Winding stairs, which change direction using winders, can incorporate landings or follow a circular or curved path.

Stairs can be constructed using a wide range of materials, including stone, brick, timber, steel, and concrete, or combinations thereof. Stone, historically one of the earliest materials used for purpose-made stairs, boasts a rich heritage evident in ancient Egyptian, Greek, and Roman structures. Spiral stone stairs were particularly popular in medieval castles and modern architectural marvels like Antonio Gaudi's Sagrada Familia in Barcelona.

Building Steps into a Slope

Building steps into a slope requires careful planning and execution to ensure stability, functionality, and aesthetic appeal. The layout of the slope often dictates the design, with options such as two flights of steps at right angles, separated by a landing. To prevent soil erosion and provide stability, low brick retaining walls may be necessary, especially on slopes with loose soil at the sides.

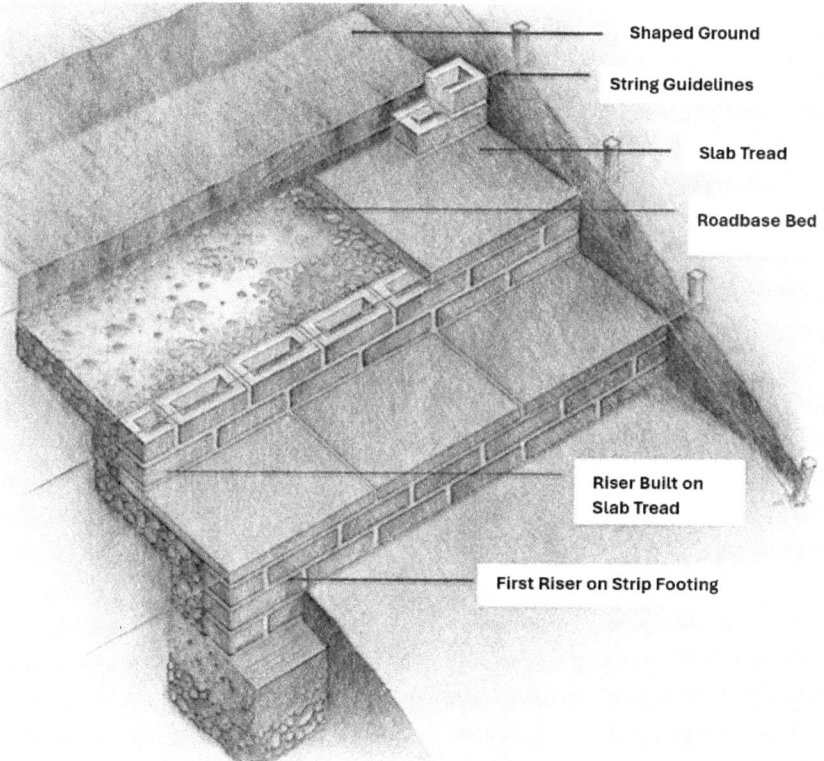

Figure 134: Stair structure.

Regardless of the specific design, the construction process typically involves several steps, starting with the preparation of the ground and the calculation of dimensions for treads and risers. Stringlines are fixed to mark the front edge of each step, ensuring even spacing and right angles to the length lines.

The ground is then shaped for each step using a spade, beginning at the bottom to maintain a flat working area. A trench is dug at the base of the flight to create a footing strip for the first riser. Roadbase is then added to the trench and compacted before filling it with concrete, creating a solid foundation for the steps.

After allowing time for the concrete to set, the construction of the steps proceeds with the laying of the first riser and the first tread behind it. Paving slabs are used to create the surface of each tread, with mortar providing a stable base and a slight slope for drainage. Care is taken to ensure that each riser is vertical and that the top tread is level with the surrounding ground.

Finally, any gaps between the tread slabs are filled with mortar or sharp sand, with a waiting period of about 24 hours for the mortar to set before the steps can be used. Throughout the construction process, precise measurements, proper alignment, and attention to detail are essential to ensure the safety and longevity of the steps built into the slope.

Chapter Eight
Constructing Stone Structures and Features

The use of stone and stone structures in landscaping offers a myriad of benefits and aesthetic possibilities, making it a popular choice for designers and homeowners alike. Stones, whether natural or man-made, can be employed in various ways to enhance the beauty, functionality, and sustainability of outdoor spaces.

One of the primary advantages of incorporating stone into landscaping is its durability and longevity. Natural stone, such as granite, limestone, or slate, can withstand harsh weather conditions and environmental stressors, ensuring that the landscape features built with stone will remain intact for many years. Additionally, stone requires minimal maintenance compared to other materials, making it a cost-effective option in the long run.

Figure 135: Use of stone in landscaping. CC0 Public Domain via PxHere.

In terms of aesthetics, stone adds a timeless and rustic charm to outdoor spaces. Whether used for pathways, retaining walls, or decorative elements like rock gardens or water features, stone blends seamlessly with natural surroundings and can complement any landscape style, from traditional to contemporary. Moreover, stones come in a wide range of colours, textures, and shapes, providing endless design possibilities and allowing landscapers to create unique and personalized outdoor environments.

In landscaping, stones are often used to create hardscape features such as pathways, patios, and retaining walls. Stone pathways add visual interest to the landscape while providing functional walkways that guide visitors through the garden or yard. Patios constructed with stone offer versatile outdoor living spaces for dining, entertaining, or relaxation, and they can be customized to suit the homeowner's preferences in terms of size, shape, and design.

LANDSCAPE DESIGN AND CONSTRUCTION

Figure 136: Use of stone in landscaping. stonescape, CC BY-SA 2.0, via Flickr.

Retaining walls built with stone serve both practical and aesthetic purposes. They help to prevent soil erosion, manage drainage, and create terraced levels in sloped areas, allowing for better utilization of space in the landscape. Additionally, retaining walls made of natural stone add texture and character to the garden or yard, serving as focal points or decorative elements within the overall design.

Beyond functional features, stones can be used creatively to enhance the visual appeal of the landscape. Rock gardens, for example, incorporate various sizes and shapes of stones along with drought-tolerant plants to create low-maintenance and visually striking garden beds. Water features such as fountains, ponds, or waterfalls can also be constructed using stone, adding a sense of tranquillity and natural beauty to the outdoor space.

The use of stone and stone structures in landscaping offers numerous benefits, including durability, versatility, and aesthetic appeal. Whether used for pathways, patios, retaining walls, or decorative elements, stones add texture, character, and a timeless elegance to outdoor environments, transforming them into inviting and captivating spaces for relaxation, recreation, and enjoyment.

The use of stone in construction works encompasses a broad spectrum of geological, physical, and chemical classifications, each playing a crucial role in determining the suitability and performance of stones for various applications. Geologically, stones are categorized into igneous, sedimentary, and metamorphic rocks. Igneous rocks, such as granite and basalt, form from the cooling and solidifying of molten materials, resulting in durable and crystalline surfaces. Sedimentary rocks, like sandstone and limestone, are formed from deposits of eroded and pre-existing rock, while metamorphic rocks undergo changes due to pressure and internal heat, transforming into new materials like marble or gneiss.

Physical classification of stones is based on their structure, with stratified rocks exhibiting layers or stratification that allows for easy splitting, and unstratified rocks lacking this layered structure, such as granite. Foliated rocks, commonly found among metamorphic rocks, exhibit a tendency to split along specific directions, similar to stratified rocks. Chemical classification categorizes stones based on their composition, with siliceous rocks containing silica, argillaceous rocks containing clay, and calcareous rocks containing calcium carbonate, each possessing unique properties and applications.

When selecting stones for engineering works, various properties must be considered, including structure, texture, density, appearance, strength, hardness, percentage wear, porosity, weathering resistance, toughness, resistance to fire, ease of finishing, and seasoning. Structured stones are preferred for superstructure construction, while unstructured stones are suitable for foundations. Texture affects the appearance and durability of stones, with fine-grained stones being attractive and strong. Density influences strength, with denser stones being stronger, while appearance is enhanced by uniform colour and compact grains.

Strength and hardness are critical properties for stones used in construction, with crushing strength and Dory's testing machine used to assess these characteristics. Percentage wear and absorption indicate durability and resistance to weathering and water absorption, respectively. Stones with good weather resistance and toughness are preferred for outdoor applications, while resistance to fire varies depending on the stone's composition. Ease of finishing and seasoning are also important considerations, as they affect the cost and performance of stone masonry.

Understanding the geological, physical, and chemical properties of stones, along with their various characteristics and classifications, is essential for selecting suitable materials for civil engineering projects. By evaluating these properties, engineers can ensure the durability, functionality, and aesthetic appeal of stone structures in landscaping and construction works.

The requirements of good building stones encompass a range of characteristics crucial for their suitability in construction projects. Strength is paramount, as stones must resist the loads imposed on them, especially in large structures where the weight distribution is significant. Durability is another vital aspect, ensuring that stones can withstand the adverse effects of natural forces such as wind, rain, and heat over extended periods. Hardness is essential for stones used in floors and pavements, as they must endure abrasive factors like foot traffic and the movement of heavy materials without deteriorating.

Toughness is a measure of a stone's ability to withstand stress and vibrations caused by machinery or loads moving over them. Stones used in road construction, for example, require high toughness to withstand the constant impact of vehicles. Specific gravity is also crucial, with heavier stones preferred for construction projects such as dams, retaining walls, and harbors due to their increased stability and resistance to displacement.

Porosity and absorption are critical considerations, as porous stones allow water to penetrate, weakening the stone and making it susceptible to freeze-thaw cycles, where water expands upon freezing, causing the stone to disintegrate. Stones should ideally have low porosity to minimize water ingress and subsequent damage. Finishing plays a significant role in the appearance and functionality of stones, with easy workability important to reduce costs while maintaining strength and durability.

Appearance is a key factor, particularly for facade works, where the colour and polish of the stone contribute to the aesthetic appeal of the building. Seasoning is necessary to remove quarry sap and stabilize the stone's properties before use, with laterite stones requiring a period of seasoning to rid them of quarry sap through exposure to natural elements.

Cost considerations are also vital, with proximity to the quarry site impacting transportation costs and overall expenses. While not all stones may meet every requirement, builders and contractors can conduct various tests such as crushing strength, water absorption, abrasion, impact, and acid tests to assess their suitability for specific applications. Ultimately, selecting the right building stone involves balancing these requirements to ensure optimal performance and longevity in construction projects.

Landscaping projects often incorporate a variety of stones to enhance outdoor spaces, adding visual appeal, functionality, and durability. Common stones used in landscaping include:

- **Flagstone**: Flagstone is a popular choice for pathways, patios, and outdoor flooring due to its natural appearance and flat, smooth surface. It comes in various colours and shapes, providing versatility in design. Flagstone is durable and can withstand outdoor elements, making it suitable for both residential and commercial landscaping projects.

- **Cobblestone**: Cobblestones are rounded stones typically used for driveways, walkways, and edging. They offer a rustic and traditional look, adding charm and character to outdoor areas. Cobblestones are durable and can withstand heavy foot traffic and vehicular loads, making them ideal for high-traffic areas in landscaping projects.

- **Gravel**: Gravel is a versatile landscaping material available in various sizes and colours. It is commonly used for pathways, driveways, ground cover, and drainage solutions. Gravel provides excellent drainage and erosion control, making it suitable for both practical and decorative purposes in landscaping projects.

- **River Rock**: River rock, also known as pebbles or creek stones, are smooth, rounded stones often found along riverbeds. They come in various sizes and colours, ranging from earthy tones to vibrant hues. River rock is commonly used for decorative purposes in landscaping, such as garden borders, water features, and rock gardens, adding texture and visual interest to outdoor spaces.

- **Boulders**: Boulders are large, natural stones typically used as focal points or accents in landscaping projects. They come in various shapes, sizes, and colours, ranging from small to oversized. Boulders can be strategically placed in gardens, around water features, or along pathways to create visual interest and add a sense of natural beauty to outdoor environments.

- **Limestone**: Limestone is a versatile natural stone used in landscaping for retaining walls, steps, and edging. It is available in various colours and textures, ranging from soft beige to warm earth tones. Limestone is durable, weather-resistant, and easy to work with, making it a popular choice for both residential and commercial landscaping projects.

- **Slate**: Slate is a fine-grained metamorphic rock known for its distinctive texture and colour variations. It is commonly used for pathways, patios, and retaining walls due to its durability and slip-resistant surface. Slate adds a contemporary and elegant look to outdoor spaces, making it a popular choice for modern landscaping designs.

- **Granite**: Granite is a durable and versatile natural stone used in landscaping for pathways, steps, and outdoor countertops. It is known for its strength, resilience, and resistance to weathering, making it suitable for high-traffic areas and outdoor applications. Granite comes in various colours and finishes, providing flexibility in design and aesthetic appeal in landscaping projects.

These are just a few examples of the common stones used in landscaping projects. Each type of stone offers unique characteristics and benefits, allowing landscape designers and homeowners to create beautiful and functional outdoor spaces tailored to their specific needs and preferences.

Selecting the right stone for a project involves considering both its appearance and performance. Stone offers a wide range of colours, textures, and finishes, providing ample opportunities for expressing individual style and personality. Whether used for flooring, walls, or outdoor landscaping, the unique character of stone adds a distinctive touch to any space. When choosing stone, it's essential to prioritize durability and resistance to staining and wear. Understanding the strengths and challenges of different types of stone is crucial in making an informed decision.

The vast array of colours, textures, and finishes available in stone now rivals those of more traditional floor coverings. This variety allows homeowners and designers to find a stone that not only complements the overall aesthetic of a space but also reflects the personal style and preferences of the occupants. Whether seeking a sleek and modern look with polished granite or a rustic charm with rough-hewn slate, there's a stone option to suit every taste and design concept.

Beyond aesthetics, the performance of the chosen stone is paramount. For flooring applications, durability and resistance to wear and tear are essential factors to consider. Stone that is prone to scratching or staining may not be suitable for high-traffic areas or households with pets and children. Additionally, the stone's ability to withstand moisture, heat, and other environmental factors should be evaluated, especially for outdoor applications where exposure to the elements is inevitable.

Understanding the basic properties of stone is key to making an informed decision during the selection process. Different types of stone have varying levels of hardness, porosity, and resistance to abrasion and weathering. For example, granite is known for its durability and resistance to scratching, making it an excellent choice for high-traffic areas such as kitchens and entryways. On the other hand, limestone may be more susceptible to staining and erosion over time, requiring more maintenance and care.

By assessing the specific needs and requirements of a project, homeowners and designers can narrow down their options and select the most suitable stone for the job. Whether prioritizing aesthetics, durability, or practicality, choosing the right stone ensures that the finished space not only looks beautiful but also performs well over time. Consulting with experts in stone selection and installation can also provide valuable insights and guidance in making the best choice for a particular project.

Sandstone

Sandstone, a sedimentary rock primarily composed of quartz cemented together with clay and secondary silica, possesses unique characteristics due to the presence of minor minerals such as iron and manganese. These soluble minerals can migrate within the stone, resulting in distinctive banding patterns or uniform colours. Sandstone's gritty nature typically precludes the development of a polished finish, although some dense varieties can be honed to a smooth texture. Common surface finishes include sawn, sandblasted, bush hammer, and rock-face textures.

In terms of appearance, sandstone exhibits a wide range of colours, including white, gold, brown, red, purple, grey, green, and black. Its versatility makes it a popular choice for various applications, including pedestrian paving, internal and external cladding, statuary, and masonry construction. Sandstone's ability to be easily cut and shaped into different forms makes it highly adaptable to diverse design requirements. Additionally, most surface finishes of sandstone comply with rigorous slip resistance standards, making it suitable for areas with high foot traffic.

Figure 137: Seaworn sandstone brick. Dimitrios Savva (Photography), CC0, via Wikimedia Commons.

One of the notable advantages of sandstone is its ability to remain cool underfoot, making it ideal for outdoor entertaining areas. However, there are some considerations to take into account when using sandstone. Certain types may contain expansive clays, which can lead to problems such as decay or bowing of tiles when exposed to repetitive wet-dry cycles. Sandstone also has relatively high water absorption, ranging from 2% to 8% by weight, making it susceptible to staining and salt attack. Its low resistance to wear can result in the production of gritty residue, which may be harmful to softer floor coverings like marble or carpet.

When selecting a specific type of sandstone, it's essential to evaluate its performance in the intended location. Basic physical properties such as water absorption, density, compressive strength, and modulus of rupture are crucial factors to consider for assessing stain resistance and durability. Sandstone's strength should be evaluated in both wet and dry conditions, as it can lose more than 50% of its strength when wet. Resistance to salt attack and dimensional stability following soaking are also important criteria to determine the stone's suitability for specific applications. Abrasion resistance testing is beneficial, especially for commercial paving projects, to ensure long-term durability and performance. Proper evaluation of these performance criteria helps ensure the successful use of sandstone in various construction and landscaping projects.

Figure 138: Quartz Sandstone. Huhulenik, CC BY 3.0, via Wikimedia Commons.

Granite

Granite, an igneous rock formed at depth, is renowned for its durability and versatility. True granites typically contain quartz, mica, and feldspar, although in the commercial sense, the term encompasses various igneous rocks capable of taking a polish. The colour and texture of granite vary widely, depending on the stone's mineral composition and rate of cooling during formation. This variability contributes to the unique aesthetic appeal of granite.

Figure 139: Granite in various textures. Adoscam, CC BY-SA 4.0, via Wikimedia Commons.

In terms of appearance, granite offers unparalleled versatility, with the ability to be processed into a wide range of finishes. These include highly reflective polished surfaces, rough exfoliated (flamed) textures, honed finishes, sandblasted textures, antiqued appearances, and water-jet blasted designs. The extensive colour range of granite spans the spectrum from jet black to ice white, with common colours including red, brown, green, grey, yellow-gold, and blue. Granite is inherently granular, but the grain size can vary significantly from less than 1mm to over 5cm.

Granite finds widespread usage in various applications, including paving, internal and external cladding, wall and floor tiles, benchtops, and monuments. Its selection is often driven by its reputation as one of the most durable stone types, characterized by strength and resilience. With relatively low water absorption capacity and chemically inert minerals, granite exhibits excellent resistance to stains, making it a preferred choice for areas prone to spills and moisture.

However, certain characteristics of granite warrant consideration when selecting and using it. Dark-coloured granites may have a tendency to show oil stains, while light-coloured varieties are more susceptible to rust stains from external sources or altered minerals within the stone. Proper design of expansion joints is crucial, especially in exposed locations, to accommodate thermal expansion and prevent cracking. Poor extraction techniques, such as blasting, can introduce stress cracks into the granite, compromising its strength and integrity.

Figure 140: Sample of natural black cloud-patterned granite. Daoplathanoi, CC BY-SA 4.0, via Wikimedia Commons.

Performance evaluation criteria for granite include water absorption, density, and flexural strength, which provide insights into its freshness and general strength. The coefficient of thermal expansion is essential for determining the stone's expansion properties upon heating, guiding the design of expansion joint spacing. Petrographic examination offers a detailed analysis of the stone's composition, identifying potential issues such as micro-cracks or staining minerals that may affect its long-term performance. By considering these factors, architects, designers, and builders can make informed decisions when selecting and using granite in various construction projects.

Limestone

Limestone is primarily a sedimentary rock composed mainly of calcium carbonate. Its formation often occurs through the deposition and compaction of marine fossil debris, such as shells, coral, and bones. However, limestone can also originate from freshwater and aeolian (wind-blown) deposits, which are commercially available. The process of deposition and compaction over time results in the formation of limestone rock.

The density of limestone varies significantly, influencing the available surface finishes. High-density limestone, like Jura from Germany, can undergo processing to achieve a "satin" honed finish. In contrast, coarser and less dense types of limestone are typically limited to sawn or coarse-honed finishes due to their composition and texture.

Limestone exhibits a predominantly white, cream, or tan coloration, often with golden highlights attributed to the presence of limonite, an iron hydroxide. Additionally, limestone can occur in shades of blue-grey, grey, and black, offering a diverse range of aesthetic possibilities.

Limestone finds application in various construction and landscaping projects, including paving, internal and external cladding, and floor and wall tiles. Its versatility and aesthetic appeal make it a popular choice in architectural design.

Limestone possesses a sensory appeal, visually and tactilely pleasing. Its subtle pastel and natural colours complement contemporary minimalist design trends while providing warmth and texture. Moreover, limestone is generally resistant to salt attack, making it suitable for use in environments such as pool surrounds.

Figure 141: Weathered limestone from the Cambrian of Nevada, USA. James St. John, CC BY 2.0, via Wikimedia Commons.

Despite its aesthetic appeal, limestone has certain vulnerabilities to consider. Due to its composition of calcium carbonate, limestone is sensitive to acid, which can cause surface etching on polished or fine-honed surfaces. Additionally, limestone is relatively soft compared to granite, leading to surface wear and loss of polish in high-traffic areas. Certain types of limestone may contain linear features known as stylolites, which, if lined with clay, can weaken the stone, particularly when exposed to moisture.

Several criteria are essential for evaluating the performance of limestone, including water absorption, density, compressive strength, modulus of rupture, resistance to salt attack (particularly for low-density stone), dimensional stability, abrasion resistance, and petrographic examination. These evaluations help ensure that limestone meets the necessary standards for durability, longevity, and suitability for specific applications.

Travertine

Travertine is a sedimentary rock formed by the precipitation of calcium carbonate from mineral springs. This process often occurs over long periods, during which the calcium carbonate is deposited onto vegetation such as moss or algae. The interaction between the mineral-rich water and organic matter contributes to the development of the typical porous nature of travertine.

Commercially available travertine typically exhibits a relatively high density, allowing for various surface finishes. It is commonly processed to achieve a "satin" honed finish, providing a smooth texture. Travertine can also be utilized with its pores either unfilled or filled with a stable cementitious or polymer filler, depending on the desired aesthetic and functional requirements. Additionally, textured finishes such as sandblasted or bush-hammered finishes are possible with travertine.

Travertine is known for its predominantly white, cream, or tan coloration, sometimes featuring subtle golden or blue-grey tones. The appearance of travertine can vary significantly based on the cutting orientation. Vein-cut travertine, cut across the "grain," highlights tonal variations in deposition layers and exposes large, elongated pores. In contrast, cross-cut or fleuri-cut travertine, cut parallel or along the grain, presents variations in layers as a flowery, blotchy, or circular pattern.

Travertine finds widespread application in both internal and external cladding, as well as floor and wall tiles. Its versatility, durability, and aesthetic appeal make it a popular choice in architectural and landscaping projects.

Figure 142: Travertine Paver Deck. Casata, CC BY-SA 3.0, via Wikimedia Commons.

The unique patterning and texture of travertine have been admired for thousands of years. Beyond its aesthetic qualities, travertine is generally dense and durable while also possessing a soft texture. Its ability to remain cool underfoot makes it particularly suitable for areas such as bathrooms or pool surrounds, where barefoot comfort is desired.

If left unfilled, the characteristic porous nature of travertine may lead to the entrapment of dirt and grime, requiring regular maintenance. Additionally, while travertine is relatively strong, the elongated pores within vein-cut travertine can significantly reduce flexural strength compared to cross-cut material. Like limestone, travertine is composed of calcium carbonate, making it susceptible to acid attack.

Performance evaluation of travertine involves assessing criteria such as water absorption, density, flexural strength, and abrasion resistance. These evaluations help ensure that travertine meets the necessary standards for durability, longevity, and suitability for specific applications.

Marble

Marble is a metamorphic rock primarily composed of calcite, which forms from limestone under the influence of heat and/or pressure. This transformation occurs deep within the Earth's crust over extended periods. Commercially, the term "marble" is also extended to high-density limestone varieties that can be polished to a smooth finish.

Due to its high density and low porosity, marble can be processed to achieve a high polish, imparting a luxurious sheen to its surface. Other available surface finishes include honed, sawn, and sandblasted, each offering distinct textures and visual effects.

Marble typically exhibits a white base colour, often accented by minor veining in various hues. However, it is also available in a range of colours such as black, blue-grey, red, and pink. Marble is known for its fine-grained texture, although some varieties with larger grains exceeding 5cm are also found.

Figure 143: Marble Fountain Vase. Игорь Гордеев, CC BY-SA 4.0, via Wikimedia Commons.

Marble finds widespread application in paving, both internal and external cladding, as well as in the fabrication of bench and vanity tops, and floor and wall tiles. Its elegant appearance and versatile colour options make it a popular choice for enhancing the aesthetic appeal of architectural and interior design projects.

The translucent quality and pearly lustre of marble are unparalleled, evoking a sense of elegance and sophistication. Its availability in a variety of colours and patterns allows for customization, catering to diverse design preferences. Whether chosen for uniform colours, subtle veining, or dramatic mosaic effects, marble lends an air of refinement to any space.

Most types of marble primarily consist of calcium carbonate, rendering them susceptible to acid attack. Additionally, marble is relatively soft, making it prone to scratching and surface wear, particularly in high-traffic areas. Textured finishes, while adding visual interest, may lead to polishing over time, potentially reducing slip resistance. Certain types of marble may also exhibit warping when used in large format panels outdoors.

Performance evaluation of marble involves assessing criteria such as water absorption, density, compressive strength, flexural strength, dimensional stability, and petrographic examination. These evaluations help ensure that marble meets the necessary standards for durability, longevity, and suitability for specific applications, aiding in informed decision-making during material selection.

Slate

Slate, a fine-grained metamorphic rock, undergoes significant pressure, resulting in the development of foliation or sheet-like layers. Its primary composition includes quartz and muscovite, accompanied by lesser amounts of chlorite, hematite, and pyrite. Additionally, trace minerals may influence the stone's colour profile, contributing to its diverse aesthetic appeal.

Slate's natural foliation lends itself to a rough split-face finish, highlighting its inherent texture and character. Depending on processing techniques, slate can also be honed, sawn, or subjected to a bush-hammered finish, offering versatility in design applications.

Typically, slate exhibits various shades of grey, although commercial options also encompass black, green, red, and purple variants. Its colour diversity allows for creative expression in architectural and interior design projects, contributing to visually striking environments.

Slate finds extensive use in wall, floor, and roof tiles, as well as internal and external paving applications. Additionally, large slates can be processed to create bench or billiard table tops, showcasing its adaptability across diverse contexts.

The natural split-face finish of slate simplifies processing while offering high slip resistance, ensuring safety in various settings. Its low porosity and chemically inert composition make it resistant to staining, enhancing its appeal for both indoor and outdoor paving projects. Moreover, slate's durability and longevity make it a popular choice for architectural elements requiring robust materials.

Slate containing pyrite may decay over time, leading to rust stains and compromising its aesthetic integrity. Quality concerns may arise, as poor-grade slates may experience delamination or softening with age, potentially resulting in structural failure. Additionally, the lack of calibration in many slate varieties necessitates additional effort during installation to achieve a level surface.

Evaluation of slate's performance involves assessing criteria such as water absorption, density, modulus of rupture, and resistance to acid attack. These metrics ensure that slate meets quality standards, offering durability, reliability, and suitability for intended applications. By considering these factors, stakeholders can make informed decisions when selecting slate for construction and design projects.

Figure 144: Slate path. Michael Coghlan, CC BY-SA 2.0, via Flickr.

Bluestone

Bluestone encompasses a diverse range of stone types, typically characterized by their resistance to easy dressing, akin to sandstone, which is often classified as a 'freestone'. In Victoria, basalt earns the moniker of bluestone, while South Australia's definition extends to metamorphic rocks like schists and siltstone. Porphyry sourced from Queensland also falls under the bluestone classification.

Bluestone products are commonly marketed with natural split or rock face finishes, enhancing their rugged aesthetic. Victorian bluestone, or basalt, is often utilized with a sawn finish, lending a more refined appearance. Additionally, some bluestone variants are available with honed and sandblasted finishes, offering versatility in design applications.

Victorian bluestone exhibits a spectrum from black to dark grey-blue hues, characterized by large pores colloquially termed 'cats paws'. In contrast, South Australian bluestone primarily showcases grey-blue tones with autumn color highlights. Porphyry presents options in grey-blue shades as well as golden autumn colors, adding variety to architectural palettes.

Bluestone finds extensive use in masonry construction, where it is processed into cubic materials, as well as in pedestrian and vehicular paving applications, where it is utilized as setts or flags. Victorian bluestone, owing to its versatility, can be sawn into calibrated slabs and tiles for paving and cladding purposes, further expanding its utility.

Bluestone is favoured for its perceived strength, density, durability, and stain resistance, making it a reliable choice for various construction projects. In regions like Victoria and South Australia, bluestone holds cultural significance, seamlessly integrating into local history and blending contemporary and natural environments with its earthy color range.

Most bluestone variants undergo minimal calibration during processing, resulting in significant thickness variations that necessitate careful consideration during installation to ensure uniformity and stability.

Evaluation of bluestone's performance involves assessing criteria such as water absorption, density, modulus of rupture, and secondary mineral content. These metrics enable stakeholders to gauge bluestone's suitability for specific applications, ensuring durability, longevity, and aesthetic appeal in construction endeavours.

Figure 145: Variegated Bluestone Patio. Pistils Landscape Design + Build, CC BY-SA 2.0, via Flickr.

Bluestone available in the USA shares some similarities with its counterparts in other regions while also presenting unique features specific to its geological origin and commercial processing.

Formation and Composition: Bluestone in the USA comprises various types of stone known for their resistance to easy dressing, similar to sandstone's classification as a 'freestone'. While the term bluestone is loosely used, it typically encompasses materials like basalt, which is prevalent in regions like Pennsylvania and New York. Basalt, characterized by its dense and durable nature, earns the designation of bluestone due to its distinct blue-grey hue and suitability for construction purposes.

Surface Finishes: Bluestone products available in the USA often feature natural split or rock face finishes, highlighting their rugged aesthetic appeal. Sawn finishes may also be employed to achieve a more refined appearance, particularly with basalt varieties. Additionally, honed and sandblasted finishes provide versatility in design applications, catering to diverse aesthetic preferences and project requirements.

Appearance: Bluestone sourced from regions like Pennsylvania and New York typically exhibits grey-blue tones, with variations in colour intensity and texture. The stone's appearance may vary depending on factors such as geological composition, weathering processes, and commercial processing techniques. The characteristic 'cats paws' or large pores, reminiscent of Victorian bluestone, contribute to its distinctive appearance.

Common Usage: Bluestone in the USA finds widespread use in masonry construction, paving applications for both pedestrian walkways and vehicular surfaces, as well as in landscaping projects. Its versatility allows for processing into various forms, including cubic materials for masonry and calibrated slabs for paving and cladding purposes, catering to the diverse needs of construction projects across different sectors.

Reasons for Selection: Bluestone is favoured in the USA for its perceived strength, durability, and aesthetic appeal, making it a preferred choice for architects, designers, and contractors. Its dense composition and resistance to staining and wear make it suitable for high-traffic areas, while its natural beauty adds a touch of elegance to outdoor and indoor spaces alike.

Characteristics to Consider: Similar to bluestone elsewhere, variants available in the USA may exhibit thickness variations due to minimal calibration during processing. This necessitates careful planning and installation to ensure uniformity and stability in construction projects. Additionally, evaluating factors such as water absorption, density, and secondary mineral content is essential to assess bluestone's suitability for specific applications.

Performance Evaluation Criteria: Evaluation of bluestone's performance in the USA involves assessing metrics like water absorption, density, modulus of rupture, and secondary mineral content. These criteria enable stakeholders to make informed decisions regarding the stone's durability, longevity, and aesthetic appeal in various construction endeavours, ensuring optimal outcomes for projects.

Rockeries

Rocks play a crucial role in enhancing the natural ambiance of gardens, infusing them with character and charm. Their versatile use allows for the creation of diverse and attractive effects, reminiscent of natural rocky features like alpine outcrops, cliff rockfalls, or rocky creek beds. In Europe and America, the tradition of incorporating rockeries featuring low-growing alpine plants has endured for many years, adding to the timeless allure of garden landscapes.

Constructing a rockery entails several fundamental considerations. First and foremost, rocks should be firmly embedded in the ground, ideally with at least half of their mass buried to ensure stability. Careful selection of rocks is essential, prioritizing those naturally weathered or adorned with moss or lichen, which lend authenticity to the arrangement. Clustering rocks closely together, ensuring they touch and interlock seamlessly, fosters the illusion of naturally occurring formations.

Figure 146: Hortus Haren. Acer palmatum in the rock garden. Agnes Monkelbaan, CC BY-SA 4.0, via Wikimedia Commons.

One key principle in rockery construction is to reveal only the weathered or moss-covered surfaces of rocks, concealing the remainder beneath the soil or adjacent rocks. This practice contributes to a more organic and harmonious aesthetic, except when simulating recent rockfalls, where exposed rocks can evoke a sense of spontaneity and drama.

Beyond traditional rockeries, rocks find broader application in landscaping. They serve as erosion control measures when arranged in sloping areas, create focal points or contrasts with surrounding vegetation, and adorn pools or ponds, offering both aesthetic appeal and functional benefits. Additionally, rocks can form natural walkways, provide stability for plants, and retain moisture in soil, enhancing garden resilience.

Various rockery ideas can be explored to suit different garden styles and preferences. From dry creek beds featuring native plants to formal Japanese rock gardens characterized by meticulous rock placement, the possibilities are diverse. Drystone walls and wet stone falls offer alternatives for boundary delineation or soil retention, each requiring distinct construction techniques and aesthetic considerations.

Figure 147: Rock garden, Brno, Troubsko, Ostopovická. I.Sáček, senior, CC0, via Wikimedia Commons.

For those seeking to simulate the appearance of rocks without sourcing natural materials, artificial rocks made of concrete offer a practical solution. Constructing artificial rocks involves molding concrete over wire mesh frameworks, allowing for customized shapes, textures, and sizes. This method affords creative freedom while minimizing the environmental impact associated with extracting natural rocks.

In planting rockeries, careful consideration should be given to plant selection to complement the rocky theme and ensure long-term harmony. Native plants adapted to rocky environments are ideal choices, chosen based on their suitability for the specific conditions and their ability to coexist harmoniously with the rock formations.

The incorporation of rocks in garden design not only enhances visual appeal but also fosters a connection with nature, evoking a sense of tranquillity and timelessness. Whether constructing traditional rockeries or experimenting with innovative landscaping techniques, rocks remain indispensable elements in shaping outdoor spaces into serene and captivating retreats.

Planting in rockeries requires careful consideration to ensure the health and vitality of the chosen flora, particularly when situated close to rockwork treated with concrete or mortar. It's essential to bear in mind that these materials are alkaline, possessing a high pH level, which can influence the pH of the surrounding soil as chemical components leach out over time. In sandy soils, this effect may dissipate after approximately six months, but it's prudent to conduct pH tests and mitigate any potential issues. One preventive measure involves washing the surface of the rocks with a solution of vinegar and water, which helps neutralize alkalinity and creates a more hospitable environment for plants.

Just as with rock selection, careful consideration of plant varieties is crucial for optimal results. Observing naturally occurring rocky habitats can provide valuable insights into the types of plants thriving in such conditions, aiding in the selection of species that complement the rocky theme of the garden. It's essential to choose plants that won't obscure the rocks as they mature, striking a balance between aesthetic appeal and practicality. Several plant varieties have demonstrated success in rockeries, offering a diverse range of colours, textures, and growth habits to suit various preferences.

For tropical regions, a selection of non-native plants suitable for rockeries provides additional options for landscaping diversity. These species, while not native to the area, exhibit adaptability to rocky environments and can thrive alongside indigenous flora. With careful planning and consideration of environmental factors, such as sunlight exposure and soil moisture levels, these non-native plants can contribute to the overall aesthetic appeal and biodiversity of the garden.

Native plant species, on the other hand, offer inherent advantages in terms of adaptation to local climate and soil conditions. They often require less maintenance and are better suited to the ecological context of the region. By incorporating native plants into rockeries, gardeners can promote biodiversity, support local ecosystems, and create landscapes that reflect the natural beauty of the surrounding environment.

Overall, the planting process in rockeries involves a thoughtful approach that integrates knowledge of soil chemistry, plant biology, and environmental factors. By selecting suitable plant varieties and implementing appropriate planting techniques, gardeners can establish vibrant and sustainable rock gardens that thrive in harmony with their surroundings, enriching the aesthetic appeal and ecological value of outdoor spaces.

Stone Steps

Building stone steps in a garden not only enhances the aesthetic appeal of the landscape but also improves accessibility, allowing for easier navigation through uneven terrain. While stone may not always be the most economical option, its versatility and ease of use make it a popular choice for DIY projects. With basic tools and materials, laying stone steps can be accomplished in just a few hours, making it a feasible endeavor for homeowners looking to enhance their outdoor spaces.

Figure 148: Stone step example. Field Outdoor Spaces, CC BY 2.0, via Flickr.

Choosing the right stone is crucial and involves considerations such as budget, size, colour, and texture. Each step must be carefully selected, positioned, and occasionally shaped by hand to ensure a cohesive and visually appealing design. Stone steps typically have a riser height between 150-180mm and treads around 1200x350x30mm, providing a comfortable and safe walking surface.

Incorporating thematic elements into the design can further enhance the beauty and functionality of the stone steps. For example, surrounding the steps with lush greenery and tropical plants like succulents can create a vibrant and inviting atmosphere. Mixing different sizes and shapes of stone adds character and visual interest to the garden, breaking away from the monotony of straight, rectangular designs.

Stone steps can also serve as pathways to hidden areas or features within the garden, adding an element of mystery and discovery. Lining the steps with colourful plants or flowers adds to the intrigue and beauty of the space, enticing visitors to explore further.

Sandstone, while more expensive, offers a luxurious and architectural look, perfect for creating a harmonious and upscale garden design. Stone steps can also lead to various outdoor amenities such as pools or seating areas, enhancing the overall functionality and enjoyment of the outdoor space.

Figure 149: Spiral steps with stonework and sandstone. R3dus-01, CC BY-SA 4.0, via Wikimedia Commons.

Surrounding stone steps with water features like ponds or streams creates a tranquil ambiance, while lighting along the steps adds both functionality and visual appeal, transforming the garden into a magical oasis, especially at night. Greenery like moss can be added to blend the steps seamlessly into the environment, creating a natural and organic feel.

Ultimately, stone steps in a garden not only serve a practical purpose but also contribute to the overall beauty, tranquillity, and functionality of the outdoor space, creating a welcoming and inviting atmosphere for homeowners and visitors alike.

Stone Paths

Designing and installing a stone path in the garden can significantly enhance its visual appeal while adding a timeless charm that makes it appear as though it has been a part of the landscape for decades. Stone pathways offer a unique aesthetic as each piece varies slightly in colour and texture, lending a sense of character and authenticity to the outdoor space. While laying stone is relatively straightforward, the weight of the stones makes them challenging to lift and may require resetting if they become unstable or dip over time.

To lay flagstones, which are large, irregularly shaped stones, one method involves positioning them on a lawn and using a shovel to cut around them. After removing the turf, a 25mm bed of paving sand is laid, and the stones are positioned so that their tops are about 25mm above the ground level. For smaller stones known as steppers or cut stone, the process involves digging out any turf, laying a 25mm bed of sand, and positioning the stones on top, filling the gaps with sand or gravel as needed. Using a timber board and spirit level helps ensure that the stones are laid evenly and securely.

Figure 150: Rock garden with flagstone pathway. Oceanflynn, CC BY-SA 4.0, via Wikimedia Commons.

There are various types of stone paths to choose from, each offering its own set of advantages and considerations. Steppers, for example, are small, irregularly shaped stones that are best laid tightly together with sand, gravel, or soil in between. While they are less stable than flagstones, steppers are typically the least expensive option. Cut stone, on the other hand, is the priciest variety but offers a neat appearance with minimal gaps between stones. This option may require cutting stones to fit with a diamond saw, making it suitable for paths that require steps or precise fitting. Flagstones, characterized by their irregular shape and large size, are laid in a line and offer stability due to their weight. They are spaced approximately 450mm apart in the centre, providing a sturdy and visually appealing pathway through the garden.

In addition to the type of stone chosen, factors such as budget, aesthetics, and intended use should be considered when designing a stone path. Whether opting for the rustic charm of steppers, the precise elegance of cut stone, or the classic appeal of flagstones, a well-designed and properly installed stone path can elevate the beauty and functionality of any garden space, creating a welcoming and visually stunning environment for homeowners and visitors alike.

Stone Walls

Stone walls are versatile elements in landscaping, offering both functional and aesthetic benefits. Here are some common ways stone walls are used:

- **Retaining Walls**: Stone walls are often used to hold back soil on sloped terrain, preventing erosion and creating level areas for gardens, patios, or walkways. They provide structural support while enhancing the visual appeal of the landscape.

- **Garden Borders**: Stone walls can define borders between different areas of the landscape, such as separating flower beds from lawns or delineating outdoor living spaces from natural areas. They add structure and organization to the garden while complementing the overall design.

- **Privacy Barriers**: Taller stone walls can offer privacy by blocking views from neighbouring properties or busy streets. By strategically placing them around outdoor living areas or secluded gardens, they create intimate spaces for relaxation and enjoyment.

- **Terracing**: Stone walls are often used to create terraced gardens on steep slopes, allowing for multiple levels of planting beds or seating areas. This not only maximizes usable space but also adds visual interest to the landscape.

- **Water Features**: Stone walls can be incorporated into water features such as fountains, ponds, or waterfalls, adding texture and natural beauty. They can serve as retaining structures for water bodies or as decorative elements around them, enhancing the overall aesthetic appeal.

- **Architectural Features**: Stone walls can be used to define architectural features such as entryways, gateways, or focal points in the landscape. They provide a sense of permanence and craftsmanship, adding character and charm to outdoor spaces.

- **Seating Walls**: Low stone walls can double as seating areas, offering a place for relaxation or socializing. When integrated into patios or outdoor entertainment areas, they provide additional seating options while blending seamlessly with the surrounding landscape.

- **Decorative Accents**: Stone walls can serve as decorative accents in the landscape, adding texture, colour, and visual interest. They can be used to frame garden beds, highlight specimen plants, or create artistic patterns and designs.

Overall, stone walls play a crucial role in landscaping by providing structural support, defining spaces, enhancing privacy, and adding aesthetic appeal to outdoor environments. Their versatility and durability make them a popular choice for both residential and commercial landscaping projects.

Undulating Fieldstone Wall: An undulating stone wall offers both functionality and style, serving as a barrier while adding visual interest to the landscape. Fieldstone, whether dry stacked or held together with mortar, provides a natural and timeless material for garden walls. Its rustic charm creates a classic backdrop for gardens, blending seamlessly with the surrounding environment.

Figure 151: Fieldstone terraced yard. CLK Hatcher, CC BY-SA 2.0, via Wikimedia Commons.

Curved Flagstone Wall: Breaking away from the traditional straight lines, a gracefully curved flagstone wall introduces elegance to the backyard patio. This circular wall not only adds a sense of enclosure and privacy but also incorporates a small fountain, enhancing the aesthetic appeal. Quartz, granite, and limestone are popular choices for flagstone, offering durability and versatility in design.

Low Stone Wall: A low stone wall offers a subtle yet effective barrier along property lines without obstructing views. Using stones of different shapes and sizes adds texture and visual interest to the landscape design. Additionally, topping the wall with pots and containers allows for further customization and functionality.

Stacked-Stone Entryway: In this entryway garden, a stacked-stone wall provides structural support for a garden bed, showcasing a blend of flat stones for a secure fit. Mixing masonry types, such as light stone with red brick, adds contrast and character to the landscape, creating a visually appealing focal point.

Dry-Stacked Stone Wall: The natural appearance of a dry-stacked stone wall makes it an attractive option for landscaping. The spaces between stones allow for drainage, reducing pressure on the retaining wall. Moreover, the design enables the creation of planting pockets for small rock garden plants, enhancing the wall's functionality.

Mortared Stone Wall: Adaptable to various landscapes, a mortared stone wall offers strength and stability, particularly for terraced slopes. Ideal for garden walls, stone provides a durable and aesthetically pleasing building material, blending seamlessly with the natural surroundings.

Varied-Size Stone Wall: Combining large and small stones, a lattice-topped stone wall showcases the beauty and diversity of natural stone. Mortaring stones together creates a textural wall perfect for cottage or country gardens. Additionally, the bamboo lattice trellis offers plants a place to climb, adding another dimension to the landscape.

Stone Block Wall: Incorporating large stacked stones, an informal stone block wall serves as both a functional boundary and a piece of landscape art. This stone structure separates the lawn from the garden, adding character and visual appeal to the front yard.

Building a Dry Stone Wall

Low to mid-height stone retaining walls serve multiple purposes in landscaping, offering both practical and aesthetic benefits. They can be utilized to edge driveways, lawns, vegetable patches, or to create structured spaces within a garden, effectively delineating different areas while adding visual interest. One of the most popular construction techniques for these walls is the "dry stack" method, favoured by homeowners looking for a DIY project. This technique involves stacking stones without the use of mortar, relying on the careful arrangement of stones to create a stable structure.

One of the key advantages of dry stack retaining walls is their mortarless construction, which naturally facilitates drainage. The gaps between the stones allow water to seep through, aiding in the garden's natural drainage system. This feature not only prevents water build-up behind the wall but also mitigates the risk of damage, even during heavy rainfall. Additionally, the absence of mortar simplifies the construction process and eliminates the need for specialized masonry skills.

Constructing a stone retaining wall typically requires careful planning and preparation. Before starting the project, it's essential to ensure compliance with any local regulations and to check for buried pipes or cables in the area. Accurately measuring the dimensions of the wall and calculating the required materials is crucial to avoid running out of supplies midway through the project. Some homeowners find it helpful to use a garden hose to visualize the layout and shape of the wall before beginning construction.

Figure 152: Dry stone fences in the Yorkshire Dales, England. Peter K Burian, CC BY-SA 4.0, via Wikimedia Commons.

Selecting the right stones is paramount to the success of the project. Stackable stones with flat sides are recommended for ease of construction, while heavier stones provide greater stability over time. It's advisable to procure materials from a reputable supplier or showroom, opting for delivery to minimize lifting and transportation efforts. In terms of tools, basic equipment such as tape measures, spirit levels, shovels, and wheelbarrows are essential for the construction process.

Once the materials and tools are ready, the construction process begins with marking the outline of the wall and establishing the desired height and levels using stakes and strings. Digging out the footing for the first step and pouring concrete to create a solid foundation is a critical step in ensuring the stability and longevity of the wall. Careful attention to detail during each stage of construction is essential to achieve a level, structurally sound retaining wall that enhances the beauty and functionality of the landscape.

Building a stone wall requires careful planning and preparation to ensure a sturdy and visually appealing structure. The first step in the process involves preparing the foundation. This begins by establishing the line of the wall using pegs and a stringline, followed by cutting back the slope at the base. A trench is then dug, measuring 200mm deep and 600mm wide, which will serve as the foundation for the wall. It's essential to separate the topsoil and subsoil nearby for easy backfilling later. The trench is filled with a 100mm bed of 20mm aggregate to provide stability and drainage.

Once the foundation is prepared, construction of the wall can commence. Large, square or rectangular stones are chosen for the bottom layer, providing a solid base for the structure. Care is taken to place these stones flush with the proposed face of the wall, angling them slightly forward to facilitate water runoff. As the wall is built, any gaps behind it are backfilled with rubble or scree to provide additional support.

Adjusting the stringline to the height of the second stone layer ensures that the wall remains straight and level. Successive layers of stones are then added, with joints staggered and angled slightly backward for stability. Stones may need to be shaped or cut to fit using a stone hammer and wedges. Care is taken to ensure each stone is firm and stable before proceeding to the next layer.

Figure 153: Wedging gaps.

As construction progresses, the top layer of stones is carefully selected to fit together snugly, providing a smooth finish. If desired, capstones can be fixed into a bed of premixed mortar on the penultimate course for added security. Finally, the area behind the wall is backfilled with gravel or other suitable materials up to the level of the capstones to complete the construction.

In subsequent steps, additional courses of stones are laid, with wider courses than the previous ones to provide stability. Geotextile landscape fabric is tucked in behind the stones to prevent soil erosion, and backfilling is done after each course to ensure the wall remains stable. Chinking stones or wedge stones are driven into the face of the wall to fill any gaps or secure loose rocks, and capstones are laid to bring the wall to the desired height. Mortar may be used to secure small capstones in place permanently, and the area is backfilled and topped with topsoil to finish the construction process. Throughout the process, attention to detail and adherence to proper techniques are essential to ensure the durability and longevity of the stone wall.

Dry-Stone Raised Bed

Building a raised bed involves several steps to create a sturdy structure that provides adequate drainage and support for plants. The first step is to excavate the base trench, which is marked using a rope or line-marking aerosol paint to outline the bed's shape. A square shovel is then used to dig a trench about 200mm deep and 250mm wide. The base of the trench is levelled, and 100mm of gravel is added to ensure good drainage.

Next, landscape fabric is rolled out along the trench, with one edge kept in the centre and weighted down with bricks to hold it in place. The base course of stones is installed over the edge of the fabric and gravel, and each stone is firmly pressed down using a rubber mallet, checking for level from stone to stone.

As the wall is built, centre stones are laid, offsetting the joints between the courses to give the wall greater strength. The landscape fabric is lifted tight against the back of the stones as they are installed, and topsoil is backfilled against the wall up to the top of the last installed course to stabilize the stones.

In the next step, capstones are laid along the top of the wall, roughly checking for level. Three or four stones are removed at a time, and a bed of mortar is spread both under and over the fabric using a trowel. The capstones are then repositioned and tapped with a mallet until they are level.

Once the capstones are in place, mortar is packed into the joints on the top and front of the capstones using a small pointing and brickie's trowel. The joints are overfilled, and the mortar is rounded over with the pointing trowel for a neat finish. Excess mortar is brushed away, and the stone surface is sponged to prevent staining. The mortar is left to set overnight.

Finally, the raised bed is ready for planting. Plants are arranged in the bed, with enough room between each for their mature size. Holes are dug twice as wide as the rootballs using a spade, and the plants are positioned and backfilled with topsoil, gently firming them in. A 100mm layer of mulch is added, and the entire raised bed is given a deep watering to settle the soil and encourage plant growth.

Laying a Stepping Stone Path

Creating a walkway with individual stepping stones offers both practicality and a touch of timeless cottage charm to a garden. The process requires basic tools such as a solid rubber mallet, a spade, a trowel, and some sand to ensure the stones remain stable and don't sink into the ground. Depending on the weight of the stones or pavers, you may need assistance to lift them into place, especially if they are particularly heavy.

To achieve a polished look, it's essential to fill in any gaps around the edges of the stones with a mixture of sand and soil. This not only enhances the appearance of the path but also helps to stabilize the stones and prevent them from shifting over time. Once filled, the area can be gently patted down to ensure the mixture settles evenly.

In areas where the path intersects with the lawn, it's common for bare patches to form around the stepping stones. To remedy this, grass seed can be sown or runners can be planted to encourage new growth. It's important to water these areas with a fine rose attachment until the new grass becomes established, ensuring that they blend seamlessly with the surrounding lawn.

The process of laying stepping stones begins with cutting the turf around the edges of each stone using a serrated knife. Care must be taken to ensure that the cuts are precise and allow enough space for the stones to sit comfortably without overlapping. Once the turf is cut, it can be carefully lifted out of the hole, revealing the underlying soil.

With the turf removed, the next step involves digging holes that are three to five centimetres deeper than the thickness of the stones. This provides enough space to accommodate the stones while ensuring they sit flush with the ground once installed. Once the holes are dug, a layer of sand, approximately five to eight centimetres thick, is spread evenly within each hole and levelled out.

After preparing the holes, each stone is carefully placed back into its designated spot and secured in place using the rubber mallet. The stones are driven into the sand, wedging them securely so that they are level with the ground surface. This process is repeated for each stepping stone until the entire path is complete, providing a charming and functional addition to the garden landscape.

Before laying the pavers, it's essential to set the stride width to ensure comfortable and balanced walking. A few pavers are initially laid spaced about 100 to 200mm apart, and the spacing is adjusted as needed to accommodate the average stride width. Each step should ideally land in the centre of each paver, promoting a natural and ergonomic walking experience.

The process of laying the pavers begins with marking the spacing, setting a laying line using taut string lines, and mixing the mortar. The mortar mixture, comprising fine beach sand, cement, water, and a plasticizer, is spread at each paver location to create a stable base. The pavers are then carefully lifted into position, aligned with the string line, and levelled using a spirit level and rubber mallet.

Once the pavers are set in place, the mortar is allowed to cure for 24 hours before crushed rock or pebbles are barrowed in and spread around the pavers. A rake and square-nosed shovel are used to evenly distribute the crushed rock, ensuring a finished height approximately 10mm below the top of the pavers. This final step not only enhances the aesthetic appeal of the pathway but also adds stability and support to the stepping stones, creating a functional and visually pleasing addition to the landscape.

Building a Feature Rockery

Incorporating plants among rocks in a garden landscape offers several advantages, making it a popular choice among gardeners. Firstly, rocks, along with the mosses and lichens that often grow on their surfaces, introduce an array of interesting textures and colours, adding visual appeal to the garden. They create a dynamic contrast against the greenery of plants, enhancing the overall aesthetic. Secondly, rocks can serve as visual dividers, effectively separating different pockets of plants and creating distinct areas within the garden, adding structure and organization to the landscape design.

Moreover, rocks play a crucial role in soil erosion control, especially on sloping ground. By strategically placing rocks, gardeners can prevent soil from washing away from plant roots during heavy rains, ensuring the stability of the garden beds. Additionally, rocks help suppress weed growth among the plants, reducing the need for frequent weeding and maintenance. They create a physical barrier that inhibits weed growth, contributing to a cleaner and more manageable garden space.

Furthermore, rocks provide insulation for plant roots, creating a conducive environment for plant growth. The shade and moisture provided by rocks create microclimates that are beneficial for certain plant species, allowing them to thrive even in challenging conditions. As a result, incorporating rocks into garden landscapes can support a diverse range of plant life, enhancing biodiversity and ecological resilience.

When it comes to choosing the location for building a rockery, slopes are the most obvious choice, as rocks can serve the dual purpose of retaining soil and creating a naturalistic rock outcrop. However, rockeries can also be constructed on flat ground to provide visual relief and add interest to the garden. Careful consideration is required to seamlessly integrate the rockery into the existing landscape, ensuring it complements the overall design aesthetic.

Selecting the right type of rock is essential for the success of a rockery project. Common options include basalt, sandstone, and granite, each offering unique characteristics and aesthetic qualities. Natural-shaped rocks are preferred by most gardeners for their authenticity, but cut blocks can also be used to create interesting effects. It's important to consider factors such as cost, size, and availability when choosing rocks for the project.

Moving rocks, especially large and heavy ones, requires careful planning and the right tools. Hiring machinery like loaders or tractors can expedite the process, but caution must be exercised to avoid damaging the rocks' surfaces. Alternatively, medium to large rocks can be moved by hand with the assistance of crowbars, ramps, wheelbarrows, or hand trolleys. Proper handling techniques are essential to ensure the safety of both the workers and the rocks.

In arranging rocks for a rockery, attention to detail is crucial to achieve a naturalistic and visually pleasing result. Rocks should be securely anchored and positioned to imitate natural contours and formations. Start building from the bottom of the slope, ensuring that each rock is firmly embedded in the ground to prevent future instability. Careful consideration of rock placement, alignment, and orientation is essential to create a harmonious and aesthetically pleasing rockery that seamlessly blends into the surrounding landscape.

Building a Gabion Wall

Gabions, wire mesh containers filled with rock, have become increasingly popular in landscaping due to their versatility and effectiveness in various applications. These structures serve as excellent solutions for constructing retaining walls, garden beds, rock wall features, seating areas, and numerous other landscape elements. The concept behind gabions is simple yet ingenious: the weight of the internal fill, typically rock or stone, provides the necessary strength to withstand pressures from earth retention, making them highly durable and reliable.

There are two primary types of gabions: woven wire baskets and weld mesh cages. Woven wire baskets are commonly used in civil projects due to their cost advantages, while weld mesh cages offer superior aesthetics and stronger panels, making them more suitable for architectural projects. Regardless of the type, gabions have proven to be cost-effective for projects of various scales, from small residential gardens to large infrastructure developments.

Gabion walls, in particular, have gained popularity as fencing solutions in both residential and commercial landscapes. These walls consist of a series of wire cages filled with rocks, providing a solid and visually appealing barrier. The wire cages play a crucial role in retaining the shape and structural integrity of the gabion wall. Therefore, choosing superior welded steel wire panels for constructing gabion baskets or mesh cages is essential for ensuring durability and longevity.

Figure 154: Gabion support wall. Globetrotter19, CC BY-SA 4.0, via Wikimedia Commons.

The versatility of gabion walls extends beyond mere functionality; they offer numerous options for character landscaping. For instance, gabion walls can be used to create impressive statements flanking property driveways or defining banks and separating sections of gardens, even on a small scale in backyard landscapes. Moreover, gabion walls make excellent additions to patio areas, serving as attractive surrounds for seating arrangements or as low garden borders. They can also be integrated into water features or used as the foundation for rock-solid letterboxes, showcasing the endless potential uses of gabion walls in landscaping design.

In addition to their aesthetic appeal and functional benefits, gabion walls are also effective in erosion control and are commonly used in major infrastructure projects such as railways, bridges, and highways. Their ability to withstand environmental pressures while maintaining their structural integrity makes them a preferred choice for various landscape and civil engineering applications. Overall, gabions offer a durable, cost-effective, and visually appealing solution for a wide range of landscaping projects, making them increasingly popular among homeowners, landscapers, and architects alike.

Gabions offer several key advantages that make them highly desirable for a wide range of landscaping and civil engineering projects. Firstly, gabions have a long life cycle when properly constructed and maintained. It's important to note that galvanized gabions are not recommended for longevity, nor are those imported from Asia, as they may not conform to Australian standards and may not last as long as locally sourced materials. However, when constructed using high-quality materials and according to established standards, gabions can provide a durable solution that withstands the test of time.

One of the most appealing aspects of gabions is that they require minimal maintenance once installed. Unlike many other types of structures, gabions do not need regular upkeep or repairs, making them a convenient and cost-effective choice for landscaping projects. This low maintenance requirement contributes to their overall longevity and cost-effectiveness over time.

Another significant advantage of gabions is their ability to provide free drainage. The open mesh design of gabion structures allows water to pass through the structure rather than building up behind it. This feature is particularly beneficial in areas prone to heavy rainfall or soil erosion, as it helps to prevent water damage and maintain the stability of the surrounding landscape.

From an aesthetic standpoint, gabions offer architectural appeal, particularly when used to create dry stack stone walls. These walls have a natural and rustic appearance that can enhance the visual appeal of any outdoor space. Whether used for retaining walls, garden borders, or decorative features, gabions can add a touch of elegance and sophistication to landscaping designs.

Additionally, gabions feature a modular design that makes them easy to construct and customize to suit specific project requirements. The individual wire mesh baskets or cages can be assembled and filled with rock or stone on-site, allowing for flexibility in design and construction. This modular approach also simplifies transportation and installation, making gabions a practical choice for a variety of applications.

Furthermore, gabions require limited footings compared to traditional masonry walls or concrete structures. The weight of the gabion structure, combined with its design and construction, helps to distribute the load evenly, reducing the need for extensive foundation work. This not only saves time and labour during installation but also minimizes the environmental impact of the project.

Lastly, gabions are resistant to graffiti and vandalism, making them a practical choice for public spaces or high-traffic areas. The sturdy construction and durable materials used in gabions make them difficult to damage or deface, providing added security and peace of mind for property owners and developers.

The key advantages of using gabions include their long life cycle, minimal maintenance requirements, free drainage capability, architectural appeal, modular design, limited footings required, and resistance to graffiti and vandalism. These qualities make gabions an attractive and practical choice for a wide range of landscaping and civil engineering projects, offering durability, versatility, and aesthetic appeal in equal measure.

Gabion foundations play a crucial role in ensuring the stability and longevity of gabion walls, particularly in landscaping and civil engineering projects. The process of establishing a solid foundation for gabion walls involves several key steps to ensure that the structure can withstand the forces exerted upon it and remain structurally sound over time.

The first step in constructing gabion foundations involves the removal of topsoil and soft subsoils from the area where the wall will be built. This helps to create a stable base for the wall and prevents potential issues such as settlement or erosion. The thickness of the road base required for the foundation depends on the specific subsoil conditions of the site. In general, topsoil, organic material, and softer subsoils are removed and replaced with compacted hardfill or road base.

Foundation testing is often conducted to assess the subsoil bearing strength and determine the requirements for the foundation. While small, non-engineered retaining walls may not require extensive testing, it's essential to consult with a local civil engineer or construction professional if there are any uncertainties regarding the foundation's requirements.

Proper compaction of the road base is essential to ensure the stability and longevity of the gabion wall. Using a plate compactor to compact the road base helps to eliminate future consolidation and settlement, reducing the risk of structural issues over time. Some contractors may also opt to place a thin layer of sand over the road base for final foundation leveling, although this practice is not suitable for sites with high groundwater flows.

Stepped foundations are commonly used for gabion walls built on sloping sites. This technique involves creating stepped levels in the foundation to accommodate the slope of the terrain and ensure that the wall remains level and stable. Concrete ledges may be cast into the bedrock to provide additional support and stability for the gabion baskets.

In some cases, double-width base gabions may be used to improve wall stability and reduce the bearing load on the subsoil. By spreading the load over a larger area, double-width base gabions allow for the construction of gabion walls on weaker subsoils without the need for expensive or extensive foundations.

Overall, gabion foundations are essential for ensuring the stability, durability, and longevity of gabion walls in various landscaping and civil engineering applications. By following proper construction techniques and consulting with experts as needed, gabion walls can be built to withstand the test of time and provide effective erosion control, retaining wall solutions, and architectural features for both residential and commercial projects.

Step 1 of building gabion walls involves preparing the base level, a critical step to ensure the stability and longevity of the structure. Typically, compact road base is used for this purpose, as it provides a solid foundation for various types of gabion walls, including retaining walls, fences, and other features. However, in locations with high water flow or specific soil conditions, additional preparation may be necessary to ensure optimal performance and durability. The choice of road base ensures that the foundation is sturdy enough to support the weight of the gabion structure and withstand external forces such as erosion and settlement.

In Step 2, the assembly and installation of the gabion cages take place. This step is crucial for ensuring that the gabion walls remain structurally sound and visually appealing. It begins with assembling the gabion cages, ensuring that each component is installed correctly and securely. The use of bracing wire helps to reinforce the structure and maintain its shape during installation. Following a string line is essential to ensure that the gabion walls remain perfectly straight and aligned throughout the construction process. This meticulous attention to detail not only enhances the structural integrity of the walls but also contributes to the aesthetic appeal of the finished project.

During assembly and installation, each gabion cage is linked together to create a single, cohesive structure. This interconnected design helps to distribute the weight evenly across the entire length of the wall, minimizing the risk of sagging or instability. By linking the gabion cages together, the individual components work together to form a unified barrier that provides effective erosion control, retention, or delineation of spaces within the landscape. Additionally, this integrated approach simplifies the construction process and ensures that the gabion walls meet the desired specifications and requirements of the project.

Overall, Steps 1 and 2 of building gabion walls are essential for laying the groundwork and establishing the structural framework necessary for a successful construction project. By carefully preparing the base level and meticulously assembling and installing the gabion cages, builders can create sturdy, durable, and visually appealing walls that enhance the functionality and aesthetics of any landscape. Whether used for retaining soil, defining boundaries, or creating architectural features, gabion walls offer versatility, durability, and aesthetic appeal in a wide range of landscaping applications.

The 2:1 ratio serves as a guideline for the construction of free-standing or retaining walls, helping to ensure structural stability and prevent collapse. This ratio specifies that the height of the wall should not exceed twice its base width. Adhering to this ratio helps distribute the weight of the wall evenly and reduces the risk of structural failure, particularly in situations where the ground may be uneven or subject to external pressures. By limiting the height of the wall relative to its base width, builders can create walls that are both visually appealing and structurally sound.

Gabion retaining walls, especially those with flat ground behind them or slopes of less than 5 degrees, should also adhere to the 2:1 ratio to maintain stability and prevent potential issues such as bulging or collapse. These walls rely on the weight of the gabion baskets and the friction between the stones to retain soil and withstand external forces. Exceeding the 2:1 ratio in such cases could compromise the integrity of the wall and increase the risk of failure, particularly in areas with poor soil conditions or high water pressure.

For non-retaining walls that fall below the 2:1 ratio, internal supports may be necessary to prevent collapse. These supports help reinforce the structure and provide additional stability, particularly in situations where the wall may be subject to lateral pressure or other external forces. By incorporating internal supports, builders can ensure that the wall remains structurally sound and resistant to deformation or failure over time.

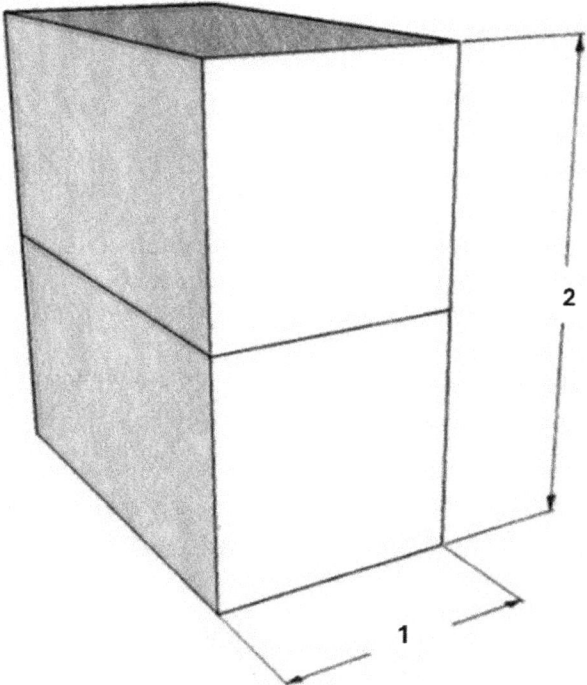

Figure 155: Non retaining walls less than the 2:1 ratio, will need internal supports to prevent collapse.

In cases where retaining walls bear additional loads, such as driveways, buildings, or elevated banks, extra thickness may be required to accommodate the increased weight and pressure. Additionally, an engineer's design may be necessary to ensure that the wall can safely support these additional loads without compromising its integrity or stability. By working with an engineer and adhering to established design principles, builders can create retaining walls that meet the specific requirements of their project while maintaining safety and structural integrity.

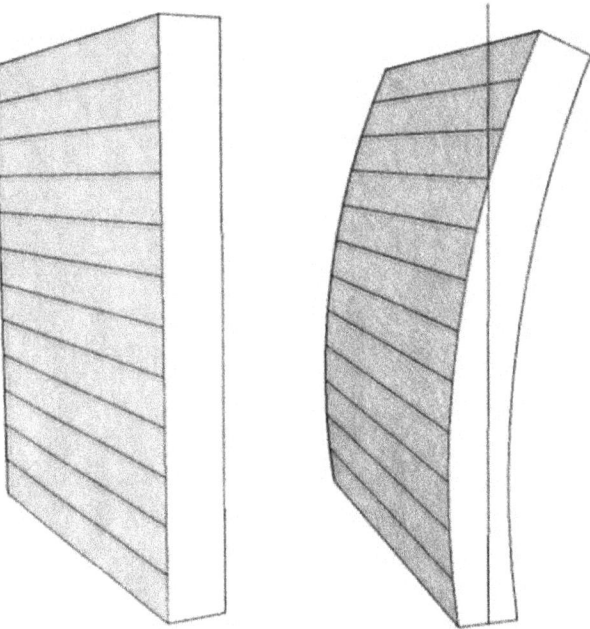

Figure 156: Gabion support posts must extend to at least 1.5 x Depth from the top of the gabion basket.

Gabion support posts play a crucial role in ensuring the stability of gabion walls, particularly in taller or load-bearing structures. These posts must extend to a sufficient depth from the top of the gabion basket to provide adequate support and prevent sagging or collapse. Additionally, the support posts need to be strong enough to withstand the weight of the gabion wall without snapping or bending under pressure. By properly sizing and reinforcing the support posts, builders can create gabion walls that are durable, stable, and resistant to deformation or failure over time.

Using geo-fabric in the construction of gabion walls serves multiple purposes, contributing to their longevity and effectiveness as retaining structures. By installing a quality non-woven geo-fabric material under and behind the gabion baskets, builders can enhance the wall's durability and performance over time. This fabric allows water to flow through the gabion structure, preventing pressure build-up behind the wall while still containing soil particles. This is crucial for maintaining the stability of the wall and preventing erosion, as it ensures proper drainage without compromising the integrity of the structure. Additionally, the geo-fabric helps to prevent the migration of soil or fines through the gabion baskets, preserving the aesthetic appeal and functionality of the wall.

Selecting the right type of rock for gabion walls is essential for ensuring their longevity and stability. It's recommended to choose stones such as granite, basalt, or bluestone in sizes ranging from 100 to 200mm. These types of stones are known for their durability and resistance to degradation over time, making them ideal for use in gabion construction. Their angular shapes also facilitate tight stacking within the gabion baskets, ensuring a secure and stable structure. Furthermore, these stones are readily available through landscape yards and are relatively low-cost compared to decorative stone options, making them a practical choice for building gabion walls.

Taking the time to properly fill gabion baskets with stone is crucial for achieving a structurally sound and aesthetically pleasing result. While gabions are relatively easy to assemble and set up, it's important not to rush the process of filling them with stone. Builders should carefully check the facing panels regularly to ensure they are straight and even, as this will contribute to the overall appearance and stability of the wall. Packing the stone tightly without leaving gaps is essential for maximizing the strength and durability of the gabion structure. By following a sweeping sequence and spreading stone evenly from one cage to the next, builders can ensure that the gabions remain even and aligned, which is particularly important when installing lids or finishing touches. Taking the time to fill gabion baskets properly will result in a well-constructed wall that is both functional and visually appealing.

Stone around the Pool

Pools have evolved from mere swimming spots to central features of outdoor entertainment areas, with the surrounding paving and landscaping now holding equal importance to the pool itself. When selecting paving materials for poolside areas, there is a vast array of options available, including natural and engineered products. While aesthetics play a significant role in the selection process, it is crucial to also consider the fitness for purpose of the chosen product to maintain the desired appearance and functionality. To aid in this decision-making process, it is advisable to review the five S's: stain resistance, slip resistance, salt tolerance, strength, and stability.

Stain resistance is paramount when it comes to poolside paving, as these areas are susceptible to a wide range of staining agents, including spilled drinks, oil from barbecues, and tannin from fallen leaves. Pavers with low absorption capacity are preferable, as stains are less conspicuous on materials with a uniform appearance. High-density limestone, granite, slate, and bluestone are typically effective at resisting stains. Additionally, the judicious use of an oil repellent impregnating sealer in high-risk areas can help preserve the appearance of the stone.

Safety is a primary concern around pools, making slip resistance a critical factor in paving selection. Various surface textures, such as sawn, grit blasted, flamed (exfoliated), and split face, can provide slip resistance and enhance safety. While rough texture surfaces may trap grime, regular cleaning with a hose and stiff-bristled broom can mitigate this issue.

Given the aggressive environment of pool surrounds, salt tolerance is essential for paving materials. Resistance to salt attack can be determined by specific standards, and materials with excellent salt resistance include granite, high-density limestone, bluestone, and certain types of slate and sandstone. Textured finishes can help conceal minor surface decay, but it's crucial to avoid sealers that may trap salt within the stone, leading to accelerated decay.

Strength is vital for paving to withstand service loads, both in dry and wet conditions. Sedimentary stone types like sandstone and limestone can lose strength when wet, highlighting the importance of choosing materials with adequate strength characteristics. Doubling the thickness of the paver or using square paving units can increase breaking load and reduce the risk of breakage.

Figure 157: Stones around pool. CC0 Public Domain, via PxHere.

Lastly, stability is crucial to prevent warping and decay caused by expansion and contraction of minerals within the stone due to frequent wetting and drying. Long, thin pavers and those with high clay content or expansive minerals are at greater risk of warping. Regular expansion joints, rapid-setting adhesives, and square paving units can help improve dimensional stability and reduce the risk of warping, ensuring the longevity of poolside paving.

Cutting Rocks for Landscaping

Cutting rocks can significantly enhance the versatility of your landscaping endeavours, offering the choice between clean, straight lines for borders or a more natural, rugged appearance. This flexibility allows for precise placement of multi-coloured rocks, enabling you to achieve your desired colour scheme. Rock cutting becomes particularly invaluable when constructing rock steps and walls, as it facilitates the creation of both straight and curved structures.

Before embarking on rock cutting, it's essential to prioritize safety by adjusting your respirator and goggles to ensure proper fitting and protection. Cutting rocks with a saw generates a considerable amount of dust, making respiratory and eye protection imperative.

Determining the direction of the grain in your rock piece is crucial for successful cutting. The grain refers to the lines visible within the rock. Conducting two test cuts—one against the grain and another with the grain—allows you to assess the saw's ability, blade effectiveness, and the reaction of your specific rock type. While cutting against the grain may be easier, some rocks may fall apart prematurely due to vibrations when cut with the grain. Most rocks can be cut using a standard circular saw with a masonry blade, but the ease of operation depends on the rock type. For instance, limestone is softer and more manageable to cut compared to granite.

When cutting rocks, it's essential to stop before the blade penetrates entirely. Typically, rocks can be cut less than 1 inch deep, after which tapping the backside with a hammer breaks them the rest of the way. This tapping process along the backside of the cut allows the rock to break in line with the saw cut. If the break deviates from the saw cut, adjusting the depth of the cut and repeating the process may be necessary.

After cutting, any uneven portions of the rock can be chipped away using a hammer. Some rocks can even be entirely cut using the hammer alone. By tapping the rock along the desired breaking line, you can gradually chip away uneven sections, following the natural contours of the rock. With experience, you'll develop a sense of the breaking characteristics unique to the type of rock you're working with, allowing for more precise and efficient cutting over time.

Cutting stone for a wall requires careful preparation and the right tools. Before beginning the cutting process, ensure you have all the necessary supplies on hand. You'll need a chisel and an electric grinder equipped with a diamond cutting blade. If your project is small, renting the grinder may be a cost-effective option. Additionally, a stone mason's hammer is essential for shaping the stone. Safety gear is paramount, so make sure to wear protective goggles, a full face shield, and hearing protection to prevent injuries.

Once you've gathered your supplies, measure the dimensions of the stone you need. Whether you're aiming for uniform sizes or specific dimensions to fit into particular spaces in the wall, accurate measurements are crucial. Use a measuring tape to determine the required dimensions before proceeding with the cutting process.

Next, mark the stone where you intend to make your cuts. This ensures precision and helps maintain consistency in the size and shape of the stones for your wall.

To start cutting, focus on the "face side" of the stone—the side that will be outward-facing on the wall. Using a chisel and sledgehammer, create a groove along the marked line. The chisel allows for a cleaner break than the grinder wheel, resulting in a smoother finish. Work systematically along the marked line, making small marks about an inch apart with the chisel and hammer. Continue until you've formed a groove along the entire length of the face side.

Before proceeding further, don protective gear, including a face mask and hearing protection, as you'll be working with an electric grinder for the next steps. Rotate the stone so that one of the other sides is facing upward, and use the grinder to cut a straight line across it. Repeat this process for each side of the stone other than the face side until you've created a groove on each side.

Finally, use the chisel to finalize the cuts. Starting with the face side, deliver three to four firm blows with the hammer along the groove to break the stone. Rotate to the next face and repeat the process until the stone breaks along the marked line. Continue this method for each side of the stone until you've achieved the desired shape and size. While the process may be time-consuming, patience and precision will yield satisfactory results for your stone wall project.

Laying Stone Pavers

Installing pavers can indeed be a complex task, and navigating the plethora of opinions on the "correct" or "best" method can be overwhelming. To ensure a successful outcome for your landscaping project, it's essential to consider various factors and seek advice from experienced professionals in the industry. Cutting corners to save costs in the short term may lead to significant maintenance issues or expensive repairs down the line.

When it comes to laying natural stone pavers, several methods are commonly used, each with its own set of advantages and considerations. The first method involves laying a concrete slab as a base, typically 50-60mm thick [80]. It's crucial to allow sufficient time for the concrete to cure before proceeding with the installation of the pavers. Waterproofing the concrete surface is also recommended to prevent issues such as efflorescence, which can mar the appearance of the pavers over time. Flexible glue is used to adhere the pavers to the concrete slab, and pre-sealing highly textured surfaces helps facilitate the grouting process.

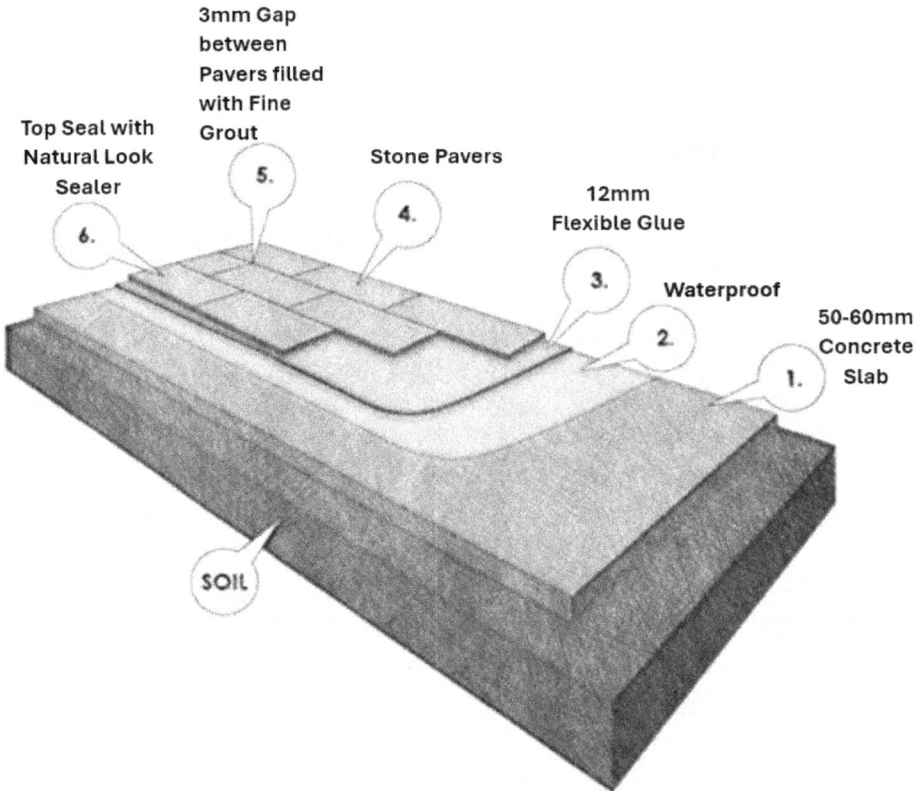

Figure 158: Laying pavers, method 1.

Alternatively, the second method offers a more cost-effective solution by using compacted road base and a sand-cement screed. This method reduces the cost per square meter compared to a concrete slab but still provides a strong and stable base for the pavers. After laying the road base and screed, the pavers are glued directly to the substrate, offering a quality installation at a lower cost [80].

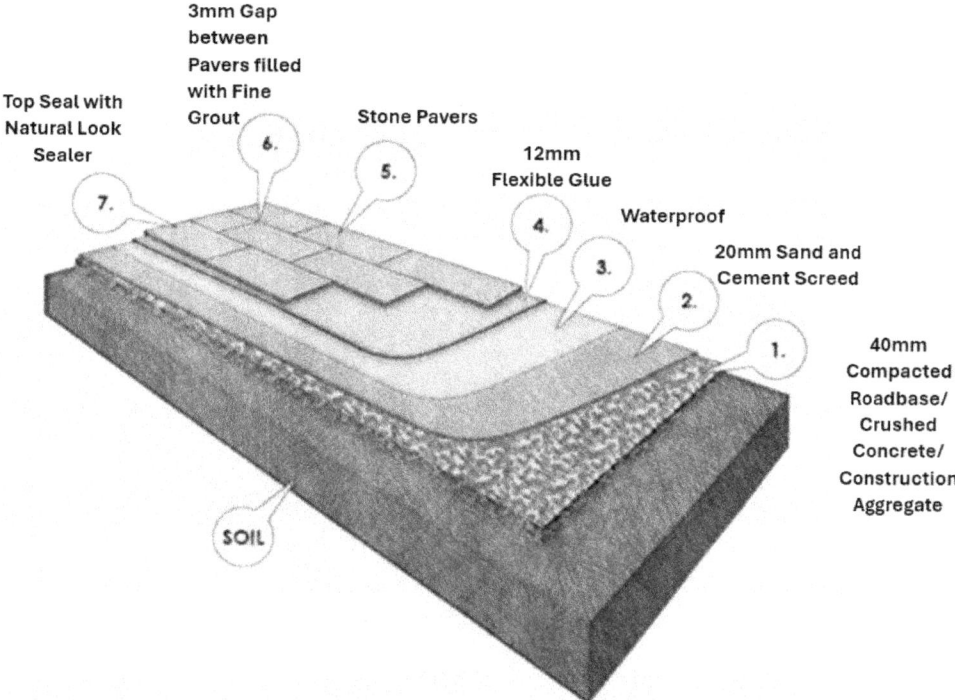

Figure 159: Laying pavers, method 2.

The third method, known as the "wet-bed" approach, is another cost-effective option widely adopted in the industry. Similar to the second method, it involves laying a base of compacted road base followed by a layer of sand and cement. This flexible surface allows for easy manoeuvring and adjustment of the pavers during installation. Once the pavers are in place and grouted, the final step is to apply a sealer to protect and enhance their appearance [80].

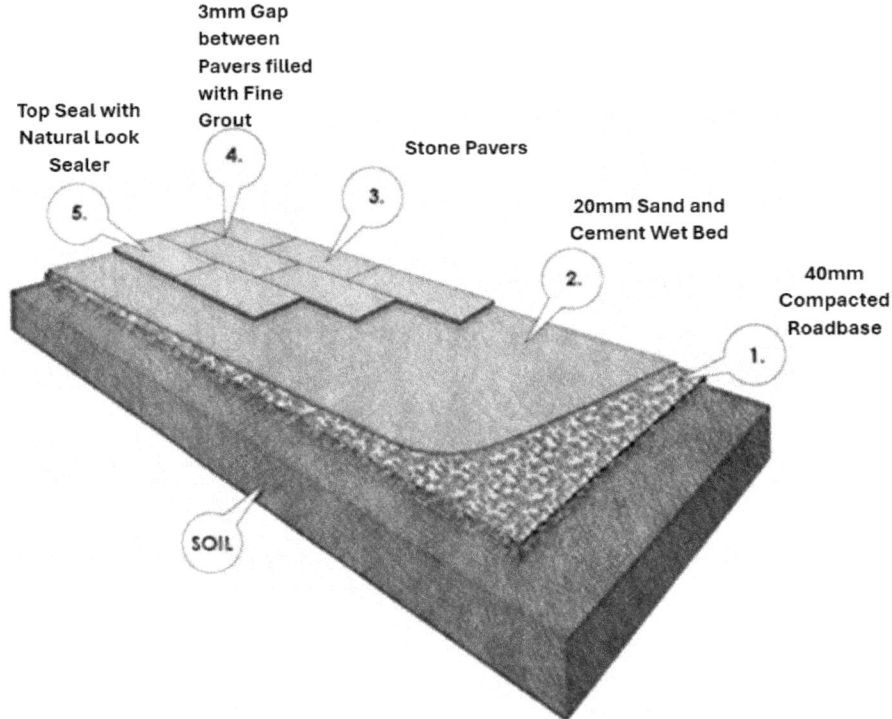

Figure 160: Laying pavers, method 3.

Choosing the right method for installing stone pavers depends on various factors, including budget, project requirements, and personal preferences. Regardless of the method chosen, attention to detail and proper execution are crucial for achieving a professional-looking result that will stand the test of time. By following industry best practices and using quality materials, you can create a stunning outdoor space to enjoy with family and friends for years to come [80].

The process of laying stone pavers involves several crucial steps to ensure a successful installation. Beginning with the delivery, stone pavers are typically transported to the site using specialized equipment such as an all-terrain forklift or crane truck. The driver assesses potential risks and determines the safest location for pallet placement, although the customer's instructions may also be considered. It's essential to inspect the product upon delivery for any discrepancies or defects, reporting them promptly to avoid issues during installation.

Handling and storing the stone pavers require careful attention to prevent damage. Each paver comes with a protective layer between them, and these sheets should be utilized during restacking to avoid surface damage. It's important to note that stacking the pavers in a criss-cross formation should be avoided as it can cause permanent surface variations. Additionally, extended storage may lead to shadowing and surface variations due to weathering, which are not the responsibility of the manufacturer.

Accepting a certain level of deviation in colour and surface finish is crucial when working with natural stone pavers. Minor marks and chipping are considered acceptable unless they significantly affect the structural integrity or appearance of the pavers. Therefore, it's advisable to inspect the products thoroughly before installation to ensure they meet expectations.

Proper foundation preparation is key to a durable and long-lasting installation. Stone pavers should be installed on a foundation of concrete or compacted crushed rock, with the thickness varying based on the intended use of the area. Attention should be paid to slope requirements to facilitate rainwater runoff and prevent water accumulation, which can cause damage over time.

Cutting stone pavers requires the use of appropriate tools and safety equipment to ensure precision and minimize the risk of accidents. Mortar bed compound and bonding slurry compound are recommended for laying stone pavers, providing a strong and stable base for the installation. Control and expansion joints should be included in the design to accommodate natural movement and prevent cracking.

Two primary laying methods, rigid and flexible, are commonly used for installing stone pavers. The rigid method involves laying the pavers on a concrete base, while the flexible method allows for some movement and is suitable for smaller products. Regardless of the method chosen, attention to detail and adherence to industry best practices are essential for a successful installation.

When laying stone pavers as tiles, different considerations apply, and appropriate tile adhesive products designed for external use should be utilized. Overall, following recommended guidelines and seeking professional assistance when necessary can help ensure a durable and visually appealing outcome for your stone paver installation project.

Laying stone pavers using Pedestal Support Systems offers a versatile method commonly employed in various settings such as balconies, decks, and rooftop gardens. Determining the appropriate number of supports and their sizes and thicknesses for this application typically requires consultation with stone experts to ensure optimal performance and stability. Utilizing a high-grade pre-bagged grouting compound suitable for external use is recommended for filling grout joints ranging between 7-10mm. Following the manufacturer's instructions for mixing and applying the grout is essential to achieve a uniform and durable finish. It's crucial to keep the pavers clean throughout the grouting process and promptly remove any excess grout before it dries completely to avoid unsightly residue.

Sealing stone pavers is advisable to enhance their durability and resistance to oil-based stains, making them easier to clean. Opting for a penetrating sealer is recommended, and seeking assistance from professional sealing applicators can ensure proper application and effectiveness. Cleaning the pavers after laying and grouting is essential to remove any grout and mortar residue. This process involves wetting the area, applying an acid water mix (20 parts water to 1 part Hydrochloric acid), gently agitating the surface with a stiff broom, and thoroughly washing the surface. It's important to work on small areas at a time and avoid applying the acid mix to dry pavers to prevent over etching or burning. Wearing appropriate safety protection such as gloves and eye protection is crucial when handling acid, and it's essential to add acid to water, not the other way around, to avoid dangerous reactions.

Maintenance of stone pavers typically involves minimal effort, primarily consisting of regular sweeping and cleaning with a high-pressure water wash. Sealing the paving with an appropriate sealer can help prolong its lifespan and simplify maintenance. For stubborn stains that cannot be removed by regular cleaning methods, such as organic stains, using a household bleach product or repeating the acid wash process may be necessary. Alternatively, professional cleaning companies specializing in paver cleaning can provide assistance in removing stubborn marks and restoring the pavers to their original condition. Regular maintenance and prompt cleaning of stains can help preserve the appearance and integrity of stone pavers, ensuring they remain an attractive and functional feature in outdoor spaces for years to come.

Avoiding mistakes in paving installation requires a comprehensive understanding of the long-term implications of various factors on the durability and appearance of the pavement. While paving may initially look pristine, it is subjected to a range of environmental factors over time, including exposure to acidic rain, alkaline tap water, sunlight, tree roots, and subsurface pressures. Within the project site itself, pavers may encounter soil, compost, leaf litter, cleaning chemicals, grease, and more. To ensure the longevity and performance of the pavement, it's crucial to anticipate these conditions, educate project stakeholders, and take appropriate actions.

One significant mistake to avoid is failing to plan for movement in the pavement. The earth's surface undergoes continuous expansion and contraction due to seasonal changes and temperature fluctuations, while tree roots exert pressure on structures. Paving materials, including concrete and natural stone, are also subject to expansion, contraction, and warping. Proper planning for movement involves determining the placement of construction joints, contraction joints, and expansion joints before construction begins. Creating a plan, having it checked by a construction professional, and executing it diligently during construction can prevent failures caused by inadequate accommodation of movement.

Another common mistake is the avoidance or incorrect use of mortar additives, particularly concerning large format paving sizes. Mortar additives are essential for improving elasticity, workability, and adhesion, especially for large format pavers. Failure to use appropriate additives can result in pavers becoming detached from their foundation, known as de-bonding, leading to costly repairs and replacements. Additionally, large format pavers behave differently than small format ones and require specialized installation methods to ensure proper adhesion and performance over time.

Improper storage of pavers on-site is another mistake to avoid. Engineered paving stone is susceptible to irreversible staining if stored incorrectly before installation. It's essential to keep pavers dry, ideally stored undercover or in a protected space, and avoid stacking them prematurely across the project site. If storing on-site is necessary, leaving the shrink wrap intact, keeping the pavers dry, and installing small batches at a time can help prevent staining and maintain their appearance.

Incorrect mortar ratios and mixing methods are also common pitfalls to avoid. Mixing mortar is a delicate balance between art and science, requiring adherence to correct ratios, thorough mixing, and consideration of environmental factors. Insufficient mixing time, incorrect sequence of adding water, and using grey cement instead of white can lead to poor adhesion and structural issues. Following approved mortar ratios, using quality mortar additives, and ensuring thorough mixing are essential for a successful paving installation.

Lastly, neglecting acid washing after installation is a mistake that can mar the appearance of the pavement. Proper cleaning of mortar and grout residues is crucial for maintaining the pristine appearance of the pavers. Acid washing effectively removes deposits and stains, restoring the pavers to their original condition. By avoiding these common mistakes and adhering to best practices in paving installation, project stakeholders can ensure the longevity, performance, and aesthetic appeal of their paved surfaces.

Chapter Nine
PAVING PROJECTS

Setting up the area for paving is a critical step that significantly influences the outcome of the project. Proper preparation ensures a professional result and extends the longevity of the paved surface. The first step is to excavate the area to be paved to the depth of the pavers plus an additional 30 mm for the bedding sand. If the underlying soil is unstable or contains a high clay content, further excavation of 50 mm may be necessary to create a stable base using coarse material like quarry rubble. String lines are then placed around the area, sloped away from nearby structures to facilitate water runoff, with a recommended drop of 20 mm for every meter of pavers.

After setting up the string lines, the base of coarse material is laid if required and compacted to a depth of 50 mm using a rubber mallet and board or a plate compactor. This step ensures a stable foundation for the paving. Next, bedding sand is spread evenly over the area to a depth of about 40 mm using a rake. It's essential to avoid using beach sand or fine sand for this purpose as they may not provide adequate support for the pavers. Wooden rails are then placed along the sides of the area, and the bedding sand is levelled using a screeding rail to achieve a smooth and even surface.

Before starting the actual paving process, it's crucial to clear the site of any existing vegetation, including roots, to prevent future sinking of the paved surface. The area should be excavated to a depth of around 150 mm below the desired finished height of the pavers and the bottom of the work area should be scraped flat with a shovel. Stakes are then driven into the ground at the extremities of the proposed paved area, and string lines are run between them at the desired finished surface level using a string level, water level, or spirit level.

Once the paving level is established, the string lines are adjusted to allow for surface drainage, typically with a minimum fall of 1:60. It's important to ensure that the finished paving is below the damp-proof course level of any nearby buildings and that the paving slopes away from the building to prevent water accumulation. The prepared ground must be even and parallel to the finished paver surface level to avoid unevenness in the paved surface. Any soft or wet spots should be removed and replaced with road base, which may need to be stabilized with cement and well compacted to ensure a solid foundation for the paving. By following these steps meticulously, you can set up the area for paving effectively and lay the groundwork for a successful paving project.

The base for paving is a critical component that provides stability and support for the pavers, ensuring the longevity and durability of the paved surface. The type of base required depends on the intended use of the paved area. For driveways, the Australian Standard dictates a minimum sub-base thickness of 100 mm of 25 Mpa cured concrete with F72 mesh. This robust base is necessary to withstand the weight and pressure exerted by vehicles. On the other hand, for pedestrian areas, a sub-base of compacted crushed rock to a depth of 75 mm is recommended, with stabilization using cement preferred for added strength.

Before proceeding with the paving project, it's essential to calculate the area to be paved accurately. This involves measuring the length and width of the area and multiplying these measurements to determine the square meters of the paved area. Additionally, it's advisable to allow for a 10% margin for wastage, considering cuts and breakages during installation. Once the area is calculated, the quantity of pavers needed can be determined based on the area to be paved.

Calculating the materials required for the base and bedding is crucial for creating a stable foundation for the paving. Road base, typically laid at a depth of 100 mm, is necessary for driveways and unstable sites. The amount of road base required can be calculated by multiplying the area in square meters by 0.1 to obtain the cubic meters needed. Similarly, bedding sand, laid at a depth of 50 mm when compacted, is essential for providing a level surface for the pavers. The amount of bedding sand required can be calculated using the same method as for road base.

After establishing the base and bedding, joint filling sand is needed to fill the gaps between the pavers. This sand is swept into the gaps to provide stability and prevent shifting of the pavers. The amount of joint filling sand required depends on the area of paving and the size of the gaps between the pavers. Finally, sand cement mix may be needed for edge restraints to keep the pavers from shifting. This mix, typically consisting of sand and cement, is essential for securing the perimeter of the paved area. By accurately calculating the materials required for the base and bedding, you can ensure a solid foundation for your paving project and achieve a professional result.

Good drainage is crucial for the longevity and durability of outdoor paving areas. Poorly designed sub-bases can lead to water retention, which in turn can cause weathering of the pavers over time. Moreover, inadequate drainage can result in water penetrating the sub-base and pooling in the joints, leading to issues like efflorescence and dark staining of the pavers. To prevent such problems, it's essential to prioritize rainwater runoff in the design of the outdoor flooring area. This involves ensuring that water and moisture are not trapped on the surface of the floor, which can be achieved through perfect levelness and effective slope.

The design of the outdoor flooring area should incorporate drainage surfaces to facilitate the efficient removal of water. Inadequate drainage can lead to the build-up of dirt and the development of saltpetre efflorescence and rings, which can detract from the appearance of the paved area. Recommended gradients for effective drainage are greater than 1% for small areas and greater than 2% for larger areas. By incorporating proper drainage into the design, you can prevent water-related issues and ensure the longevity of your paved surface.

When laying pavers, it's important to use a suitable mortar bed to provide stability and support. A typical mortar bed consists of 4 parts sand, 1 part lime per 100, 1 part cement, 1 part water, and bonding agent. The mortar bed should be between 15-25 mm thick and made with well-graded and washed sand. It's crucial to use only enough water to make the mix workable, as excess water can decrease the strength of the mortar. The consistency of the mortar mix is sufficient when the paver does not settle when placed on the screed. Additionally, scoring the surface of the mortar with a pattern or light markings enhances bonding between the mortar and the paver.

The quality of the cement used is also essential for the durability of the mortar bed. General Purpose (GP) cement is recommended, and blended cements should be avoided. It's important to follow the manufacturer's directions when using cement products, and it's not recommended to use them when the outside temperature exceeds 30°C. Thoroughly mixing the mortar to ensure it is free of lumps and well blended is crucial for achieving a strong and durable mortar bed.

Bedding sand is another important component used to provide a medium for the pavers to bed down into and form a firm position. This sand should be spread evenly over the paving area to a depth of 30 mm to ensure proper support and stability for the pavers. By following these guidelines for slope, drainage, and mortar bed preparation, you can ensure the successful installation and long-term durability of your paved surface.

Preparing the Area to be Paved

Marking out the area to be paved is the first crucial step in ensuring a successful paving project. This is typically done using a string line and timber pegs, which are placed 50mm beyond the end of the paving area to minimize any impact on the string line during excavation. Excavation is then carried out to prepare the ground for paving, with the depth of the excavation being crucial for a stable foundation. Typically, the area is excavated to a depth of the paver plus 100mm for the compacted road base and an additional 50mm for the compacted bedding sand, totalling 150mm in depth.

Preparation of the sub-grade, or the underlying ground, is essential to ensure a stable base for the pavement. This process involves removing surface vegetation and root zones, typically around 50mm in depth, to prevent organic material from decomposing and causing voids in the covering layers, which could lead to settlement. For most paving projects, some degree of digging down to a 'formation level' is required to accommodate the finished levels of the paving work and remove any bad ground, topsoil, or soft spots.

The formation level of the sub-grade serves as the base of the construction and will be overlain by other pavement layers. In cases where the ground is structurally weak or likely to be subjected to exceptional loads, a capping layer may be required. This layer consists of a selected fill material, often crushed rock, laid in layers and thoroughly compacted before placing further layers, up to the sub-base layer.

When determining the finished paved surface level, it's essential to consider factors such as the slope away from the building, the depth of the base layer, bedding sand, and pavers themselves. Proper drainage is critical to prevent water build-up on the paving, which can lead to issues like efflorescence and staining. Therefore, the paving should slope away from the building at a rate of about 20mm per meter to ensure adequate drainage.

Additionally, if the paving is against the side of a building, it's important to leave a gap of at least 25mm below the damp proof course to prevent rising damp problems in the home. The damp proof course and air vents should never be covered by paving materials. By carefully preparing the ground and ensuring proper drainage, you can create a stable and durable base for your paving project.

Setting out clay pavers requires careful planning and attention to detail to ensure that the pattern of the pavement remains in line despite slight variations in the size of the pavers. The most effective way to achieve this is by using a grid of string lines spaced at exact intervals. While this may sound complicated, it is a straightforward process that ultimately saves time and effort in the long run.

To begin, it's essential to determine the average width of the pavers. This can be done by selecting 30 pavers at random, placing them tightly side by side, and measuring their overall width. Dividing this figure by 30 provides the average width of the pavers. Adding 2.5 mm to this average width, to account for the joint between the pavers, and then multiplying by 10 gives the spacing for the grid of string lines. For example, if the average paver width is 112.5 mm, the grid spacing would be 1150 mm (115 mm x 10).

Maintaining the squareness of the job is crucial, and a ratio of 3:4:5 can be used to achieve this. It's also important to blend pavers from two or three pallets to ensure a full blending of colour. Additionally, leaving a 2-4 mm gap between pavers is recommended to prevent chipping, and working to a string line as the job progresses allows for adjustments using a screwdriver or trowel.

Throughout the process, it's necessary to cut pavers to fit the desired pattern. While cutting pavers by hand may seem daunting, it's not difficult with the right tools—a sharp bolster and a heavy club hammer. Alternatively, pavers can be cut using a hydraulic cutter or a diamond saw. The process involves scoring the face of the paver with the bolster and club hammer, repeating this for the other three sides, and then firmly hitting the scored mark with the bolster to crack the paver. Finally, the face of the best half should be cleaned to ensure a neat finish.

Patterns can be further enhanced by utilizing angles and incorporating header courses, providing flexibility for creative designs while maintaining the integrity of the pavement. By following these steps and paying attention to detail, you can achieve a beautifully laid clay paver pavement that stands the test of time.

Preparing the base for paving is a critical step in ensuring the longevity and stability of the pavement. The process begins with tipping the road base into the area to be paved and spreading it evenly to a specified depth, usually around 110mm. This depth accounts for future settlement, ensuring that the base remains level even after compaction. Compacting the road base thoroughly is essential, as it creates a solid foundation for the pavers. Using a tamping tool and thoroughly wetting the road base aids in achieving optimal compaction.

Following the compaction of the road base, the bedding sand is spread on top to a depth of approximately 60mm. This layer also allows for some settlement, typically around 10mm, as the pavers are placed on top. Setting up screed rails at each end of the area ensures that the bedding sand is levelled uniformly, providing a smooth surface for laying the pavers.

The base layer, consisting of road base material or well-graded crushed rock, is spread evenly over the prepared ground before compaction. Raking ensures an even thickness of the base layer, crucial for achieving uniform compaction. Compaction is typically performed using a mechanical plate compactor, which applies force evenly across the surface, eliminating air voids and creating a stable base for the pavers. Compacting in 2-3 layers, rather than a single layer, helps achieve uniform compaction and prevents an uneven base, which could lead to an uneven surface for the pavers.

Vibrating plate compactors play a vital role in the compaction process, especially for concrete, asphalt, or soil substrates. They use vibration to compact the substrate downwards, filling air or water spaces between particles and creating a dense and flat base. Different types of vibrating plate compactors are available, each designed for specific substrate applications, such as concrete or asphalt. However, operating these machines requires training and expertise to ensure safety and optimal results.

Figure 161: Using a vibrating plate compactor. CC0 1.0, via Rawpixel.

Once the base is properly compacted and levelled, the corners are marked out with stakes, and string lines are tied between them at the desired level. Ensuring the corners are square using a builder's square is essential for maintaining the accuracy of the layout. Adjusting the string lines to allow for proper slope, typically about 25mm over 3 meters for water runoff, is crucial for drainage away from the house.

Finally, the top layer of grass or dirt is removed to the required depth, typically allowing for 10cm of hardcore, a thin layer of sand, and the thickness of the chosen pavers. Distributing the hardcore evenly across the area, leveling it out, and compacting it to create a solid base completes the preparation process. A thin layer of sand is then spread and levelled to provide a smooth surface for laying the pavers.

Bonding Slurry Compound

Bonding slurry compound is a crucial element in ensuring the stability and adhesion of pavers to the concrete slab. This compound can be created using either cement and water or cement and bonding agent, mixed to a paste-like consistency that is easily workable. It's essential to achieve the right balance in the mixture, adding only enough water to create the desired paste. This ensures proper adhesion without compromising the strength of the compound.

Before laying the pavers, it's imperative to prepare the concrete slab properly. Ensuring it is free of dust and debris is essential for optimal adhesion. The slab can be swept and hosed if necessary. Etching and bonding of the slab can assist in eliminating dust and increase adhesion, ensuring a strong bond between the pavers and the concrete base.

Dampening the area of the concrete slab where the pavers will be laid helps create an ideal environment for bonding. A 20mm thick layer of mortar mix is then evenly spread over the dampened slab, ensuring there are no voids in the mortar layer. Cleaning the base of the pavers is also crucial, as any dust or scale can affect adhesion. Using a wire brush to remove any debris ensures a clean surface for proper bonding. It's also essential to rinse off any residue or sediment from cut pavers before placing them to prevent staining.

Carefully bedding down the pavers with a good quality rubber mallet ensures that they are properly seated and eliminates any air voids underneath. Using a white mallet for light-coloured pavers and a black one for darker colours helps prevent staining. Tapping the pavers into place ensures they are securely set in the mortar layer. Any voids should be filled with a trowel, and excess mortar should be removed and discarded.

Once the pavers are in place, it's crucial to clean the surface thoroughly with clean water and a sponge to remove any excess material. Working cleanly and in small controlled areas ensures that the pavers are laid before the mortar dries, preventing any issues with adhesion or alignment.

In setting out the paving pattern, using set out lines is essential for maintaining alignment. A grid of string lines spaced at exact intervals around the perimeter of the job helps ensure the paving pattern stays in line. Using two string lines at right angles keeps the paving joints straight. Leaving a gap of 2-3mm between each paver, unless they have nibs, prevents chipping and ensures proper alignment. Disturbing the bed of sand as little as possible during this process helps maintain stability and alignment while laying the pavers.

Laying Process

Laying pavers around swimming pools requires careful consideration to ensure stability and prevent differential movement between the pool and the paving. It's recommended to lay pavers on concrete slabs to provide a sturdy foundation. Additionally, expansion joints should be incorporated to accommodate any movement, with an expansion joint approximately every 4-5 meters. These joints should match existing joints in the underlying concrete slab and be filled with flexible mastic to prevent debris build-up.

After laying the pavers, it's essential to adhere to certain guidelines. Pedestrian areas should not bear any load for at least 48 hours, while areas laid with mortar on a concrete base should not bear any load for at least 3 weeks. Grouting the pavers involves wetting them prior to grouting and using a stiff mix of washed sand and cement or a pre-bagged grouting compound. The grout should be trowelled into joints between 7-10mm, ensuring there are no voids and that it extends along the entire depth of the paver. Excess grout should be cleaned immediately to avoid sticking or staining, especially with polymer-based grouts.

In the laying process, it's important to dry lay the pavers first to ensure they fit well and you're satisfied with the layout. Beginning in one corner and working along the edges, allow for a gap of 2-4mm for mortar joints. Any necessary cuts can be made using an angle grinder. Once satisfied with the layout, remove the pavers and add a layer of mortar for the first paver, ensuring it is carefully placed and levelled. Spacers should be used between pavers, and the slabs tapped into position using a timber and rubber mallet. The entire area should be completed in this manner, with at least 24 hours allowed for the mortar to set before filling the spaces between tiles using mortar and a trowel.

Haunching the edges of the paving locks the pavers into place, preventing loosening or dislodging. This involves digging a trench along the edge of the paving deeper than the bedding sand and road base, then mixing concrete and water to create a haunching mixture. This mixture is placed up against the side of the pavers in the trench, with the surface angled halfway up the side of the paver and smoothed using a wooden float. After allowing the haunching to set for 24 hours, the pavers can be compacted.

When placing the pavers, they should be laid evenly, ensuring they are square with the starting edge. A minimum gap of 2mm should be left between pavers, and if laying them against a structure, they should be below the damp proof course with a plastic membrane between the structure and the paved area. Finally, the squareness and alignment of the pavers should be checked, and adjustments made as needed.

Edge restraints play a crucial role in the stability and longevity of paved areas. By acting as a boundary, they retain and restrain both the paving units and the sand used in the installation process. Without proper edge restraints, there's a risk of paving failure, which can manifest in various ways such as shifting, spreading, or sinking of the pavers.

One essential aspect of installing edge restraints is ensuring that they are finished approximately 10mm below the level of the uncompacted pavers. This depth allows for adequate compaction of the pavers and the bedding sand. By positioning the edge restraints slightly below the surface level of the pavers, it helps to prevent any interference during the compaction process, ensuring a uniform and stable surface.

The primary function of edge restraints is to prevent lateral movement of the paving units. This lateral restraint is crucial, especially in areas subject to heavy traffic or external forces, such as vehicular loads or soil pressure. Without proper restraint, the pavers may shift or spread over time, leading to uneven surfaces, trip hazards, and potential damage to surrounding structures or landscape features.

Additionally, edge restraints help to contain the bedding sand within the paved area, preventing erosion and displacement. This containment ensures that the sand remains in place, providing crucial support and stability to the pavers. It also helps to maintain the integrity of the paved surface by reducing the risk of gaps or voids forming between the pavers, which can compromise the structural integrity of the pavement.

Edge restraints are essential components of any paved area, providing both structural support and aesthetic enhancement. By properly installing edge restraints at the appropriate depth and ensuring their alignment and stability, you can significantly extend the lifespan of your paved surface while maintaining its functionality and visual appeal.

Cutting Paving

Cutting precast concrete blocks, flags, and kerbs is a common practice in construction, but it comes with health risks associated with exposure to crystalline silica dust. Silica, a natural component found in construction materials like concrete, can lead to serious respiratory issues such as silicosis if inhaled over time. Therefore, it's crucial to assess the risks involved in cutting concrete and implement measures to minimize exposure to silica dust.

The Workplace Exposure Limits (WELs) for respirable crystalline silica (RCS) have been set to mitigate health risks, with exposures controlled below 0.1 mg/m3 carrying a very low risk of developing silicosis. However, research has shown that cutting concrete with handheld power saws without dust suppression can result in RCS exposure levels far exceeding the WEL within seconds. This not only poses a risk to the operator but also to bystanders nearby. Therefore, it's imperative to adopt safer cutting practices and equipment to mitigate these risks.

The guidelines emphasize the importance of avoiding or minimizing the need for cutting concrete whenever possible. Techniques such as designing layouts using modular dimensions and utilizing closure units or half blocks can help reduce or eliminate the need for cutting. When cutting is unavoidable, it's essential to control dust generation effectively.

Mechanical splitting with block splitters is recommended as an alternative to power saw cutting, as it produces satisfactory results without dispersing excessive dust. However, when power saws are necessary, using bench power saws with dust suppression is preferred over handheld ones to minimize dust generation. Proper placement of the concrete to be cut on a firm, level surface is crucial to ensure safe cutting practices.

Similar precautions apply to cutting flag paving and precast concrete kerbs. Techniques to avoid or minimize cutting include selecting modular dimensions for flag paving layouts and utilizing small unit 'kerbing blocks' for forming curves and transitions in kerbs. Power saws with dust suppression should be used for cutting, and appropriate personal protective equipment, including suitable dust masks, must be worn at all times.

Cleaning Pavers

Cleaning pavers is an essential step in maintaining their appearance and longevity. After laying and grouting the pavers, it's recommended to wash them using a dilute acid solution. This solution helps remove any residual grout, mortar stains, or other contaminants on the surface of the pavers before sealing. However, it's crucial to test the solution in a small, inconspicuous area first to ensure it doesn't cause patchiness or discoloration.

The cleaning process begins by dampening the pavers with water to prepare them for the acid solution. The Cleaner 304 is then diluted with water at a ratio of 1:15 to prevent any damage to the concrete. Using a stiff broom, scrubber, or brush, the solution is applied to the surface of the pavers and gently agitated for about 20 seconds to ensure thorough coverage. It's essential not to leave the solution on the pavers for more than a total of 3 minutes to prevent any adverse effects.

After applying the Cleaner 304 solution, the pavers should be rinsed immediately and thoroughly with a high-pressure hose to remove any residue. It's recommended to work in small areas of no more than 3 or 4 meters to ensure thorough cleaning. The acid wash process should be carried out from the highest point to the lowest point of the paved area, and the surface of the pavers should not be allowed to dry out during the cleaning process.

Once the pavers have been cleaned, it's important to neutralize the surface using a soap and water solution to ensure that any remaining acid residue is removed. Safety precautions, including wearing appropriate protective equipment such as goggles and rubber gloves, should always be followed when handling acidic or chemical solutions to avoid any accidents or injuries.

Additionally, it's essential to follow correct cleaning methods to avoid damaging the pavers. Acid cleaning with hydrochloric acid (HCl) should only be used to remove mortar stains and should be done with caution to prevent any unsightly staining. Proper pre-wetting of the pavers, correct application of the acid solution, and thorough rinsing afterward are crucial steps in ensuring effective and safe cleaning.

After cleaning, sealing the pavers is optional but can make future cleaning easier and provide some protection against oil-based stains. Premier Pavers offer a twelve-month warranty against faulty workmanship or materials, but it's essential to inspect the pavers upon delivery and report any discrepancies within two working days to ensure any warranty claims are addressed promptly.

Adding Drainage

Proper drainage in a garden is essential to prevent issues such as boggy spots on the lawn or flooding, which can result from poorly designed or installed drains or a complete lack of drainage infrastructure. Addressing these concerns involves implementing effective drainage solutions that efficiently capture water and direct it away from problematic areas, ensuring it does not accumulate and cause damage. The goal is to guide water swiftly and effectively to a dispersal or stormwater system, while avoiding any connection to the sewer system to prevent contamination.

One common method for installing drainage is through surface drainage systems, which involve laying low-profile drains and dispersion systems. This approach requires specific tools and materials, including grated drainage channels, unslotted ag pipes, premixed concrete, silicone sealant, and a trenching shovel. The process begins with marking out the location for the drain using a stringline and set-out paint, followed by digging a trench of appropriate depth and width to accommodate the drainage system.

Securing end caps to the drain and sealing them with silicone sealant ensures a watertight connection, while any necessary adjustments to the length of the drain or connections to output pipes can be made using a handsaw. Another trench may be required for the output pipe, depending on the layout of the drainage system. Careful attention to detail during the installation process is crucial to ensure the effectiveness and longevity of the drainage system.

By following these steps and utilizing the appropriate tools and materials, homeowners can successfully install discreet drains in their gardens to prevent flooding and maintain proper drainage. Effective surface drainage not only protects the property from water damage but also contributes to a healthier and more aesthetically pleasing outdoor environment.

Installing sub-surface drainage is a comprehensive solution for managing water at its source, effectively preventing water accumulation and dispersing it away from problematic areas. This method requires specific materials and careful planning to ensure its effectiveness. Essential components include trench liner, end caps, drain matting, and blue metal aggregate, with optional additions such as decorative gravel, timber edging, and a drainage pipe. Before proceeding, it's advisable to consult local council guidelines on drainage and stormwater management to ensure compliance with regulations.

The first step in installing sub-surface drainage involves excavating a trench in the affected area, ensuring it is at least 100mm deeper than the height of the trench liner. If planning to add a garden bed, the trench may need to be deeper to accommodate the additional soil. The trench liner serves as a barrier that allows water to disperse while providing the option to install a drainage pipe or slotted ag pipe if necessary, particularly for areas where garden beds will be incorporated into the design.

Once the trench is prepared, the next step is to cover the entire trench liner with drain matting to provide additional filtration and protection. Following this, the trench is backfilled using blue metal aggregate, ensuring that the liner is completely covered by a layer at least 30mm deep. This aggregate layer facilitates water drainage and prevents soil erosion while promoting optimal water flow through the drainage system. Another layer of drain matting is then placed on top of the blue metal to enhance filtration and prevent clogging.

To conceal the drainage system, various options are available depending on aesthetic preferences and landscaping requirements. One approach is to add a layer of decorative river pebbles over the drain, secured by timber edging to create a visually appealing finish. Alternatively, turf or a garden bed can be laid over the drain to integrate seamlessly with the surrounding landscape. When incorporating a garden bed, it's essential to dig the drain deeper to accommodate soil depth and choose shallow-rooted plants to avoid damaging the drainage system.

Chapter Ten

Constructing Landscape Features Using Concrete

Concrete is a versatile material commonly used in landscaping for various purposes due to its durability, versatility, and ease of customization. Here are some common ways concrete is used in landscaping:

- **Patios and Pathways:** Concrete can be poured and shaped into various designs to create functional and visually appealing patios and pathways in outdoor spaces. Decorative techniques such as stamping, staining, and scoring can be applied to enhance the appearance of concrete surfaces, mimicking the look of natural stone, brick, or wood.

- **Retaining Walls:** Concrete retaining walls are commonly used to create terraced landscapes, prevent soil erosion, and define outdoor spaces. These walls provide structural support and can be customized with textures, colours, and finishes to complement the overall design aesthetic.

- **Driveways and Parking Areas:** Concrete is a popular choice for driveways and parking areas due to its strength and durability. It can withstand heavy vehicle traffic and is available in various finishes, including exposed aggregate and brushed concrete, to enhance traction and aesthetics.

- **Decorative Features:** Concrete can be molded into a wide range of decorative features such as planters, benches, statues, and water features. These elements add visual interest to outdoor spaces and can be customized to suit specific design themes and preferences.

- **Outdoor Furniture:** Concrete furniture, such as tables, benches, and seating areas, offers durability and stability for outdoor use. These pieces can be cast or molded into various shapes and sizes, providing functional seating and gathering areas in gardens, patios, and other outdoor settings.

- **Fire Pits and Barbecues:** Concrete fire pits and barbecues are popular additions to outdoor living spaces, providing a focal point for social gatherings and entertaining. These features can be built-in or freestanding and customized with decorative elements to enhance their aesthetic appeal.

- **Pool Decks:** Concrete is often used to create pool decks due to its slip-resistant properties and ability to withstand exposure to water and chlorine. Decorative techniques such as stamping and staining can be applied to create custom designs that complement the surrounding landscape.

- **Raised Planters and Garden Borders:** Concrete can be used to construct raised planters and garden borders, providing defined spaces for planting and landscaping. These structures offer durability and longevity, helping to contain soil and plants while adding visual interest to garden beds.

Figure 162: Flagstone Concrete Patio. Decorative Concrete Kingdom, CC BY 2.0, via Flickr.

Overall, concrete offers a versatile and durable solution for various landscaping applications, allowing homeowners and landscapers to create functional and aesthetically pleasing outdoor spaces that withstand the test of time.

Concrete Basics

Concrete is a fundamental material in landscaping due to its strength, durability, and versatility. It offers unlimited design flexibility in terms of shape, colour, and texture, making it a preferred choice for enhancing outdoor spaces. From patios and driveways to decorative elements like countertops and fireplaces, concrete finds extensive use in landscaping projects due to its numerous advantages.

One of the primary reasons for choosing concrete in landscaping projects is its durability. Concrete is more long-lasting and resistant to extreme weather conditions and heavy foot traffic compared to many other building materials. It can withstand the abrasion caused by outdoor furniture and maintains its structural integrity over time.

Moreover, concrete offers exceptional versatility, making it suitable for various applications both in and around the home. While it's commonly used as a paving material for pathways and driveways, it can also be utilized to create countertops, sinks, fireplaces, and outdoor waterscapes. Its ability to be cast in nearly any form or shape allows for creative customization in landscaping designs.

Another advantage of concrete is its easy maintenance. It is a solid surface that is easy to clean and resistant to debris and weed growth. Regular washing and resealing every few years can keep concrete surfaces looking good for decades, reducing the need for frequent repairs or replacements.

In terms of cost-effectiveness, concrete often proves to be more economical compared to other paving materials like brick and natural stone. Its ease of installation and availability make it a cost-effective option for landscaping projects, especially when working within a budget.

However, concrete does have its limitations. One of the main drawbacks is its tendency to crack due to expansion and contraction. To mitigate this issue, control joints can be installed during concrete placement to minimize cracking. Additionally, regular sealing every two to three years is recommended to protect concrete from staining and wear.

Despite its limitations, concrete remains a popular choice for landscaping projects, especially with the advent of decorative concrete techniques. Gone are the days when concrete was considered boring and grey. Today, concrete can be transformed with a variety of colours, textures, and surface treatments such as stamping and staining. Homeowners often opt for decorative concrete for their patios, paths, or driveways to achieve a high-end look at a reasonable cost.

Concrete is a composite material widely used in construction and landscaping due to its strength, durability, and versatility. It is composed of several key ingredients, with aggregate being a crucial component. Aggregate refers to crushed rock or stone, which provides the bulk and structural integrity to concrete. This aggregate is typically clean, sharp, and hard, with a coarse texture and sharp edges that allow it to bond effectively with other ingredients, resulting in a stronger mix. The selection of aggregate size depends on the specific requirements of the project, with larger sizes used for civil engineering structures and smaller sizes for paving work.

Modern concrete as we know it traces its origins back to the introduction and manufacture of Portland Cement in England around 1842. Since then, various formulations and mixtures of concrete have been developed, but the basic composition remains consistent. In addition to aggregate, concrete typically contains standard grade, general-purpose grey Portland Cement, which serves as the binding agent. This cement is usually sold in bags of around 20 kilograms and is a critical component in the concrete mixture.

In addition to aggregate and cement, concrete mixtures also include water and sometimes additives or admixtures to enhance specific properties. The water used in concrete should be clean and freshwater, as it plays a crucial role in the hydration process that transforms the cement into a solid mass. The proper ratio of water to cement is essential to ensure the desired strength and workability of the concrete.

Sand is another important ingredient in concrete mixtures, serving as the smallest aggregate size and providing fine particles that fill the gaps between larger aggregates. This helps create a more homogeneous mixture and improves the overall cohesion and strength of the concrete.

The process of mixing concrete involves combining these ingredients in specific proportions to achieve the desired properties for the intended application. Whether delivered from a local batching plant by a transit mixer or mixed on-site, concrete mixtures must be carefully prepared to ensure consistency and quality. The resulting mixture should have enough cement paste to coat every piece of aggregate thoroughly, creating a uniform and cohesive mass.

Placing concrete efficiently and effectively is crucial for the success of any construction project. Whether it's for a foundation, slab, or other structural elements, concrete must be delivered and positioned correctly to ensure structural integrity and quality. The process begins with careful planning to determine the best method of placement based on site conditions, accessibility, and the specific requirements of the project.

Direct delivery from a mixer truck is often the most straightforward method for placing concrete. This requires clear access to the site, allowing the truck to back up to two or three sides of the job. Adequate space must be provided to accommodate the truck's movement, ensuring that site huts, excavated soil, and other obstructions do not hinder the delivery process. Clear signage and directions should be provided to guide the truck driver to the designated placement area.

In cases where site access is limited, alternative methods may need to be considered. Superplasticised concrete, which flows easily and can be pushed further using a shovel, is an option for overcoming accessibility challenges. However, it imposes higher loads on formwork and may require stronger reinforcement to maintain structural integrity. Regardless of the type of concrete used, proper compaction is essential to ensure uniformity and strength.

When a mixer truck cannot reach the desired placement area directly, various transportation methods may be employed. These include pumps, tippers, dumpers, wheelbarrows, and mobile cranes with hoppers or buckets. Concrete pumps, equipped with hydraulic booms, are particularly useful for placing concrete on restricted sites, as they can reach significant heights and distances with ease. Cranes with buckets offer a versatile solution for delivering concrete to inaccessible or elevated areas, requiring minimal site clearance.

Pre-mixed concrete is a convenient option available in both metropolitan and rural areas. When ordering pre-mixed concrete, it's essential to specify the quantity, purpose, and desired delivery time. Higher-grade concrete may cost more but offers advantages such as quicker setting times and improved surface finish. It's crucial to begin placing and compacting the concrete as soon as the truck arrives, as pre-mixed concrete sets relatively quickly.

Before placing concrete, proper ground preparation is necessary to ensure a stable and level base. This involves removing topsoil, levelling and compacting the subsoil, and addressing any sloping terrain. Formwork must be securely installed to define the shape and dimensions of the concrete slab, with careful attention to detail to ensure accuracy and rigidity. Double-checking the level dimensions and shape of the formed area is essential before proceeding with concrete placement, as any errors at this stage can affect the integrity of the final structure.

Installing Service Pipes

Installing service pipes, such as drainage and water-supply pipes, is a crucial step in the construction process, particularly when preparing for the placement of a concrete slab. These pipes are essential for facilitating proper drainage and supplying water to the building, ensuring that it functions efficiently and effectively once construction is complete. Typically, a qualified plumber is responsible for installing these pipes, as they require specialized knowledge and expertise to ensure proper installation and functionality.

One important consideration when installing service pipes is the need to protect against termite infestation, especially in regions where termites pose a significant risk. Termite collars must be fitted to all pipes that pass through the slab, serving as a barrier against termite attacks. These collars are designed to prevent termites from accessing the building through the service pipes, helping to safeguard the structure from potential damage and infestation.

Figure 163: Service pipe installation. CC0 Public Domain, via PxHere.

Once the service pipes are installed and fitted with termite collars, it's essential to ensure that they are securely positioned and properly aligned. Concreters must exercise great care to avoid disturbing or moving the drainage pipes once they have been set in position. Any disruption to the placement of these pipes can compromise their functionality and integrity, leading to potential issues with drainage or water supply once the concrete slab is poured.

Proper coordination between the plumbing team and the concreters is crucial during this stage of construction to ensure seamless integration of the service pipes with the concrete slab. Clear communication and adherence to established guidelines and standards are essential to prevent errors or oversights that could result in costly rework or delays. By taking care to install service pipes correctly and securely, construction teams can lay the groundwork for a successful and functional building that meets the needs of its occupants for years to come.

Laying Concrete Underlay

Laying a concrete underlay is a critical step in the construction process, particularly when preparing for the placement of a concrete slab. The underlay serves as a vapor barrier membrane, designed to prevent moisture from seeping into the concrete from the ground below. It must be constructed from impermeable material that is resistant to ultraviolet deterioration and capable of withstanding impacts during construction activities. To ensure reliability and effectiveness, it's recommended to use a reputable brand of underlay that is specifically labelled as suitable for use as a concrete underlay.

The process of laying the concrete underlay begins with preparing the ground surface where the slab will be poured. The underlay is then placed over this prepared ground, covering the entire area where the concrete will be poured. It's essential to extend the underlay up over the edge formwork, ensuring that it fully encapsulates the area where the concrete will be contained. Using as wide an underlay as possible is advisable, as this minimizes the need for joints, which can be potential weak points in the vapor barrier.

At joints in the underlay, it's crucial to overlap the sheets by at least 200 millimetres to create a secure seal. Small pieces of tape should be used to hold the overlapping sections in place, with continuous taping of joints often required by local regulations to maintain the integrity of the vapor barrier. Ideally, these overlaps should occur within the trenches of the beam layout, further enhancing the barrier's effectiveness.

In areas where drainage and service pipes penetrate through the concrete slab, special care must be taken to ensure that the underlay provides adequate protection. The underlay should be carefully cut to accommodate the pipes, with the edges turned up and securely taped around the pipe penetrations. Additionally, to prevent debris from entering the pipes during construction, a piece of underlay should be placed over the pipe penetration and taped securely to the turned-up underlay.

By meticulously laying the concrete underlay according to these guidelines, construction teams can effectively safeguard the integrity of the concrete slab against moisture intrusion, ensuring the longevity and performance of the structure. This attention to detail during the underlay installation process is essential for creating a reliable vapor barrier that will protect the concrete slab and the building above it for years to come.

Fixing Reinforcement in the Beams

Reinforcing is a fundamental aspect of concrete construction, used to enhance the strength, durability, and structural integrity of concrete elements. The process involves incorporating various types of reinforcing materials, such as steel bars, mesh, fibres, or other composite materials, into the concrete mix to counteract tensile forces, control cracking, and improve overall performance. Reinforcing is utilized in several ways in concreting:

- **Steel Reinforcement**: Steel reinforcement, commonly referred to as rebar, is the most widely used form of reinforcement in concrete construction. Rebar is typically made of steel rods or bars and is placed within the concrete to provide tensile strength and resist bending forces. It helps to counteract the weak tensile strength of concrete, which is particularly important in structural elements subjected to bending or tension, such as beams, columns, and slabs.

- **Mesh Reinforcement**: Mesh reinforcement consists of sheets or rolls of steel wire mesh or fabric, often used in applications where large areas of concrete need to be reinforced, such as slabs-on-ground or pavements. Mesh reinforcement helps distribute loads more evenly across the concrete surface, control cracking, and improve structural integrity. It is particularly effective in preventing the propagation of shrinkage cracks in concrete.

- **Fibre Reinforcement**: Fibre reinforcement involves adding discrete fibres, such as steel, synthetic, or glass fibres, to the concrete mix to improve its toughness, impact resistance, and durability. Fiber reinforcement can enhance the performance of concrete in various applications, including flooring, shotcrete, and precast elements. Fibers act as micro-reinforcement within the concrete matrix, providing additional strength and preventing crack propagation.

- **Composite Reinforcement**: Composite reinforcement combines different materials, such as fibres or polymers, with traditional steel reinforcement to create hybrid reinforcement systems. These systems leverage the unique properties of each material to enhance specific performance characteristics of the concrete, such as corrosion resistance, ductility, or lightweight construction. Composite reinforcement is often used in specialty applications or in environments where traditional steel reinforcement may be susceptible to corrosion or degradation.

- **Placement and Fixing**: Reinforcing materials are strategically placed within the concrete formwork or moulds before pouring the concrete mix. The placement and fixing of reinforcement involve careful positioning to ensure proper coverage, spacing, and alignment within the concrete element. This process requires skilled labour and adherence to engineering specifications and design requirements to achieve the desired structural performance.

Fixing reinforcement in the beams and slabs is a crucial step in the construction process, particularly for structures like slabs-on-ground that require thickened edges or internal beams for support and stability. These beams play a critical role in distributing the load of the structure and resisting forces such as bending and shear. Properly placed steel reinforcement, commonly referred to as bottom-steel for beams and top-steel for slabs, enhances the structural integrity and durability of these elements.

In edge-beams and internal beams of slabs, bottom-steel reinforcement is fixed near the bottom of the concrete section. This reinforcement, typically in the form of trench mesh, consists of a single or double layer of steel bars separated by a fitment or ligature, as specified by the building plans. It is essential to provide adequate concrete cover to the reinforcement, typically a minimum of 40 millimetres, to protect it from corrosion and ensure its effectiveness in reinforcing the concrete. In areas with aggressive groundwater, a greater depth of concrete cover, up to 75 millimetres, may be necessary.

To maintain the proper positioning of the bottom-steel reinforcement, it is placed on bar chairs or trench mesh spacers. These supports elevate the reinforcement to the required height within the concrete section, ensuring that it is adequately embedded and positioned to provide structural support. Additionally, proper overlap of trench mesh sections, with a minimum half-meter overlap and full-width overlap at corners, helps ensure continuity and integrity of the reinforcement throughout the beam.

Figure 164: Reinforcement in place prior to pour. CC0 Public Domain, via PxHere.

Similarly, in the case of slabs, top-steel reinforcement is essential to control cracking that may occur as the concrete dries out. This reinforcement, typically in the form of fabric sheets, is laid over the entire area of the slab-on-ground. The fabric sheets are placed on bar chairs with bases to maintain the required distance from the slab surface, ensuring a minimum concrete cover of 20 millimetres above the reinforcement. Adequate reinforcement is vital to control cracking and enhance the structural performance of the slab.

During the fixing of reinforcement in slabs, provisions should also be made for embedding services such as floor heating systems or electrical wiring conduit. Additionally, if hot water heating pipes are to be embedded within the slab, adjustments may need to be made to the slab thickness to accommodate these elements. Proper lap splicing of slab fabric sheets ensures continuity of reinforcement across the slab and enhances its effectiveness in controlling cracking and distributing loads.

Furthermore, this stage of construction also involves positioning holding down bolts for wind bracing and other ancillary fixtures. These bolts are strategically located to facilitate the installation of additional structural elements and fixtures, ensuring the overall stability and functionality of the structure. Overall, the proper fixing of reinforcement in beams and slabs is crucial for ensuring the structural integrity, durability, and performance of the concrete elements in a construction project.

Placing, Compacting, Finishing and Curing Concrete

Placing and compacting concrete is a critical stage in the concrete construction process, influencing the structural integrity, durability, and surface finish of the final product. To ensure optimal performance, several key considerations must be taken into account during this phase.

Firstly, the concrete mix must be carefully ordered based on the required strength-grade and slump. Strength-grade refers to the compressive strength of the concrete, typically denoted by an "N" value followed by a number indicating the strength in megapascals (MPa). Slump, on the other hand, is a measure of the consistency of the concrete mix, indicating its workability and fluidity. It's crucial to order concrete with the appropriate strength-grade and slump to meet the structural requirements of the project. For instance, N20 grade concrete with a slump between 80-100 mm is commonly used for many applications.

During placement, each load of concrete should be placed adjacent to the previous load to ensure uniformity and continuity in the concrete surface. It's essential to start at one end and systematically work along the slab, integrating each new load seamlessly with the previous one. Additionally, pouring concrete on hot, windy days should be avoided, as adverse weather conditions can compromise the quality of the concrete. Seeking advice from the concrete supplier regarding weather conditions and placement techniques can help mitigate potential issues.

When placing concrete, it's crucial to prevent free-falling from heights exceeding one meter, as this can cause segregation and honeycombing, leading to weakened concrete structures. Leveling the concrete surface with a screeding board helps achieve a smooth, even finish. The screeding board should be moved in a sawing and chopping motion to compact the concrete effectively and remove excess material.

To further enhance concrete compaction, mechanical vibrators are commonly employed. These vibrators are inserted into the concrete at regular intervals along the beam length, helping to consolidate the mix and eliminate air voids. Care must be taken to hold the vibrator vertically and avoid disturbing the steel reinforcement, underlay, or formwork. Proper compaction is essential for improving concrete density, strength, and resistance to cracking, ensuring the long-term performance and durability of the structure.

Figure 165: Flattening of just poured concrete by vibration. Wouter Hagens, CC BY-SA 3.0, via Wikimedia Commons.

Finishing the surface of a concrete slab is a crucial step in the construction process, as it not only enhances the appearance but also improves the durability and functionality of the concrete structure. After the initial compaction and leveling of the concrete, the slab should be floated with a trowel to achieve a smooth surface. This process helps to fill any voids or imperfections in the concrete and prepares it for the final finishing.

Once the slab has been floated, it needs to set to a sufficient hardness before proceeding with the final finishing. This ensures that the surface can withstand further manipulation without being damaged. Typically, the concrete should be firm enough that a person standing on their heels will not sink more than 5 mm into the surface.

During the setting period, free water, known as bleed water, will rise to the surface of the slab. It's important to allow this water to evaporate naturally before proceeding with the final finishing. On colder days, the bleed water may need to be removed manually using a rope or hose dragged across the surface. It's crucial to avoid using dry cement or sand to absorb the bleed water, as this can weaken the finished surface and result in a dusty, unsatisfactory appearance.

For achieving a professional-quality finish, mechanical tools such as a concrete helicopter are often used. A helicopter is a power trowel equipped with rotating blades that smooth the surface of the concrete efficiently and evenly. When using a helicopter, it's essential to make two passes over the entire slab, starting from where the concrete was first placed and working systematically across the surface. Avoid spending too much time in one area to prevent overworking the concrete and creating unevenness.

In the absence of a helicopter, hand tools such as wood or steel floats and trowels can also be used to achieve a smooth finish. Regardless of the tools employed, it's crucial to work the entire surface of the slab twice to ensure uniformity and consistency in the finish. The level of finishing required may vary depending on the intended use of the concrete slab. For instance, if the slab will be covered with tiles set in mortar, a simple screed finish may suffice. However, for surfaces intended for carpeting or glued tiles, a more refined finish using steel or sponge trowels may be necessary to achieve the desired result.

Figure 166: Finishing a concrete pathway by hand. Master Sgt. Mike R. Smith, Public Domain, via Picryl.

Curing is a critical step in the concrete construction process that involves protecting the concrete against premature drying out, which can lead to various issues such as loss of strength, surface cracking, and dust formation. Proper curing is essential for allowing the concrete to achieve its full strength and durability over time. As soon as the concrete surface is sufficiently hard to resist damage, curing measures must be initiated to maintain adequate moisture levels within the concrete.

One common method of curing involves covering the concrete slab with sheets of plastic or building paper and securing them in place with planks or weights. This creates a barrier that helps to retain moisture within the concrete, allowing it to continue curing properly. It's recommended to leave the curing cover in place for at least three days to ensure sufficient moisture retention. In some cases, additional water may need to be gently sprayed under the covering after the first day to replenish any moisture loss.

This curing method not only helps to prevent moisture loss but also protects the slab from potential damage due to rain or external factors. Failure to properly cure the concrete can have detrimental effects on the overall quality and longevity of the concrete structure, making it susceptible to premature deterioration and reduced performance.

Alternatively, curing compounds can be applied to the surface of the concrete to prevent moisture loss. These compounds are specially formulated chemicals designed to slow down the evaporation of water from the concrete, thus allowing for proper curing to take place. It's crucial to use high-quality curing compounds to ensure effective curing and optimal results.

When applying curing compounds, it's essential to follow the manufacturer's instructions and apply a double coat evenly over the entire surface immediately after finishing the concrete. Some curing compounds may have specific requirements or limitations, especially if future floor coverings such as tiles or adhesives are planned for the concrete surface.

Proper curing is essential for achieving the desired strength and durability of the concrete slab. Failure to adequately cure the concrete can result in significant strength loss and compromise the structural integrity of the construction. Therefore, contractors must prioritize curing as an integral part of the concrete placement process to ensure long-lasting and high-performance concrete structures.

Formwork and Falsework

Formwork and falsework are crucial components in concrete construction, providing support and structure during the pouring and curing process until the concrete has gained sufficient strength to support itself.

Formwork refers to the system of moulds or frameworks that are used to contain and shape wet concrete until it sets and becomes self-supporting. It encompasses not only the physical forms into which concrete is poured but also the supporting structures, including frames, braces, and other elements that provide stability to the formwork assembly. The formwork system must be sturdy and precise to ensure that the concrete retains the desired shape and dimensions as it cures.

Various materials can be used for formwork, including wood, steel, aluminium, and prefabricated plastic or composite materials, depending on the specific requirements of the project. The choice of formwork material often depends on factors such as the complexity of the structure, the desired finish of the concrete surface, and the number of times the formwork will be reused.

Falsework, on the other hand, refers to the temporary support structures used to hold up the formwork, as well as any other temporary structures needed during construction until the permanent structure becomes self-supporting. While formwork directly shapes the concrete, falsework provides the essential support and stability required during the concrete placement and curing process.

Falsework systems are typically constructed from steel or timber components and are designed to withstand the weight of wet concrete, as well as any additional loads imposed during construction, such as equipment, materials, and workers. These temporary structures must be carefully engineered and installed to ensure the safety and integrity of the construction process.

The primary purpose of falsework is to provide temporary support to the formwork and other construction elements until the concrete has cured sufficiently to support its weight independently. Once the concrete has hardened and gained the necessary strength, the falsework can be removed, leaving behind the permanent structure.

Both formwork and falsework play critical roles in the success of concrete construction projects, ensuring that concrete structures are built safely, accurately, and according to design specifications. Proper planning, design, and installation of formwork and falsework are essential to the overall quality and integrity of the finished concrete structure.

Concreting Project Planning

Concreting project planning involves a systematic approach to ensure that the concrete construction process proceeds smoothly and efficiently. Several key points need to be considered to ensure the success of the project.

Firstly, the area to be concreted must be decided upon, and a detailed plan should be drawn up, including all measurements. The site should then be pegged out, and cord lines stretched to define the area accurately. Any turf or vegetation should be removed from the site to prepare it for concreting.

The finished levels of the work need to be determined, taking into account any required drainage slopes. It is crucial to ensure that water will not run towards any sensitive areas, such as house footings, garages, or neighbouring properties. The thickness of the concrete should also be determined based on the intended use of the area being concreted.

Formwork is essential for containing the concrete during pouring, and it must be properly constructed and braced to support the weight of the concrete. Joints between formwork boards should be watertight to prevent cement slurry leakage. Additionally, drainage and other requirements indicated on the plan should be accounted for, and the ground should be levelled and compacted before laying the formwork.

Decisions regarding the surface finish of the concrete should be made, considering factors such as durability and aesthetic appeal. Reinforcement requirements and the positioning of control joints should also be determined and marked on the plan.

Labour and equipment requirements need to be assessed to ensure that the project can be completed efficiently. The delivery time of the concrete to the site should be determined, and arrangements should be made for mixing the concrete on-site or using pre-mixed concrete. Equipment such as mechanical mixers should be hired in advance, and materials should be ordered and delivered according to the project timeline.

Before commencing work, it is essential to ensure that all aspects of the project have been considered, and any necessary preparations, such as installing a vapor barrier or conducting trial placements, have been completed. If the project appears too large to handle independently, it may be advisable to seek assistance from a professional concrete contractor.

Finally, concrete should be placed, finished, and cured according to best practices to ensure the integrity and longevity of the structure. It is crucial to follow proper procedures and avoid adding water to batched concrete, as this can compromise its final strength.

In addition to project-specific considerations, matters related to construction site management should also be addressed, including building schedules, site storage, traffic management, and public safety measures. These considerations help to ensure that the construction site operates efficiently and safely throughout the project duration.

Placing concrete is a critical step in the construction process that requires careful attention to detail to ensure the integrity and quality of the finished structure. When placing concrete, it is essential to handle the material with care to avoid damaging or moving the formwork and reinforcement. Concrete should be placed as close to its final position as possible to minimize the risk of segregation and ensure uniformity in the finished product.

It is advisable to start placing concrete from the corners of the formwork or, in the case of sloping sites, from the lowest level, working towards the source of concrete supply. Delays in the placement process can lead to the concrete drying out and stiffening, particularly on hot and windy days. Therefore, it is crucial to plan ahead and ensure that all necessary preparations are completed before the concrete is delivered to the site.

Adding extra water to concrete to make it more workable is not recommended, as it can compromise the strength and durability of the finished product. It is essential to use the correct mix of concrete for the intended application and to avoid segregation, which can weaken the concrete and result in a poor surface finish.

To prevent segregation, concrete should not be allowed to fall freely from a height of more than 1.5 meters. When pouring concrete on sloping surfaces or into enclosed spaces, such as basements or stairs, care must be taken to ensure that the concrete is placed evenly and does not segregate.

Compaction is a crucial step in the concrete placement process, as it ensures that the concrete is properly consolidated and free of air voids. Mechanical vibration or hand rodding is typically used to compact the concrete, depending on the size and complexity of the project. It is essential to compact the concrete while it is still in a workable (plastic) state to achieve the desired density and strength in the finished product.

Screeding is another important step in the concrete placement process, as it levels and compacts the surface of the concrete. Mechanical screeds are commonly used to achieve a smooth and even finish, but hand screeding may be necessary for smaller projects or areas with limited access.

Internal vibration, using a mechanical vibrator or poker vibrator, is used to consolidate the concrete from within, ensuring that it is evenly compacted throughout. It is important to use the correct size and type of vibrator for the specific application and to follow proper procedures to avoid damaging the concrete or formwork.

Overall, careful planning and attention to detail are essential when placing concrete to ensure the success of the construction project and the longevity of the finished structure. By following best practices and adhering to safety guidelines, construction professionals can achieve high-quality results and avoid costly mistakes.

Finishing concrete is a crucial step in the construction process, aimed at screeding, floating, and trowelling the surface to densify and compact the concrete layer while achieving the desired aesthetic appearance. It involves two main stages: initial finishing and final finishing. During the initial finishing stage, concrete is screeded to the level of the formwork, bull floated, and left to set. This process may suffice for certain applications, especially if floor coverings will be used over the concrete. Bleed water, which appears on the surface of the concrete as it sets, should be carefully managed to avoid weakening the surface in the long run. Excess bleed water can be removed by using a garden hose, but using stone dust or cement for drying is not recommended.

Floating is a crucial aspect of the initial finishing stage, helping to compact and level the surface while closing minor cracks. It can be done either by hand or with a power float, with the latter typically producing a better finish. The final finishing stage involves additional steps such as trowelling, edging, grooving, jointing, or patterning the concrete surface to achieve the desired texture and appearance. Trowelling, in particular, leaves a dense, hard, and smooth surface that enhances durability but can be slippery when wet. Edging tools are used to finish the edges of the slab, providing a neater and stronger edge less prone to chipping.

Proper planning and execution of finishing techniques are essential to ensure the quality and longevity of the concrete surface. It is important to follow best practices for achieving a smooth and durable finish, whether by hand or using power tools such as trowels and floats. Control joints are also essential to manage cracking in the concrete, allowing for controlled movement and preventing random cracks from forming. These joints weaken the concrete intentionally, ensuring that cracks occur where desired rather than randomly throughout the surface.

In terms of practical implementation, setting up the formwork at the exact finish height is a common practice, allowing for accurate placement and screeding of the concrete. Temporary screeding rails may be required for wider pours to ensure uniformity across the surface. Additionally, various tools and techniques, such as laser levels or dumpy levels, can be used to achieve precise finish heights and surface levels. Overall, attention to detail and adherence to best practices are essential for achieving high-quality concrete finishes that meet both functional and aesthetic requirements.

Building a Basic Concrete Path

Gathering the necessary supplies is the first step in preparing for a concrete project. Essential items include timber pegs, 90 x 25mm timber lengths for formwork, and concrete, which can be either bagged or premixed depending on the project's volume. For easy transport of materials, a wheelbarrow with inflated rubber tires is recommended. Additional tools and equipment required for the job include a stringline, shovel, screed board, tape measure, drill, power saw, edging tool, concrete groover, mallet, spirit level, bricks or pavers, bull-nose float, suitable screws, steel trowel, brickie's trowel (optional), and rubber boots for personal protection.

The next step involves marking out the path and excavating the area to a depth of 100mm. It's essential to ensure that the ground slopes away from any buildings and sits below the internal floor level. If grading the path away is not feasible, a surface drain should be installed and connected to stormwater to prevent water buildup.

Using a stringline, set to the required height of the finished path, and ensure it is taut. Check the excavated ground's consistency in height from the stringline using a tape measure and adjust if necessary. For curved paths, use a power saw to cut evenly spaced grooves halfway through the forms, a technique known as kerfing, which allows the timber to bend.

Hammer timber pegs into the ground at each corner of the path area and position the forms along the edges, fixing them to the pegs. Additional pegs should be hammered into the ground inside and outside the forms, with the outside pegs screwed to the forms. If forms need to be joined end-to-end, reinforce with pegs and screws, ensuring the formwork is at the correct height.

Mix the concrete according to the package instructions and shovel it into the formwork, spreading it evenly over the ground and up the sides and into the corners of the formwork. If using premixed concrete, be prepared to work quickly as the truck's arrival signals a limited time for unloading.

Use a screed board to move the concrete back and forth to smooth it to the correct level. Any excess concrete can be moved along with a shovel. Use a steel trowel to remove any air pockets gently. Once the concrete has started to dry but is still wet enough to leave an imprint, smooth the surface using a bull-nose float.

Round off the edges using an edging tool, and if necessary, create a gap between the concrete and formwork using the point of a brickie's trowel. For paths longer than 3m, divide them into sections and create grooves or dummy joints across the path to help prevent cracking using a concrete groover.

To cure the concrete, keep it wet for a few days by hosing with water or covering it with plastic. Finally, remove the formwork once the concrete has set overnight.

Edging and Grooving

The finishing touches applied to the edges of a concrete slab play a crucial role in both its aesthetics and structural integrity. Utilizing a special edging tool ensures that the edges are neatly defined and less prone to chipping, enhancing the overall appearance of footpaths, patios, kerbs, and steps. By creating a quarter-round arris along the perimeter of the concrete, edging trowels achieve this desired effect. These trowels, typically made of steel, feature a quarter-round forming edge and are available in various widths and with different diameter quadrants. This meticulous edging not only improves the visual appeal of the concrete but also fortifies its edges against potential damage.

Furthermore, planning and incorporating joints into the concrete during finishing are essential practices. Joints serve to control cracking by allowing the concrete to expand and contract without causing structural issues. By strategically placing joints before pouring the concrete and integrating them seamlessly during the finishing process, contractors ensure the long-term durability of the slab.

Once the surface of the concrete is finished, proper curing becomes imperative to preserve its strength and integrity. Among the various finishing techniques, brooming offers both functional and aesthetic benefits. By using brooms of varying stiffness, contractors can achieve finishes that are not only visually appealing but also provide slip and skid resistance, making them suitable for various applications ranging from footpaths to industrial floors.

The choice of broom and technique used significantly impacts the final texture of the surface. Polypropylene and horsehair bristles are suitable for creating light textures, while poly fibre bristles are ideal for medium and coarse textures. Special soft plastic bristles are utilized for texturing over long distances to minimize the risk of mortar drag or bristle clogging. Contractors may employ brooms to create a variety of patterns, including straight lines, curved designs, wavy finishes, and sawtooth patterns, depending on the desired aesthetic effect.

Achieving consistent finishes requires careful attention to factors such as timing, angle of broom placement, and pressure applied during the process. Additionally, ensuring uniformity across the entire surface is crucial to prevent issues such as 'balling' of loose matrix material in shaded areas. For industrial applications where heavier traffic is anticipated, a medium to coarse broomed texture is recommended to ensure longevity and skid resistance over the design life of the pavement or floor.

Coloured Concrete

Colour plays a significant role in the aesthetics and functionality of concrete floors and pavements, and several methods can be employed to introduce colour into these structures. One approach involves using off-white or white cements, which can alter the colour of the concrete. Off-white cement, particularly prevalent in Australia, is often preferred for architectural finishes due to its tendency to produce a more consistent colour. However, variations in shade may still occur, making the use of pigments advisable for achieving precise and vibrant colours. White cement, though imported and relatively costly, can also be used or supplemented with white titanium oxide pigment for enhanced brightness and colour consistency.

Another method, integral colouring, involves adding pigments directly to the concrete mix to uniformly colour the entire volume of concrete. These pigments, available in various forms such as powders, granules, or liquids, are chemically inert and resistant to degradation, providing a permanent colouring solution. Pigmented concrete takes on the colour of these ultra-fine particles, which become bound within the concrete matrix. Careful consideration of factors such as mixing procedures, pigment proportions, and curing techniques is essential to achieve consistent and durable results.

Dry-shake toppings, comprised of cement, sand, and pigments, offer an alternative method for introducing colour to concrete surfaces. These toppings, available as pre-made products or mixtures prepared on-site, are applied to fresh concrete surfaces and worked into the surface using trowels. Dry-shake toppings can enhance the strength and durability of the finished surface while providing a range of colour options.

Chemical stains offer yet another approach to colouring concrete, reacting with excess calcium in the concrete to produce permanent coloration. This method often results in unique mottled finishes and is particularly suited for flatwork construction. However, careful planning and skilled application are required to achieve satisfactory results, especially when applying stains to existing concrete surfaces.

Dyes and tints, available in water or solvent solutions, provide vibrant colours and can be used to correct or enhance the results of chemical staining. Unlike stains, dyes and tints do not react with concrete, offering predictable results and a wider range of colour options.

Surface coatings, including paving paint, urethane, epoxy, and cementitious materials, offer uniform colour coverage and can protect concrete surfaces from abrasion and staining. These coatings may require reapplication over time due to wear and may need to be compatible with sealers for optimal performance.

Lastly, exposed aggregates can provide permanent colour in concrete finishes, albeit with limitations dictated by the available aggregates. Each method of colouring concrete offers unique benefits and considerations, making it essential to select the most appropriate approach based on factors such as colour requirements, surface type, and desired durability.

Patterned concrete

Surface texturing and patterning in concrete pavements have evolved over the years, incorporating a range of techniques and tools to achieve desired visual and functional outcomes. Traditionally, stiff-bristle brooms, wood floats, and sponges have been utilized to create textures and patterns on concrete surfaces. However, modern advancements have introduced purpose-made rubber moulds, metal dies for stamping impressions, and cardboard stencils for applying dry-shake toppings, expanding the possibilities for decorative concrete finishes.

The success of these techniques hinges on meticulous planning and precise timing during the brief window when concrete is workable. Ordering 'low-bleed' concrete reduces waiting time for bleedwater to evaporate, extending the period available for finishing. Additionally, the inclusion of polypropylene fibres in the mix can enhance cohesion and minimize bleeding. Effective curing practices are paramount for achieving the desired appearance and durability of the pavement.

Stencilling involves altering the concrete surface after it has stiffened but before it has fully hardened. Cardboard stencils laid on the surface mask areas from subsequent colour application, resulting in patterns with contrasting colours between the base concrete and the applied colorant. Various stencil patterns, such as brick bonds or stone-like finishes, can be achieved, with the surface texture further diversified using brooms to enhance slip resistance on slopes.

Figure 167: Concrete being stamped with ashlar slate pattern. ChicagoConcrete, Chicagoland Concrete, Inc., CC BY-SA 3.0, via Wikimedia Commons.

The stencilling process begins with protecting adjacent surfaces to prevent staining from cement or oxide splashes during concrete placement. Once the concrete is levelled and smoothed, stencils are carefully positioned and embedded into the surface. Proper stencil placement ensures clean edges and consistent colour application. After colouring and texturing, stencils are removed, and the concrete is cured to optimize the finish's durability.

Similarly, stamped concrete involves pressing patterns into the concrete surface using metal moulds or rubber mats after the concrete has stiffened. The process begins with concrete placement and levelling, followed by colouring and application of surface hardener. Coloured release agents are then applied to prevent adhesion between the concrete and stamping moulds, creating two-tone effects and enhancing pattern details.

Careful planning of stamping sequences ensures seamless pattern transitions and clean edges. After curing, the release agent is removed, and the surface is sealed to protect against contaminants and enhance appearance. Joints are strategically planned to align with pattern grooves and accommodate structural movements, contributing to the overall aesthetics and functionality of the stamped concrete.

In both stencilling and stamping, attention to detail, precise timing, and adherence to best practices are essential for achieving high-quality decorative concrete finishes. From surface preparation to curing and joint installation, each step plays a crucial role in ensuring the longevity and visual appeal of the pavement.

Concrete Control Joints

Concrete control joints serve as strategic points of weakness in concrete flatwork to manage shrinkage and control cracking. Also known as weakened plane joints, contraction joints, or crack inducers, these joints have been integral in concrete construction for years, with new variations continuously emerging.

The positioning of concrete control joints is crucial for effective functionality. Typically, a control joint should be placed in a slab at least every 3000mm. However, other criteria may dictate spacing, such as the thickness of the slab. For instance, a common guideline suggests that joint spacing should not exceed 30 times the thickness of the slab. Additionally, for slabs wider than footpaths, the length of any section should not exceed 1.5 times the width of the shorter side.

Exceptions exist, particularly for thinner slabs or those with specific requirements, like termite reticulation pipes. In these cases, control joints may need to be placed at shorter intervals to ensure proper control of cracking. The careful placement of control joints is essential to prevent undesirable cracking and maintain structural integrity.

Various types of joints are employed in concrete control joint applications. One method involves using jointing tools to create joints by cutting into the concrete surface. This technique, while time-consuming, is suitable for narrower sections like footpaths and requires a plank support across wider slabs. Alternatively, proprietary metal inserts and crack inducers offer efficient and precise control joint solutions, particularly in stencilled and exposed aggregate concrete finishes.

Saw cuts have become a preferred method for larger projects, thanks to advancements in diamond saw technology. This technique allows concrete work to proceed steadily without immediate consideration of control joints, as sawing can be performed the following day. However, timing is critical, as sawing too early or too late can result in unwanted outcomes such as aggregate plucking or cracking.

Proprietary metal inserts and key joints provide a more definitive break in the concrete, offering greater control over vertical movement and ensuring neat finishes. These options are particularly suitable for decorative finishes, as they can be customized with coloured rubber caps to enhance aesthetics. Additionally, crack inducers, in conjunction with other types of joints, provide a more accurate and positive break, minimizing the risk of uncontrolled cracking.

Overall, proper planning, precise placement, and selection of appropriate joint types are essential considerations in the effective utilization of concrete control joints. By adhering to best practices and leveraging advancements in jointing technology, contractors can ensure the durability, functionality, and aesthetic appeal of concrete flatwork structures.

Exposed-aggregate Finishes

Exposed-aggregate finishes in concrete offer aesthetic appeal and durability, achieved by revealing selected stones on the surface. This can be accomplished through seeding the concrete with aggregates or ordering a specialized mix containing aggregates. The key lies in removing the thin layer of cement mortar covering the stones soon after the concrete stiffens. Various methods such as water washing, abrasive blasting, acid etching, and honing can be employed for this purpose, each offering distinct results.

The choice of aggregates is crucial, as they come in different colours, textures, and sizes, ranging from smooth river gravels to coarse crushed rocks. The selection depends on the desired application and aesthetic effect. Additionally, the concrete itself can be coloured to complement or contrast with the aggregates. Before proceeding with large-scale projects, it's advisable to create sample panels to assess techniques, surface finish, stone distribution, and colour consistency. Moreover, it's essential to execute exposed-aggregate finishes under the supervision of experienced professionals familiar with these techniques.

Figure 168: Exposed-aggregate finish. TXTR, via Pexels.

Seeded aggregates involve sprinkling the selected stones over the concrete surface after screeding and bull floating. The aggregates are then embedded into the surface by tamping and repeated floating. Aggregate exposure begins when the surface can bear weight without making impressions deeper than 2 mm. Water washing, often accompanied by the use of surface set-retarders, is a common method to remove the cement mortar and reveal the aggregates. After exposure, proper curing and surface treatment, such as acid washing, may be necessary to enhance the appearance of the stones.

Abrasive blasting and acid etching are alternative methods to achieve aggregate exposure, each with its own advantages and considerations. Abrasive blasting utilizes sand or grit to erode the surface cement mortar, while acid etching removes the surface cement to varying depths. Honing, on the other hand, involves grinding the concrete surface with abrasives to achieve a smooth, low-maintenance finish. The final appearance depends on factors like aggregate colour and hardness, matrix colour, concrete quality, and depth of grinding.

Environmental considerations are paramount when dealing with coloured and exposed-aggregate finishes due to potential water runoff containing cement or acid. Proper measures must be taken to prevent environmental contamination, such as providing filters at strategic points, diverting runoff to catchment areas, and temporarily capping drainage inlets. Careful planning and execution are essential to minimize environmental impact while achieving desired aesthetic results in concrete finishes.

Constructing Concrete Stairs

Poured concrete steps offer durability and longevity, serving as a reliable transition between outdoor surfaces like a patio and the entry to your home. However, determining the appropriate height and depth of each step can be challenging. This is where some basic math comes in handy, enabling you to calculate the unit rise (vertical height) and run (horizontal length) of each step.

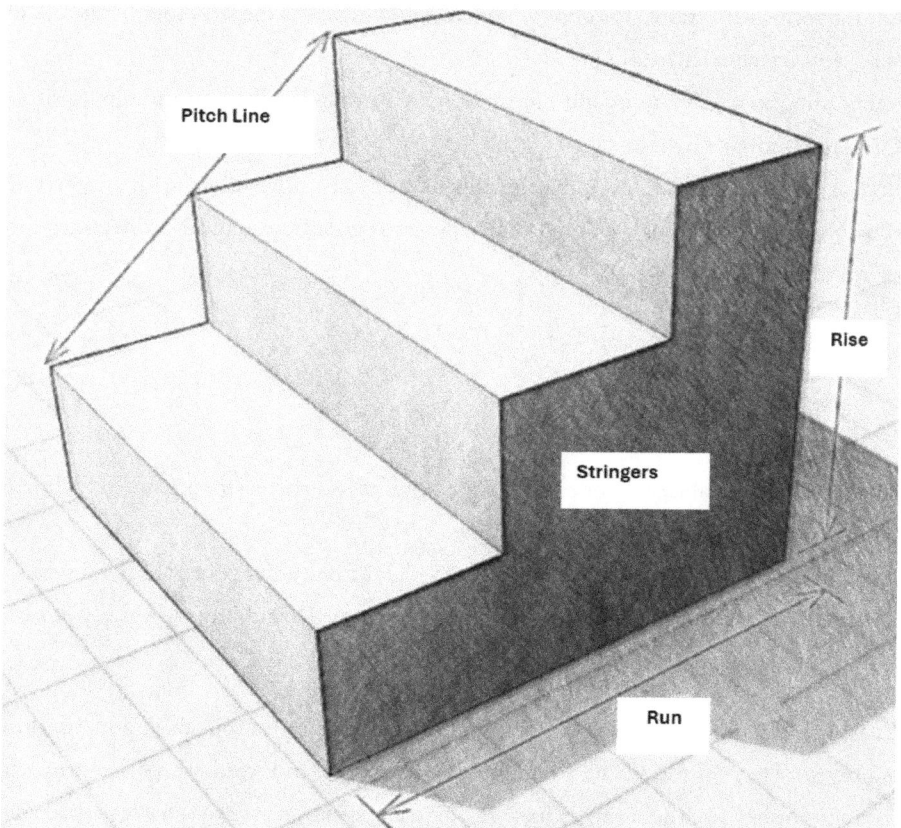

Figure 169: Stair terms.

Before diving into the construction process, it's crucial to understand local building codes governing step construction. Failure to adhere to these codes may result in the need to redo the steps according to regulations. Codes often dictate specific requirements regarding step dimensions, reinforcement placement, and concrete mix composition [81].

Planning and executing concrete steps typically require two to three days, excluding curing time. Following a systematic approach is essential for a successful outcome. Here's a breakdown of the necessary steps and materials required for the project:

Firstly, accurately measure the rise (vertical distance) and run (horizontal distance) of the area where the steps will be located. Drive stakes to mark the base of the bottom step and compute the unit rise and run for each step based on these measurements. This involves dividing the total rise by a standard step height (usually 7 inches) and determining the number of steps needed [81].

Next, lay out footings wider than the steps and excavate to the required depth according to local codes. Pour concrete footings, insert rebar for reinforcement, and allow them to cure. Dig a trench between the footings and fill it with compacted gravel.

For added stability, consider anchoring the concrete steps to the foundation wall, depending on local requirements.

Outline the steps on plywood sheets based on the computed dimensions, ensuring accuracy and precision. Set the forms in place, ensuring they are square, level, and plumb. Secure them with stakes and screws, and cut riser forms to size, attaching them to the side forms.

Install angled braces for support and reinforcement, ensuring the forms remain stable throughout the pouring process. Additionally, incorporate expansion strips and reinforcement rebar for added strength.

Fill the space inside the forms with rubble to conserve concrete and reinforce the structure further. Add lengths of rebar at intervals for additional reinforcement and support.

Mix the concrete according to specifications and fill the forms starting from the bottom step. Ensure the concrete settles evenly and tap the forms to remove air bubbles.

Once the concrete has set sufficiently, remove the riser forms and finish the surface with a trowel. Edge the risers for a smooth appearance and broom the treads for traction. Install railings as needed and allow the concrete to cure completely before removing side forms and addressing any voids [81].

Paving Coatings

There are several paving coatings available, each offering unique benefits and characteristics suited to different paving materials and desired outcomes. Some common paving coatings include:

- **Sealers**: Sealers are applied to paving surfaces to protect them from water penetration, oil stains, UV rays, and other forms of damage. They can enhance the colour of the paving material and provide a glossy or matte finish. Sealers are commonly used on concrete, brick, and natural stone pavements.

- **Acrylic Coatings**: Acrylic coatings are versatile and can be used on various paving materials, including concrete, asphalt, and pavers. They offer excellent durability, UV resistance, and weatherproofing properties. Acrylic coatings come in different finishes, such as matte, satin, and glossy, and can be tinted to achieve desired colours.

- **Epoxy Coatings**: Epoxy coatings are highly durable and resistant to chemicals, abrasion, and staining, making them suitable for high-traffic areas. They are commonly used on concrete surfaces and provide a smooth, glossy finish. Epoxy coatings can also be customized with decorative elements like coloured flakes or aggregates.

- **Polyurethane Coatings**: Polyurethane coatings offer exceptional durability and flexibility, making them ideal for outdoor paving applications. They provide protection against UV rays, moisture, and heavy foot traffic. Polyurethane coatings are available in various formulations, including solvent-based and water-based options.

- **Anti-Slip Coatings**: Anti-slip coatings are designed to improve traction on paved surfaces, reducing the risk of slips and falls, especially in wet or icy conditions. These coatings contain additives or textures that create a non-skid surface without compromising the appearance of the pavement.

- **Penetrating Sealers**: Penetrating sealers are absorbed into the pores of the paving material, forming a protective barrier against moisture and contaminants while allowing the surface to breathe. They are commonly used on porous materials like concrete, brick, and natural stone, providing long-lasting protection without altering the appearance of the pavement.

- **Colour Enhancers**: Colour enhancers are coatings specifically formulated to deepen and enrich the natural colour of paving materials like concrete, brick, and stone. They penetrate the surface to highlight the texture and character of the pavement while providing protection against fading and weathering.

When selecting a paving coating, it's essential to consider factors such as the type of paving material, the desired level of protection and aesthetics, environmental conditions, and maintenance requirements. Consulting with a professional contractor or supplier can help determine the most suitable coating for your specific paving project.

Determining the most durable paving coating depends on various factors, including the specific conditions of the pavement, the type of material being coated, and the intended use of the paved surface. However, based on their inherent properties, some coatings may generally offer greater durability than others.

1. **Epoxy Coatings**: Epoxy coatings are known for their exceptional durability and resistance to chemicals, abrasion, and staining. They form a strong bond with the substrate, creating a hard, impermeable surface that can withstand heavy foot traffic and harsh environmental conditions. Epoxy coatings are commonly used in industrial and commercial settings where durability is paramount.

2. **Polyurethane Coatings**: Polyurethane coatings also offer high durability and flexibility, making them suitable for outdoor paving applications. They provide excellent protection against UV rays, moisture, and heavy foot traffic, while their flexible nature allows them to withstand temperature fluctuations and minor substrate movements without cracking or peeling.

3. **Acrylic Coatings**: Acrylic coatings are versatile and offer good durability, UV resistance, and weatherproofing properties. While they may not be as durable as epoxy or polyurethane coatings, acrylic coatings still provide adequate protection for most paved surfaces, including concrete, asphalt, and pavers. They are often used in residential and light commercial applications.

Among these options, epoxy coatings are typically considered the most durable due to their superior resistance to wear, chemicals, and environmental factors. However, it's essential to consider the specific requirements of your paving project and consult with a professional to determine the most suitable coating for your needs.

To rejuvenate and enhance the appearance of a driveway, painting it can be a rewarding project, but it requires careful preparation and execution to ensure a long-lasting finish. Before you begin, it's crucial to gather all the necessary tools and materials, including an outdoor broom, pole sander, scrub brush, pressure washer, bucket, paint brush, paint roller on a pole, paint tray, cleaner, mineral turpentine, paving paint, and painter's tape. Having these items ready will streamline the process and help achieve professional results.

The first step in painting the driveway is to thoroughly clean the surface to ensure proper adhesion of the paint. Start by sweeping away loose debris such as gravel and dirt using an outdoor broom or leaf blower. Additionally, remove any weeds or moss growing between the pavers to create a clean canvas for painting. Cleaning the surface not only improves the paint's adhesion but also enhances the overall aesthetic appeal of the driveway.

If the driveway has been previously painted, it's essential to sand the surface to remove any remnants of the old paint. Using a pole sander is recommended for this task, as it provides efficient and uniform sanding. Sanding the surface helps create a smooth and even base for the new paint, ensuring better adhesion and a professional finish.

After sanding, address any stains on the driveway surface, such as petrol, oil, or grease marks. Use an oil and grease remover to effectively lift and eliminate these stains, following the instructions provided on the product label. Thoroughly cleaning the surface ensures that the paint adheres evenly and prevents unsightly blemishes from showing through the new coat of paint.

Once the surface is clean and free of stains, proceed to pressure wash the driveway to remove any remaining grime and dirt. A pressure washer is an effective tool for this task, as it provides high-pressure water jets that can penetrate and lift stubborn dirt and debris from the surface. Allow the driveway to dry completely before moving on to the next step to ensure optimal paint adhesion and durability.

Before applying the paint, it's essential to properly prepare the paint according to the manufacturer's instructions. Choose an exterior paint suitable for driveways and concrete floors and consider adding a slip-resistant additive for safety in wet conditions. Follow the instructions on the paint tin carefully to ensure proper mixing and application for the best results.

When you're ready to start painting, begin by cutting in the edges and corners of the driveway using a paintbrush. This ensures that you cover all areas evenly and neatly, especially those that are difficult to reach with a roller. Then, use a paint roller to apply the paint to the rest of the driveway, working from one edge to the other in smooth, overlapping strokes. Applying the paint evenly with a roller helps achieve a uniform finish and minimizes visible brush or roller marks.

After the first coat of paint has dried, apply a second coat to ensure adequate coverage and durability. Allow the paint to dry completely for approximately seven days before driving on it to prevent premature damage or marring of the finish. Following these steps meticulously will result in a beautifully painted driveway that enhances the curb appeal of your home and withstands the test of time.

Chapter Eleven

Implementing a Retaining Wall Project

A retaining wall is a structure built to hold back soil and prevent erosion, especially on slopes and hillsides. They are commonly used in landscaping to create level areas, terrace sloping landscapes, and add structural support to outdoor spaces. Retaining walls can be constructed from various materials such as concrete blocks, natural stone, brick, timber, or even gabion baskets filled with rocks.

Figure 170: Redi-Rock retaining wall. Redi-Rock International, CC BY 2.0, via Flickr.

In landscaping, retaining walls serve several purposes:
- **Erosion Control**: One of the primary functions of a retaining wall is to prevent soil erosion on sloped terrain. By holding back soil, they help stabilize the landscape and prevent landslides or washouts, especially during heavy rainfall or storms.

- **Creating Level Areas**: Retaining walls are often used to create level or terraced areas on steep slopes. This allows for the installation of gardens, patios, walkways, or other functional spaces that would otherwise be difficult to establish on uneven terrain.

- **Maximizing Usable Space**: By creating level areas, retaining walls maximize the usable space in a landscape. This can be particularly beneficial in small yards or properties with limited flat areas, allowing homeowners to make the most of their outdoor space.

- **Visual Appeal**: Retaining walls can enhance the aesthetic appeal of a landscape by adding texture, depth, and dimension. They can be designed to complement the overall style of the outdoor space and can incorporate various materials, colours, and patterns to create visual interest.

- **Supporting Structures**: In addition to soil retention, retaining walls can provide structural support for other landscape features such as driveways, pathways, or garden beds. They help distribute weight evenly and prevent soil movement, ensuring the stability and longevity of these structures.

- **Water Management**: Retaining walls can also be designed to manage water runoff and drainage in a landscape. By incorporating proper drainage systems and backfill materials, they can redirect water away from buildings, foundations, and other sensitive areas, reducing the risk of water damage and flooding.

Before embarking on a retaining wall project, thorough consideration of various jobsite factors is essential to ensure a successful outcome. Adequate site access is paramount, as it dictates the movement of construction equipment and materials. For sites with restricted access, meticulous planning regarding the staging and storage of blocks, wall rock, and other materials is necessary to streamline the construction process. Additionally, ensuring that the site is easily reachable facilitates the efficient execution of the project.

The selection and preparation of wall rock are crucial components in building a durable and stable retaining wall. Utilizing clean, granular rock beneath the base course creates a solid foundation for the wall. Optimal drainage and compaction further enhance the quality and performance of the finished structure. The term "wall rock" refers to the material utilized for the base, within, and behind the block. Ideal wall rock consists of crushed or smooth stone, well-graded, compactable aggregate, typically ranging in size from 0.25 to 1.5 inches (6 to 38 mm).

Having the necessary tools and equipment on hand is essential for a smooth construction process. Prioritizing safety, workers should be equipped with appropriate personal protective equipment, including safety glasses, gloves, dust masks, and ear protection. Hand tools such as levels, tape measures, chisels, tamps, and hammers are indispensable for precise construction. Power tools like plate compactors and concrete saws, along with rental equipment such as skid loaders and transit levels, significantly aid in the construction of retaining walls and can be obtained from equipment rental centres.

Effective planning is fundamental to the success of any retaining wall project. Factors such as lot lines, utility lines, permits, and neighbour considerations must be carefully evaluated during the planning phase. A detailed site plan drawn to scale serves as a valuable tool for foreseeing design and construction challenges, as well as estimating project costs accurately. Lot surveys obtained from city halls provide critical information regarding property lines and site layout, facilitating informed decision-making during the planning process. Additionally, contacting local utility companies to mark buried utility lines mitigates the risk of accidents and ensures compliance with regulations. Obtaining necessary building permits and adhering to local building codes are imperative, particularly for retaining walls exceeding certain height thresholds. Lastly, communicating with neighbours about the project fosters goodwill and minimizes potential disruptions during construction.

On-site Soil

Understanding the properties of on-site soils is crucial when undertaking a retaining wall project, as different soil types exert varying pressure on the wall structure. Clay soils, for instance, hold moisture and thus impose more pressure on the wall compared to sandy soils. To accurately identify the soils at the site, a simple test involves picking up a handful of soil from at least 12 inches below the surface and squeezing it to form a ball.

Clay soils, characterized by their cohesive nature, will stick together to form a ball. While they are commonly found and can be used in projects, they require careful consideration due to their moisture-retaining properties, which can exert additional pressure behind the walls. Sandy soils, on the other hand, are granular and do not stick together, offering good drainage and making them ideal for wall construction. Organic soils may stick together initially but lack cohesion once pressure is released. They should only be used for finishing the top layer of the wall and must never be employed in wall construction due to their poor structural integrity.

The soils utilized beneath and behind the retaining wall play a pivotal role in its overall stability. In addition to retaining wall blocks and geogrid reinforcement, the properties and characteristics of the infill soils significantly impact the wall's performance. Granular soils, such as sand and gravel, are preferable over clay soils due to their better compaction, drainage, and lower reinforcement requirements. The friction angle, representing the internal strength of the soil, influences soil classification and dictates construction methods. Consulting a geotechnical engineer for accurate soil classification is recommended.

Proper soil selection is imperative for achieving optimal wall performance. If on-site soils are of low quality, particularly heavy clays or organic soils, they should be removed and replaced with stronger soils to reduce reinforcement needs and ensure long-term stability. Compaction of infill soils is a critical step in construction, necessitating placement in layers or "lifts" of less than 8 inches to facilitate thorough compaction. Properly sized compaction equipment must be utilized, with compacting carried out after each block course placement. The consolidation zone, extending 3 feet into the infill soil from the back of the block, requires specific compaction procedures to achieve adequate soil strength.

Incorporating existing vegetation into the wall layout and adding new plantings can enhance the overall landscape. However, careful consideration must be given to plantings behind the wall to avoid disturbing any reinforcement added during construction. By addressing these soil-related considerations and adhering to proper construction techniques, retaining walls can be built to withstand the pressures exerted by varying soil types while enhancing the aesthetic appeal of the landscape.

Cut and Fill

When constructing a retaining wall on a hill or slope, careful consideration of the wall's placement is essential, as it directly impacts the amount of soil management required for the project. The two primary scenarios involve cut sites and fill sites, each presenting distinct challenges and necessitating different approaches to soil management.

A cut site involves cutting into the hillside to create a level area for the wall's installation, thereby removing excess soil in the process. Before undertaking this approach, it's crucial to decide how to handle the excavated soil. Depending on the project requirements and local regulations, options may include redistributing the soil elsewhere on-site, hauling it away, or repurposing it for other landscaping needs. Proper planning ensures efficient soil removal and minimizes disruptions to the surrounding environment.

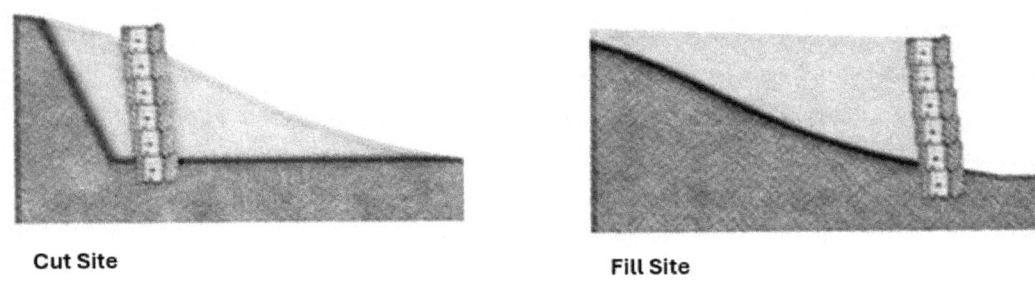

Figure 171: Cut and fill sites.

On the other hand, a fill site entails the need for additional soil to be brought onto the site to fill in behind the entire wall. This approach is typically employed when the existing slope is insufficient to support the wall's construction without additional backfill material. Planning ahead is vital for fill sites, as it involves arranging for the transportation and delivery of suitable backfill materials to the site. Factors such as soil type, compaction requirements, and drainage considerations must be taken into account when selecting backfill materials to ensure optimal wall stability and performance.

Both cut and fill sites require careful planning and coordination to manage soil effectively and ensure the success of the retaining wall project. Factors such as site topography, soil composition, environmental regulations, and project specifications all influence the decision-making process. By carefully assessing the site conditions and determining the appropriate approach for soil management, construction teams can minimize potential challenges and achieve successful outcomes in building retaining walls on hills or slopes.

Base Preparation

Starting the layout of a retaining wall project involves careful planning and precise marking of the wall's location. This begins by placing stakes to represent the front of the retaining wall and using tools like string lines or paint to outline the entire length accurately. For curved walls, a garden hose proves to be a valuable tool in achieving smooth and precise curves. Once the layout is established, the excavation phase begins by removing all surface vegetation and organic materials from the area, ensuring a clean surface for construction.

Excavation is a critical step in preparing the site for the retaining wall. If reinforcement such as geogrid is required, excavation behind the wall must accommodate the design length specified in the approved plans. Starting at the lowest point of the wall, a base trench is dug along the length of the wall. The dimensions of the base trench are determined based on the height of the wall, with a width of 24 inches (600 mm) and a depth calculated at 6 inches (150 mm) plus an additional 1 inch (25 mm) for every 1 foot (300 mm) of wall height.

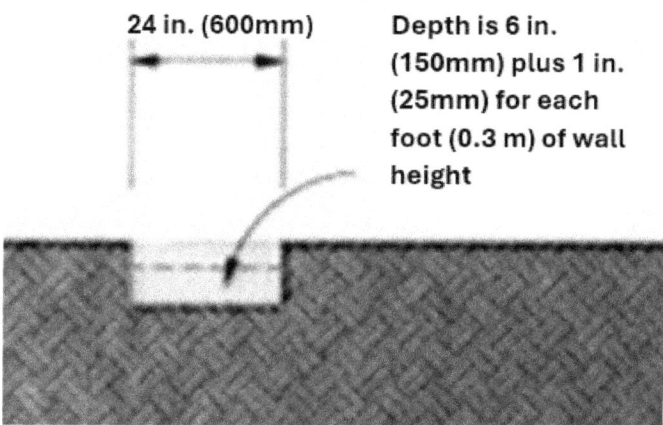

Figure 172: Base trench.

Compacting the base trench is essential for ensuring a stable foundation for the retaining wall. A minimum of two passes with a walk-behind plate compactor is recommended to achieve proper compaction. In cases where the foundation soils at the bottom of the base trench are not firm or solid, especially if composed of heavy clay or wet soils, it may be necessary to remove and replace this material with granular material, compacting it in lifts of 8 inches (200 mm) or less.

Base material placement is the next step, and it involves several important considerations. For reinforced walls or walls over 4 feet (1.2 m) tall, a drain pipe is required, placed at the lowest possible point toward the back of the trench and vented to daylight every 50 feet (15 m). A minimum of 6 inches (150 mm) of wall rock is then placed in the base trench and raked smooth before compacting it with a plate compactor. Throughout this process, it's crucial to check the entire length for level and make adjustments as necessary to ensure the wall's stability and integrity.

Building Courses

Building a retaining wall requires careful attention to detail and precise execution to ensure its stability and longevity. The process begins by starting the base course at the lowest wall elevation. All blocks are placed with the raised front lip facing up and forward on the base material near the front of the base trench. Each block is checked and adjusted for level and alignment as it is installed. Minor adjustments can be made by tapping the blocks with a dead blow hammer or by placing up to 0.5 inches (13 mm) of coarse sand under the blocks. It's crucial to maintain a straight and level base course to ensure a quality finished wall, as irregularities in the base course can become more pronounced as the wall stacks up.

Once the base course is laid, the backfilling and compaction process begins. The area in front of the blocks is filled with on-site soils to prevent the base course blocks from shifting during filling and compacting. The hollow cores of the base course and 12 inches (300 mm) behind the block are filled with wall rock to the height of the block. Infill or approved on-site soils are then used to backfill behind the wall rock in lifts of no more than 8 inches (200 mm). A plate compactor is used to consolidate the wall rock directly behind the block and compact the area parallel to the wall, working from the back of the block to the back of the excavated area with a minimum of 2 passes. This process is repeated for every course after the first course, with compaction starting on the block.

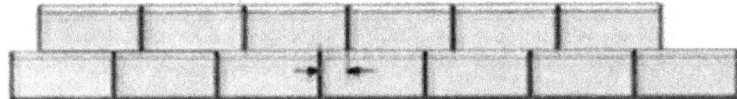

Figure 173: Laying courses.

Additional courses are installed by stacking blocks with vertical seams offset from the blocks below by at least 1/4 the length of the block. Each block is checked for level and alignment, and adjustments are made as needed. The hollow cores and 12 inches (300 mm) behind the block are filled with wall rock to the height of the block, and infill or approved on-site soils are used to backfill behind the wall rock in lifts of no more than 8 inches (200 mm). From the second course and above, a plate compactor is used to compact directly on the blocks as well as the area behind the blocks in lifts of 8 inches (200 mm) or less. This process is repeated until the wall reaches the desired height, with organic soils used to fill behind the blocks on the last course to assist in plantings above the wall and direct water away from the blocks.

Installing wall rock and backfill materials is a crucial step in ensuring the stability and integrity of a retaining wall. This process begins by backfilling the hollow cores and a minimum of 12 inches (300 mm) behind the wall with wall rock. It's essential to install the wall rock to be level or below the receiving notch of the anchoring unit to prevent interference with the placement of subsequent courses of blocks. Wall rock provides structural support and helps with drainage behind the wall, contributing to its overall stability.

Once the wall rock is in place, approved soils are used to backfill behind the wall rock and in front of the base course. These soils should be carefully selected to ensure proper compaction and drainage. Backfilling with approved soils helps to provide additional support to the wall and creates a stable foundation for the landscaping above.

After backfilling with wall rock and approved soils, a plate compactor is used to consolidate the area behind the blocks. This compaction process helps to ensure that the backfill materials are properly compacted and provides additional stability to the wall. It's important to compact in lifts of 8 inches (200 mm) or less to achieve optimal compaction and prevent settling over time.

Overall, the installation of wall rock and backfill materials is a critical step in the construction of a retaining wall. Proper placement and compaction of these materials are essential for ensuring the stability, longevity, and performance of the wall, as well as the safety of the surrounding area. Following best practices for installing wall rock and backfill materials will help to create a durable and reliable retaining wall that effectively retains soil and enhances the aesthetic appeal of the landscape.

Building Retaining Wall Step-Ups into the Slope

When constructing step-up retaining walls, careful planning and precise execution are essential to ensure structural integrity and stability. The process begins by establishing the base course at the lowest elevation of the wall. A base trench, typically 24 inches (600 mm) wide, is excavated to accommodate the foundational elements of the wall. The depth of this trench is calculated based on the wall's height, with 6 inches (150 mm) plus an additional 1 inch (25 mm) for each foot (300 mm) of wall height considered for the amount of buried block required. This ensures proper support and stability for the structure.

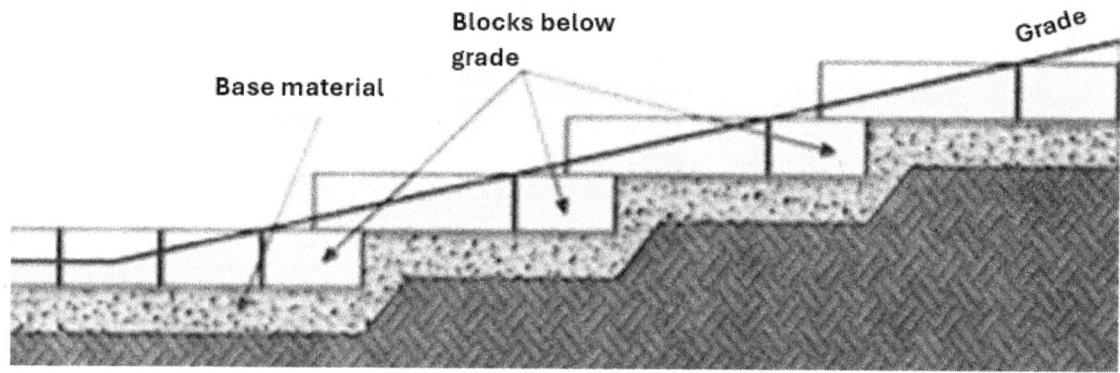

Figure 174: Step-up retaining wall into slope.

In cases where a slope exists below the wall, consulting a local engineer is recommended to address any specific challenges or considerations related to the site's topography. Once the trench is excavated, it is compacted and levelled using a plate compactor to create a firm and stable base for the wall. Additionally, a drain pipe is positioned at the lowest point within the trench to facilitate proper drainage and prevent water build-up behind the wall.

After preparing the base trench, a layer of wall rock, typically 6 inches (150 mm) thick, is placed and levelled within the trench. This layer provides additional support and helps to ensure proper drainage within the wall structure. The base course of blocks is then installed on top of the wall rock, with careful attention paid to levelling and alignment to maintain structural integrity.

As the construction progresses upwards, each subsequent step-up is excavated, compacted, and levelled to accommodate the base material and buried block. The base course of blocks is then installed on the prepared surface, and the process of filling the hollow cores and surrounding areas with wall rock and backfill materials is repeated. This ensures that each step-up is properly supported and integrated into the overall structure of the retaining wall.

Throughout the construction process, it is crucial to compact the wall rock and backfill materials behind the blocks and within the step-up areas to minimize the risk of settlement and ensure long-term stability. This is achieved by making a minimum of two passes with a plate compactor, effectively consolidating the materials and creating a solid foundation for the wall.

It's important to note that maintaining proper burial depth for each block at the step-ups is critical to prevent erosion and potential wall failure. By adhering to these guidelines and best practices, step-up retaining walls can be effectively constructed to provide reliable support and stability in sloped terrain.

Using Geogrid

Geogrids play a crucial role in slope stabilization and earth retention projects, offering flexibility, strength, and durability. These synthetic meshes are specifically designed to reinforce soil structures and prevent erosion, making them essential components in retaining wall construction. Geogrids come in various materials, sizes, and strengths, with options ranging from high tensile strength plastics to woven polyester yarns. Typically packaged in rolls at the factory, geogrids provide a versatile solution for reinforcing soil structures in diverse terrain.

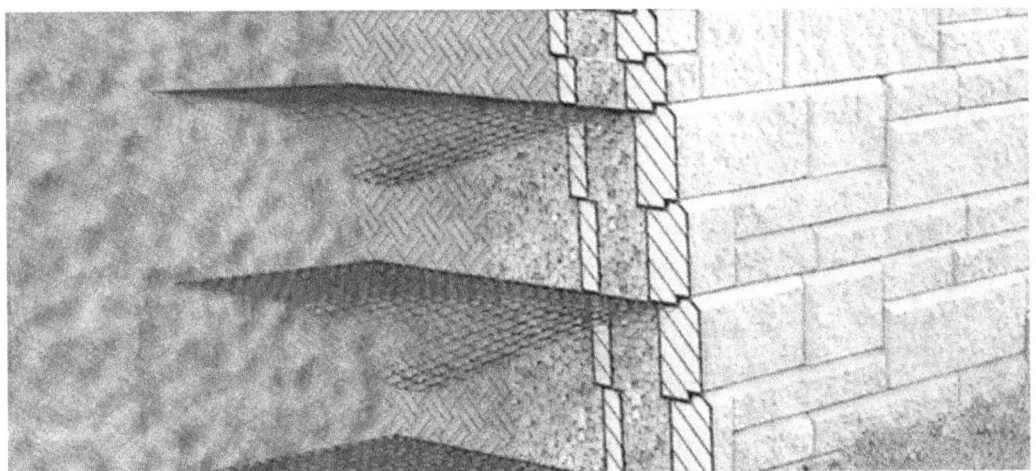

Figure 175: Using Geogrid in retaining wall construction.

The effectiveness of geogrids in reinforcing soil structures can be demonstrated through the sand castle test, a method that evaluates the performance of soil under vertical force. This test involves two cylinders of soil, with the first containing compacted material only and the second incorporating mesh screens to simulate geogrid reinforcement. By subjecting these cylinders to vertical force, the test assesses how the soil performs with and without geogrid reinforcement, highlighting the significant role of geogrids in enhancing soil stability and preventing erosion.

During the installation of geogrid reinforcement in retaining wall construction, several key steps are followed to ensure proper integration and functionality. After completing the base course of the retaining wall, the first layer of geogrid is installed, with careful attention paid to avoiding direct compaction on top of the grid. Instead, the next course of blocks is stacked so that the vertical seams are offset from the blocks below, maintaining structural integrity and alignment along the retaining wall line.

Once the geogrid is in place, it is important to remove any slack by pulling on the back of the grid and securing it in position if necessary. Compaction of wall rock and infill soils behind the retaining wall is then carried out using a plate compactor, ensuring proper consolidation and stability of the soil structure. Compaction is performed in lifts of 8 inches or less, starting on the block and working in a path parallel to the block to achieve solid, movement-free soil.

As additional courses of blocks are installed, geogrid reinforcement is incorporated according to approved plans, typically on every other course of the retaining wall. This strategic placement ensures optimal reinforcement while minimizing material usage and construction costs. Finally, the retaining wall is completed to the desired height, with organic soils used to fill behind the blocks on the last course, facilitating plantings above the wall and directing water away from the structure.

Curves and Serpentines

Curves add an elegant touch to any landscape design, offering a visually appealing contrast to straight lines and angles. They are relatively simple to design and construct, requiring careful consideration of the desired curvature and the selection of suitable building materials. When planning curved retaining walls, it's essential to determine whether you prefer tight or gentle curves and choose blocks or combinations of blocks that best complement your design vision.

Building curves in retaining walls typically involves minimal cutting, making the construction process straightforward and efficient. One key aspect to consider is offsetting the vertical seams of the blocks to maintain structural integrity and aesthetic appeal. For both inside and outside curves, it's advisable to maintain an offset of at least one-quarter of the block length from the courses below. This can be achieved by cutting a block in half or using half-width blocks to ensure a seamless and visually pleasing curve.

Figure 176: Example of a curved retaining wall. Armcon Precast, CC BY 2.0, via Flikr.

Before constructing the retaining wall, it's helpful to lay out the design using a garden hose or paint to visualize the curves accurately. Measuring the radius of each curve is crucial, and referring to the radius chart provided by the block manufacturer can guide the selection of appropriate blocks or adjustments to fit the chosen design. In general, gentle sweeping curves tend to produce more aesthetically pleasing results, enhancing the overall appeal of the retaining wall.

When building inside curves, maintaining a flowing and consistent alignment of the front of the blocks while fanning them out at the back helps create a smooth and visually appealing curve. On the other hand, constructing smooth outside curves involves removing one or both of the "wings" from the back of the blocks to tighten the radius of the curve. This can be achieved by hitting the back of the wings with a hammer or using a hammer and chisel along the existing score line for a clean break.

To start the curve, mark the centre point where the curve will begin and drive a stake into the ground. Attach a string line to the stake, extending it to the required radius length and rotating it around to mark the location of the base course. Install the blocks along the marked line, ensuring that the front of the blocks align with the designated mark. Transitioning the curve back into a straight wall or another curve can be accomplished by laying out the curve and the first few blocks of the next section, making adjustments as necessary for a seamless transition.

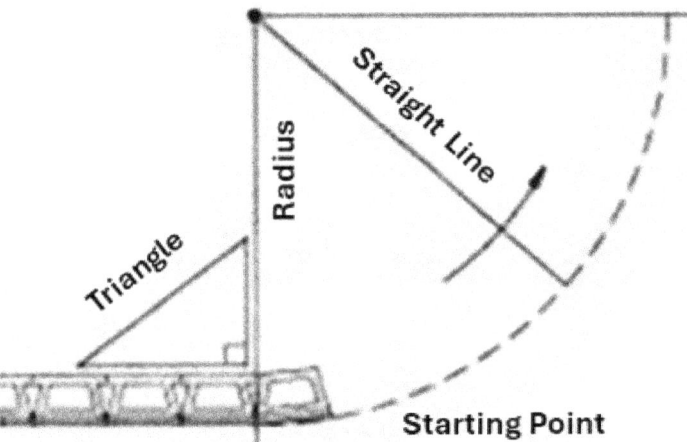

Figure 177: Starting a curve.

When incorporating curves into reinforced retaining walls, proper placement of geogrid becomes crucial to ensure structural stability and longevity. Geogrid, a flexible synthetic mesh designed for slope stabilization and earth retention, needs to follow the curvature of the retaining wall while maintaining 100% coverage to effectively reinforce the structure. Whether dealing with inside or outside curves, specific techniques are employed to accommodate the geogrid and ensure optimal performance.

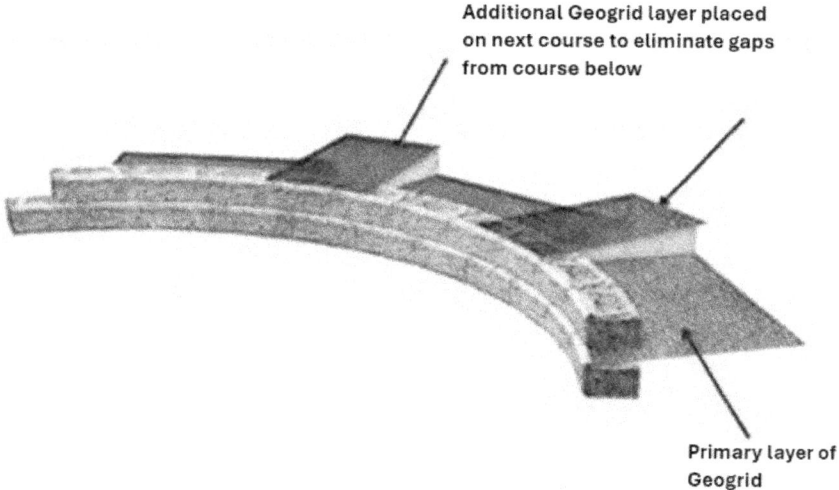

Figure 178: Inside curves with Geogrid.

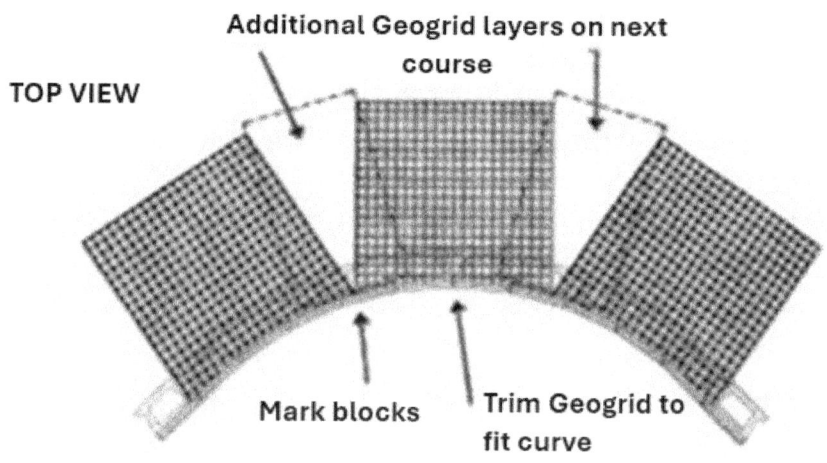

Figure 179: Inside curves with Geogrid.

Inside curves present a unique challenge when it comes to geogrid placement. To address this, the geogrid should be rolled out behind the wall, with its edge snug against the front of the blocks. As voids may appear between pieces of geogrid at the back, these areas need to be marked or noted for reference. On the subsequent course of blocks, additional layers of geogrid are placed over the marked areas to cover the voids effectively. In cases of patterned walls, efforts are made to fit the grid through the coursing as best as possible to fill the voids from the course below.

For outside curves, a similar approach is taken to ensure proper geogrid coverage. The reinforcement grid is rolled out around the curve, trimmed to fit along the front lip of the blocks, and lifted where it overlaps to insert infill material, which helps separate geogrid layers. It's essential to avoid compacting directly on the geogrid, and the entire curved area must be covered to maintain structural integrity.

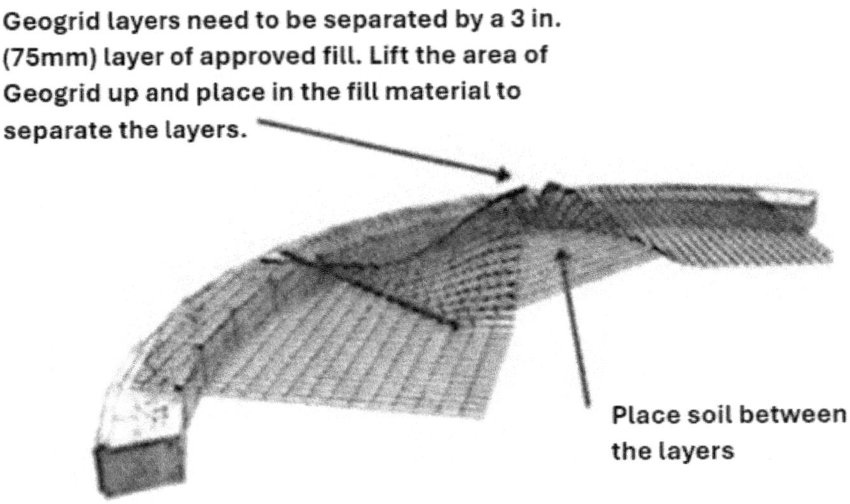

Geogrid layers need to be separated by a 3 in. (75mm) layer of approved fill. Lift the area of Geogrid up and place in the fill material to separate the layers.

Place soil between the layers

Figure 180: Outside Curves with Geogrid.

Capping curves requires careful consideration to ensure a seamless finish that complements the curvature of the retaining wall. For standard curves, two caps are initially placed on top of the wall, leaving space for a third cap to fit snugly between their widest points. Once positioned, the centre cap is marked where it overlaps the bottom of the other two caps, and it's then cut accordingly to create a tight fit. This process is repeated as needed to cap the entire curve, and using high-strength construction adhesive to secure the caps is advisable for added stability.

For tighter curves, particularly those with outside radii, a different approach is taken to achieve a precise fit. After placing two caps with their backs together, the distance of the gap between them at the front of the wall is measured. This measurement is then halved, and corresponding marks are made on the back of each cap. Using a masonry saw, the caps are cut along the marked lines, ensuring a perfect match for the curvature of the wall. These steps are applicable to both inside and outside radiuses, providing a tailored solution for capping curves with precision and accuracy.

Corners and Angles

When it comes to designing and constructing retaining walls, corners and angles pose unique challenges that often require custom cutting of blocks. However, it's generally recommended to opt for curves instead of corners whenever possible, as curved retaining walls offer better stability and a more aesthetically pleasing appearance in landscape design. While corners are feasible, curved walls provide a smoother flowing look to the landscape, enhancing the overall visual appeal.

Inside corners, although requiring some modification of standard Allan Block units, can be constructed relatively easily. By removing part of the lip from one block and a portion from another, the blocks can be overlapped to create a strong interlock. This process begins at the base course, where modified blocks are set in place, ensuring that the raised lip on one block aligns with the raised lips on the opposite retaining wall. As the construction progresses upward, the alternating placement of modified blocks continues, facilitating a seamless integration of inside corners into the retaining wall structure. Additionally, cutting caps at 45-degree angles further enhances the custom finished look of inside corners, providing a clean and polished appearance to the wall.

For outside corners, corner blocks are employed to streamline the construction process. These blocks, designed with a setback, offer a solution for creating stable outside corners without the need for extensive custom cutting. Beginning at the corners and working outward, corner blocks are set in place, and perpendicular base courses are installed, levelled, backfilled, and compacted. Alternate corner blocks are then placed on subsequent courses, ensuring a secure and structurally sound outside corner. Similar to inside corners, cutting caps at 45-degree angles adds a touch of sophistication to the finished appearance of outside corners, elevating the overall aesthetic appeal of the retaining wall.

While outside corners may require more time and skill compared to inside corners, utilizing corner blocks streamlines the process, allowing for efficient construction without compromising on stability or visual appeal. By adhering to proper construction techniques and incorporating thoughtful design elements, retaining walls can seamlessly integrate into the landscape, enhancing both functionality and aesthetics.

Building a Timber Retaining Wall

Building a timber retaining wall is an effective solution for levelling out sloping blocks while creating additional usable space in the landscape. Before starting the project, it's essential to gather all the necessary materials and tools. The materials required typically include treated sleepers for posts, galvanized nails, geo-fabric, agricultural coil pipe, drainage gravel, and bags of cement. Meanwhile, the tools needed for the project may include a mattock, tape measure, circular saw, club hammer, square, sledgehammer, angle grinder, wheelbarrow, spirit level, string line, and marking paint.

The first step in building a timber retaining wall is to mark the placement of the wall using a string line as a guide. This helps ensure accuracy and alignment during the construction process. It's crucial to choose the type of timber that suits your aesthetic preferences and budget. Rectangular hardwood sleepers or round logs are popular choices for low-load applications like garden beds due to their natural appearance, affordability, and low maintenance requirements.

Once the placement is marked, the post spacing should be determined according to the length of the timber. Typically, posts should be spaced at intervals of 1.2 meters apart for 2.4-meter-long sleepers or 1.5 meters apart for 3-meter-long sleepers. The timber used must be treated to hazard level H4 or better to ensure durability and longevity.

Next, postholes should be dug to a depth of 700mm and a width of 300mm. The bottom 100mm of each hole should be filled with coarse gravel to facilitate drainage. The posts should be cut to the appropriate length, with the tops cut at a slight slope to shed water, and all cut ends should be sealed with an appropriate timber preservative.

Once the posts are in place and set in concrete, a string should be tied between them to align the other posts accurately. Horizontal timbers can then be installed and secured to the upright posts using galvanized spikes or nails. Additional layers of logs or sleepers can be stacked on top to reach the desired height, securing them with nails or spikes as needed. It's important to ensure that the sleepers are placed behind the posts for stability.

Behind the second layer of timber, slotted agricultural pipe should be laid for drainage, surrounded by coarse gravel. Porous geotextile should be lined inside the wall to filter seepage and reduce soil erosion. Plastic sheeting should be avoided as it can cause water buildup and potential wall collapse. Finally, the area behind the wall should be backfilled, creating a spoon drain on top to assist with runoff, before stepping back to admire the completed work.

Chapter Twelve

PLANTS AND PLANT CULTURE

Plant identification is crucial for landscaping for several reasons:

- **Selection**: Identifying plants allows landscapers to choose the most appropriate species for a particular environment or design. Factors such as climate, soil type, sunlight exposure, and available space all influence plant selection. By accurately identifying plants, landscapers can ensure they choose species that will thrive in the intended location, leading to healthier and more visually appealing landscapes.

- **Maintenance**: Different plants have different maintenance requirements. Some may need regular pruning, watering, fertilizing, or pest control, while others may be more self-sufficient. Knowing the specific needs of each plant helps landscapers plan and execute maintenance tasks more effectively, reducing the risk of over- or under-caring for plants.

- **Aesthetics**: Plant selection plays a significant role in the overall aesthetics of a landscape design. Identifying plants allows landscapers to create harmonious combinations of colours, textures, shapes, and sizes that enhance the visual appeal of outdoor spaces. By understanding the characteristics of each plant, landscapers can design landscapes that achieve the desired aesthetic goals.

- **Functionality**: Plants serve various functions in landscaping, such as providing shade, privacy screening, erosion control, noise reduction, or attracting wildlife. Proper plant identification ensures that the chosen species fulfill these functional requirements effectively. For example, selecting fast-growing, dense foliage plants for privacy screening or choosing deep-rooted plants for erosion control can contribute to the functionality and long-term success of the landscape design.

- **Environmental Considerations**: Some plants may have invasive tendencies or be susceptible to local pests and diseases. By accurately identifying plants, landscapers can avoid introducing invasive species that may harm local ecosystems or selecting plants that are vulnerable to prevalent pests or diseases. This promotes environmental sustainability and reduces the need for chemical interventions.

- **Safety**: Certain plants may pose risks to human health or property if not properly identified. For example, some plants may have thorns, spines, or toxic properties that could cause injury or illness if touched or ingested. Identifying potentially hazardous plants allows landscapers to take appropriate precautions, such as placing them away from high-traffic areas or selecting alternative species.

Plants can be identified by:

- **Observation**: Begin by observing the plant in its natural habitat or where it is growing. Take note of its overall size, shape, and growth habit. Pay attention to features such as leaf arrangement, leaf shape, flower characteristics, stem structure, and any other distinctive features.

- **Use Field Guides**: Field guides are valuable resources that provide detailed descriptions and illustrations of plant species. Look for field guides specific to your region or the type of plants you're trying to identify. These guides typically organize plants based on their characteristics, making it easier to narrow down potential matches.

- **Online Resources**: There are numerous online platforms and databases dedicated to plant identification. Websites and mobile apps like iNaturalist, PlantSnap, and PictureThis allow users to upload photos of plants and receive suggestions or identifications based on image recognition technology or community expertise.

- **Botanical Keys**: Botanical keys are systematic guides that use a series of questions or characteristics to help identify plants. These keys often require knowledge of botanical terminology but can be effective for accurately identifying plants. Botanical keys are commonly found in botanical textbooks or field guides.

- **Consult Experts**: If you're having difficulty identifying a plant, consider seeking assistance from experts. Botanists, horticulturists, gardeners, or staff at botanical gardens or nurseries may be able to help identify plants based on their knowledge and experience.

- **Take Detailed Photos**: When attempting to identify a plant using online resources or consulting experts, take clear, detailed photos from multiple angles. Capture close-up shots of leaves, flowers, fruits, and any other distinguishing features. Providing multiple images can improve the accuracy of the identification.

- **Consider the Habitat**: Take into account the plant's habitat and ecological context. Certain plants are characteristic of specific environments or ecosystems. Understanding where the plant is growing can provide clues to its identity.

- **Compare and Confirm**: Once you have a potential identification, compare the plant to known images or descriptions in field guides, online databases, or botanical keys. Look for matches in terms of overall appearance, leaf shape, flower colour, and other characteristics. Confirm the identification by cross-referencing with multiple sources if possible.

- **Be Patient and Persistent**: Plant identification can sometimes be challenging, especially for beginners. Don't be discouraged if you're unable to identify a plant right away. Keep exploring, learning, and refining your observation skills over time.

Providing Client Plant Advice

Providing thorough client advice for safety in the garden is essential to minimize the risk of accidents and injuries. This includes:

- **General Garden Safety**: Clients should be made aware of common garden hazards to prevent accidents. For instance, stepping on the upturned teeth of a rake can lead to injuries, such as the handle hitting the head or the teeth causing cuts. It's crucial to keep garden tools, hoses, and solid objects properly stored to avoid tripping hazards. Steps and paths should be stable and have a non-skid surface to prevent slips and falls. Additionally, when using ladders, ensuring their stability before climbing is essential to avoid accidents.

- **Safe Handling of Sharp Tools**: Sharp gardening tools like rakes, forks, and shears pose a risk of injury if not handled properly. Clients should store these tools out of children's reach and ensure they are secured to prevent accidents. Any cuts received from garden tools should be promptly cleaned with warm water and disinfectant to prevent infection.

- **Rotary Mower Safety**: Using rotary mowers requires caution to avoid accidents. Before mowing, clients should remove stones or pebbles from the lawn to prevent them from being caught in the blades and causing injury. Wearing appropriate footwear like solid boots or gumboots is recommended, and clients should always push the mower forward rather than pulling it backward to prevent accidents.

- **Safe Use of Chemicals**: Clients should understand the proper handling and storage of garden chemicals and fertilizers to prevent accidents and environmental damage. Chemicals should be stored out of reach of children and pets in a secure, dry, and cool location. Clients should read and follow the instructions on the product label carefully, paying special attention to the rate of application and safety directions. It's important not to use kitchen utensils for measuring pesticides and to avoid spraying chemicals under adverse weather conditions. Clients should only mix enough chemicals for the intended job to avoid excess disposal issues. Unused chemical mixtures should not be stored, as they can deteriorate over time. It's also illegal to transfer chemicals into containers not designed for that purpose.

Providing comprehensive client advice for the safe use of chemicals, plant nutrition, and potting mix is essential for ensuring the health and well-being of both individuals and the environment. This includes:

- **Chemical Use Safety**: Clients should be informed about the importance of carefully reading and following the directions on garden chemical labels. This includes understanding safety directions and using the products only for their intended purpose. It's crucial to avoid contact with the skin, eyes, and mouth when handling concentrated sprays or dusts. Clients should also refrain from using chemicals on windy or rainy days and should not eat, drink, or smoke while using garden chemicals. After use, all mixing and spray equipment should be thoroughly rinsed, and chemicals must be stored in their original containers, out of reach of children and pets, in a secure and locked cupboard.

- **Plant Nutrition and Feeding**: Clients should understand the role of fertilizers in supplying nutrients to plants for healthy growth. The three major ingredients of plant food are nitrogen (N), phosphorus (P), and potassium (K). Different plants have varying nutrient requirements, and fertilizers are available in balanced forms known as N.P.K. mixtures. Clients should be advised on selecting the appropriate fertilizer based on the needs of their plants. Additionally, clients should be informed about the importance of not over-fertilizing, avoiding application to dry soil, and using fertilizers suitable for specific plant types, such as delicate ferns or Australian native plants.

- **Potting Mix Use**: Clients should be guided on the importance of using quality potting mix for potted plants. Ordinary garden soil may contain weed seeds and be too heavy for pots. Australian Standards for potting mixes ensure quality and safety. These standards include tests for air-filled porosity, water holding capacity, pH levels, soil salinity, and nutrient levels. Quality potting mixes are typically composed of composted pine bark, recycled material, or green waste, along with screened river sand for drainage. Clients should be advised on proper potting techniques, such as not covering drainage holes, watering plants after potting, and washing hands after handling potting mix to avoid ingestion of dust or mist.

Providing comprehensive client advice for watering, growing vegetables, and growing lawn involves understanding the specific needs of plants and turf, as well as the environmental conditions they thrive in. This includes:

- **Watering Advice**:

  - Timing: Watering established plants and lawns is best done in the early morning or late afternoon to maximize water absorption and minimize evaporation. For seedlings and seed beds, watering earlier in the day helps the soil surface dry by evening, reducing the risk of fungal diseases and deterring pests like slugs and snails.

  - Frequency: Seedlings, young transplants, and vegetable crops require frequent and evenly distributed watering to thrive. Adequate moisture levels are crucial, especially during hot weather, to prevent wilting and ensure proper growth.

  - Methods: Watering should be done with a fine spray to avoid mechanical damage to plants and soil crusting. Thorough watering followed by allowing the soil to dry out slightly promotes root health and oxygenation.

- **Growing Vegetables Advice**:

  - Seasonal Considerations: Vegetables are grouped based on their growing season, with cool-season, intermediate-season, and warm-season varieties requiring specific temperature ranges for optimal growth.

  - Cultivation Practices: Proper positioning in sunny areas, well-draining soil with good structure, and adequate nutrient supply are essential for successful vegetable cultivation. Attention to pH levels, mulching, and crop rotation helps maintain soil health and fertility.

  - Vegetable Selection: A diverse range of vegetables can be grown at home, offering nutritional benefits and culinary versatility. From leafy greens to root crops, each vegetable has unique requirements for growth and development.

- **Growing Lawn Advice**:

  - Grass Selection: Choosing the right grass species for the climate and conditions ensures a healthy and resilient lawn. Warm-season and cool-season grasses have different growth patterns and water requirements.

  - Establishment: Proper soil preparation, whether seeding or laying turf, sets the foundation for a lush lawn. Adequate watering during the establishment phase promotes root development and turf health.

- Maintenance: Regular fertilizing, mowing, and watering are essential for maintaining a vibrant lawn. Light, frequent fertilization is preferred over heavy applications, and proper mowing height and frequency support healthy grass growth.

- Watering Practices: Lawns should be watered in the morning to minimize evaporation and promote deep root penetration. Thorough watering, less frequently, encourages root growth and drought tolerance.

Providing comprehensive client advice for growing fruit and citrus trees involves understanding the specific needs of these plants and offering practical guidance for their care and maintenance. This includes:

- **Where to Grow**:

  - Sunlight Requirement: Citrus trees thrive in full sun, so it's essential to plant them in sunny spots in the garden. For those with limited sunlight, growing citrus in pots offers flexibility as they can be moved to take advantage of changing sunlight patterns.

  - Container Options: When growing citrus in pots, lightweight and durable containers like Yates Tuscan pots are recommended. These pots offer the Mediterranean aesthetic that complements citrus trees while being more manageable and cost-effective than traditional terracotta pots.

- **Good Drainage**:

  - Soil Preparation: Citrus trees require well-draining soil, especially varieties like the 'Eureka' lemon, which are susceptible to water-related issues. In heavy clay soils, it's essential to improve drainage by raising the bed level, incorporating gypsum, and adding plenty of organic matter like compost or aged manure.

- **Fertilization**:

  - Before Planting: Incorporating Dynamic Lifter organic pellets into the soil before planting provides gentle nourishment without risking root burn. This organic fertilizer enhances soil health and supports root development.

  - Established Citrus: Regular feeding with Thrive Granular Citrus Food at least twice a year ensures that citrus trees receive essential nutrients for healthy growth and fruit production. Alternating with Dynamic Lifter organic pellets maintains soil microbial activity.

  - Potted Citrus: Slow-release fertilizers like Dynamic Lifter or controlled-release Nutricote pellets are suitable for potted citrus to minimize the risk of root burn and provide consistent nourishment.

- **Pests & Diseases Management**:

  - Scale: Identified by lumps on fruit and leaves, scale infestations can be controlled with treatments like Yates PestOil or horticultural white oil.

  - Fruit Fly: Grubs inside fruit indicate fruit fly infestation. Using products like Yates Nature's Way Fruit Fly Control, combined with proper sanitation practices, helps manage fruit fly populations.

- Gall Wasp: Lumps in branches are signs of gall wasp infestation. Promptly removing and destroying affected branches before the end of August prevents further spread.

- Cold Damage: Curled-up leaves and reddish-brown patches indicate cold damage. Moving potted citrus to warmer locations during colder periods helps mitigate damage.

- Citrus Leaf Miner: Trails and twists in newer leaves signal citrus leaf miner activity. Treatments with PestOil or physical removal of affected leaves help control infestations.

Plant Diseases

Understanding and addressing plant diseases is an essential aspect of gardening, as plants, like humans, are susceptible to illnesses. It's common for gardeners to initially feel dismayed when their carefully tended plants suddenly show signs of sickness. However, with experience, they learn to recognize and manage these issues effectively. Diseases manifest in various forms, including powdery blooms, sooty molds, or shot holes on leaves and fruit, indicating the presence of a garden disease.

The distinction between natural variegation and variegation caused by plant diseases like viruses is crucial for gardeners in diagnosing and managing plant health. While variegated leaves in some plants result from natural mutations, others may signal underlying issues. These natural mutations, resulting in paler and mottled effects due to reduced chlorophyll, have been selectively bred for in certain plants, despite potential reductions in vigor and lifespan. However, variegation caused by plant diseases, particularly viruses, presents a more serious concern.

Plant viruses, often transmitted by vectors like aphids or thrips, pose significant threats to cultivated plants, especially food crops. Unlike their wild counterparts, cultivated plants are susceptible to various virus infections, disrupting normal plant functions like photosynthesis and growth. Symptoms of virus infections can manifest as leaf color variegation, ringspots, bronzing, malformations, or wilting, with young foliage typically exhibiting the most obvious signs.

The classification of plant viruses typically relies on common names derived from the first plant studied, the prominent symptom, and the virus group. Spread primarily occurs through vectors, sap transmission, or contaminated plant material like seeds, bulbs, or cuttings. Control measures are limited, emphasizing prevention through practices such as removing infected plants, weed management, personal hygiene, tool sterilization, and utilizing disease-resistant varieties. Professional growers often employ insect-proof greenhouses to mitigate virus transmission via vectors.

Given the potential economic and ecological consequences of introducing new virus diseases, strict quarantine measures are crucial to prevent their spread. Adherence to quarantine legislation helps safeguard against the inadvertent introduction of harmful viruses through plant or seed imports. With no chemical or biological controls available, prevention remains the most effective strategy in managing plant virus diseases, underscoring the importance of vigilance and proactive measures in maintaining plant health and productivity.

Preventing many diseases begins with growing plants in suitable conditions, including the appropriate spot with the right soil pH, water, light, and soil preparation. Adequate soil preparation and proper plant care practices can often prevent disease outbreaks. However, if an outbreak occurs, correctly identifying the problem is crucial. Once the issue is identified, gardeners can seek appropriate solutions to treat the problem effectively.

Simple and sustainable solutions often exist for plant diseases. For example, ensuring plants are well-fed with compost and manure and avoiding wetting leaves can mitigate disease spread. These methods are preferable as they do not involve the use of chemicals that may harm beneficial insects or amphibians or pollute waterways.

Specific diseases, such as Early Blight of Tomatoes, have distinct characteristics and preferences. Early Blight, a fungal disease, affects tomato plants, causing brown spots with yellow halos on leaves and stems. This disease thrives in temperatures over 15°C and moist conditions, spreading rapidly in humid environments with poor air circulation. Understanding its preferences helps gardeners implement targeted control measures.

Figure 181: Early blight on tomato leaves. Dwight Sipler from Stow, MA, USA, CC BY 2.0, via Wikimedia Commons.

Effective control methods for Early Blight include homemade remedies like milk-and-water solutions, bicarbonate of soda sprays with fish emulsion, and seaweed sprays. These solutions alter the leaf surface pH, strengthen cell walls, and create conditions unfavourable for fungal growth. Additionally, low environmental impact fungicides are available, although their success may vary.

Other preventive measures include destroying infected plants and dropped leaves, rotating crops, and avoiding planting susceptible crops in the same area each season. These strategies help minimize disease recurrence and maintain garden health. By understanding the characteristics of specific diseases and implementing appropriate control measures, gardeners can effectively manage plant diseases and maintain thriving gardens.

During the winter months, when fruit trees appear dormant, the microscopic world of fungi is actively preparing to wreak havoc come spring. Peach Leaf Curl, a prevalent fungus, is notorious for disfiguring leaves and fruit on peach, nectarine, apricot, and almond trees. This fungal menace, along with others like Shot Hole, Freckle Spot, Rust, and Powdery Mildew, lie dormant, waiting to multiply once the weather warms up. To combat these fungal problems, winter spraying is recommended to minimize their incidence.

Peach Leaf Curl manifests as blistered and puckered new growth on trees, with severe cases leading to pimpled fruit and premature fruit drop. In the cool, moist conditions of early spring, the fungus proliferates, perpetuating the cycle of infestation year after year if left unchecked. Apart from Peach Leaf Curl, other fungal diseases may also plague stone fruit trees during this time.

To mitigate the spread of Peach Leaf Curl and other fungal diseases, several measures can be taken. Good garden hygiene involves removing fallen leaves and damaged or rotten fruit, while keeping trees pruned to an open vase shape enhances air circulation. Planting trees in well-prepared soil with adequate sunlight and air circulation, along with maintaining a regular fertilizing and watering schedule, also helps prevent fungal issues.

Figure 182: Leaf curl on peach leaves. Freshclover, CC BY-SA 4.0, via Wikimedia Commons.

Winter washing, a technique involving the application of low-impact fungicides such as copper oxychloride or lime sulphur, is highly effective in controlling fungal diseases. Spraying should commence in late autumn at leaf fall, just before the tree enters dormancy, and repeated at bud swell or bud burst in late winter or early spring. Once the leaves have opened, it's too late to spray for Peach Leaf Curl and many other fungal diseases, necessitating spraying at the end of the following summer.

However, when spraying fruit trees, caution must be exercised to minimize the potential impact of spray drift on surrounding vegetation, soil microorganisms, pets, and humans. Spraying is typically carried out until runoff, where the spray liquid completely covers the tree surface and runs off onto the ground. Using spray sheets to protect non-targeted areas is advisable. Additionally, only preparing enough spray for immediate use helps avoid disposal issues.

While spraying may not guarantee 100% effectiveness, vigilance during summer is crucial. Any leaves showing signs of fungal disease should be promptly removed to prevent further spread. By implementing these measures, gardeners can effectively manage fungal diseases in fruit trees and ensure healthy yields come harvest time.

Black Spot of Rose, a fungal disease notorious among gardeners, manifests as round, black spots with fringed margins on the upper surfaces of rose leaves, typically reaching up to 12mm wide. Despite its unappealing nature, this fungus thrives on various types of roses, especially in conditions conducive to its growth, such as high humidity and over-fertilization. It particularly relishes environments lacking in air movement and with excess moisture on leaves, making crowded gardens its ideal habitat. However, it despises well-mulched garden beds, sunlight, and diligent gardeners who monitor their plants regularly.

Figure 183: Black Spot (Diplocarpon rosae). Stephen James McWilliam, CC BY 4.0, via Wikimedia Commons.

The detrimental impact of Black Spot becomes evident through the telltale signs of irregular black spots covering rose leaves, ultimately leading to leaf drop. This fungal menace perpetuates its infestation by dispersing spores onto the ground, ensuring its continuous presence in the garden. Combatting Black Spot requires a multi-faceted approach aimed at disrupting its life cycle and minimizing its spread.

Various home remedies offer effective means of controlling Black Spot. These include spraying a mixture of fat-free milk and water onto clean rose leaves, which stimulates the growth of beneficial fungi that antagonize Black Spot. Additionally, a concoction of water, bicarbonate of soda, and fish emulsion, when applied weekly, suffocates pests like mites and aphids while inhibiting fungal growth. Addressing potassium deficiency in roses by regularly adding sulphate of potash can bolster their resistance to Black Spot.

Furthermore, seaweed sprayed onto rose leaves alters the leaf surface pH, making it less hospitable to fungal spores while fortifying cell walls against invasion. Lime sulphur serves as a preventive fungicide on leafless roses during winter, offering protection against Black Spot before its resurgence in the following growing season. By incorporating these preventive measures into their gardening routines, enthusiasts can effectively manage and mitigate the impact of Black Spot on their beloved roses, ensuring their continued health and beauty.

Powdery Mildew, a fungal disease prevalent in warm summer evenings, thrives in shady, humid areas with poor air circulation. Recognizable by its white, powdery appearance on leaves, this fungus can rapidly cover plants, particularly affecting lower, more sheltered regions where humidity is higher. As it progresses, affected leaves yellow and eventually die off, depriving the plant of vital nutrients. Powdery Mildew typically emerges in summer and autumn, with older leaves often bearing the brunt of the infestation.

The growth of Powdery Mildew is fuelled by humid nights with temperatures around 15°C, especially following warm days. Light breezes facilitate spore dissemination, with dry, warm, and shaded areas of the garden posing particular risk. Watering leaves in the afternoon increases night-time humidity, further promoting spore spread. Certain plants like pumpkins, cucumbers, roses, and grapes are especially susceptible, though various types of mildew can affect different plants concurrently.

Figure 184: Powdery mildew on a squash leaf. Dmitry Brant, CC BY-SA 4.0, via Wikimedia Commons.

While uncontrollable factors like weather conditions can influence Powdery Mildew incidence, proactive measures can mitigate its impact. Early morning watering at the roots, proper plant spacing to ensure adequate air circulation, and removal of fallen leaves can all help prevent Powdery Mildew. Additionally, using balanced organic fertilizers and seaweed-based plant tonics can bolster plant health, potentially reducing fungal issues.

Home remedies like milk sprays, which slow down Powdery Mildew progression, can prolong plant productivity if applied early in the morning. Furthermore, natural predators like the Fungus Eating Ladybird can aid in controlling Powdery Mildew by consuming the fungus, albeit sparing the leaves beneath. By adopting these preventive strategies and leveraging natural solutions, gardeners can effectively manage Powdery Mildew and safeguard their plants from its detrimental effects.

Blossom End Rot, despite its name, isn't a disease but rather a disorder that affects the blossom end of fruits, causing them to appear brown, tough, and sunken. It gives the impression of being water-soaked and can significantly impact crops like tomatoes, capsicums, eggplants, watermelons, and zucchinis. This disorder tends to thrive in environments where watering practices are inconsistent, leading to fluctuations in soil moisture levels. Additionally, over-fertilization with nitrogen and potassium, acidic soils, and calcium deficiencies exacerbate the likelihood of Blossom End Rot.

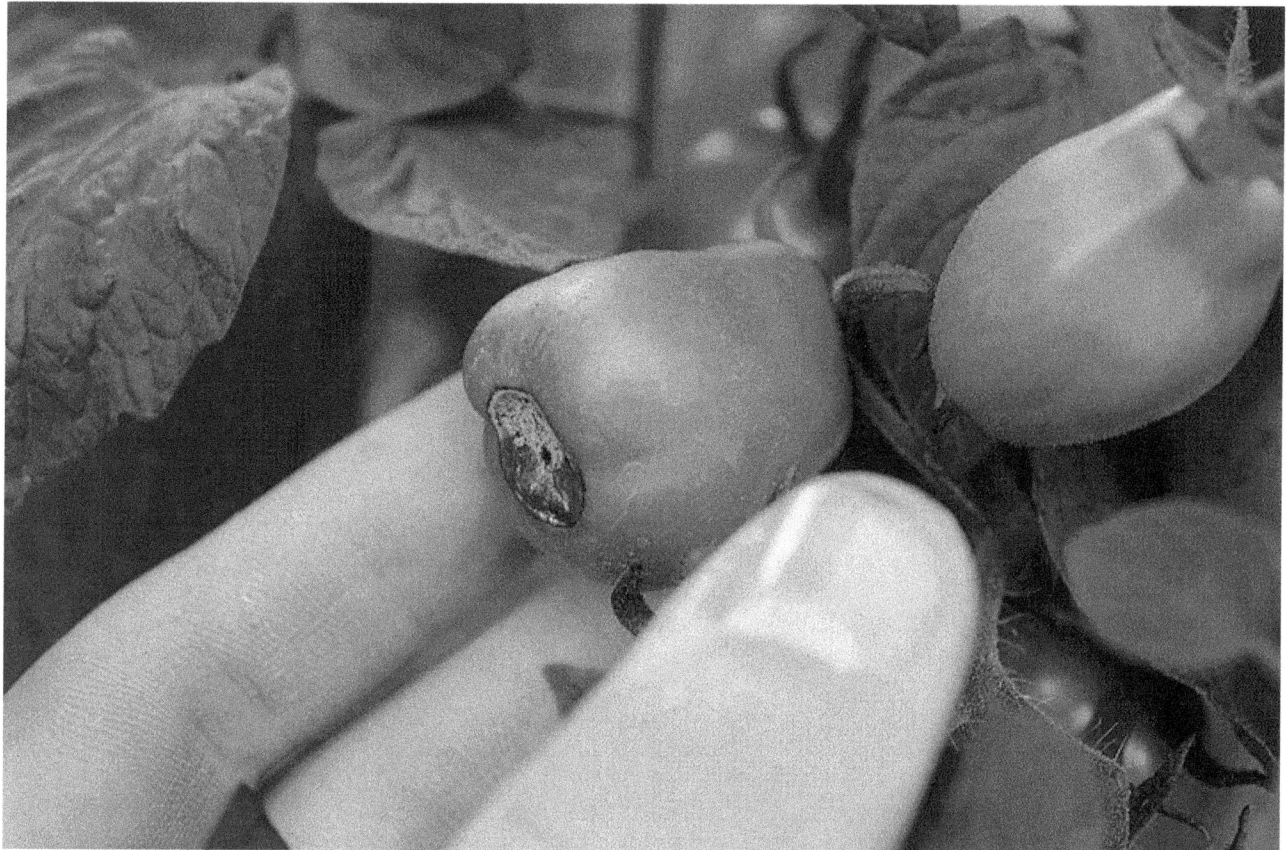
Figure 185: Blossom end rot (calcium deficiency) on a tomato. A13ean, CC BY-SA 3.0, via Wikimedia Commons.

The disorder spreads its undesirable affection by manifesting in fruits that are inadequately watered, creating ideal conditions for its development. Gardens that lack proper pH balance, effective watering practices, mulching, and windbreaks to prevent excessive drying of plants are particularly vulnerable. Its presence becomes unmistakable when one end of the fruit becomes discoloured, appearing brown and somewhat squishy. Even the presence of tiny hairs on the fruit can indicate the onset of Blossom End Rot, often accompanied by fungal growth.

Traditional methods of controlling Blossom End Rot involve the application of chelated calcium, aiming to address calcium deficiencies that contribute to the disorder. However, modern approaches focus on preventive measures to minimize its occurrence. Protecting crops with suitable windbreaks, adjusting soil pH with lime amendments, and improving soil drainage with gypsum applications are among the recommended strategies. Additionally, incorporating organic matter like poultry manure into sandy soils enhances their moisture-retention capacity, reducing water stress during hot weather.

A well-balanced fertilization program is crucial, with low applications of fertilizers applied frequently to mitigate their salting effect on the soil. On sandy soils with high salt levels, increasing watering frequency helps leach out salts, safeguarding against Blossom End Rot. Adequate watering, particularly during fruiting stages and hot days, is essential for maintaining optimal soil moisture levels. Furthermore, mulching serves as a protective barrier, conserving soil moisture and moderating temperature fluctuations, thereby reducing the risk of Blossom End Rot. By adopting these proactive measures, gardeners can effectively manage this disorder and safeguard their fruit crops from its detrimental effects.

Sooty Mould, aptly named for its resemblance to black soot or charcoal, is a fungus that thrives on the sweet honeydew secreted by sap-sucking pests like aphids, scale insects, or mealybugs. This fungus doesn't directly harm plants but can make them unsightly by covering leaves and stems with a gray to black layer. Its presence often indicates an underlying pest issue that needs attention, making it more of an indicator than a direct threat to plant health. Sooty Mould's main hobby is making plants appear unattractive, but it relies entirely on the exudates of sap-sucking insects for sustenance.

Figure 186: Sooty mould and larval cuticle of Ommatissus lybicus - taken on date palm in Oman. Roy Bateman, CC BY-SA 4.0, via Wikimedia Commons.

Almost any plant is susceptible to Sooty Mould, making it a potential nuisance in gardens where sap-sucking pests are prevalent. However, it has a strong aversion to gardeners who diligently manage pest problems and practice good garden hygiene, as these practices limit its food source and prevent its proliferation. Recognizing Sooty Mould is relatively straightforward; affected foliage looks as though it's been dusted with charcoal, often feeling sticky to the touch, and can be easily wiped off.

Controlling Sooty Mould is primarily about addressing the underlying pest infestation. Removing or treating the honeydew-producing insects will cause the Sooty Mould to disappear over time. Additionally, physically removing the fungus by wiping affected foliage with a damp cloth is a temporary solution but will be ineffective if the pest issue persists. Fallen leaves affected by Sooty Mould should be collected and disposed of in the bin rather than composted, as composting may inadvertently spread the fungus.

Controlling ant populations is also crucial, as ants tend to protect and cultivate honeydew-producing insects, facilitating the growth of Sooty Mould. Planting ant-repellent species like tansy nearby can help deter ants from colonizing plants. Regularly checking the base of plants for ant nests and mulching with tansy can further discourage ants and, consequently, the growth of Sooty Mould. By addressing both the pest issue and the conditions favourable to Sooty Mould, gardeners can effectively manage this fungus and maintain the health and appearance of their plants.

Phytophthora root rot, caused by the fungus Phytophthora, has a notorious history of causing agricultural disasters worldwide. One of its species, P. infestans, famously triggered the Irish potato famine in the 1800s, devastating potato crops and leading to widespread hunger and population decline in Ireland. Another devastating species, P. cinnamomi, has made its home in Australia, likely introduced during European settlement. This fungus has spread across several Australian states, including Western Australia, Victoria, Tasmania, South Australia, and coastal Queensland, where it's wreaking havoc on vast hectares of native vegetation.

In Western Australia, the impact of Phytophthora root rot has been particularly severe, affecting majestic jarrah forests and other vegetation. The fungus infiltrates the plant's root system, and sometimes the stem, with its presence only detectable under a microscope. By destroying the roots, Phytophthora prevents the plant from absorbing essential water and nutrients, leading to wilting, nutrient deficiency, and ultimately, death. While some plants can survive the disease, many succumb to the lack of vital resources caused by root damage.

Figure 187: Rhododendron-Phytophthora Root Rot. Jerzy Opioła, CC BY-SA 4.0, via Wikimedia Commons.

Phytophthora releases spores into the soil, which spread through soil water to infect neighbouring plants, perpetuating its destructive cycle. Interestingly, Phytophthora root rot tends to cause less damage in undisturbed vegetation, especially in regions with annual rainfall below 600 mm. However, diagnosing the disease accurately can be challenging without laboratory tests, as symptoms such as brown patches on leaves and foliage yellowing can resemble other stress-related issues like drought. In severe cases, where large mature trees are affected, it may take years for the disease to kill the plant, contributing to long-term environmental damage and habitat loss.

Insects and Plants

Insects play a crucial role in shaping plant communities through various interactions that can have both positive and negative impacts on plants. One significant positive impact is pollination, where insects like bees, butterflies, and beetles facilitate the reproduction of flowering plants by transferring pollen, essential for seed and fruit production [82]. Without insect pollinators, many plant species, including important food crops, would struggle to reproduce, leading to a decline in plant populations and ecosystem diversity. On the other hand, herbivorous insects can have a negative impact by feeding on plant tissues, causing damage that ranges from reduced growth to severe yield losses and even plant death in extreme cases [83].

In addition to direct effects like pollination and herbivory, insects can also act as vectors for plant diseases, transmitting pathogens from infected plants to healthy ones as they feed. For instance, aphids are known to transmit viruses to crops, resulting in diseases like mosaic viruses in tomatoes and cucumbers [84]. This transmission of diseases by insects can significantly impact plant health, leading to yield losses and economic damage in agricultural settings. However, not all insect-plant interactions are detrimental; some insects serve as beneficial predators and parasitoids that help control pest populations, thus protecting plants from damage [85].

Plants, in response to insect feeding or damage, can activate defence mechanisms to protect themselves. These defence responses can involve the release of chemical compounds that repel or deter herbivorous insects, as well as changes in morphology such as producing thicker leaves or forming galls [86]. Understanding these plant defence mechanisms is crucial for developing effective pest management strategies that aim to promote beneficial insect populations while minimizing the damage caused by pests. The interplay between plants and insects is complex and multifaceted, influencing plant health, reproduction, and overall ecosystem dynamics [87].

Research has shown that the impact of insects on plants can vary depending on factors such as the type of insect, the plant species involved, and environmental conditions. Studies have highlighted the importance of considering the ecological interactions between plants and insects to develop sustainable pest management strategies [88]. For example, the response of native insect communities to invasive plants can shed light on how different plant species may experience varying levels of herbivore damage, influencing their overall health and survival [89]. Additionally, the phylogenetic isolation of host plants has been found to affect the species richness, composition, and specialization of insect herbivores, highlighting the intricate relationships between plants and their herbivorous counterparts [90].

Furthermore, the performance of herbivorous insects can be influenced by factors such as plant water stress and previous herbivore damage, emphasizing the interconnectedness of abiotic and biotic factors in shaping insect-plant interactions [91]. Studies have also explored how herbivores mediate competitive and facilitative responses of native and invasive plant populations, indicating the dynamic nature of these interactions [92]. The specificity of induced plant responses to different herbivore species underscores the complexity of plant-insect relationships and the need to consider the diverse mechanisms at play [93].

Ants, though not directly harmful to plants, can still have significant implications for gardening enthusiasts. While they don't cause direct damage to plants, ants may engage in certain behaviours that can indirectly affect plant health and garden ecosystems. For instance, ants are known to pilfer freshly sown seeds from garden beds and seed boxes, potentially compromising the success of seed germination and plant establishment. This behaviour can be frustrating for gardeners who have painstakingly prepared their soil and planted seeds, only to find them disturbed or missing due to ant activity.

Furthermore, ants have a symbiotic relationship with sap-sucking insects like aphids and scale. These insects secrete a sugary substance known as honeydew, which ants eagerly consume as a food source. In return, ants protect aphids and scale from natural predators, ensuring a steady supply of honeydew. This mutualistic relationship between ants and sap-sucking insects can lead to increased pest populations in the garden, as ants actively defend and nurture these pests. As a result, plants infested with aphids or scale may attract ants, which can serve as a warning sign of potential pest problems in the garden.

Figure 188: Black garden ants on leaves. Judgefloro, CC0, via Wikimedia Commons.

Observing ants in specific locations within the garden can provide valuable insights into soil conditions and moisture levels. Ants are often found on the stems and undersides of leaves, where sap-sucking insects like aphids and scale tend to congregate. Additionally, ants may be observed near the base of plants or on the soil surface. Their presence in these areas can indicate underlying issues such as soil dryness or water repellency. Ants may be attracted to dry soil conditions, prompting gardeners to assess and address moisture levels in their garden beds. Treating dry or water-repellent soil with a wetting agent can help improve water penetration and distribution, creating a more hospitable environment for plants and discouraging ant activity.

While ants themselves may not directly harm plants, their presence in the garden can signal potential issues such as seed theft, pest infestations, and soil dryness. By understanding the behaviours and interactions of ants in the garden, gardeners can take proactive measures to mitigate any negative impacts and promote a healthy and thriving garden ecosystem.

Aphids, belonging to the family Aphididae, are small insects that can cause significant damage to plants in gardens and agricultural settings. These soft-bodied insects typically measure between 2 to 4 millimetres in length and come in various colours, including white, green, yellow, and black. They are commonly found clustered on young shoots, flower buds, or underneath older leaves. Aphids have a wide range of host plants, including fruit trees, roses, camellias, chrysanthemums, ornamentals, and many vegetables. Their ability to transmit virus diseases, such as broad bean wilt, further adds to their threat to plant health.

One of the distinctive features of aphids is their rapid reproduction rate, especially in warm weather. Small aphid colonies can quickly multiply and develop into large infestations within a short span of time. Therefore, it's essential for gardeners to monitor their plants regularly, especially during warmer periods, to detect and control aphids when their populations are still relatively small. Natural predators such as ladybirds and parasitic wasps play a crucial role in controlling aphid populations. Ladybird larvae, resembling tiny bird droppings, are particularly voracious eaters of aphids, while parasitic wasps lay eggs inside aphids, leading to their demise.

Figure 189: Aphids, Mike Lewinski from Tres Piedras, NM, United States, CC BY 2.0, via Wikimedia Commons.

Symptoms of aphid infestation include distorted and twisted leaves, buds failing to open properly, and stunted new growth. Additionally, aphids excrete a sugary substance called honeydew, which can create an environment conducive to the growth of sooty mold fungus. This black, powdery mold can cover plant surfaces and inhibit photosynthesis if left unchecked. Fortunately, controlling aphids can help alleviate the problem of sooty mold, as eliminating the source of honeydew removes the fungal growth's supporting environment.

Aphids pose a significant threat to plant health due to their rapid reproduction, ability to transmit diseases, and potential for causing physical damage to plant tissues. Regular monitoring of plants, promotion of natural predators, and prompt intervention when aphid populations are detected are essential strategies for managing aphid infestations and protecting garden plants from their detrimental effects.

Caterpillars, the larval stage of moths and butterflies belonging to the order Lepidoptera, encompass a diverse group of insects that can wreak havoc on plants in gardens and agricultural settings. Common examples include cabbage moth, cabbage white butterfly, potato moth, and tomato moth. These pests lay their eggs on the underside of leaves, and upon hatching, the caterpillars emerge and begin to feed voraciously on foliage or fruit. Some notorious caterpillars, such as the armyworm, are active mainly at night, causing extensive damage to crops and lawns. Unlike their destructive offspring, adult moths are typically nocturnal and less frequently observed.

Symptoms of caterpillar infestation often manifest as irregularly shaped holes in leaves or fruit, indicative of the feeding activity of these voracious larvae. Additionally, the presence of black or brown droppings, known as frass, is a telltale sign of caterpillar presence. These pests can quickly defoliate plants if left unchecked, posing a significant threat to crop yields and ornamental plants in gardens.

On the other hand, curl grubs, the larvae of beetles, represent another category of garden pests that cause considerable damage to lawns, gardens, and potted plants. These cream-colored larvae with light brown heads range in size from 4mm to 40 mm when fully grown. Often confused with 'witchetty grubs,' curl grubs feed on plant roots in large numbers, particularly during mid-spring to mid-summer. Their feeding activity can lead to yellowing and browning of grass in affected lawns, ultimately resulting in the death of grass patches. Notably, curl grubs exhibit a distinctive behaviour of curling up when disturbed, making them somewhat recognizable to gardeners.

Figure 190: A Curl Grub larvae. CSIRO, CC BY 3.0, via Wikimedia Commons.

Symptoms of curl grub infestation in lawns include the yellowing, browning, and eventual death of grass patches. Severely affected areas may exhibit the unsettling phenomenon of the lawn being easily lifted and rolled back, resembling the lifting of a carpet. This characteristic damage pattern underscores the significant economic and aesthetic impact that curl grubs can have on turfgrass areas. Effective management strategies, such as biological controls or targeted insecticides, are crucial for mitigating the damage caused by caterpillars and curl grubs, thereby safeguarding the health and vitality of garden plants and lawns.

Cutworms, the larval stage of night-flying moths belonging to the family Noctuidae, are notorious garden pests known for their destructive feeding habits on young plants and seedlings. These caterpillars emerge from eggs laid in the soil by adult moths, and upon hatching, they feed voraciously on tender plant stems at ground level. The name "cutworm" originates from their characteristic behaviour of chewing through plant stems, causing the affected plants to collapse or be cut off near the soil surface. Ranging in size from light grey or pinkish brown to almost black, cutworms can grow up to 40mm in length and exhibit a distinct defensive mechanism of curling up into a flat coil when disturbed.

Cutworms are primarily nocturnal feeders, actively consuming plant tissue during the night and seeking shelter in the soil during the day. They pose a significant threat to young seedlings and soft fruits like strawberries, particularly after periods of rain when they are more likely to be active. To prevent cutworm infestation and protect vulnerable plants, gardeners employ various tactics such as placing small, open-ended plastic cups around plant bases or wrapping them with aluminium foil. These physical barriers disrupt the cutworms' access to plant stems and deter their feeding activity.

Given their nocturnal behaviour, gardeners can conduct nocturnal patrols with a torchlight to detect and remove cutworms actively feeding on plants. By identifying and removing these pests promptly, gardeners can mitigate the damage caused by cutworms and safeguard the health and vitality of their garden plants. Effective management strategies, including cultural controls and targeted interventions, are essential for minimizing the impact of cutworm infestations and preserving the integrity of garden crops and ornamentals.

Hibiscus flower beetles, scientifically known as Aethina concolor, are small oval-shaped insects measuring around 3mm in size. Despite their diminutive size, these beetles can have a significant impact on the health and aesthetics of hibiscus and related plants such as abutilon. One notable characteristic of hibiscus flower beetles is their elusive nature; they tend to be shy and often conceal themselves within the folds of flowers, making them challenging to detect.

These flower beetles are notorious for their feeding habits, which involve chewing holes in both the flowers and foliage of hibiscus plants. As a result of their feeding activity, affected flowers may exhibit visible chew holes upon opening, detracting from the plant's overall appearance. Additionally, the foliage of infested plants can display signs of damage, appearing tattered and unhealthy. The cumulative effect of beetle damage can stress the plants, leading to reduced vigour and compromised growth.

One telltale symptom of hibiscus flower beetle infestation is the premature dropping of flower buds by healthy plants. This response is triggered by the plant's natural defence mechanisms, which detect the presence of the beetle and prompt the shedding of damaged or compromised flower buds. Therefore, if gardeners observe a significant number of flowers falling prematurely from their hibiscus plants, it may serve as an indication of hibiscus flower beetle activity. Prompt identification and management of these pests are crucial for preserving the health and vitality of hibiscus and related ornamental plants, ensuring they continue to thrive and flourish in the garden.

Lace bugs, belonging to the Corythucha and Stephanitis species, are tiny soft-bodied insects measuring around 3mm in size. Despite their small stature, these pests can cause significant damage to ornamental plants. Lace bugs are characterized by their distinctive appearance, featuring large lacy wings that distinguish them from other insect species. These insects are typically found clinging to the underside of leaf surfaces, where they feed on plant sap.

One of the challenges in detecting lace bugs is their small size, which often leads to their presence going unnoticed until signs of damage become apparent on the leaves. Lace bugs overwinter as eggs on the mid veins of leaves and hatch in the spring, making early detection and proactive management crucial for preventing infestations. These pests are attracted to a wide range of ornamental plants, including azaleas, rhododendrons, viburnums, flowering quince, crabapple, and cotoneaster.

Symptoms of lace bug infestation manifest as white or yellow spots or marks on the upper surface of leaves, resulting from the insects' feeding activity. Over time, continued feeding by lace bugs can lead to a silvery mottled appearance across the entire leaf surface. Additionally, lace bugs leave behind tiny black, hard varnish-like droppings as they feed, further indicating their presence. Once leaf damage occurs, it cannot be reversed, underscoring the importance of implementing proactive control measures to mitigate lace bug infestations and minimize the impact on ornamental plants.

Figure 191: Fringetree Lace Bug. Katja Schulz from Washington, D. C., USA, CC BY 2.0, via Wikimedia Commons.

Mealybugs, belonging to the order Pseudococcus, are small insects adorned with a white mealy coating, with some species also featuring white hairs attached to their bodies. These pests sustain themselves by sucking on plant juices, causing damage to the host plant. One of the distinctive characteristics of mealybugs is their excretion of a sticky substance known as honeydew. This honeydew serves as a food source for ants and creates an ideal environment for the growth of sooty mold, further exacerbating the damage to plants. Mealybugs thrive in mild temperatures and high humidity, conditions that are conducive to their breeding cycle, with eggs hatching approximately every 2-3 weeks. However, prolonged periods of hot weather can suppress their population numbers.

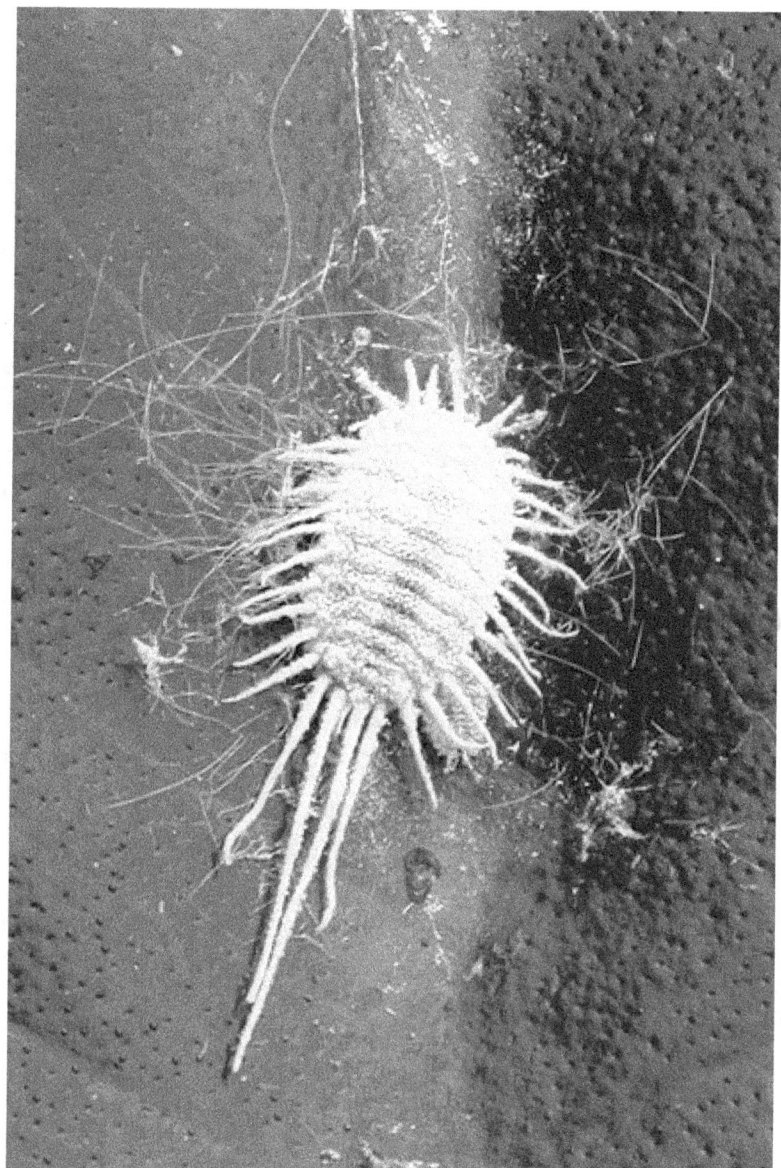

Figure 192: A Mealybug (Pseudococcidae). D-Kuru, CC BY-SA 3.0 AT, via Wikimedia Commons.

Figure 192: A Mealybug (Pseudococcidae). D-Kuru, CC BY-SA 3.0 AT, via Wikimedia Commons.

Symptoms of mealybug infestation typically manifest as distorted new growth on plants, accompanied by the presence of a whitish substance in the leaf axils. Upon closer inspection, the mealybugs themselves can often be observed on the affected plant parts. These pests can quickly proliferate and spread throughout the plant and surrounding areas, posing a threat to plant health and vitality. Effective management strategies are essential for controlling mealybug infestations and preventing further damage to plants in affected areas.

Psyllids, belonging to the family Psyllidae within the order Hemiptera, are diminutive sap-sucking insects primarily known for their predilection for native plants such as lilly pilly. These minuscule pests bear a resemblance to miniature cicadas and are typically only visible through the aid of a microscope or hand lens. Both the juvenile and adult stages of psyllids contribute to plant damage by extracting sap from the leaves. Some species of psyllids construct protective coverings composed of wax and honeydew. It's important to note that while there are numerous species of psyllids, each tends to exhibit a relatively specific host plant preference.

Figure 193: Psyllid on alder. S. Rae from Scotland, UK, CC BY 2.0, via Wikimedia Commons.

Symptoms of psyllid infestation commonly include dimpling or pockmarks on new growth leaves, as well as distortion and dieback of terminal shoots. In more severe cases of psyllid infestation, leaf defoliation may occur, further compromising the health and aesthetics of the affected plant. Additionally, the crystal-like honeydew produced by psyllids serves as a substrate for the growth of sooty mold, which can further exacerbate the damage. Discoloration of leaves may also be evident in plants afflicted by psyllids. Effective management strategies are essential for controlling psyllid populations and mitigating their impact on plant health and vitality.

Rust is a fungal disease that manifests as distinctive orange, yellow, or red pustules on the leaves or stems of plants, which eventually rupture and release large quantities of spores. These pustules typically develop on both sides of the leaf, with the fungus thriving within the leaf tissue. Each strain of rust is specific to certain host plants, meaning that rust affecting one type of plant is unlikely to spread to others. Commonly affected plants include calendulas, roses, snapdragons, geraniums, gerberas, and beans, while even turf can fall victim to rust infestations. In recent years, the emergence of myrtle rust has posed a significant threat to plants like lilly pillies and other native species.

Figure 194: Rust on young garlic plant after record-breaking rains (6 days almost nonstop) in Los Angeles, California. Downtown-gal, Public domain, via Wikimedia Commons.

Symptoms of rust are easily identifiable by the presence of the characteristic orange, yellow, or red pustules on the leaves or stems of infected plants. These pustules serve as the primary sites for spore production and dissemination, contributing to the spread of the disease within and between plants. Effective management strategies are essential for controlling rust outbreaks and minimizing their impact on plant health and aesthetics.

Scale insects, belonging to the order Hemiptera, are plant pests that spend the majority of their lives as immobile adults concealed under a protective coating. These insects sustain themselves by feeding on the sap of plants, typically targeting stalks, leaves, and stems. There are two main types of scale: hard scale, which features a protective covering resembling an oyster shell, and soft scale, which tends to settle on the mid-rib of leaves and stalks. Among the soft scale varieties, white wax scale is particularly common, often observed as large patches of white waxy material along plant stems and shoots. Beneath this wax, the insects feed on the plant's sap. Adult female scale insects are prolific egg layers, capable of depositing up to 1000 eggs, which hatch into mobile nymphs known as crawlers. These crawlers seek out nearby feeding sites on the plant, where they establish themselves and continue feeding on sap. The crawler stage represents the most vulnerable phase of the scale's life cycle, as they lack the protective wax coating found in the adult stage.

Symptoms of scale infestation may include various signs of plant distress, such as leaf drop, twig and branch dieback, and stunted or distorted fruit growth. In the case of citrus trees, specific symptoms like small yellow spots on leaves, leaf drop, and distorted fruit may indicate an infestation of citrus scale pests. Additionally, visual cues such as white patches on stems or the presence of pink or brown raised dome-like structures measuring approximately 3-5mm on leaves and stalks can signal a scale infestation. Furthermore, the presence of sooty mold, a black fungal growth that thrives on the sugary excretions of scale insects, may also accompany scale infestations, serving as an additional indicator of their presence on plants. Effective management strategies are necessary to control scale infestations and mitigate their impact on plant health and vitality.

Snails and slugs, classified under the class Gastropoda, are notable members of the mollusk group, characterized by their soft-bodied nature, with or without a protective shell. Unlike segmented organisms, these creatures lack segmentation and exhibit a preference for moist environments. They thrive in habitats rich in decaying organic matter, including animal debris, algae, and various plant materials such as leaves and stems. Slugs and snails are most active during cool, wet, and humid conditions, particularly favouring nocturnal activity when moisture levels are optimal for their survival and movement.

Figure 195: Baby Garden Snail (Cornu aspersum). Matthew T Rader, CC BY-SA 4.0, via Wikimedia Commons.

Identifying the presence of snails and slugs often involves observing distinctive signs indicative of their activity. One of the most recognizable indications is the presence of silvery trails left behind by these creatures as they move, which can sometimes dry and appear akin to gold dust. These trails are formed by the mucus secretions produced by snails and slugs to facilitate their locomotion. Additionally, damage to plants is a common symptom of snail and slug infestations, characterized by the presence of holes in leaves and instances of seedlings being chewed off at the base. Such feeding behavior can result in significant damage to vegetation, particularly in garden settings where these pests can rapidly multiply and wreak havoc on cultivated plants. Effective management strategies are often necessary to control snail and slug populations and mitigate their detrimental impact on plant health and aesthetics.

Thrips, belonging to the order Thysanoptera, encompass a vast array of species, totalling approximately 7,400 worldwide, with many posing significant threats as pests. Among the well-known varieties are greenhouse thrips, Western flower thrips, and plague thrips. These tiny insects typically measure between 0.5mm to 1.5mm in length and exhibit a diverse range of colours, spanning from white and yellow to black. Due to their diminutive size, thrips are often only visible under magnification. They target various parts of plants, including flowers, fruit, and foliage, affecting a wide range of species such as roses, fruit trees, azaleas, gladioli, and numerous vegetables like tomatoes, onions, and beans.

Thrips employ a distinctive mode of attack, laying their eggs inside plant tissue, where the ensuing pupae feed on the plant's juices. This characteristic behaviour poses challenges for control efforts, particularly as thrips also deposit eggs within unopened buds, complicating detection and management. Moreover, thrips are notorious vectors for plant viruses, with examples such as tomato thrips and Western flower thrips implicated in the transmission of the tomato spotted wilt virus.

Figure 196: Thysanoptera, thrips. xpda, CC BY-SA 4.0, via Wikimedia Commons.

Identifying thrips infestations often involves recognizing telltale symptoms indicative of their presence. One common manifestation is the visible damage caused by thrips as they scrape the surface of leaves and petals while feeding on sap, resulting in a distinctive white mottled appearance on affected foliage. Additionally, affected plants may exhibit browning on petals and fruit, accompanied by premature flower drop. Left unchecked, thrips infestations can lead to more severe consequences, including the deformation and stunting of leaves, new shoots, and flowers. Instances of wilting and browning may also occur, further exacerbating the detrimental impact of thrips on plant health and vitality. Effective management strategies are essential for mitigating thrips populations and minimizing their detrimental effects on cultivated plants.

Two-Spotted Mites, scientifically known as Tetranychus urticae, belong to the family of arachnids and are closely related to spiders, possessing four pairs of legs. These minuscule pests, often appearing in clusters, exhibit a pinkish-red hue and are typically found congregating on the undersides of leaves, where they may produce fine webbing. During the winter months, Two-Spotted Mites seek shelter in protected areas, emerging during hot, dry weather when their life cycle, spanning from eggs to adults, can be completed in as little as a week.

One notable characteristic of Two-Spotted Mites is their propensity to develop resistance to pesticides relatively quickly, owing to the rapid completion of their life cycle under favourable environmental conditions. Unlike some pests, Two-Spotted Mites thrive in arid conditions and exhibit a dislike for moisture and humidity. As a result, employing overhead watering techniques can prove effective in controlling mite populations, particularly in dry environments such as indoor settings.

Identifying the presence of Two-Spotted Mites often involves recognizing certain symptomatic manifestations on affected plants. Yellow mottling or bronzing of the leaves, reminiscent of lace bug damage, is a common indicator of infestation. Additionally, significant distortion of flower and leaf buds may occur, further signalling the presence of these pests. In cases of heavy infestations, fine webbing may be visible, serving as a visual cue for the severity of the mite population. If left unchecked, Two-Spotted Mites can cause defoliation of affected plant parts, leading to detrimental consequences for plant health and overall vitality. Employing appropriate management strategies is crucial for mitigating Two-Spotted Mite infestations and safeguarding plant health.

Whiteflies, despite their name, are not true flies but rather small, white-winged sap-sucking insects resembling tiny moths, typically with a wingspan of about 3mm. In recent years, they have become increasingly prevalent and are considered major pests for home gardeners. These pests have several different types, and when a plant is disturbed, a cloud of tiny insects can be observed flying out, only to settle back onto the same plant shortly thereafter. Both the adult and juvenile stages, known as nymphs, feed on plant juices, making them particularly detrimental to a wide range of plants favoured by home gardeners, including hibiscus, poinsettia, gerberas, and various herbs and vegetable seedlings such as squash, melon, eggplant, cabbage, beans, tomatoes, and broccoli.

Figure 197: Aleyrodidae, whiteflies. xpda, CC BY-SA 4.0, via Wikimedia Commons.

Identifying the presence of whiteflies often involves observing symptomatic manifestations on affected plants. Common symptoms include wilting and stunting of new shoots, which can severely impact the overall growth and vigour of the plant. Additionally, whiteflies may cause silvering and yellowing of leaves, particularly evident in plants like squash, and can lead to uneven ripening of tomatoes. In severe infestations, whiteflies can even contribute to plant death. Furthermore, the presence of whiteflies may also be accompanied by the development of sooty mold, a black fungal growth that thrives on the honeydew excreted by whiteflies as they feed on plant tissue. This combination of symptoms underscores the damaging impact that whiteflies can have on plants and underscores the importance of implementing effective management strategies to control their populations and mitigate their detrimental effects on plant health.

Accounting for insect control in landscape design involves implementing various strategies to minimize pest populations and their impact on plants while creating a balanced and sustainable ecosystem. Here are some key considerations and techniques:

- **Plant Selection**: Choose plant species that are resistant or less susceptible to common pests in your area. Native plants, for example, are often more adapted to local conditions and may have built-in defences against pests. Additionally, diversity in plant species can help prevent the rapid spread of pests by disrupting their feeding and breeding patterns.

- **Companion Planting**: Incorporate companion plants that repel or deter pests naturally. For instance, aromatic herbs like basil and rosemary can help deter certain insects, while flowers such as marigolds and nasturtiums can attract beneficial insects that prey on pests.

- **Habitat Management**: Create habitats that attract natural predators of pests, such as ladybugs, lacewings, and predatory wasps. Providing shelter, water sources, and nectar-rich flowers for these beneficial insects encourages them to stay in the area and control pest populations naturally.

- **Cultural Practices**: Adopt good cultural practices that promote plant health and vigour, making them more resilient to pest attacks. This includes proper irrigation, fertilization, pruning, and mulching techniques. Avoid over-fertilization, as it can stimulate excessive plant growth, making them more susceptible to pests.

- **Integrated Pest Management (IPM)**: Implement an IPM approach that combines multiple pest control methods, including biological, cultural, mechanical, and chemical strategies. IPM focuses on monitoring pest populations, using least-toxic control methods first, and minimizing environmental impact.

- **Physical Barriers**: Install physical barriers such as row covers, netting, and screens to protect plants from insect pests. This is particularly useful for preventing pests like caterpillars and birds from accessing vulnerable plants.

- **Regular Monitoring**: Regularly inspect plants for signs of pest infestation, such as chewed leaves, distorted growth, or the presence of eggs and larvae. Early detection allows for timely intervention and prevents pest populations from escalating.

- **Natural Predators**: Introduce or encourage natural predators of pests into the landscape. This can include releasing beneficial insects like ladybugs or introducing insect-repelling plants that attract predators.

- **Sanitation**: Practice good garden hygiene by removing plant debris, fallen leaves, and weeds, as these can harbor pest populations and provide breeding grounds for insects. Proper disposal of infested plant material also helps prevent the spread of pests to other areas.

Lawns

Bindii, scientifically known as Soliva pterosperma, is an annual weed characterized by its small ferny rosette, measuring about 20mm in diameter. Its flowers are inconspicuous, appearing as tiny greenish-yellow blooms. Bindii seeds germinate in autumn but exhibit minimal growth until spring. By mid-spring, each rosette produces flower heads adorned with numerous spines, eventually maturing and dispersing seeds by mid-summer. The spread of bindii seeds is facilitated by foot traffic or animal fur. Effective control of bindii is most achievable during its growth spurt in spring. Once seed heads form, herbicide uptake becomes limited, reducing the efficacy of control measures.

African Black Beetles, scientifically termed Heteronychus arator, pose a threat to various plants, particularly grasses, in both their adult and larval stages. Adult beetles emerge in spring, laying copious eggs, necessitating prompt treatment. While adult beetles may inflict some damage, it is their larvae, known as curl grubs, that are voracious feeders, causing substantial harm if left unchecked. Symptoms of black beetle infestation include patchy lawn areas with discoloured or browned grass, indicative of damaged root systems. Severe infestations can result in grass dying off and becoming easily liftable, akin to a rolled-back carpet.

Broadleaf or flat weeds encompass a range of common weed species like marshmallow, dandelion, and chickweed, characterized by their wide leaves and varying growth patterns. These weeds can be either summer or winter perennials, with dormant periods at different times of the year. Effective control of broadleaf weeds involves timely intervention, preferably targeting small, actively growing weeds before they mature and produce seeds. Selective herbicides tailored to specific lawn types can aid in weed management, ensuring minimal impact on desired vegetation.

Figure 198: Dandelion. Humoyun Mehridinov, CC BY-SA 4.0, via Wikimedia Commons.

Capeweed, scientifically known as Arctotheca calendula, is an annual weed that emerges from late summer to early autumn, forming rosettes of grey-green leaves with yellow daisy-like flowers in spring and early summer. Capeweed seeds exhibit dormancy, remaining viable in the soil for several years until conducive conditions trigger germination. Controlling capeweed involves preventing seed formation by either manual removal or spot treatment with glyphosate herbicides. By preventing capeweed from flowering and seeding, its spread can be curtailed effectively.

Clover, belonging to the Trifolium genus, is a common lawn weed with characteristic trifoliate leaves and creeping stems that root upon contact with the ground. Clover favours nitrogen-deficient lawns, as it can fix nitrogen from the air, promoting its growth. Preventing clover invasion involves ensuring strong lawn growth through proper fertilization and maintenance practices. However, for homeowners intentionally growing clover lawns, selective herbicides should be avoided, as they can harm desirable clover species.

Curl grubs, often misidentified as witchetty grubs, are the larvae of various beetle species with cream bodies and light brown heads. These grubs feed on plant roots, particularly active during mid-spring to mid-summer, causing extensive damage to lawns, gardens, and potted plants. Symptoms of curl grub infestation include yellowing and browning of grass, eventually leading to lawn deterioration. Effective control methods include targeted pesticide application and maintaining optimal lawn health to minimize susceptibility to infestation.

Dandelions, scientifically known as Taraxacum officinale, are perennial herbs characterized by long taproots and yellow petal heads. After flowering, dandelions produce fluffy seed heads, dispersing seeds widely. Moss, algae, and lichen often thrive in shaded, damp, or compacted areas of lawns and gardens. Eradicating these growths requires improving drainage, increasing sunlight exposure, and, in the case of moss, applying iron sulphate solutions regularly. While moss and lichen are non-parasitic and do not harm trees, their presence may indicate underlying health issues in plants.

Onion weed, scientifically referred to as Nothoscordum inodorum, is a perennial weed with thin green leaves and white flowers. It is considered a noxious weed in several regions due to its invasive nature and prolific seed production. Effective control involves preventing seed formation and repeatedly treating the weed with glyphosate-based herbicides. Similarly, oxalis species, including creeping oxalis and soursob, exhibit aggressive growth habits, spreading through seeds or bulbils. Control measures include manual removal or targeted herbicide application, coupled with improving lawn health to minimize weed establishment.

Paspalum, a tough perennial grass with extensive root systems, poses challenges for eradication due to its resilient growth habit. Effective control involves targeted herbicide application or physical removal by cutting clumps at ground level. Thistles, characterized by rosettes of leaves and tall flowering stems, are best controlled through early intervention during active growth stages. Herbicides are most effective when applied during the spring to autumn period, targeting thistle rosettes before flowering. Manual methods such as hoeing or digging out plants can also aid in thistle management, particularly for individual plants in garden beds.

Vegetables

Aphids, belonging to the family Aphididae, are small, soft-bodied insects typically measuring between 2 to 4 mm in length. These pests come in various colors, including white, green, yellow, and black, and are commonly found clustering on young shoots, flower buds, or beneath older leaves. Aphids are known to attack a wide range of plants, including fruit trees, roses, ornamentals, and vegetables, and they can quickly multiply, leading to large infestations, especially in warm weather. Aside from causing direct damage to plants, aphids also pose a risk by transmitting virus diseases such as broad bean wilt.

To control aphids effectively, regular monitoring of plants during warm weather is essential to detect and manage infestations early when populations are relatively small. Natural predators like ladybirds and parasitic wasps can help keep aphid numbers in check. Ladybird larvae and parasitic wasp eggs inside aphids are effective biological controls, reducing aphid populations rapidly once they appear. Symptoms of aphid infestation include distorted leaves, stunted growth, and the presence of honeydew, which can lead to the growth of sooty mold fungus. Removing aphid colonies promptly can prevent the development of sooty mold.

Cabbage moth and cabbage butterfly caterpillars, including species like Plutella xylostella and Pieris rapae, are common pests that target various crops such as cabbage, broccoli, and celery. The adult moths and butterflies lay eggs on the underside of leaves, and the hatched larvae feed on foliage and fruit, causing damage. Symptoms of infestation include large holes in outer leaves and the presence of frass, the caterpillars' excrement, on or inside leaves. Control measures involve manually removing caterpillars or applying targeted sprays before they tunnel into the heart of plants.

Caterpillars, which are the larval stage of moths and butterflies, pose a threat to many plants, including vegetables and lawns. Species like the cabbage moth, cabbage white butterfly, and armyworm feed on leaves, buds, and fruit, causing irregular-shaped holes and leaving behind droppings. Control strategies include manual removal, targeted pesticide application, or cultural practices like maintaining a healthy lawn to minimize infestation. Corn earworms, another caterpillar species, target a variety of vegetables, with symptoms including holes in buds and new leaves and damage to corn ears.

Fruit flies, characterized by reddish-brown bodies and yellow markings, are attracted to ripening fruits and vegetables. The adult flies lay eggs on the fruit's surface, and the hatched larvae tunnel into the fruit, causing it to rot. Control methods involve spraying plants with insecticides before fruit ripens or using protein and sugar-based baits to attract and kill adult flies. Symptoms of fruit fly infestation include sting marks on fruit and the presence of larvae inside affected fruits.

Figure 199: Fruit Fly (Drosophila melanogaster). Parent Géry, CC BY-SA 4.0, via Wikimedia Commons.

Green vegetable bugs, bright green insects about 1.5 cm long, attack a variety of crops and ornamentals, sucking sap from stalks and leaves and causing wilting and fruit distortion. These bugs emit an unpleasant odour when disturbed, making them a nuisance. Control measures may involve manually removing bugs or using physical barriers to protect plants. Powdery mildew, a fungal disease that affects many plants, spreads a white or ash-grey film over leaves, causing distortion and blackening of new growth. Control involves regular spraying with fungicides in warm and humid conditions.

Rats and mice are notorious pests that cause damage to agricultural crops and homes by eating seeds, plants, and stored food. They are particularly problematic in cooler and wetter weather, causing structural damage and spreading diseases. Control methods include trapping, baiting, and sealing entry points to prevent infestation. Snails and slugs, soft-bodied mollusks, feed on decaying matter and plant material, leaving behind silvery trails and chewed leaves. Control measures involve physical barriers, baits, or cultural practices like reducing moisture to deter these pests.

Fruit Trees

Aphids, members of the family Aphididae, are ubiquitous pests found on a variety of plants, recognizable by their small size and soft bodies ranging in colours from white, green, yellow to black. These insects, typically measuring between 2 to 4 mm in length, tend to gather on young shoots, flower buds, or beneath older leaves. With numerous species varying in colour, aphids pose a threat to fruit trees, roses, ornamental plants, and various vegetables. Their rapid multiplication, especially in warm weather, can lead to substantial infestations within days. Besides direct damage to plants, aphids are vectors for virus diseases like broad bean wilt.

Control measures for aphids involve regular monitoring of plants during warm weather to catch and manage infestations early when populations are still small. Natural predators such as ladybirds and parasitic wasps offer effective biological control. Ladybird larvae and parasitic wasp eggs inside aphids can rapidly reduce aphid numbers once they arrive. Symptoms of aphid infestation include twisted and distorted leaves, stunted growth, and the presence of honeydew, which can lead to the growth of sooty mold fungus. Removing aphid colonies promptly can prevent the development of sooty mold.

Bronze Orange Bugs, also known as Stink Bugs, are notorious pests that damage citrus trees by sucking sap from young shoots, causing fruit drop and discoloration of stems. These bugs emit a foul-smelling, acidic liquid when disturbed, posing a risk to human health. Symptoms of infestation include wilting of young shoots, blackened flower stalks, and shrivelled growth. Control methods involve the use of registered insecticides specifically designed for citrus pests, applied cautiously to avoid contact with the bug's defensive secretions.

Brown rot, predominantly affecting stone fruits like peaches and nectarines, is caused by a fungus that overwinters in mummified fruit or cankers on stems. During blossom time, fruiting bodies develop, shedding spores that spread easily. Symptoms include wilted, brown flowers, and fruit with powdery tan-coloured spores that quickly rot. Preventive measures involve removing mummified fruit and applying fungicides during spring and summer, especially during wet weather conditions.

Citrus collar rot, a fungal root disease affecting citrus trees, manifests as bark death around the trunk base, oozing gum, and yellowing leaves. Improved air circulation and soil drainage, along with preventive fungicide sprays, can help manage this disease. Citrus leafminer, the larvae of a tiny moth, causes curling and distortion of new citrus growth, leaving silvery trails on leaves. Chemical control and pruning can mitigate leafminer damage. Citrus rust mite infestations result in blemished fruit with greyish-brown patches, impacting fruit quality and appearance.

Other citrus diseases and pests, including lemon scab, mealybugs, and passionfruit fungal spots, require specific control measures tailored to each infestation. Sooty mold, a fungus often secondary to insect infestations like aphids and scale, covers plant surfaces with a black, sticky substance, reducing photosynthesis. Control methods involve addressing the underlying insect problem. Vine moth caterpillars and white louse scale are additional pests requiring specific management strategies to protect plants from damage and maintain overall plant health.

Identifying Plant Nutrient Deficiencies

Not all plant issues stem from insect infestations or diseases; sometimes, the culprit is a nutrient deficiency or excess. Nutrient deficiencies typically manifest as foliage discoloration or distortion. It's essential to diagnose and address these issues promptly to prevent further damage. The first step is to rule out insect pests or diseases as the cause of plant distress.

Foliage discoloration and stunted growth may also result from environmental factors such as excessively wet or compacted soil, which hinders root growth. Extreme temperatures, either too cold or too hot, can also impede plant growth and affect flowering and fruit set. Additionally, over-fertilization can lead to salt injury, causing plants to appear scorched or wilted, even when the soil is adequately moist.

Plants require a balanced mix of nutrients to thrive. Macronutrients, such as nitrogen, potassium, phosphorus, calcium, sulphur, and magnesium, are essential elements needed in relatively large quantities for healthy plant growth. However, there are also micronutrients, including boron, copper, iron, manganese, molybdenum, and zinc, which are required in smaller amounts but are equally vital for plant development.

These nutrients are absorbed by the plant roots from the soil, with water serving as the medium for nutrient transfer. Therefore, sufficient plant nutrition relies on both adequate water availability and the appropriate soil pH. Each plant species has its preferred pH range to access nutrients effectively. If the soil pH deviates from this range, either too acidic or alkaline, the plant's ability to absorb essential nutrients is compromised, regardless of the soil's richness. Thus, maintaining the correct soil pH is crucial for optimal plant health and nutrient uptake.

Plant nutrient deficiencies can manifest in various symptoms, indicating a lack of essential macronutrients and micronutrients crucial for healthy plant growth and development. Macronutrients, such as calcium, nitrogen, magnesium, phosphorus, potassium, and sulphur, are needed in relatively large quantities, while micronutrients, including boron, copper, manganese, molybdenum, and zinc, are required in smaller amounts but are equally vital.

Calcium deficiency symptoms typically present as distorted or hook-shaped new leaves, with the growing tip potentially dying off. In tomatoes, it contributes to blossom end rot, while in cabbage and celery, it may lead to tip burn and brown/black heart, respectively. Sources of calcium include compounds containing the word 'calcium' and gypsum. However, excessive calcium can inhibit the absorption of other nutrients.

Nitrogen deficiency is indicated by yellowing of older leaves, particularly at the bottom of the plant, with remaining foliage appearing light green. Stems may also yellow and become spindly, and overall growth slows down. Nitrogen sources include compounds containing 'nitrate,' 'ammonium,' or 'urea,' as well as manure. However, many forms of nitrogen are water-soluble and can wash away.

Magnesium deficiency results in slow growth, with leaves turning pale yellow, especially on the outer edges. New growth may be yellow with dark spots. Sources of magnesium include compounds containing the word 'magnesium,' such as Epsom salts.

Phosphorus deficiency symptoms include small leaves with a reddish-purple tint, burnt-looking leaf tips, and older leaves turning almost black. Reduced fruit or seed production may also occur. Phosphorus sources include compounds containing 'phosphate' or 'bone,' as well as greensand, with its availability heavily dependent on pH range.

Potassium deficiency is characterized by older leaves appearing scorched around the edges or wilted, along with interveinal chlorosis (yellowing between leaf veins). Sources of potassium include compounds containing 'potassium' or 'potash.'

Sulphur deficiency symptoms involve new growth turning pale yellow, while older growth remains green, ultimately stunting growth. Sulphur sources include compounds containing 'sulphate,' with deficiencies more prevalent in dry weather.

Among micronutrients, boron deficiency may lead to poor stem and root growth, with terminal buds dying off and the formation of witches' brooms. Copper deficiency manifests as stunted growth, with leaves becoming limp, curling, or dropping, along with seed stalks bending over. Manganese deficiency results in slowed growth, pale yellowing of younger leaves, and diminished size of leaves, shoots, and fruit. Molybdenum deficiency symptoms include yellowing of older leaves and distortion of remaining foliage. Zinc deficiency is characterized by yellowing between veins of new growth, sometimes forming a rosette in terminal leaves.

Chapter Thirteen
Recognising Plants

Understanding plant communities is crucial for comprehending the intricate dynamics of ecosystems and the diverse habitats they support. Plants play multifaceted roles in any environment, serving as a source of food and natural products, providing habitats for numerous animals and birds, protecting soils from erosion, combating salinity issues, enhancing air quality through oxygen production and carbon dioxide removal, and participating in the natural cycle of decay, which replenishes valuable nutrients in the soil.

A plant community encompasses all the plant species within a given area, and its composition and structure vary significantly based on factors such as climate, drainage, soil type, and topography. These factors influence the adaptation of plant species to specific environmental conditions. For instance, certain plants thrive in cold climates, while others prefer warmer temperatures. Similarly, some plants are adapted to high rainfall areas, whereas others exhibit drought tolerance. Soil composition also plays a crucial role, as plants adapted to sandy soils may not flourish in clay or loam.

Environmental conditions further shape plant communities. For example, plants growing in coastal dunes often develop tough outer layers to withstand sand-blasting and salt spray. Additionally, events like bushfires and land clearing significantly impact plant communities, altering the types and abundance of plant species present.

Plant communities are classified based on the structure of their vegetation, which consists of different layers or strata varying in height and density. The tallest layer of vegetation determines the community's name. For instance, a community dominated by trees with a dense canopy is classified as a forest, while a community with scattered trees and visible sky is termed a woodland.

Figure 200: The image depicts a towering layer of trees, ranging from 10 to 30 meters in height, with the majority closely spaced and interconnected, creating a thick canopy. This particular ecosystem is classified as a forest. Donar Reiskoffer, CC BY-SA 3.0, via Wikimedia Commons.

Other classifications include scrub, shrubland, heath, and herbland, based on the height and density of the dominant vegetation. Scrub communities are characterized by dense shrubs, while heath communities feature stunted shrubs in dense canopies. Shrublands have sparse canopies with fewer shrubs touching, and herblands consist mainly of grasses, herbs, or sedges without trees or shrubs.

Understanding plant communities goes beyond their names; it involves recognizing the environmental factors influencing their composition and structure. Observing plant communities in their natural habitats provides insights into the intricate relationships between plants, soil, climate, and other ecological factors, fostering a deeper appreciation for the complexity and resilience of ecosystems.

Classification and Naming of Plants

Plants are named and classified based on their characteristics, evolutionary history, and genetic relationships. The process of naming and classifying plants is known as taxonomy. Here's how it typically works:

- **Observation and Description:** Taxonomists, scientists who specialize in plant classification, observe and study plants in their natural habitats. They collect data on various features such as leaf shape, flower structure, fruit type, and growth habits.

- **Morphological Characteristics:** Taxonomists analyse the physical characteristics of plants to identify similarities and differences. These characteristics can include the shape and arrangement of leaves, the structure of flowers and fruits, the presence of specialized organs like thorns or tendrils, and overall plant structure.

- **Genetic Analysis:** With advancements in technology, genetic analysis has become an integral part of plant classification. DNA sequencing allows taxonomists to compare the genetic makeup of different plant species, providing insights into their evolutionary relationships.

- **Classification Hierarchies:** Plants are classified into a hierarchical system that includes several levels:

  - **Kingdom:** Plants belong to the kingdom Plantae, which includes all living organisms that are capable of photosynthesis.

  - **Division/Phylum:** Within the plant kingdom, plants are further divided into divisions or phyla based on major evolutionary differences. For example, flowering plants belong to the division Magnoliophyta, while non-flowering plants like ferns belong to the division Pteridophyta.

  - **Class, Order, Family, Genus, Species:** Plants are then classified into increasingly specific categories, including class, order, family, genus, and species. These categories represent increasingly narrower groups based on shared characteristics. For example, within the family Rosaceae (roses), there are various genera such as Rosa (true roses) and Malus (apples), each containing multiple species.

- **Binomial Nomenclature:** Each plant species is given a unique scientific name using binomial nomenclature, which consists of two parts: the genus name (capitalized) and the species name (lowercase), both italicized or underlined. For example, the scientific name for the common sunflower is Helianthus annuus, where "Helianthus" is the genus and "annuus" is the species.

- **Taxonomic Keys:** Taxonomists use identification tools called taxonomic keys to help classify and identify plants based on their characteristics. These keys consist of a series of questions or statements that lead to the identification of a particular plant species.

The naming and classification of plants rely on a combination of morphological characteristics, genetic analysis, and a hierarchical system of classification to organize and categorize the vast diversity of plant life on Earth.

Scientific names are crucial for accurately identifying and categorizing plants. These names consist of two parts: the generic (or genus) name and the specific name or epithet, forming a binomial. The generic name represents a group of plants with shared characteristics, ideally evolving from a common ancestor, while the specific name distinguishes between different organisms within the genus. Binomial names always begin with the generic name capitalized, followed by the specific epithet in lowercase, such as "Grevillea victoriae." These names are typically derived from Latin or Latinized words from other languages like Greek, Aboriginal names, or acronyms, and must adhere to certain grammatical rules.

Above the genus and species levels, there are hierarchical levels of classification, with one of the most significant being the family. Families group several genera together based on shared characteristics. For example, "Grevillea victoriae" belongs to the family Proteaceae, alongside genera like Banksia and Hakea. Family names start with a capital letter and often end in "...ceae."

Below the species level, there are additional classifications like subspecies and varieties. These subdivisions allow for further differentiation within plant groups to reflect variations observed in nature. Subspecies and varieties are abbreviated as 'subsp.' and 'var.,' respectively. For instance, within "Grevillea victoriae," three subspecies are recognized, each reflecting distinct variations from the original species description.

When a subspecies, variety, or other subdivision below the species level is published, an autonym is automatically generated. An autonym refers to the original species description and serves to differentiate it from newly described subdivisions. For example, the publication of "Grevillea victoriae subsp. nivalis" in 2000 created the autonym "Grevillea victoriae subsp. victoriae," representing the typical form of the species.

In cases where the exact species is unknown, the generic name followed by 'sp.' is used, such as "Grevillea sp." When referring to multiple species within a genus collectively, 'spp.' is added to the generic name, as in "Grevillea spp." Scientific names are typically italicized within a sentence or written in a different typeface or underlined to distinguish them from other words. However, family names and abbreviations like 'subsp.' or 'sp.' are not italicized.

The process of naming plants, known as botanical nomenclature, operates under a set of internationally recognized rules and regulations outlined in the International Code of Botanical Nomenclature, abbreviated as the 'Code.' Initially formulated in 1905, this code undergoes revisions approximately every six years, guided by the consensus of taxonomic botanists worldwide. The most recent version, known as the Vienna Code, was adopted at the Seventeenth International Botanical Congress in Vienna, Austria, in July 2005. When a plant name adheres to the rules outlined in the Code, it is considered a valid publication.

A fundamental aspect of plant nomenclature revolves around type specimens, commonly referred to as 'types.' These specimens, typically preserved in herbarium collections, serve as the standard reference for a particular author's interpretation of a published plant name. Types play a crucial role in determining how names should be applied, though this process can be intricate due to various factors. To accommodate this complexity, the International Code of Botanical Nomenclature recognizes several types, each denoted by a prefix before the term '-type,' such as holotype, lectotype, or neotype.

Cultivar names, referring to cultivated varieties, follow a separate set of rules established by the International Code of Nomenclature for Cultivated Plants, last updated in 2004. These names are added after a valid scientific name at the genus or species level, not Latinized, enclosed in single quotes, and not italicized. For example, "Grevillea 'Robyn Gordon'" denotes a cultivar resulting from a hybridization process between two species, while "Grevillea rosmarinifolia 'Rosy Posy'" represents a selected form of a valid species. Alternatively, "Grevillea 'Rosy Posy'" provides a less informative but acceptable way of naming the plant. These rules ensure consistency and clarity in naming cultivated varieties within the botanical community.

Figure 201: Grevillea rosmarinifolia. Frank Vincentz, CC BY-SA 3.0, via Wikimedia Commons.

Common names, unlike scientific names governed by international conventions, lack standardized rules and regulations. They typically emerge from everyday usage by individuals who interact with the plants, often without any awareness of the scientific taxonomy. These true "common names" span various languages, scripts, and cultural contexts, reflecting the diverse linguistic and cultural landscapes across regions. Consequently, the same plant species may possess entirely different common names in different geographical areas, and even within the same locality, distinct groups of people might assign different common names to the same plant species.

The evolution of common names can be influenced by cultural interactions, where names used by one group may be adopted or adapted by another. This process sometimes leads to variations in pronunciation or even alterations in the original name's form. For instance, the aquatic fern known scientifically as Marsilea drummondii has acquired the common name "Nardoo," derived from an attempt to Anglicize the spoken Aboriginal name for the plant in one region of Australia. This demonstrates how common names can undergo transformation as they are transmitted across different cultural and linguistic contexts.

Unlike scientific names, which provide a universally recognized and standardized system for identifying and classifying organisms, common names are inherently dynamic and context-dependent. They reflect the intricate relationships between humans and the natural world within specific cultural and geographical contexts. While common names facilitate communication about plants within local communities, their variability and lack of standardization can pose challenges for scientific communication and research, highlighting the importance of using scientific names as a reliable and unambiguous means of reference in botanical studies and conservation efforts.

As such, plants are named around the world using a combination of scientific nomenclature and common names, each serving different purposes and reflecting different cultural and linguistic contexts.

Scientific names, also known as botanical names or Latin names, are assigned to plants according to a standardized system governed by international conventions. These names consist of two parts: the genus name and the specific epithet. Together, they form a binomial name unique to each plant species. Scientific names are typically in Latin or Latinized form and are universally recognized across languages and regions. They provide a precise and unambiguous means of identifying and classifying plant species, making them essential for scientific communication, research, and conservation efforts.

Common names, on the other hand, are vernacular names used by people in everyday language to refer to plants. These names often vary widely depending on the region, language, culture, and even local traditions within a particular area. Common names may reflect cultural significance, ecological attributes, physical appearance, or historical context associated with the plant. While common names facilitate communication about plants within local communities and are often deeply rooted in cultural traditions, their variability and lack of standardization can sometimes lead to confusion, especially in scientific contexts or across different language groups.

In addition to scientific and common names, some plants may also have indigenous names used by specific indigenous communities or ethnic groups. These names are often closely tied to traditional knowledge systems and reflect the intimate relationship between indigenous peoples and their natural environments. Indigenous names may offer valuable insights into the ecological, medicinal, or cultural significance of plants within indigenous cultures and can contribute to broader efforts in ethnobotany and conservation.

Flowers and Leaves

Botany, the scientific study of plants, delves into the intricacies of plant structures and functions, both internally and externally. By understanding these features, botanists can better recognize and classify different plant species. A fundamental aspect of botany involves examining the various layers or whorls of flowers, which play essential roles in plant reproduction and pollination.

The outermost layer of a flower consists of sepals, collectively known as the calyx. Sepals often resemble leaves and serve to protect and enclose the unopened flower bud. They can either be separate or fused together, exhibiting different characteristics across plant species.

Moving inward, the second whorl comprises petals, forming the corolla. Petals can be free, fused, or partially overlapping (imbricate), displaying a variety of colors, patterns, and shapes. Their vibrant hues attract pollinators like bees, butterflies, and birds, facilitating the transfer of pollen for reproduction.

Stamens, the third whorl, represent the male reproductive organs of a flower. Located inside the petals, stamens consist of a filament and an anther, where pollen grains develop. These structures may be separate or united and play a crucial role in pollen production and dispersal.

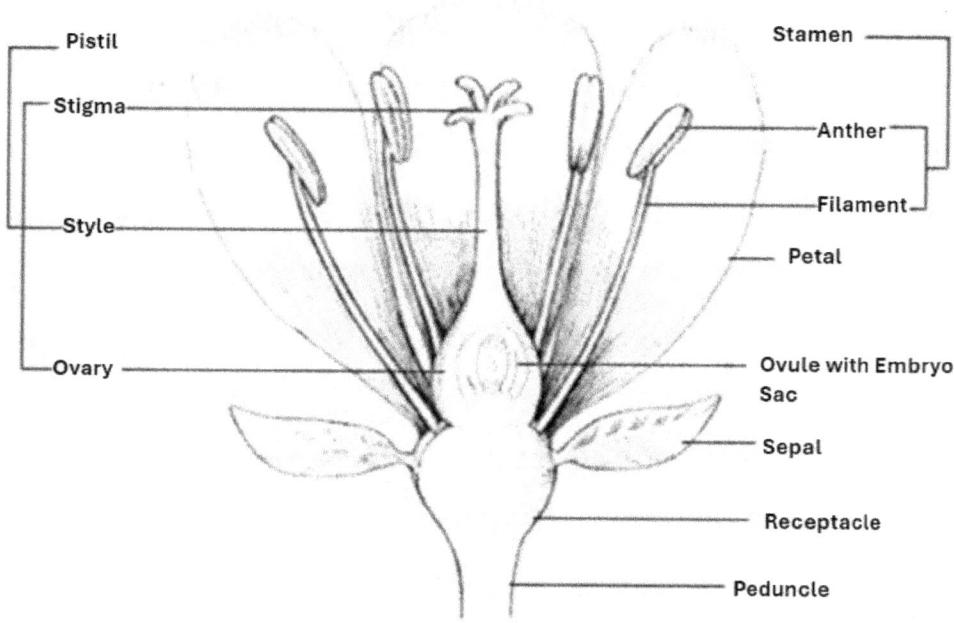

Figure 202: Parts of a flower. Back image Anjubaba, CC BY-SA 4.0, via Wikimedia Commons.

The innermost whorl, the pistil, constitutes the female reproductive organs. Comprising three main parts—the stigma, style, and ovary—the pistil facilitates fertilization and seed development. The ovary, the swollen base of the style, houses ovules attached by the placenta. Following fertilization, ovules develop into seeds within the ovary, eventually maturing into fruits.

The position of the ovary within the flower—whether superior (above) or inferior (below)—provides valuable information for flower identification. Additionally, the structure and arrangement of the ovary walls, as well as the presence of dividing walls (septa), contribute to the classification of plant species.

Leaves, the primary organs of photosynthesis in plants, exhibit a diverse range of characteristics that aid in their identification and classification. One of the fundamental features used to describe leaves is their shape, which varies widely across plant species. Leaf shapes can range from simple, such as ovate, lanceolate, or elliptical, to more complex forms like palmate or lobed, each contributing to the plant's overall appearance and function.

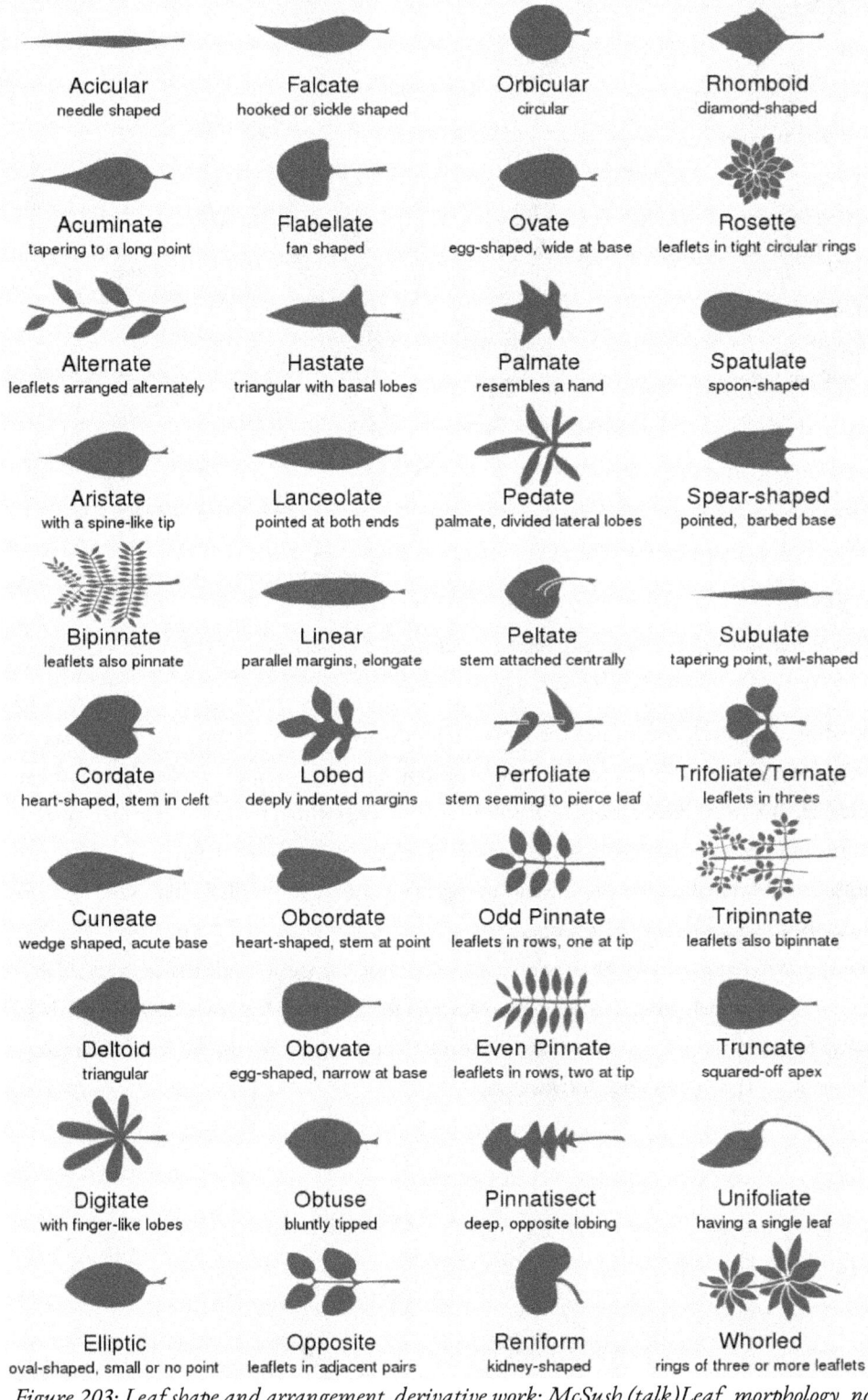

Figure 203: Leaf shape and arrangement. derivative work: McSush (talk)Leaf_morphology_no_title.png: User: Debivort, CC BY-SA 3.0, via Wikimedia Commons.

Another crucial aspect of leaf morphology is the margin, or edge, of the leaf. Margins can be smooth, serrated, toothed, or lobed, providing further distinctions among different plant species. The margin type often plays a role in the plant's defence mechanisms and adaptation to its environment.

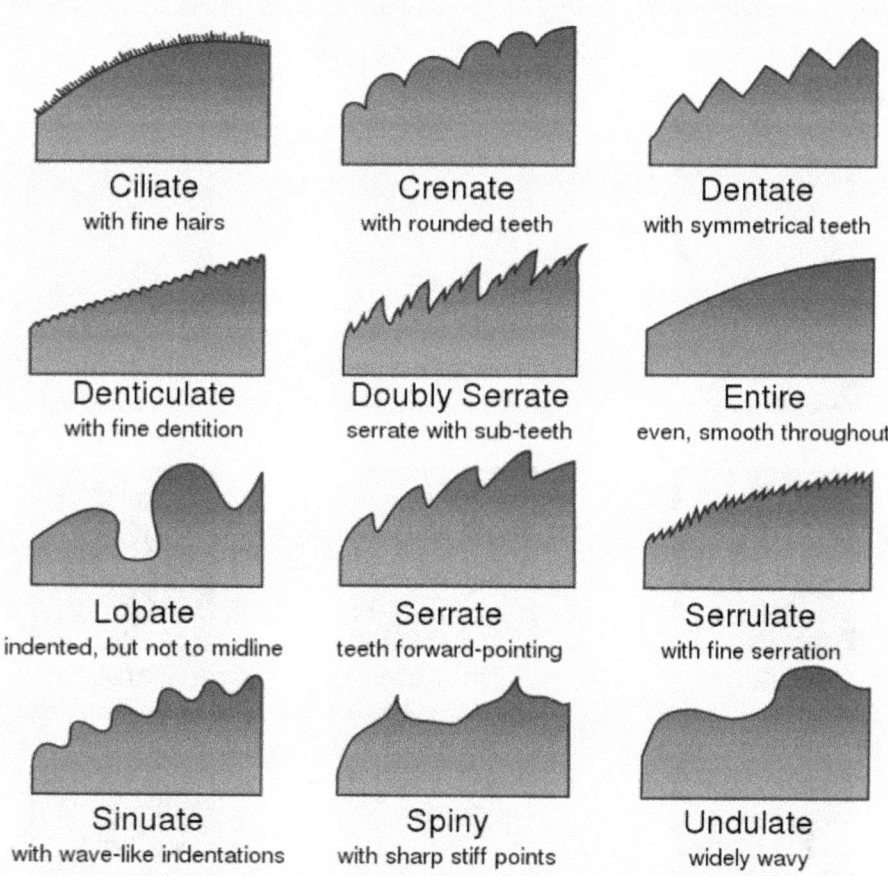

Figure 204: Leaf margin. derivative work: McSush (talk)Leaf_morphology_no_title.png: User: Debivort, CC BY-SA 3.0, via Wikimedia Commons.

Furthermore, the arrangement of leaves on the stem offers valuable insights into plant structure and growth patterns. Leaves can be categorized as opposite, alternate, or whorled based on their spatial orientation along the stem. Opposite leaves emerge in pairs directly opposite each other, while alternate leaves alternate positions along the stem. In contrast, whorled leaves cluster in a circular arrangement around the stem, with multiple leaves originating from the same point.

Leaf venation refers to the pattern of veins in a leaf, which serve as the vascular system for transporting water, nutrients, and sugars throughout the plant. This intricate network of veins provides structural support to the leaf and facilitates efficient resource distribution, contributing to the overall function and health of the plant.

There are two main types of leaf venation: parallel and reticulate (or pinnate). Parallel venation occurs when the primary veins run parallel to each other from the base to the tip of the leaf, with little to no branching. This type of venation is commonly found in monocotyledonous plants, such as grasses and lilies.

On the other hand, reticulate venation, also known as pinnate venation, features a branching network of veins that form a intricate pattern resembling a net or web. In this type of venation, the primary veins branch off into smaller veins, creating a hierarchical structure that enhances the efficiency of nutrient transport and provides greater surface area for photosynthesis. Reticulate venation is characteristic of dicotyledonous plants, including most trees, shrubs, and flowering plants.

Leaf venation patterns can vary significantly among different plant species and even within the same species, reflecting adaptations to environmental conditions, evolutionary relationships, and ecological niches. By studying leaf venation, botanists can gain insights into the evolutionary history, ecological strategies, and physiological adaptations of plants, contributing to our understanding of plant diversity and ecosystem dynamics.

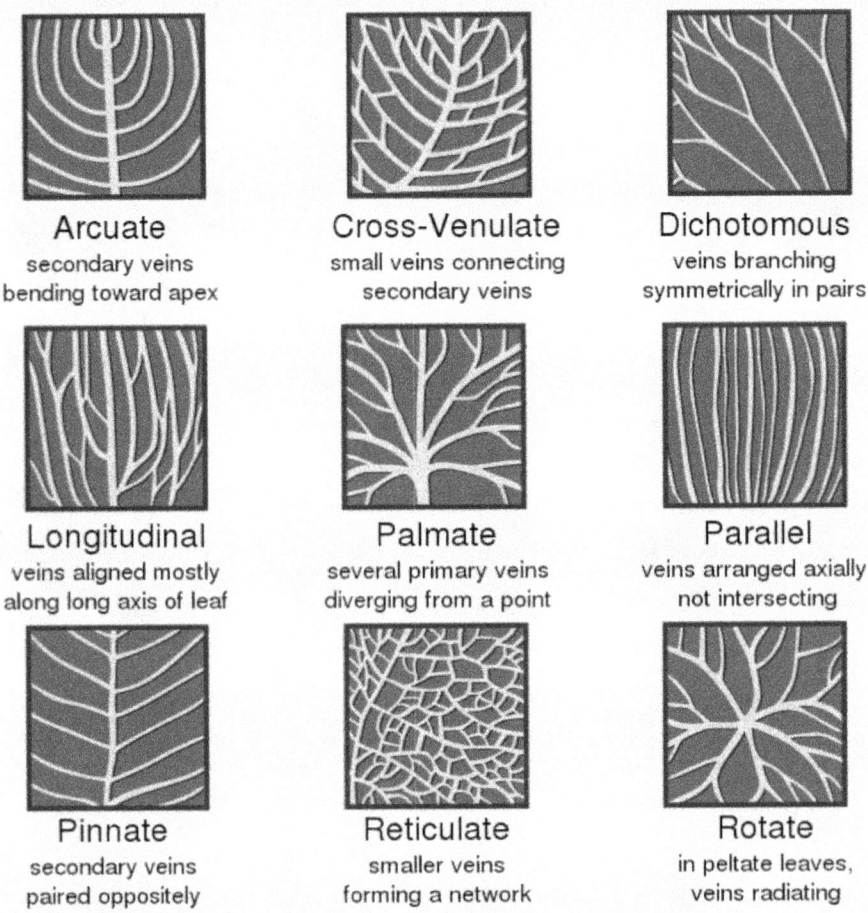

Figure 205: Leaf venation. derivative work: McSush (talk)Leaf_morphology_no_title.png: User: Debivort, CC BY-SA 3.0, via Wikimedia Commons.

Additionally, the smell or aroma emitted by leaves can serve as a distinguishing characteristic, contributing to the overall sensory experience of interacting with plants. For example, the distinctive aroma of eucalyptus leaves is a well-known feature of many species within the genus.

In terms of classification, leaves are broadly categorized into two groups: simple and compound. Simple leaves consist of a single blade attached to the stem by a petiole, whereas compound leaves comprise multiple leaflets arranged along a common petiole. This division reflects the structural diversity and complexity observed in leaf morphology across plant taxa.

Simple leaves are characterized by their singular structure, consisting of one continuous piece attached to the stem. The main part of the leaf, known as the blade, typically exhibits a flat surface and is connected to the stem either by a sheathing leaf base or a petiole, which acts as a stalk. At the base of the petiole, where it meets the stem, an axillary bud is often present, representing a potential point of future growth. In some cases, simple leaves lack a distinct petiole, and they are referred to as sessile leaves, directly attached to the stem without a stalk. Examples of plants featuring simple leaves include gum trees and banksias, showcasing the diversity of this leaf structure within the plant kingdom.

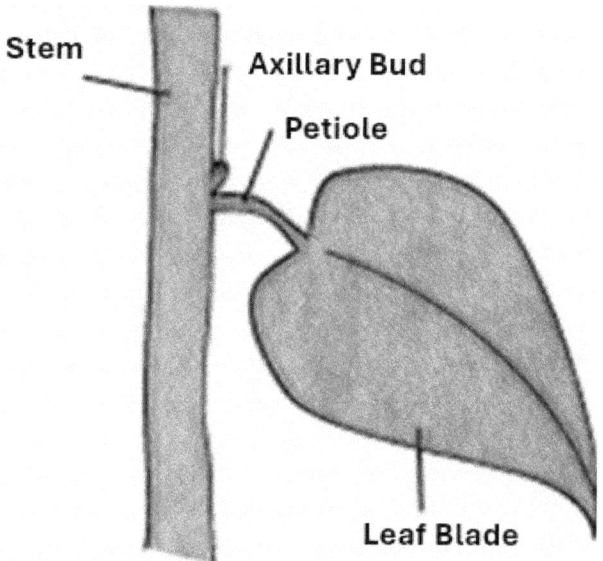

Figure 206: Simple leaf.

In contrast, compound leaves exhibit a more intricate arrangement, where the leaf blade is divided into multiple leaflets. Instead of a single continuous piece, the blade is segmented into distinct units, with the axis beyond the petiole termed the rachis, serving as the central axis for the leaflets. Despite their segmented nature, compound leaves typically possess only one axillary bud, reflecting the unified growth potential of the entire leaf structure. Compound leaves come in various forms, including pinnate, bipinnate, palmate, and ternate, each characterized by specific arrangements and configurations of leaflets along the rachis.

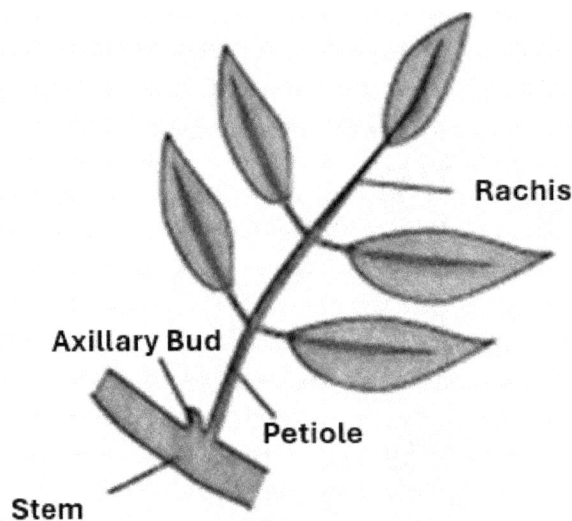

Figure 207: Compound leaves.

Pinnate compound leaves feature leaflets arranged along the central axis, resembling the structure of a feather, while bipinnate leaves exhibit a secondary level of leaflet division, creating a doubly compound appearance. Palmate compound leaves radiate leaflets outward from a central point, akin to the structure of a palm frond, whereas ternate leaves consist of three leaflets stemming from a single point of attachment. Many plants belonging to the pea family, such as Kennedia and Hardenbergia, showcase compound leaves, demonstrating the adaptability and versatility of this leaf structure across different plant species. Overall, the distinction between simple and compound leaves reflects the diverse strategies employed by plants to optimize photosynthesis, resource acquisition, and environmental adaptation.

Leaves, the primary organs of photosynthesis in plants, serve essential functions vital for the growth, development, and survival of plant life. Among the key roles performed by leaves, two primary functions stand out: photosynthesis and transpiration. Photosynthesis, facilitated by the presence of chlorophyll, the green pigment within leaves, harnesses solar energy to convert water and carbon dioxide into oxygen and sugar. This process not only produces oxygen, crucial for sustaining life on Earth, but also generates sugar molecules that serve as building blocks for plant growth and provide energy for metabolic processes. Excess sugar may be converted into starch for storage in the roots, ensuring a reserve of energy for future use.

Transpiration, the process by which plants lose water through leaf surfaces via evaporation, serves multiple functions essential for plant health. While transpiration aids in cooling the leaves, preventing overheating and potential damage, it also facilitates the uptake of water and essential nutrients from the soil through the roots, maintaining hydration and nutrient balance within the plant. Furthermore, transpiration plays a critical role in the water cycle, contributing to the movement of water vapor from the Earth's surface into the atmosphere, where it condenses to form clouds and eventually returns to the ground as precipitation, completing the cycle.

In botanical classification, flowering plants, or angiosperms, are categorized into two major groups: monocotyledons (monocots) and dicotyledons (dicots), distinguished by specific morphological characteristics. Monocots typically exhibit non-woody structures, with fibrous root systems lacking a distinct taproot. Their stems are generally non-woody, containing scattered vascular bundles, and their flowers often feature floral parts arranged in multiples of three. Leaves of monocots are typically long, slender, and characterized by parallel veins, lacking a petiole and instead attached to the stem by a sheathing leaf base. Examples of monocots include grasses, lilies, and orchids, each showcasing unique adaptations suited to their ecological niches.

On the other hand, dicots encompass a broader range of plant forms, including both woody and herbaceous species. Dicots often develop a taproot system, with a main root extending deeper into the soil and giving rise to lateral roots. Their stems may be woody or non-woody, featuring vascular bundles arranged in a ring formation. Floral parts of dicots typically occur in fours or fives, and their leaves exhibit greater variability in size, shape, and margin characteristics. Veins in dicot leaves form a network pattern, and leaves may be attached to the stem via a petiole or directly without a stalk. Examples of dicots encompass trees, shrubs, herbs, and vines, such as gum trees, wattles, and daisies, illustrating the diverse forms and adaptations within this group.

In addition to their roles in photosynthesis and transpiration, roots play crucial roles in anchoring plants in the soil, absorbing water and nutrients, and storing reserves for future growth and development. The root cap at the tip of each root protects the delicate growing tip as it penetrates the soil, while tiny root hairs enhance water and nutrient absorption by increasing surface area. As roots extend and proliferate, they provide structural support to the plant and facilitate resource uptake essential for overall plant health and vitality.

Buds, the underdeveloped or unopened reproductive structures of plants, play crucial roles in the growth and development of various species. These buds can be classified as either terminal, located at the tip of a stem, or axillary, situated between a leaf and the stem. While terminal buds typically give rise to new growth, such as leaves or flowers, axillary buds have the potential to develop into new branches or flowers, contributing to the overall architecture and reproductive capacity of the plant.

Stems, the structural axes of plants, fulfill numerous functions essential for plant survival and reproduction. They provide support for leaves and flowers, allowing these organs to access sunlight for photosynthesis and facilitating the movement of water and nutrients from the roots to other parts of the plant. In their youth, stems are often green and relatively soft, gradually changing in colour and texture as they mature. Along with providing structural support, stems can develop various features such as leaves, buds, lenticels (pores facilitating gas exchange), nodes (points of attachment for leaves or buds), and bark, the protective outer layer of woody plants.

The appearance and characteristics of stems vary widely among plant species, with certain traits aiding in plant identification. For instance, the trunk morphology of trees, such as gnarled shapes in many banksias or bottle-like structures in boab trees, can be distinctive identifiers. Similarly, twisted or contorted forms, like those seen in river red gum or alpine snow gum, offer unique visual cues for plant recognition. Additionally, bark characteristics, including texture, colour, and shedding patterns, provide valuable diagnostic features. For example, the deeply furrowed bark of ironbark or the rough, peeling bark of stringybark are recognizable traits used in plant identification.

Bark, the protective outer layer of woody stems and branches, serves as a barrier against environmental stresses such as fire, drought, and physical damage from animals or pathogens. It also helps regulate temperature and moisture levels within the plant. Bark can exhibit a wide range of textures, colours, and patterns, which can be instrumental in distinguishing between different plant species. Thick, deeply furrowed bark, such as that found in ironbarks, provides resilience against fire and mechanical damage, while smooth, papery bark, as seen in many melaleucas, offers protection against desiccation and herbivory. Understanding the diverse characteristics of bark can aid botanists and enthusiasts in accurately identifying plant species and understanding their ecological roles.

Fruits and Seeds

Fruits and seeds are fundamental components of plant reproduction and play crucial roles in the dispersal and propagation of plant species. While fruits available in grocery stores are familiar to most, those from wild or bush environments can exhibit diverse forms and functions, reflecting the ecological adaptations of various plant species.

The term "fruit" refers specifically to the mature ovary of a flower, which contains the seeds. Originally, the fruit was the ovary itself, while the seeds were the ovules before fertilization. Understanding the different types of fruits is essential for botanists and enthusiasts alike, as it provides insights into plant evolution and ecological interactions.

There are three primary types of fruits: fleshy, dry dehiscent, and dry indehiscent. Fleshy fruits, such as lilly pilly and blackberry, become soft and often change color as they ripen. They may contain one large seed or numerous small seeds and are typically dispersed by birds and animals that consume the fruit and then spread the seeds through their droppings. Collecting seeds from fleshy fruits requires timing, as it is best done when the fruits are ripe but before they naturally fall from the plant.

Dry dehiscent fruits, exemplified by capsules found in eucalypts and legumes like peas, open spontaneously upon maturity to release their seeds. These fruits become dry and split open, sometimes violently, dispersing the seeds to nearby locations. Timing is crucial when collecting seeds from dry dehiscent fruits, as they must be harvested before seed release to prevent loss.

Dry indehiscent fruits, which include structures like wings or hairs for wind dispersal, do not open to release their seeds. Instead, the seeds remain enclosed within the fruit structure, facilitating dispersal mechanisms like wind or animal attachment. Examples of dry indehiscent fruits include those with awns, such as grasses, which easily attach to passing animals or clothing for dispersal. Collecting seeds from dry indehiscent fruits requires careful consideration of ripeness, ensuring seeds are mature but collected before natural dispersal occurs.

Understanding the diversity of fruit types and their associated seed dispersal mechanisms is essential for plant conservation efforts and ecosystem management. By recognizing the characteristics of different fruit types and their roles in plant reproduction, botanists can make informed decisions regarding seed collection, propagation, and habitat restoration initiatives.

Resources and Equipment

Resources and equipment play pivotal roles in the process of plant recognition and identification, particularly for those venturing into the field of botany. For novices, assistance from colleagues and access to various resources like libraries, websites, and expert advice are indispensable. Public libraries offer a wealth of botanical literature, ranging from field guides to scientific journals, aiding enthusiasts in their quest for plant knowledge. The accessibility of online platforms further expands the horizon, enabling individuals to explore vast databases of botanical information tailored to their region or specific interests.

Field guides stand out as invaluable companions for plant identification, providing concise descriptions, illustrations, and keys for accurate classification. These portable references facilitate on-the-spot identification, making them essential tools for botanical enthusiasts and professionals alike. Moreover, organizations and training providers often maintain specialized libraries or collections tailored to their respective fields, offering valuable resources for research and learning.

In addition to traditional resources, interpersonal connections form a crucial aspect of botanical exploration. Suppliers, contractors, and colleagues within one's organization can offer practical insights and firsthand knowledge about plant species encountered in the field. Supervisors, with their wealth of experience, serve as invaluable mentors, guiding novices through the intricacies of plant identification and fostering a deeper understanding of botanical principles.

When venturing into the field for specimen collection or observation, equipped with the appropriate tools and equipment is essential. Hand tools such as loppers and pruning saws facilitate the collection of plant samples, while bags made of paper or cloth provide suitable storage for specimens. Cameras serve as indispensable tools for documenting plant species and their habitats, aiding in subsequent identification and research endeavours. Hand-held lenses enhance observation capabilities, allowing for detailed examination of plant parts and features.

Careful planning and preparation are paramount when embarking on botanical excursions, ensuring that the necessary equipment is readily available and properly maintained. By equipping oneself with the requisite resources and knowledge, enthusiasts and professionals alike can embark on a fulfilling journey of plant discovery, contributing to our collective understanding and appreciation of the botanical world.

Common Plant Varieties

Acacia

Acacia is a diverse genus of trees and shrubs belonging to the Fabaceae family, commonly known as the pea, bean, or legume family. With over 1,400 species distributed across various habitats worldwide, Acacia is one of the largest genera of flowering plants. These plants exhibit remarkable adaptability, thriving in diverse ecosystems ranging from arid deserts to tropical rainforests.

One of the defining characteristics of Acacia species is their distinctive foliage, typically comprising small, often bipinnate leaves with numerous leaflets arranged along a central stem. The leaves may vary in size, shape, and texture depending on the species and environmental conditions. Additionally, many Acacia species feature thorns or spines, which serve as a deterrent against herbivores and browsing animals.

Acacia plants are renowned for their vibrant and often fragrant flowers, which vary in colour from creamy whites and soft yellows to vibrant oranges and reds. These showy blossoms are typically arranged in dense clusters or spikes, attracting a wide array of pollinators, including bees, butterflies, and birds. The flowers give way to distinctive seed pods, which come in various shapes and sizes, ranging from elongated and cylindrical to flattened and disc-shaped.

Ecologically, Acacia species play vital roles in their respective ecosystems, providing food, shelter, and nesting sites for a diverse array of wildlife. Many species have symbiotic relationships with nitrogen-fixing bacteria in their root nodules, enabling them to thrive in nutrient-poor soils and contribute to soil fertility. Additionally, Acacia trees are often prized for their durable wood, which is used in furniture-making, construction, and various handicrafts.

Culturally, Acacia holds significance in many societies around the world. In Aboriginal Australian culture, several Acacia species, such as Acacia aneura (mulga) and Acacia pycnantha (golden wattle), are revered as sacred plants and hold symbolic importance in ceremonies and traditions. The golden wattle, in particular, is Australia's national floral emblem, representing unity, resilience, and the spirit of the Australian people.

Figure 208: Acacia retinodes Schltdl., wild source: southern Australia, picture taken in Munich Botanial Garden. Pharaoh han, CC BY-SA 3.0, via Wikimedia Commons.

Despite their ecological and cultural significance, some Acacia species are considered invasive in certain regions, where they can outcompete native vegetation and disrupt local ecosystems. Efforts to manage and control invasive Acacia populations often involve strategic measures such as targeted herbicide application, mechanical removal, and ecological restoration initiatives.

Banksia

Banksia is a genus of woody shrubs and trees native to Australia, belonging to the Proteaceae family. Named after the botanist Sir Joseph Banks, who first collected specimens during Captain James Cook's 1770 voyage to Australia, Banksia species are renowned for their distinctive flower spikes, unique foliage, and ecological significance.

There are around 170 species of Banksia, ranging from prostrate shrubs to tall trees, with diverse forms and adaptations to various habitats across Australia, from coastal dunes to mountainous regions. They are most abundant in southwestern Australia, where they dominate the landscape in many areas, but they can also be found in other parts of the country, including the east coast and tropical north.

One of the most striking features of Banksia plants is their inflorescence, which consists of cylindrical or cone-shaped flower spikes composed of numerous tiny individual flowers. These flower spikes come in a wide range of colors, including shades of yellow, orange, red, and pink, and they often produce copious amounts of nectar, attracting a diverse array of pollinators, such as birds, insects, and mammals.

Banksia foliage is typically leathery and serrated, with various adaptations to survive in nutrient-poor soils and dry, fire-prone environments. Some species have specialized root structures, such as lignotubers, which allow them to resprout after bushfires, ensuring their survival in fire-prone landscapes. Additionally, Banksia leaves often have adaptations, such as hairy undersides or thick cuticles, to reduce water loss and withstand harsh environmental conditions.

Ecologically, Banksia species play vital roles in their respective ecosystems, providing food and habitat for a wide range of wildlife. The nectar-rich flowers are a valuable food source for nectar-feeding birds, such as honeyeaters and lorikeets, as well as insects like bees and butterflies. The woody cones also contain seeds that are an important food source for seed-eating birds and small mammals.

Figure 209: Banksia menziesii. Photographs by Gnangarra, CC BY 2.5 AU, via Wikimedia Commons.

Culturally, Banksia holds significance in Indigenous Australian culture, where it has been used for various purposes for thousands of years. Indigenous Australians used Banksia flowers as a food source, either by eating the nectar directly or by soaking the flower spikes in water to make a sweet beverage. The hard, woody seed cones were also used to make tools, containers, and musical instruments.

In horticulture, Banksia species are valued for their ornamental beauty, unique foliage, and drought tolerance, making them popular choices for gardens and landscaping in Australia and other countries with similar climates. Cultivated varieties of Banksia are available in nurseries, offering a wide range of colours, sizes, and growth habits to suit different landscaping needs.

Overall, Banksia is a diverse and ecologically important genus of plants with a rich cultural heritage and aesthetic appeal. From their stunning flower spikes and unique foliage to their ecological resilience and cultural significance, Banksia species continue to captivate and inspire people worldwide, highlighting the intrinsic connection between plants and human society.

The Boronia Family

The Boronia family, formally known as the Rutaceae family, is a diverse group of flowering plants that includes a wide range of species, many of which are highly valued for their ornamental, aromatic, and medicinal properties. This botanical family is distributed worldwide, with a particularly strong presence in tropical and subtropical regions.

Taxonomy and Diversity: The Boronia family belongs to the order Sapindales and comprises approximately 160 genera and over 2,000 species. Some of the most well-known genera within the Rutaceae family include Citrus (which includes oranges, lemons, and limes), Boronia, Ruta, and Murraya.

Characteristics: Plants in the Boronia family exhibit a variety of growth forms, including trees, shrubs, and herbs. They are often characterized by simple or compound leaves, typically with glandular dots or oil glands that produce aromatic oils. The flowers are usually bisexual and have a variable number of petals and sepals, often arranged in clusters or inflorescences. Many species in this family produce fruits known as capsules or berries.

Distribution and Habitat: The Rutaceae family is widely distributed across the globe, with representatives found in both temperate and tropical regions. They are particularly abundant in regions with Mediterranean climates, such as the Mediterranean Basin, South Africa, and parts of Australia. Within these regions, they occupy diverse habitats ranging from forests and woodlands to grasslands and coastal areas.

Ecological and Economic Importance: Plants in the Boronia family play significant ecological roles as sources of food, shelter, and habitat for a wide range of animals, including insects, birds, and mammals. Many species are also valued for their economic importance. Citrus fruits, for example, are one of the most economically important fruit crops worldwide, providing essential vitamins, minerals, and nutrients to human diets. Additionally, essential oils derived from Rutaceae plants are used extensively in perfumery, cosmetics, and aromatherapy due to their pleasing fragrances and therapeutic properties.

Cultural Significance: Several species within the Rutaceae family hold cultural significance in various societies around the world. Citrus fruits, for instance, have been cultivated for thousands of years and are deeply intertwined with cultural practices and culinary traditions in many regions. In addition to their culinary uses, citrus fruits and other Rutaceae plants have also been used in traditional medicine for their purported health benefits.

Challenges and Conservation: While many species within the Rutaceae family are abundant and widely cultivated, others face threats from habitat loss, deforestation, and overexploitation. Conservation efforts are underway to protect endangered species and their habitats, particularly in regions with high levels of biodiversity. Additionally, research into sustainable cultivation practices and the development of alternative crops may help alleviate pressure on wild populations and promote the conservation of Rutaceae plants for future generations.

Figure 210: Dictamnus dasycarpus (Rutaceae). Dr. Alexey Yakovlev, CC BY-SA 2.0, via Wikimedia Commons.

In summary, the Boronia family, or Rutaceae, is a diverse and ecologically important group of plants with global distribution and cultural significance. From their economic importance as food crops and sources of essential oils to their ecological roles as providers of habitat and biodiversity, Rutaceae plants play a vital role in ecosystems and human societies worldwide.

Callistemon

Callistemon, commonly known as bottlebrushes, is a genus of flowering plants in the family Myrtaceae. This genus is native to Australia and includes around 40 species of evergreen shrubs and trees known for their distinctive bottlebrush-shaped flower spikes. Callistemons are widely cultivated for their ornamental value, and many species are popular in gardens and landscapes around the world.

Taxonomy and Distribution: The genus Callistemon belongs to the family Myrtaceae, which also includes eucalypts and paperbarks. These plants are endemic to Australia, where they are found in a variety of habitats, from coastal regions to mountain ranges and arid inland areas. While the majority of Callistemon species are native to Australia, a few species are also found in New Guinea and nearby islands.

Characteristics: Callistemon plants are characterized by their distinctive bottlebrush-shaped flower spikes, which consist of numerous individual flowers densely packed together in cylindrical or conical clusters. These flower spikes come in various colours, including shades of red, pink, purple, yellow, and cream, depending on the species and cultivar. The flowers are typically rich in nectar, attracting pollinators such as birds, bees, and butterflies.

In addition to their showy flowers, Callistemons have narrow, lance-shaped leaves that are often aromatic when crushed. The foliage is typically dense and evergreen, providing year-round interest in the garden. Depending on the species, Callistemon plants can range in size from compact shrubs to small trees, with some species reaching heights of up to 10 meters (33 feet).

Figure 211: Callistemon bottlebursh flowers. Sridhar Rao, CC BY-SA 4.0, via Wikimedia Commons.

Cultivation and Uses: Callistemons are popular ornamental plants valued for their attractive flowers, foliage, and drought tolerance. They are commonly grown in gardens, parks, and public landscapes, where they add colour and texture to mixed borders, hedges, and native plantings. Many cultivars have been developed with specific flower colors, sizes, and growth habits to suit different landscaping needs.

These plants are relatively easy to grow and prefer sunny positions in well-draining soil. They are adaptable to a range of soil types, including sandy, loamy, and clay soils, and are tolerant of coastal conditions and moderate frost. Callistemons generally require minimal maintenance once established, although regular pruning after flowering can help promote bushy growth and enhance flowering performance.

In addition to their ornamental value, Callistemon species have several other uses. Indigenous Australian peoples used various parts of the plants for medicinal purposes, including treating coughs, colds, and skin ailments. The flowers are also attractive to nectar-feeding birds and insects, making them valuable additions to wildlife gardens and habitat restoration projects.

Notable Species: Some of the most commonly cultivated species and hybrids of Callistemon include:

- Callistemon citrinus (Crimson Bottlebrush): Known for its bright red flower spikes and compact growth habit.

- Callistemon viminalis (Weeping Bottlebrush): Characterized by its pendulous branches and pink or red flower spikes.

- Callistemon 'Captain Cook': A popular dwarf cultivar with vibrant red flowers and a bushy growth habit.

- Callistemon pallidus (Lemon Bottlebrush): Noted for its pale yellow to cream-colored flower spikes and lemon-scented foliage.

Overall, Callistemons are versatile and attractive plants that bring a touch of Australian beauty to gardens around the world. With their colourful flowers, aromatic foliage, and low-maintenance nature, they are valued by gardeners and landscapers for their aesthetic appeal and ecological benefits.

Eremophila and Relatives

Eremophila is a genus of flowering plants in the family Scrophulariaceae, which is now often included in the family Plantaginaceae. This genus is native to Australia, where it is widespread and diverse, with over 200 recognized species. Eremophilas are commonly known as emu bushes or poverty bushes and are valued for their attractive flowers, aromatic foliage, and drought tolerance.

Figure 212: Photo of Eremophila maculata flowers at the Desert Demonstration Garden in Las Vegas. Stan Shebs, CC BY-SA 3.0, via Wikimedia Commons.

Taxonomy and Distribution: The genus Eremophila belongs to the family Plantaginaceae, which also includes plants such as plantains and foxgloves. These plants are endemic to Australia, where they are found in a variety of habitats, from arid deserts to woodlands and coastal regions. Eremophilas exhibit a wide range of growth habits, from low-growing shrubs to small trees, depending on the species and environmental conditions.

Characteristics: Eremophila plants are characterized by their small, tubular flowers, which come in a variety of colours, including shades of red, purple, pink, yellow, and white. The flowers are often highly fragrant and are attractive to pollinators such as bees, butterflies, and birds. They typically bloom in clusters along the stems, creating a striking display of colour during the flowering season.

In addition to their showy flowers, Eremophilas have narrow, lance-shaped leaves that are often covered in fine hairs, giving them a silvery or grayish appearance. The foliage is usually aromatic when crushed, emitting a pleasant scent that is reminiscent of sage or eucalyptus. Many species also have woody stems and branches, which may be densely branched or sparsely foliated depending on the species.

Cultivation and Uses: Eremophilas are popular ornamental plants valued for their drought tolerance, low maintenance requirements, and ornamental value. They are commonly grown in gardens, parks, and public landscapes, where they add colour and texture to mixed borders, rockeries, and native plantings. Many cultivars and hybrids have been developed with specific flower colours, sizes, and growth habits to suit different landscaping needs.

These plants are relatively easy to grow and prefer sunny positions in well-draining soil. They are adapted to a wide range of soil types, including sandy, loamy, and rocky soils, and are tolerant of dry conditions once established. Eremophilas generally require minimal pruning and fertilization, although deadheading spent flowers can help promote continuous blooming and maintain a tidy appearance.

In addition to their ornamental value, Eremophila species have several other uses. Some species have been used in traditional Aboriginal medicine for their medicinal properties, while others have cultural significance as food sources or ceremonial plants. The foliage and flowers of certain species may also be used in dried flower arrangements or potpourri, adding fragrance and visual interest to indoor spaces.

Notable Species: Some of the most commonly cultivated species and hybrids of Eremophila include:

- Eremophila nivea (Silky Eremophila): Known for its silver-gray foliage and clusters of lilac-purple flowers.

- Eremophila glabra (Tar Bush): Characterized by its narrow, lance-shaped leaves and clusters of yellow or orange flowers.

- Eremophila maculata (Spotted Emu Bush): Noted for its colorful flowers, which may be shades of pink, purple, red, or white, often with contrasting spots or streaks.

- Eremophila hygrophana (Blue Emu Bush): Valued for its striking blue to purple flowers and aromatic foliage.

Overall, Eremophilas are versatile and attractive plants that bring a touch of Australian beauty to gardens around the world. With their colourful flowers, aromatic foliage, and tolerance of harsh growing conditions, they are valued by gardeners and landscapers for their aesthetic appeal and resilience in challenging environments.

Eucalyptus, Corymbia and Angophora

Eucalyptus, Corymbia, and Angophora are three closely related genera within the family Myrtaceae, commonly known as the gum tree family. These genera are native to Australia and are well-known for their iconic appearance, diverse species, and economic importance. While they share many characteristics, each genus has its own unique features and adaptations.

Eucalyptus: Eucalyptus is the largest genus in the Myrtaceae family, comprising over 700 species. These trees and shrubs are widely distributed throughout Australia, with some species also found in neighboring countries such as Indonesia and the Philippines. Eucalyptus trees are known for their distinctive bark, which often peels away in strips or patches to reveal smooth, colorful bark beneath. The leaves are typically leathery, lance-shaped, and arranged alternately along the stems.

One of the most notable features of Eucalyptus is its oil-rich foliage, which contains volatile compounds known as essential oils. These oils give the leaves their characteristic aroma and are responsible for many of the medicinal and commercial uses of eucalyptus. Eucalyptus oil is commonly extracted from the leaves and used in products such as cough drops, chest rubs, and aromatherapy oils.

Figure 213: Eucalyptus tereticornis buds, capsules, flowers and foliage, Rockhampton, Queensland. Ethel Aardvark, CC BY 3.0, via Wikimedia Commons.

In addition to their economic value, eucalyptus trees play important ecological roles in their native habitats. They provide food and shelter for a wide range of wildlife, including koalas, possums, and various bird species. Eucalyptus forests also help regulate local climates, control erosion, and maintain soil fertility.

Corymbia: Corymbia is a genus of eucalypts that was formerly included within the genus Eucalyptus until recent taxonomic revisions separated them into distinct genera. Corymbia species are characterized by their smooth or tessellated bark, which may be shed in irregular patches, and their often large, showy flowers arranged in corymbs (flat-topped clusters). The leaves are similar to those of Eucalyptus, being typically lance-shaped and leathery, with a glossy green color.

Corymbia trees are commonly found in northern and eastern Australia, particularly in tropical and subtropical regions. They are adapted to a wide range of environmental conditions, from arid inland areas to coastal plains and wetlands. Some species are highly valued for their timber, which is used in construction, furniture making, and paper production.

Angophora: Angophora is another genus of eucalypts that is closely related to Eucalyptus and Corymbia. These trees are native to eastern Australia and are known for their rough, fibrous bark, which often extends to the smaller branches and may form decorative patterns or "scribbles" caused by insect activity. The leaves of Angophora species are similar to those of Eucalyptus and Corymbia, being lance-shaped and aromatic when crushed.

One of the distinguishing features of Angophora is its distinctive flower buds, which are often arranged in clusters and have a characteristic urn-like shape. The flowers are typically white or cream-colored and are pollinated by bees, butterflies, and other insects. Angophora trees are commonly found in woodland and forest habitats, where they contribute to the biodiversity and ecological resilience of these ecosystems.

Chamelaucium and Relatives

Chamelaucium and its relatives belong to the family Myrtaceae and are native to Australia. Chamelaucium is a genus of flowering plants commonly known as waxflowers or Geraldton wax. These plants are renowned for their attractive, waxy flowers and aromatic foliage. Along with Chamelaucium, some other notable genera in the Myrtaceae family include Leptospermum and Melaleuca.

Chamelaucium: Chamelaucium comprises several species of evergreen shrubs, with the most well-known being Chamelaucium uncinatum. These shrubs are native to the southwestern region of Western Australia and are often cultivated for their ornamental value. Chamelaucium species typically have small, lance-shaped leaves and produce clusters of flowers at the ends of their branches. The flowers are characterized by their waxy texture, which gives them a glossy appearance, and they come in various colors including white, pink, and purple. These flowers are popular in floral arrangements and are prized for their long-lasting freshness.

Figure 214: Chamelaucium uncinatum (flowers and leaves). Location: Maui. Forest & Kim Starr, CC BY 3.0, via Wikimedia Commons.

Leptospermum: Leptospermum, commonly known as tea trees, is another genus within the Myrtaceae family. These evergreen shrubs or small trees are native to Australia, New Zealand, and Southeast Asia. Leptospermum species are known for their small, five-petaled flowers, which resemble those of chamelaucium but are typically smaller and less showy. The foliage of Leptospermum plants varies from species to species, with some having aromatic leaves similar to chamelaucium, while others have needle-like or lance-shaped leaves. One species in particular, Leptospermum scoparium, is famous for its antibacterial properties and is used to produce tea tree oil, which has numerous medicinal and cosmetic applications.

Melaleuca: Melaleuca is a diverse genus of plants within the Myrtaceae family, commonly known as paperbarks or honey myrtles. These plants are native to Australia and nearby islands, as well as Southeast Asia and the Pacific Islands. Melaleuca species range from small shrubs to tall trees and are characterized by their distinctive bark, which peels away in thin, papery layers. The flowers of Melaleuca plants are small and usually white, cream, or pink in color, and they are arranged in dense clusters at the ends of the branches. Some species of Melaleuca, such as Melaleuca alternifolia, are highly valued for their essential oils, which have antiseptic and anti-inflammatory properties and are used in various medicinal and cosmetic products.

Grevillea

Grevillea is a diverse genus of flowering plants belonging to the family Proteaceae, native to Australia, New Guinea, and nearby islands. Named after Charles Francis Greville, a patron of botany, the genus consists of over 360 species, ranging from small shrubs to large trees. Grevilleas are renowned for their unique and often intricate flowers, which come in a variety of colours, shapes, and sizes. These plants are highly valued in horticulture for their ornamental appeal, drought tolerance, and ability to attract birds and pollinators to the garden.

Characteristics: Grevillea species exhibit a wide range of growth habits and foliage characteristics. They can be evergreen or deciduous, and their leaves vary from small and needle-like to large and lobed. The foliage is often leathery in texture and may be serrated or smooth-edged. Grevillea flowers are typically arranged in clusters or spikes, known as inflorescences, and are composed of numerous small, tubular flowers. The flowers often feature prominent styles and stamens, giving them a unique and striking appearance.

Cultivation: Grevilleas are popular garden plants in Australia and other regions with Mediterranean or dry climates. They are valued for their tolerance to drought, poor soil, and coastal conditions, making them suitable for a wide range of garden settings. Grevilleas thrive in full sun and well-drained soil, although they can tolerate partial shade and a variety of soil types. These plants are relatively low-maintenance once established, requiring minimal watering and pruning. Some species may benefit from occasional fertilization to promote healthy growth and flowering.

Horticultural Varieties: Grevillea cultivars have been developed for their ornamental flowers, foliage, and growth habits. These cultivars come in a wide range of colors, including shades of red, orange, yellow, pink, and white. Some popular cultivars include Grevillea 'Robyn Gordon', known for its vibrant red flowers, and Grevillea 'Moonlight', prized for its creamy white blooms. In addition to their aesthetic value, many Grevillea cultivars are selected for their compact growth habit, making them suitable for small gardens or container planting.

Ecological Importance: Grevilleas play an important ecological role in their native habitats, serving as food sources for a variety of birds, insects, and mammals. The nectar-rich flowers attract honeyeaters, lorikeets, and other nectar-feeding birds, while the foliage provides shelter and nesting sites for small mammals and insects. Grevilleas are also important host plants for butterflies and moths, with some species serving as larval food plants for specific butterfly species.

Conservation: While many Grevillea species are widespread and common in their native habitats, some are considered threatened or endangered due to habitat loss, invasive species, and other environmental threats. Conservation efforts are underway to protect and preserve these species, including habitat restoration, seed banking, and captive propagation programs. Botanic gardens and conservation organizations play a key role in these efforts, working to conserve Grevilleas and their diverse ecosystems for future generations.

In summary, Grevillea is a diverse and charismatic genus of flowering plants native to Australia and other regions with Mediterranean climates. Known for their ornamental flowers, drought tolerance, and ecological importance, Grevilleas are valued in horticulture, conservation, and landscaping, contributing to the beauty and biodiversity of gardens and natural landscapes around the world.

Figure 215: Silky Oak (Grevillea Robusta) in Athens. George E. Koronaios, CC BY-SA 2.0, via Wikimedia Commons.

Hakea

Hakea is a genus of flowering plants in the family Proteaceae, native to Australia. Named after Baron Christian Ludwig von Hake, a German patron of botany, the genus comprises over 150 species, ranging from small shrubs to tall trees. Hakeas are characterized by their distinctive foliage, unique flowers, and woody fruits, known as follicles or woody pods. These plants are valued for their ornamental appeal, drought tolerance, and wildlife habitat value, making them popular choices in Australian gardens and landscapes.

Characteristics: Hakea species exhibit a diverse range of growth habits and foliage characteristics. The foliage can be needle-like, linear, or lobed, and is often leathery in texture. The leaves are typically arranged alternately along the stems and may be toothed or smooth-edged. Hakea flowers are borne in clusters or spikes and are composed of small, tubular flowers surrounded by colourful bracts. The flowers vary in colour from white and cream to pink, red, and yellow, depending on the species. After flowering, woody fruits develop, containing two seeds enclosed in hard, woody follicles.

Cultivation: Hakeas are popular garden plants in Australia and other regions with Mediterranean or dry climates. They are valued for their drought tolerance, low maintenance requirements, and ornamental flowers. Hakeas thrive in full sun and well-drained soil, although they can tolerate a range of soil types, including sandy, gravelly, and clay soils. These plants are relatively low-maintenance once established, requiring minimal watering and pruning. Some species may benefit from occasional fertilization to promote healthy growth and flowering.

Horticultural Varieties: Several Hakea species and cultivars are cultivated for their ornamental flowers, foliage, and growth habits. Some popular species include Hakea laurina, known as the "Pincushion Hakea," prized for its unique, globular flower heads surrounded by pink or red bracts. Another favourite is Hakea sericea, commonly known as the "Silky Hakea," valued for its silver-gray foliage and cream-colored flowers. In addition to species, several cultivars have been developed for their compact growth habit, profuse flowering, and attractive foliage.

Figure 216: Pincushion Hakea (Hakea laurina). Unspecified, CC BY-SA 3.0, via Wikimedia Commons.

Ecological Importance: Hakeas play an important ecological role in their native habitats, providing food and habitat for a variety of wildlife. The nectar-rich flowers attract pollinators such as bees, butterflies, and birds, while the foliage provides shelter and nesting sites for small mammals and insects. Hakea fruits, with their hard, woody follicles, are adapted for dispersal by animals, particularly birds and mammals that consume the seeds and transport them to new locations.

Conservation: While many Hakea species are widespread and common in their native habitats, some are considered threatened or endangered due to habitat loss, invasive species, and other environmental threats. Conservation efforts are underway to protect and preserve these species, including habitat restoration, seed banking, and captive propagation programs. Botanic gardens and conservation organizations play a key role in these efforts, working to conserve Hakeas and their diverse ecosystems for future generations.

Kangaroo Paw Family

The Kangaroo Paw Family, scientifically known as Haemodoraceae, is a distinctive group of flowering plants native to Australia. This family is named after its most iconic member, the Kangaroo Paw plant (Anigozanthos), which is renowned for its unique and vibrant flowers resembling the paw of a kangaroo. While Kangaroo Paws are the most well-known representatives, the family also includes other genera with diverse characteristics and ecological roles. Here's a detailed overview of the Kangaroo Paw Family:

Figure 217: Kangaroo Paw. Davidwilcox, CC BY-SA 3.0, via Wikimedia Commons.

Taxonomy and Classification: The Kangaroo Paw Family, Haemodoraceae, belongs to the order Commelinales within the monocotyledons (monocots), a large and diverse group of flowering plants. The family comprises several genera, including Anigozanthos, Conostylis, Macropidia, and Haemodorum, among others. These genera vary in their morphology, habitat preferences, and geographic distribution.

Morphology and Characteristics: Members of the Kangaroo Paw Family exhibit a range of morphological characteristics, but they share some common features. Most species in this family are herbaceous perennials with rhizomatous or tuberous root systems. The leaves are typically linear or sword-shaped, often forming basal rosettes. The flowers are the most distinctive feature, with tubular, often brightly colored tepals arranged in clusters or spikes. In Kangaroo Paw plants, the flowers are adapted for pollination by birds, with prominent, brush-like styles that contain nectar.

Habitat and Distribution: The Kangaroo Paw Family is primarily found in Australia, with the highest diversity occurring in the southwestern region of Western Australia. These plants inhabit a variety of ecosystems, including heathlands, shrublands, woodlands, and grasslands. They are often associated with sandy or gravelly soils and are adapted to a range of environmental conditions, from coastal to inland habitats. Some species are endemic to specific regions, while others have broader distributions across Australia.

Ecological Importance: Plants in the Kangaroo Paw Family play important ecological roles in their native habitats. The distinctive flowers attract pollinators such as birds, bees, and insects, contributing to plant reproduction and genetic diversity. Additionally, the foliage provides habitat and food sources for a variety of wildlife, including insects, reptiles, and small mammals. Some species are adapted to fire-prone environments and may resprout from underground structures after bushfires, contributing to ecosystem resilience.

Cultural Significance: Kangaroo Paw plants hold cultural significance for Indigenous Australian communities, who have used them for various purposes for thousands of years. Traditionally, the flowers, roots, and rhizomes of these plants were utilized for food, medicine, and ceremonial purposes. Today, Kangaroo Paw plants are celebrated for their ornamental value in gardens, landscapes, and floral arrangements, both in Australia and internationally. They are popular choices for native gardens, providing colour, texture, and wildlife habitat.

Conservation Status: While some species in the Kangaroo Paw Family are common and widespread, others are threatened or endangered due to habitat loss, invasive species, and other anthropogenic factors. Conservation efforts are underway to protect and conserve these species, including habitat restoration, seed banking, and captive propagation programs. Botanic gardens, conservation organizations, and government agencies play key roles in these efforts, working to safeguard the biodiversity and ecological integrity of Australia's native flora.

Leptospermum and Relatives

Leptospermum, commonly known as Tea Tree, is a genus of flowering plants belonging to the Myrtaceae family. This diverse genus consists of around 80 species of evergreen shrubs or small trees native to Australia, New Zealand, and Southeast Asia. Leptospermum plants are renowned for their aromatic foliage, profuse flowering, and medicinal properties. Here's a detailed overview of Leptospermum and its relatives:

Taxonomy and Classification: Leptospermum is classified within the family Myrtaceae, which also includes other well-known genera such as Eucalyptus, Melaleuca, and Callistemon. The genus name "Leptospermum" is derived from the Greek words "leptos," meaning slender, and "sperma," meaning seed, referring to the small, slender seeds characteristic of these plants. Leptospermum species are sometimes colloquially referred to as Tea Trees due to their historical use in brewing tea-like infusions.

Morphology and Characteristics: Leptospermum plants are typically small to medium-sized shrubs with dense foliage and slender branches. They often have small, linear to elliptical leaves that are arranged alternately along the stems. The foliage is aromatic, with a distinctive herbal or resinous scent when crushed. The flowers of Leptospermum species are solitary or clustered, with five petals and numerous stamens, giving them a delicate and intricate appearance. Flower colours vary among species and can include white, pink, red, or purple hues. The fruits are small, woody capsules containing numerous tiny seeds.

Figure 218: Leptospermum scoparium. KENPEI, CC BY-SA 3.0, via Wikimedia Commons.

Habitat and Distribution: Leptospermum species are widely distributed across diverse habitats, including coastal areas, heathlands, woodlands, and montane regions. They are particularly abundant in Australia and New Zealand, where they occupy a variety of ecological niches. In their native habitats, Leptospermum plants are often found in sandy or rocky soils, where they are adapted to tolerate nutrient-poor conditions and periodic drought. Some species exhibit adaptations to fire-prone environments, resprouting vigorously after wildfires.

Ecological Importance: Leptospermum plants play important ecological roles in their native ecosystems. They provide food and habitat for a variety of wildlife, including birds, insects, and small mammals. The flowers attract pollinators such as bees, butterflies, and birds, contributing to plant reproduction and genetic diversity. Additionally, the dense foliage and intricate branching structure of Leptospermum shrubs provide shelter and nesting sites for wildlife, helping to maintain biodiversity.

Cultural and Medicinal Uses: Throughout history, Indigenous Australian communities have utilized various parts of Leptospermum plants for medicinal, culinary, and cultural purposes. Infusions made from the leaves and flowers were used as traditional remedies for ailments such as colds, coughs, and skin conditions. The antimicrobial properties of Tea Tree oil, extracted from certain Leptospermum species, have been recognized and utilized in modern herbal medicine and skincare products. Additionally, Leptospermum plants are valued in landscaping and horticulture for their ornamental foliage and flowers, often used in gardens, parks, and revegetation projects.

Conservation Status: While many Leptospermum species are widespread and common, some are threatened or endangered due to habitat loss, invasive species, and other environmental pressures. Conservation efforts are underway to protect and conserve these species, including habitat restoration, seed banking, and captive propagation programs. Botanic gardens, conservation organizations, and government agencies play key roles in these efforts, working to safeguard the biodiversity and ecological integrity of Leptospermum and its relatives.

Melaleuca

Melaleuca is a diverse genus of flowering plants belonging to the Myrtaceae family, commonly known as the myrtle family. This genus comprises around 200 species of evergreen shrubs and trees, many of which are native to Australia. Melaleuca plants are renowned for their aromatic foliage, colourful flowers, and adaptable nature. Here's a detailed overview of Melaleuca:

Taxonomy and Classification: Melaleuca is classified within the family Myrtaceae, which also includes other well-known genera such as Eucalyptus, Callistemon, and Leptospermum. The genus name "Melaleuca" is derived from the Greek words "melas," meaning black, and "leukos," meaning white, referring to the contrasting colours of the bark and flowers in some species. Melaleuca species are sometimes colloquially referred to as "paperbarks" due to their characteristic bark texture.

Morphology and Characteristics: Melaleuca species exhibit a wide range of growth habits, ranging from small shrubs to tall trees. They typically have slender branches, linear to lance-shaped leaves, and often bear clusters of small, cylindrical or bottlebrush-shaped flowers. The flowers are usually white, cream, yellow, pink, or red in colour and are composed of numerous tiny stamens. The bark of Melaleuca plants is distinctive, often peeling away in thin, papery layers, which provide insulation and protection for the underlying stem tissue.

Habitat and Distribution: Melaleuca species are distributed across diverse habitats, including coastal areas, wetlands, woodlands, and heathlands. They are particularly abundant in Australia, where they occur in a variety of ecological settings, from tropical rainforests to arid deserts. Melaleucas are also found in other regions with warm climates, including Southeast Asia, Africa, and the Pacific Islands. Many species are adapted to waterlogged or saline soils and are commonly found in wetland ecosystems such as swamps, marshes, and riverbanks.

Figure 219: Melaleuca uncinata. Margaret Donald, CC BY-SA 2.0, via Wikimedia Commons.

Ecological Importance: Melaleuca plants play important ecological roles in their native ecosystems. They provide food and habitat for a variety of wildlife, including birds, insects, and small mammals. The flowers attract pollinators such as bees, butterflies, and birds, contributing to plant reproduction and genetic diversity. Additionally, the dense foliage and bark of Melaleuca plants provide shelter and nesting sites for wildlife, helping to maintain biodiversity and ecosystem resilience.

Cultural and Medicinal Uses: Throughout history, Indigenous Australian communities have utilized various parts of Melaleuca plants for medicinal, culinary, and cultural purposes. Infusions made from the leaves and flowers were used as traditional remedies for ailments such as colds, coughs, and skin conditions. The aromatic essential oils extracted from Melaleuca species, commonly known as tea tree oil, have been valued for their antimicrobial, anti-inflammatory, and antiseptic properties. Tea tree oil is widely used in modern herbal medicine, aromatherapy, skincare products, and household cleaners.

Landscaping and Horticulture: Melaleuca plants are valued in landscaping and horticulture for their ornamental foliage, colourful flowers, and low-maintenance characteristics. Many species are cultivated as ornamental shrubs or small trees in gardens, parks, and urban landscapes. They are well-suited to a variety of garden styles, including native gardens, coastal gardens, and waterwise landscapes. Melaleucas are also used in land rehabilitation and revegetation projects to stabilize soil, control erosion, and restore degraded habitats.

Conservation Status: While many Melaleuca species are widespread and common, some are threatened or endangered due to habitat loss, invasive species, and other environmental pressures. Conservation efforts are underway to protect and conserve these species, including habitat restoration, seed banking, and captive propagation programs. Botanic gardens, conservation organizations, and government agencies play key roles in these efforts, working to safeguard the biodiversity and ecological integrity of Melaleuca and its relatives.

Waratah and Relatives

The Waratah (Telopea) and its relatives are a group of flowering plants belonging to the Proteaceae family, which is predominantly found in Australia. Renowned for their striking beauty, these plants are highly valued in horticulture and are iconic symbols of the Australian bush. Here's a detailed overview of the Waratah and its relatives:

Taxonomy and Classification: The genus Telopea, commonly known as Waratah, is a small group of shrubs and small trees native to southeastern Australia. They are classified within the family Proteaceae, which also includes other well-known genera such as Banksia, Grevillea, and Hakea. The name "Telopea" is derived from the Greek words "telos," meaning end, and "opeos," meaning eye or sight, referring to the flowers' conspicuous position at the end of the stems.

Morphology and Characteristics: Waratahs are characterized by their large, showy flower heads, which consist of numerous small individual flowers densely packed into a rounded or globular inflorescence. The inflorescence is surrounded by colourful bracts, which are modified leaves that resemble petals and contribute to the overall attractiveness of the flower. Waratah flowers typically range in colour from deep red to crimson, but there are also varieties with pink or white flowers. The leaves of Waratah plants are dark green, leathery, and often have serrated edges.

Habitat and Distribution: Waratahs are endemic to the eastern and southeastern regions of Australia, where they are found in a variety of habitats, including heathlands, woodlands, and sclerophyll forests. They are particularly abundant in the states of New South Wales, Victoria, and Tasmania, where they thrive in well-drained soils with good sunlight exposure. Waratahs are adapted to a range of environmental conditions, from coastal dunes to mountain slopes, and are often associated with nutrient-poor soils.

Ecological Importance: Waratahs play important ecological roles in their native ecosystems by providing food and habitat for a variety of wildlife, including birds, insects, and small mammals. The nectar-rich flowers attract pollinators such as honeyeaters, bees, and butterflies, facilitating cross-pollination and seed production. Additionally, the dense foliage and complex structure of Waratah plants provide shelter and nesting sites for wildlife, contributing to biodiversity and ecosystem stability.

Cultural Significance: Waratahs have long held cultural significance for Indigenous Australian communities, who valued the plants for their beauty, medicinal properties, and spiritual significance. The flowers were used in traditional ceremonies, rituals, and storytelling, and were sometimes worn as adornments or used to decorate ceremonial objects. Waratahs also feature prominently in Aboriginal art, folklore, and oral traditions, symbolizing resilience, strength, and connection to the land.

Horticultural Uses: Waratahs are highly prized in horticulture for their ornamental value and are cultivated as garden plants, cut flowers, and landscaping features. They are popular choices for native gardens, wildlife habitats, and public parks, where their vibrant flowers add colour and visual interest to the landscape. Cultivated varieties of Waratah plants are available in nurseries and garden centres, offering a range of flower colours, sizes, and growth habits to suit different garden styles and climates.

Figure 220: Telopea truncata, Mount Field National Park, Tasmania, Australia. JJ Harrison, CC BY-SA 3.0, via Wikimedia Commons.

Conservation Status: While Waratahs are not currently listed as threatened or endangered species, some populations may be at risk due to habitat loss, land clearing, and urbanization. Conservation efforts are underway to protect and conserve natural habitats where Waratahs occur, including national parks, reserves, and private land conservation initiatives. Seed banking, habitat restoration, and public education programs are important components of these conservation efforts, aimed at preserving the biodiversity and ecological integrity of Waratah and its relatives for future generations.

Eastern Redbud

Eastern Redbud (Cercis canadensis) is a small to medium-sized deciduous tree native to eastern North America. It is highly valued for its ornamental beauty, especially in the spring when it produces clusters of pink to purple flowers along its branches before the emergence of its heart-shaped leaves.

Figure 221: Eastern Redbud (Cercis canadensis). Ввласенко, CC BY-SA 4.0, via Wikimedia Commons.

Here's a detailed overview of the Eastern Redbud:

- **Description**:

    - Size: Eastern Redbud typically grows to a height of 20 to 30 feet (6 to 9 meters) tall, with a similar spread.

    - Bark: The bark is thin, smooth, and reddish-brown when young, becoming darker and developing ridges as the tree matures.

    - Leaves: The leaves are alternate, simple, and broadly heart-shaped, with a smooth margin. They emerge after the flowers and turn yellow in the fall before dropping.

    - Flowers: The flowers are small, pea-like, and appear in clusters along the branches before the leaves emerge in early spring. They can range in color from light pink to deep purple and attract pollinators like bees and butterflies.

    - Fruits: After flowering, slender green pods develop, which eventually mature into flattened, brown seed pods. These pods persist into the winter and can add visual interest to the tree.

- Growth Habit: Eastern Redbud has a spreading, often multi-trunked growth habit, forming an irregularly shaped crown.

- **Habitat and Range**:
  - Eastern Redbud is native to eastern and central North America, ranging from southern Ontario and Quebec in Canada to Florida and Texas in the United States.
  - It is often found growing in open woodlands, along woodland edges, in ravines, and on slopes.

- **Cultivation**:
  - Soil: Eastern Redbud prefers moist, well-drained soils but can tolerate a range of soil types, including clay, loam, and sand.
  - Light: It thrives in full sun to partial shade, with full sun exposure promoting the best flowering.
  - Maintenance: Once established, Eastern Redbud is relatively low-maintenance, requiring little pruning other than to remove dead or damaged branches.

- **Landscaping Use**:
  - Ornamental: Eastern Redbud is widely planted as an ornamental tree in residential landscapes, parks, and along streetscapes for its showy spring flowers and attractive foliage.
  - Wildlife Value: The flowers provide nectar for pollinators, while the seeds are eaten by birds and small mammals.

- **Cultural Significance**:
  - Native Americans: Indigenous peoples used various parts of the Eastern Redbud for medicinal purposes, and the wood was used for making tools and dyes.
  - State Tree: Eastern Redbud is the state tree of Oklahoma.

Overall, Eastern Redbud is a charming and versatile tree prized for its early spring blooms, attractive foliage, and adaptability to a variety of growing conditions, making it a popular choice for gardens and landscapes throughout its native range and beyond.

Eastern White Pine

Eastern White Pine (Pinus strobus) is a large evergreen conifer native to eastern North America. It is one of the most important timber trees in the region and is prized for its majestic appearance, fast growth, and valuable wood. Here's a detailed overview of the Eastern White Pine:

- **Description**:
  - Size: Eastern White Pine is a tall, straight-growing tree that can reach heights of 50 to 80 feet (15 to 24 meters) or more, with a trunk diameter of 1.5 to 3 feet (0.5 to 1 meter).

- Bark: The bark of young trees is smooth and gray-green, becoming deeply furrowed and reddish-brown with age.

- Needles: The needles are soft, flexible, and bluish-green, occurring in bundles of five. They are typically 2.5 to 5 inches (6 to 13 cm) long.

- Cones: The cones are cylindrical and slender, ranging from 3 to 8 inches (7 to 20 cm) long. They mature in their second year and release winged seeds that are dispersed by the wind.

- Growth Habit: Eastern White Pine has an open, pyramidal crown when young, becoming more rounded and irregular with age.

- **Habitat and Range**:

  - Eastern White Pine is native to eastern North America, ranging from eastern Canada (Newfoundland to Manitoba) south to the Appalachian Mountains and west to the Great Lakes region.

  - It typically grows in mixed hardwood-conifer forests, often on moist, well-drained soils, but it can also tolerate a range of soil types and moisture conditions.

- **Cultivation**:

  - Soil: Eastern White Pine prefers moist, well-drained soils with a slightly acidic pH but can grow in a variety of soil types, including sandy, loamy, and rocky soils.

  - Light: It thrives in full sun but can tolerate partial shade, especially when young.

  - Maintenance: Eastern White Pine requires minimal maintenance once established, although pruning may be necessary to remove dead or diseased branches.

- **Uses**:

  - Timber: Eastern White Pine is highly valued for its lightweight, straight-grained wood, which is easy to work with and resistant to warping and splitting. It is used for a wide range of construction purposes, including framing, siding, trim, and interior panelling.

  - Landscaping: Eastern White Pine is planted as an ornamental tree in parks, gardens, and large landscapes for its graceful form and soft, feathery foliage.

  - Wildlife Habitat: The tree provides food and habitat for various wildlife species, including birds, squirrels, and deer. The seeds are an important food source for many birds and small mammals.

- **Cultural Significance**:

  - Historical Importance: Eastern White Pine played a significant role in American history, particularly during the colonial era, when it was prized for shipbuilding and exported to Europe for use in masts and spars.

- Symbolism: In some Native American cultures, Eastern White Pine is considered a sacred tree and is associated with peace and spirituality.

Figure 222: Pinus strobus foliage and cones, weighed down with glazed ice. Washington DC, USA. F Delventhal from Outside Washington, D.C., US, CC BY 2.0, via Wikimedia Commons.

Eastern White Pine is an iconic and ecologically important tree species valued for its beauty, versatility, and role in supporting diverse ecosystems throughout its native range. Despite challenges such as habitat loss and pests like the invasive pine beetle, efforts are underway to conserve and sustainably manage this valuable resource for future generations.

Black-eyed Susan

Black-eyed Susan (Rudbeckia hirta) is a popular herbaceous perennial plant native to North America, known for its bright and cheerful flowers.

Figure 223: Black-eyed Susan blossom. G. Edward Johnson, CC BY-SA 3.0, via Wikimedia Commons.

Here's a detailed overview:

- **Description**:

    - Flowers: Black-eyed Susan produces daisy-like flowers with golden-yellow petals surrounding a dark brown or black central cone. The cone resembles a 'black eye,' hence the common name.

    - Foliage: The plant has hairy, lance-shaped leaves that grow in basal rosettes and along the stems.

    - Height: Depending on the variety, Black-eyed Susan typically grows 1 to 3 feet (30 to 90 cm) tall, with a spread of about 1 to 2 feet (30 to 60 cm).

    - Growth Habit: It has an upright, clumping growth habit.

- **Habitat and Range**:

    - Black-eyed Susan is native to various regions of North America, including the eastern United States, the Midwest, and parts of Canada.

- It is commonly found in meadows, prairies, open woodlands, and along roadsides and disturbed areas.

- **Cultivation**:

    - Soil: Black-eyed Susan thrives in well-drained soil with average fertility. It can tolerate a wide range of soil types, including sandy, loamy, and clay soils.

    - Light: It prefers full sun but can tolerate partial shade, although too much shade may result in fewer flowers.

    - Water: Once established, Black-eyed Susan is drought-tolerant and only requires occasional watering during dry periods.

    - Maintenance: This plant is relatively low-maintenance and does not require regular fertilization. Deadheading spent flowers can prolong the blooming period and prevent self-seeding.

- **Propagation**:

    - Black-eyed Susan can be propagated from seeds, divisions, or nursery-grown transplants.

    - Seeds can be sown directly in the garden in the spring or fall, or started indoors 6 to 8 weeks before the last frost date.

    - Division of mature plants can be done in the spring or fall to create new plants and rejuvenate older ones.

- **Uses**:

    - Garden Ornamental: Black-eyed Susan is a popular choice for gardens and landscapes due to its vibrant flowers, long bloom period, and easy care.

    - Pollinator Plant: The nectar-rich flowers attract bees, butterflies, and other pollinators, making it a valuable addition to pollinator gardens.

    - Cut Flowers: The long-lasting flowers make excellent cut flowers for floral arrangements and bouquets.

    - Naturalization: Black-eyed Susan can be used for naturalizing meadows and wildflower gardens, where it adds colour and attracts wildlife.

- **Cultural Significance**:

    - Symbolism: Black-eyed Susan is often associated with qualities such as encouragement, motivation, and optimism. It is a symbol of cheerfulness and resilience.

    - Folklore: The plant's name is believed to have originated from a poem by English poet John Gay, titled "Black-eyed Susan," written in 1720.

Black-eyed Susan is a versatile and attractive plant that adds a splash of colour to gardens and natural areas throughout North America. With its bright flowers, easy care requirements, and ability to support pollinators, it is a favourite among gardeners and nature enthusiasts alike.

Eastern Red Cedar

Eastern Red Cedar, scientifically known as Juniperus virginiana, is a species of coniferous tree native to eastern North America. Despite its common name, it is not a true cedar but belongs to the Cypress family (Cupressaceae).

Figure 224: Eastern Red Cedar at South Riding Golf Course in South Riding, Virginia. Famartin, CC BY-SA 3.0, via Wikimedia Commons.

Here's a detailed overview:

- **Description**:

  - Size: Eastern Red Cedar is a medium-sized tree that typically grows to heights of 30 to 40 feet (9 to 12 meters), occasionally reaching up to 90 feet (27 meters) in optimal conditions.

  - Shape: It has a pyramidal to columnar crown when young, which becomes more irregular and rounded with age.

  - Bark: The bark is reddish-brown and exfoliates in thin strips, revealing reddish inner bark.

  - Foliage: The tree has scale-like leaves arranged in opposite pairs or whorls of three. The foliage is typically dark green and aromatic.

  - Cones: Female trees produce small, bluish-green seed cones that mature to dark blue or purple berries known as "juniper berries." These cones are an important food source for wildlife.

- **Habitat and Range**:

  - Eastern Red Cedar is native to a wide range of habitats across eastern North America, including open woodlands, fields, prairies, and disturbed areas.

  - It is commonly found in regions with well-drained soils, including sandy, rocky, and clay soils.

- **Cultural Significance**:

  - Landscape Use: Eastern Red Cedar is valued for its ornamental qualities and is often planted as a specimen tree in landscapes and gardens. Its dense foliage provides year-round interest and serves as a windbreak or privacy screen.

  - Wildlife Habitat: The tree provides food and shelter for various wildlife species, including birds (such as cedar waxwings), mammals, and insects. The berries are an important winter food source for many bird species.

  - Wood Uses: The wood of Eastern Red Cedar is highly durable and naturally resistant to decay and insect damage. It is used for a variety of purposes, including fence posts, outdoor furniture, chests, closets (as aromatic cedar), and decorative woodwork.

- **Ecological Role**:

  - Succession: Eastern Red Cedar is often one of the first trees to colonize abandoned fields and disturbed areas. Its ability to thrive in poor soils and withstand drought makes it a pioneer species in ecological succession.

  - Allelopathy: The tree produces chemicals that inhibit the growth of other plant species, creating dense stands of cedar known as "cedar glades" or "cedar barrens."

  - Wildlife Habitat: Eastern Red Cedar provides nesting sites and cover for birds and small mammals. It also serves as a larval host plant for certain butterfly species.

- **Cultivation**:
    - Eastern Red Cedar is relatively easy to grow and adaptable to a wide range of soil types and growing conditions.
    - It prefers full sun but can tolerate partial shade.
    - The tree is drought-tolerant once established and requires little maintenance.
- **Conservation Status**:
    - While Eastern Red Cedar is not considered globally threatened, its abundance in some areas has led to concerns about its ecological impact, particularly in grassland and prairie ecosystems where it can become invasive.

Eastern Red Cedar is a versatile and ecologically important tree with cultural, ecological, and economic significance. Its attractive appearance, wildlife value, and durable wood make it a valuable asset in natural and cultivated landscapes across its native range.

Purple Coneflower

Purple Coneflower, scientifically known as Echinacea purpurea, is a herbaceous perennial plant native to eastern and central North America. It is a member of the Asteraceae family and is renowned for its medicinal properties and ornamental value. Here's a detailed overview:

- **Description**:
    - Appearance: Purple Coneflower is characterized by its showy, daisy-like flowers with prominent, spiny, coppery-orange central cones surrounded by purple to pinkish-purple ray florets. Each flower head can measure 3 to 4 inches (7.6 to 10 cm) in diameter.
    - Foliage: The plant features lance-shaped, coarse-textured leaves arranged alternately along sturdy, hairy stems. The leaves have a rough texture and serrated margins.
    - Height: Purple Coneflower typically grows to heights of 2 to 5 feet (0.6 to 1.5 meters) tall, with a spread of 1.5 to 2 feet (0.5 to 0.6 meters).
    - Blooming Period: The plant produces flowers from early to midsummer, attracting pollinators such as bees, butterflies, and hummingbirds.
- **Habitat and Range**:
    - Purple Coneflower is native to a variety of habitats, including prairies, meadows, open woodlands, and roadsides, across the eastern and central regions of North America.
    - It prefers well-drained soils and full sun but can tolerate a wide range of soil types, including sandy, loamy, and clay soils.
- **Cultural Significance**:

- Medicinal Use: Purple Coneflower has a long history of medicinal use by Native American tribes, who used various parts of the plant to treat ailments such as infections, wounds, and respiratory issues. Today, it is a popular herbal remedy believed to support immune function and overall wellness.

- Ornamental Value: Purple Coneflower is widely cultivated as an ornamental plant in gardens and landscapes for its attractive flowers, drought tolerance, and ease of care. It adds colour and texture to perennial borders, wildflower gardens, and naturalistic landscapes.

- Wildlife Attraction: The flowers provide nectar and pollen for pollinators, while the seeds are a food source for birds, particularly finches and sparrows.

- **Cultivation**:

  - Growing Conditions: Purple Coneflower thrives in full sun to partial shade and well-drained soil. It is drought-tolerant once established and prefers slightly acidic to neutral pH levels.

  - Propagation: The plant can be propagated from seeds, division of established clumps, or root cuttings. Seeds can be sown directly in the garden in fall or spring, while division is best done in early spring or fall.

  - Maintenance: Purple Coneflower requires minimal maintenance once established. Deadheading spent flowers can prolong the blooming period, while division every few years can rejuvenate overcrowded clumps.

- **Conservation Status**:

  - While Purple Coneflower is not considered globally threatened, certain varieties or populations may face threats from habitat loss, urbanization, and agricultural practices. However, its widespread cultivation in gardens and restoration projects helps maintain genetic diversity and support pollinator populations.

Purple Coneflower is a versatile and attractive perennial plant valued for its medicinal properties, ecological benefits, and aesthetic appeal. Whether grown for its therapeutic benefits or as a garden ornamental, it remains a beloved and cherished plant in horticulture and herbalism.

Figure 225: Purple Coneflowers (Echinacea purpurea). Andrew C, CC BY 2.0, via Wikimedia Commons.

Switchgrass

Switchgrass, scientifically known as Panicum virgatum, is a warm-season perennial grass native to North America. It is a member of the Poaceae family and is valued for its adaptability, drought tolerance, and ecological benefits. Here's a detailed overview:

- **Description**:

    - Appearance: Switchgrass is a tall, upright grass with sturdy stems that can reach heights of 3 to 7 feet (0.9 to 2.1 meters) at maturity. The stems are topped with airy panicles of tiny flowers that bloom in late summer to early fall.

    - Foliage: The plant features linear, lance-shaped leaves that are typically blue-green in colour. The leaves are alternate and can grow up to 2 feet (0.6 meters) in length.

    - Root System: Switchgrass has deep, fibrous roots that can extend several feet into the soil, making it highly effective at soil stabilization and erosion control.

- **Habitat and Range**:

    - Native Range: Switchgrass is native to the tallgrass prairies of North America, where it once dominated vast expanses of the central and eastern United States.

- ○ Habitat: It thrives in a variety of habitats, including prairies, savannas, open woodlands, and disturbed areas with well-drained soils.

- ○ Range: Switchgrass is found across much of the United States, from the eastern seaboard to the Rocky Mountains, as well as parts of southern Canada.

- **Ecological Importance**:

  - ○ Soil Conservation: Switchgrass plays a crucial role in soil conservation and erosion control due to its extensive root system, which helps stabilize soil and prevent nutrient runoff.

  - ○ Wildlife Habitat: The dense foliage and seed heads of switchgrass provide cover and nesting sites for a variety of wildlife, including birds, small mammals, and insects.

  - ○ Carbon Sequestration: Switchgrass is a carbon-neutral crop that sequesters carbon dioxide from the atmosphere into its roots and soil, helping mitigate climate change.

  - ○ Biodiversity: Native switchgrass populations support diverse plant and animal communities, contributing to overall ecosystem health and resilience.

- **Cultural and Agricultural Uses**:

  - ○ Forage Crop: Switchgrass is commonly used as a forage crop for livestock grazing and hay production. It provides nutritious feed for cattle, sheep, and horses, particularly in regions with hot summers and limited rainfall.

  - ○ Biomass Production: Switchgrass is also cultivated for biomass production and bioenergy purposes. It can be harvested and converted into biofuels, such as ethanol and cellulosic ethanol, through processes like fermentation and enzymatic hydrolysis.

  - ○ Landscaping and Restoration: Switchgrass is increasingly used in landscaping and ecological restoration projects due to its aesthetic appeal, wildlife value, and ability to thrive in diverse environments.

- **Cultivation**:

  - ○ Growing Conditions: Switchgrass prefers full sun and well-drained soils but can tolerate a wide range of soil types, including sandy, loamy, and clay soils. It is drought-tolerant once established and requires minimal water and fertilizer.

  - ○ Propagation: Switchgrass can be propagated from seeds or vegetative cuttings. Seeds are typically sown in spring or fall, while vegetative propagation involves dividing established clumps or planting stem cuttings.

  - ○ Maintenance: Once established, switchgrass requires minimal maintenance. It should be mowed or grazed periodically to promote new growth and prevent lodging. In agricultural settings, fertilization and weed control may be necessary to optimize yield.

Figure 226: Panicum virgatum. Dinkum, CC0, via Wikimedia Commons.

Switchgrass is a versatile and valuable native grass species with numerous ecological, agricultural, and cultural benefits. Its adaptability, resilience, and multifunctional uses make it a valuable asset in sustainable land management and conservation efforts.

American Beech

American Beech, scientifically known as Fagus grandifolia, is a majestic deciduous tree native to eastern North America. It belongs to the Fagaceae family and is renowned for its stately appearance, smooth gray bark, and dense, spreading canopy.

Figure 227: American Beech Tree, Fagus grandifolia. Specimen tree at Morton Arboretum, Lisle, Illinois, USA. Bruce Marlin, CC BY-SA 2.5, via Wikimedia Commons.

Here's a detailed overview of this iconic tree:

- **Description**:

  - Size and Shape: American Beech trees typically grow to heights of 50 to 80 feet (15 to 24 meters), with some specimens reaching over 100 feet (30 meters). They have a broad, rounded crown and a straight, tall trunk that often forks near the ground.

  - Leaves: The foliage consists of simple, ovate-shaped leaves with pointed tips and serrated edges. The leaves are lustrous dark green in summer and turn a golden bronze in fall, adding to the tree's ornamental value.

  - Bark: One of the distinguishing features of the American Beech is its smooth, pale gray bark, which remains relatively unblemished even as the tree matures. Over time, the bark develops distinctive horizontal ridges and fissures.

- **Habitat and Range**:

- Native Range: American Beech is indigenous to the eastern United States and southeastern Canada, where it occurs in mixed hardwood forests, moist woodlands, and along stream banks.
- Habitat: It thrives in well-drained, fertile soils with adequate moisture, although it can tolerate a range of soil types, including clay and loam. Beech trees prefer sheltered sites with partial shade but can also grow in full sun.

- **Ecological Importance**:
  - Wildlife Habitat: American Beech trees provide habitat and food for a variety of wildlife species. The nuts, known as beechnuts, are an important food source for birds, squirrels, chipmunks, and other small mammals.
  - Soil Stabilization: The dense root system of American Beech helps stabilize soil and prevent erosion, making it valuable for soil conservation in riparian zones and steep slopes.
  - Canopy Cover: The broad, spreading canopy of mature Beech trees creates a cool, shaded environment beneath, which benefits understory plants, soil microorganisms, and stream ecosystems.

- **Cultural and Economic Uses**:
  - Timber: American Beech wood is valued for its strength, hardness, and fine grain, making it suitable for furniture, flooring, cabinetry, and veneer. However, beech wood is prone to warping and is less commonly used than other hardwoods like oak and maple.
  - Landscaping: American Beech is often planted as an ornamental tree in parks, estates, and urban landscapes due to its graceful form, attractive foliage, and year-round interest.
  - Wildlife Plantings: Landowners may plant Beech trees to enhance wildlife habitat on their property, providing food and cover for birds and mammals.

- **Challenges and Conservation**:
  - Pests and Diseases: American Beech trees are susceptible to a variety of pests and diseases, including beech bark disease, which is caused by a combination of scale insects and fungal pathogens. This disease has devastated Beech populations in some areas, leading to declines in tree health and vigor.
  - Conservation Efforts: Efforts to conserve American Beech trees include monitoring for signs of disease, promoting genetic diversity through selective breeding programs, and preserving mature stands of Beech in protected areas and wildlife reserves.

American Beech is a cherished native tree species valued for its ecological importance, cultural significance, and aesthetic appeal. Despite facing challenges from pests and diseases, efforts to conserve and manage Beech populations are essential for ensuring the continued health and vitality of this iconic tree species.

Wild Bergamot

Wild Bergamot, scientifically known as Monarda fistulosa, is a perennial herbaceous plant native to North America. Belonging to the mint family (Lamiaceae), it is also commonly referred to as Bee Balm, Horsemint, or Oswego Tea.

Figure 228: Monarda fistulosa. Lazaregagnidze, CC BY-SA 4.0, via Wikimedia Commons.

Here's a detailed overview of this versatile and attractive wildflower:

- **Description**:

    ○ Appearance: Wild Bergamot typically grows to heights of 2 to 4 feet (0.6 to 1.2 meters) and features square stems with lance-shaped, aromatic leaves arranged opposite each other along the stem. The foliage is dark green and emits a pleasant minty fragrance when crushed.

    ○ Flowers: The showy flowers of Wild Bergamot bloom from mid to late summer and are highly attractive to pollinators such as bees, butterflies, and hummingbirds. The flowers are tubular and arranged in dense, spherical clusters at the ends of the stems. They come in various shades of pink, lavender, and purple, adding vibrant color to meadows, prairies, and garden borders.

    ○ Roots: The plant develops a deep taproot system, which helps it withstand drought conditions and makes it well-adapted to a variety of soil types, including sandy, loamy, and clay soils.

- **Habitat and Range**:

- Native Range: Wild Bergamot is indigenous to much of North America, including the eastern United States, the Great Plains, and parts of Canada. It is commonly found in open woodlands, prairies, meadows, and along roadsides and stream banks.

- Habitat Preferences: This adaptable plant thrives in full sun to partial shade and prefers moist, well-drained soils. While it can tolerate periods of drought, it benefits from regular moisture, especially during the growing season.

- **Ecological Importance**:

  - Pollinator Magnet: The nectar-rich flowers of Wild Bergamot attract a wide range of pollinators, including bees, butterflies, moths, and hummingbirds. As a result, it plays a vital role in supporting pollinator populations and promoting biodiversity in natural habitats and home gardens.

  - Medicinal Uses: Traditionally, various Native American tribes used Wild Bergamot for its medicinal properties. It was brewed into teas or infusions to treat ailments such as colds, sore throats, and digestive issues. The leaves and flowers were also used topically as poultices to soothe skin irritations and minor wounds.

  - Culinary Uses: The leaves of Wild Bergamot can be dried and used to make a fragrant herbal tea known as Oswego Tea. The tea has a slightly citrusy flavor and was popularized by the Oswego Native American tribe in the northeastern United States.

- **Cultural Significance**:

  - Gardening: Wild Bergamot is a popular choice for native plant gardens, pollinator gardens, and wildflower meadows due to its attractive flowers, aromatic foliage, and wildlife-friendly attributes. It is easy to grow from seed or transplants and requires minimal maintenance once established.

  - Cultural Symbolism: In addition to its practical uses, Wild Bergamot holds cultural significance for various Indigenous peoples, who value it for its medicinal, culinary, and ceremonial purposes. It is also celebrated for its beauty and resilience in natural landscapes.

- **Conservation and Management**:

  - Conservation Status: While Wild Bergamot is not considered threatened or endangered at the species level, it faces threats from habitat loss, fragmentation, and invasive species encroachment in some regions. Efforts to conserve and protect its native habitats are important for maintaining healthy populations and supporting pollinator diversity.

  - Garden Cultivation: Home gardeners can contribute to the conservation of Wild Bergamot by incorporating it into their landscape designs and providing suitable habitat for pollinators. Choosing native plants like Wild Bergamot helps support local ecosystems and fosters ecological resilience.

Wild Bergamot is a valuable native plant species cherished for its beauty, ecological importance, and cultural significance across North America. Whether gracing natural meadows or cultivated gardens, this versatile wildflower continues to captivate and inspire admiration for its many virtues.

Eastern Hemlock

Eastern Hemlock, scientifically known as Tsuga canadensis, is a majestic coniferous tree native to eastern North America. Belonging to the pine family (Pinaceae), it is one of the most iconic and ecologically significant tree species in the region. Here's an in-depth overview of this magnificent evergreen:

- **Description**:

  - Appearance: Eastern Hemlock is a large, long-lived tree that typically grows to heights of 50 to 70 feet (15 to 21 meters) and occasionally exceeds 100 feet (30 meters) in optimal growing conditions. It has a pyramidal or conical crown with gracefully drooping branches, giving it an elegant and stately appearance.

  - Foliage: The needles of Eastern Hemlock are flat, short, and arranged in two rows along the stems. They are dark green above and pale green beneath, creating a distinctive bicolored effect. The foliage remains on the tree year-round, providing cover and shelter for wildlife during the winter months.

  - Cones: The seed cones of Eastern Hemlock are small, egg-shaped, and hang downward from the branches. They mature in late summer or early fall, releasing tiny seeds that are dispersed by wind and animals.

- **Habitat and Range**:

  - Native Range: Eastern Hemlock is indigenous to the eastern United States and southeastern Canada, where it occurs in moist, cool forest habitats with well-drained soils. It is commonly found in mixed deciduous-coniferous forests, ravines, and along stream banks.

  - Habitat Preferences: This shade-tolerant tree thrives in cool, humid climates and prefers sheltered, north-facing slopes or valleys where it can retain moisture and avoid exposure to direct sunlight. It is often associated with other moisture-loving species such as yellow birch, sugar maple, and American beech.

- **Ecological Importance**:

  - Keystone Species: Eastern Hemlock plays a crucial role in forest ecosystems as a keystone species, influencing the structure and composition of plant and animal communities. Its dense foliage provides habitat and nesting sites for a variety of wildlife, including birds, squirrels, and deer. Additionally, fallen hemlock logs contribute to nutrient cycling and soil enrichment.

  - Riparian Buffer: Along stream banks and riparian zones, Eastern Hemlock helps stabilize soil, prevent erosion, and regulate water temperature, creating optimal conditions for aquatic organisms such as trout and amphibians. Its presence can enhance water quality and protect sensitive aquatic habitats from sedimentation and runoff.

- **Threats and Conservation**:

- Invasive Pests: One of the most significant threats to Eastern Hemlock is the invasive hemlock woolly adelgid (Adelges tsugae), a tiny aphid-like insect that feeds on the tree's sap and can cause widespread mortality, especially in stressed or weakened trees. Efforts to control and manage adelgid infestations are critical for preserving hemlock populations and mitigating ecological impacts.

- Habitat Loss: Urbanization, land development, and logging activities have contributed to habitat loss and fragmentation, reducing the availability of suitable habitat for Eastern Hemlock and other forest-dwelling species. Conservation measures such as land protection, habitat restoration, and sustainable forestry practices are essential for maintaining healthy hemlock populations and preserving biodiversity.

- **Cultural and Historical Significance**:

  - Indigenous Uses: Eastern Hemlock has a long history of cultural and medicinal use by Indigenous peoples, who valued its bark, needles, and resin for various purposes. It was traditionally used for making baskets, cordage, dyes, and herbal remedies for treating colds, fevers, and skin ailments.

  - Logging Industry: During the 19th and early 20th centuries, Eastern Hemlock was extensively harvested for its valuable timber, which was prized for its strength, durability, and resistance to decay. It was used in construction, shipbuilding, tanning, and pulp and paper production, contributing to the economic development of the region.

Eastern Hemlock is a keystone species of eastern North American forests, renowned for its ecological significance, cultural heritage, and aesthetic beauty. Despite facing threats from invasive pests and habitat degradation, efforts to conserve and protect this iconic tree species are essential for safeguarding the integrity of forest ecosystems and maintaining biodiversity for future generations.

Figure 229: Tsuga canadensis. Laval University, CC BY-SA 4.0, via Wikimedia Commons.

Common Milkweed

Common milkweed, scientifically known as Asclepias syriaca, is a herbaceous perennial plant native to North America. It belongs to the milkweed family (Asclepiadaceae), comprising around 140 species distributed across the continent.

Figure 230: Asclepias syriaca. Аимаина хикари, CC0, via Wikimedia Commons.

Common milkweed is a fascinating plant with a rich ecological significance, cultural history, and unique botanical features:

- **Description**:

    ◦ Appearance: Common milkweed typically grows between 3 to 6 feet (0.9 to 1.8 meters) tall and features a stout, upright stem with broad, lance-shaped leaves arranged oppositely along the stem. The leaves are dark green and slightly hairy, emitting a milky sap when damaged. In summer, the plant produces clusters of showy, pink to purplish flowers resembling umbrellas. Each flower consists of five petals and a central crown or "corona" of hooded structures. After flowering, elongated seed pods called follicles develop, containing numerous seeds attached to silky white fibres.

- **Habitat and Range**:

    ◦ Native Range: Common milkweed is native to eastern and central North America, where it occurs in a variety of habitats, including fields, meadows, prairies, roadsides, and disturbed areas. It is particularly abundant in open, sunny sites with well-drained soils.

- Distribution: This species ranges from southern Canada and the eastern United States to the Great Plains and parts of the Midwest. It is considered naturalized in some western states and has been introduced to other regions outside its native range.

- **Ecological Importance**:

    - Host Plant for Monarchs: Common milkweed is perhaps best known as a critical host plant for the monarch butterfly (Danaus plexippus) and other milkweed-associated insects. Monarch caterpillars feed exclusively on milkweed foliage, ingesting toxic compounds known as cardiac glycosides, which make them unpalatable to predators. Milkweed is essential for the survival of monarch populations, providing food and habitat for all stages of their life cycle.

    - Pollinator Magnet: The fragrant flowers of common milkweed are highly attractive to a wide range of pollinators, including bees, butterflies, moths, and hummingbirds. These insects visit the flowers to feed on nectar and inadvertently transfer pollen between individuals, facilitating pollination and seed production.

    - Soil Stabilization: Common milkweed plays a role in soil stabilization and erosion control, thanks to its deep, fibrous root system, which helps bind soil particles and prevent erosion, especially on sloping terrain and disturbed sites.

- **Cultural and Historical Significance**:

    - Indigenous Uses: Indigenous peoples of North America have long utilized common milkweed for various purposes. They used the fibrous stems to make cordage, nets, and textiles, while the young shoots and flower buds were harvested as food. Additionally, the milky sap was applied topically as a medicinal remedy for warts, skin conditions, and other ailments.

    - Folklore and Traditions: Common milkweed has been the subject of numerous folk beliefs and traditions. In some cultures, it was thought to possess magical properties or protective qualities against evil spirits. Its association with the monarch butterfly has also led to symbolic interpretations, representing transformation, renewal, and the cycle of life.

- **Conservation and Management**:

    - Invasive Potential: While common milkweed is valued for its ecological role and cultural significance, it can also exhibit invasive tendencies in certain contexts, particularly in agricultural settings or disturbed habitats. Its aggressive growth habit and ability to spread via wind-dispersed seeds can result in its dominance and displacement of native vegetation.

    - Habitat Restoration: In conservation and restoration projects aimed at supporting monarch butterflies and other pollinators, common milkweed is often included as a key component. Efforts to enhance habitat quality, reduce pesticide use, and promote the planting of native milkweed species can help conserve populations of this iconic plant and the species that depend on it.

In summary, common milkweed is a charismatic and ecologically important plant species native to North America. Its role as a host plant for monarch butterflies, along with its cultural significance and diverse ecological contributions, underscores the importance of conserving and appreciating this remarkable plant in its natural habitat.

Common Oak

Common oak (Quercus robur) is a majestic deciduous tree that holds a significant place in European landscapes, forests, and cultural heritage. Belonging to the Fagaceae family, it is one of the most widespread tree species in Europe, thriving in a variety of habitats from lowlands to upland regions. Common oak is known for its impressive stature, often reaching heights of 20-40 meters (65-130 feet) and living for several centuries, with some specimens exceeding 1,000 years old.

One of the distinctive features of the common oak is its deeply lobed leaves, which typically have 5-7 lobes and are dark green on the upper surface and paler beneath. These leaves turn a rich golden-brown in autumn, creating a stunning display of colours before they drop to the forest floor. The bark of mature oaks is characterized by deep fissures and ridges, providing habitat for a diverse range of organisms, including insects, fungi, and lichens.

Figure 231: Pedunculate oak (Quercus robur) with acorns. Robert Flogaus-Faust, CC BY 4.0, via Wikimedia Commons.

Common oak is a monoecious species, meaning it has separate male and female reproductive structures on the same tree. The flowers appear in spring, with male catkins releasing pollen and female flowers developing into characteristic acorns. Acorns are encased in cup-like structures called cupules, and they mature over the course of several months, eventually dropping to the ground in autumn. These acorns are an important food source for numerous wildlife species, including squirrels, deer, and birds.

In addition to its ecological importance, common oak has long been valued for its high-quality timber, which is durable, strong, and resistant to decay. It has been used for centuries in construction, shipbuilding, furniture making, and various other applications. The oak's timber is also highly prized for its attractive grain patterns, making it a favoured material for woodworking and decorative purposes.

Beyond its practical uses, common oak holds a deep cultural significance in many European societies. It has been revered in folklore, mythology, and literature for centuries, often symbolizing strength, longevity, and wisdom. In many cultures, the oak tree is associated with deities or considered sacred, and ancient rituals and customs often centred around venerating these majestic trees.

Despite its resilience and widespread distribution, common oak faces various threats, including habitat loss, climate change, pests, and diseases. Efforts to conserve and protect these iconic trees are essential to safeguard their ecological, cultural, and economic value for future generations. Through sustainable management practices, reforestation initiatives, and public awareness campaigns, common oak can continue to thrive and enrich Europe's landscapes for centuries to come.

Common Hawthorn

Common hawthorn, scientifically known as Crataegus monogyna, is a small deciduous tree or shrub native to Europe, North Africa, and Western Asia. Belonging to the Rosaceae family, it is widely distributed across various habitats, including woodlands, hedgerows, scrublands, and coastal areas. Commonly referred to as hawthorn, maythorn, or whitethorn, this species is renowned for its dense, thorny branches, fragrant blossoms, and vibrant red berries.

One of the distinguishing features of common hawthorn is its deeply lobed, serrated leaves, which are bright green in spring and summer, turning to shades of orange and red in autumn before they are shed for winter. The tree produces clusters of small, fragrant flowers in late spring, typically white or pink in colour, which attract a wide range of pollinators, including bees, butterflies, and hoverflies. These blossoms give way to spherical, bright red fruits known as haws, which ripen in late summer and persist on the tree well into winter, providing a valuable food source for birds and small mammals.

Figure 232: Common hawthorn with mature fruit. Muséum de Toulouse, CC BY-SA 4.0, via Wikimedia Commons.

In addition to its ecological role as a wildlife habitat and food source, common hawthorn has a long history of cultural and medicinal use. In folklore and mythology, hawthorn has been associated with various superstitions, beliefs, and rituals, often symbolizing protection, fertility, and love. Traditionally, hawthorn was used in herbal medicine for its purported cardiovascular benefits, with preparations made from its flowers, leaves, and berries believed to support heart health and circulation. While modern scientific research has yet to fully validate these traditional uses, hawthorn extracts are still commonly used as herbal supplements for cardiovascular support.

Common hawthorn is also valued for its ornamental qualities, with cultivated varieties prized for their showy blossoms, attractive foliage, and compact growth habit. It is frequently planted in gardens, parks, and urban landscapes as a hedging plant, specimen tree, or wildlife-friendly addition to mixed borders. Its dense, thorny growth habit makes it an effective barrier plant for security and privacy, while its spring blossoms and autumn berries add seasonal interest and colour to the landscape.

Despite its numerous virtues, common hawthorn can also be considered invasive in some regions, particularly in North America, where it has been introduced as an ornamental plant. Its ability to form dense thickets and outcompete native vegetation can lead to ecological imbalances and biodiversity loss. Therefore, careful management and monitoring are essential to prevent its spread in areas where it is not native.

Overall, common hawthorn is a versatile and valuable species with ecological, cultural, and aesthetic significance. Its role as a wildlife habitat, medicinal plant, and ornamental species underscores its importance in both natural and cultivated landscapes, making it a cherished component of Europe's botanical heritage.

English Ivy

English ivy, scientifically known as Hedera helix, is a species of evergreen climbing vine native to Europe and Western Asia. Belonging to the Araliaceae family, it is characterized by its vigorous growth habit, glossy green leaves, and ability to climb and adhere to various surfaces using aerial rootlets. Commonly referred to as ivy, this versatile plant has been widely cultivated for its ornamental value, as well as for its ability to provide ground cover, stabilize soil, and add greenery to landscapes.

The leaves of English ivy are dark green, leathery, and typically three to five-lobed, although some varieties may have entire leaves. In mature plants, the foliage can develop a mottled or variegated pattern, adding visual interest to its appearance. English ivy produces small, inconspicuous flowers in late summer or early autumn, followed by clusters of dark berries that provide a valuable food source for birds during the winter months.

English ivy is known for its adaptability to various growing conditions, thriving in both sun and shade, as well as in a wide range of soil types. It is commonly found growing along fences, walls, trees, and other vertical surfaces, where it can provide natural insulation, reduce noise pollution, and enhance aesthetic appeal. However, its vigorous growth and ability to spread rapidly make it a potentially invasive species in some regions, where it can outcompete native vegetation and disrupt natural ecosystems.

Despite its invasive potential, English ivy remains a popular choice for landscaping and garden design, valued for its versatility, low maintenance requirements, and year-round greenery. It is frequently used to cover unsightly structures, create living walls, and add texture and dimension to garden beds and borders. In addition to its ornamental uses, English ivy has also been utilized for its medicinal properties, with extracts from the plant traditionally used in herbal remedies for various ailments, including respiratory conditions, skin disorders, and inflammation.

When growing English ivy, it is important to consider its potential to become invasive and to take steps to prevent its spread into natural areas. This may include regular pruning to control growth, avoiding planting near sensitive ecosystems, and using alternative ground cover options in areas where ivy may pose a threat. Additionally, selecting non-invasive cultivars and practicing responsible garden management can help minimize the environmental impact of this popular plant.

Figure 233: Hedera helix 'Merion Beauty'. Agnieszka Kwiecień, Nova, CC BY-SA 4.0, via Wikimedia Commons.

Overall, English ivy is a versatile and attractive plant with a long history of cultivation and use in landscaping and horticulture. Its ability to thrive in diverse conditions, provide year-round greenery, and enhance the beauty of outdoor spaces has cemented its status as a beloved garden favourite, despite concerns about its potential invasiveness in certain environments. With careful management and responsible cultivation practices, English ivy can continue to be enjoyed for its many benefits while minimizing its impact on native ecosystems.

European Holly

European Holly, scientifically known as Ilex aquifolium, is a species of evergreen tree native to western and southern Europe, including the British Isles. Belonging to the Aquifoliaceae family, it is one of the most iconic and recognizable holly species, known for its glossy, dark green leaves, bright red berries, and spiny foliage. European Holly is a slow-growing, long-lived tree that can reach heights of up to 15 meters (50 feet) tall, with a dense, pyramidal or rounded crown.

The leaves of European Holly are alternate, leathery, and glossy, with a distinctive shape characterized by a waxy, dark green upper surface and spiny margins. The foliage provides year-round interest and serves as an important source of shelter and food for wildlife, including birds and small mammals. Inconspicuous white flowers bloom in late spring or early summer, giving way to clusters of vibrant red berries that persist throughout the winter months, adding color to the landscape and providing valuable nutrition for birds during the colder seasons.

European Holly is valued for its ornamental qualities and is commonly used in landscaping and garden design for its evergreen foliage, attractive berries, and ability to provide year-round interest. It is often planted as a specimen tree, used as a hedge or screen, or incorporated into mixed borders and woodland gardens. The tree's dense growth habit and spiny foliage make it an effective choice for creating privacy barriers or deterring unwanted intruders.

In addition to its ornamental uses, European Holly has a long history of cultural and symbolic significance. In ancient Celtic and Druidic traditions, holly was revered as a symbol of protection, fertility, and rebirth, and was often associated with winter solstice celebrations and rituals. The tree's association with Christmas and other winter holidays persists to this day, with holly branches and berries commonly used to decorate homes and festive arrangements during the holiday season.

Figure 234: Ilex aquifolium L. (European holly). Jardin des Plantes, Paris. Jebulon, CC0, via Wikimedia Commons.

Despite its popularity as an ornamental tree, European Holly can be challenging to grow and maintain in certain environments. It prefers moist, well-drained soils and partial shade but can tolerate a wide range of soil types and light conditions. Pruning may be necessary to maintain a desired shape or size, and the tree's spiny foliage requires careful handling to avoid injury. Additionally, European Holly is dioecious, meaning that male and female flowers are borne on separate trees, so both male and female specimens are needed to produce berries.

European Holly is a versatile and attractive tree with a rich cultural history and a range of practical and aesthetic uses in landscaping and garden design. Its glossy foliage, vibrant berries, and enduring symbolism make it a beloved addition to gardens and natural landscapes throughout Europe and beyond, providing beauty, wildlife habitat, and seasonal interest for generations to come.

Common Hazel

Common Hazel, scientifically known as Corylus avellana, is a deciduous shrub native to Europe and parts of Asia and North Africa. Belonging to the Betulaceae family, it is one of the most familiar and widely distributed hazel species, known for its distinctive catkins, edible nuts, and coppiced growth habit. Common Hazel typically grows in a variety of habitats, including woodlands, hedgerows, and scrublands, and is often found in association with other tree and shrub species.

The shrub typically reaches heights of 3 to 8 meters (10 to 26 feet) tall, although it can grow taller under favourable conditions. Common Hazel has a spreading, multi-stemmed growth habit, with slender branches that form dense thickets. The leaves are alternate, roundish or heart-shaped, with doubly serrated margins and a soft, hairy texture. In autumn, the foliage turns yellow before dropping off, adding a splash of colour to the landscape.

One of the most distinctive features of Common Hazel is its flowers, which appear in late winter or early spring before the leaves emerge. Male catkins are long and pendulous, while female flowers are tiny and inconspicuous, located at the base of the same branch. Wind pollination is common in hazels, with pollen from the male catkins carried by the wind to fertilize the female flowers. After pollination, the female flowers develop into clusters of nuts encased in protective husks, known as hazelnuts or cobnuts.

Hazelnuts are an important food source for a variety of wildlife, including birds, squirrels, and small mammals, which feed on the nuts and help to disperse them. In addition to their ecological role, hazelnuts have been a valuable food source for humans for thousands of years, with evidence of their consumption dating back to prehistoric times. Today, hazelnuts are widely cultivated for commercial purposes, prized for their rich flavour and versatility in cooking and baking.

Common Hazel has a long history of human use and has been utilized for a variety of purposes throughout the ages. The flexible branches were traditionally used for thatching, weaving, and basketry, while the wood was prized for its strength and durability. In addition to its practical uses, Common Hazel has also played a role in folklore, mythology, and superstition, with hazel branches often associated with protection, divination, and magic.

In terms of cultivation, Common Hazel is relatively low-maintenance and adaptable to a range of soil types and environmental conditions. It prefers well-drained, fertile soils and thrives in full sun to partial shade. The shrub can be propagated from seeds, cuttings, or suckers, and responds well to pruning and coppicing. Coppicing, or the practice of periodically cutting the shrub down to ground level to promote vigorous regrowth, has been used for centuries to harvest hazel wood for fuel, fencing, and other purposes.

Figure 235: Corylus avellana, Betulaceae, Common Hazel, habitus; Karlsruhe, Germany. H. Zell, CC BY-SA 3.0, via Wikimedia Commons.

Overall, Common Hazel is a versatile and valuable shrub with a rich cultural and ecological significance. From its distinctive catkins and edible nuts to its historical uses and associations, Common Hazel continues to play a multifaceted role in the natural world and human society, providing food, habitat, and inspiration for generations to come.

European Elder

European Elder, scientifically known as Sambucus nigra, is a deciduous shrub or small tree native to Europe, North Africa, and Southwest Asia. Belonging to the Adoxaceae family, it is one of the most widespread elder species, known for its fragrant flowers, clusters of small black berries, and traditional medicinal uses. European Elder typically grows in a variety of habitats, including woodlands, hedgerows, and disturbed areas, and is often found in association with other shrub and tree species.

Figure 236: Sambucus nigra. Willow, CC BY-SA 2.5, via Wikimedia Commons.

The shrub typically reaches heights of 3 to 10 meters (10 to 33 feet) tall, although it can grow taller under favourable conditions. European Elder has a spreading, multi-stemmed growth habit, with stout branches that form dense thickets. The leaves are compound, opposite, pinnate, with 5 to 9 leaflets, each with serrated margins and a dark green colour. In autumn, the foliage turns yellow before dropping off, adding a splash of colour to the landscape.

One of the most striking features of European Elder is its flowers, which appear in late spring to early summer in large, flat-topped clusters known as corymbs. The creamy white flowers have a sweet, musky fragrance and are highly attractive to pollinators, including bees, butterflies, and hoverflies. After pollination, the flowers develop into clusters of small, dark purple to black berries, each containing several small seeds. The berries ripen in late summer to early autumn and are a valuable food source for birds and small mammals.

In addition to its ecological role, European Elder has a long history of human use and has been utilized for a variety of purposes throughout the ages. The flowers and berries are edible and have been used in traditional European cuisine to make wines, syrups, jams, and cordials. Elderflower cordial, in particular, is a popular beverage made from the fragrant flowers and is enjoyed for its refreshing taste and aromatic qualities.

In traditional herbal medicine, various parts of the European Elder plant, including the flowers, berries, leaves, and bark, have been used to treat a wide range of ailments, including colds, flu, fever, and inflammation. Elderberry syrup, in particular, is believed to have immune-boosting properties and is commonly used as a natural remedy for respiratory infections and other common illnesses. While scientific research on the medicinal properties of European Elder is ongoing, anecdotal evidence and traditional knowledge support its use as a herbal remedy.

European Elder is relatively easy to cultivate and is often grown for its ornamental value as well as its culinary and medicinal uses. It prefers well-drained, fertile soils and thrives in full sun to partial shade. The shrub can be propagated from seeds, cuttings, or root divisions, and responds well to pruning and shaping. In addition to its practical uses, European Elder is also valued for its wildlife habitat value, providing food and shelter for a variety of bird and insect species.

European Elder is a versatile and valuable shrub with a rich cultural and ecological significance. From its fragrant flowers and edible berries to its traditional medicinal uses and wildlife habitat value, European Elder continues to play a multifaceted role in the natural world and human society, providing sustenance, healing, and beauty for generations to come.

Common Yarrow

Common Yarrow, scientifically known as Achillea millefolium, is a widespread and versatile flowering plant native to Europe, Asia, and North America. Belonging to the Asteraceae family, it is a hardy perennial herbaceous plant with a long history of medicinal and cultural uses. Common Yarrow typically grows in a variety of habitats, including grasslands, meadows, roadsides, and disturbed areas, and is known for its feathery, fern-like foliage and clusters of small, white or pink flowers.

Figure 237: Common yarrow (Achillea millefolium). Allen Browne, CC BY 4.0, via Wikimedia Commons.

The plant typically reaches heights of 30 to 100 centimetres (12 to 40 inches) tall, although it can vary depending on environmental conditions. Common Yarrow has a basal rosette of finely divided leaves that give it a delicate, lacy appearance. The leaves are aromatic when crushed and have a characteristic spicy scent. In summer, the plant sends up tall, erect stems topped with flat-topped clusters of small, daisy-like flowers. The flowers can range in colour from white to pink, and occasionally yellow, and are highly attractive to pollinators, including bees, butterflies, and hoverflies.

One of the most remarkable features of Common Yarrow is its adaptability and resilience. It is tolerant of a wide range of soil types, pH levels, and moisture conditions, making it a common sight in both natural and cultivated landscapes. In addition, Common Yarrow has a deep, fibrous root system that helps it withstand drought and stabilize soil, making it useful for erosion control and habitat restoration projects.

Common Yarrow has a long history of traditional medicinal uses, dating back thousands of years. It has been used by various indigenous cultures around the world to treat a wide range of ailments, including wounds, fever, digestive disorders, and menstrual problems. The plant contains several bioactive compounds, including flavonoids, alkaloids, and volatile oils, which are believed to have anti-inflammatory, antimicrobial, and analgesic properties. Common Yarrow is commonly used externally as a poultice or wash for wounds and bruises, and internally as a tea or tincture for colds, fevers, and digestive complaints.

In addition to its medicinal uses, Common Yarrow has also been valued for its culinary and cosmetic applications. The young leaves and flowers are edible and can be used fresh or dried as a flavouring agent in salads, soups, and teas. The flowers are also used to make natural dyes and cosmetics, including soaps, lotions, and hair rinses. Common Yarrow is also a popular ornamental plant in gardens and landscapes, valued for its attractive foliage, long-lasting flowers, and low-maintenance requirements.

From its medicinal properties and culinary uses to its ecological benefits and ornamental value, Common Yarrow continues to be a valuable and versatile plant with a rich cultural and ecological significance. Whether growing wild in natural habitats or cultivated in gardens and landscapes, Common Yarrow serves as a reminder of the interconnectedness of humans and the natural world, providing sustenance, healing, and beauty for generations to come.

Common Bluebell

Common Bluebell, scientifically known as Hyacinthoides non-scripta, is a charming and iconic spring-flowering perennial native to western Europe, particularly abundant in the British Isles. Belonging to the family Asparagaceae, this plant is renowned for its delicate, nodding bell-shaped flowers and its ability to carpet woodland floors with a sea of vibrant blue hues during the spring months. Common Bluebells typically bloom from April to May, heralding the arrival of spring with their enchanting floral display.

The plant typically grows from bulbs, which are underground storage organs that allow it to survive harsh environmental conditions and periods of dormancy. Each bulb produces a clump of narrow, strap-like leaves that emerge in early spring and provide a lush green backdrop for the flowers. The flower spikes, known as racemes, arise from the centre of the foliage and bear numerous drooping, tubular flowers that hang gracefully from slender stems. The flowers are usually a deep violet-blue colour, although they can occasionally be pink or white, and they emit a sweet, delicate fragrance that attracts pollinators such as bees, butterflies, and hoverflies.

Common Bluebells are typically found in deciduous woodlands, where they thrive in the dappled shade provided by mature trees. They prefer moist, well-drained soils with a rich humus layer, where they can form extensive colonies known as "bluebell woods." These woodlands are often characterized by their dense, lush vegetation and rich biodiversity, providing important habitat for a wide range of woodland flora and fauna.

In addition to their aesthetic beauty, Common Bluebells hold a special place in British culture and folklore. They are often associated with ancient woodlands and are celebrated in poetry, literature, and art as symbols of springtime and renewal. In folklore, it was believed that bluebells had magical properties and were associated with fairies and woodland spirits. It was said that anyone who heard the ringing of bluebells would be led astray by fairies and would never be seen again.

Despite their cultural significance and ecological importance, Common Bluebells face threats from habitat loss, habitat fragmentation, and competition from invasive species. In some areas, they are also threatened by over-collection for use in floral arrangements and garden plantings. Conservation efforts are underway to protect and restore bluebell woodlands, including habitat restoration, habitat conservation, and public education initiatives.

Figure 238: Common Bluebell - Hyacinthoides non-scripta. Björn S, CC BY-SA 2.0, via Wikimedia Commons.

Common Bluebells are cherished for their beauty, cultural significance, and ecological importance, serving as a symbol of the natural heritage and biodiversity of western Europe. As guardians of the woodland floor, they continue to captivate and inspire all who encounter them, reminding us of the delicate balance and interconnectedness of the natural world.

Plant Selection

The exact number of plant species on Earth is difficult to determine precisely due to several factors, including the vastness and complexity of ecosystems, the continual discovery of new species, and the challenges associated with accurately cataloguing and classifying existing species. However, scientists estimate that there are anywhere from 300,000 to 400,000 known plant species worldwide [94].

It's important to note that this estimate is constantly evolving as scientists discover and describe new species, particularly in biodiverse regions such as tropical rainforests, remote islands, and unexplored habitats. Additionally, advancements in DNA sequencing and molecular techniques have facilitated the identification of previously unknown species and have provided insights into the evolutionary relationships among plants [94].

Furthermore, the number of plant species is likely much higher when considering undiscovered or yet-to-be-described species, as well as cryptic species that may appear similar but possess distinct genetic differences. As scientific research and exploration continue, our understanding of plant diversity will continue to expand, contributing to our knowledge of ecosystems, conservation efforts, and sustainable resource management.

Selecting plants for landscaping involves careful consideration of various factors to create a harmonious and aesthetically pleasing outdoor environment that suits the specific needs and preferences of the homeowner or designer. Here are some steps to guide the selection process:

- **Assess the Site Conditions**: Begin by evaluating the environmental conditions of the site where the landscaping will take place. Consider factors such as sunlight exposure, soil type and quality, moisture levels, drainage patterns, and microclimates (e.g., areas with high wind exposure or frost pockets). Understanding these conditions will help determine which plants are suitable for the site.

- **Identify Functional Requirements**: Determine the purpose and function of the landscaping. Are you creating a garden for visual appeal, privacy screening, shade, erosion control, wildlife habitat, or food production? Identifying the primary functions of the landscape will help narrow down plant choices and layout options.

- **Consider Maintenance Needs**: Take into account the level of maintenance you are willing and able to commit to. Some plants require frequent pruning, watering, fertilizing, and pest control, while others are low-maintenance and more tolerant of neglect. Choose plants that match your maintenance preferences and skill level.

- **Select a Plant Palette**: Based on the site conditions, functional requirements, and maintenance considerations, develop a plant palette that includes a variety of species with different sizes, shapes, colors, textures, and seasonal interest. Aim for diversity to create visual interest and resilience in the landscape.

- **Research Plant Characteristics**: Before making final selections, research the specific characteristics of each plant on your list. Consider factors such as mature size, growth habit (e.g., spreading, upright), foliage type (e.g., evergreen, deciduous), flower color and bloom time, fragrance, wildlife attractants, and potential allergens or toxicities.

- **Ensure Compatibility**: Ensure that selected plants are compatible with each other and with existing landscape elements such as hardscapes, structures, and other vegetation. Consider factors like root spread, canopy size, and growth rate to prevent overcrowding, competition for resources, and maintenance issues down the line.

- **Account for Seasonal Changes**: Plan for seasonal changes in the landscape by selecting plants that provide interest and beauty year-round. Incorporate a mix of evergreen and deciduous plants, as well as species with sequential bloom times, to ensure visual appeal across different seasons.

- **Evaluate Local Regulations and Considerations**: Check local regulations, zoning ordinances, and homeowners' association guidelines that may impact plant selection, placement, and landscaping practices. Consider factors such as invasive species regulations, water conservation requirements, and native plant recommendations.

- **Seek Professional Advice if Needed**: If you're unsure about plant selection or landscaping design, consider consulting with a professional landscape designer, horticulturist, or arborist. They can offer expert advice, site assessments, and personalized recommendations tailored to your specific needs and goals.

Chapter Fourteen

Implementing a Plant Establishment Program

Establishing plants in challenging environments requires special attention and care, especially during the critical first year. Newly planted vegetation faces numerous risks and vulnerabilities compared to established plants, making it essential to nurture them through the establishment phase. Several factors contribute to the vulnerability of new plants, including their susceptibility to drying out, limited foliage mass to withstand damage, and the need to adapt to new environmental conditions. Additionally, transplant shock, which occurs when plants are damaged during the planting process, further complicates their establishment [95].

One key strategy for plant establishment is providing support and protection to help plants acclimate gradually to their new surroundings. This involves implementing measures to shield them from extreme conditions while gradually reducing support, allowing plants to build resilience over time. Here are some methods to aid in plant establishment:

Trickle and Drip Irrigation [95]: Trickle and drip irrigation systems offer a practical and cost-effective solution for delivering consistent moisture to plants, supporting their establishment and growth. These systems utilize flexible plastic piping and various nozzles to provide targeted irrigation to individual plants, minimizing water waste and reducing disease risks associated with foliage moisture. While trickle irrigation offers several advantages, such as ease of installation and water conservation, it may be prone to issues like blocked nozzles and periodic maintenance requirements.

Mulches [95]: Mulches play a crucial role in promoting plant establishment by offering multiple benefits, including weed suppression, moisture retention, nutrient enrichment, temperature moderation, and erosion control. Both organic and inorganic mulches are available, with organic options providing additional benefits like soil improvement as they decompose. Organic mulches, such as compost, leaf litter, straw, and bark, contribute essential nutrients and humus to the soil while reducing weed competition and conserving moisture. Mat mulches, such as plastic or weed mats, and bulk mulches, like sawdust or grass clippings, offer different advantages and considerations based on factors like cost, availability, and ease of application.

When applying mulch, it's essential to ensure adequate thickness to provide effective coverage without smothering plants or impeding water penetration. Typically, bulk mulches should be 5-7cm thick, while thicker layers of 10-15cm may be necessary in weed-prone areas [95]. Additionally, mulches should be kept clear of plant stems or trunks to prevent moisture retention and potential rot. Overall, selecting appropriate establishment methods and providing ongoing care and maintenance are crucial for ensuring the successful establishment and long-term health of newly planted vegetation in challenging environments.

Mulches offer numerous benefits for plant health and soil quality, but they can also present challenges if not used correctly. Several common problems associated with mulches include:

1. Nitrogen Depletion: Mulches containing wood or bark products, such as sawdust or pine bark, may initially draw nitrogen from the soil as they decompose. This can lead to nutrient deficiencies in plants unless nitrogen fertilizers are added to compensate for the depletion.

2. Water Repellence: Some mulch materials, especially those with fine particles like sawdust, can compact together, forming a barrier that repels water and reduces moisture penetration to plant roots. Combining mulch materials or composting them before use can help mitigate this issue.

3. Toxicity: Bark and sawdust from certain tree species, such as Pinus and Eucalyptus, may contain toxins harmful to other plants. Fresh material from these trees should be composted for several weeks to allow toxins to leach out before use.

4. Wind Displacement: Lightweight mulches are prone to blowing away or being dislodged by wind. Mixing them with heavier materials or securing them with stakes can prevent displacement.

5. Weed Establishment: Mat-type mulches used for plantings should have small slits and overlapping edges to minimize weed growth around the base of plants.

Tree guards are essential for protecting young trees from environmental stressors and grazing animals. When selecting tree guards, consider the following factors:

1. Necessity: Determine if tree guards are truly needed based on the plant's ability to establish and grow in its environment without protection.

2. Functionality: Choose guards that effectively fulfill their intended purpose, whether it's protecting against animals, wind, frost, or machinery damage.

3. Cost: Evaluate the cost-effectiveness of different guard options, considering upfront expenses versus long-term protection benefits.

4. Durability: Opt for guards made of durable materials that can withstand environmental conditions and provide long-term protection.

5. Ease of Installation: Select guards that are easy to erect, repair, or replace as needed, considering factors like stake requirements and maintenance access.

Common types of tree guards include:

- Plastic Tubes: UV-stabilized plastic tubes offer durable protection and create a favourable microclimate for plant growth. They require stakes for support.

- Plastic Mesh: Available in flexible and rigid forms, plastic mesh guards provide effective protection and require stakes for support.

- Plastic Pipe: Flexible plastic pipes can be placed around young plants to protect them from frost. They should be removed once the danger of frost has passed.

- Wire Mesh: Chicken wire or similar materials provide a barrier against grazing animals and are relatively inexpensive and long-lasting.

- Hessian: Hessian bags or cloth offer wind and sun protection but may sag over time. They require tying around stakes for support.

- Tyres: Old car tyres can be placed around seedlings as a cheap barrier against rabbits and hares.

- Milk Cartons: Useful for marking seedling locations and providing limited protection against pests and frost, milk cartons last for a couple of years.

Figure 239: Young Nyssa ogeche (Ogeechee tupelo) protected by a tree guard. Hameltion, CC BY-SA 4.0, via Wikimedia Commons.

Techniques for Planting Sloped Areas

Pocket planting is a method used to establish vegetation on slopes, particularly in areas prone to erosion. It involves creating a small basin or pocket on the slope, using the excavated soil to build a retaining wall around the pocket, especially on the downslope side. This retaining wall helps to retain water and prevent soil erosion. An overflow spillway in the wall allows excess water to drain away during heavy rains. While effective, pocket planting may require periodic reformation until the plants are fully established. However, it's important to note that this technique is not suitable for steep slopes due to the risk of instability.

Slope serration is another technique used to stabilize sloping sites and promote plant establishment while reducing erosion. This method involves terracing the slope into steps, with each step sloping back toward the hill to retain water. Over time, these steps may erode, but by then, the plants are usually well established. The loose soil from the eroded steps also provides favourable germination sites for seeds dropped by nearby plants.

Wattling is a traditional method of erosion control that involves using bundles of branches placed on slopes to prevent soil erosion. These bundles are tied together and partially buried in contoured trenches across the slope, or spread across the surface of the slope. Wattling can be done using branches from species that root easily, such as willows or poplars, which then become part of the slope stabilization. Alternatively, dried brush or straw can be used, held in place with wire mesh securely pegged down. While less common, this technique can be effective, especially on degraded sites, to enable native species to regenerate.

In arid environments, establishing vegetation can be particularly challenging due to water scarcity. Mulching, controlling weeds, wide plant spacing, and creating saucers of soil to retain water are simple methods used to overcome water shortage issues. Planting smaller-sized plants and using condensation traps to capture moisture can also aid in establishment. Direct seeding is a low-cost method of reestablishing vegetation, but it requires careful weed control and follow-up maintenance. Spray seeding, on the other hand, involves mixing seeds into a slurry of water and cellulose materials, then spraying the mixture onto the ground surface. This method provides a protective mulching surface for seeds and is useful for steep slopes or areas with limited access. Overall, these methods play crucial roles in stabilizing slopes, preventing erosion, and promoting plant growth in challenging environments.

Planting and Establishment Processes

Site preparation prior to planting is crucial for the success of revegetation projects. It involves several key steps aimed at creating optimal conditions for plant establishment and growth.

Firstly, fencing out stock is essential to protect newly planted vegetation from grazing animals, which can cause damage and inhibit growth. Testing the soil pH is also important, as it helps determine the acidity or alkalinity of the soil, which can impact plant health. Based on the results, soil additives like acid, lime, or dolomite may be necessary to balance pH levels and create favorable growing conditions.

Before planting, it's important to spray out weeds to reduce competition during the critical establishment phase. Dead weeds left in situ can protect the soil surface, contribute to soil organic matter, and create a litter layer (mulch) that aids in moisture retention and weed suppression.

When preparing to plant, several steps are taken to ensure the successful establishment of vegetation. Tubestock is sprayed with Envy™ 24 hours prior to planting to enhance root growth and reduce transplant shock. Pre-soaking tubestock facilitates extraction from the tube and helps minimize transplant shock.

Planting holes are dug to accommodate the root system of the tubestock, with the depth of the hole matching the level of the rootball in the tube. Soil conditioners like natramin, gypsum, lime, or dolomite may be added to the planting holes to improve soil structure and fertility. Fertilizer pellets are placed at the bottom of the planting holes to provide nutrients to the young plants.

When extracting plants from their tubes, care must be taken to avoid damaging the stems. Proper techniques include turning the tube upside down, tapping the base to release the plant, and gently sliding the tube from the rootball.

Once planted, tubestock should be positioned in the center of the hole, with the stem at the same level as it was in the tube. Soil is backfilled around the rootball, and the planting hole is shaped into a saucer-shaped depression to catch rainfall and runoff.

Mulch is applied around the base of the plant to conserve moisture, suppress weeds, and improve soil health. Tree guards and stakes are installed to protect young plants from wildlife and provide support during establishment.

Finally, watering is critical for the survival of newly planted vegetation. A minimum of 10 liters of water is recommended per plant, delivered directly to the root zone. Organic fertilizers like Organic Xtra™ are preferred for their ability to add organic matter to the soil without causing harm to the plants.

Overall, proper site preparation ensures the success of revegetation projects by creating optimal conditions for plant establishment and growth.

Post-planting care is essential for the successful establishment of newly planted vegetation. Adequate watering, especially during the initial 6-week period, is crucial to ensure the survival and growth of young plants. Monitoring the watering schedule and adjusting it based on weather conditions is important for optimal plant health. Stake and prune leggy plants as needed to promote proper growth and development. Protecting plants from pests and diseases is also essential, preferably through natural means rather than chemical interventions. Regular monitoring of plantings and timely actions to address issues like weed control are necessary for the long-term success of revegetation projects.

Pests and diseases pose significant threats to the health and vitality of plants, affecting almost all species to varying degrees. However, employing certain strategies can help minimize the risk and impact of these issues. One effective approach is to prioritize the selection of locally occurring native species for planting projects. Indigenous plants have evolved alongside their native pests and pathogens, often developing natural resistance or tolerance to them. As a result, when native species are planted, pest and disease outbreaks tend to be less severe compared to introducing non-native species.

Furthermore, it is advisable to avoid the indiscriminate use of chemical pesticides and herbicides to control outbreaks. While these chemicals may provide short-term relief, they can have detrimental effects on the environment, disrupting ecosystems and harming beneficial organisms. Instead, it is preferable to allow natural predators such as birds, reptiles, mammals, and insects to regulate pest populations. Natural predators play a crucial role in maintaining ecological balance by preying on pest species, helping to keep their populations in check.

Although occasional severe outbreaks of pests and diseases may occur, it is essential not to intervene hastily. Often, nature has its way of restoring balance over time if left undisturbed. By refraining from interference, a natural equilibrium between pests and their predators can be reestablished. This approach aligns with principles of ecological sustainability and promotes the long-term health and resilience of plant ecosystems. Through thoughtful plant selection and reliance on natural control mechanisms, the negative impacts of pests and diseases on vegetation can be mitigated effectively, contributing to the overall success of landscaping and revegetation efforts.

Planting Plan

A planting plan serves as the blueprint for creating a cohesive and visually appealing landscape by strategically placing plants to optimize available resources. This comprehensive plan takes into account various factors such as the available space, soil conditions, aspect (orientation to the sun), and desired aesthetic outcomes. By considering these elements, the planting plan aims to maximize the potential of the garden area while ensuring the long-term health and vitality of the vegetation.

One of the primary functions of a planting plan is to provide a graphical representation of the proposed landscape design. It delineates the exact locations, sizes, and species of both existing and new plants within the garden. This visual map helps landscapers, gardeners, or homeowners to understand the spatial arrangement of plants and envision how the garden will look once established. Additionally, the plan may include annotations or symbols to indicate key features such as paths, ponds, seating areas, or other landscape elements.

In addition to the graphical layout, a planting plan typically includes a plant schedule for easy reference. This schedule provides detailed information about each plant, including botanical and common names, quantities, sizes, and placement locations. Having this organized reference allows for efficient procurement of plants and ensures that the intended design is implemented accurately. Moreover, a comprehensive plant reference sheet may accompany the plan, featuring thumbnail photos and descriptions of each plant to aid in visualizing the garden's composition and appearance.

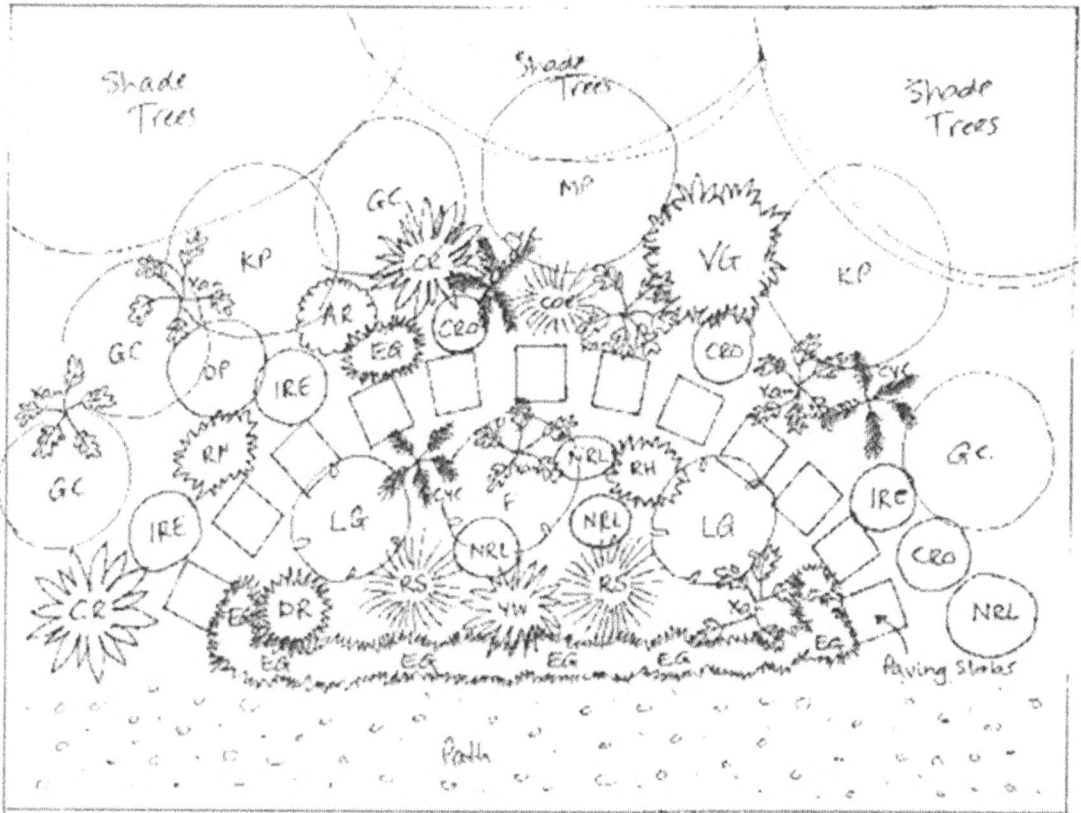

Figure 240: Sample Planting Plan for a tropical garden.

Key to Figure 240 (adapted from Dawsons Garden World [96]):

- AR = Ardisia

- CORD = Cordyline

- CR = Crinum (Spider flower)

- CROT = Croton (Joseph's Coat)

- CYC = Cycad
- DR = Dracaena
- EG = Evergreen Giant
- GC = Golden Cane Palm
- F = Frangipani
- LG = Magnolia Little Gem
- IRE = Iresine (Blood Leaf Plant)
- KP = Kentia Palm
- MP = Majestic Palm
- OP = Oyster Plant
- RH = Rhoeo (Moses in the Cradle)
- RS = Cordyline Red Sensation
- NRL = New Zealand Rock Lily
- VG = Variegated Ginger
- Xan = Xanadu
- YW = Yellow Wave Flax

A well-executed planting plan serves as an indispensable tool for anyone undertaking garden rejuvenation or renovation projects. Whether it's a small backyard garden or a larger landscape design, having a clear and detailed plan enhances the efficiency of the planting process and contributes to the successful realization of the desired garden vision. By following the guidance provided in the plan, gardeners can create beautiful and functional outdoor spaces that harmonize with their surroundings and meet their aesthetic preferences and practical needs.

Interpreting symbols on a planting plan is essential for understanding the layout and composition of the proposed landscape. These symbols typically represent different types of trees and shrubs that are to be planted on the site. Each symbol is designed to convey specific information about the plant species, helping landscapers, gardeners, or homeowners accurately implement the design envisioned by the planner or designer.

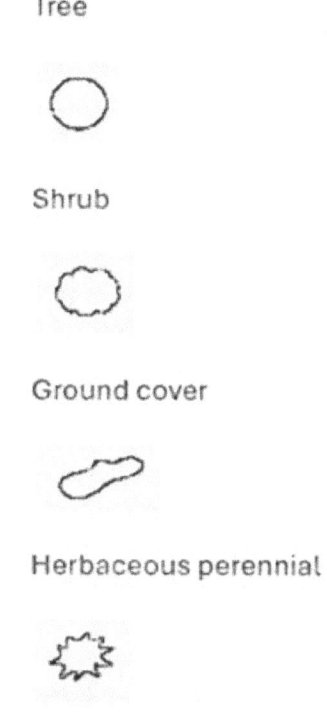

Figure 241: Plan symbols.

Commonly used symbols on planting plans include various shapes and sizes to denote different plant types. For instance, tree symbols often resemble simplified representations of trees, while shrub symbols may depict smaller, bushier forms. These symbols are strategically placed on the plan to indicate where each type of plant should be positioned within the landscape. By referring to these symbols, individuals can visualize the distribution and arrangement of vegetation throughout the garden or outdoor space.

The numbers enclosed within these symbols serve as identifiers that correspond to specific plant species listed on the planting plan. This numerical labelling system helps link each symbol to its corresponding plant name, facilitating accurate placement during the planting process. For example, if a tree symbol contains the number "1," it indicates that a particular tree species, such as Callistemon viminalis, should be planted at the corresponding location marked on the plan.

To effectively interpret the symbols on the planting plan, it's important to refer to the legend or key provided on the plan itself. The legend typically provides a visual reference guide that explains the meaning of each symbol used on the plan, along with corresponding plant names and numbers. By consulting the legend, individuals can easily identify the types of trees and shrubs designated for planting and understand their specific locations within the landscape.

Interpreting symbols on a planting plan is a crucial step in implementing a successful landscape design. By understanding the meaning of each symbol and its associated plant species, gardeners can ensure that the intended design is executed accurately and that the resulting landscape reflects the desired aesthetic and functional goals. Effective communication between planners, designers, and implementers is key to translating the vision outlined in the planting plan into a thriving and visually appealing outdoor environment.

Locating trees and shrubs according to the planting plan involves a methodical approach to ensure that each plant is placed in its intended location to achieve the desired design and growth patterns in the garden bed.

Figure 242: Sample layout plan.

Here is a detailed explanation of the process:

Understanding the Planting Plan

- **Plan Layout**: The planting plan is a carefully designed blueprint of the garden bed. It shows where each type of plant should be placed. This ensures the garden will have the correct balance, appearance, and growth space.

- **Symbols and Key**: The plan uses symbols or numbers to represent different types of plants. There is a key provided which explains what each symbol or number corresponds to:

    - 1: Large tree

    - 2: Smaller tree

    - 3: Large shrub

    - 4: Medium-sized shrub

    - 5: Small shrubs

    - 6: Groundcover

    - 7: Large herbaceous perennials

    - 8: Small herbaceous perennials

Matching Plants to Symbols

The plant species are matched to these symbols to ensure each plant is correctly placed according to its size and growth habit. Here's how the matching is done:

- **Large Tree**:
    - **Plant**: Callistemon viminalis
    - **Symbol**: 1

- **Smaller Tree**:
    - **Plant**: Eucalyptus torquata
    - **Symbol**: 2

- **Large Shrub**:
    - **Plant**: Grevillea 'Robyn Gordon'
    - **Symbol**: 3

- **Medium-sized Shrub**:
    - **Plant**: Grevillea 'Honey Gem'
    - **Symbol**: 4

- **Small Shrubs**:
    - **Plant**: Correa Mannii
    - **Symbol**: 5

- **Groundcover**:
    - **Plant**: Myoporum parvifolium
    - **Symbol**: 6

- **Large Herbaceous Perennial**:
    - **Plant**: Anigozanthus viridus
    - **Symbol**: 7

- **Small Herbaceous Perennial**:

- **Plant**: Conostylis candicans
- **Symbol**: 8

Steps to Locate Plants

1. **Review the Plan**: Carefully study the planting plan to understand where each type of plant should be placed. Pay attention to the symbols and their corresponding locations.

2. **Identify Plants**: Use the key to identify which plant corresponds to each symbol.

3. **Mark Locations**: In the garden bed, mark the locations for each plant according to the plan. This can be done using stakes, flags, or paint to ensure accurate placement.

4. **Planting**:
    - **Large Trees and Shrubs**: Start by planting the large trees and shrubs as they will be the focal points and take up the most space.
    - **Medium and Small Shrubs**: Next, plant the medium and small shrubs around the larger plants, ensuring they have enough space to grow.
    - **Groundcover and Herbaceous Perennials**: Finally, plant the groundcover and herbaceous perennials. These plants usually fill in the gaps and add layers to the garden.

5. **Check and Adjust**: After planting, step back and check if the arrangement matches the planting plan. Make any necessary adjustments to ensure the design is accurate.

By following these steps, you can effectively locate and plant trees and shrubs according to the planting plan, creating a well-organized and aesthetically pleasing garden bed.

Preparing the Garden Bed for Planting

Preparing a garden bed for planting involves several steps to ensure the site is clean, levelled, and ready to accommodate the planned vegetation. Before digging begins, it's crucial to clear out the site by removing weeds, rubbish, and any debris that may impede the planting process. Neil's instructions emphasize the importance of thorough cleaning, especially considering that some of the weeds may have prickles and burrs, posing potential hazards to those handling them. Therefore, selecting the appropriate tools and equipment is essential for completing the task efficiently and safely.

To remove weeds and rubbish effectively, you'll need tools specifically designed for this purpose. Handheld tools like garden trowels, weed pullers, and pruning shears can help you tackle different types of weeds, including those with prickles and burrs. It's essential to wear protective gloves to shield your hands from potential injuries and to avoid direct contact with hazardous materials.

Levelling out the soil is the next step in preparing the garden bed. For this task, you'll need a tool suitable for smoothing and levelling the ground, such as a garden rake or a levelling tool. Ensuring that the soil surface is even and free of bumps or depressions is crucial for providing a stable and uniform planting environment.

Once the site is cleared and levelled, marking out the positions for planting becomes necessary. This involves using markers or stakes to indicate where each plant will be positioned according to the measurements provided on the planting plan. Marking out the planting locations accurately ensures that the spacing between plants aligns with the intended design and allows for proper growth and development.

Measuring the distance between plants is essential for maintaining consistency and adherence to the planting plan's specifications. You'll need a measuring tool, such as a tape measure or a ruler, to ensure that the spacing between plants meets the requirements outlined in the plan. This ensures that plants are adequately spaced to optimize their growth and prevent overcrowding.

Finally, transporting the selected tools and equipment to the planting site requires some form of carrying or transportation mechanism. This could be a garden cart, wheelbarrow, or even a bucket depending on the volume and weight of the items. Having a reliable means of transporting the equipment ensures that you have everything you need readily available at the site, minimizing disruptions and maximizing efficiency during the preparation process.

Figure 243: Preparing for planting. Pacific Southwest Region 5, Public domain, via Wikimedia Commons.

Planting safety is paramount when undertaking gardening tasks, as it involves various activities that can pose risks to personal well-being if not approached with caution. Neil's guidelines outline essential safety measures to minimize the likelihood of accidents and injuries during the planting process. One fundamental rule emphasized is to never dig without knowing what lies underground, highlighting the importance of using services like the dial-before-you-dig service to identify potential hazards such as buried cables or pipes.

Taking a slow and steady approach to gardening tasks is crucial to prevent injuries and mistakes. Rushing through tasks can lead to overexertion and strain, increasing the risk of muscle injuries. Neil stresses the importance of recognizing personal limitations and seeking assistance for lifting heavy objects or operating machinery. Being mindful of how certain activities, like digging or using vibrating equipment, can strain muscles unknowingly is essential for preventing injuries.

Wearing appropriate work clothes and protective gear is essential for safeguarding against potential hazards in the garden. Wearing a back brace while lifting and digging helps support the spine and reduces the risk of back injuries. Additionally, wearing heavy closed-toe shoes, long pants, and gloves protects against cuts, scratches, and other injuries. Proper attire, including a wide-brimmed hat and sunscreen, helps prevent sunburn and dehydration when working outdoors for extended periods.

Maintaining awareness of potential dangers in the garden is crucial for ensuring safety. Neil advises against entering trenches deeper than knee-level due to the risk of collapse, emphasizing the importance of having someone nearby in case of emergencies. Implementing safety measures like wearing reflective vests and marking work areas with witches' hats ensures visibility and alerts others to keep clear, reducing the risk of accidents involving passing vehicles or pedestrians.

Ensuring safe access to the work site involves considerations for personal safety, the safety of others, and protection of existing plants and garden features. Neil emphasizes the importance of cordoning off work areas near footpaths or public access points to prevent accidents and injuries. Taking care to avoid trampling on plants or damaging garden features while working demonstrates respect for the environment and minimizes the risk of unintentional damage.

Prioritizing safety during planting activities is essential for preventing accidents, injuries, and damage to property. By following Neil's guidelines and adopting a cautious approach to gardening tasks, individuals can create a safe and conducive environment for successful planting while minimizing risks to personal well-being and the surrounding environment.

Digging Holes and Planting

Digging a hole may seem like a straightforward task, but the process can vary significantly depending on the type of soil encountered. Soil composition plays a crucial role in determining the ease or difficulty of digging, as each soil type presents its own set of challenges and considerations. From loamy soils to sandy beaches, clay-rich earth, and gravelly terrain, understanding the characteristics of each soil type is essential for effective hole digging and successful planting.

Loamy soil, characterized by its balanced mixture of sand, silt, and clay, is often preferred by gardeners for its ease of cultivation. Loam offers good drainage and nutrient retention, making it relatively straightforward to dig and prepare for planting. With its friable texture, loam allows for easy penetration of roots and facilitates essential soil aeration, providing an optimal environment for plant growth.

Conversely, sandy soil poses unique challenges due to its coarse texture and low nutrient retention capacity. When dry, sandy soil tends to collapse easily, complicating the digging process. However, dampened sandy soil can stick together, making it more manageable for planting. To enhance water retention and soil structure in sandy areas, gardeners may incorporate organic materials and soil wetters into planting holes to improve moisture retention and promote root development.

Clay soil presents perhaps the most daunting obstacles for diggers, resembling hardened concrete when dry and sticky mud when wet. Digging in clay requires considerable effort and may result in compacted, glazed surfaces that impede root penetration. Gardeners often employ strategies such as gouging the sides of the hole with a fork to alleviate compaction and facilitate root growth. Adding organic matter to clay soil can help improve drainage and aeration, mitigating the challenges posed by its dense composition.

Gravelly soils, characterized by the presence of small rocks and larger stones, present their own set of challenges for hole digging. The presence of rocks makes digging laborious and may necessitate adjusting the hole's location to avoid obstacles. Gardeners may need to incorporate organic matter into planting holes to improve soil fertility and provide a conducive environment for plant roots to establish and thrive.

Digging planting holes is a fundamental task in gardening or landscaping, but it's essential to approach it with caution and careful consideration to ensure safety and success. Here are some detailed tips to guide you through the process:

- **Prioritize Safety**: Safety should always be the top priority when digging planting holes. It's crucial to learn proper digging, lifting, and turning techniques to avoid injuries, particularly to the back. Many individuals in the landscaping trade sustain back injuries due to improper lifting and digging methods. Implementing safety procedures and using ergonomic tools can significantly reduce the risk of injury.

- **Identify Underground Services**: Before digging, it's essential to identify and locate any underground services or utilities that may be present in the area. This includes irrigation pipes, electrical wires, or other cables. Accidentally damaging these services can lead to costly repairs and potential safety hazards. Utilizing tools such as ground-penetrating radar or contacting relevant utility companies for information can help prevent accidents.

Preparing Planting Holes: Once the appropriate precautions have been taken, and the correct-sized holes have been dug, the next step is to prepare the soil in these holes to ensure optimal conditions for plant growth. Proper soil preparation is vital for the healthy establishment of new trees and plants. Here are some considerations for preparing planting holes:

- **Soil Assessment**: Before adding any amendments or fertilizers, assess the quality of the soil in the planting holes. Factors such as texture, drainage, and nutrient content can influence plant growth. Conducting a soil test can provide valuable information about pH levels and nutrient deficiencies, guiding the selection of suitable amendments.

- **Amendments**: Depending on the soil's composition and the specific needs of the plants being installed, amendments may be necessary to improve soil structure and fertility. Common amendments include organic matter such as compost, aged manure, or peat moss, which can enhance soil moisture retention, aeration, and nutrient availability. Incorporating amendments into the soil thoroughly ensures uniform distribution and benefits for plant roots.

- **Backfilling**: Carefully backfill the planting holes with the amended soil, ensuring that the roots of the new trees or plants are adequately covered. Avoid compacting the soil excessively, as compacted soil can restrict root growth and water infiltration. Tamp the soil gently to remove air pockets and promote good soil-to-root contact.

- **Watering**: After backfilling, thoroughly water the newly planted trees or plants to settle the soil around the roots and provide essential moisture for establishment. Monitor soil moisture levels regularly and adjust watering frequency as needed, particularly during dry periods or hot weather.

By following these tips for digging planting holes and preparing the soil effectively, gardeners and landscapers can create an optimal environment for plant growth and ensure the long-term health and vitality of their landscape installations.

Planting a tree is a process that requires careful attention to detail to ensure the successful establishment and long-term health of the tree. The first step in planting a tree is to soak the root ball while you work. This helps ensure that the roots are thoroughly moistened, as a dry root ball could potentially reject water from the surrounding soil. Adding a seaweed product to the water can further aid in preventing transplant shock and promoting healthy root growth.

Next, it's time to dig the hole for planting. The hole should be at least twice the size of the existing root ball of the tree. While depth is more critical than width in most cases, it's essential to dig enough to ensure that the existing roots can be completely covered. While a bigger, deeper hole is generally better, there's no need to go to extreme lengths.

Once the hole is dug, it's important to improve the soil to support the tree's long-term survival. In clay soils, adding gypsum can help improve soil structure and drainage, while well-rotted compost provides organic matter and further enhances soil structure. In sandy soils, compost is essential for holding moisture around the roots. Additionally, using a good fertilizer, such as a slow-release fertilizer with microbial coating or blood and bone, can help provide essential nutrients for the tree's growth.

After preparing the soil, carefully decant the tree from its pot, taking care to keep the roots as intact as possible. Root disturbance can shock the plant, so minimizing disruption is crucial for the tree's health. If the plant is pot-bound or has poor root structure, consider teasing out the bottom of the roots to encourage healthy growth.

Once the tree is ready, place it in the hole and backfill with soil to cover the roots. Ensure that the soil around the plant is firm, leaving a slight well at the top to catch water directly above the roots. This technique maximizes the effectiveness of rainfall, which is particularly important in climates where water availability may be limited.

Finally, water the plant thoroughly to settle the soil around the roots and provide essential moisture. This initial watering helps establish good contact between the roots and the soil and provides the tree with its first drink in its new environment. Even if the soil is already damp, watering ensures deeper moisture penetration, which is vital for the tree's ongoing health and growth. By following these steps, you can help ensure that your newly planted tree has the best possible start and thrives in its new home for years to come.

Removing plants from pots is a crucial step in the planting process and should be done carefully to avoid damaging the roots and disrupting the plant's growth. Here's a step-by-step guide on how to properly remove plants from pots:

- **Prepare the Work Area**: Before you begin, ensure you have a clean and spacious area to work in. Lay down a tarp or some newspapers to catch any soil that may spill during the process.

- **Water the Plant**: It's helpful to water the plant thoroughly a few hours before you plan to remove it from the pot. Moist soil will hold together better, and the roots will be less likely to break during the removal process.

- **Choose the Right Time**: The best time to remove a plant from its pot is when the soil is slightly moist, not completely dry or overly wet. This ensures that the soil will hold together but won't be too compacted.

- **Tap the Pot**: Gently tap the sides and bottom of the pot to loosen the soil and roots. This helps release the root ball from the container without causing damage.

- **Support the Plant**: Hold the plant securely at the base of the stem or trunk, depending on the type of plant. If it's a small plant, you can also hold it gently by the leaves or branches.

- **Turn the Pot**: Carefully turn the pot upside down, holding the plant steady with one hand while supporting the pot with the other. You may need to tap or gently squeeze the sides of the pot to loosen the root ball.

- **Remove the Pot**: Once the pot is loosened, carefully slide it off the root ball. If the pot is plastic, you can gently squeeze the sides to help release it. For ceramic or clay pots, you may need to tap or gently pry the pot away from the root ball.

- **Inspect the Roots**: Once the plant is out of the pot, take a moment to inspect the roots. Look for any signs of damage or disease, and gently tease out any roots that are circling around the root ball.

- **Plant Immediately**: Once the plant is out of the pot, it's important to plant it in its new location as soon as possible. Leaving the roots exposed to air for too long can cause them to dry out and become damaged.

Dealing with root-bound plants is essential for their health and successful transplantation. When a plant becomes root-bound, its roots grow densely in a circular pattern within the pot, potentially restricting their growth and nutrient uptake. To deal with root bound plants:

- **Identify Root-Bound Plants**: Before you start the transplantation process, carefully inspect the plant's root system. Signs of being root-bound include roots circling around the pot's edges, appearing crowded, and emerging from drainage holes at the bottom.

- **Prepare the Plant**: If you've identified a root-bound plant, gently remove it from its pot. Tap the sides of the pot to loosen the soil and roots. You may also need to gently squeeze the pot or run a knife around the inner edges to loosen the root ball.

- **Assess the Root Ball**: Once the plant is out of the pot, assess the condition of the root ball. If the roots are tightly packed and circling around the soil, the plant is root-bound and requires intervention.

- **Loosen the Roots**: Carefully loosen the roots to encourage outward growth and prevent them from continuing to circle in the new planting location. You can use your fingers to gently tease apart the outer layer of roots, or a gardening tool like a fork to gently break up the root ball.

- **Trim Excess Roots**: In severe cases of root-binding, where the root ball is excessively dense, you may need to trim away some of the outer roots. Use clean and sharp pruning shears to trim any circling or damaged roots. Make clean cuts to avoid injuring the plant further.

- **Prune the Top Growth**: Root pruning can shock the plant, so it's often beneficial to prune back the top growth as well. This reduces the plant's demand for water and nutrients while it recovers from root pruning. Trim back any excessively long or damaged stems or foliage, but avoid removing too much greenery.

- **Prepare the Planting Hole**: Before replanting the root-bound plant, prepare the planting hole in the new location. Dig a hole that's wide and deep enough to accommodate the plant's root system comfortably.

- **Replant Carefully**: Once the planting hole is ready, carefully place the root-bound plant in the centre, spreading out the roots in a natural position. Backfill the hole with soil, gently pressing it down to eliminate air pockets around the roots.

- **Water Thoroughly**: After replanting, water the plant thoroughly to help settle the soil and hydrate the roots. Keep the soil consistently moist in the following weeks to support the plant's recovery and establishment in its new environment.

Staking and tying

Staking newly planted trees and shrubs can be an important step in ensuring their successful establishment, particularly in areas prone to strong winds or where there's a risk of damage from mowers or whipper-snippers. While most plants grow stronger and develop better shapes without staking, certain circumstances necessitate providing external support to prevent them from being blown over or damaged. Standard ornamentals, like standard iceberg roses, are examples of plants that typically require staking throughout their lifespan due to their top-heavy growth.

When staking and tying a plant, it's essential to adhere to specific rules to avoid causing damage to the plant and to ensure effective support. First and foremost, the stake should be placed in the planting hole at the time of planting to avoid damaging the roots during insertion. This ensures that the stake is firmly anchored in the soil without disturbing the plant's delicate root system.

Figure 244: Tree stake. Fructibus, CC0, via Wikimedia Commons.

Furthermore, the choice of tying material is crucial. It's important to select a soft material that won't cut into or damage the stem of the plant. Additionally, the tying material should be positioned in a way that prevents rubbing against the stem, which can cause abrasions or wounds. If using wire as tying material, it's recommended to thread it through a short length of hose to act as a cushion against the stem. Alternatively, there are many commercial tying materials available specifically designed for this purpose.

When tying the plant to the stake, it's advisable to use a figure-8 method. This technique provides support to the plant while allowing for some movement in the wind, which encourages the development of a stronger root system and stem. It's crucial not to tie the stem too tightly against the stake, as this can restrict movement and potentially cause the stem to snap in strong winds. By following these guidelines, staking and tying can effectively support newly planted trees and shrubs without causing harm, promoting their healthy growth and establishment in their new environment.

Care After Planting

After planting trees or shrubs, proper care and maintenance are essential to ensure their successful establishment and long-term health. One important aspect of post-planting care is staking, particularly if the area is prone to strong winds. Staking helps prevent the newly planted tree from being whipped about by the wind, which can cause root damage and hinder establishment. The stake should remain in place until the tree is well established, typically for a period ranging from 6 to 24 months. It's important to periodically check and adjust the ties to prevent them from cutting into the trunk as the tree grows.

Mulching is another crucial step in caring for newly planted trees. Mulch helps to regulate soil temperature, retain moisture, and suppress weed growth, all of which are beneficial for the tree's health. However, it's essential to leave a gap of 150-200 mm in the mulch around the tree trunk to prevent moisture build-up, which can lead to rotting of the trunk.

In addition to staking and mulching, providing wind and sun protection may be necessary for young trees, especially those exposed to harsh environmental conditions. Methods such as using old fertilizer bags or painting the trunk with a protective coating can help shield the tree from excessive sun exposure or wind damage.

Proper watering is critical for the establishment of newly planted trees, especially during hot and dry weather. Until the tree develops an active root system, it relies on the volume of the pot and surrounding soil for water. Watering frequency depends on weather conditions, with trees needing to be watered 2-3 times per week in hot weather and 1-2 times per week in cooler weather. Once the tree has produced new growth, watering once a week should be sufficient.

Fertilizer application is another aspect of post-planting care that requires attention. It's essential to distribute fertilizer evenly in a band around the tree, avoiding concentrated application close to the base, as this can damage or kill the tree. As the tree matures, the width of the fertilizer band should increase, with applications watered in to prevent root damage.

Regular maintenance tasks such as pruning, weed control, and monitoring for pest and disease issues are also important for the overall health and vitality of newly planted trees. By following these guidelines and providing proper care and attention, newly planted trees can establish successfully and thrive in their new environment.

Pruning

Tree pruning is a fundamental aspect of tree maintenance that contributes to the safety, health, and aesthetic appeal of landscape trees. At Valley Tree Managers, our team of skilled professionals is well-versed in the art and science of pruning, ensuring that each cut made to your trees enhances their longevity and overall well-being.

There are various objectives behind tree pruning, all aimed at maintaining the health, beauty, safety, and functionality of trees in the landscape. Among the most common reasons for pruning ornamental and shade trees are promoting healthy growth, correcting structural defects, and improving aesthetics. It's crucial to understand that every pruning action has the potential to influence a tree's growth, hence pruning should be undertaken for specific purposes.

Pruning for structure focuses on enhancing various structural elements of a tree, such as spacing, growth rate, attachment strength, and ultimate branch and stem size. This type of pruning, typically performed on young and medium-sized trees, reduces the risk of tree failure by fostering a structurally sound trunk and branch architecture.

Cleaning the canopy involves removing crowded, weakly attached, dead, cracked, or broken branches, as well as low-vigor branches. This type of pruning, commonly practiced on mature trees, helps maintain their health by eliminating unnecessary dead or diseased branches while preserving live ones.

Thinning entails selectively removing small live branches to reduce crown density, allowing better light penetration and air circulation throughout the tree's canopy. It also helps lighten heavy limbs and preserve the tree's natural shape. Thinning is particularly beneficial when additional sunlight or airflow is needed for underlying vegetation.

Raising the canopy involves selectively removing the lowest branches to create vertical clearance over structures like buildings, signs, and pathways. This encourages upward growth of middle and top branches, elevating the entire canopy. Maintaining a balanced structure is essential when raising the canopy to avoid creating imbalances that could compromise the tree's stability.

Reducing the tree's height or spread is done to provide clearance from objects such as buildings and utility lines. This involves selectively pruning back leading branches to maintain the tree's structural integrity and form while achieving the desired reduction.

Lastly, trees that have suffered severe damage from storms, vandalism, or improper pruning can undergo restorative pruning to improve their structure, form, and appearance. This involves selectively pruning damaged or misshapen branches to encourage healthy regrowth and restore the tree's overall vitality.

By understanding the various objectives and techniques of tree pruning, we ensure that each pruning action contributes to the long-term health and beauty of your landscape trees.

Chapter Fifteen

Implementing Soil Improvements for Garden and Turf Areas

Garden and Turf Soil

The soil in which your lawn grows plays a crucial role in determining its success. Understanding soil composition and structure is essential for effective lawn care and maintenance. Soil is composed of various components, including organic matter, minerals, air, water, and living organisms. Organic matter, derived from decomposing plants and animals, improves soil structure and provides essential nutrients. Minerals, resulting from the weathering of rocks, also contribute nutrients necessary for plant growth. Air pockets within the soil allow oxygen to reach plant roots and facilitate water penetration and drainage. Additionally, living organisms such as microorganisms and earthworms play vital roles in soil health by aiding in decomposition and nutrient cycling.

Soils exhibit considerable variation due to differences in the proportions and arrangement of these components. Analysing soil composition helps determine the necessary improvements to optimize lawn performance. Conducting a soil analysis involves assessing its colour, texture, and particle size distribution. The ribbon test is a common method used to determine soil texture, indicating the presence of sand, silt, or clay particles and their respective proportions. Sandy soils have larger, coarser particles and drain quickly but may lack essential nutrients. Clay soils, on the other hand, have finer particles and retain water and nutrients but may become compacted and poorly drained.

Soil structure refers to the arrangement of soil particles and aggregates, which influences water retention, aeration, and root penetration. Well-structured soils have firm aggregates that allow for adequate water and air movement, promoting healthy root growth. In contrast, poorly structured soils are often compacted, impeding water infiltration and root development. Understanding soil pH is also crucial, as it affects nutrient availability to plants. Soil pH can range from acidic to neutral to alkaline, with each pH level influencing nutrient uptake differently.

Improving soil quality may be necessary to address specific issues and enhance lawn performance. For sandy soils, adding organic matter and clay-containing soil can improve nutrient retention and water-holding capacity. Mixing these amendments thoroughly into the soil helps create a balanced growing environment. Conversely, clay soils benefit from the addition of organic matter and gypsum to improve drainage and soil structure. Cultivating the soil to incorporate these amendments is essential, but timing and moisture levels must be carefully considered to avoid compaction or waterlogging.

In cases where soil quality is severely compromised, such as on new housing developments or heavily compacted areas, extensive soil improvement may be required. Bringing in new soil and raising the ground level can help address drainage issues and provide a suitable growing medium for healthy turf establishment. Contouring the existing soil and incorporating drainage solutions are essential steps in creating an optimal environment for lawn growth.

Soil Sampling and Testing on a Small Property

Soil testing is a fundamental practice for small landholders aiming to optimize soil health and enhance agricultural productivity. By conducting accurate soil tests, landholders can gain valuable insights into their soil's physical, chemical, and biological components, allowing them to make informed decisions about fertilization strategies and soil management practices. Understanding soil limitations and nutrient deficiencies enables landholders to develop tailored action plans to address specific issues and maximize crop and pasture yields.

Healthy soil encompasses a balance of various factors, including nutrient levels, pH, salinity, and organic matter content. Regular soil testing serves as a vital monitoring tool to track soil nutrient levels over time and ensure that inputs match the needs of crops and pastures. A soil imbalance can hinder plant growth and nutrient uptake, leading to reduced yields and wasted resources. Therefore, soil testing plays a crucial role in maintaining soil fertility and optimizing agricultural productivity.

Before purchasing farming land, it is advisable to request soil tests from the current owner to identify any underlying soil health issues. Understanding the soil composition and nutrient levels can provide valuable insights into the farm's potential and help inform management decisions. Similarly, for landholders with limited soil testing history, conducting regular soil tests is essential to monitor soil health and track changes over time.

The soil testing process involves collecting representative soil samples, laboratory analysis, interpretation of test results, and record-keeping. Accurate soil sampling is crucial to ensure reliable test results. Samples should be collected from various locations within individual paddocks, considering factors such as soil type and land use history. Sampling should be timed appropriately, ideally before planting crops or establishing pastures, to provide an accurate assessment of soil fertility.

Soil test results are only as accurate as the samples collected and handled leading up to laboratory analysis. Incorrect sampling techniques, inadequate sample size, or sampling at the wrong time of year can result in misleading test results. Therefore, it is essential to follow proper sampling protocols and guidelines to ensure representative soil samples are collected. Additionally, recording and monitoring soil test results over time allows landholders to track changes in soil health and evaluate the effectiveness of soil management practices.

Soil testing is a comprehensive process that involves more than just analysing the nutrient status of the soil. It encompasses various stages, including sampling, analysis, and interpretation of results, leading to informed recommendations for soil management. Consulting with local agronomists or soil experts before collecting samples is advisable to ensure the appropriateness of the sampling procedure and to discuss the need for additional tests, such as deep soil nitrogen tests. It's crucial to collect samples consistently to a specific depth, typically the top 10cm of soil, where nutrients are often concentrated.

The timing of soil sample collection is critical, as soil moisture, plant growth stage, and organic matter decomposition can influence soil nutrient levels. For instance, nutrient availability may be low in spring-collected soil samples as nutrients are still within plants and have not yet been returned to the soil through decomposition. Mid-summer, when the soil is dry, is often considered an optimal time for soil sampling, but consulting with local experts for region-specific guidance is essential.

Regular soil testing is recommended to account for the various factors that can influence soil test results, such as subtle differences in soil type and nutrient availability. Testing at the same time each year enhances result comparison between years and helps build a clear profile of soil health over time. Additionally, sending samples to the same laboratory for testing ensures consistency and facilitates result interpretation.

Sampling sites should be selected carefully to ensure representativeness and accuracy of test results. Soil sampling should be conducted across the entire paddock, with consideration given to factors like soil type, land use history, and potential sources of contamination. It's essential to avoid sampling near areas with potential sources of variation, such as fences, trees, stock camps, and recent fertilization or soil management activities.

Accounting for soil variability is crucial, as many soils exhibit differences in texture, depth, and nutrient levels across relatively short distances. Sampling protocols should be adapted to address variations within paddocks, with separate samples taken from different soil types or management zones. Proper handling of soil samples, including labelling, storage, and transport, is essential to prevent contamination and ensure accurate test results.

Interpreting soil test results requires careful consideration of laboratory recommendations and consultation with agricultural consultants or agronomists. Different laboratories may offer varying services, including result interpretation and soil management recommendations. Properly interpreting soil test results is essential for developing effective soil management strategies to optimize soil health and productivity.

Soil Structure

The structure of soil plays a crucial role in various soil functions, including drainage, water retention, nutrient availability, compaction, and infiltration rate. Soil consists of four primary components: water, air, organic matter, and solid mineral particles. Water and air occupy the pore spaces within the soil, while organic matter comprises living and decaying plant material. Solid mineral particles, which vary in size from gravel to clay, form the solid framework of the soil.

Particle size distribution determines soil texture, which influences its characteristics and behaviour. Soil particles range from large gravel particles to tiny clay particles, with varying diameters. Soil texture is categorized based on the percentage of sand, silt, and clay particles present. For instance, sandy loam contains higher proportions of sand particles compared to clay loam, which has a higher clay content.

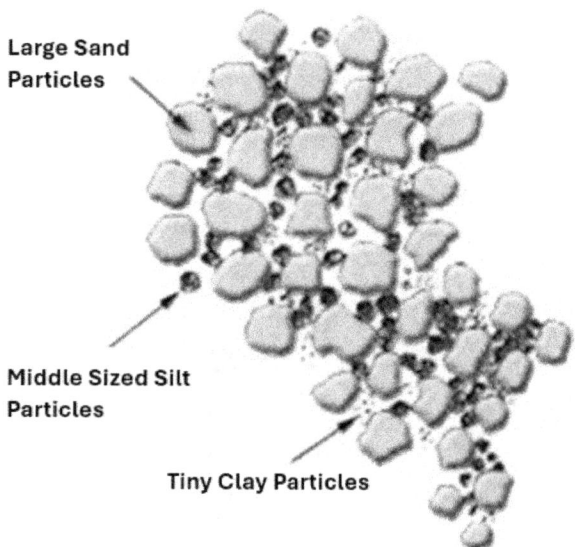

Figure 245: Soil composition.

Pore spaces within the soil provide pathways for water movement and root growth. These spaces hold water and air, essential for plant growth. Larger pore spaces facilitate better drainage, allowing excess water to drain away quickly, while smaller pore spaces retain more water. Capillary forces, influenced by pore size, determine the soil's ability to retain water against gravity. Soils with larger pore spaces have smaller capillary forces and can hold less water, while those with smaller pore spaces retain more water.

Soil structure, viewed up close, reveals a complex arrangement where approximately half of the soil is comprised of solid material, while the rest consists of pore spaces. These spaces serve as crucial zones for various activities: water storage, habitat for organisms, and accumulation of organic matter and nutrients. The arrangement of solids and pores, as depicted in a magnified diagram, showcases the porosity of soil, demonstrating the importance of both small and large pores within aggregates. Small pores offer storage and refuge, while larger pores and fissures between aggregates serve as pathways for liquids, gases, roots, and organisms. Understanding soil structure enables us to anticipate how management practices might alter it. For instance, pondering the impact of a weighted wheel passing over the surface, a tyne dragging through it, or the removal of organic matter prompts insight into soil dynamics.

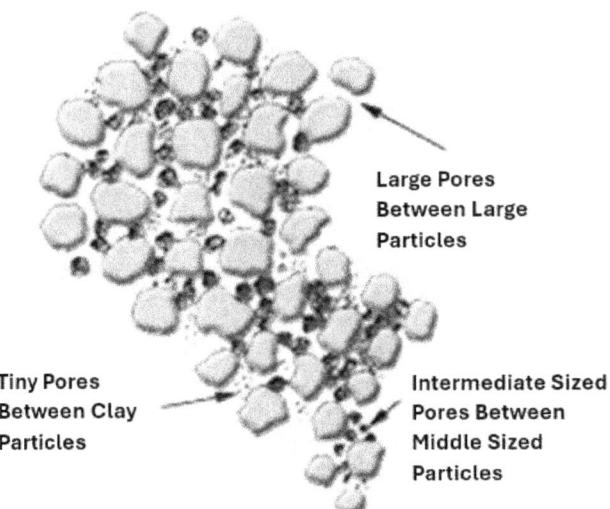

Figure 246: Pore spaces.

Water holding capacity refers to the maximum amount of water soil can retain after saturation. After rainfall saturates the soil, excess water drains away, leaving water held against gravity in the soil's pore spaces. This retained water, known as field capacity, varies depending on soil particle and pore size. Larger pores hold air at field capacity, while smaller pores retain water. As plant roots extract water from the soil, they reach a point where the soil retains water too tightly for roots to access, leading to wilting. This stage, known as the permanent wilting point, varies among soils due to differences in particle and pore space size.

Understanding soil structure and its components is vital for effective soil management practices. Farmers and land managers utilize this knowledge to optimize soil health, water management, and crop productivity. By assessing soil texture, water holding capacity, and pore space characteristics, they can tailor management strategies to improve soil structure, fertility, and overall health. Additionally, recognizing the relationship between soil structure and plant growth aids in sustainable agricultural practices and environmental stewardship.

The significance of soil structure can be likened to that of a city layout, dictating the functionality, pace, and sustainability of soil processes. Several characteristics help evaluate soil performance, including porosity, permeability, bonding, aggregation, soil strength, friability, tillage, and trafficability. These factors collectively influence a soil's ability to aerate, store water, resist compaction, and support plant growth. Soil structure encompasses various types, ranging from granular and aggregated structures with high permeability to platey and massive structures with low permeability. Damaged soil structure manifests in root restriction, compacted layers, plough pans, and surface crusting, impairing soil functionality and agricultural productivity.

Compaction poses a significant challenge in soil management, particularly in the topmost layer where mechanical pressures from equipment operations and trampling activities exert force, diminishing pore spaces crucial for soil health. While compaction issues are more pronounced in loam and clay soils, even sandy soils are susceptible to its effects. Certain conditions exacerbate the likelihood of compaction occurrence, such as heavy traffic areas, wet soil, and poor grass cover. In essence, compaction alters the soil's physical structure by compressing soil particles, thereby reducing pore spaces and replacing them with smaller particles.

The consequences of compaction reverberate throughout the soil ecosystem, disrupting vital processes like aeration, water infiltration, and drainage. As pore spaces shrink, capillary forces intensify, leading to greater water retention and diminished air content, consequently impeding plant respiration. This compromised aeration adversely affects plant health and nutrient uptake, rendering turf thin and unresponsive to fertilization. Moreover, the altered soil environment favours weed growth, as weeds possess higher tolerance levels for compaction compared to turf, ultimately leading to their dominance in affected areas.

Mitigating compaction necessitates strategic interventions aimed at restoring soil structure and functionality. Specially designed aerators, such as corers and verti-drains, offer effective solutions by creating holes in the turf, thereby alleviating compaction. Coring involves the removal of soil plugs, while verti-drains penetrate the soil, shattering its profile. These operations should be conducted under specific conditions, ensuring optimal soil moisture levels and turf growth. Typically, turf is cored shortly after irrigation to facilitate soil retention within coring implements. Active turf growth periods, like spring or autumn, provide conducive environments for remedial actions. Ultimately, addressing compaction requires a proactive approach guided by timely interventions and meticulous soil management practices.

Soil colour serves as a conspicuous yet significant characteristic that offers valuable insights into the soil environment, playing a pivotal role in assessment and classification endeavours. In a well-drained soil, colours like white, red, brown, and black hold sway, each indicative of distinct soil properties and constituents. White signifies the prevalence of silica or the presence of salts, while red hints at iron oxide accumulation, and brown/black points towards the level and type of organic matter. Employing a colour triangle aids in illustrating the relationships between these influential hues, facilitating a nuanced understanding of soil composition and dynamics.

Several factors converge to determine soil colour, with mineral matter derived from parent material constituting a primary influencer. Rocks contribute to soil coloration, often imparting their hues to the soil, while compounds like iron play a crucial role in colour formation. Additionally, organic matter, particularly humus, significantly impacts soil colour, transitioning from various shades of brown to black as it undergoes breakdown stages. Sodium content further influences organic matter colour depth, with higher sodium levels promoting darker soil appearance.

The nature and abundance of iron are pivotal in dictating soil colour variations, with red, yellow, grey, and bluish-grey hues manifesting depending on iron's chemical states and environmental conditions. Under well-drained or dry circumstances, iron oxide formation leads to red or yellow soil colours, while waterlogged conditions foster the emergence of greyish tones due to reduced iron states. Furthermore, moisture content significantly affects soil colour, with darker hues observed in moist conditions, aiding in identifying water-related soil issues such as waterlogging or leaching.

Accurate measurement of soil colour necessitates meticulous procedures, including assessments on freshly broken, moist soil surfaces. Observation throughout the entire soil profile is imperative, with attention to mottle characteristics and contrast variations. Utilization of standardized tools such as the Munsell Soil Colour Chart offers a systematic approach to soil colour assessment, facilitating consistency and comparability across analyses. The Munsell system categorizes colour into hue, value, and chroma, delineating wavelength, tone, and saturation, respectively, to ensure comprehensive colour evaluation.

In essence, soil colour serves as a multifaceted indicator of soil health and dynamics, offering insights into historical, chemical, and hydrological aspects. By discerning the nuances of soil coloration and employing standardized assessment methodologies, researchers and practitioners can glean invaluable information vital for informed decision-making in soil management endeavours.

Soil colour serves as a comprehensive indicator of various soil properties and environmental conditions, with four primary factors influencing soil coloration: mineral matter, organic matter, iron content, and moisture levels. Mineral matter, derived from parent material, contributes significantly to soil colour, with rocks imparting their hues to the soil. However, iron compounds predominantly dictate soil coloration, with varying states of iron oxidation resulting in red, yellow, grey, or bluish-grey hues. Organic matter, particularly humus, also plays a crucial role, transitioning from browns to black as it undergoes decomposition stages. Additionally, moisture content affects soil colour, with soil darkening as moisture levels increase, thereby facilitating observations regarding water relations, such as waterlogging or leaching issues.

Assessing soil colour entails employing standardized methodologies such as the Munsell system, which categorizes colour into hue, value, and chroma, ensuring consistency and comparability across analyses. Bright colours and strong reds in soils indicate adequate drainage or minimal saturation, while dull colours like yellows and greys, often found in mottled horizons, signify poor drainage and prolonged saturation. Blue-grey and blue-green colours indicate prolonged saturation, with reduced iron states and potential sulphur presence contributing to their formation. Moreover, the precipitation of iron compounds, typically orange or dull red, suggests oxidation in waterlogged environments, with iron movement processes playing a pivotal role in soil colour dynamics.

Various soil characteristics and processes manifest through distinct colorations, providing valuable insights into soil history, chemistry, and hydrology. For instance, white or grey horizons between topsoil and clay subsoil result from leaching processes, indicating soil washout and reduced clay content. Such horizons, known as A2 horizons, contribute to rapid waterlogging, albeit rarely being saline due to extensive leaching. Similarly, white subsoil colours often denote the presence of calcium carbonate, with its depth indicating the extent of leaching throughout soil formation. Soil colour thus serves as a powerful diagnostic tool, facilitating informed decision-making in soil management practices and environmental assessments.

Soil particles, derived from rocks and sediments, are integral to soil structure and function, with their size and composition influencing various soil properties. Coarser materials typically originate from fragmented parent materials, while finer materials, such as clay, result from extensive weathering processes. Particle size distribution categorizes soil particles into four groups: gravel (>2 mm), sand (0.02 – 2 mm), silt (0.002 – 0.02 mm), and clay (<0.002 mm). The surface area per unit volume increases with decreasing particle size, significantly impacting bonding and aggregation processes. Clay-sized particles, especially when moist, exhibit plasticity, whereas silts adhere well but lack plasticity, and sands do not knead and tend to disintegrate easily.

Clay minerals, characterized by their small, flat, plate-like structure and negative charge, exhibit high surface activity, influencing soil aggregation profoundly. The degree of aggregation varies depending on clay mineral composition and the availability of cations within the soil environment. Bonding and aggregation within soils are primarily determined by the mineral component (sand, silt, and clay), with sandy soils weakly aggregated and clay soils exhibiting stronger bonding. Organic matter plays a critical role in augmenting and modifying soil bonding, enhancing aggregation, and contributing to soil health.

Aggregation occurs through gravitational, electrostatic, and chemical interactions, involving factors such as soil texture, clay mineral type, soluble ions, organic matter, chemical cements, and environmental conditions. Different clay minerals produce distinct aggregation patterns, with some exhibiting stable bonding while others are susceptible to dispersion upon wetting. Plant material and root exudates contribute significantly to organic matter content, promoting microbial activity and adhesive by-product production, further enhancing aggregate stability.

The importance of clay particles lies in their minute size, large surface area relative to weight, and negative charge, influencing soil permeability, drainage, water availability, and erosion susceptibility. The resilience of soil aggregation, dictated by bonding strength between soil aggregates, determines soil strength, consolidation under pressure, resistance to disintegration, and erosion susceptibility. Evaluating aggregation involves assessing aggregate stability, often measured by how well aggregates hold together in water, with poorly aggregated soils prone to dispersion, crusting, compaction, and waterlogging.

Improving aggregate stability necessitates modifications to soil properties and management practices. Strategies include retaining crop stubble to increase organic matter, limiting vehicle traffic to prevent soil degradation, applying gypsum to correct sodicity, incorporating green manure or compost to enhance organic matter content, using raised beds to alleviate waterlogging, and adopting minimum tillage practices to preserve soil structure. By understanding the dynamics of soil particles and aggregation, practitioners can implement effective strategies to improve soil health and productivity while mitigating environmental degradation.

Assessing aggregate stability is crucial for understanding soil health and its capacity to resist degradation. This assessment involves observing the behaviour of soil aggregates when immersed in water. The method typically employs air-dried aggregates, approximately the size of a green pea, which are submerged in rainwater or distilled water. Over time, the aggregates may exhibit different responses: remaining unchanged, swelling, slaking (breaking into smaller fragments), or dispersing into a fine milky suspension. The presence or absence of dispersion indicates the stability of soil aggregates. Highly dispersive soils may suffer from severe crusting and poor drainage, while non-dispersive soils exhibit excellent aggregate stability and are less prone to structural problems.

The evaluation of aggregate stability provides insights into soil porosity, which refers to the pore space between mineral particles filled with air or water. Pores vary in diameter, ranging from a few millimetres to fractions of a micron, with different types serving distinct functions. Transmission pores, also known as macropores, facilitate root growth, air, and water movement, promoting soil aeration and drainage. Storage pores, or micropores, retain water for plant use, contributing to soil moisture availability. Residual pores hold water tightly, rendering it inaccessible to plants or soil organisms. Understanding pore size distribution aids in comprehending soil behaviour and function, highlighting the importance of soil structure in supporting vegetation and maintaining soil health.

Soil strength, influenced by cohesive forces and frictional resistance between particles, is another critical aspect of soil assessment. It determines the soil's ability to resist deformation, breakage, and slippage, impacting root penetration, trafficability, and erosion susceptibility. Soil engineers measure soil strength by applying shear forces or assessing penetration resistance, providing insights into soil compaction, crusting, and plow pans. Consistence, evaluated by testing the force required to deform soil aggregates, serves as an indicator of soil strength and condition, with moisture content influencing soil response.

The moisture content of soil significantly affects its strength, with clay type and content playing a crucial role in cohesion. As water content increases, cohesion decreases due to enhanced separation of clay particles and softening of soil cements. Compaction of wet soils leads to more severe structural changes than dry soils, emphasizing the importance of moisture management in maintaining soil stability and productivity. Consistence ratings, ranging from loose to rigid, provide a standardized approach to assessing soil strength and condition, aiding in soil management decisions and predicting soil behaviour under different conditions.

Test Results

Understanding the results of soil tests is crucial for effective soil management, but it's equally essential to seek guidance from horticulturists or agronomists to interpret and apply this information appropriately. One key parameter assessed in soil testing is pH, which measures soil acidity or alkalinity. North Coast soils are naturally acidic, with a preferred pH range of 5.0–5.5 (measured in $CaCl_2$ solution) for most agricultural and horticultural purposes. Soil acidity influences nutrient availability and microbial activity, impacting plant growth. Cation exchange capacity (CEC) is another critical aspect, indicating the soil's ability to hold essential nutrients like calcium, magnesium, and potassium. Soils with CEC above 10 are considered fertile, ideal for supporting plant growth.

Exchangeable cations, including calcium, magnesium, potassium, sodium, and aluminium, play vital roles in soil fertility. Preferred percentages and suggested quantity values help assess soil nutrient levels and balance. The calcium/magnesium ratio, typically above 3, influences nutrient uptake and soil structure. Soil amendments like lime or gypsum may be necessary to adjust cation ratios and optimize plant growth. Phosphorus levels, assessed through Bray or Colwell tests, vary with land use and soil texture. Maintaining optimal pH levels is crucial for phosphorus availability, especially in acidic soils where phosphorus may become unavailable to plants.

Nitrate nitrogen levels fluctuate seasonally and depend on factors like rainfall and land management practices. While specific calibrated levels are not established for the North Coast, agronomists generally recommend certain thresholds for pasture and horticultural crops. Electrical conductivity (EC) measures soil salt content, with values below 0.15 dS/m preferred for productive soils. Soil salinity problems can arise from excessive fertilization or saline irrigation water, affecting plant growth and productivity.

Trace elements, essential for plant growth in small quantities, require careful monitoring. Soil tests provide information on trace element levels, with preferred ranges varying according to crop requirements. Organic carbon, indicative of soil organic matter content, influences nutrient retention, soil structure, and microbial activity. Declining organic carbon levels may necessitate soil management practices like green manure crops or minimum tillage to enhance soil health.

While laboratory tests offer valuable insights into soil fertility and nutrient status, they may not detect issues like soil compaction, erosion, or structural decline. Field observations, including soil surface condition, topsoil depth, root penetration, and soil structure, provide additional information crucial for assessing soil health. Soil health cards serve as simple tools for ongoing soil examination and management. Collaborating with soil specialists ensures informed decision-making and effective soil management strategies tailored to specific agricultural or horticultural needs.

Chemical Properties

The chemical properties of soil play a pivotal role in releasing essential nutrients for plant growth. These properties are influenced by various factors, including the soil's parent rock composition, leaching history, and management practices. Soil nutrient proportions can vary widely, affecting plant growth differently. Understanding plant nutrient requirements is essential, as they can vary based on plant type and life cycle stage. Major nutrients like carbon, oxygen, hydrogen, nitrogen, phosphorus, potassium, sulphur, and calcium are required in larger quantities, while minor or trace elements like magnesium, iron, copper, zinc, manganese, molybdenum, boron, and chlorine are needed in smaller amounts. Plants may also require traces of elements like aluminium, sodium, silicon, cobalt, nickel, and vanadium. While some elements may not directly participate in plant biochemical processes, their presence in soil is crucial for overall plant health, as they are essential for animals that consume these plants.

Soil acidity or pH is a fundamental chemical property that significantly influences nutrient availability. The pH scale ranges from 0 to 14, with values below 7 indicating acidity and values above 7 indicating alkalinity. Nutrient availability can be affected by soil pH, with certain nutrients becoming chemically bound and unavailable to plants at extreme pH levels. Most plants thrive in a pH range between 6 and 7, but preferences may vary among different plant species. Extreme pH levels can damage plant roots, affecting nutrient uptake and overall plant health. Therefore, adjusting soil pH through amendments like lime or sulphur is essential for optimizing nutrient availability and plant growth.

Identifying nutrient deficiencies or toxicities in plants is crucial for effective soil management. Different nutrients play specific roles in plant biochemistry, and deficiencies can disrupt these processes, leading to visible symptoms in plants. Symptoms vary based on the mobility of nutrients within plants, with deficiencies in mobile nutrients appearing first on older leaves and deficiencies in immobile nutrients affecting newer leaves and shoots. Recognizing these symptoms and understanding nutrient roles can help gardeners address deficiencies through appropriate soil management practices.

The capacity of soil to store and release nutrients is influenced by its composition, particularly clay and humus content. Clay and humus particles have charged surfaces that attract and hold nutrient ions, facilitating nutrient uptake by plant roots. The cation exchange capacity (CEC) measures the soil's ability to hold nutrient ions, with higher CEC indicating greater nutrient retention capacity. Increasing soil organic matter through practices like composting enhances CEC, improving nutrient availability for plants.

Biological properties of soil, including its diverse microbial life, are essential for nutrient cycling and plant health. Soil organisms, such as earthworms, bacteria, fungi, and protozoa, play crucial roles in decomposing organic matter and releasing nutrients in forms accessible to plants. Organic gardening practices aim to maintain healthy soil biology by avoiding chemical inputs that harm soil organisms and promoting natural interactions within soil ecosystems. Composting and earthworm cultivation are common methods used by gardeners to enhance soil biology and nutrient cycling.

Plant Nutrients in the Soil

Soil serves as a vital reservoir of nutrients crucial for plant growth, with nitrogen (N), phosphorus (P), and potassium (K) being the primary elements, collectively known as NPK. Additionally, calcium (Ca), magnesium (Mg), and sulphur (S) are essential nutrients, while iron (Fe), manganese (Mn), zinc (Zn), copper (Cu), boron (B), and molybdenum (Mo) are required in trace amounts. Each nutrient plays a specific role in plant development, from supporting cellular structure to aiding metabolic processes. While the significance of these nutrients in plant growth is complex, understanding their roles is fundamental for effective soil management and maximizing crop productivity [97].

Nitrogen, a fundamental component of plant proteins, hormones, and chlorophyll, is crucial for overall plant growth. While some plants can fix atmospheric nitrogen, others rely on nitrogen supplied through fertilizers like ammonium sulphate, ammonium nitrate, or urea [97]. Phosphorus facilitates energy transfer in plants and stimulates early root and plant growth. Superphosphate, derived from rock phosphate and sulfuric acid, is a common phosphorus source, along with phosphorus-rich manures.

Potassium enhances plant vigour, disease resistance, and fruit quality, making it essential for crop health. However, sandy soils, common in regions like the North Coast, often suffer from potassium deficiency, necessitating supplementation through fertilizers like muriate of potash or sulphate of potash. Calcium is crucial for root health and leaf development, but its availability may be limited in acidic soils. Lime, gypsum, dolomite, and superphosphate are common calcium sources used to address deficiencies [97].

Magnesium, a component of chlorophyll, is vital for photosynthesis and is often deficient in sandy, acidic soils. Sulphur, responsible for various flavour and odour compounds in plants, is crucial for protein synthesis and energy production. While sulphur deficiency is less common in soils rich in organic matter, supplementation through fertilizers like superphosphate or gypsum may be necessary.

Trace elements like iron, manganese, copper, zinc, boron, and molybdenum play essential roles in various biochemical processes within plants. While deficiencies of these elements can adversely affect plant growth, excessive levels can also lead to toxicity. Management strategies such as soil amendments and targeted fertilization are employed to address nutrient imbalances and ensure optimal plant nutrition [97].

Understanding the nutrient requirements of crops and the factors influencing nutrient availability in soil is essential for sustainable agriculture. By effectively managing soil nutrients, farmers can optimize crop yields, enhance plant health, and contribute to overall agricultural productivity and food security.

Repairing Soil

Good soil is not a one-size-fits-all concept; its quality depends on various factors, including the types of plants it supports and its history over time. For resilient plants, good soil may mean minimal friability and adequate nutrition, while water-loving plants thrive in soils with limited drainage. However, for most plants, ideal soil characteristics include good drainage, fertility, moisture retention, and a loose, friable texture that facilitates root growth and nutrient uptake.

Treating soil over the winter months requires careful attention, especially in areas prone to waterlogging. To improve waterlogged soil, avoid heavy machinery or foot traffic that can compact it further. Instead, apply clay breaker solutions to sodic clay soils and add layers of organic matter to protect against erosion and compaction. Installing drainage systems can prevent future waterlogging issues.

Soil improvement strategies vary depending on soil type. Clay soils, although nutrient-rich, often suffer from poor drainage and waterlogging. Cultivating the soil and adding gypsum can help break up clay particles and improve drainage. Sandy soils, with their excellent drainage but low nutrient levels, benefit from organic matter additions to enhance fertility and moisture retention. Rocky soils pose unique challenges, and building garden beds on top of existing soil using no-dig methods or imported soil may be the most practical solution.

Maintaining soil fertility is crucial for sustained plant growth. Regular additions of compost, manure, or mulch replenish soil nutrients as organic matter decomposes. While fertilizers can supplement nutrient requirements, they should not be relied upon solely, as overuse of inorganic fertilizers can lead to environmental harm.

Compacted soils, common in clay soils, restrict root growth and water infiltration. Aerating compacted soils by incorporating organic matter and sand can improve soil structure and oxygen availability to plant roots. When building structures on soil, stability is paramount. Seek advice from professionals to ensure stable ground and prevent structural damage.

Erosion is a significant concern, especially on steep slopes. Measures such as retaining walls, terracing, drainage installation, or soil grading can stabilize soil and prevent erosion. With proper planning and soil management techniques, even challenging soils can be improved over time, providing a fertile foundation for healthy plant growth.

Soil Preparation

Soil serves as the fundamental growing medium for almost all open space turf areas, playing a crucial role in turf management. Comprised of minerals, organic matter, water, air, and living organisms, healthy soil provides physical support, water retention, and essential nutrients to plants. The characteristics of soil profoundly impact various aspects of turf management, including watering requirements, root depth and efficiency, drainage, nutrient supply, and susceptibility to weeds, pests, and diseases. Consequently, current turf management practices emphasize irrigation and fertilization schedules, but the need for these can be minimized with suitable soil texture and preparation.

The preparation of soil depends on its type and prevailing site conditions, which typically fall into three main categories: sandy soils, clay soils, and loamy soils. Sandy soils, known for their rapid drainage, may require frequent watering, while clay soils, with their water-holding capacity, can lead to waterlogging if not managed properly. Loamy soils, characterized by a balanced mixture of coarse and fine particles along with organic matter, offer ideal conditions for plant growth. Understanding soil texture is essential for determining its water retention capacity and suitability for different plant types.

Local soil conditions and testing play a crucial role in determining suitable plant choices and soil management strategies. Rather than adding superficial layers of garden mix, it's advisable to select plants adapted to the site's existing soil conditions. Deep-rooted plants can help break up compacted or poor soils, while the addition of organic matter encourages microbial activity and improves soil structure and moisture retention. Potential issues such as acid sulphate soils and salinity require specialized attention and management techniques to mitigate their effects on turf areas.

Soil additives can further enhance soil performance, addressing specific challenges such as hydrophobicity or excessive clay dispersion. Wetting agents can alleviate water repellency in sandy or organic-rich soils, while gypsum may be necessary to counteract dispersion in sodic clay soils. Water-storing crystals offer a reservoir of moisture during dry periods, benefiting plant root systems. Construction or landscaping activities that disturb soil subgrades necessitate careful restoration using saved topsoil, with attention to surface roughening and adequate drainage.

For landscaping projects, compliance with standards ensures soil quality and suitability for intended plant types. Turf can thrive on a variety of soils, but each may require different levels of management. For instance, pure sand demands more attention compared to a sandy loam soil type commonly found in sports fields. By understanding soil characteristics and implementing appropriate management practices, turf managers can optimize growing conditions and maintain healthy turf in open space areas.

The soil texture triangle is a graphical tool used by soil scientists, agronomists, and gardeners to determine the textural classification of a soil based on its relative proportions of sand, silt, and clay. It helps in understanding soil properties such as water retention, drainage, and nutrient availability, which are crucial for effective soil management and crop productivity.

Here's how to use the soil texture triangle:

- **Collect Soil Sample**: Begin by collecting a representative soil sample from the area of interest. Take samples from various locations within the area to ensure accuracy, especially if there are variations in soil texture across the site.

- **Determine Soil Texture Fractions**: In the laboratory, the soil sample is analysed to determine its texture fractions: sand, silt, and clay. This is typically done using methods such as the hydrometer method or the sieve method.

- **Calculate Percentages**: Calculate the percentage of each texture fraction in the soil sample. This is usually expressed as a percentage of the total soil mass. For example, if a soil sample contains 40% sand, 30% silt, and 30% clay, these percentages are used in the next step.

- **Locate Points on the Triangle**: On the soil texture triangle, locate the percentage of sand on the horizontal axis and the percentage of clay on the vertical axis. Find the intersection point of the sand percentage and clay percentage lines.

- **Identify Soil Texture**: Once you've located the intersection point, draw a line from this point parallel to the silt axis. The point where this line intersects the edge of the triangle represents the soil texture classification. The triangle typically divides soil textures into categories such as sand, loamy sand, sandy loam, loam, silt loam, silty clay loam, clay loam, sandy clay loam, silty clay, and clay.

- **Interpret Results**: Based on the soil texture classification obtained from the soil texture triangle, interpret the soil properties and their implications for soil management. For example, sandy soils tend to have good drainage but low water and nutrient retention, while clay soils have poor drainage but high water and nutrient retention.

- **Adjust Soil Management Practices**: Understanding the soil texture helps in determining appropriate soil management practices. For instance, sandy soils may require more frequent irrigation and fertilization to compensate for their low nutrient retention, while clay soils may benefit from practices that improve drainage, such as soil amendment or raised beds.

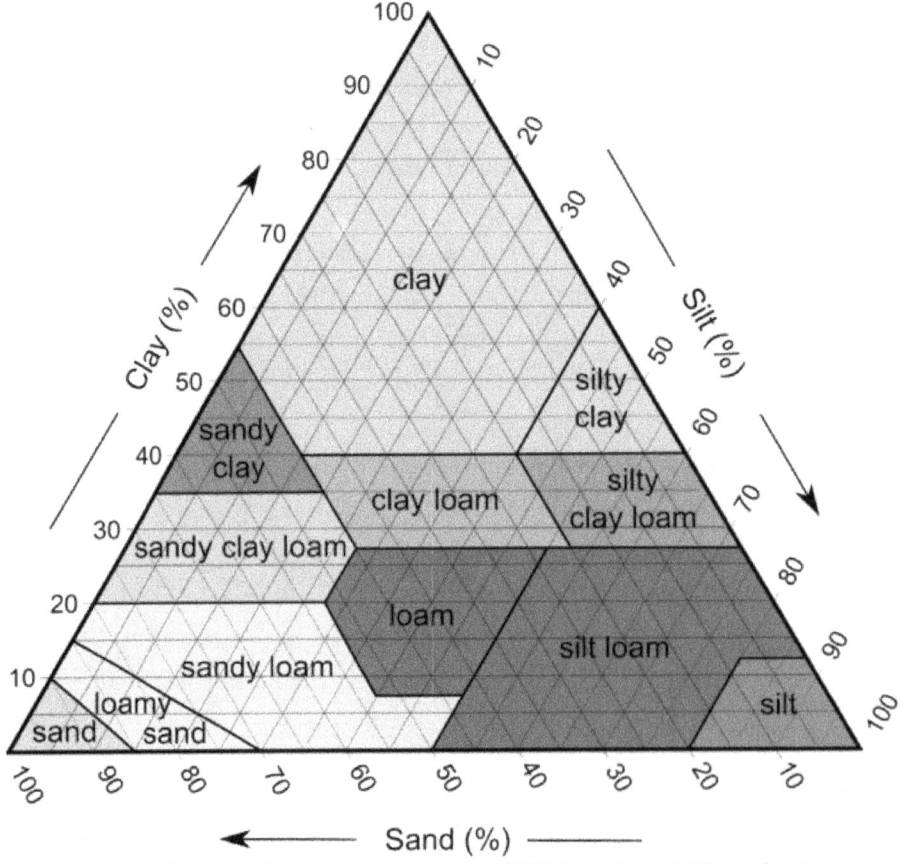

Figure 247: A soil texture diagram. Mikenorton, CC BY-SA 3.0, via Wikimedia Commons.

Sandy soils present both advantages and challenges for turf management, requiring careful attention to ensure optimal growth conditions. While turf managers appreciate sandy soils for their resistance to compaction, quick recovery after rain, and firm surface, they also acknowledge their limitations, such as low nutrient and water retention capacities.

The low nutrient-holding capacity of sandy soils can pose challenges for turf health and growth. However, with proper field construction techniques and fertilizer practices, these challenges can be overcome. Constructing turf profiles on sand requires attention to the base layer to prevent excessive water drainage and ensure adequate moisture retention within the root zone. Organic or controlled-release fertilizers can supplement nutrient deficiencies, while building up organic matter in the soil helps improve its overall fertility and water-holding capacity. Additionally, irrigating with smaller, more frequent applications helps minimize water loss below the root zone.

Silty soils, on the other hand, are prone to compaction due to their high silt content. Without regular irrigation and aeration, they can become excessively dense, hindering turf growth.

Heavy clays and weathered shale present significant challenges for turf management, as they are prone to compaction and waterlogging, limiting water availability for turf uptake. In cases where sites are already constructed using these unsuitable soils, importing an alternative growing medium becomes necessary. Consulting a soil scientist can provide valuable insights into soil quality assessment and appropriate remediation strategies.

Healthy, deep topsoil with a well-structured texture is essential for optimal turf health. Deep topsoils offer greater water retention capabilities compared to shallow soils, promoting healthier turf growth. It's imperative not to compromise on topsoil depth, ensuring a minimum depth of 250 mm to support robust turf growth and resilience against compaction, waterlogging, and weed infestation. Turf growing on shallow topsoil faces increased water requirements, compaction risks, and susceptibility to weed infestation, ultimately compromising its overall performance.

Despite the critical role of soil in turf performance, it's not uncommon to find turf laid directly on inadequate substrates such as shale, clay, or builder's rubble. This practice undermines turf health and resilience, highlighting the importance of proper soil assessment and preparation in turf management practices.

The water-holding capacity of soil is a critical factor in determining its suitability for plant growth and turf management. Soil acts as a reservoir for water, much like a sponge or a tank, but the amount it can hold varies significantly depending on its texture.

Sandy soils, characterized by their larger particle size, typically have a low capacity to hold water for plant uptake. This limitation can pose challenges for turf management, as sandy soils may require more frequent irrigation to maintain adequate soil moisture levels for healthy turf growth.

In contrast, loam and clay soils have the ability to retain larger amounts of water for plant uptake, making them more conducive to turf management. However, this capacity is contingent upon the soil being adequately aerated and uncompacted. Compacted clay loam soils, for example, may have reduced water-holding capacities due to restricted pore spaces. Aerating compacted soils can effectively double their capacity to store water, improving conditions for turf growth.

One cost-effective technique to increase the water-holding capacity of soils is through soil texture and depth amendments. By modifying the soil's texture and increasing its depth, it's possible to enhance its ability to retain water. This not only benefits turf health and playing surface quality but also contributes to water conservation efforts.

Implementing soil improvements can lead to significant enhancements in turf conditions, particularly on unirrigated sites. By increasing the soil's capacity to capture and retain water, turf managers can achieve healthier turf growth without the need for expensive irrigation systems. This approach not only promotes sustainable turf management practices but also offers economic benefits by reducing water usage and associated costs.

Fungal Soil

Ramial wood chips, particularly those derived from the outer branches of deciduous trees, offer numerous benefits for soil health and plant growth, especially for woody plants. These chips are rich in live tissue and nutrients, providing an optimal balance of carbon to nitrogen for fungal dominance in the soil. The term "ramial" originates from the French word "rameal," meaning related to small branches, highlighting its focus on younger, nutrient-rich plant material. This type of mulch encourages the proliferation of beneficial fungi, fostering symbiotic relationships with woody plants.

The significance of fungi in soil health cannot be overstated. Beneficial fungi play a crucial role in protecting plants from diseases, creating a healthy soil biology, and offering direct protection through the production of anti-pathogens. Mycorrhizal fungi, in particular, form symbiotic relationships with plant roots, extending their reach for water and nutrients in exchange for food sugars produced by the plants. This intricate network of fungi, facilitated by chemical communication, not only benefits individual plants but also connects nearby plants, contributing to the overall resilience of ecosystems.

Figure 248: Mushrooms found growing in Miracle-Gro potting soil. WDavis1911, CC BY-SA 3.0, via Wikimedia Commons.

The revelations about the interconnectedness of plants and fungi challenge previous paradigms of competition and highlight the importance of holistic ecosystem management. By fostering healthy soil conditions rich in microbial activity, including beneficial fungi, we can promote resilience and vitality in plant communities. The parallels drawn between soil health and human gut microbiota underscore the interconnected nature of ecosystems, emphasizing the need for responsible stewardship of natural resources.

These insights into soil biology prompt us to reconsider our approaches to gardening and landscaping. Instead of viewing plants and fungi as separate entities, we recognize their symbiotic relationships and strive to create environments conducive to their mutual flourishing. Encouraging fungal dominance in soil through the use of ramial wood chips represents a tangible step toward fostering resilient ecosystems.

Soil Improvement

Soil improvement is a fundamental aspect of gardening and agriculture, encompassing various methods aimed at enhancing soil quality for optimal plant growth and health. This process involves modifying soil characteristics through targeted interventions to create a more hospitable environment for plants. One of the most common approaches to soil improvement involves the regular addition of organic matter, which serves as a cornerstone for nurturing soil health.

Organic matter, derived from living organisms such as plants and animals, plays a pivotal role in enriching soil fertility and structure. Examples of organic matter sourced from animals include manure and blood and bone fertilizers, while plant-derived organic matter includes compost and mulches. Incorporating organic matter into the soil offers a multitude of benefits essential for robust plant growth and vitality.

Firstly, organic matter enhances the soil's water retention capacity, allowing it to hold moisture more effectively. This is particularly advantageous during dry periods, as adequate soil moisture is crucial for sustaining plant hydration and physiological processes. Additionally, organic matter acts as a reservoir for essential nutrients, gradually releasing them into the soil as plants require, thereby fostering nutrient availability for optimal plant nutrition.

Moreover, organic matter plays a pivotal role in improving soil structure across all soil types. In clay soils, organic matter helps to alleviate compaction and improve aeration, facilitating root penetration and growth. On the other hand, in sandy soils, organic matter acts as a binding agent, enhancing soil aggregation and water retention. By enhancing soil structure, organic matter promotes better root development and nutrient uptake, ultimately contributing to healthier and more resilient plants.

Furthermore, organic matter promotes improved drainage in heavy soils by enhancing soil porosity and permeability. This mitigates issues associated with waterlogging and facilitates excess water drainage, reducing the risk of root rot and other water-related plant diseases. Additionally, the presence of organic matter fosters the proliferation of earthworms and beneficial microorganisms in the soil, which play integral roles in nutrient cycling, soil aeration, and pest regulation.

In essence, the incorporation of organic matter into soil serves as a multifaceted approach to soil improvement, addressing various soil deficiencies and promoting overall soil health. By harnessing the benefits of organic matter, gardeners and farmers can create an optimal growing environment that supports vigorous plant growth, resilience to environmental stresses, and sustainable agricultural practices.

Maintaining soil health and vitality requires a delicate balance of various soil organisms, each playing unique roles in the soil ecosystem. Earthworms, often regarded as nature's engineers, are crucial contributors to soil health due to their tunnelling activities and role in decomposing organic matter. These humble creatures aerate the soil as they tunnel through it, facilitating the movement of air, water, and nutrients to plant roots. Moreover, earthworms feed on decomposing organic matter, breaking it down into nutrient-rich castings that enrich the soil, promoting fertility and overall soil health. While earthworms are invaluable allies in soil management, their presence alone does not guarantee optimal soil health.

In addition to earthworms, a diverse array of soil organisms, including Springtails, Ants, Centipedes, and Flatworms, contribute to the overall health and vitality of the soil ecosystem. Each of these organisms plays a unique role in nutrient cycling, soil structure formation, and pest regulation, collectively contributing to the resilience and functionality of the soil ecosystem. Springtails, for example, help decompose organic matter and improve soil aeration, while ants aid in soil mixing and nutrient distribution through their tunnelling activities. Centipedes and flatworms also contribute to nutrient cycling and soil structure enhancement, albeit through different mechanisms.

The presence of mushrooms in the garden or compost is often a sign of a healthy soil ecosystem. Mushrooms, the fruiting bodies of fungi, play a vital role in breaking down woody material and organic matter, thereby facilitating nutrient recycling and soil organic matter decomposition. Fungi are integral components of the soil food web, forming symbiotic relationships with plant roots and contributing to soil aggregation, nutrient uptake, and disease suppression. The presence of mushrooms indicates a thriving fungal community in the soil, which is essential for maintaining soil health and fertility.

Ultimately, the key to fostering a healthy soil ecosystem lies in continuous soil improvement practices. By incorporating organic matter, practicing crop rotation, minimizing tillage, and avoiding the excessive use of synthetic fertilizers and pesticides, gardeners and farmers can create conducive environments for beneficial soil organisms to thrive. As soil health improves, the diversity and abundance of beneficial soil organisms, including earthworms, microbes, and fungi, will naturally increase, further enhancing soil fertility, structure, and resilience. Therefore, by nurturing a harmonious balance of soil organisms, gardeners can promote sustainable soil management practices and cultivate vibrant, productive gardens and agricultural landscapes.

Soil composition plays a critical role in determining the health and productivity of plants, as different soil types possess distinct characteristics that impact water retention, nutrient availability, aeration, and workability. Understanding the various soil types and their properties is essential for effective soil management and plant growth.

Sandy soils are characterized by their large particle size and substantial pore spaces between particles. These soils drain water rapidly, making them well-aerated and easy to cultivate. Due to their light texture, sandy soils are often preferred for their workability. However, their porous nature means they struggle to retain water and nutrients, posing challenges for plant growth. Improving sandy soils typically involves enhancing their water and nutrient retention capacity through the addition of organic matter and soil amendments.

On the opposite end of the spectrum are clay soils, composed of fine particles with minimal pore spaces. Clay soils exhibit excellent water retention properties, holding moisture and nutrients effectively. However, their dense structure hinders drainage and aeration, leading to issues such as waterlogging and compaction. Improving clay soils often involves enhancing drainage and aeration through practices like soil amendment with organic matter, gypsum application to alleviate compaction, and proper soil management techniques to prevent waterlogging.

Loam soils represent a balance between sandy and clay soils, consisting of a mixture of coarse and fine particles. These soils are highly versatile and offer optimal water retention, drainage, and nutrient availability for plant growth. Sandy loam, with a higher proportion of sand, tends to be well-draining but may require additional organic matter to improve nutrient retention. Conversely, clay loam, with a higher clay content, may benefit from amendments to enhance drainage and prevent compaction. Improving loam soils typically involves maintaining their balanced composition through regular soil testing, organic matter addition, and proper irrigation and fertilization practices.

Identifying the soil type in a garden or agricultural field can be done through simple observations of its physical properties. Sandy soils feel coarse and gritty, do not stick together, and are easily crumbled. In contrast, clay soils feel sticky and plastic, with a tendency to form hard clumps when dry. Loam soils exhibit intermediate characteristics, displaying good crumbliness and moderate stickiness. Understanding the characteristics of different soil types allows gardeners and farmers to tailor their soil management practices to optimize plant growth and productivity, ensuring healthy and thriving landscapes.

Improving sandy soil is crucial for enhancing its ability to retain water and nutrients, thereby fostering better conditions for plant growth and health. Sandy soil, while easy to work with due to its coarse texture and good drainage, often struggles with water retention and nutrient deficiencies. Fortunately, several strategies can be employed to improve sandy soil and make it more conducive to plant growth.

One effective method to improve sandy soil is by incorporating organic matter. Organic matter, such as compost, well-rotted manure, or leaf mold, can significantly enhance the soil's water-holding capacity and nutrient retention. When organic matter is mixed into sandy soil, it helps to bind the particles together, reducing pore spaces and preventing water from draining too quickly. Additionally, organic matter serves as a reservoir for essential nutrients, releasing them gradually to plants as they decompose, thereby enriching the soil fertility.

Another approach to improving sandy soil is through the addition of soil amendments. Substances like peat moss, coco coir, or vermiculite can be mixed into sandy soil to enhance its water retention capabilities. These amendments act as sponges, absorbing and holding moisture within the soil, thereby reducing the risk of water runoff and allowing plants more time to access water. Additionally, soil amendments can improve soil structure by increasing its ability to hold onto nutrients, promoting healthier root growth and overall plant development.

Furthermore, incorporating clay-based materials into sandy soil can help improve its water and nutrient retention. Clay particles have a smaller size than sand particles and can effectively bind together to form aggregates, thereby reducing pore spaces and increasing water retention. Adding clay-based amendments, such as bentonite clay or kaolin clay, to sandy soil can help improve its structure and water-holding capacity over time. However, it's essential to monitor the application rates carefully to avoid over-amending the soil and creating unfavourable conditions for plant growth.

In addition to organic matter and soil amendments, practicing proper soil management techniques is crucial for improving sandy soil. Mulching the soil surface with organic materials, such as wood chips or straw, can help conserve moisture, regulate soil temperature, and prevent erosion. Regularly incorporating organic matter into the soil through composting or cover cropping can also contribute to long-term soil improvement. Furthermore, practicing crop rotation and diversifying plant species can help replenish soil nutrients and prevent nutrient depletion over time.

Improving clay soil presents a unique set of challenges due to its dense, compacted nature, which often leads to poor drainage and aeration. However, with the right strategies, clay soil can be transformed into a more hospitable environment for plants to thrive. Several approaches can be employed to improve clay soil, each targeting different aspects of soil structure and fertility.

One effective method for improving clay soil is by incorporating organic matter. Organic materials such as compost, well-rotted manure, or leaf mold can help break up clay particles, improve soil structure, and increase its water-holding capacity. When organic matter is added to clay soil, it acts as a sponge, absorbing excess water during wet periods and releasing it slowly during dry spells. Additionally, organic matter provides essential nutrients to plants as it decomposes, thereby enhancing soil fertility and promoting healthy root development.

Furthermore, incorporating soil amendments can help alleviate the compacted nature of clay soil and improve its drainage and aeration. Adding materials like gypsum, perlite, or coarse sand can help break up clay particles, reduce compaction, and create channels for water and air to penetrate the soil. Gypsum, in particular, can be beneficial for clay soils with high levels of sodium, as it helps to displace sodium ions and improve soil structure. However, it's essential to use soil amendments judiciously and follow recommended application rates to avoid over-amending the soil.

Another approach to improving clay soil is through mechanical cultivation techniques such as tilling or double digging. These methods involve loosening the soil to break up compacted layers, improve soil structure, and promote better root penetration. However, it's important to exercise caution when tilling clay soil, as excessive cultivation can lead to further compaction and soil degradation over time. Instead, focus on aerating the soil gently and incorporating organic matter into the top few inches to encourage beneficial soil biology and improve soil health.

In addition to organic matter and soil amendments, implementing proper soil management practices is essential for long-term clay soil improvement. For example, practicing minimum tillage techniques and avoiding heavy machinery on wet soil can help prevent compaction and preserve soil structure. Implementing cover crops or green manures can also help improve soil fertility, prevent erosion, and add organic matter to the soil over time. Furthermore, rotating crops and diversifying plant species can help break pest and disease cycles, reduce soil erosion, and maintain soil health.

Soil pH plays a crucial role in plant health and growth, as it directly affects the availability of essential nutrients in the soil. Understanding soil pH is essential for gardeners and farmers to provide optimal conditions for their plants. The pH scale ranges from 1 to 14, with values below 7 considered acidic and those above 7 considered alkaline. A pH of 7 is considered neutral. Most plants thrive in soil with a slightly acidic to neutral pH range of 6.5 to 7.5. However, soil pH outside this range can lead to nutrient deficiencies or toxicities, adversely affecting plant growth and development.

Testing soil pH is the first step in determining its acidity or alkalinity level. Soil pH test kits are readily available and provide a simple way to measure soil pH. It's essential to collect soil samples from different areas of the garden to ensure accurate results, as pH can vary significantly within a single property. Once the soil pH is determined, appropriate measures can be taken to adjust it to the desired level.

For soils with pH levels below 6.0, commonly referred to as acidic soil, the aim is to increase pH and make the soil more alkaline. One effective method to correct acidic soil is by applying lime or dolomite. Lime, usually in the form of calcium carbonate, helps raise soil pH by neutralizing acidity. Dolomite, which contains both calcium carbonate and magnesium carbonate, serves a similar purpose but also provides magnesium to the soil. Products like Yates Hydrangea Pinking Liquid Lime & Dolomite offer a convenient way to apply these amendments to the soil. It's recommended to apply lime or dolomite every 3-4 weeks until the desired pH level is achieved.

It's important to note that while adjusting soil pH, gardeners should consider the specific requirements of the plants they intend to grow. Some plants, known as acid-loving plants, prefer slightly acidic soil conditions with pH levels ranging from 5 to 6.5. Examples of acid-loving plants include azaleas, camellias, rhododendrons, and blueberries. For these plants, maintaining a slightly acidic soil pH is crucial for optimal growth and flowering. Gardeners should take care not to raise the soil pH excessively, as it may negatively impact the health and performance of acid-loving plants.

Soil drainage is a critical factor that significantly influences plant health and growth. Adequate drainage ensures that excess water can move away from the root zone, preventing waterlogging and the associated problems such as root rot and reduced oxygen availability in the soil. While some plants may tolerate wet conditions, most plants thrive in well-drained soil. The importance of soil drainage becomes particularly evident in heavy clay soils, which are prone to poor drainage due to their fine particle size and tendency to compact.

Heavy clay soils present a particular challenge when it comes to drainage. Their tightly packed particles restrict water movement, leading to water pooling on the soil surface and slow infiltration rates. As a result, plant roots may suffocate due to waterlogged conditions, and soil-borne diseases may proliferate in the waterlogged environment. In contrast, sandy soils, with their larger particle size and better aeration, generally have superior drainage properties compared to clay soils.

To improve soil drainage and create a more hospitable environment for plants, various strategies can be employed. One approach is to incorporate organic matter into the soil, such as compost or well-rotted manure, to enhance soil structure and porosity. Organic matter improves soil drainage by increasing soil aggregation, which creates larger pore spaces for water to drain freely through the soil profile. Products like Yates Dynamic Lifter, a rich source of organic matter, can be incorporated into the soil to improve its structure and drainage capacity.

In addition to organic amendments, other techniques can be employed to address drainage issues effectively. Raised beds offer a practical solution, particularly in areas with poorly drained soil. By elevating the planting area above ground level and filling it with free-draining soil, raised beds provide optimal growing conditions for plants while avoiding the challenges associated with waterlogged soil. Raised mounds of good quality soil can also be created for planting trees and shrubs, ensuring adequate drainage around their root systems.

For more complex drainage problems, such as persistent waterlogging or areas prone to flooding, additional measures may be necessary. Installing drainage channels or trenches can help divert excess water away from the soil and prevent water build-up. These drainage systems are designed to facilitate the efficient removal of excess water, ensuring that plant roots remain healthy and oxygenated even during periods of heavy rainfall or irrigation.

Chapter Sixteen

ERECTING TIMBER STRUCTURES AND FEATURES

Timber stands out as a versatile material for garden and landscaping projects, offering both functionality and aesthetic appeal. Its natural appearance allows it to seamlessly blend with the surrounding environment, enhancing the beauty of outdoor spaces while serving practical purposes. Whether used to construct decks, screens, bench seats, pergolas, or retaining walls, timber garden features can become focal points that elevate the overall design of a landscape.

Combining different timber species, including both hardwoods and softwoods, can create visually stunning effects while adding texture and warmth to outdoor areas. The varied tones and grain patterns of different wood types contribute to a natural, inviting atmosphere, allowing outdoor spaces to harmonize with existing architectural elements and the surrounding landscape. Timber structures have the unique ability to integrate outdoor rooms with indoor living spaces, extending the functional and aesthetic qualities of a home into the garden.

One of the most popular timber structures in garden design is the deck, which serves as a versatile outdoor living space. Whether used for relaxation, entertaining guests, or enjoying the poolside ambiance, a well-designed deck enhances the outdoor lifestyle. Sunken decks, built slightly below ground level, offer a unique seating area that adds depth and character to the garden, creating inviting spaces for relaxation and socializing.

Figure 249: A raised wood decking with outdoor furniture. Acabashi, CC BY-SA 4.0, via Wikimedia Commons.

Timber screens provide practical solutions for concealing unsightly areas, creating privacy, or defining separate zones within outdoor spaces. These screens can serve as decorative features, highlighting plants or water features, while also serving functional purposes such as hiding fences or storage areas. Bench seating made from timber not only offers comfortable seating options but also adds visual interest to garden design, with many benches providing additional storage space for cushions and accessories.

Retaining walls constructed from timber sleepers or poles offer effective solutions for managing slopes and creating terraced garden beds. These walls provide structural support while adding rustic charm and texture to the landscape. However, it's essential to consider factors such as bushfire risk when using timber in outdoor structures, particularly in regions prone to wildfires. Selecting fire-resistant timber species and adhering to building regulations can help mitigate potential risks and ensure the safety of timber garden features.

In summary, timber garden features play a vital role in landscape design, offering versatility, warmth, and aesthetic appeal to outdoor spaces. By incorporating timber structures into garden projects, homeowners can create functional, visually pleasing environments that complement their lifestyle and enhance the beauty of their surroundings. Whether used for relaxation, entertainment, or practical purposes, timber remains a timeless choice for landscaping projects, adding natural beauty and charm to outdoor living spaces.

A pergola serves as an elegant outdoor structure designed to provide both aesthetic appeal and functional utility. Comprising columns that support a roofing grid of beams and rafters, pergolas can be open-air or covered, offering shelter from the elements while still allowing for an open, airy ambiance. These structures can vary in size and design, ranging from freestanding installations to those attached to a house, seamlessly blending indoor and outdoor living spaces.

To better understand what distinguishes a pergola from other similar outdoor structures, it's helpful to compare it with arbors, gazebos, trellises, lattice, and carports. While arbors share similarities with pergolas, such as supporting vines and providing a sheltered space, they typically feature simpler designs and smaller dimensions. Arbors often boast curved arches and are freestanding, lacking the architectural flourishes and larger scale commonly associated with pergolas.

In contrast, gazebos are fully enclosed structures with raised floors and rounded shapes, offering a more substantial sheltered space compared to pergolas. Carports, on the other hand, are primarily designed for vehicle storage, featuring a roof supported by posts, although some may resemble pergolas in design.

Pergolas have a long history rooted in architectural traditions, with origins dating back to grand masonry structures of the Italian Renaissance. While traditional pergolas feature flat tops and may incorporate masonry columns, modern interpretations often utilize wood construction and can be attached to houses, creating seamless extensions of indoor living areas into outdoor environments. Landscape architects may distinguish pergolas from arbors by noting that pergolas form a "colonnade" with their columns, creating a linear structure over garden pathways.

One of the defining features of pergolas is their ability to support vines, creating lush green canopies that offer shade and enhance the natural beauty of outdoor spaces. Vines such as Dutchman's pipe, Virginia creeper, and wisteria thrive when trained to climb pergola structures, providing shade and visual interest. While some homeowners prefer open-air pergolas with vines covering the roofing grid, others opt for covered designs, utilizing materials like fiberglass or retractable shade canopies to provide complete shade and protection from rain.

Figure 250: Hard-Top pergola. Aleš Pajek, CC BY-SA 4.0, via Wikimedia Commons.

Arbors and pergolas are both charming landscaping structures that add character and functionality to outdoor spaces, but they possess distinct characteristics that set them apart. While they share similarities in their purpose and design, such as providing shade and supporting climbing plants, understanding the subtle differences between the two can help homeowners make informed decisions when selecting the right structure for their gardens.

Figure 251: The rose arbor on the grounds of Bland Cottage. Richardelainechambers at en.wikipedia, Public domain, via Wikimedia Commons.

Garden arbors, in essence, are simpler and more modest in scale compared to pergolas. These structures often lack elaborate architectural details like masonry columns and are typically smaller in size. One of the defining features of arbors is their curved arches at the top, which lend them a romantic and whimsical aesthetic. Traditionally, arbors were crafted from wood or metal, but modern variations are increasingly being made from materials like vinyl, offering durability and low maintenance.

Unlike pergolas, which may be attached to a house or serve as extensions of indoor living spaces, arbors are freestanding structures. They are commonly found as standalone features in gardens, parks, and outdoor pathways, serving as focal points or entryways. While arbors are not usually affixed to buildings, they may be attached to fences, particularly when serving as gateways to delineate entrances or pathways within a garden.

The simplicity and versatility of garden arbors make them popular choices for homeowners seeking to add a touch of elegance and charm to their outdoor landscapes. Whether adorned with climbing roses, wisteria, or other flowering vines, arbors create picturesque passageways and provide a sense of enclosure while maintaining an open, airy feel. With their timeless appeal and understated beauty, arbors continue to be cherished elements of garden design, inviting visitors to wander through enchanting outdoor spaces filled with natural beauty and tranquillity.

The gazebo, another outdoor wooden structure closely related to pergolas, serves a distinct purpose and possesses unique features that set it apart. Unlike pergolas, gazebos are characterized by their closed roofs, providing complete shelter from the elements. This enclosed design offers protection from rain, sun, and wind, creating a cosy and intimate outdoor space for relaxation and entertainment. While pergolas typically have an open-roof design that allows for partial shade and ventilation, gazebos offer a more enclosed environment, making them ideal for various outdoor activities regardless of the weather.

In addition to their closed roofs, gazebos often feature other distinguishing characteristics that differentiate them from pergolas. Many gazebos have raised floors, elevating the structure above ground level and providing a defined platform for seating, dining, or socializing. This raised design not only enhances the aesthetic appeal of the gazebo but also helps to keep the interior space clean and dry, especially during wet weather conditions. Furthermore, gazebos commonly have a rounded shape, with curved or domed roofs that add elegance and architectural interest to the structure. This distinctive shape sets gazebos apart from the more linear and open design of pergolas, contributing to their unique charm and appeal.

Figure 252: Gazebo. Chris Light, CC BY-SA 4.0, via Wikimedia Commons.

While both gazebos and pergolas serve as outdoor structures for enhancing the beauty and functionality of outdoor spaces, they cater to different needs and preferences. Gazebos offer a fully enclosed and sheltered environment, making them ideal for intimate gatherings, outdoor dining, or relaxing in comfort. In contrast, pergolas provide a partially shaded and open-air space that allows for greater ventilation and interaction with the surrounding landscape. Each structure offers its own set of benefits and design possibilities, allowing homeowners to create personalized outdoor retreats that suit their lifestyle and preferences.

Another outdoor structure mentioned in relation to pergolas is the carport, which serves a practical purpose rather than solely focusing on aesthetics or leisure. Unlike gazebos and pergolas, which are primarily designed for outdoor living and entertainment, carports are intended to provide shelter for vehicles, protecting them from the elements and minimizing exposure to harsh weather conditions. While the basic design of a carport typically consists of a roof supported by posts, some homeowners may opt for more elaborate carport designs that resemble pergolas in appearance. These carports combine functionality with aesthetic appeal, offering a stylish solution for car storage while complementing the overall design of the outdoor space.

Planning and Preparing the Workspace

The construction process initiates with a thorough understanding of the project requirements, often conveyed through a set of drawings. These drawings serve as a blueprint, guiding the construction process by illustrating the desired outcome and specifications. It is essential for workers to carefully read and interpret these drawings to comprehend the intricacies of the job. Additionally, site inspection plays a crucial role in identifying specific job requirements, especially in restoration projects where the existing structure needs to be preserved or matched. Through on-site assessment, workers can gain valuable insights into the scope of work and ensure that the new construction aligns seamlessly with the original structure.

Instructions for the construction process can manifest in various formats, including written documents or verbal communication from supervisors or project managers. Regardless of the format, it is imperative to extract all pertinent information necessary for the successful completion of the project. This includes understanding the nature of the work to be performed, the location of the work site, required materials, tools, equipment, and the construction sequence.

Determining the type of work to be done is paramount as it dictates the approach and preparations needed for the construction process. Whether it involves constructing partition walls or installing fixtures, comprehending the scope of work enables workers to plan effectively and allocate resources accordingly. Similarly, understanding the work site's location, whether onsite or offsite, is essential for logistical planning, including material delivery, equipment access, and utility requirements such as electricity and water supply.

Furthermore, identifying the materials required for the job is crucial for procurement and logistical planning. Workers must ascertain the types, dimensions, and quantities of materials needed to execute the construction tasks efficiently. Similarly, understanding the requisite tools and equipment ensures that workers are adequately equipped to handle various aspects of the construction process, from measuring and marking to shaping and cutting materials.

Understanding the construction sequence is pivotal for organizing tasks and optimizing workflow. By delineating the sequence of activities involved in the project, workers can strategically plan tool placement, material stacking, and task execution to streamline operations and minimize downtime. Additionally, awareness of other tradespeople or contractors working on-site is essential for coordinating activities, avoiding conflicts, and ensuring a safe working environment. Factors such as shared access to resources, potential hazards, and logistical challenges must be considered to facilitate smooth collaboration and project execution.

Handling, stacking, and storing materials are critical aspects of construction logistics that require careful consideration to ensure efficiency, safety, and the preservation of materials. When handling building materials, several factors must be taken into account to minimize the risk of injury and damage. Firstly, understanding the size, shape, weight, and nature of the load is essential for determining the appropriate lifting and carrying techniques. Workers need to assess whether they can safely lift and transport the materials without straining themselves or risking injury.

Moreover, the route taken to transport materials must be evaluated to identify potential hazards and obstacles. Factors such as slippery surfaces, trip hazards, narrow passages, stairs, and elevators can impede the safe movement of materials. Workers must ensure that the pathway is clear and free from obstructions to facilitate smooth material handling. Additionally, considering the physical capabilities of workers, including their size, strength, and age, is crucial for assigning tasks and determining the appropriate workload to prevent overexertion or injury.

Once materials are received at the construction site, proper stacking and storage procedures must be implemented to maintain their integrity and prevent damage. Designating a specific storage area for materials helps organize the site and facilitates easy access during construction. When stacking materials, particularly timber, it is essential to provide even support and elevation to prevent bowing, sagging, or contact with the ground, which can compromise their structural integrity. In cases of extreme weather conditions, such as rain or heat, protective measures like wrapping or covering materials with plastic or canvas sheeting may be necessary to prevent deterioration.

Furthermore, the organization of stacked materials plays a vital role in optimizing workflow and efficiency on the construction site. Grouping materials according to type and length facilitates easy selection and distribution during the construction process. By separating timbers needed for different components into distinct stacks, workers can quickly access the required materials without unnecessary delays or confusion. Implementing systematic storage and stacking practices not only enhances productivity but also minimizes the risk of errors and material wastage, contributing to overall project success.

Measuring and marking off are fundamental processes in construction, crucial for ensuring accuracy and precision in the assembly of structural components. Plans and specifications provide detailed instructions regarding partition framing components, including measurements and the quantity of materials required, such as top and bottom plates, studs, and noggings. Before proceeding with construction, a pattern stud is set out, with all stud and nogging sizes marked for reference.

To prepare materials for cutting and assembly, marking off is essential. This involves accurately delineating the dimensions on the timber components using measuring tools such as steel retractable measuring tapes, folding rules, T-squares, or combination squares. The choice of tool depends on the specific requirements of the task and the preferences of the worker. These tools provide the necessary precision for marking out lengths, angles, and other specifications outlined in the construction plans.

When commencing the setting out process, selecting the best timber is paramount to ensure structural integrity and aesthetic appeal. Workers rely on visual inspection to identify straight and flat surfaces, using their line of sight along the surface edges to assess the timber's quality. Top plates, in particular, must be chosen from the straightest lengths available, while bottom plates can be straightened during installation.

The most commonly used tools for measuring and marking off are steel retractable measuring tapes and carpenter's pencils. These tools offer versatility and accuracy, making them indispensable for various tasks on the construction site. Measuring tapes provide precise measurements, while carpenter's pencils allow for clear and visible marking on timber surfaces. Together, these tools enable workers to execute the marking off process efficiently and accurately, laying the groundwork for successful construction projects.

Wood Materials

Hardwood and softwood are terms used to classify different types of trees based on their botanical characteristics, wood structure, and various properties. Despite the common misconception that hardwoods are necessarily harder than softwoods, the distinction between the two is primarily based on their reproduction, rather than the actual hardness of the wood.

One of the primary differences between hardwoods and softwoods lies in their botanical origins. Hardwoods are derived from angiosperm trees, which are characterized by seeds enclosed within fruits or nuts. These trees typically shed their leaves annually and are known for their broad, flat leaves. Examples of hardwood trees include oak, maple, mahogany, and cherry. Softwoods, on the other hand, originate from gymnosperm trees, which typically bear cones and have needle-like or scale-like leaves. Softwood trees, such as pine, cedar, spruce, and fir, often retain their needles year-round.

In terms of wood structure, hardwoods generally have a more complex cellular arrangement compared to softwoods. Hardwoods typically have vessels or pores in their structure, which are visible to the naked eye and contribute to their characteristic grain patterns. The presence of vessels gives hardwoods their distinctive appearance and contributes to their overall density. Softwoods, on the other hand, lack vessels and instead have simpler structures composed mainly of longitudinal cells called tracheids. This structural difference contributes to the varying physical and mechanical properties of hardwoods and softwoods.

The physical properties of hardwoods and softwoods differ significantly due to their distinct cellular structures. Hardwoods are typically denser and heavier than softwoods, making them well-suited for applications requiring strength and durability. Hardwoods also tend to have higher resistance to wear, abrasion, and decay, making them ideal for furniture, flooring, cabinetry, and other high-quality woodworking projects. In contrast, softwoods are generally lighter and less dense, with lower resistance to wear and decay. Softwoods are commonly used in construction, framing, outdoor decking, and pulp and paper production.

Another important distinction between hardwoods and softwoods lies in their growth rates and ecological characteristics. Hardwood trees tend to grow more slowly and are often found in temperate regions with distinct seasonal changes. Softwood trees, on the other hand, typically grow faster and are abundant in boreal and temperate forests. The rapid growth rate of softwoods makes them a more sustainable and cost-effective choice for various commercial applications, such as timber production and construction.

While hardwoods and softwoods differ in their botanical origins, wood structure, physical properties, and ecological characteristics, both types of wood have unique qualities that make them valuable resources in construction, woodworking, and various other industries. Understanding the differences between hardwoods and softwoods is essential for selecting the appropriate material for specific applications based on factors such as strength, durability, appearance, and environmental sustainability.

Below are some examples of hardwood and softwood species from various regions around the world:

Hardwoods:

- **Oak (Quercus spp.):** Found throughout North America, Europe, and Asia, oak is valued for its strength, durability, and attractive grain patterns. It is commonly used in furniture making, flooring, and cabinetry.

- **Mahogany (Swietenia spp.):** Native to tropical regions of the Americas, mahogany is prized for its rich reddish-brown colour and excellent workability. It is often used in high-quality furniture, musical instruments, and boat building.

- **Teak (Tectona grandis):** Native to Southeast Asia, particularly India, Myanmar, and Indonesia, teak is highly durable and resistant to decay, making it ideal for outdoor furniture, boat decks, and construction.

- **Cherry (Prunus avium):** Found in North America, Europe, and parts of Asia, cherry wood is known for its warm colour and fine grain. It is commonly used in cabinetry, fine furniture, and woodworking projects.

- **Maple (Acer spp.):** Native to North America, Europe, and Asia, maple wood is prized for its strength, hardness, and attractive grain patterns. It is used in furniture making, flooring, and musical instruments.

Softwoods:

- **Pine (Pinus spp.):** Widely distributed across North America, Europe, and Asia, pine is one of the most common softwoods used in construction. It is valued for its affordability, ease of workability, and versatility. Pine is used for framing, flooring, panelling, and furniture.

- **Spruce (Picea spp.):** Native to northern temperate regions, spruce is known for its strength, straight grain, and light colour. It is commonly used in construction, particularly for framing, sheathing, and millwork.

- **Cedar (Cedrus spp.):** Found in various regions around the world, including North America, Europe, and Asia, cedar wood is prized for its natural resistance to decay and insects. It is often used for outdoor applications such as siding, decking, and fencing.

- **Fir (Abies spp.):** Native to temperate regions of the Northern Hemisphere, fir wood is valued for its strength, stiffness, and light weight. It is commonly used in construction for framing, sheathing, and interior finishing.

- **Douglas Fir (Pseudotsuga menziesii):** Native to western North America, Douglas fir is one of the most important softwood species in the region. It is used in construction for framing, flooring, and plywood production, as well as in woodworking projects.

Radiata Pine (Pinus radiata): Radiata pine, also known as Monterey pine, is a large softwood originating from the west coast of North America and Canada. It has become widely grown around the world, including in places like South Africa, South America, New Zealand, Spain, Italy, and India. Introduced to Australia during the gold rush days of the 1850s, radiata pine features a pale yellow to brown colour with darker areas due to its high resin content. Despite being a softwood, it tends to be rather hard and is fairly lightweight, making it easy to nail. Radiata pine is plantation-grown and regenerates quickly after harvesting. It is versatile, used in residential wall and roof framing, furniture, mouldings, plywood, particleboard, fibreboard, and paper production. Treated with preservatives like Copper Chromium Arsenic (CCA), it can be used for outdoor applications like posts, cladding, and landscaping.

Figure 253: Pinus radiata, Huckleberry Hill, Monterey, California. RyanGWU82 at Flickr, CC BY 2.0, via Wikimedia Commons.

Douglas Fir (Pseudotsuga menziesii): Also known as Oregon, Douglas fir is a commonly grown native softwood of North America, with small plantations in New Zealand and Australia. It features a pale yellow-brown to pale reddish-brown colour that darkens with age. Despite its versatility, it is not very durable and tends to crack and become brittle over time, especially in hot roof spaces. Surprisingly dense for a softwood, it has an average density of around 530 kg/m³. Douglas fir has been widely used for structural framing, joinery, door and window frames, cupboard frames, and boat building. However, its poor durability rating (Class 4) and higher cost compared to alternatives like radiata pine have led to a decline in its extensive use.

Figure 254: Douglas fir growing at the top of the Triple Tree trail, Gallatin Range, Gallatin County, Montana. Matt Lavin, CC BY-SA 2.0, via Wikimedia Commons.

Cypress Pine (Callitris glauca): Cypress pine, specifically the white variety, is a small to medium-sized softwood grown in inland areas of New South Wales (NSW) and Queensland, Australia. It features a pale yellow sapwood and variegated brown heartwood with a striped appearance and distinctive knots. Cypress pine is known for its hardness and density, with an average density of around 680 kg/m^3. Slow-growing, taking approximately 50 years to mature to a height of 10m, cypress pine is highly durable (Class 1) and naturally resistant to termite attacks. It finds application in tongue and groove flooring boards, weatherboard cladding, timber framing, decking, posts, poles, and panelling.

Figure 255: Callitris columellaris (syn. C. glauca; White Cypress-pine), Lightning Ridge, NSW. Cgoodwin, CC BY-SA 3.0, via Wikimedia Commons.

Western Red Cedar (Thuja plicata): Native to North America and British Columbia, western red cedar is a large softwood imported into Australia. It should not be confused with Australian red cedar, which is a hardwood. Featuring a variety of colours ranging from pale cream/brown to dark brown, it has a distinct odour that becomes evident when worked. Despite its softness and lightweight nature, with an average density of around 350 kg/m^3, it has a fairly good durability rating (Class 2). Western red cedar is used for weatherboards, roof shingles, window and door frames, wall linings, joinery, outdoor furniture, and other applications.

Figure 256: Thuja plicata experimental forest in Rogów Arboretum, Poland. Crusier, CC BY-SA 3.0, via Wikimedia Commons.

These examples illustrate the diverse range of timbers available for various construction and woodworking purposes, each with its unique characteristics, uses, and regional availability.

Timber, as a building material, is a versatile resource derived from trees, primarily composed of cellulose, hemicellulose, extractives, and lignin. Trees, the source of timber, are classified into two main groups: softwoods and hardwoods. Softwoods, also known as conifers, are older and simpler in structure, comprising around 600 species worldwide. Hardwoods, evolved from softwoods, have a more complex structure and encompass thousands of species, some of which have been transported to various regions by early explorers. This broad classification enables the utilization of timber from a diverse range of tree species, including those like eucalyptus found in Australia and even in distant places like Portugal.

Old growth forests, characterized by naturally occurring diverse species, have existed for thousands of years, with some trees reaching ages exceeding three hundred years. These forests rely on natural processes like fire, wind, and animals for regeneration and seed dispersal. However, logging in old growth forests often involves the use of heavy machinery, leading to habitat destruction, soil erosion, and the displacement or extinction of indigenous flora and fauna. Sustainable logging in old-growth forests necessitates meticulous planning to minimize ecological impact, a challenging endeavour due to the intricacies of forest ecosystems.

In contrast, plantation forests are artificially cultivated, with trees grown from seedlings in controlled conditions. These forests are characterized by neat, evenly spaced rows of trees, facilitating efficient harvesting and maximizing yield. Fast-growing species like Radiata pine and Hoop pine are commonly planted, offering a sustainable alternative to logging old growth forests.

The managed growth and harvesting in plantation forests result in a renewable timber resource with reduced environmental impact and lower production costs.

The availability, cost-effectiveness, and characteristics of specific softwood and hardwood species make them popular choices for various construction and finishing applications. Softwood species like Radiata pine, Hoop pine, and Slash pine are favoured for their quick regeneration and suitability for construction. Hardwood species, prized for their durability and aesthetic appeal, are often used for finishing and fixing out timber in cottage construction.

Timber remains a valuable building material, offering a renewable and environmentally friendly alternative to traditional construction materials. Sustainable practices in both old-growth and plantation forests are essential to ensure the long-term viability of timber as a building resource while preserving natural ecosystems.

Conversion of Timber

Sawn timber represents the initial stage in the manufacturing process of timber products. It involves the conversion of raw logs into roughly squared pieces suitable for further processing. This conversion is typically achieved using large circular breakdown saws or band saws, which cut through the logs to create individual timber pieces. Sawing is preferably conducted soon after the tree has been felled, as freshly cut or "green" timber is easier to saw compared to seasoned wood. Sawn timber is usually cut to nominal sizes, such as 25mm, 50mm, or 100mm, though slight variations in dimensions may occur.

Following sawing, timber may undergo the process of dressing. Dressed timber refers to wood that has been passed through a planning machine, such as a jointer or thicknesser, to smoothen one or more of its surfaces. This planning process results in a reduction of the nominal sizes of the timber pieces. For instance, a piece of timber with a nominal size of 25mm may be planed to a finished size of 19mm, while a 50mm nominal piece may be planed down to 42mm, and so forth. Dressing not only enhances the aesthetic appeal of the timber but also ensures uniformity in thickness, facilitating its use in construction and woodworking applications.

Milled timber represents the next stage in the manufacturing process and involves the refinement of timber surfaces to achieve specific decorative or functional characteristics. This process typically utilizes milling or moulding machines equipped with various cutting heads and profiles. Milled timber may exhibit features such as tongue and groove edges for interlocking joints, fluted or grooved faces for decorative purposes, classical moulded edges for architectural embellishments, rebates for joining or framing, and changes in shape such as quads or cavettos for aesthetic enhancements. By milling timber, manufacturers can create a diverse range of profiles and finishes tailored to the requirements of different applications, including flooring, panelling, mouldings, and furniture components.

Overall, these manufacturing terms—sawn timber, dressed timber, and milled timber—represent sequential stages in the transformation of raw logs into refined timber products. Each stage involves specific processes aimed at enhancing the usability, appearance, and functionality of the timber, catering to the diverse needs of construction, manufacturing, and design industries. By understanding these terms and processes, stakeholders in the timber industry can effectively navigate the production chain and select products that meet their desired specifications and standards.

Conversion is a critical process in timber production, involving the sawing of logs into marketable sizes. Ideally, this should be done soon after felling to minimize the loss of usable timber due to end splitting. While the primary objective is to maximize recovery, timber can be cut to suit specific needs within a structure. For instance, finishing timbers may be cut to highlight the natural attributes of the grain, while structural timber may prioritize producing long grains to minimize shrinkage.

Various methods are employed in log conversion, each with its advantages and limitations. Live sawing, for example, yields a large number of wide boards but can pose challenges in controlling shrinkage and warping due to the diverse end grain shapes produced. Back sawing, another common method, results in boards with relatively straight grain on the edge and the best figure on the face, though end grain appears as a series of arcs. Quarter sawing, while producing fewer usable boards, offers straight grain on the edge and face, with short end grain arcs across the thickness.

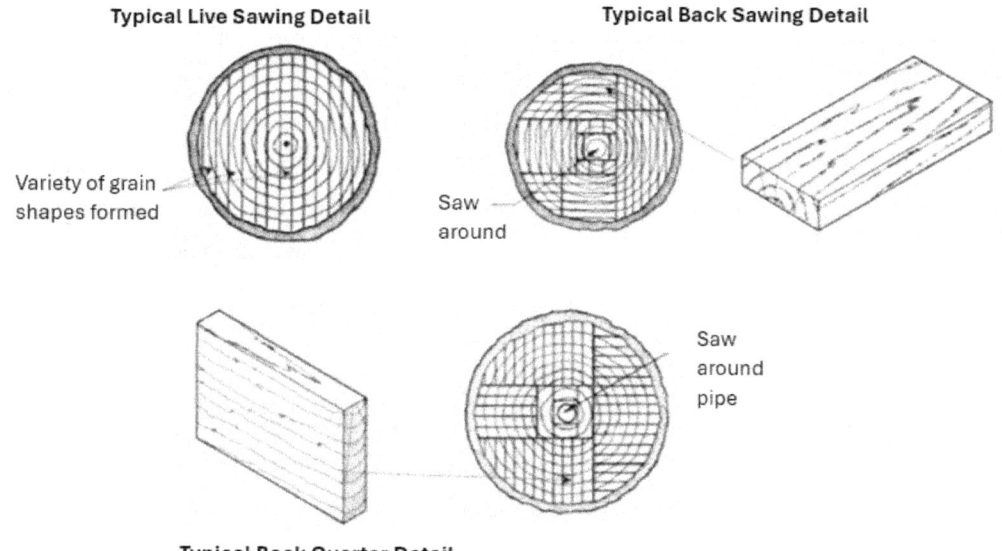

Figure 257: Methods of converting a log to marketable sizes.

Timber shrinkage is a natural phenomenon that occurs as timber dries out, leading to potential issues like warping and splitting. Shrinkage is not uniform in all directions, complicating matters. Longitudinal shrinkage, along the length of the growth rings, is minimal and usually disregarded. Radial shrinkage occurs along the direction of the medullary rays, most noticeable across the width of quarter-sawn boards. Tangential shrinkage, along the growth rings, is the most significant and can cause back-sawn boards to shorten and result in cupping of the timber face. Understanding these directional variations in shrinkage is crucial for managing timber effectively and minimizing associated problems during the drying process and in subsequent applications.

Timber seasoning, also known as timber drying or timber curing, is a critical process that involves removing moisture from freshly cut green timber to stabilize it for various applications. Green timber contains a significant amount of free water in its cells, as well as combined water in the cell walls. The primary objective of seasoning is to eliminate excess free water while retaining just enough combined water to prevent the collapse of timber cells. This controlled process is essential to avoid problems such as excessive shrinkage, cracking, and loss of natural properties like colour, odour, durability, and workability.

Retaining a small percentage of moisture in timber is crucial to keeping it "alive" and maintaining its structural integrity and properties. The equilibrium moisture content typically ranges from around 8% in dry environments to approximately 12% in moist environments. Timber with a moisture content exceeding 18% becomes vulnerable to decay and insect infestation.

Natural seasoning is one of the traditional methods used, involving stacking timber outdoors off the ground and covering it to allow air circulation. This gradual drying process is aided by factors such as a slightly pitched roof covering to regulate exposure to sunlight and prevent rain from saturating the timber. The stack is structured with separators like timber strips to prevent warping and bending, and the ends of timber pieces are sealed to prevent excessive splitting. The duration of natural seasoning varies depending on factors such as timber species, size, stack position, and weather conditions, typically ranging from 6 months to 2 years.

Artificial seasoning, also known as kiln drying, offers a more controlled and accelerated drying process. Timber is stacked on trolleys and placed in kilns where temperature and humidity levels can be precisely controlled. There are different types of kilns, including progressive kilns and compartment kilns, each with its advantages. Heat, often applied through steam coils, accelerates the drying process. Skilled operators are crucial to monitor and adjust the process to prevent defects like warping, checking, or collapse. Artificial seasoning typically takes 7 to 21 days, depending on conditions.

Combined seasoning combines elements of both natural and artificial methods. Timber undergoes initial air drying to remove excessive water before being transferred to a kiln for controlled drying to achieve the desired moisture content.

Other specialized methods of seasoning include chemical seasoning and microwave seasoning, which are tailored for specific timber uses such as carvings and golf club heads. These methods offer unique advantages but are less commonly used compared to traditional and kiln drying methods. Overall, timber seasoning plays a vital role in enhancing the quality, durability, and usability of timber products across various industries.

Timber grading is a systematic method used to classify timber based on its quality, characteristics, and suitability for various applications. Different countries and regions have developed their own timber grading systems to ensure consistency, reliability, and safety in the use of timber products. These grading systems typically take into account factors such as wood species, structural properties, appearance, and manufacturing defects. Here's an overview of timber grading around the world:

- **North America (United States and Canada):**

    - In North America, the most commonly used timber grading system is established by organizations like the American Lumber Standard Committee (ALSC) and the National Lumber Grades Authority (NLGA) in Canada.

    - Softwood lumber is typically graded based on the appearance of the wood and its structural properties. Grades such as Select Structural, No.1, No.2, No.3, Stud, and Utility are used to classify softwood lumber based on its strength, appearance, and suitability for different applications.

    - Hardwood lumber grading often involves a combination of grades based on appearance and defect tolerance. Grades like FAS (Firsts and Seconds), Selects, No.1 Common, and No.2 Common are commonly used for hardwood lumber.

- **Europe:**

    - In Europe, timber grading systems vary by country but often follow the guidelines set by the European Committee for Standardization (CEN).

    - Common grading systems include the C16, C24, and C30 strength classes for softwood timber, which are based on the timber's bending strength and stiffness.

- Appearance grading is also used for softwood lumber, with grades such as A, B, and C indicating the quality of the wood's appearance.

- Some countries, like Sweden and Finland, have their own grading systems tailored to their local timber species and industry standards.

- **Australia and New Zealand:**

  - Australia and New Zealand use grading systems that are similar to those in North America and Europe but adapted to local timber species and industry requirements.

  - In Australia, softwood lumber is graded based on its structural properties, appearance, and potential defects. Grades such as F5, F7, and F17 are commonly used to classify softwood timber based on its strength and stiffness.

  - Appearance grading for softwood lumber in Australia includes grades like Standard and Better, Select, and Feature Grade, which indicate the quality of the wood's appearance and surface finish.

  - New Zealand follows similar grading standards for softwood lumber, with grades like SG8, SG10, and SG12 indicating the timber's structural strength and stiffness.

- **Asia:**

  - In countries like Japan and China, timber grading systems are tailored to local timber species and industry requirements.

  - Grading systems in Asia often focus on structural properties and strength classes for softwood and hardwood lumber, with grades based on bending strength, stiffness, and density.

  - Appearance grading may also be used for select timber species, particularly for high-quality finishes and specialty applications.

Overall, timber grading systems around the world serve to ensure consistency, quality, and safety in the use of timber products across various industries, from construction to furniture manufacturing. These systems help consumers and industry professionals make informed decisions about the selection and use of timber based on their specific needs and requirements.

In North America, particularly in the United States and Canada, the timber industry relies heavily on standardized grading systems to ensure consistency and quality in the production and use of lumber. Two prominent organizations, the American Lumber Standard Committee (ALSC) and the National Lumber Grades Authority (NLGA) in Canada, play significant roles in establishing and maintaining these grading standards.

Softwood lumber, which includes wood from coniferous trees such as pine, spruce, and fir, is typically graded based on both its appearance and structural properties. This dual approach ensures that the lumber meets the requirements for various applications, ranging from structural framing to finishing. Grades such as Select Structural, No.1, No.2, No.3, Stud, and Utility are commonly used to classify softwood lumber based on factors such as strength, knot content, warp, and overall appearance. For example, Select Structural grade is reserved for lumber with minimal defects and high strength, making it suitable for demanding structural applications, while Utility grade may include more defects but still meets the minimum strength requirements for less critical uses.

On the other hand, hardwood lumber grading often involves a nuanced combination of grades that take into account appearance and defect tolerance. Hardwood species, which come from deciduous trees like oak, maple, and cherry, exhibit a wide range of grain patterns, colors, and natural characteristics that influence their grading. Grades such as FAS (Firsts and Seconds), Selects, No.1 Common, and No.2 Common are commonly used for hardwood lumber. FAS grade, for instance, indicates lumber with the highest quality and minimal defects, suitable for premium applications like furniture making and cabinetry. No.1 Common and No.2 Common grades allow for more defects but are still suitable for a variety of applications, from flooring to millwork.

In Europe, timber grading systems exhibit variations across different countries, although many adhere to the guidelines established by the European Committee for Standardization (CEN). These standards provide a framework for assessing the quality and performance of timber products, ensuring consistency and reliability across the region's diverse timber industry.

Softwood timber grading in Europe often revolves around strength classes, which indicate the lumber's bending strength and stiffness. Common strength classes include C16, C24, and C30, with each class representing different levels of structural performance. For instance, C16 timber possesses sufficient strength for typical construction applications, while C24 and C30 grades offer higher levels of strength and durability, suitable for more demanding structural requirements. These strength classes help builders and engineers select the appropriate timber for specific construction projects, ensuring structural integrity and safety.

In addition to strength-based grading, appearance grading is also prevalent in Europe's timber industry, particularly for softwood lumber. Appearance grades such as A, B, and C are used to assess the quality of the wood's surface appearance, including factors like knots, splits, and overall grain pattern. Grade A typically represents lumber with minimal defects and a smooth, uniform appearance, suitable for visible applications such as furniture and trim work. Grade C, on the other hand, may include more pronounced defects and variations in appearance, making it suitable for less visible or structural uses where aesthetics are less critical.

While European countries often adhere to overarching standards set by organizations like CEN, some nations have developed their own grading systems tailored to their local timber species and industry practices. For example, countries like Sweden and Finland, known for their extensive forest resources and timber processing industries, have established national grading systems that reflect the unique characteristics of their indigenous timber species. These localized grading systems ensure that timber products meet the specific requirements and preferences of domestic markets while also aligning with broader European standards for quality and performance.

In Australia and New Zealand, timber grading systems bear similarities to those used in North America and Europe but are adapted to suit the local timber species and industry requirements prevalent in the region. These grading systems serve as essential frameworks for assessing the quality, strength, and suitability of timber products for various construction and woodworking applications.

In Australia, softwood lumber grading encompasses considerations of structural properties, appearance, and potential defects. Grades such as F5, F7, and F17 are commonly employed to classify softwood timber based on its strength and stiffness. For instance, F5 timber may be suitable for lighter structural applications, while F17 timber offers greater strength and durability, suitable for more demanding construction projects. These grades enable builders and engineers to select timber that meets the specific structural requirements of their projects, ensuring safety and performance.

Appearance grading is also integral to timber assessment in Australia, particularly for softwood lumber. Grades such as Standard and Better, Select, and Feature Grade are used to evaluate the wood's surface appearance and finish. Grade Standard and Better typically denote lumber with minimal defects and a uniform appearance, suitable for visible applications like furniture and cabinetry. In contrast, Feature Grade may include more pronounced defects, knots, or variations in appearance, making it suitable for structural or less visible uses where aesthetics are less critical.

Similarly, New Zealand adheres to comparable grading standards for softwood lumber, with grades like SG8, SG10, and SG12 indicating the timber's structural strength and stiffness. These grades mirror the principles of strength-based grading seen in other regions, with higher numbers indicating greater levels of strength and durability. By employing these grading systems, New Zealand ensures that its softwood lumber meets the necessary performance standards for diverse construction applications, from residential framing to commercial infrastructure projects.

In countries like Japan and China, timber grading systems are intricately tailored to accommodate the specific characteristics of local timber species and the unique demands of the regional industry. These grading systems are essential for ensuring the quality, reliability, and suitability of timber products for various construction, manufacturing, and woodworking applications prevalent in these regions.

Grading systems in Asia, particularly in Japan and China, tend to prioritize the assessment of structural properties and strength classes for both softwood and hardwood lumber. These systems typically involve the classification of timber based on factors such as bending strength, stiffness, density, and other mechanical properties crucial for determining their performance under load-bearing conditions. By categorizing timber into different strength classes, these grading systems enable builders, engineers, and manufacturers to select materials that meet the specific structural requirements of their projects, ensuring safety, longevity, and resilience in construction and manufacturing endeavours.

In addition to structural grading, appearance grading may also play a significant role in assessing select timber species in Asian countries, particularly for applications requiring high-quality finishes and specialty aesthetics. Appearance grading involves evaluating the surface characteristics, colour, texture, and overall visual appeal of timber products, ensuring that they meet the desired standards for architectural, interior design, and furniture-making purposes. By incorporating appearance grading into the overall assessment of timber quality, Asian grading systems accommodate the diverse aesthetic preferences and functional requirements prevalent in the region's construction and woodworking industries.

Furthermore, timber grading systems in Japan and China are continuously evolving to align with advancements in technology, changes in industry practices, and emerging trends in sustainable forestry and timber utilization. These systems often undergo periodic revisions, incorporating new standards, methodologies, and quality control measures to enhance the accuracy, reliability, and consistency of timber grading processes. By staying abreast of these developments and ensuring adherence to established grading standards, Japan and China uphold the integrity and competitiveness of their timber industries while meeting the evolving needs and expectations of domestic and international markets.

Timber defects encompass a wide range of irregularities and imperfections that can affect the quality, strength, and appearance of wood products. These defects originate from various sources, including natural processes during tree growth, environmental factors, poor handling or processing practices, and biological agents such as insects and fungi. Understanding the nature and causes of these defects is crucial for identifying and mitigating their impact on timber quality and performance.

One common category of defects arises from natural characteristics inherent in the tree itself. Trees may exhibit features such as ribboned or wavy grain, knots, gum veins, and burls, which can transfer to the timber during processing. These natural defects contribute to the uniqueness and aesthetic appeal of timber but may also affect its structural integrity and workability, depending on their size, density, and distribution within the wood.

External factors such as insect infestations, fungal decay, and environmental stresses can also lead to timber defects. For example, cup shakes can occur due to poor drying techniques or crystallization of resin between growth rings, resulting in fibre separation. Heart shakes and star shakes involve splitting of fibres around medullary rays, often caused by rapid changes in moisture content or physical trauma during tree growth or processing.

Gum pockets form when resin accumulates between growth rings, causing fibre separation and weakening of the wood. Felling shakes occur when a falling tree impacts a hard object, leading to fine fractures within the trunk. These defects may not be immediately apparent but can compromise timber integrity over time, especially under load or environmental stress.

Knots represent another common defect found in timber, resulting from the presence of branches within the tree trunk. Different types of knots, such as spike knots, live knots, decayed knots, loose knots, and pin knots, can affect wood strength, appearance, and workability to varying degrees. Collapse occurs when rapid drying causes cell flattening and uneven shrinkage, leading to surface irregularities and structural weaknesses.

Cupping and wane refer to deformations in timber edges or surfaces due to uneven moisture content or poor cutting practices. Grain defects, including spring, bow, and twist, arise from irregularities in wood grain caused by growth patterns, processing techniques, or environmental factors. These defects can affect timber straightness, flatness, and dimensional stability, impacting its suitability for structural or aesthetic applications.

Timber Decay and Fungal Attack

Timber decay is a common issue that arises from the interaction of oxygen, water, and fungi. Unlike plants, fungi do not possess chlorophyll and cannot produce food through photosynthesis. Instead, they feed on organic materials by breaking them down and absorbing nutrients. Fungi reproduce through spores, which can remain dormant in the environment or spread through wind and rain. Timber decay can occur both in exposed areas, such as external fascia corners with water leaks, and in protected spaces, like under suspended timber floors where moisture accumulates due to poor ventilation.

For fungal attack to occur, timber must have a moisture content of 18% or higher, making it susceptible to decay. Timber with moisture levels below 18% remains resistant to fungal decay. Therefore, maintaining low and consistent moisture levels is crucial in preventing timber decay in buildings. Decay in timber ceases when moisture content reaches 150% or greater, as the wood becomes waterlogged and no longer conducive to fungal activity.

Two main types of timber decay are wet rot and dry rot. Wet rot is caused by various types of fungi, including brown rot, white rot, and soft rot fungi. It is the most common form of fungal attack in residential and commercial structures. Dry rot, while less common in Australia, requires high moisture content (above 30%) and cooler conditions to thrive. It can spread from sub-floor areas to roof spaces, posing significant structural risks.

Decaying timber exhibits high moisture content (above 20%) and visible fungal activity, while decayed timber has lost moisture, shrunk in size, and may be falling apart. The main types of timber-destroying fungi include brown rot fungi, which leave timber with a characteristic brown colour and cubical texture; white rot fungi, which produce white fibrous growth and attack both cellulose and lignin; soft rot fungi, which leave timber with a carrot-like texture and a darker colour; and dry rot fungi, which require higher moisture content to establish and can spread rapidly under suitable conditions.

Preventing timber decay involves using durable timbers with a Class 1 or 2 durability rating, maintaining low moisture levels, and ensuring adequate ventilation. Rising damp, caused by moisture drawn up through masonry walls, can also contribute to timber decay by transferring moisture to structural components. Installing a damp-proof course (DPC) during construction and repairing any existing damp issues using physical or chemical methods can mitigate the risk of rising damp and subsequent timber decay. Physical repairs involve replacing damaged DPCs, while chemical methods involve injecting waterproof barriers into walls to create a new DPC layer. Care must be taken during application to minimize fire hazards posed by evaporating solvents. Overall, proactive measures to control moisture and address damp issues are essential for preserving timber integrity and structural stability in buildings.

Dampness in buildings and timber can stem from various sources, posing significant risks to structural integrity and durability. Leaking taps against walls, drainage pipes in the sub-floor area, poor sub-floor ventilation, and leaking stormwater pipes are common culprits. Additionally, rusted or leaking downpipes and gutters, degraded or non-existent damp-proof courses (DPCs), and leaking appliances like dishwashers and washing machines can contribute to moisture ingress. Other factors include leaking shower recesses, rainwater running freely in sub-floor areas, and cracked or broken roof tiles. Neglecting building maintenance exacerbates these issues over time, leading to timber decay, shortened material life, and expensive repairs.

To enhance timber durability and longevity, various preservation methods and materials are employed. Some timbers naturally resist insect and environmental attacks, such as White Cypress pine, Tallowwood, Ironbark, and Turpentine, while others, like Mountain ash and Radiata pine, have poor resistance. Pressure treating green timber with preservatives is a common and effective method. Copper sulphate, chromium sulphate, and arsenic pentoxide (CCA salts) are vacuum-pressure impregnated into the timber cells at approximately 1400 kPa for sixty minutes. As the timber seasons and loses free water, the salts act as insecticides and fungicides, deterring termites, borers, and various fungi. Treated timbers are recognizable by their characteristic green colour.

Surface treatments are also utilized to seal and protect timber from weathering and fungal attacks. Linseed oil, a natural oil that dries completely and penetrates timber, provides a base for paint coats and seals internal and external joinery items. Tung oil, another natural oil, serves a similar purpose but tends to yellow timber if left raw. Semi-drying oils like safflower, sunflower, and soybean oils, which do not yellow timber, are used as bases for gloss alkyd enamels. Natural resins and gums, derived from pine extracts or the excretions of the Lac beetle, are favoured for internal joinery and furniture. Primers play a crucial role in forming strong bonds between timber surfaces and topcoats, sealing pores, and providing water repellency. Modern primers use oils mixed with pigments to create white or pink variants and are available in water and oil-based preparations for application on fascias, weatherboards, window and door frames, and external structures prior to undercoat and topcoat application. These preservation methods and treatments are vital for maintaining timber integrity and prolonging its service life amidst varying environmental conditions and potential threats.

Transport and Delivery of Timber

Considerations for transporting timber to construction sites involve several factors, including length, width, height, and weight restrictions. It's essential to adhere to these limits to ensure safe and efficient transportation. Transporting timber flat and unloading it carefully, rather than dumping it, helps prevent damage and maintain the integrity of the material.

During transport, employing soft slings and protective measures for timber corners minimizes the risk of damage. Load spreaders are beneficial for slender assemblies, ensuring even weight distribution and stability. Seasoned timber should be protected from moisture to prevent deterioration during transit.

When arranging delivery, it's crucial to coordinate with the construction sequence. For example, large members for bearers should be delivered first and placed on top of stacks to avoid damage. Different deliveries of floor, wall, and roof timber can streamline construction and minimize on-site storage requirements. Internal appearance timber, such as flooring, should only be delivered once the roof is in place to protect it from exposure to the elements.

Storing timber on-site requires careful consideration to maintain its quality. Stacking timber off the ground using high durability gluts reduces the risk of termite attacks and keeps the timber dry, away from pooled water. Stacking timber flat helps preserve its straightness and makes handling safer and more manageable.

Seasoned timber should be covered to prevent partial seasoning and minimize moisture changes, reducing the risk of distortion and shrinkage. This also promotes better paint adhesion and overall quality. Internal appearance timber, such as flooring and stairs, should be stored indoors to allow it to acclimate to the ambient conditions of its future environment, minimizing later shrinkage and cracking.

During construction, protecting seasoned timber from exposure to adverse weather conditions is essential. Partially completed work should be covered wherever possible to prevent damage. Similarly, internal appearance timber should be shielded from rain and sunlight to maintain its quality and appearance. Ambient conditions should be controlled to mimic service conditions before installation to minimize future issues.

Exposed timber requires additional protection, particularly against moisture movement. Sealing timber against moisture with paint is essential, paying particular attention to end grain, which is more susceptible to damage. By implementing these measures, the integrity and longevity of timber can be preserved, ensuring its durability and quality throughout construction and beyond.

Fixings and Fastenings

Nails serve as one of the primary wood fasteners employed by carpenters in various construction tasks. Typically made of metal, nails feature a pointed end for easy insertion into wood and a flat or rounded end on the other side. Process nails, often used with pine, are coated with adhesive to enhance their grip within the wood. Understanding the different types and sizes of nails is crucial, as their selection depends on the specific application and the size of the component being fastened. For instance, when securing wall plates of varying thicknesses, nails ranging from 75 mm to 100 mm may be employed.

Two common nails used in house framing include large bullet head nails, which prioritize strength over appearance, and bronze-coloured nails intended for use with nail guns, typically featuring an adhesive coating for added stability. Various nail types are designed for specific purposes in construction. For instance, common nails are ideal for rough framing, while box nails are suitable for toenailing and lighter framing work. Casing nails are utilized in finished carpentry to secure doors, window casings, and other trim elements, while finishing nails and brads are employed for light wood-trim materials and can be easily driven below the surface of lumber.

The size of a nail is denoted in a unit known as a penny, represented by the lowercase letter "d," indicating the length of the nail. For example, a 6d nail is 2 inches long, while a 10d nail is 3 inches long. It's essential to drive nails at least three times the thickness of the wood being fastened, with two-thirds of the nail's length driven into the other piece of wood for proper anchorage. Protruding nails should be bent over to prevent damage and injury.

Several general rules govern the use of nails in building. Nails should be driven at an angle toward each other to enhance their holding power, and careful placement is necessary to maximize their effectiveness. Nails driven across the grain provide better holding power than those driven with the grain. Additionally, a few nails of the appropriate type and size, strategically placed and properly driven, are often more effective than numerous nails driven closely together. Nails are generally considered the most economical and straightforward fasteners to apply in construction projects.

Specialized nails, including those coated with zinc, cement, or resin materials, as well as annular and spiral nails threaded for greater holding power, cater to specific construction needs. These nails are made from various materials such as iron, steel, copper, bronze, aluminium, and stainless steel. Roofing nails, drywall nails, and power nails for nail guns are among the specialized varieties available, each designed for specific applications and offering unique features tailored to their intended use. Additionally, staples, available in various shapes and sizes, serve as alternatives to nails for specific fastening requirements, with heavy-duty staples used for plywood sheeting and subflooring, while lighter-duty staples are suitable for interior trim applications.

Screws, characterized by their threaded shanks, serve as versatile metal fasteners in construction and carpentry tasks. Wood screws, categorized by their length and diameter, are crucial components in various applications, whether driven in manually with a hand screwdriver or with the assistance of electric or battery drills equipped with screwdriver tips. These screws come in different types and sizes, with the diameter designated by the screw gauge. They can be tailored for specific uses, such as fixing timber to timber or attaching materials to treated pine.

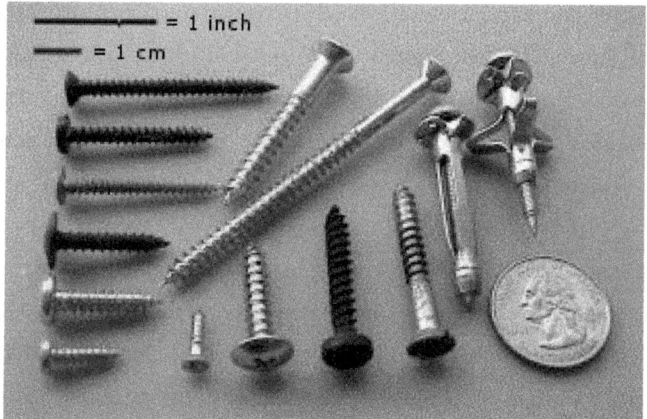

Figure 258: Various screws: differing sizes and colours, several Phillips, a flathead, and a Torx. Also included: wall anchor screws (one expanded), and a US quarter for scale. Brianiac, Public domain, via Wikimedia Commons.

Masonry anchors play a vital role in securing bottom plates of frames or partitions to concrete slab floors or affixing timber members to brick or concrete walls. The use of these anchors, like Dyna bolts, involves drilling a hole through the timber and concrete to accommodate the anchor's size and length, driving in the anchor until the washer reaches the top of the timber, and then tightening the washer securely.

The preference for screws over nails as fasteners may stem from various factors, including the need for superior holding power, aesthetic considerations, and specific project requirements. Although screws may be more costly and time-consuming to use compared to nails, their advantages lie in their ability to provide enhanced holding power, facilitate secure tightening of fastened items, present a neater appearance, and allow for easy removal without damaging the material.

Wood screws typically consist of unhardened steel, stainless steel, aluminium, or brass, with various finishes available, including bright finishes, bluing, or plating with zinc, cadmium, or chrome. Threaded from a gimlet point for approximately two-thirds of their length, wood screws feature slotted or Phillips heads designed for insertion by an appropriate driver. These screws are designated according to head style, with common types including flathead, oval head, and roundhead.

Preparation of wood for receiving screws involves drilling a body hole of the screw's diameter and a starter hole in the base wood with a diameter smaller than that of the screw threads. This meticulous preparation ensures accuracy in screw placement, reduces the risk of wood splitting, and facilitates the driving process. Lag screws, also known as lag bolts or wood screws, feature coarser threads and are utilized in larger construction projects where ordinary wood screws would be insufficient.

Expansion shields, also referred to as expansion anchors, are essential components for inserting into predrilled holes, typically in masonry, to provide a secure anchor for screws, bolts, or nails. These shields expand when a fastener is driven into them, firmly wedging them against the hole's surface. For metal assemblies, sheet metal screws with flat, round, oval, or fillister heads are commonly employed.

Screw sizes range from 1/4 inch to 6 inches, with variations in length and shaft size. The proper nomenclature of a screw includes the type, material, finish, length, and screw size number, which indicates the wire gauge of the body and drill or bit sizes for the body and starter holes. Tables outlining screw sizes, lengths, diameters, and applicable drill bit sizes provide comprehensive guidance for selecting and using screws effectively in construction and carpentry projects.

Bolts are essential components in construction projects where exceptional strength is required or when the structure may need frequent disassembly. They are typically used in conjunction with nuts for fastening, and washers are sometimes employed to protect the material's surface and allow for additional torque during tightening. The selection of bolts is based on specific requirements regarding length, diameter, threads, head style, and type, ensuring both structural integrity and aesthetic appeal in construction projects.

Carriage bolts, categorized into square neck, finned neck, and ribbed neck varieties, feature round heads and partially threaded shafts. Unlike other bolts, carriage bolts are not designed to be driven; instead, they are inserted into pre-drilled holes and secured with nuts. The threads on carriage bolts typically extend two to four times the diameter of the bolt in length, providing ample grip and preventing rotation when the nut is tightened or removed. Finned carriage bolts feature fins extending from the head to the shank, while ribbed carriage bolts have longitudinal ribs, splines, or serrations on the shoulder beneath the head.

During installation, holes bored to receive carriage bolts are sized to fit snugly around the bolt's body and counterbored to accommodate the head, allowing it to sit flush with or below the material's surface. Carriage bolts are primarily used for wood-to-wood applications but can also be utilized for wood-to-metal connections. When used in wood-to-metal applications, the bolt's head should be embedded into the wood component. In some cases, metal surfaces are predrilled and countersunk to facilitate the use of carriage bolts in metal-to-metal connections.

Carriage bolts are available in various diameters ranging from 1/4 inch to 1 inch and lengths spanning from 3/4 inch to 20 inches. When fastening carriage bolts, it is recommended to use a flat washer between the nut and the surface to distribute the load and prevent damage to the material. These bolts offer reliable fastening solutions in construction projects, ensuring structural stability and facilitating efficient assembly and disassembly processes when necessary.

Self-drilling screws offer a convenient solution for fastening applications, as they are designed to drill their own holes and tap their own threads. Specifically developed for various construction needs, Buildex® self-drilling screws boast high pullout strength, shear strength, and maximum thread engagement, making them suitable for both structural steel and timber constructions. One of the primary advantages of self-drilling screws is their time-saving capability, significantly reducing assembly and on-site labour time by eliminating the need for alignment or pre-drilling holes. This efficiency often cuts down the time required for roofing, cladding, and assembly tasks by half compared to conventional methods.

Figure 259: Hex-head self-drilling screw. Zheer16 @ Pixabay, CC0, via Wikimedia Commons.

Ease of use is another key benefit of self-drilling screws, as they eliminate the need for skilled labour and the selection of various tools. With the engineering design of these fasteners, unskilled workers can quickly and effortlessly install them, providing tradesmen with the advantages of speed and ease of installation. Additionally, as the fastening process is reduced to a single operation, alignment issues are eliminated, contributing to greater efficiency and cost-effectiveness compared to traditional methods that involve drilling, tapping, and fastening or using nuts and bolts separately.

To achieve optimal results when using self-drilling screws, it is recommended to use electric screw drivers (TEK Guns) with a wattage rating between 380 and 650 watts, operating at 2500 rpm. The Buildex® range of screws is categorized based on gauge, threads per inch (TPI), and length, allowing for easy identification and selection according to specific project requirements. The gauge of a screw is determined by the basic size of the thread outside diameter, with standard gauges ranging from 6 to 15. Threads per inch (TPI) indicate the number of thread crests along a linear measurement of 1 inch (25.4mm).

Self-drilling screws come in various types of threads to suit different applications. Coarse threads, also known as spaced threads, are typically used for timber applications and thin steel, while fine threads, known as metal threads, are reserved for thicker steel materials. Buttress threads provide superior holding power in thin metal, while Taptite threads are ideal for steel and plastics, forming their own threads during installation. Twin start threads offer faster installation by moving forward at twice the speed, catering to efficient assembly processes.

Head styles of self-drilling screws vary to accommodate diverse fastening needs. These include hexagon head, hexagon head with washer face, wafer head, pan head, bugle head, countersunk head, self-embedding head, countersunk rib head, button head, tamper-resistant head, special pan head, Headlok® security head screws, and designer head screws. Each head style serves specific purposes, ranging from providing greater strength and torque input to achieving flush or recessed finishes and offering tamper-proof features for security applications. With their versatility, ease of use, and efficiency, self-drilling screws have become indispensable in modern construction practices, offering reliable and effective fastening solutions across various applications.

Corrugated fasteners play a crucial role in securing joints and splices in small timber and boards, with a particular emphasis on mitre joints. Typically made from 18- to 22-gauge sheet metal, corrugated fasteners feature alternating ridges and grooves, with ridges ranging from 3/16 to 5/16 inch in width, centre to centre. One end of the fastener is cut square, while the other end is sharpened with bevelled edges. There are two main types of corrugated fasteners: those with parallel ridges and those with ridges running at a slight angle to one another. The latter type, with angled ridges, has a tendency to compress the material due to the variation in ridge spacing from top to bottom.

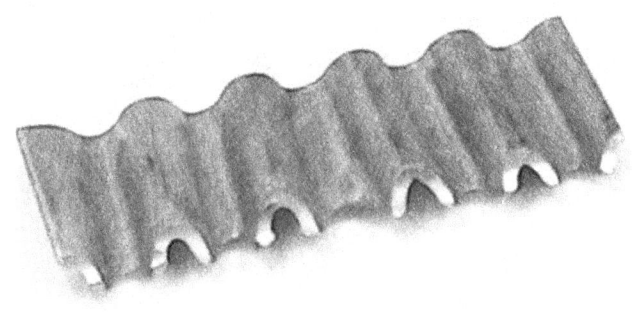

Figure 260: Corrugated fastener.

Corrugated fasteners come in various lengths and widths to accommodate different applications. The width typically ranges from 5/8 to 1 1/8 inches, while the length varies from 1/4 to 3/4 inch. Additionally, these fasteners are manufactured with different numbers of ridges, typically ranging from three to six ridges per fastener. Their versatility allows them to be used in multiple ways, such as fastening parallel boards together, creating various types of joints, and serving as an alternative to nails in situations where nails may cause splitting of the timber.

In small timber applications, corrugated fasteners offer greater holding power compared to nails, making them a preferred choice for securing joints. Their design and construction allow for efficient and reliable fastening, especially in scenarios where traditional fasteners may not provide adequate strength or may compromise the integrity of the material. The proper method of using corrugated fasteners involves careful placement and alignment, as illustrated in figure 3-84, ensuring optimal performance and structural stability in the assembled components. Overall, corrugated fasteners are indispensable components in woodworking and carpentry, providing secure and durable connections in various construction projects.

Glue serves a fundamental role in woodworking, primarily by creating strong bonds between joints in millwork and cabinetry. Modern glues typically feature a plastic base and are available in both powder and liquid forms. These glues are often sold under various brand names, each offering unique properties tailored to specific applications. Here, we'll explore some of the popular types of glue commonly used in woodworking.

Polyvinyl resin, commonly known as white glue, is a liquid adhesive packaged in convenient plastic squeeze bottles. It excels in bonding wood together and sets quickly after application. However, white glue is not waterproof, so it's unsuitable for projects exposed to constant moisture or high humidity. Despite this limitation, its ease of use and fast drying make it a preferred choice for many woodworking tasks.

Urea resin, available in powder form, requires mixing with water to activate. This adhesive forms strong bonds with wood and offers fair water resistance. While not as quick-drying as white glue, urea resin remains a popular choice due to its reliable performance and versatility in various woodworking applications.

Phenolic resin glue stands out for its exceptional resistance to temperature extremes and water. It finds extensive use in bonding the veneer layers of exterior-grade plywood, where durability and weather resistance are paramount. The robust nature of phenolic resin glue makes it ideal for outdoor projects or applications exposed to harsh environmental conditions.

Resorcinol glue boasts excellent water and temperature resistance, making it suitable for demanding woodworking tasks. This adhesive forms a remarkably strong bond and is often employed in bonding the wood layers of laminated timbers. Its superior performance in challenging environments makes it a preferred choice for structural applications where strength and durability are critical.

Contact cement, featuring a neoprene rubber base, is specifically designed for bonding plastic laminates to wood surfaces. This adhesive bonds rapidly upon contact, eliminating the need for clamping and enabling efficient assembly of parts that cannot be easily secured with traditional clamps. Its fast-setting nature and strong adhesion make it a valuable tool for laminate work and similar applications in woodworking.

The diverse range of glues available in the market offers woodworkers a plethora of options to suit their specific needs and preferences. From fast-drying white glue to resilient phenolic resin, each type of adhesive brings unique characteristics and benefits to woodworking projects, ensuring strong and reliable bonds that withstand the test of time.

Mastics are versatile adhesives widely employed across the construction industry, prized for their thicker consistency derived from asphalt, rubber, or resin bases. These adhesives are typically available in cans, tubes, or canisters compatible with hand-operated or air-operated caulking guns, facilitating easy application and handling.

One of the primary uses of mastics is to bond materials directly to masonry or concrete walls, offering an alternative to conventional fastening methods like concrete nails. For instance, furring strips can be securely affixed to uneven concrete walls using mastic, bypassing the complexities associated with driving nails into concrete. Additionally, mastics provide an effective means to attach insulation materials to masonry or concrete surfaces, enhancing thermal performance and energy efficiency.

Mastics also find extensive application in the installation of drywall (gypsum board), offering a reliable bonding solution for attaching gypsum board directly to wall studs or masonry surfaces. This eliminates the need for nails, resulting in a smoother finish without nail indentations that would require filling. Moreover, mastics enable the bonding of gypsum board to furring strips or directly to concrete or masonry walls, offering flexibility in construction projects.

One notable advantage of using mastic adhesives is the ability to apply panelling with minimal or no nails at all. Wall panels can be securely bonded to studs, furring strips, or directly against concrete or masonry walls using mastics, providing a clean and seamless appearance. Additionally, mastics can be combined with nails or staples to fasten plywood panels to floor joists, effectively reducing squeaks, bounce, and nail popping. Furthermore, the use of mastic adhesives enhances the stiffness and strength of the floor unit, contributing to overall structural integrity and performance.

Pressed metal plates serve as coverings for butt-joints, which occur when two components, such as beams, are aligned at right angles against each other. These plates are typically made of metal and are designed to conceal the joint between the two components, providing both functional and aesthetic benefits to the structure.

The installation process involves fitting the pressed metal plate over the joint and securing it in place using metal spikes. These spikes are hammered down over the joint, effectively fastening the plate and ensuring that it remains securely in position. This method of attachment helps to maintain the integrity of the joint and prevents the plate from becoming dislodged over time.

Pressed metal plates offer several advantages in construction applications. Firstly, they provide a seamless and visually appealing finish to joints, enhancing the overall appearance of the structure. Additionally, they help to protect the joint from external elements such as moisture and debris, reducing the risk of damage or deterioration over time.

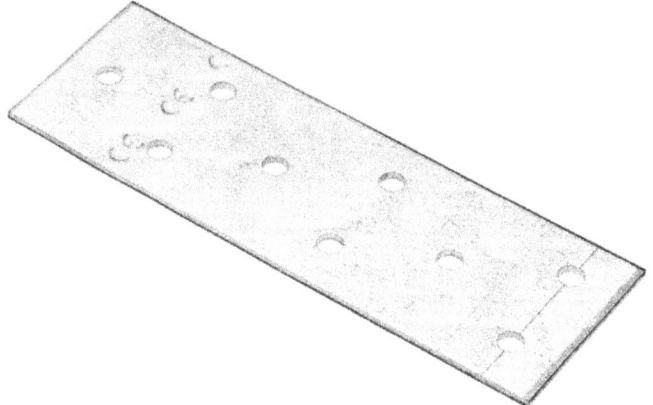

Figure 261: Metal joining plate.

Moreover, pressed metal plates contribute to the structural stability of the joint by providing an additional layer of reinforcement. By covering the joint and securing it firmly in place, these plates help to distribute loads more evenly across the joint, reducing the risk of structural failure or weakness.

Carpentry Tools

In timber landscape construction projects, a variety of cutting tools, including crosscut saws, drop saws, circular saws, reciprocating saws, routers, and panel saws, are employed to accomplish different tasks efficiently and accurately.

Crosscut saws are used for cutting structural and finishing timbers in landscape projects, such as constructing pergolas, fences, or wooden decks. They provide clean and precise cuts, ensuring that the timber pieces fit together seamlessly.

Drop saws, also known as mitre saws, are essential for making accurate and angled cuts in timber, which is often necessary for framing structures like gazebos, trellises, or raised garden beds. They offer the ability to cut timber to precise lengths with minimal effort, making them ideal for repetitive cutting tasks.

Circular saws are versatile tools commonly used in landscape construction projects for cutting timber into various shapes and sizes. From cutting timber boards for pathways or retaining walls to shaping wood for custom-built features like benches or arbors, circular saws provide the flexibility and power needed to handle a wide range of cutting tasks.

Reciprocating saws are valuable for rough cutting or removing sections of timber quickly, making them useful for tasks such as removing old timber structures or trimming branches on trees during landscape renovations or maintenance.

Routers are indispensable for shaping and edging timber in landscape construction projects. They can be used to create decorative edges on timber boards for pathways or garden borders, as well as for carving intricate designs or patterns into wooden surfaces for aesthetic enhancement.

Panel saws, with their ability to cut small sections of timber accurately and smoothly, are useful for cutting timber panels or boards to specific dimensions for constructing features like planter boxes, seating areas, or decorative screens in landscape designs.

In addition to cutting tools, electric drills are essential for boring holes in timber for fastening or assembling various landscape structures, such as attaching timber boards together or securing fixtures like hooks, brackets, or hinges.

Further, in timber landscape construction projects, a variety of hand tools and power tools are essential for accurate measurements, precise cuts, and secure fastening of timber components. Here's how some of the tools mentioned are used in such projects:

Panel Saw: Panel saws are indispensable for cutting small sections of timber, plywood, or cornice accurately and smoothly. In landscape construction, panel saws are commonly used for tasks such as cutting timber boards for decking, constructing garden beds, or shaping wooden structures like pergolas or trellises.

One Metre Folding Rule: Used for measuring short distances accurately, folding rules are handy tools in landscape construction projects for laying out designs, marking cutting lines on timber, and ensuring precise dimensions for various structures and features.

Steel Square: Steel squares are utilized for setting out or testing small right-angle corners in timber landscape construction. They ensure that corners are perfectly perpendicular, which is crucial for the structural integrity and aesthetics of timber components such as garden beds, fences, or seating areas.

Combination Square: Combination squares are versatile tools that find numerous applications in timber landscape construction projects. From testing for squareness and marking lines at 90 or 45 degrees to gauging parallel lines, combination squares ensure accuracy and consistency in measurements and cuts.

Chalk Line Reel: Chalk line reels are indispensable for marking straight lines accurately over long distances. In landscape construction, they are commonly used for laying out the boundaries of paved areas, marking cut lines on timber, or delineating planting beds.

Steel Tape: Steel tapes are essential for measuring larger distances accurately, making them invaluable in landscape construction projects for setting out and checking wall dimensions, building sizes, or distances between features in the outdoor space.

Tee Square or T-Square: Tee squares are specifically designed for cutting plasterboard across its width with a knife. While not directly used in timber landscape construction, they may find application in related indoor renovation or construction tasks.

Extension/Power Leads: Power leads are vital for connecting electrically-driven power tools, such as saws or drills, to the power source. They ensure uninterrupted power supply during various construction tasks, enhancing efficiency and productivity on the job site.

Saw Stool/Horse: Saw stools or horses provide stable support for timber pieces while cutting or sawing. In landscape construction, they facilitate safe and accurate cutting of timber components for various structures or features.

Screwdrivers and Nail Punch: Screwdrivers are used for inserting and removing screws, while nail punches are handy for driving nails beneath the surface of timber components to achieve a smooth finish. Both tools are essential for assembling timber structures in landscape construction projects.

These tools, whether hand tools like saws and squares or power tools like nailers and sanders, play crucial roles in ensuring precision, efficiency, and safety in timber landscape construction projects. By using them skilfully and adhering to safety protocols, construction professionals can achieve high-quality results in outdoor spaces.

Joining Techniques

In landscape construction projects, various types of carpentry joints are utilized to create strong and durable connections between timber components. These joints not only provide structural integrity but also contribute to the aesthetic appeal of outdoor structures. Some common types of carpentry joints used in landscape construction include:

- **Butt Joint:** The simplest and most basic joint, where the ends of two timber pieces are butted together and fastened with nails, screws, or adhesives. Butt joints are often reinforced with metal plates or brackets for added strength.

- **Mortise and Tenon Joint:** A traditional joint where a projecting tenon on one timber piece fits into a corresponding mortise (hole) in another piece. Mortise and tenon joints are commonly used in landscape construction for assembling timber frames, pergolas, and garden structures due to their strength and stability.

- **Dovetail Joint:** A joint characterized by interlocking wedge-shaped projections (dovetails) on one timber piece that fit into corresponding slots on another piece. Dovetail joints are known for their decorative appearance and are often used in constructing outdoor furniture, planter boxes, and decorative features.

- **Half-Lap Joint:** A joint where half the thickness of each timber piece is removed to create a flush surface when the pieces are joined together. Half-lap joints are commonly used in landscape construction for assembling timber frames, benches, and raised garden beds.

- **Mitre Joint:** A joint formed by cutting two timber pieces at an angle, usually 45 degrees, so that they fit together to form a 90-degree corner. Mitre joints are often used in constructing outdoor trim work, decking, and decorative features where precise angles are required.

- **Dowel Joint:** A joint where holes are drilled into the mating surfaces of two timber pieces, and wooden dowels are inserted to align and secure the pieces together. Dowel joints provide strong and inconspicuous connections and are commonly used in landscape construction for joining timber panels, gates, and fences.

- **Bridle Joint:** A joint where a half-lap joint is cut in one timber piece, and a corresponding notch is cut in the end of the mating piece to create a snug fit. Bridle joints are used in landscape construction for assembling timber frames, pergolas, and outdoor seating where strength and stability are essential.

- **Tongue and Groove Joint:** A joint where a protruding tongue on one timber piece fits into a corresponding groove on another piece to create a tight-fitting, interlocking connection. Tongue and groove joints are often used in constructing outdoor flooring, decking, and cladding for their weather-resistant and durable properties.

These are just a few examples of the carpentry joints commonly employed in landscape construction projects. The choice of joint depends on factors such as the design requirements, structural considerations, and aesthetic preferences of the project.

Forming a butt joint is a fundamental technique in woodworking, commonly used to join two timber pieces together at their ends. Despite its simplicity, creating a strong and durable butt joint requires careful attention to detail and proper execution.

Figure 262: Butt Joint.

To form a butt joint:

- **Selecting Suitable Timber:** Begin by choosing timber pieces that are suitable for your project in terms of size, species, and quality. Ensure that the timber is straight, free from defects like knots or splits, and properly seasoned to minimize the risk of warping or shrinking over time.

- **Preparing the Timber:** Before cutting, inspect the timber pieces to ensure they are clean, square, and of the correct dimensions for your project. Use a measuring tape, pencil, and square to mark the desired length on each piece of timber accurately.

- **Cutting the Timber:** With the timber properly marked, use an appropriate saw – such as a hand saw, circular saw, or miter saw – to make the cuts. It's crucial to ensure that the cuts are straight, clean, and square to the timber's edges to achieve a tight fit when joining the pieces.

- **Aligning the Timber Pieces:** Once the timber pieces are cut to size, place the cut ends together to form the joint. Carefully align the pieces, ensuring that they are flush and properly seated against each other. Clamps or a vice can be used to hold the pieces securely in place during assembly, particularly for larger or heavier timber.

- **Reinforcing the Joint (Optional):** Depending on the application and the desired strength of the joint, consider reinforcing it with additional support. This can be done using mechanical fasteners such as screws, nails, or dowels, or by applying wood glue to the mating surfaces before joining them together.

- **Fastening the Joint:** With the pieces properly aligned, proceed to fasten the joint using the chosen method. If using screws or nails, pre-drill pilot holes to prevent splitting and ensure accurate placement. Drive the fasteners through one piece of timber and into the end grain of the other, ensuring a tight and secure connection.

- **Checking Alignment and Stability:** After fastening the joint, double-check the alignment and stability of the assembled pieces. Ensure that the joint is flush, tight, and free from gaps or misalignments. Test the joint's strength by applying gentle pressure or tapping on the joined area to ensure it feels solid and secure.

- **Finishing and Sanding (Optional):** Depending on the project requirements, you may choose to finish the timber pieces to enhance their appearance and provide protection against moisture and wear. Sand the joint and surrounding areas to remove any rough edges, splinters, or imperfections, creating a smooth and professional finish.

Forming a mortise and tenon joint is a classic woodworking technique renowned for its strength, durability, and versatility. This joint consists of two main parts: the mortise, which is a cavity or hole cut into one piece of timber, and the tenon, a protruding tongue or tab on the end of the other piece that fits snugly into the mortise.

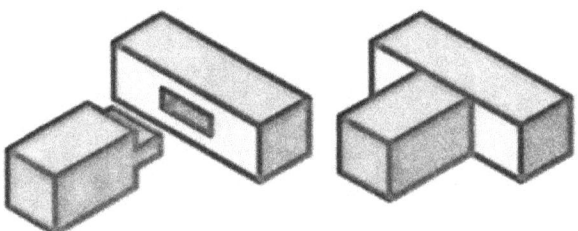

Figure 263: Mortise and Tenon Joint.

To form a mortise and tenon joint:

- **Selecting Suitable Timber:** Begin by selecting high-quality timber pieces that are straight, clean, and free from defects like knots, splits, or warping. Choose timber species with suitable hardness and strength for your project, ensuring they are properly seasoned to minimize the risk of movement over time.

- **Measuring and Marking:** Use a measuring tape, pencil, and square to mark the location and dimensions of the mortise and tenon on the timber pieces. The tenon should typically be one-third to one-half the thickness of the timber and extend at least one-third the width of the joint.

- **Cutting the Tenon:** With the timber properly marked, use a saw – such as a tenon saw, bandsaw, or table saw – to cut the tenon on one end of the piece. Ensure that the cuts are straight, clean, and accurate, and use a square to ensure that the shoulders of the tenon are perpendicular to its cheeks.

- **Forming the Mortise:** With the tenon cut, proceed to form the mortise in the corresponding piece of timber. This can be done using various tools, including a chisel and mallet, router, or mortising machine. Carefully remove material to create a cavity that matches the size and shape of the tenon, ensuring a snug fit.

- **Fitting the Tenon:** Once the mortise is formed, test-fit the tenon to ensure that it fits snugly and securely into the mortise. The fit should be tight enough to hold the joint together without gaps but loose enough to allow for easy assembly and disassembly.

- **Reinforcing the Joint (Optional):** Depending on the application and the desired strength of the joint, consider reinforcing it with additional support. This can be done by applying wood glue to the mating surfaces before joining them together or by inserting wooden or metal dowels, pegs, or wedges into the joint for added stability.

- **Assembling the Joint:** With the tenon properly fitted into the mortise, apply wood glue to the mating surfaces to create a strong bond between the two pieces. Carefully align the pieces and gently tap them together using a mallet or hammer, ensuring that the joint is flush and properly seated.

- **Clamping and Drying:** Once assembled, use clamps to hold the joint securely together while the glue dries. Follow the manufacturer's instructions for the recommended drying time, ensuring that the joint remains undisturbed during this period to allow the glue to set properly.

- **Finishing and Sanding (Optional):** After the glue has dried, remove any excess glue squeeze-out and sand the joint and surrounding areas to create a smooth and professional finish. This step helps to remove any rough edges, splinters, or imperfections, enhancing the appearance and feel of the joint.

Forming a dovetail joint is a woodworking technique known for its strength, durability, and aesthetic appeal. This joint, characterized by its interlocking teeth resembling the shape of a dove's tail, is widely used in fine woodworking for joining two pieces of timber at right angles. To form a dovetail joint:

- **Selecting Suitable Timber:** Begin by selecting high-quality timber pieces that are straight, clean, and free from defects. Choose timber species with suitable hardness and strength for your project, ensuring they are properly seasoned to minimize the risk of movement over time.

- **Measuring and Marking:** Use a measuring tape, pencil, and square to mark the location and dimensions of the dovetail joints on the timber pieces. Dovetails typically consist of a series of tails and pins, with the tails cut into one piece and the pins into the other. The spacing and size of the tails and pins will depend on the desired strength and appearance of the joint.

- **Cutting the Tails:** With the timber properly marked, use a dovetail saw or bandsaw to cut the tails on one end of the piece. The tails are typically cut at an angle, with the depth of the cut equal to half the thickness of the timber. Ensure that the cuts are straight, clean, and accurately angled, following the marked lines closely.

- **Transferring the Tail Layout:** Once the tails are cut, transfer their layout onto the corresponding piece of timber by placing them against the end grain and tracing their outlines with a pencil or marking knife. This will serve as a guide for cutting the pins later.

- **Cutting the Pins:** With the tail layout transferred, use a coping saw, dovetail saw, or bandsaw to carefully cut out the waste material between the tails, following the marked outlines closely. Take care to cut straight and accurately to ensure a tight fit between the tails and pins.

- **Fine-Tuning the Fit:** Once the tails and pins are cut, test-fit them together to ensure that they fit snugly and securely without gaps. Use a chisel, rasp, or file to fine-tune the fit as needed, removing any excess material and adjusting the angles or depths of the cuts as necessary.

- **Assembling the Joint:** With the tails and pins properly fitted, apply wood glue to the mating surfaces to create a strong bond between the two pieces. Carefully align the pieces and gently tap them together using a mallet or hammer, ensuring that the joint is flush and properly seated.

- **Clamping and Drying:** Once assembled, use clamps to hold the joint securely together while the glue dries. Follow the manufacturer's instructions for the recommended drying time, ensuring that the joint remains undisturbed during this period to allow the glue to set properly.

- **Finishing and Sanding (Optional):** After the glue has dried, remove any excess glue squeeze-out and sand the joint and surrounding areas to create a smooth and professional finish. This step helps to remove any rough edges, splinters, or imperfections, enhancing the appearance and feel of the joint.

Forming a half-lap joint is a straightforward yet effective method for joining two pieces of timber along their edges. This joint is widely used in woodworking and carpentry for its simplicity, strength, and versatility.

Figure 264: Half-Lap Joint.

To form a half-lap joint:

- **Selecting Suitable Timber:** Begin by selecting timber pieces that are straight, clean, and free from defects. Choose pieces with consistent thickness and width to ensure a tight fit and strong joint. It's essential to use timber species with suitable hardness and strength for your project, ensuring they are properly seasoned to minimize the risk of movement over time.

- **Measuring and Marking:** Use a measuring tape, pencil, and square to mark the location and dimensions of the half-lap joint on both timber pieces. Determine the width and depth of the lap joint, ensuring that it is appropriately sized for the intended application and provides sufficient surface area for gluing and fastening.

- **Cutting the Lap:** With the timber properly marked, use a saw, such as a table saw, circular saw, or handsaw, to carefully cut along the marked lines to remove half of the material from each piece. The depth of the cut should be equal to half the thickness of the timber, ensuring that both pieces fit together flush and evenly.

- **Fine-Tuning the Fit:** Once the laps are cut, test-fit the two pieces together to ensure that they fit snugly and securely without gaps. Use a chisel, rasp, or file to fine-tune the fit as needed, removing any excess material and adjusting the mating surfaces to ensure a tight and flush joint.

- **Assembling the Joint:** Apply wood glue to the mating surfaces of the half-lap joint to create a strong bond between the two pieces. Carefully align the pieces and press them together firmly, ensuring that the joint is flush and properly seated. If additional strength is required, you can reinforce the joint with screws, nails, or dowels.

- **Clamping and Drying:** Once assembled, use clamps to hold the joint securely together while the glue dries. Follow the manufacturer's instructions for the recommended drying time, ensuring that the joint remains undisturbed during this period to allow the glue to set properly.

- **Finishing and Sanding (Optional):** After the glue has dried, remove any excess glue squeeze-out and sand the joint and surrounding areas to create a smooth and professional finish. This step helps to remove any rough edges, splinters, or imperfections, enhancing the appearance and feel of the joint.

Forming a mitre joint involves joining two pieces of timber or other materials at an angle, typically 45 degrees, creating a clean and seamless corner joint. It's commonly used in woodworking and carpentry for applications such as picture frames, trim work, and moulding.

Figure 265: Mitre Joint.

To form a mitre joint:

- **Selecting Suitable Timber:** Begin by selecting timber pieces that are straight, clean, and free from defects. It's essential to ensure that the pieces have consistent thickness and width to achieve a tight and precise joint. Choose timber species that match your project requirements in terms of strength, hardness, and appearance.

- **Measuring and Marking:** Use a measuring tape, pencil, and square to mark the location and angle of the mitre joint on both timber pieces. Typically, mitre joints are cut at a 45-degree angle, but this can vary depending on the desired angle for your project. Ensure that the angle is consistent and accurate for both pieces to create a seamless joint.

- **Cutting the Mitre:** With the timber properly marked, use a mitre saw, table saw with a mitre gauge, or handsaw to carefully cut along the marked lines to create the mitre angles on each piece. It's crucial to ensure that the cuts are clean, straight, and precise to achieve a tight and seamless joint. Take your time and double-check the angles to ensure accuracy.

- **Dry-Fitting:** Once the mitre cuts are made, dry-fit the two pieces together to ensure that the angles match up perfectly and create a tight joint without gaps or unevenness. Make any necessary adjustments to the cuts using a fine-toothed saw or sandpaper to achieve a snug and flush fit.

- **Gluing and Assembling:** Apply wood glue to the mitre surfaces of both pieces, ensuring even coverage along the entire joint. Carefully align the pieces at the correct angle and press them together firmly to create a strong bond. Use clamps to hold the joint securely while the glue dries, following the manufacturer's instructions for drying time.

- **Reinforcing the Joint (Optional):** Depending on the application and desired strength of the joint, you may choose to reinforce it with additional fasteners such as nails, screws, or biscuits. These can be inserted through the joint at an angle to provide extra stability and support, particularly for load-bearing or structural applications.

- **Finishing and Sanding (Optional):** After the glue has dried, remove any excess glue squeeze-out and sand the joint and surrounding areas to create a smooth and professional finish. This step helps to remove any rough edges, splinters, or imperfections, enhancing the appearance and feel of the joint.

Forming a dowel joint involves joining two pieces of timber by inserting dowels, cylindrical rods typically made of wood, metal, or plastic, into corresponding holes drilled in the pieces to be joined. This method creates a strong and durable connection, often used in furniture making, cabinetry, and woodworking projects.

Figure 266: Dowel Joint.

To form a dowel joint:

- **Selecting Suitable Timber:** Begin by selecting timber pieces that are straight, clean, and free from defects. Ensure that the pieces have consistent thickness and width to achieve a tight and precise joint. Choose timber species that match your project requirements in terms of strength, hardness, and appearance.

- **Measuring and Marking:** Use a measuring tape, pencil, and square to mark the location and spacing of the dowel holes on both timber pieces. It's essential to ensure accurate and consistent spacing between the holes to create a strong and evenly distributed joint. Mark the centre points for drilling the dowel holes on both surfaces to be joined.

- **Drilling Dowel Holes:** Use a drill press or handheld drill equipped with a dowel jig and drill bit to carefully drill the dowel holes at the marked locations on both timber pieces. The diameter of the drill bit should match the diameter of the dowels to create a snug fit. Drill the holes to the appropriate depth, ensuring that they are straight and perpendicular to the surface.

- **Cutting Dowel Inserts:** Cut dowel inserts to the appropriate length using a handsaw or dowel cutting jig. The length of the dowels should match the depth of the drilled holes to ensure a flush fit. It's crucial to cut the dowels accurately to achieve a tight and secure joint.

- **Applying Glue:** Apply wood glue to the inside of the dowel holes and along the surface of the dowel inserts. Ensure even coverage of the glue to create a strong bond between the dowels and timber pieces. Use a brush or dowel to spread the glue evenly and remove any excess.

- **Inserting Dowels:** Insert the dowel inserts into the drilled holes on one of the timber pieces, ensuring that they are fully seated and flush with the surface. Repeat the process for the other timber piece, aligning the dowel holes with the dowel inserts to create a tight and precise joint.

- **Assembling the Joint:** Carefully join the two timber pieces together, ensuring that the dowels are properly aligned and seated in the corresponding holes. Apply gentle pressure to the joint to ensure a tight fit and squeeze out any excess glue. Use clamps to hold the joint securely while the glue dries, following the manufacturer's instructions for drying time.

- **Finishing and Sanding (Optional):** After the glue has dried, remove any excess glue squeeze-out and sand the joint and surrounding areas to create a smooth and professional finish. This step helps to remove any rough edges, splinters, or imperfections, enhancing the appearance and feel of the joint.

Forming a bridle joint involves creating a strong and durable connection between two pieces of timber by interlocking them with corresponding notches or slots. Also known as a open tenon joint, this woodworking technique is commonly used in cabinetry, furniture making, and joinery projects. To form a bridle joint:

- **Selecting Suitable Timber:** Begin by selecting timber pieces that are straight, clean, and free from defects. Ensure that the pieces have consistent thickness and width to achieve a tight and precise joint. Choose timber species that match your project requirements in terms of strength, hardness, and appearance.

- **Measuring and Marking:** Use a measuring tape, pencil, and square to mark the location and dimensions of the notches or slots on both timber pieces. It's essential to ensure accurate and consistent measurements to create a strong and evenly distributed joint. Mark the width and depth of the notches on both surfaces to be joined.

- **Cutting the Notches:** Use a saw, chisel, or router equipped with a straight bit to carefully cut the notches or slots at the marked locations on both timber pieces. The width and depth of the notches should match the dimensions specified in your design plans to ensure a snug and precise fit. Take your time to cut the notches accurately, ensuring that they are straight and perpendicular to the surface.

- **Test Fitting:** After cutting the notches, perform a test fit by inserting one timber piece into the corresponding notch on the other piece. Ensure that the fit is snug and that the joint aligns properly without gaps or misalignments. Make any necessary adjustments to the notches to achieve a tight and precise fit.

- **Applying Glue (Optional):** Depending on the specific requirements of your project, you may choose to apply wood glue to the mating surfaces of the joint to create a stronger bond. Apply the glue evenly to the surfaces using a brush or roller, ensuring full coverage. Use a damp cloth to remove any excess glue squeeze-out.

- **Assembling the Joint:** Carefully join the two timber pieces together, ensuring that the notches interlock properly and that the joint aligns accurately. Apply gentle pressure to the joint to ensure a tight fit and squeeze out any excess glue. Use clamps to hold the joint securely while the glue dries, following the manufacturer's instructions for drying time.

- **Reinforcing (Optional):** To further strengthen the joint, you may choose to install dowels, screws, or nails through the sides of the joint. Pre-drill pilot holes to prevent splitting and ensure accurate placement of the fasteners. Drive the fasteners carefully into the timber, countersinking them below the surface if necessary.

- **Finishing and Sanding (Optional):** After the glue has dried and any reinforcements have been added, remove any excess glue squeeze-out and sand the joint and surrounding areas to create a smooth and professional finish. This step helps to remove any rough edges, splinters, or imperfections, enhancing the appearance and feel of the joint.

Forming a tongue and groove joint involves creating a snug and interlocking connection between two pieces of timber, commonly used in flooring, panelling, and cabinetry. This joint is characterized by a protruding tongue on one piece and a corresponding groove on the other, allowing for precise alignment and a strong bond.

Figure 267: Tongue and Groove Joint.

To form a tongue and groove joint:

- **Selecting Suitable Timber:** Begin by selecting timber pieces that are straight, clean, and free from defects. Ensure that the pieces have consistent thickness and width to achieve a tight and precise joint. Choose timber species that match your project requirements in terms of strength, hardness, and appearance.

- **Measuring and Marking:** Use a measuring tape, pencil, and square to mark the location and dimensions of the tongue and groove on both timber pieces. It's essential to ensure accurate and consistent measurements to create a strong and evenly distributed joint. Mark the width, depth, and length of the tongue and groove on each piece.

- **Cutting the Groove:** Use a router equipped with a straight bit or a table saw with a dado blade to carefully cut the groove along the edge of one timber piece. The width and depth of the groove should match the dimensions specified in your design plans to ensure a snug fit for the tongue. Take your time to cut the groove accurately, ensuring that it is straight and centred along the edge.

- **Cutting the Tongue:** After cutting the groove, use a router, table saw, or tongue and groove plane to cut the corresponding tongue along the edge of the other timber piece. The width and thickness of the tongue should match the dimensions of the groove to ensure a precise fit. Take care to cut the tongue accurately, ensuring that it aligns properly with the groove.

- **Test Fitting:** Perform a test fit by inserting the tongue of one timber piece into the groove of the other piece. Ensure that the fit is snug and that the joint aligns properly without gaps or misalignments. Make any necessary adjustments to the tongue and groove to achieve a tight and precise fit.

- **Applying Glue (Optional):** Depending on the specific requirements of your project, you may choose to apply wood glue to the mating surfaces of the joint to create a stronger bond. Apply the glue evenly to the surfaces using a brush or roller, ensuring full coverage. Use a damp cloth to remove any excess glue squeeze-out.

- **Assembling the Joint:** Carefully join the two timber pieces together, ensuring that the tongue slides smoothly into the groove and that the joint aligns accurately. Apply gentle pressure to the joint to ensure a tight fit and squeeze out any excess glue. Use clamps to hold the joint securely while the glue dries, following the manufacturer's instructions for drying time.

- **Finishing and Sanding (Optional):** After the glue has dried, remove any excess glue squeeze-out and sand the joint and surrounding areas to create a smooth and professional finish. This step helps to remove any rough edges, splinters, or imperfections, enhancing the appearance and feel of the joint.

Excavations

Excavations are often necessary for timber landscaping projects for several reasons:

- **Foundation Preparation:** Excavations are essential for preparing the ground and creating a stable foundation for timber structures such as decks, pergolas, and retaining walls. Digging down to the required depth allows for the removal of topsoil, rocks, roots, and other debris that could compromise the stability and integrity of the structure.

- **Levelling and Grading:** Excavations help to level and grade the terrain to ensure that the timber landscape features are installed on a flat and even surface. This is crucial for ensuring the structural integrity of the timber elements and preventing issues such as uneven settling, shifting, or instability over time.

- **Drainage Installation:** Excavations allow for the installation of drainage systems such as French drains, surface drains, or trench drains to manage water runoff and prevent waterlogging or erosion around timber structures. Proper drainage is essential for preserving the integrity of timber materials and preventing water damage or decay.

- **Utility Installation:** Excavations may be required to install underground utilities such as irrigation systems, electrical wiring, or drainage pipes to support various timber landscaping features. These utilities may need to be buried beneath the surface to provide essential services without detracting from the aesthetics of the landscape.

- **Tree and Planting Preparation:** Excavations may be necessary for preparing planting beds, tree pits, or root zones for the installation of trees, shrubs, and other vegetation within the timber landscape design. Excavating soil to the appropriate depth and volume ensures that plants have adequate space for root growth and access to essential nutrients and water.

- **Structural Support:** Excavations may be required to create footings, piers, or support posts for timber structures such as decks, pergolas, or retaining walls. Digging below the frost line or to a specified depth allows for the installation of support elements that provide stability and prevent settling or shifting of the structure over time.

- **Access and Clearance:** Excavations provide access to underground areas and allow for clearance of obstacles or obstructions that may hinder the installation or construction process. This includes removing rocks, boulders, tree stumps, or other debris that could interfere with the placement of timber landscape features.

Excavations play a critical role in the preparation, construction, and installation of timber landscaping projects, ensuring that the site is properly prepared, levelled, drained, and supported to accommodate the desired design elements and achieve long-lasting, functional, and visually appealing results.

Excavation work for timber landscaping projects encompasses a range of tasks and methods, each requiring careful consideration of safety measures and planning. The choice of excavation method and the establishment of a safe system of work are crucial steps in mitigating risks associated with the project. Particularly when the excavation involves more than shallow trenching or deals with significant quantities of material, health and safety issues must be prioritized.

Figure 268: Landscaping excavation. Christine, CC BY-SA 2.0, via Flickr.

Trenching is a common aspect of excavation work, especially for projects requiring deep excavations. To minimize the risk of trench collapse, various methods such as shoring, benching, or battering must be employed. In built-up areas or streets, additional precautions like sheeting may be necessary to prevent collapse due to vehicle movement. Regardless of depth, if there's a risk of engulfment, appropriate risk controls must be in place.

A geotechnical engineer's report is often required to assess the stability and safety of trench excavations. This report provides crucial information about soil conditions, support requirements, and potential long-term effects on stability. Engineers or competent persons should design support systems based on this report's recommendations, ensuring the implementation of effective risk controls.

Excavation preparation and execution typically involve the use of heavy equipment such as bulldozers, scrapers, and excavators. Manual work may also be necessary, especially for finer tasks like trimming. Safety measures, including fall protection and traffic management, must be in place to mitigate risks associated with manual labour and powered mobile plant operation.

Tunnelling work presents its own set of challenges and requires specialized engineering expertise throughout the planning, design, and construction phases. Adequate pre-construction investigation and accurate interpretation of ground conditions are essential for safe tunnel construction. Designers must consider excavation methods, ground conditions, and support requirements to develop a comprehensive tunnel design that prioritizes safety.

Common hazards in tunnel construction include stability issues, changing ground conditions, confined spaces, air contamination, and the use of heavy machinery. Risk control measures such as ground support, fall protection, and ventilation systems are crucial for mitigating these hazards and ensuring worker safety.

Shafts, often constructed for access or ventilation to tunnels, pose unique risks related to limited workspace, falling objects, and hoisting equipment. Proper stabilization, continuous lining during excavation, and fall protection measures are essential for safe shaft construction.

After completing excavation work, loose materials must be removed using appropriate hand tools and disposed of properly to avoid contamination. Checking the completed excavation against specifications or work instructions ensures that the project meets safety and quality standards, with additional surveys conducted if necessary to verify the accuracy of the work. Overall, careful planning, adherence to safety protocols, and ongoing monitoring are essential for successful excavation in timber landscaping projects.

Digging Post Holes

Installing posts for projects like mailboxes or fences requires careful planning and precise execution to ensure stability and longevity. Simply digging a hole is not sufficient; specific tools and techniques are necessary for the task. Assuming the post locations have been laid out using string and stakes, which serve as the starting and center points for the holes, the excavation process begins.

Depth is a critical consideration for post holes, with the rule of thumb being one-third of the fence height. For example, a 1.8-meter fence would require a hole depth of 600mm. While opinions on hole diameter vary, a wider hole facilitates upright post installation but requires more concrete for stability.

The tools required for post hole excavation include shovels, digging shovels, post hole diggers, reciprocating saws, steel crowbars, and post hole augurs or a bobcat for larger projects. The six-step process for digging the perfect hole involves starting with a shovel to centre the hole around the stake, using a digging shovel to slice through roots and turf, employing post hole diggers to penetrate the soil and extract dirt, and widening the hole as necessary while stabilizing the post.

Figure 269: Auger and post hole. Btwashburn, CC BY 2.0, via Flickr.

Troubleshooting tips include wetting hard or sandy soil for easier extraction, using a steel crowbar to dislodge rocks, and covering holes when leaving the site to prevent accidents. Additionally, caution should be exercised with powerful digging equipment like post hole augurs, as they require strength to operate and may be less effective in certain soil conditions. Sawing through large roots with a reciprocating saw is recommended for easier excavation. Finally, it's essential to check for underground utilities before digging and to use lightweight post hole diggers to avoid unnecessary exhaustion.

Working with Lattice

Lattice has become a popular choice for outdoor landscaping projects, primarily made from treated pine due to its durability and resistance to decay, termites, and fungi. Treated pine lattice panels come in various pre-made sizes, making them versatile for different applications. One of the significant advantages of treated pine lattice is its low maintenance requirement; it typically does not need protective painting or staining unless desired for aesthetic reasons. The natural greenish colour of treated pine blends seamlessly with outdoor environments, complementing the earthy tones of plants, woodwork, bricks, and paving.

Figure 270: Use of lattice panels. Andrea_44 from Leamington, Ontario, Canada, CC BY 2.0, via Wikimedia Commons.

In addition to treated pine, hardwood and western red cedar lattice panels are also available for outdoor use. Cedar lattice, in particular, can be used indoors as well, serving as a decorative feature or room divider. Furthermore, lattice made from fibre cement sheets offers a modern alternative, providing the same design attributes as timber lattice but with added benefits such as ease of painting with a roller. However, fibre cement lattice is prone to cracking, requiring careful handling during installation.

Traditionally, timber lattice comes in two main patterns: square and diagonal, with variations in the grid spacing. The square pattern is the most popular today, offering a classic look suitable for various landscaping styles. For those seeking a more contemporary option, cement sheet lattice may be preferred.

To begin the installation process, marking the line of the wall and ensuring all posts are set in a straight line is crucial. Corner posts are marked first, followed by driving stakes and running a stringline to mark the intermediary post positions. Post holes are then dug approximately 500mm deep and 300mm square. Using an auger-type post hole digger can simplify this task.

The next step involves notching the posts for the cross rails before setting them in the ground. The top rail is flush with the top of the post, while the bottom rail sits approximately 100mm above the ground. Middle rail notches are spaced accordingly to accommodate the width of the lattice panels. Notches for the top and bottom rails are made to the thickness of the rail and chiselled out to provide a flush fit, while middle rail post notches are created to the width of the rail and set 15mm deep on the inside of each corner post and both sides of any intermediary posts. This meticulous approach ensures a secure and visually appealing installation of lattice panels for landscaping projects.

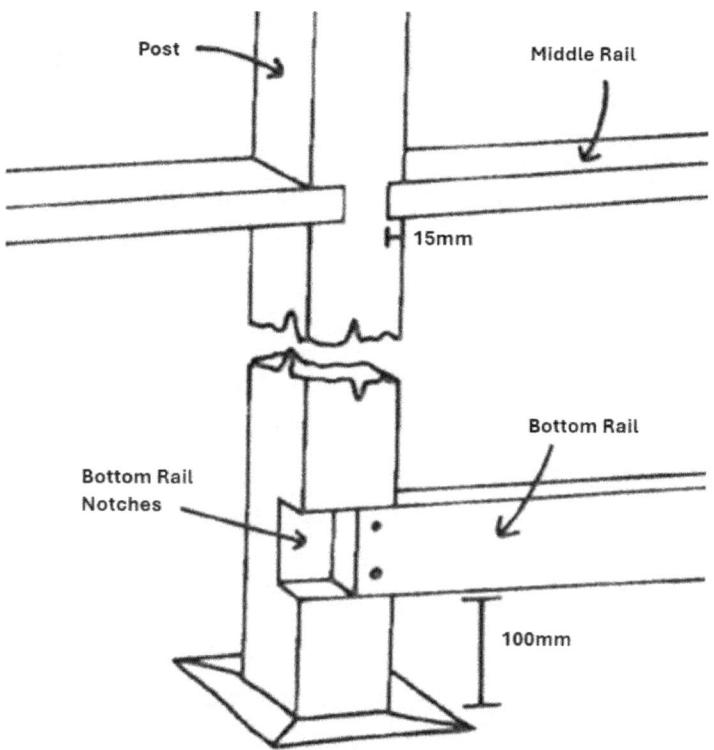

Figure 271: Cutting rail notches.

Setting the posts is a critical step in ensuring the stability and alignment of the lattice wall. After digging the post holes and preparing them with timber sole plates or concrete, the next step is to establish a straight line between the corner posts using a stringline. This stringline is fixed to the height of the bottom rail notch, ensuring consistency in height along the entire length of the wall. A spirit level is then used to confirm that the stringline is level, making adjustments as needed to accommodate uneven ground. It's essential to ensure that the bottom of the notch aligns precisely with the stringline to avoid crooked lattice installation.

To keep the posts upright and straight during installation, temporary bracing with 50 x 25mm battens is necessary. In sandy soil conditions, special post struts may be required to provide additional support. Once the posts are correctly positioned, the holes are filled with a mixture of soil and dry cement, compacted firmly to stabilize the posts. The top of the mixture is sloped away from the post above ground level to facilitate water runoff. Water is then added to set the cement in the soil, allowing it to cure overnight.

The following day, the rails are cut and fixed into the post notches using galvanized bullet head nails. The temporary braces are left in place to provide support during this process. Rail joins should be positioned in the middle of the posts to ensure stability, avoiding multiple joins in the same post where possible. Once the rails are secured, the lattice panels are attached using galvanized flat head nails, with attention paid to maintaining the straightness of the midrail during nailing.

For a professional finish, adding a capping to the lattice wall is recommended. An angled capping that sheds water effectively is chosen, and it is fixed to the rails using galvanized nails spaced approximately 600mm apart. These nails should be driven at least 35mm into the rail to ensure a secure attachment. Overall, these steps ensure that the lattice wall is not only structurally sound but also visually appealing, enhancing the aesthetic appeal of outdoor spaces.

Lattice offers a myriad of creative possibilities to enhance both the aesthetic appeal and functionality of garden and home spaces. Its versatility makes it a popular choice for various applications, from adding privacy to creating charming garden features. One common use is as an attractive screen atop a paling fence, providing both privacy and a supportive structure for climbing plants. By fixing uprights to the fence rails and attaching lattice panels to them, a visually appealing and functional barrier is created, ideal for fostering the growth of creepers.

Imagine a handsome arbor gracing your garden landscape, serving as a focal point adorned with climbing roses. These structures are not only sturdy but also easy to install, offering a beautiful addition to any outdoor space. Lattice can also be repurposed into a quick and simple shelving unit by cutting lattice panels to size, attaching battens at the top and bottom, and adding ready-made shelves, providing both storage and visual interest.

For those in need of occasional privacy screens, lattice panels can be joined together with hinges to create portable Chinese garden screens. These screens offer a versatile solution for adding privacy, concealing unsightly areas, or corralling straying pets with ease. Additionally, lattice can be used as garden screens, dividers, or wall attachments for climbing plants, offering shade on exposed verandas or patios and enclosing ferneries for added ambiance.

Beyond its decorative uses, lattice serves practical purposes as well. It can be employed to screen carports, conceal vehicles, trailers, and boats from public view, or partition utility areas from entertainment spaces. The versatility of lattice knows no bounds, limited only by one's imagination. With its wide range of applications, lattice allows homeowners to customize and enhance their living spaces, creating environments that are both functional and visually pleasing.

Building a Trellis

Creating an inviting front yard doesn't have to break the bank; sometimes, all it takes is some strategic landscaping and thoughtful additions to transform a plain patch of ground into a welcoming entrance. One effective way to achieve this transformation is by incorporating a stone wall and arbours, which can lend a sense of character and elegance to the exterior of a home. The use of primed treated pine for the arbour gateway and stone blocks for the walls offers a cost-effective solution that can mimic the appearance of more expensive materials while expediting the construction process.

Figure 272: Garden Trellis. Virginia State Parks staff, CC BY 2.0, via Wikimedia Commons.

To complete the look and enhance the functionality of the space, adding a paved patio and pathway leading to the gateway, along with carefully selected landscape features and new plants, can significantly elevate the aesthetic appeal of the front yard. These elements not only contribute to the overall visual impact but also create a cohesive and inviting outdoor environment for homeowners and visitors alike.

Building the arbours is a crucial step in defining the access to the front door and adding architectural interest to the landscape. Constructed from primed exterior finger-jointed pine, the decorative arbours consist of pairs of posts clad on all sides, supporting lintels on either side, with the trellis arbour featuring an integrated lattice panel. It's important to adapt the size of the arbours to ensure they are proportional to the home's scale, and applying an exterior acrylic finish ensures durability and weather resistance.

The construction process begins with laying out the arbour positions using a temporary timber frame, followed by marking post locations and digging post holes. Sink the posts into the holes, ensuring they are plumb, and secure them to the frame before filling the holes with fast-set concrete. Next, attach the lintels using offcuts for support and secure them with bugle screws, ensuring equal height on all sides. Then, add the cladding, starting from the base and working upwards, ensuring equal overhang on both sides.

For the trellis panel, leave off two sides of cladding and position the rails accordingly, securing them with screws and adding spacers at regular intervals. Finish the trellis by attaching slats centred on the markings and secured with galvanized nails. Finally, complete the arbours by adding the remaining cladding, ensuring a seamless and polished finish.

Overall, by following these steps and utilizing cost-effective materials, homeowners can create an inviting front yard that enhances the curb appeal of their property without breaking the budget.

Building a Timber Paling Fence

Building a timber paling fence requires careful planning, precise measurements, and the right tools and materials. Before starting the construction process, it's essential to gather all the necessary items. This includes hardwood timber posts, treated pine fencing rails, plinth boards, timber palings of varying sizes, framing nails, paling nails, cement (GP Cement), and a set of tools such as a crowbar, shovel, stringline, level, circular saw, hammer, chisel, set square, pencil, framing gun, paling gun, and an air compressor.

Figure 273: Timber piling fence example. Andy Beecroft, CC BY 2.0, via Wikimedia Commons.

The construction process begins with dismantling the old fence, which involves cutting it into manageable sections for removal. It's crucial to handle this task carefully to avoid injury and ensure efficient disposal. When loading the sections onto a trailer, alternating the orientation of the sections can maximize space and minimize tipping costs.

Setting the stringline is the next step, which involves establishing a straight line for the new fence. This is achieved by attaching a stringline between the front and back posts at the desired height. The stringline must be pulled tightly to prevent sagging, ensuring a straight fence alignment. While not all old fence holes may line up perfectly, the goal is to align the majority of them as closely as possible with the stringline.

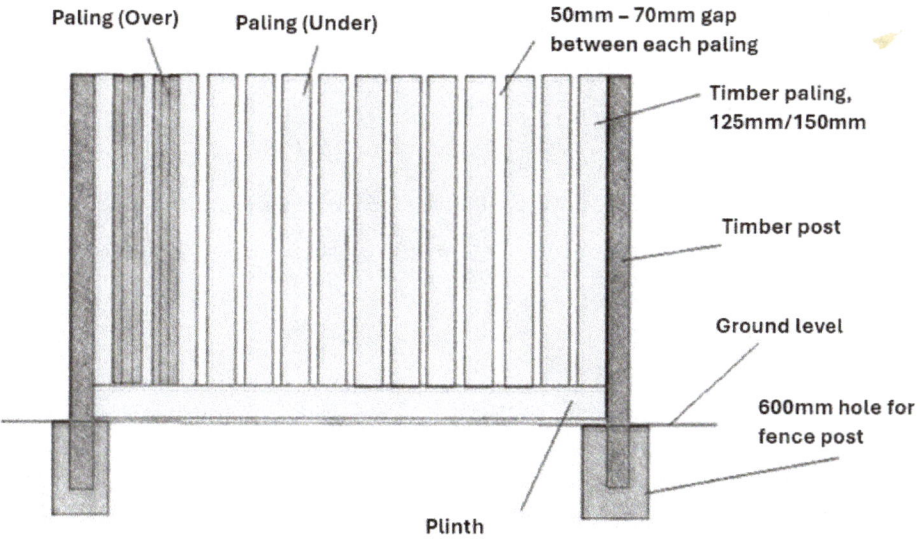

Figure 274: Timber Fence Diagram Front.

Once the stringline is in place, marking out and digging the fence post holes can begin. These holes should be dug approximately 600mm deep and 250mm in diameter, with the aim of positioning the posts as close to the stringline as possible. A mixture of soil and cement is used to secure the posts in place, ensuring stability and alignment. Bracing the posts temporarily during this process can help maintain their upright position.

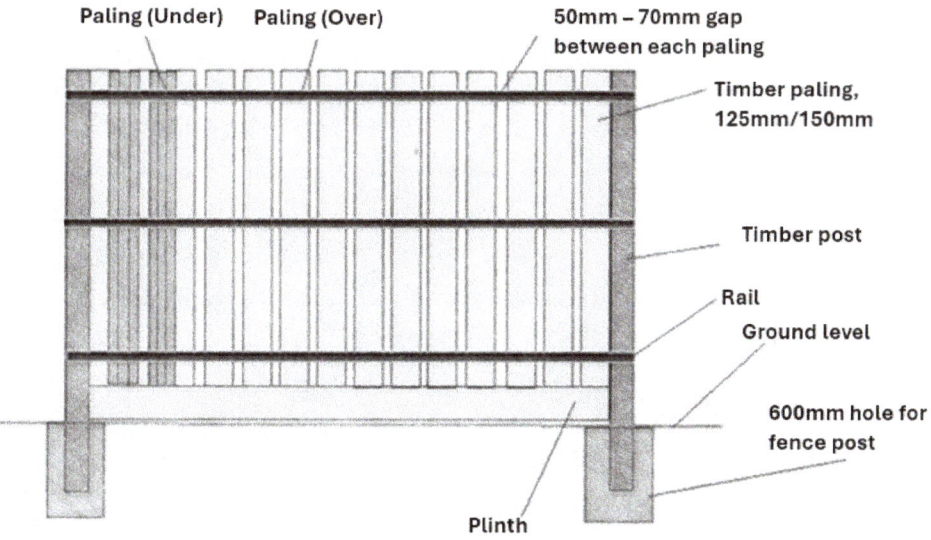

Figure 275: Timber Paling Fence Diagram Back.

After the posts are set, the construction of the fence can proceed by attaching the rails and palings. Cutting the checkouts for the fence rails ensures a snug fit, while nailing the plinth board and fencing rails into place provides structural support. Careful measurement and alignment are crucial at this stage to ensure the fence is straight and level.

Finally, attaching the timber palings completes the construction process. This involves placing the palings onto the rails, ensuring even spacing and alignment. The under palings are secured with one nail in the top and bottom rails, while the over palings require two nails in each rail. Using a level periodically can help maintain the straightness of the palings and ensure a professional finish.

Overall, building a timber paling fence requires attention to detail, precision, and patience. By following these steps and utilizing the appropriate tools and materials, homeowners can construct a sturdy and visually appealing fence that enhances the aesthetics and security of their property.

Building a Pergola

A pergola serves as an oasis of relaxation in a backyard, particularly during the summer months when the sun is shining brightly. It offers shade from the intense heat when covered with bamboo or a shade cloth, and during the winter, the covering can be removed to allow sunlight to filter through, providing a versatile outdoor space for year-round enjoyment. In the case of this example project, the pergola was strategically built above a freestanding deck adjacent to a sunny poolside area, creating a luxurious resort-style relaxation spot right in the backyard [98].

The foundation of the pergola consists of seven sturdy 90 x 90mm posts, with an additional existing shed corner post serving as the eighth post on the front right. These posts provide the structural support needed for the pergola. The rear beam is supported by four back posts, ensuring stability and strength for the entire structure. Rafters are then installed to span the beams, with battens fixed perpendicular to the rafters to provide support for the bamboo roofing or shade cloth.

Before construction begins, careful site preparation is necessary. The deck area is measured and pegged out, with any vegetation and debris removed to create a clean canvas for building. The positioning of the pergola posts is measured from the corner of the existing shed, following the angled pool paving header course to ensure a seamless integration with the existing landscape. Concrete footings are then prepared by excavating holes to the appropriate dimensions using a posthole digger or powered auger. The posts are set in concrete, with gravel added for drainage, ensuring a stable foundation for the pergola.

Building the deck involves securing bearers to the pergola posts, raising the deck adjacent to the existing paving. The deck is constructed using treated-pine bearers and joists of specific dimensions, with the bearers supported by the pergola posts and central stumps equally spaced between the posts. This design provides structural integrity while creating a step-up effect from the ground level to the deck surface.

Several tips are provided for building a low deck effectively. These include grading the ground for proper surface drainage, ensuring ventilation and access underneath and around the deck for maintenance, selecting appropriate timber species that meet building regulations, using high-quality fixings such as hot-dipped galvanized or stainless-steel nails and screws, and implementing bracing techniques to prevent lateral movement and enhance stability. Double diagonal braces are suggested for additional reinforcement at the top corners of the posts, ensuring that the deck and pergola remain secure and durable over time.

Positioning the front posts of the pergola is a crucial step in ensuring the overall alignment and aesthetic appeal of the structure. To achieve precise positioning, specific measurements and techniques are employed. Firstly, the front posts are aligned with the edge of the header course, which refers to the row of pavers or stones that serve as the border or edging of the paved area. This alignment helps maintain symmetry and visual harmony with the existing landscape features, such as pathways or paved areas, creating a seamless integration of the pergola into the outdoor space.

The process begins by lifting four pavers at each designated front post location. This allows access to the ground beneath, where the post holes will be excavated. By removing the pavers, the construction team gains direct access to the ground surface, facilitating the digging of holes to accommodate the pergola posts. These holes are typically dug to a specific depth and width, ensuring adequate support and stability for the posts once they are installed.

Figure 276: Position the front posts.

Once the holes are excavated to the appropriate dimensions, the front posts are positioned carefully to align with the edge of the header course. It's essential to maintain a precise distance between the posts and the paving line to achieve a visually pleasing result. In this case, the posts are positioned approximately 10mm outside the paving line, providing a slight buffer to ensure that the pergola remains slightly detached from the paved surface.

After the posts are positioned correctly, the next step involves filling the excavated holes with concrete to secure the posts in place. The concrete serves as a solid foundation, anchoring the posts firmly into the ground and providing stability to the entire structure. Once the concrete has set and cured, typically over a period of several days, the pavers are re-laid around the base of the posts. This final step ensures that the paved area maintains its integrity and appearance while seamlessly integrating with the newly installed pergola.

Setting the pergola posts marks a significant milestone in the construction process, laying the foundation for the entire structure. The process begins by positioning the corner posts in their designated locations. These corner posts serve as the primary supports for the pergola, anchoring it securely to the ground. Careful consideration is given to their placement, ensuring they are accurately positioned according to the predetermined layout and design of the pergola.

Once the corner posts are in place, the next crucial step is to ensure they are perfectly upright or plumb. This is essential for the structural integrity and stability of the pergola. To achieve this, plumb bobs or levels may be used to check the vertical alignment of each post. Any necessary adjustments are made to ensure that the posts are perfectly vertical before proceeding further.

Cross-bracing is then employed to reinforce the corner posts and prevent lateral movement or instability. This involves attaching 40 x 19mm braces to the posts and securing them to ground pegs. These braces provide additional support and rigidity, especially during the concrete pouring process and while the concrete sets.

With the corner posts securely in place and cross-braced, the next step is to concrete around the posts. This involves filling the holes excavated for the posts with concrete, ensuring that the posts are firmly anchored to the ground. Tamping the concrete helps to compact it and remove any air pockets, enhancing its strength and stability.

During the concrete pouring process, attention is also paid to sloping the tops of the concrete around the posts. This sloping helps to facilitate drainage, ensuring that water does not pool around the base of the posts. Proper drainage is essential for preventing water damage and prolonging the lifespan of the pergola.

Once the corner posts are set in concrete, the process is repeated for any intermediate posts that are required for additional support along the length of the pergola. These intermediate posts are positioned according to the design specifications and spaced at regular intervals to evenly distribute the weight of the structure.

Cutting the posts marks a crucial step in the construction process, ensuring that they are precisely trimmed to the required height and align with the overall design and dimensions of the pergola. This step typically follows the setting of the posts in concrete, allowing for adjustments to be made based on the actual ground level and other site-specific considerations.

Figure 277: Cutting the posts.

To begin the process of cutting the posts, the desired height for each post is transferred from the design plans to the actual posts themselves. This is typically done using a straight edge and a spirit level to ensure accuracy and consistency across all posts. By marking a square line around each post at the designated height, the construction team establishes a clear guideline for cutting away any excess material.

The use of a circular saw is typically employed to cut the posts to the desired height along the marked square lines. Circular saws offer precision and efficiency, allowing for clean and straight cuts to be made with relative ease. However, it's important to exercise caution during this process to ensure safety and accuracy.

One useful tip to enhance the accuracy of the cutting process is the use of a water level. A water level provides a highly accurate means of measuring and transferring heights between posts, especially in situations where the ground may not be perfectly level or consistent. By using a water level in conjunction with traditional leveling tools, construction teams can ensure that each post is cut to the precise height required for the pergola.

The process of housing and notching the posts is a crucial step in the construction of a pergola, as it involves creating specific features in the posts to accommodate the beams and rafters of the structure. This step requires precision and attention to detail to ensure that the components fit together seamlessly and securely, ultimately contributing to the structural integrity and aesthetic appeal of the pergola.

To begin, the top of the back corner posts and the left front corner post are "housed" to accommodate the beams of the pergola. This involves cutting a precise groove or recess into the top of each post, typically measuring 190 x 45mm in size. This housing provides a secure and stable connection point for the beams, allowing them to rest flush with the tops of the posts and providing structural support for the entire pergola framework.

In addition to housing the posts for the beams, a 45 x 45mm notch is cut from the outside edge of certain posts to accommodate the outside rafters of the pergola. This notch is strategically positioned to allow the outside rafters to slot over the beams securely, creating a smooth and uniform appearance along the edges of the pergola structure. By carefully cutting and fitting these notches, construction teams ensure that the rafters are properly supported and aligned, minimizing the risk of sagging or structural instability over time.

Figure 278: Housing and notching the posts.

One important tip to keep in mind during this process is to seal all cut treated-pine surfaces. Treated pine is commonly used in pergola construction due to its durability and resistance to rot and decay. However, cutting and exposing untreated surfaces can compromise the protective properties of the wood, potentially leading to moisture damage and deterioration over time. By applying a suitable sealant or protective coating to all cut surfaces, construction teams can help prolong the lifespan of the pergola and maintain its structural integrity for years to come.

When it comes to housing intermediate posts for a pergola, precision is key. This step involves creating grooves or recesses in the posts to accommodate the beams of the pergola structure. By housing the intermediate posts, you ensure a secure and stable connection between the posts and beams, contributing to the overall strength and integrity of the pergola.

To begin the process, a circular saw blade is set to a depth of 45mm, which matches the depth of the housing required for the beams. Careful adjustments are made to ensure the blade is set accurately, as any deviation could result in an improper fit between the posts and beams. Once the saw blade is properly set, a series of cuts are made into the posts, spaced approximately 7mm apart. These cuts are made to the height of the housing, ensuring that the recess is deep enough to accommodate the beams securely.

After making the series of cuts with the circular saw, the next step is to remove the waste material from the housing using a sharp chisel and hand plane. This requires careful and precise work to ensure that the housing is clean, smooth, and properly sized to fit the beams. The chisel is used to carefully chip away at the wood between the cuts, while the hand plane helps to smooth out any rough edges and refine the surface of the housing. This meticulous process may take time and patience, but it is essential for creating a snug and secure fit between the posts and beams.

A helpful tip during this process is to test-fit a beam offcut into the housing to ensure it sits flush. This allows you to confirm that the housing is the correct size and depth to accommodate the beams properly. If adjustments are needed, they can be made before proceeding further with the construction of the pergola. By test-fitting the beams, you can identify any potential issues early on and address them before they become more challenging to correct.

Preparing the beam ends is a crucial step in the construction of a pergola, as it ensures that the beams are properly sized and positioned to support the rafters effectively. This step involves cutting the beams to the correct length and shape, allowing for a 500mm overhang at each end for aesthetic purposes and to provide adequate coverage.

Using a circular saw, the beams are carefully cut to match the template for the rafter ends. The template serves as a guide for shaping the ends of the beams to create a uniform and visually appealing look for the pergola. Precision is key during this process to ensure that the beams are cut accurately and to the correct dimensions.

Once the beams are cut to size, they are lifted into place and positioned on the posts. The next step involves marking the position of the rafters on the face of the beam. This marking serves as a guide for attaching the rafters later in the construction process, ensuring that they are evenly spaced and properly aligned.

To secure the beams in place, they are clamped to the posts using sturdy clamps. This helps to hold the beams securely in position while additional work is carried out on the pergola structure. Clamping the beams also helps to ensure that they remain level and properly aligned, contributing to the overall stability and structural integrity of the pergola.

Overlapping the beams is a critical step in the construction of a pergola, as it helps to reinforce the structure and ensure its stability over time. This process involves strategically positioning the beams along the front and back lines of the posts, with one end of each beam overlapping the other. The overlap creates a stronger connection between the beams and distributes the weight of the pergola more evenly, reducing the risk of sagging or structural failure.

To begin, a short and long beam is selected for each line of posts. These beams are carefully positioned so that they overlap at the centre-line of the housing on the posts. The centre-line alignment ensures that the load-bearing forces are evenly distributed across the beams, helping to prevent any weak points in the structure.

Once the beams are properly aligned, the next step is to secure them in place using galvanized cup-head bolts. These bolts are drilled through the centre of the overlap, creating a strong and durable connection between the beams. The use of galvanized bolts helps to protect against rust and corrosion, ensuring that the connection remains secure over time, even in harsh outdoor conditions.

The clearance holes drilled for the bolts allow for any minor adjustments to be made during the installation process, ensuring that the beams are aligned correctly and securely fastened to the posts. Once the bolts are in place, they are tightened securely to hold the beams firmly in position.

Positioning the end rafters is a crucial step in the construction of a pergola as it sets the framework for the roof structure. These rafters, typically placed perpendicular to the beams, play a significant role in providing support and stability to the overall structure.

To begin, the end rafters are positioned across the beams, aligning them with the edges of the beams to mark the notches. This ensures that the rafters are evenly spaced and properly aligned with the beams, creating a symmetrical and structurally sound framework for the roof.

Figure 279: Positioning end rafters.

Once positioned, a template is laid on the ends of the rafters to mark out the notches accurately. This template serves as a guide for cutting the notches, ensuring that they are the correct size and shape to fit securely over the beams. Careful attention is paid to ensure that the notches are positioned correctly and aligned with the beams to prevent any gaps or inconsistencies in the roof structure.

After marking out the notches, the end rafters are positioned over the front and back beams, ensuring that they are flush against the lugs on the corner posts. This helps to ensure that the rafters are properly seated and securely attached to the beams, providing additional stability and support to the pergola structure.

Securing the rafters is a crucial step in the construction process of a pergola, as it ensures the stability and durability of the roof structure. Properly securing the rafters not only prevents them from shifting or moving over time but also strengthens the overall framework of the pergola.

To begin, the rafter is clamped firmly to the beam to pull it tightly against the beam. This step helps to ensure that the rafter is properly aligned and seated on the beam, minimizing any gaps or inconsistencies in the roof structure. By pulling the rafter tightly against the beam, you create a strong connection between the two components, enhancing the stability of the pergola.

Once the rafter is in the desired position, a nail is skewed through the rafter and into the beam to hold it securely in place. This nail serves as a temporary fastener, keeping the rafter in position while additional securing methods are applied. Care is taken to ensure that the nail is driven straight and securely into the beam, providing reliable support for the rafter.

To further secure the rafter, galvanized framing anchors are attached on either side of the rafter. These framing anchors are designed to provide additional reinforcement and stability to the connection between the rafter and the beam. They help distribute the weight and load evenly across the joint, reducing the risk of structural failure or damage.

Once the framing anchors are in place, they are fixed to the beam using galvanized clouts or nails. Galvanized clouts are chosen for their corrosion resistance and durability, ensuring that the connection remains strong and reliable over time, even in harsh weather conditions.

Fitting the remaining rafters is a critical phase in completing the pergola's roof structure, ensuring uniform spacing and proper alignment for a sturdy and aesthetically pleasing finish. This process involves marking the positions of the rafters on the front and back beams at maximum 900mm centres, allowing for consistent support and coverage across the pergola's width.

To begin, precise measurements are taken to determine the length of each rafter before cutting and preparing them for installation. This step ensures that the rafters fit snugly within the designated space and align properly with the existing structure, minimizing gaps or unevenness in the roof assembly.

Figure 280: Fitting remaining rafters.

Once the rafters are cut to the appropriate length and prepared for installation, they are secured in place according to the predetermined spacing marked on the front and back beams. This step involves carefully positioning each rafter along the designated centres, ensuring uniformity and structural integrity throughout the pergola's roof framework.

Proper securing of the rafters involves employing similar techniques as those used for the initial rafter installation, such as clamping, nailing, and attaching framing anchors. Each rafter is securely fastened to the beams, ensuring a tight and stable connection that can withstand external forces and environmental conditions.

Throughout the process, attention to detail is crucial to ensure that all rafters are correctly positioned, aligned, and secured to maintain the structural integrity and visual appeal of the pergola. By following precise measurements and installation techniques, you can achieve a professional-quality finish that enhances the functionality and aesthetics of the outdoor space.

Securing the battens is the next step in the construction of a pergola. Battens play a dual role in providing structural support for the roof covering and enhancing the aesthetic appeal of the pergola. These horizontal members are typically installed perpendicular to the rafters and are spaced at regular intervals across the length of the pergola.

The spacing of the battens is essential for ensuring structural integrity and evenly distributed support for the roof covering. Typically, battens are spaced at 600mm intervals along the rafters, although this spacing may vary depending on the specific design requirements and load-bearing capacity of the materials used.

A 500mm overhang is often recommended for the battens to provide adequate coverage for the roof covering and to ensure proper protection from the elements. This overhang also contributes to the overall visual appeal of the pergola by creating a balanced and harmonious aesthetic.

Figure 281: Securing the batters.

Butt-joining the battens at the centre-line of the rafters helps to create a seamless and uniform appearance, enhancing the overall aesthetics of the pergola. This method of joining ensures that the battens align neatly with the rafters, creating clean lines and a cohesive look.

Positioning the first and last batten above the front and back beams is essential for providing stability and support at the extremities of the pergola. These battens serve as anchor points for securing the roof covering and help to distribute loads evenly across the structure.

Securing the battens with stainless-steel decking screws ensures durability and weather resistance, making them suitable for outdoor applications. Stainless steel is highly resistant to corrosion, rust, and decay, making it ideal for use in pergola construction where exposure to moisture and weathering is common.

To construct a pergola, the next step involves adding the bearers, which are horizontal supports that will bear the weight of the structure. Four bearers need to be cut to the appropriate length according to the dimensions of the pergola design. These bearers will typically run parallel to each other, connecting the vertical posts of the pergola.

Once the bearers are cut to size, the next step is to ensure they are level when installed. This is crucial for the stability and aesthetics of the pergola. Using a level, the position of the bearers is adjusted relative to the pergola posts to ensure they are perfectly horizontal.

After levelling the bearers, 10mm checkouts are cut into the pergola posts to accommodate the bearers. These checkouts are essentially notches or recesses made in the posts where the bearers will fit snugly. This step ensures a secure and stable connection between the bearers and the posts.

With the checkouts in place, the bearers are then secured to the pergola posts using two offset M10 x 130mm bolts for each bearer. These bolts are inserted through pre-drilled holes in the bearers and posts and tightened to firmly attach the bearers to the structure. The offset design of the bolts helps in providing additional stability by preventing any potential movement or shifting of the bearers.

Once the bearers are securely attached to the pergola posts, the next step is to position the first and last joists on the bearers. Joists are additional horizontal supports that run perpendicular to the bearers and provide further structural integrity to the pergola. These are typically placed at the beginning and end of the bearers' span.

The joists are secured to the bearers using 75mm x 14g batten screws. These screws are driven through the joists into the bearers, ensuring a strong and durable connection between the two components. By securing the joists to the bearers, the overall stability and load-bearing capacity of the pergola are enhanced, creating a solid foundation for any additional elements such as roofing or decorative features that may be added later.

Stumps are essentially vertical supports that provide the foundation for the structure, typically placed into the ground or anchored on a solid surface. The stumps need to be spaced at maximum 1300mm centres, ensuring adequate support across the entirety of the structure. This spacing ensures that the load is evenly distributed and prevents any weak points in the foundation.

Once the spacing is determined, a 140 x 45mm housing is cut on each stump. This housing serves as a notch or recess where the intermediate bearers will fit snugly. The size of the housing is designed to accommodate the dimensions of the bearers and ensure a secure fit, preventing any movement or instability in the structure.

With the housings cut into the stumps, the next step is to position the intermediate bearers onto the stumps. Intermediate bearers are horizontal supports that run perpendicular to the stumps and provide additional structural stability to the overall framework. These bearers are placed into the housings on the stumps, ensuring that they are aligned properly and securely fitted.

To secure the intermediate bearers to the stumps, M10 x 100mm bolts are used. These bolts are inserted through pre-drilled holes in both the bearers and the stumps and then tightened to firmly attach the bearers to the stumps. This step is crucial for ensuring that the bearers are securely fastened to the stumps and will not shift or become loose over time.

Finally, once the bearers are in place and secured to the stumps, the stumps are concreted into the ground. Concrete provides additional stability and strength to the stumps, anchoring them firmly in place. During this process, the tops of the stumps are sloped to facilitate drainage. This sloping ensures that any water that accumulates on the surface of the structure can drain away efficiently, preventing water damage and prolonging the lifespan of the stumps and the entire structure.

Figure 282: Positioning stumps and attaching bearers.

To advance the construction process, the next step involves fastening the joists, which are horizontal framing members that run parallel to each other and provide the framework for the structure's flooring or decking. Firstly, the joists are cut to the required length according to the dimensions of the structure. Once cut, the spacing of the joists is marked at 450mm centres perpendicular to the bearers. This spacing ensures structural integrity and evenly distributes the load across the bearers, preventing any sagging or instability in the flooring or decking.

Figure 283: Fastening the joists.

Stringlines are then set to guide the placement of the joists. These stringlines serve as visual references to ensure that the joists are installed in a straight line and at the correct spacing. Following the stringlines, the joists are positioned on the bearers accordingly.

To secure the joists to the bearers, skew-nailing is employed. Skew-nailing involves driving nails at an angle through the joists into the bearers, providing a strong and secure connection. Galvanized bullet-head nails, typically 75mm x 3.15mm in size, are used for this purpose. These nails are resistant to corrosion, ensuring longevity and durability of the connection even in outdoor settings where exposure to the elements is common.

Each joist is skew-nailed on either side into the bearers, ensuring a firm attachment that prevents any movement or shifting of the joists. This method of fastening distributes the load evenly and reinforces the structural integrity of the flooring or decking.

Once all the joists are securely fastened to the bearers, any overhang of the joists beyond the perimeter of the structure is trimmed to be even with the posts. This step ensures a neat and uniform appearance while also eliminating any potential tripping hazards.

In the process of decking installation, ensuring clean and secure ends is essential for both structural integrity and aesthetic appeal. To address this, the next step involves attaching end trimmers. Since the ends of the decking may not be perfectly square, it's necessary to provide a fixing point for the decking boards and fascia, which is the vertical finishing piece that covers the ends of the decking. This fixing point is established by cutting two end trimmers from 90 x 45mm lumber to fit between the joists.

The end trimmers are sized to fit snugly between the joists at each end of the decking area. This provides a solid base and support for both the decking boards and the fascia, ensuring they are securely fastened and properly aligned. Cutting the trimmers to fit precisely between the joists is crucial for maintaining structural stability and preventing any potential sagging or movement of the decking over time.

Once the end trimmers are cut to size, the next step is to secure them in place. This is done by drilling 2mm pilot holes through the end trimmers and into the joists. Pilot holes help prevent the wood from splitting when screws are inserted and ensure a cleaner installation overall. After drilling the pilot holes, the end trimmers are then fastened to the joists using 50mm x 8g decking screws.

These decking screws are specifically designed for outdoor use and are corrosion-resistant, making them ideal for securing the end trimmers in place. By driving the screws through the end trimmers and into the joists, a strong and durable connection is created, effectively anchoring the end trimmers and providing a reliable fixing point for the decking boards and fascia.

Laying the decking is a pivotal step in completing a deck installation, requiring attention to detail and precision to ensure a sturdy and visually appealing result. To begin, a starter board is secured in place at one end of the deck area. This starter board serves as the initial reference point and provides a solid foundation for laying the subsequent decking boards.

Following the placement of the starter board, the next six decking boards are laid at a time. This approach allows for efficient progress while maintaining consistency in the installation process. By laying multiple boards simultaneously, the installer can ensure proper alignment and spacing between the boards, contributing to a uniform and professional finish.

Before securing the decking boards, it's essential to mark the centre-line of the joists on each board. This step helps ensure accurate placement of fasteners and promotes even weight distribution across the joists, enhancing the structural integrity of the deck. Once the centre-lines are marked, two 2mm pilot holes are drilled through each board at the centre of the joists.

Following the drilling of pilot holes, countersinking is performed using a combination bit. Countersinking involves creating recessed holes for the fasteners, allowing them to sit flush with the surface of the decking boards. This not only enhances the aesthetic appeal of the deck but also helps prevent tripping hazards and ensures a smooth walking surface.

With the pilot holes drilled and countersunk, the decking boards are ready to be secured in place. The boards are spaced appropriately using 50 x 2.0mm nails, which are driven through the pilot holes and into the joists. Additionally, each board is secured with 50mm x 8g decking screws, providing additional reinforcement and stability.

The combination of nails and decking screws ensures a secure and durable attachment of the decking boards to the joists. The nails provide initial stability and hold the boards in place during installation, while the screws offer long-term strength and resistance to loosening over time. This dual fastening approach helps maintain the structural integrity of the deck, even under heavy foot traffic and varying weather conditions.

Fitting the fascia is a crucial step in completing the visual appeal and structural integrity of a deck or a similar structure. The fascia serves as the finishing touch, covering the ends of the decking boards and providing a polished appearance to the entire project. To begin, the fascia is measured and cut to the appropriate length, ensuring it aligns perfectly with the edges of the deck.

When cutting the fascia, angled cuts are made at any change of angle along the front of the deck and at the corners. These angled cuts ensure a seamless transition between sections of the fascia and create a clean, professional finish. Careful attention is paid to the accuracy of these cuts to ensure the fascia fits snugly and maintains a uniform appearance around the perimeter of the deck.

Once the fascia is cut to size, it is positioned along the edges of the deck and aligned with the top of the decking boards. Proper positioning is essential to achieving a visually pleasing result and ensuring that the fascia covers the ends of the decking boards completely. The fascia is then secured in place using fasteners, typically two 65mm x 8g stainless-steel screws per joist.

These stainless-steel screws are chosen for their corrosion resistance, making them ideal for outdoor applications where exposure to moisture is common. By using stainless-steel screws, the risk of rust and deterioration is minimized, ensuring the longevity and durability of the fascia installation.

In addition to securing the fascia to the joists, it is also attached to the end trimmers previously installed at the ends of the decking area. This provides additional support and stability to the fascia, ensuring it remains securely in place over time.

Figure 284: Completed pergola project.

Chapter Seventeen

Implementing a Landscape Lighting System

Implementing a landscape lighting system involves several key steps to ensure proper installation and effective illumination of outdoor spaces. Here's a comprehensive guide:

- **Assessment and Planning**:
  - Evaluate your landscape: Identify key features such as pathways, trees, architectural elements, and outdoor living spaces that you want to highlight.
  - Determine lighting goals: Decide on the purpose of your lighting system, whether it's for safety, security, aesthetics, or a combination of these factors.
  - Sketch a lighting plan: Map out the locations where you intend to install lights and the type of fixtures needed for each area.

- **Choose Lighting Fixtures**:
  - Select appropriate fixtures: Consider factors such as durability, weather resistance, energy efficiency, and design aesthetics when choosing fixtures.
  - Match fixtures to features: Choose fixtures that complement the size, style, and function of the landscape elements you want to illuminate.
  - Opt for LED lights: LED technology offers energy efficiency, long lifespan, and versatility in terms of colour temperature and brightness levels.

- **Design Lighting Layout**:

- Create zones: Divide your landscape into zones based on lighting requirements and the desired effect. Common zones include pathway lighting, accent lighting, and security lighting.

- Determine light placement: Position fixtures to minimize glare, evenly distribute light, and highlight focal points effectively.

- Plan wiring: Design a wiring layout that connects all fixtures to a power source while minimizing visible wiring and avoiding potential hazards.

- **Installation**:

  - Prepare the site: Clear vegetation, debris, and obstacles from the installation area. Dig trenches for burying cables and install junction boxes or transformer units.

  - Install fixtures: Secure lighting fixtures in designated locations using stakes, mounts, or buried bases. Ensure proper alignment and orientation for optimal illumination.

  - Connect wiring: Lay low-voltage wiring according to the planned layout, burying it at a sufficient depth to prevent damage. Connect fixtures to the main power source or transformer unit.

- **Testing and Adjustment**:

  - Test the system: Turn on the lights to verify functionality and check for any issues such as flickering, uneven lighting, or malfunctioning fixtures.

  - Adjust lighting angles: Fine-tune the positioning and direction of fixtures to achieve the desired illumination levels and visual effects.

  - Make adjustments as needed: Address any deficiencies or areas that require additional lighting or modifications to enhance overall performance.

- **Maintenance and Care**:

  - Regular inspection: Periodically inspect fixtures, wiring, and connections for signs of damage, corrosion, or wear. Replace any faulty components promptly.

  - Clean fixtures: Remove dirt, debris, and accumulated grime from light fixtures to maintain optimal brightness and prolong their lifespan.

  - Trim vegetation: Prune trees, shrubs, and plants to prevent overgrowth from obstructing light output and ensure clear visibility of illuminated areas.

When contemplating landscape lighting, the initial thoughts might revolve around practicality—illumination for pathways, driveways, or near entrances. However, the potential of landscape lighting stretches far beyond mere functionality. It possesses the ability to transform outdoor spaces into enchanting realms, adding depth, texture, and ambiance to the nocturnal landscape.

With strategic garden lighting design, outdoor areas can transcend the ordinary, becoming captivating extensions of your living space [99].

The addition of lighting to landscape design holds the power to infuse a sense of magic and allure. Light, whether natural or artificial, has an innate quality of enhancing the beauty and character of its surroundings. By carefully selecting and positioning light fixtures, you can accentuate key features of your garden or landscaping. A fountain may shimmer in the moonlight, while an outdoor sculpture becomes a focal point bathed in a soft glow. Moreover, lighting can serve practical purposes, illuminating pathways to ensure safety while creating a welcoming atmosphere for evening gatherings.

Understanding the fundamentals of landscape lighting is essential for crafting an effective lighting scheme. While the transition from daylight to darkness alters the perception of outdoor spaces, certain principles of lighting design remain constant. Similar to indoor lighting, outdoor lighting can be categorized into three layers: overall lighting, task lighting, and accent lighting. Overall lighting provides a base level of illumination, ensuring adequate visibility across the entire area. Task lighting serves specific functions, such as lighting pathways or outdoor work areas, and is typically brighter than ambient lighting. Accent lighting, perhaps the most creative aspect of landscape lighting, focuses on highlighting particular features or objects within the landscape, such as trees, architectural elements, or sculptures. Through a combination of these lighting layers, outdoor spaces can be transformed into captivating environments that are both functional and aesthetically pleasing.

Landscape lighting serves not only to illuminate outdoor spaces but also to enhance safety, security, and aesthetics. Understanding the different areas where landscape lighting can be applied is essential for creating a comprehensive lighting plan that meets both functional and decorative needs.

- **Close-By-House Lighting**: This area of landscape lighting focuses on illuminating the side and rear entries of the house, as well as walls with accessible windows. By providing light in these areas, homeowners can deter potential intruders and enhance overall security. Strategically placed lights near entry points make it more challenging for prowlers and thieves to approach undetected, contributing to a safer home environment.

- **Driveway Lighting**: Lighting the driveway not only improves safety by enhancing visibility but also adds a decorative element to the property. Illuminating the driveway creates delineation and guides vehicles safely to and from the property. Moreover, driveway lighting can contribute to the overall aesthetic appeal of the landscape, creating an inviting ambiance for residents and visitors alike.

- **Rear Yard Lighting**: Floodlighting from the house or trees in the rear yard helps deter intruders and vandals by providing ample illumination in key areas. Concealing the light source where possible and opting for attractive fixtures rather than industrial ones ensures that the lighting complements the landscape design. Additionally, incorporating automatic timers, photocells, or motion sensors enhances convenience and efficiency in controlling the lighting.

- **Front Entry Lighting**: Lighting the front entry of the house serves both functional and aesthetic purposes. A well-lit front entry provides a warm welcome to residents and guests after dark, improving safety and accessibility. Selecting a wall bracket that adequately illuminates front steps, house numbers, and the keyhole enhances visibility and adds to the curb appeal of the property.

- **Steps and Paths Lighting**: Often overlooked, lighting for steps and paths is crucial for preventing accidents in dark areas. Low path lights, post lanterns, and lights attached to the house can effectively illuminate walkways and stairs, ensuring safe passage for residents and visitors. Properly placed lighting fixtures along paths and stairs enhance visibility and create a visually appealing landscape.

- **Garage Lighting**: Adequate lighting over the garage enhances safety and security, particularly when other lights are not in use. Well-lit garages deter intruders and provide added visibility for residents returning home after dark. Installing bright lights above the garage door ensures sufficient illumination in this area, contributing to overall property security.

Figure 285: Outdoor Lighting. Media Director, CC BY-ND 2.0, via Flickr.

In the realm of landscape lighting design, the array of available light fixtures offers a myriad of options to illuminate outdoor spaces creatively and effectively. Familiarizing oneself with the diverse range of light fixtures facilitates the development of nuanced and well-crafted lighting designs tailored to specific landscapes. While not all fixtures may find a place in every lighting scheme, understanding their characteristics and applications empowers designers to make informed choices. Here are some prominent light fixtures commonly employed to illuminate outdoor spaces [99]:

Spotlights: Versatile and impactful, spotlights are adept at drawing attention to focal points within the landscape. Whether illuminating majestic trees, intricate sculptures, or architectural features, spotlights add depth and drama to outdoor environments by accentuating their most striking elements.

Step Lights: Practical and understated, step lights serve a crucial role in enhancing safety and visibility along steps, stairways, and pathways. Additionally, these fixtures can be utilized to illuminate outdoor patios and decks, providing both functional lighting and atmospheric charm.

Garden Lights: With their soft, diffused glow, garden lights impart a gentle luminosity to gardens, pathways, and outdoor spaces. These fixtures blend seamlessly into natural surroundings, casting a subtle radiance that accentuates the beauty of foliage and landscaping features.

String Lights: Infusing outdoor spaces with whimsy and charm, string lights offer a playful yet enchanting lighting solution. Available in an array of shapes, sizes, and colours, these versatile fixtures can be draped across trees, pergolas, and outdoor seating areas, creating a magical ambiance that beckons guests to linger beneath their luminous canopy.

Bollard Lights: Grounded and unobtrusive, bollard lights provide discreet illumination along pathways, steps, and garden borders. Installed flush with the ground, these fixtures offer a practical and aesthetically pleasing lighting solution that guides visitors through outdoor spaces with ease.

Flood Lights: Emitting powerful beams of light, flood lights are ideal for illuminating expansive outdoor areas with uniform brightness. Whether casting light upon driveways, outdoor decks, or recreational spaces, these robust fixtures ensure ample illumination and heightened security after dark.

Up/Downlights: Offering versatility and visual interest, up/downlights illuminate both upwards and downwards, casting a wash of light that accentuates vertical surfaces and architectural details. Whether used to highlight facades, walls, or landscaping features, these fixtures add depth and dimension to outdoor environments, creating captivating visual effects.

When it comes to illuminating outdoor spaces, there are primarily two main types of landscape lighting systems: low voltage (12V) and line voltage (120V). Each type has its own set of characteristics, advantages, and applications, catering to different needs and preferences.

Low voltage landscape lighting, operating at 12 volts, is a popular choice for residential use due to its safety and ease of installation. One of the key benefits of low voltage systems is the reduced risk of electrical shock, making them ideal for DIY enthusiasts or homeowners with basic electrical knowledge. Additionally, low voltage fixtures typically use cables that can be directly buried in shallow trenches, usually at a minimum depth of 6 inches. This allows for a cleaner and more discreet installation without the need for extensive excavation. Low voltage lighting systems offer versatility and flexibility, allowing homeowners to easily adjust and customize their outdoor lighting design to suit their preferences. These systems are commonly used to enhance the aesthetic appeal of residential landscapes, highlighting architectural features, pathways, gardens, and outdoor living spaces.

On the other hand, line voltage landscape lighting operates at 120/240 volts (depending on location) and requires the expertise of a licensed electrician for installation. This type of lighting is commonly found in standard household electrical outlets and is characterized by its higher voltage and power capabilities. While line voltage systems offer increased brightness and illumination compared to low voltage alternatives, they are typically reserved for larger properties or commercial applications. Due to the higher voltage, line voltage systems require more robust wiring and fixtures, making them less suitable for DIY installation. However, they are often preferred for commercial, security, or municipal lighting projects where maximum brightness and reliability are essential.

In summary, the main types of landscape lighting, low voltage (12V) and line voltage (120V/240V), each offer distinct advantages and applications. Low voltage systems are favoured for residential use due to their safety, ease of installation, and versatility, while line voltage systems are typically employed in larger properties or commercial settings where higher brightness and power capabilities are required. Ultimately, the choice between low voltage and line voltage landscape lighting depends on factors such as the size of the property, desired illumination levels, and budget considerations.

Understanding important landscape lighting terms is crucial for selecting the right fixtures, achieving desired lighting effects, and ensuring optimal performance of your outdoor lighting system. Here are some key terms commonly used in landscape lighting:

- **Beam Spread or Beam Angle**: This term refers to the spread of light emitted from a luminaire. It is essential for determining how wide the light will spread and the coverage area it will illuminate. The beam spread is often chosen based on the specific task or application, as well as the desired lighting effect. Some fixtures have fixed beam spreads based on their design, while others offer adjustable options to customize the light distribution.

- **Colour Temperature**: Measured in Kelvin (K), colour temperature refers to the perceived warmth or coolness of light emitted by a fixture. Warm temperatures (around 2700K) produce a soft, yellowish light similar to traditional incandescent bulbs, while cooler temperatures (above 5000K) emit a brighter, bluish-white light. The choice of colour temperature can significantly impact the mood and ambiance of outdoor spaces, with warmer tones often preferred for creating a cozy, inviting atmosphere.

- **Lumen Output**: This term quantifies the amount of light produced by a fixture and indicates its brightness. Higher lumen outputs result in brighter illumination, while lower outputs produce softer, more subtle lighting effects. Understanding the lumen output of fixtures helps determine the appropriate lighting levels for different outdoor areas and activities, ensuring adequate visibility and safety.

- **Wattage**: Wattage refers to the amount of electrical power consumed by a lighting fixture. It is crucial for calculating energy consumption and determining the compatibility of fixtures with transformers or power sources. By adding up the wattage of all fixtures in a lighting system, homeowners can select an appropriately sized transformer to ensure reliable operation and prevent overloading.

- **Efficacy**: Efficacy is a measure of a lighting fixture's efficiency in converting electrical power into visible light. Expressed in lumens per watt (lm/W), efficacy indicates the effectiveness of a fixture in producing brightness relative to its power consumption. LED bulbs, known for their high efficacy, can generate more lumens per watt compared to traditional incandescent or halogen bulbs, resulting in significant energy savings and reduced operating costs. Understanding efficacy helps homeowners make informed decisions when choosing energy-efficient lighting solutions for their landscapes.

Creating an outdoor lighting plan involves a systematic approach to ensure your yard is beautifully illuminated while meeting your practical needs and enhancing the overall ambiance. This includes:

- **Start With a Drawing of the Area:** Begin by sketching a layout of your yard to visualize the space and identify key features you want to highlight. This initial step allows you to strategically plan the placement of lighting fixtures, ensuring even distribution of light and avoiding areas left in darkness.

- **Consider Your Goals:** Define your objectives for the outdoor lighting plan, whether it's to accentuate architectural features, enhance safety, bolster security, or create inviting social spaces. Understanding your goals helps determine the types of lights needed and their optimal placement to achieve the desired effects.

- **Define Your Lighting Needs:** Once you've established your goals, assess your specific lighting requirements based on the intended use of different areas in your yard. Identify potential safety hazards, social gathering spots, and architectural highlights that necessitate illumination, considering factors such as brightness, angle, and intensity of light.

- **Position Your Lighting Fixtures:** With a clear understanding of your goals and lighting needs, strategically position your fixtures to maximize their visual impact and functionality. Pay attention to optimal spacing for pathway lighting and the angle and distance for accent lighting to ensure an aesthetically pleasing and practical installation.

- **Place Your Transformers:** Determine the placement of transformers, which convert household electricity into a lower voltage for outdoor lights. Consider factors such as the transformer's wattage capacity and the combined wattage of connected lights to ensure safe operation and compliance with local building codes.

- **Determine the Wire Runs:** Plan the layout of wire runs that connect transformers and lighting fixtures, aiming for a straightforward configuration to facilitate maintenance. Bury low-voltage wires underground at a sufficient depth to avoid accidental damage and ensure safety. Consider the length of wire runs and the gauge of the wire to prevent voltage drop and optimize electrical efficiency.

When it comes to outdoor lighting systems, the choice of wire gauge plays a crucial role in ensuring efficient electricity transmission and optimal performance. The gauge of a wire refers to its diameter or thickness, with lower gauge numbers indicating thicker wires. The selection of the appropriate wire gauge depends on various factors such as the length of wire runs, voltage drop considerations, and the overall design of the lighting system.

The principle behind wire gauge selection lies in the relationship between wire thickness and electrical resistance. Thicker wires have lower electrical resistance, allowing them to carry electricity more efficiently over longer distances without experiencing significant voltage drops. In outdoor lighting applications, where wire runs can span considerable distances from transformers to individual fixtures, minimizing voltage drop is essential for maintaining consistent illumination levels throughout the system.

Standard gauges for outdoor lighting typically range from 12 gauge to 16 gauge, with 12 gauge wire being favoured for longer runs due to its thicker diameter and lower electrical resistance. This makes 12 gauge wire well-suited for applications where the distance between the transformer and lighting fixtures is significant, helping to mitigate voltage drop issues and ensure reliable performance.

In contrast, higher gauge wires, such as 16 gauge, are suitable for shorter wire runs where voltage drop is less of a concern. These thinner wires are more flexible and easier to work with, making them suitable for smaller-scale lighting installations or areas with less distance between fixtures and the power source.

When selecting the appropriate wire gauge for an outdoor lighting system, factors such as the total wattage of connected fixtures, the length of wire runs, and local building codes should be taken into account. By choosing the right wire gauge for your specific application, you can optimize the efficiency and performance of your outdoor lighting system while ensuring compliance with safety standards and regulations.

The selection of wire gauge is a critical consideration in outdoor lighting design, with thicker wires such as 12 gauge being preferred for longer runs to minimize voltage drop and maintain consistent illumination levels. By understanding the relationship between wire thickness, electrical resistance, and system performance, you can make informed decisions when planning and installing outdoor lighting systems for your home or property.

Choosing the right transformer for landscape lighting is crucial to ensuring that the system operates efficiently and effectively. Transformers are designated with a maximum wattage capacity, indicating the amount of power they can safely provide to the connected lighting circuit. For instance, a 150-watt transformer can handle a load of up to 150 watts.

Determining the power needs for landscape lighting involves a straightforward process of addition and multiplication. Each pathway light typically has a maximum bulb wattage rating, which you add up for all the lights you plan to use. The total wattage calculated from these individual lights guides you in selecting an appropriately sized transformer. For example, if you have six pathway lights, each using 18 watts, the total wattage would be 108 watts. Multiplying this total by a factor of 1.5, as a rule of thumb for safety and flexibility, yields a recommended transformer size. In this example, 108 watts x 1.5 = 162 watts, indicating that a transformer with a capacity of 162 watts or more would be suitable for the lighting system.

In addition to meeting current power requirements, it's advisable to plan for future expansion when selecting a transformer. Allowing room for growth ensures that you can easily incorporate new landscape features or additional lights into the system without the need to modify existing setups or invest in a new transformer. By choosing a transformer with a capacity slightly higher than the calculated wattage needs, you create flexibility for future enhancements to your landscape lighting design. This foresight saves time, effort, and costs associated with retrofitting or upgrading the system down the line, enabling seamless integration of new lighting elements as your outdoor space evolves.

Selecting the best wiring method for landscape lighting is crucial to ensure optimal performance and efficiency of the lighting system. There are several wiring methods available, each with its own advantages and considerations. Understanding these methods can help in making an informed decision based on the specific requirements of the project.

The first wiring method to consider is the daisy chain method. In this approach, all fixtures are connected in a linear fashion, resembling a string of daisies. The first fixture connects directly to the transformer, and subsequent fixtures are connected in sequence. While this method is simple and straightforward, one challenge is the voltage drop that occurs along the length of the wire. As the current travels further from the transformer, the voltage decreases, which may result in varying levels of brightness among the fixtures. However, for LED lights with a wide acceptable voltage range, this voltage drop is generally acceptable. The daisy chain method is suitable when fixtures are not grouped closely together and can be easily connected in a chain.

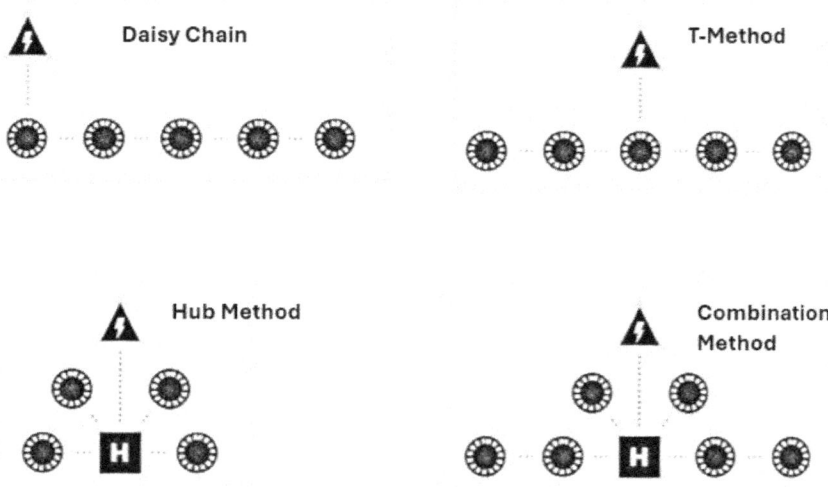

Figure 286: Wiring methods.

The T-method is similar to the daisy chain method, but with the transformer connecting to a fixture in the middle of the chain. This approach helps to save on the amount of wire used in the project while maintaining the overall voltage loss similar to the daisy chain method. The T-method is useful when a daisy chain has been established in the field, and connecting to the transformer from the middle of the chain saves on wire length.

Another wiring method is the hub method, where each wire run is connected to a central hub junction, and a single wire extends from the hub to each fixture. This method ensures equal voltage at all fixtures, making it suitable for incandescent lights. However, for LED lights with a wide acceptable voltage range, the hub method may use more wire than necessary. Nonetheless, it significantly reduces the number of splices in the field, saving time during installation. The hub method is ideal for fixtures grouped closely together in a small area, such as a garden bed.

Lastly, the combination method is a preferred choice for most LED lighting systems. This method combines elements of the other methods to conserve wire, reduce splices, and simplify installations. It offers flexibility in adapting to different project requirements and takes advantage of the wide acceptable voltage range and low wattage of LED lights. The combination method is recommended when you want to utilize various wiring techniques together, providing a balance between efficiency and ease of installation.

Optimal installation of landscape lighting requires careful planning and consideration of various factors to achieve the desired results. Here are some tips to ensure optimal installation and outcomes:

- Define your goals: Before starting the installation process, it's essential to define your lighting goals. Whether you aim to enhance safety, security, beauty, lifestyle, or energy efficiency, having clear objectives will guide your lighting design and layout decisions. For example, if safety is a priority, focus on illuminating pathways and steps to prevent trips and falls. If beauty is the goal, strategically highlight architectural features or landscaping elements to create visual interest.

- Lower loads per run: To minimize voltage drop and ensure consistent illumination, consider breaking up your lighting layout into multiple cable runs with lower loads per run. While voltage drop may not be a significant concern for LED systems, dividing the layout into smaller runs helps distribute power more evenly and reduces the risk of over-voltage or under-voltage issues.

- Break your layout into distance zones: Divide your lighting layout into distance zones based on the fixtures' proximity to the transformer. Aim to group fixtures with similar distances from the transformer on each run to maintain consistent voltage levels. By adjusting the voltage for each run to compensate for voltage drop, you can ensure uniform illumination throughout the landscape.

- Calculate cable gauge and length: Determine the appropriate cable gauge and length needed to reach the transformer based on the system's wattage and distance. Thicker wire gauges, such as 12 or 14 gauge, are suitable for shorter runs, while longer runs may require lower gauge wires to minimize voltage drop. Calculate the total wattage per zone and multiply it by the cable length in feet to determine the optimal cable gauge for each zone.

- Select the proper transformer: Choose a low voltage transformer with a wattage capacity greater than the total consumed wattage of your lighting system. Ensure that the selected transformer has at least a 20 percent buffer as maximum capacity, as recommended by most manufacturers. If the consumed wattage exceeds the transformer's capacity, opt for a larger transformer to accommodate the load.

Chapter Eighteen
Implementing a Landscape Maintenance Program

A Landscape Maintenance Program is a structured plan designed to ensure the ongoing care and upkeep of outdoor spaces such as gardens, lawns, parks, and other landscaped areas. This program outlines specific tasks, schedules, and resources needed to maintain the health, functionality, and aesthetics of the landscape over time.

There are several reasons why a Landscape Maintenance Program is needed:

- **Preservation of Investment**: Landscaping can represent a significant investment in both time and money. A Maintenance Program helps protect this investment by ensuring that the landscape remains healthy, attractive, and functional for years to come. Regular maintenance can prevent costly repairs or replacements down the line.

- **Enhanced Aesthetics**: A well-maintained landscape contributes to the overall beauty and curb appeal of a property. Regular care such as mowing, pruning, and weeding helps keep plants healthy, lawns lush, and hardscapes clean and tidy. This creates a positive impression for visitors, residents, or customers and can increase property value.

- **Health of Plants and Ecosystems**: Proper maintenance promotes the health and vitality of plants, trees, and other vegetation within the landscape. This includes tasks such as fertilization, irrigation, pest control, and disease management. By addressing issues promptly and proactively, a Maintenance Program can help prevent the spread of pests and diseases and preserve the balance of the ecosystem.

- **Safety and Accessibility**: Regular maintenance ensures that outdoor spaces are safe and accessible for users. This includes tasks such as clearing walkways, removing debris, and trimming overgrown vegetation. By addressing potential hazards, such as tripping hazards or obstructed views, a Maintenance Program helps reduce the risk of accidents and injuries.

- **Compliance and Regulations**: Many municipalities have regulations or guidelines regarding the maintenance of outdoor spaces, especially in commercial or public areas. A Maintenance Program helps ensure compliance with these regulations, avoiding fines or penalties. It may also include documentation and reporting requirements to demonstrate adherence to local standards.

- **Sustainability and Environmental Stewardship**: A well-designed Maintenance Program considers sustainable practices that minimize environmental impact. This may include strategies such as water conservation, use of native plants, and integrated pest management techniques. By promoting environmentally friendly practices, a Maintenance Program supports the long-term health of the landscape and surrounding ecosystems.

Landscape Maintenance Plan

A Landscape Maintenance Plan is a comprehensive strategy outlining the necessary activities to preserve the condition, safety, and functionality of all assets within a landscaped area. These assets are identified in the endorsed landscape plan and include elements such as vegetation, hardscapes, playgrounds, and other amenities. The primary goal of maintenance is to retain these assets in a safe and functional state, prolonging their amenity and functional life over time.

Councils and landscape managers recognize that different open space areas will have varying maintenance needs. Therefore, specific maintenance schedules are developed for each site to ensure a high level of upkeep. These schedules are tailored to meet the unique requirements of each landscape and may include tasks such as pruning, watering, fertilizing, and pest control. The landscape specifications provided represent the minimum standard for maintenance, with the goal of achieving a high-quality outcome for the community.

The Landscape Maintenance Plan establishes clear goals, objectives, and outcomes to guide the maintenance efforts. The overarching goal is to establish and maintain open space areas and streetscapes in accordance with the endorsed landscape plans. Specific objectives include maintaining open space areas, street tree plantings, playgrounds, and playing courts to a high standard. By achieving these objectives, the Landscape Maintenance Plan aims to deliver high-quality, well-managed, and aesthetically pleasing outdoor spaces for the community to enjoy.

The plan outlines several key outcomes that are expected to result from effective maintenance efforts. These include high-quality and well-managed open space areas, aesthetically pleasing streetscapes, safe and functional playground facilities, and high-quality playing courts. These outcomes contribute to the overall attractiveness, safety, and usability of the landscaped areas, enhancing the quality of life for residents and visitors alike.

In addition to outlining goals, objectives, and outcomes, the Landscape Maintenance Plan includes a detailed specification for maintenance activities. This specification provides guidance on tasks to be performed, materials to be used, and standards to be met. It serves as a reference document for contractors and maintenance personnel responsible for implementing the plan. The plan emphasizes the importance of conducting regular inventories to monitor the condition of the landscape and ensure compliance with maintenance standards. Enforcement of these standards is critical to ensuring the ongoing success of the maintenance program.

Overall, a well-developed Landscape Maintenance Plan is essential for preserving and enhancing the beauty, functionality, and value of landscaped areas. By establishing clear goals, objectives, and standards, and implementing effective maintenance practices, communities can enjoy attractive, safe, and sustainable outdoor spaces for years to come.

When reviewing such a plan, several critical components must be considered to ensure the plan is effective, clear, and feasible.

Representation of Proposed Trees

A standard practice in landscape management is to represent proposed trees at the quarters of their mature size on the plan. This means that on the initial drawings, trees are shown as smaller than they will eventually become. This practice helps visualize the initial planting stage and allows for a better understanding of the spatial arrangement and potential future growth. However, it is essential that the plant schedule within the plan clearly states the expected mature size, both in height and width, of each species. This information ensures that planners and stakeholders can anticipate the ultimate space each tree will occupy and plan accordingly for the landscape's long-term development and maintenance.

Botanical Naming

Botanical naming, or the use of scientific names for plants, is a crucial aspect of any landscape plan. These names are internationally recognized and provide a precise and unambiguous method of identifying plant species. Common names, while useful and often more accessible, can vary significantly across different regions and cultures, leading to potential confusion. Therefore, using botanical names ensures that everyone involved in the project, regardless of their background or location, can accurately identify the plants being discussed or used in the plan. This precision is particularly important for ensuring the correct species are sourced and planted, which is vital for the success of the landscape project.

Materials and Surface Treatments

A well-prepared landscape plan must detail the materials and surface treatments being used and their locations. This information is typically conveyed by labelling the specific areas or using symbolic hatches to represent different materials, accompanied by a legend or key for easy reference. This element of the plan is crucial for understanding the aesthetic and functional aspects of the landscape, including pathways, seating areas, plant beds, and other features. Clearly defined materials and treatments help ensure that the landscape is both visually appealing and practical for its intended use, and that maintenance teams understand the requirements for each type of surface.

Integration with the Surrounding Environment

Finally, a critical component of a landscape management and maintenance plan is the consideration of privacy, views, and outlook. These factors are essential for integrating the new development harmoniously within its surrounding environment. Thoughtful planning regarding these aspects can enhance the aesthetic value of the landscape, provide necessary privacy for residents or users, and ensure that views are maximized or preserved. This integration helps the landscape to blend seamlessly with its surroundings, adding to the overall appeal and usability of the space. It also helps in fostering a sense of place and continuity, making the landscape a natural extension of the existing environment rather than an intrusive addition.

In summary, a well-constructed Landscape Management and Maintenance Plan should accurately represent proposed tree sizes, use botanical names for plant identification, detail materials and surface treatments, and consider privacy, views, and outlook. These components together ensure a functional, aesthetically pleasing, and sustainable landscape that is easy to manage and maintain over time.

Maintenance Safety

Ride-On Lawn Mowers

Ride-on lawn mowers, also known as riding lawn mowers, are convenient tools for maintaining lawns, but they come with inherent risks that can lead to various injuries and accidents. These accidents can range from minor cuts and burns to severe amputations and even fatalities, especially from rollovers. In addition, prolonged exposure to the noise generated by these machines can contribute to hearing loss over time.

Figure 287: Ride-on mower operation. W.carter, CC0, via Wikimedia Commons.

Several common hazards are associated with the use of ride-on lawn mowers. These include injuries from the blades, such as cuts or amputations, as well as getting fingers, clothing, or jewellery caught in pinch or wrap points. Burns can occur from hot engine parts, and injuries like cuts, abrasions, and bruises can result from projectiles hitting the eyes, face, or exposed skin. Rollover accidents can cause major injuries or death, while refuelling can lead to fires and spills. Furthermore, prolonged exposure to the noise generated by these machines can result in hearing loss.

Examples of incidents involving ride-on lawn mowers highlight the potential dangers. For instance, a worker suffered a disfiguring facial injury when struck by a rock propelled by a mower's blade due to failure to clear debris. Another worker had two fingers amputated when attempting to clear debris without turning off the motor first.

To mitigate these risks, various safety tips should be followed. Before starting the mower, users should ensure they are familiar with its safe operation and not fatigued or under the influence of alcohol or drugs. Personal protective equipment (PPE) such as steel-toe footwear, hearing protection, safety eyewear, full-length clothing, and a hat should be worn. Additionally, thorough checks of the mower's condition and the worksite should be conducted.

During operation, precautions should be taken to avoid accidents, such as ensuring no one is in the work area, keeping hands and feet away from moving parts, and disengaging the mower blade when crossing pavement. Special attention should be paid when operating on slopes, and refuelling should be done outdoors on the ground with safety measures in place.

Loading and unloading ride-on lawn mowers also require attention to safety procedures, including working in pairs and securing the truck or trailer against movement.

Both employers and workers have responsibilities to ensure safety when using ride-on lawn mowers. Employers should maintain and repair the equipment, provide adequate training, demonstrate the safe use and storage of mowers, and ensure workers wear appropriate PPE. Workers, on the other hand, should follow safe work procedures, wear PPE, and report any defects or necessary repairs. With these measures in place, the risks associated with ride-on lawn mowers can be minimized, promoting a safer working environment.

Push Lawn Mowers

Push lawn mowers, whether standard or self-propelled, are indispensable tools for maintaining lawns, yet they come with inherent risks that can result in various injuries and accidents. These hazards range from minor cuts and burns to severe amputations and even instances of overexertion injuries, hearing loss, and eye injuries.

Several common hazards associated with push lawn mowers include injuries from the blades, such as cuts and amputations, as well as the potential for catching fingers, clothing, or jewellery in pinch or wrap points. Burns can occur from hot engine parts, and injuries like cuts, abrasions, and bruises can result from projectiles hitting the eyes, face, or exposed skin. Additionally, there's a risk of fire and spills during refuelling and prolonged exposure to the noise generated by these machines.

Examples of incidents involving push lawn mowers underscore the dangers they pose. For instance, a young worker was blinded in one eye after being struck by a rock thrown by a mower operated by a co-worker. In another case, a worker had three toes amputated when the push mower he was operating rolled back over his foot while mowing uphill on a slope, highlighting the importance of wearing approved footwear.

To mitigate these risks, various safety tips should be adhered to. Before starting the mower, users should ensure they are familiar with its safe operation, and conduct thorough checks to ensure the mower is in good working order and the worksite is clear of hazards. Personal protective equipment (PPE), including steel-toe footwear, hearing protection, safety eyewear, and appropriate clothing, should be worn.

During operation, precautions should be taken to avoid accidents, such as ensuring the transmission is out of gear and the mower blade clutch is disengaged before starting the engine. Mowing across the slope rather than up or down reduces the risk of accidents, and users should always push the mower forward rather than pulling it toward their feet. Additionally, hands and feet should be kept away from moving parts and hot components.

When finishing up or refuelling, proper shutdown procedures should be followed to ensure safety. Refuelling should only be done outdoors on the ground, with the engine turned off and allowed to cool. Employers have responsibilities to maintain and repair mowers, provide training on their safe use, and demonstrate how safety features work. Workers, in turn, are responsible for following safe work procedures, wearing appropriate PPE, and reporting any defects or necessary repairs. By adhering to these safety measures, the risks associated with push lawn mowers can be minimized, promoting a safer working environment.

Chippers and shredders

Chippers and shredders serve a crucial purpose in turning plant materials into chips or shreds, yet they pose significant risks to human safety. These machines, designed for efficient processing, can just as easily cause harm to human hands or arms, resulting in various injuries ranging from minor cuts and burns to severe amputations and even fatalities. Additionally, they present risks of overexertion injuries, hearing loss, and eye injuries, making it essential to adhere to strict safety protocols when operating them.

Figure 288: Chipper-shredder. Makinnen, CC BY-SA 4.0, via Wikimedia Commons.

Several common hazards are associated with chippers and shredders, including amputations or crush injuries from the blades or teeth, catching fingers, clothing, or jewellery in pinch or wrap points, burns from hot components, and injuries like cuts, abrasions, and bruises from projectiles striking the eyes, face, or exposed skin. Moreover, the process of refuelling these machines can also lead to fire and spills, adding to the list of potential dangers.

Real-life incidents serve as stark reminders of the risks posed by chippers and shredders. For instance, a worker lost his life when his clothing became entangled in the feeders of a chipper, pulling him into the machine. In another tragic incident, a young worker suffered compound fractures of the leg when his leg was pulled into the infeed rollers of a wood chipper.

To mitigate these risks, strict safety measures must be followed before, during, and after operating chippers and shredders. Before starting the machine, users should ensure they are familiar with its safe operation and conduct thorough checks to ensure it is in good working order. Additionally, the worksite should be barricaded, and bystanders should be kept away to prevent accidents.

During operation, personal protective equipment (PPE) is crucial, including steel-toe footwear, hearing protection, a hard hat, and a face shield. Full-length pants should be worn, and jewellery should be removed to prevent entanglement. Safe work procedures should be followed diligently, and before making any adjustments or clearing clogged materials, the machine should be shut down, allowed to stop completely, and locked out to prevent accidental start-up.

Figure 289: Feeding the chipper-shredder. Oregon Department of Transportation, CC BY 2.0, via Wikimedia Commons.

Both employers and workers have responsibilities to ensure safety when using chippers and shredders. Employers should maintain and repair the equipment, provide thorough training on its safe use, demonstrate how safety features work, and ensure adequate supervision. Workers, on the other hand, should follow safe work procedures, wear appropriate PPE, and report any defects or necessary repairs promptly. By adhering to these safety measures, the risks associated with chippers and shredders can be minimized, promoting a safer working environment for all.

Stump Grinders

Stump grinders are indispensable tools for cutting up tree stumps, yet they present significant risks to human safety if not used properly. These powerful machines, designed to tackle tough materials, can easily cause severe lacerations to feet, legs, hands, or arms. Moreover, the operation of stump grinders can send debris flying, posing risks of injury to the operator or bystanders. Additionally, they can lead to overexertion injuries, hearing loss, and eye injuries, highlighting the importance of adhering to strict safety protocols when using them.

Several common hazards are associated with stump grinders, including cuts from blades or teeth, catching fingers, clothing, or jewellery in pinch points or wrap points, burns from hot components, and injuries like cuts, abrasions, and bruises to the eyes, face, or exposed skin from flying debris. Additionally, the process of refuelling these machines can also lead to fire and spills, while holding grinders in awkward positions for long periods can result in sprains and strains.

Real-life incidents serve as poignant reminders of the dangers posed by stump grinders. For instance, a worker suffered a severe laceration to her arm when struck by a large wood chip thrown up by a stump grinder operated by a nearby co-worker.

In another incident, a worker suffered severe electrical burns when the grinder he was operating struck an underground cable, underscoring the potential dangers of not properly assessing the work area.

To mitigate these risks, stringent safety measures must be followed before, during, and after operating stump grinders. Before starting the machine, users should ensure they are familiar with its safe operation and conduct thorough checks to ensure it is in good working order. Personal protective equipment (PPE) is crucial, including steel-toe footwear, protective gloves, a hard hat, a face shield, and hearing protection. Additionally, full-length, close-fitting clothing should be worn, and jewellery should be removed to prevent entanglement.

Figure 290: A Husqvarna SG13 stump grinder in action. Charles & Hudson, CC BY-SA 2.0, via Wikimedia Commons.

During operation, users should select a firm and level work surface and stabilize the machine to prevent accidents. When working near roads, positioning the cutting head to direct wood chips away from passing traffic is essential. Operators should also be alert for coworkers or bystanders entering the work area and stop working if someone wanders into the vicinity. Proper shutdown and lockout procedures should be followed before removing clogged materials or making adjustments.

Both employers and workers have responsibilities to ensure safety when using stump grinders. Employers should maintain and repair the equipment, provide thorough training on its safe use, and demonstrate how safety features work. Workers, in turn, should follow safe work procedures, wear appropriate PPE, and report any defects or necessary repairs promptly. By adhering to these safety measures, the risks associated with stump grinders can be minimized, promoting a safer working environment for all.

Skid-steer Loaders

Skid-steer loaders, while highly versatile and efficient machines for various tasks, also pose significant risks to operator safety if not used correctly. These risks include the potential for serious injuries or even death if the machine overturns and crushes the operator, if a worker is struck by the bucket, or if a worker standing on the bucket is injured by a fall or run over by the machine. Identifying and mitigating these hazards is crucial to ensuring a safe working environment when operating skid-steer loaders.

Figure 291: Bobcat 873 - Arlington, Massachusetts, USA. Daderot, CC0, via Wikimedia Commons.

Common hazards associated with skid-steer loaders include crush injuries or death from rollovers, crush injuries from attachments, catching fingers, clothing, or jewellery in pinch points, and risks of fire and spills during refuelling. Real-life incidents serve as sobering examples of these hazards, such as a worker being killed after the loader tipped forward and fell into an excavation or another worker being pinned between the bucket and frame of a skid-steer loader when attempting to operate the controls from outside the cab.

To prevent such accidents, strict adherence to safety protocols is imperative. Before starting the machine, operators should ensure they are familiar with its safe use, conduct thorough checks to ensure it is in good operating order, and assess the worksite for potential hazards. Personal protective equipment (PPE) such as steel-toe footwear, hard hats, and hearing protection should be worn, and jewellery that might catch on controls should be removed.

During operation, operators should steer smoothly, making small adjustments and slow turns, and avoid standing, leaning, or reaching out of the cab when the engine is running. Loads should be carried as low as possible, and rough terrain should be avoided. Additionally, passengers should never be allowed on the loader, and anyone passing under a raised bucket or attachment should be prevented.

Finishing up procedures involve parking the machine safely, ensuring attachments are flat on the ground, and following manufacturer recommendations for transportation. Refuelling should be done with the engine off and after ensuring all ignition sources are extinguished.

Both employers and workers have responsibilities to ensure safety when using skid-steer loaders. Employers should maintain and repair the equipment, ensure workers are certified to operate it, and provide adequate training and supervision. Workers, on the other hand, should follow safe work procedures, wear appropriate PPE, and report any defects or necessary repairs promptly. By adhering to these safety measures, the risks associated with skid-steer loaders can be minimized, creating a safer working environment for all involved.

Trenching and Irrigation

Trenching and irrigation projects are crucial but inherently hazardous activities due to the various risks involved, including cave-ins, workers falling into trenches, and accidental severing of utility pipes. These hazards can lead to serious injuries or fatalities, making it essential to implement stringent safety measures and protocols to mitigate risks and ensure the well-being of workers.

Common hazards associated with trenching and irrigation include cave-ins, which can occur suddenly and without warning, posing grave risks to workers trapped within. Additionally, the possibility of workers falling into trenches or accidentally cutting existing utility lines further exacerbates the dangers inherent in these tasks. Hazardous atmospheres, such as natural gas or gases in the soil, also pose significant risks to worker safety and can result in suffocation deaths or other serious health issues.

Real-life incidents serve as poignant reminders of the potential dangers of trenching and irrigation projects. For instance, a landscape worker using an excavator inadvertently ruptured a natural gas line while digging a trench for an irrigation line, highlighting the importance of locating utility lines before commencing work. Another incident involved a worker being partially buried in an unsloped, unshored excavation in clay-type soil, emphasizing the critical need for proper trenching procedures and safety measures.

To prevent accidents and ensure worker safety, several safety tips should be followed. Before starting any trenching or irrigation project, it is essential to dial before you dig and obtain information on locating underground utilities. Planning for sloping or shoring the sides of trenches deeper than 1.2 meters is crucial, and consultation with a professional engineer may be necessary. Moreover, securing or removing any potential hazards near the trench and ensuring workers maintain a safe distance from trench edges are essential safety measures.

During work, wearing appropriate personal protective equipment (PPE), including steel-toe boots and work gloves, is paramount. Workers should also avoid entering trenches deeper than their knees, refrain from sitting or lying within trenches, and limit the amount of trenching done to what can be completed and backfilled in one day to prevent leaving trenches unattended.

After completing work, it is crucial to rope off or cover unattended trenches to prevent accidents. Employers have significant responsibilities in ensuring worker safety, including maintaining and repairing trenching equipment, providing adequate training on safe equipment use, and enforcing the use of appropriate PPE. Workers, in turn, must adhere to safe work procedures, wear the required PPE, and report any defects or necessary repairs promptly. By prioritizing safety and adhering to established protocols, the risks associated with trenching and irrigation projects can be minimized, fostering a safer working environment for all involved.

Chainsaws

Chainsaws are powerful tools widely used in forestry, landscaping, and construction, but they also pose significant risks to users if not handled with caution. These risks range from catastrophic injuries or death to overexertion injuries and hearing damage, especially when the equipment is used for prolonged periods. Identifying and understanding these hazards is crucial for implementing effective safety measures and preventing accidents.

Common hazards associated with chainsaw use include amputation or death from kickback, crush injuries from falling trees or branches, head injuries from falling branches, electrocution from branches hitting power lines, burns from hot points or refueling hazards, and risks of overexertion. Kickback, in particular, occurs when the saw tip touches another object or the blade is pinched, causing the saw to be thrown back towards the user, often at a speed faster than a person can react.

Real-life incident examples underscore the severity of these hazards. For instance, a landscape worker suffered continuous shocks when a tree he was cutting struck an energized power line, emphasizing the importance of proper planning and awareness of overhead hazards. Another worker suffered severe lacerations when a chainsaw kicked back and struck his leg, highlighting the need for understanding and preventing kickback incidents.

To mitigate these risks, strict adherence to safety protocols and guidelines is essential. Before starting work, operators should ensure they are familiar with the chainsaw and its safe use, conduct thorough checks to ensure the equipment is in good operating condition, and wear appropriate personal protective equipment (PPE), including chainsaw pants or chaps, steel-toe boots, hard hats, safety eyewear, hearing protection, and work gloves.

Figure 292: Chainsaw operations. Bad Kleinkirchheim, CC BY 2.0, via Wikimedia Commons.

Planning is also critical, including checking the work area for potential hazards such as power lines, buildings, vehicles, and loose branches overhead, and identifying escape routes and first aid options. Preventing kickback requires specific techniques, such as ensuring the blade's nose does not strike another object and using the top or bottom of the blade to start a cut.

During operation, caution and attentiveness are paramount. Operators should maintain a firm grip on the saw, watch for twigs that could snag the chain, and avoid straddling the limb being cut. Refuelling should be done outdoors on the ground, with all ignition sources extinguished and precautions taken to prevent spills or overfilling.

Both employers and workers share responsibilities in ensuring chainsaw safety. Employers should maintain and repair chainsaws, provide adequate training on safe equipment use, demonstrate safety features, and enforce the use of appropriate PPE. Workers, in turn, must follow safe work procedures, wear the required PPE, and promptly report any defects or necessary repairs. By prioritizing safety and adhering to established protocols, the risks associated with chainsaw use can be minimized, creating a safer working environment for all involved.

String Trimmers

String trimmers, commonly known as weed whips or whipper snippers, and edgers are essential tools for maintaining landscapes, but their hazards are often underestimated or overlooked. The whip itself can cause significant cuts, and the high-velocity projectiles produced by string trimmers can result in cuts, bruises, and eye injuries to operators, co-workers, or bystanders. Moreover, prolonged use of these tools can lead to overexertion injuries and hearing damage, making it crucial to understand and mitigate these risks.

Among the common hazards associated with string trimmers and edgers are cuts from the string, projectiles, prolonged noise exposure, muscle strain from holding the equipment in awkward positions, and the potential for fire and spills during refueling. These hazards underscore the need for comprehensive safety measures and proper training to prevent accidents and injuries.

Real-life incidents serve as sobering reminders of the potential dangers posed by these tools. For example, a worker suffered a severe laceration to his leg when struck by a piece of glass thrown by his string trimmer, highlighting the risk of projectiles. In another incident, a young worker sustained serious injuries when her hair got entangled in the fan of a string trimmer, emphasizing the importance of proper safety protocols and equipment usage.

To ensure safe operation, thorough safety measures should be implemented before starting work with string trimmers and edgers. Operators must familiarize themselves with the equipment and wear appropriate personal protective equipment (PPE), including steel-toe, non-slip footwear, hearing protection, safety eyewear or a face shield, and full-length, close-fitting clothing. Additionally, conducting site checks to remove debris, identify hazards, and ensure good ground conditions is essential for preventing accidents.

During operation, maintaining good footing and balance, keeping the cutter guard in place, and adjusting harnesses and hand grips to suit individual builds and work positions are crucial safety practices. String trimmers and edgers should only be used at ground level, and the motor should be stopped immediately if anyone enters the work area or before setting the equipment down.

Refuelling procedures should also be conducted with caution, ensuring that refuelling is done outdoors on the ground, and all ignition sources are extinguished to prevent fire hazards. Employers play a vital role in maintaining and repairing string trimmers and edgers, providing comprehensive training on safe equipment use, demonstrating safety features, and ensuring the use of appropriate PPE by workers.

In conclusion, string trimmers and edgers are valuable tools for landscape maintenance, but their hazards should not be underestimated. By implementing strict safety protocols, providing adequate training, and emphasizing the use of proper PPE, both employers and workers can mitigate risks and create a safer work environment. Regular inspection of equipment and prompt reporting of defects or necessary repairs are essential steps in ensuring continued safety and preventing accidents.

Leaf Blowers

Leaf blowers are versatile tools commonly used for clearing leaves and debris from outdoor spaces, but they come with inherent hazards that can lead to injuries if not properly managed. One of the primary dangers associated with leaf blowers is the potential for projectiles or "thrown objects," which can result in eye injuries, cuts, and bruises. Moreover, overexertion injuries and hearing damage are also common risks associated with prolonged use of these tools.

Common hazards related to leaf blowers include overuse injuries from carrying awkward weights, cuts and contusions from projectiles, burns during refuelling, and prolonged noise exposure. These hazards underscore the importance of implementing comprehensive safety measures and providing proper training to mitigate risks and prevent accidents.

Real-life incidents serve as poignant reminders of the potential dangers posed by leaf blowers. For instance, a worker suffered a scratched cornea when struck by debris thrown by her leaf blower, highlighting the risk of eye injuries when proper protective equipment is not worn. In another incident, a worker experienced permanent hearing loss after using a leaf blower without hearing protection for an extended period, emphasizing the importance of safeguarding against noise-induced hearing damage.

To ensure safe operation, it is imperative to adhere to strict safety protocols before, during, and after using leaf blowers. Operators should familiarize themselves with the equipment and wear appropriate personal protective equipment (PPE), including hearing protection and safety eyewear or a face shield. Additionally, full-length, close-fitting clothing should be worn to minimize exposure to hazards.

During operation, operators should exercise caution and vigilance, especially when working in areas with potential hazards such as blind corners or trees. Leaf blowers should only be operated at ground level, and discharge should be directed away from people, animals, and solid objects to prevent material from ricocheting and causing harm.

Refuelling procedures should be conducted with care to minimize the risk of burns and fire hazards. Employers play a crucial role in ensuring the safety of workers by maintaining and repairing leaf blowers, providing comprehensive training on safe equipment use, and demonstrating how safety features work. Adequate supervision should also be provided to ensure compliance with safety protocols.

Manual and Powered Hand Tools

Manual tools such as knives, loppers, pruning shears, and electric tools like hedge trimmers are indispensable in landscaping and gardening tasks, but they also pose significant hazards if not handled with care. These tools are often sources of cuts, lacerations, and overuse injuries due to their sharp blades and repetitive nature of use.

Common hazards associated with manual and electric tools include cuts from blades, catching fingers, clothing, or jewellery in pinch points, and overexertion injuries from repetitive use. These hazards underscore the importance of implementing robust safety measures and providing comprehensive training to minimize risks and ensure the well-being of workers.

Real-life incidents serve as poignant reminders of the potential dangers posed by these tools. For instance, a young worker severed his finger while attempting to prune a hedge with electric shears, emphasizing the risk of serious injuries when using powered hand tools without proper caution. In another incident, a landscape worker suffered an overuse injury to her wrist after several days of hand pruning, highlighting the importance of ergonomics and taking breaks to prevent repetitive strain injuries.

To mitigate risks associated with manual tools such as knives and pruners, it is essential to adhere to strict safety protocols and use appropriate personal protective equipment (PPE). Workers should choose tools that fit their hands and work style and ensure that they are sharp and in good condition before use. Proper techniques such as cutting away from oneself and using the right tool for the job should be followed to minimize the risk of accidents.

For powered hand tools like hedge trimmers, additional precautions should be taken, including using both hands to hold and guide the tool, using ground fault circuit interrupters (GFCIs) to prevent electrical hazards, and ensuring the appropriate rating of the cord for the distance. Keeping the cord behind and considering putting it through the belt can help prevent tripping hazards.

Employers play a crucial role in ensuring the safety of workers by maintaining and repairing hand tools, providing comprehensive training on safe tool use, and demonstrating how safety features work. Adequate supervision should also be provided to ensure compliance with safety protocols. Workers, on the other hand, must follow safe work procedures, wear appropriate PPE, and inspect hand tools regularly, reporting any defects or necessary repairs promptly.

While manual and electric tools are essential for landscaping and gardening tasks, they come with inherent risks that require careful management. By prioritizing safety, implementing robust safety measures, and providing proper training and supervision, both employers and workers can create a safer work environment and minimize the risk of injuries. Regular inspection of hand tools and adherence to safety protocols are essential steps in preventing accidents and ensuring the well-being of workers.

Pesticides

Exposure to pesticides poses significant risks to human health, ranging from skin irritation to severe long-term health problems and even death. While the handling of pesticides falls under specific legislation rather than the Workplace Hazardous Materials Information System (WHMIS), employers are still obligated to ensure the safety of their workers by providing access to safety data sheets (SDSs) or equivalent information for each pesticide used in the workplace.

Common hazards associated with pesticide exposure include absorption through the skin, eyes, lungs, or stomach, resulting in irritation or injury to various body parts or organs. Real-life incidents underscore the potential dangers of pesticide exposure. For instance, a worker suffered mild pesticide poisoning due to a faulty hose coupling while using a backpack herbicide applicator without wearing protective clothing. Another worker experienced severe headaches and blurred vision after applying an organophosphate pesticide without using appropriate personal protective equipment (PPE).

To mitigate the risks associated with pesticide exposure, stringent safety measures must be followed before, during, and after pesticide application. Before starting work, workers must undergo thorough training in the safe handling and use of specific pesticides. Reading and understanding the label and accompanying MSDS are essential steps to identify hazards and appropriate safety precautions. Proper storage of pesticides in a ventilated, locked area and checking weather conditions before application are crucial preventive measures.

During pesticide application, the use of recommended PPE such as respirators and protective clothing is imperative to minimize exposure. Additionally, workers must ensure that no other workers or bystanders are at risk of pesticide exposure and adhere strictly to safe work procedures.

After completing pesticide application, proper decontamination procedures must be followed. If gloves or protective clothing were used, they should be washed under water before removal, followed by immediate handwashing or showering to remove any residual pesticide. Pesticides should be returned to their designated storage facility with visible and legible labels.

Employers play a pivotal role in ensuring pesticide safety by maintaining and repairing application equipment, providing comprehensive training, reminding workers of required PPE, and offering adequate supervision. Workers, on the other hand, must hold a valid applicator certificate, follow safe work procedures, wear appropriate PPE, and promptly report any defects or necessary repairs in pesticide application equipment.

Hazardous Plants

Encountering hazardous plants is a common risk for landscape workers, as some plants possess toxic properties that can lead to severe health issues. These hazards extend beyond mere skin irritation or allergic reactions, as certain plants can cause life-threatening conditions. Common risks associated with hazardous plants include burns from sap, rash from contact, and allergic reactions or asthma triggered by specific plant species.

The sap of plants like giant hogweed, spurge laurel, or euphorbia contains toxic substances that can cause burns upon contact with the skin. In one incident, a worker experienced blistering and redness on his hands after getting sap on them while cutting down giant hogweed. Even after the blisters healed, dark blotches persisted on his hands for several months. Additionally, contact with plants such as poison ivy or cedar can result in rashes or allergic reactions, further highlighting the diverse range of hazards posed by different plant species.

Incidents involving hazardous plants can lead to severe injuries, as illustrated by an incident where a worker stepped on a prickly shrub, causing it to spring back and strike her in the face. This resulted in two prickles becoming embedded in her eye, necessitating a 40-minute surgery to remove them. Such examples underscore the importance of recognizing and effectively managing the risks associated with working around hazardous plants.

To mitigate the risks posed by hazardous plants, landscape workers must adhere to strict safety protocols. This includes ensuring they can recognize these plants, being vigilant about their surroundings, and promptly informing co-workers and supervisors if hazardous plants are encountered unexpectedly. Furthermore, wearing appropriate protective clothing and personal protective equipment (PPE) is essential to minimize the risk of exposure to toxic substances.

Workers with sensitivities to certain plants should take additional precautions, such as keeping asthma and allergy medications readily available and notifying colleagues about their sensitivities. By taking proactive measures and prioritizing safety, landscape workers can reduce the likelihood of adverse reactions when working around hazardous plants.

Employers have a crucial role in ensuring the safety of their workers by providing comprehensive training on recognizing hazardous plants and implementing preventive measures. Additionally, they should regularly remind workers about the importance of wearing appropriate PPE and provide adequate supervision to ensure compliance with safety protocols.

Poisonous plants encompass a wide variety of species found in different regions around the world. These plants contain toxic compounds that can cause harmful effects when ingested, touched, or inhaled. Here are some examples of poisonous plants categorized by their common names and toxic properties:

Poison Ivy (Toxicodendron radicans): Found in North America, poison ivy contains urushiol, a resin that causes allergic reactions upon contact with skin, resulting in itching, redness, blisters, and swelling.

Figure 293: Poison Ivy (Toxicodendron radicans). Chris Light, CC BY-SA 4.0, via Wikimedia Commons.

Poison Oak (Toxicodendron diversilobum): Similar to poison ivy, poison oak also contains urushiol and can cause skin irritation and allergic reactions in susceptible individuals.

Figure 294: Toxicodendron diversilobum (Poison Oak). Joe Decruyenaere, CC BY-SA 2.0, via Wikimedia Commons.

Poison Sumac (Toxicodendron vernix): This plant, found in wetlands and swamps in North America, contains urushiol like poison ivy and poison oak, leading to skin irritation upon contact.

Figure 295: Poison Sumac, Toxicodendron vernix. James H. Miller & Ted Bodner, Southern Weed Science Society, Bugwood.org, CC BY 3.0, via Wikimedia Commons.

Giant Hogweed (Heracleum mantegazzianum): Native to the Caucasus region, giant hogweed produces sap that contains phototoxic chemicals. Contact with the sap, followed by exposure to sunlight, can cause severe burns, blistering, and even permanent scarring.

Figure 296: Giant Hogweed (Heracleum mantegazzianum) Irvine, North Ayrshire. Rosser1954, CC BY-SA 4.0, via Wikimedia Commons.

Castor Bean Plant (Ricinus communis): Native to Africa and widely cultivated worldwide, the castor bean plant contains ricin, a highly toxic protein. Ingesting the seeds can lead to severe poisoning, causing symptoms such as abdominal pain, vomiting, diarrhoea, and potentially fatal organ damage.

Figure 297: Ricinus communis (ricino). Fernando Losada Rodríguez, CC BY-SA 4.0, via Wikimedia Commons.

Datura (Datura spp.): Also known as devil's trumpet or jimsonweed, various species of Datura contain tropane alkaloids, including scopolamine and atropine. Ingesting parts of the plant can cause hallucinations, delirium, seizures, and even death.

Figure 298: Triple-flowered Datura metel 'Fastuosa'. Flobbadob, CC BY-SA 4.0, via Wikimedia Commons.

Deadly Nightshade (Atropa belladonna): Found in Europe, Asia, and North Africa, deadly nightshade produces toxic berries containing tropane alkaloids. Ingesting the berries or other parts of the plant can lead to symptoms such as dilated pupils, rapid heartbeat, hallucinations, and respiratory failure.

Figure 299: Atropa belladonna. Agnieszka Kwiecień, Nova, CC BY-SA 4.0, via Wikimedia Commons.

Oleander (Nerium oleander): Native to the Mediterranean region and widely cultivated as an ornamental plant, oleander contains cardiac glycosides that are highly toxic when ingested. Symptoms of oleander poisoning include nausea, vomiting, abdominal pain, irregular heartbeat, and potentially fatal cardiac arrhythmias.

Figure 300: Nerium oleander. Challiyan at Malayalam Wikipedia, CC BY 3.0, via Wikimedia Commons.

Rosary Pea (Abrus precatorius): Also known as jequirity bean, rosary pea seeds contain abrin, a potent toxin similar to ricin. Ingesting even a small amount of the seeds can lead to severe poisoning, causing symptoms such as vomiting, diarrhea, organ failure, and death.

Figure 301: Abrus precatorius. Forest & Kim Starr, Public domain, via Wikimedia Commons.

Foxglove (Digitalis purpurea): Commonly grown for its ornamental flowers, foxglove contains cardiac glycosides that can cause severe poisoning when ingested. Symptoms include nausea, vomiting, dizziness, irregular heartbeat, and potentially fatal cardiac arrhythmias.

Figure 302: Common foxglove (Digitalis purpurea). Robert Flogaus-Faust, CC BY 4.0, via Wikimedia Commons.

These are just a few examples of poisonous plants found in various regions worldwide. It's essential to be aware of the toxic properties of these plants and take precautions to avoid accidental exposure, especially when working or recreating in areas where these plants grow naturally.

Maintenance Essentials

Maintaining your landscape is not just about preserving its appearance; it's about nurturing its growth and ensuring it reaches its full potential. While landscape design lays the foundation for a beautiful outdoor space, proper maintenance is essential to bring that vision to life [100]. The following is a guide to the key tasks involved in landscape maintenance and how to make the process enjoyable and rewarding.

Pruning Your Shrubs: Pruning shrubs is crucial for controlling their size and shape, maximizing flower or berry production, and promoting healthy growth. Timing is key, with early spring being ideal for most shrubs, although exceptions exist for varieties that form blossom buds in the previous season. Researching the specific needs of the shrubs in your yard is recommended to ensure optimal pruning practices.

Shaping Your Hedges: Regularly shaping hedges is a vital aspect of maintenance to prevent them from becoming unruly. Consistent shaping saves time in the long run and helps keep hedges in optimal condition. By maintaining a regular schedule, you can easily trim them back to their desired height and shape.

Weed Prevention and Control: Weeding is an unavoidable aspect of landscape maintenance, but proactive measures can help minimize its impact. Techniques such as mulching, ground cover planting, and maintaining a healthy lawn can reduce weed growth. However, regular weeding is necessary to prevent weeds from spreading and reproducing, ideally before they have a chance to seed.

Efficient Watering: Proper watering is essential for the health of your plants, but it's important to do so efficiently to conserve water and minimize costs. Understanding your plants' water needs, using timed irrigation systems, watering in the early morning to reduce evaporation, and mulching to retain moisture are all effective strategies. Grouping plants with similar water requirements can also optimize watering practices.

Maintaining Insect Balance: Insects play a crucial role in ecosystem health, but imbalances can lead to pest issues. Encouraging biodiversity, eliminating pesticides, and creating habitats for beneficial insects help maintain a healthy insect population. Companion planting and growing native plants can further support a balanced ecosystem.

Deadheading Flowers: Removing spent flowers, known as deadheading, encourages continued blooming and maintains the aesthetic appeal of your garden. This simple task can involve hand-plucking spent blooms or pruning back stems to promote new growth.

Soil Care: Healthy soil is essential for thriving plants, making soil care a fundamental aspect of landscape maintenance. Mulching provides nutrients and protects soil, while composting replenishes nutrients and supports soil microbiology.

Hardscape Maintenance: Patios, driveways, and stone pathways require regular maintenance to withstand harsh weather conditions. Cleaning, debris removal, stone replacement, and periodic resealing can extend their lifespan and keep them looking fresh.

Heritage Gardens

Maintaining gardens presents unique challenges compared to maintaining buildings, as they are subject to continual change with the seasons and the growth and decay of plant life. Despite these differences, the fundamental principles of maintenance remain consistent: understanding the significance of the garden and taking appropriate action to conserve that significance.

For heritage gardens, maintenance should prioritize horticultural best practices over contemporary trends, while also respecting the original intent of the garden and any significant modifications made over time. A well-designed maintenance program ensures the garden's viability well into the future, preserving its historical and cultural value.

Figure 303: Heritage Garden, Broughton House. Billy McCrorie, CC BY-SA 2.0, via Wikimedia Commons.

Understanding the context and significance of a garden is essential for effective maintenance. Gardens may hold importance both in their own right and as settings for heritage buildings. Given the constant evolution of landscape elements, maintaining a garden requires careful and ongoing assessment. Keeping detailed records of the garden's development and any new discoveries is crucial, as is preserving evidence that aids in understanding the site's history.

Major planting elements, such as mature trees and remnant bushland, require special attention in heritage gardens. Proper care of these features is essential for maintaining the garden's original character and significance. Strategies like tree replacement policies and bush conservation techniques help ensure the long-term survival of these vital components.

Preserving the original design and landscape features is paramount in garden maintenance. While some changes may be necessary over time, efforts should be made to retain or replicate the form, materials, and detailing of the original design. This includes maintaining pathways, lawn profiles, garden edgings, and other structural elements in line with historical authenticity.

Careful attention must also be paid to structures, furniture, and fittings within the garden. Whenever possible, original elements should be conserved or reconstructed, while modern interventions should be sympathetic to the garden's character. Lawn and tree care are essential aspects of garden maintenance, requiring regular mowing, pruning, watering, and pest control to ensure the health and vitality of the landscape.

The maintenance of heritage gardens requires a delicate balance between preservation and adaptation. By adhering to sound horticultural practices, respecting historical integrity, and implementing appropriate conservation measures, these cherished landscapes can continue to thrive and delight visitors for generations to come.

Chapter Nineteen
Sustainable Landscaping

Sustainable landscaping is an approach to landscaping that focuses on minimizing environmental impact, conserving natural resources, and promoting biodiversity while creating beautiful and functional outdoor spaces. It involves implementing eco-friendly practices that reduce water consumption, support native ecosystems, and minimize the use of harmful chemicals. Here are some key aspects of sustainable landscaping:

- **Water Conservation**: One of the primary goals of sustainable landscaping is to reduce water consumption. This can be achieved through various methods, such as installing efficient irrigation systems, using drought-tolerant plants, capturing and reusing rainwater, and implementing mulching techniques to retain soil moisture.

- **Native Plant Selection**: Choosing native plants for landscaping projects is essential for promoting biodiversity and supporting local ecosystems. Native plants are adapted to the local climate, soil conditions, and wildlife, making them more resilient and less dependent on water and chemical inputs. They also provide habitat and food sources for native wildlife, including birds, insects, and pollinators.

- **Composting**: Composting organic waste materials, such as grass clippings, leaves, and kitchen scraps, is a sustainable landscaping practice that helps enrich the soil, reduce landfill waste, and promote healthy plant growth. Compost can be used as a natural fertilizer and soil amendment, improving soil structure and fertility without the need for synthetic chemicals.

- **Minimizing Chemical Use**: Sustainable landscaping aims to minimize the use of synthetic pesticides, herbicides, and fertilizers, which can harm beneficial insects, pollute waterways, and disrupt ecosystems. Instead, natural and organic alternatives, such as compost tea, neem oil, and beneficial insects, can be used to manage pests and maintain healthy soil and plants.

- **Ecological Design**: Sustainable landscaping involves designing outdoor spaces in harmony with the surrounding environment, taking into account factors such as sun exposure, wind patterns, soil type, and existing vegetation. By designing landscapes that work with, rather than against, nature, sustainable landscapers can reduce the need for irrigation, maintenance, and chemical inputs.

- **Permeable Surfaces**: Using permeable paving materials, such as gravel, permeable concrete, or porous pavers, helps reduce stormwater runoff and allows rainwater to infiltrate into the soil, replenishing groundwater supplies and reducing the risk of flooding and erosion.

Water conservation is a fundamental aspect of sustainable landscaping, driven by the need to address water scarcity, mitigate the impacts of droughts, and minimize water wastage in outdoor environments. Sustainable landscaping practices aim to reduce water consumption through a combination of strategies designed to optimize water use efficiency while maintaining healthy and vibrant landscapes.

One key strategy for water conservation in sustainable landscaping is the installation of efficient irrigation systems. Traditional irrigation methods, such as overhead sprinklers, can result in significant water loss due to evaporation and runoff. In contrast, modern irrigation technologies, such as drip irrigation and soaker hoses, deliver water directly to the root zones of plants, minimizing waste and maximizing water uptake. These systems can be programmed with timers and moisture sensors to deliver water only when and where it is needed, further enhancing efficiency.

Another approach to water conservation in sustainable landscaping is the selection of drought-tolerant plants. Native and adapted plant species are naturally suited to local climate conditions and require less water to thrive once established. These plants have evolved to withstand periods of drought and are well-adapted to the natural rainfall patterns of their native regions. By incorporating drought-tolerant plants into landscaping designs, water usage can be significantly reduced without sacrificing aesthetic appeal.

Capturing and reusing rainwater is another effective water conservation strategy employed in sustainable landscaping. Rain barrels, cisterns, and other rainwater harvesting systems collect rainwater from rooftops and other surfaces, storing it for later use in irrigation and other outdoor applications. This reduces reliance on municipal water supplies and helps replenish groundwater reserves, particularly in regions prone to water scarcity and drought.

Mulching techniques are also commonly used in sustainable landscaping to retain soil moisture and reduce water evaporation from the soil surface. Organic mulches, such as wood chips, shredded bark, or compost, create a protective layer over the soil, helping to regulate soil temperature, suppress weeds, and improve soil structure. By conserving soil moisture and reducing the need for frequent watering, mulching contributes to water conservation efforts in landscaping.

Water conservation is a critical component of sustainable landscaping, requiring a multifaceted approach that integrates efficient irrigation practices, drought-tolerant plant selections, rainwater harvesting, and mulching techniques. By implementing these strategies, landscapers can minimize water consumption, enhance ecosystem resilience, and create beautiful and sustainable outdoor spaces for the benefit of both people and the environment.

Native plant selection is a cornerstone of sustainable landscaping practices, driven by the recognition of the numerous ecological benefits that native vegetation offers. Native plants are species that naturally occur and have evolved in a specific region over thousands of years. Choosing native plants for landscaping projects is essential for several reasons, primarily centred around promoting biodiversity, enhancing ecosystem resilience, and supporting local ecosystems.

One of the key advantages of using native plants in landscaping is their adaptation to local environmental conditions. Native plants have evolved to thrive in the climate, soil types, and precipitation patterns of their native regions. As a result, they require minimal water, fertilizer, and pesticide inputs once established, reducing the need for irrigation and chemical treatments. This inherent resilience makes native plants well-suited to sustainable landscaping practices, where the goal is to minimize environmental impact and conserve natural resources.

In addition to their environmental benefits, native plants provide critical habitat and food sources for local wildlife, including birds, insects, and pollinators. Many native plant species have co-evolved with native wildlife, forming complex ecological relationships that support biodiversity and ecosystem function. By incorporating native plants into landscaping designs, homeowners and landscapers can create wildlife-friendly habitats that attract a diverse array of beneficial organisms, contributing to the overall health and vitality of local ecosystems.

Moreover, native plants play a vital role in preserving and restoring ecosystem services, such as soil stabilization, water filtration, and carbon sequestration. Their deep root systems help prevent soil erosion, improve soil structure, and enhance water infiltration, reducing the risk of flooding and soil degradation. Native vegetation also contributes to carbon sequestration by capturing and storing atmospheric carbon dioxide in plant tissues and soil organic matter, mitigating the effects of climate change.

Furthermore, native plants offer aesthetic benefits, adding beauty, diversity, and seasonal interest to landscapes. With a wide variety of colours, shapes, and textures, native plants can be used to create visually appealing gardens, meadows, and naturalized areas that complement the surrounding environment and provide year-round enjoyment for homeowners and visitors alike.

Native plant selection is a fundamental aspect of sustainable landscaping, supporting biodiversity, ecosystem resilience, and environmental sustainability. By choosing native plants for landscaping projects, homeowners and landscapers can create beautiful, low-maintenance landscapes that benefit both people and the planet.

Composting is a key component of sustainable landscaping, offering numerous environmental and soil health benefits. It involves the decomposition of organic materials, such as kitchen scraps, yard waste, and plant residues, into nutrient-rich compost through the action of microorganisms, earthworms, and other decomposers. This natural process not only diverts organic waste from landfills, where it would otherwise contribute to methane emissions and soil degradation, but also produces a valuable soil amendment that can be used to enhance plant growth and soil fertility.

One of the primary benefits of composting is its ability to improve soil structure and fertility. Compost contains a rich array of essential nutrients, including nitrogen, phosphorus, potassium, and micronutrients, which are released slowly as organic matter decomposes. These nutrients are readily available to plants, promoting healthy root development, vigorous growth, and improved resistance to pests and diseases. Additionally, compost helps improve soil structure by increasing its water-holding capacity, drainage, and aeration, which are critical for plant growth and root health.

Moreover, composting plays a crucial role in carbon sequestration and climate change mitigation. By diverting organic waste from landfills, where it would decompose anaerobically and release methane, a potent greenhouse gas, composting helps reduce greenhouse gas emissions and mitigate climate change. Instead of contributing to atmospheric carbon dioxide levels, composting sequesters carbon in stable organic matter, which can remain in the soil for years to come, helping to offset carbon emissions and enhance soil carbon storage.

Composting also fosters a closed-loop nutrient cycle, where organic materials are recycled back into the soil, reducing the need for synthetic fertilizers and chemical inputs. By returning organic matter to the soil in the form of compost, gardeners and landscapers can replenish soil nutrients, improve soil structure, and enhance overall soil health, all while reducing reliance on environmentally harmful fertilizers and pesticides. This closed-loop approach to nutrient management helps conserve resources, protect water quality, and promote long-term sustainability in landscaping practices.

Furthermore, composting supports biodiversity and ecosystem health by providing habitat and food sources for beneficial soil organisms, such as earthworms, bacteria, and fungi. These organisms play essential roles in nutrient cycling, soil decomposition, and plant symbiosis, contributing to ecosystem resilience and stability. By creating a healthy, biologically active soil ecosystem through composting, landscapers can improve plant vigour, reduce soil erosion, and enhance overall landscape sustainability.

Minimizing chemical use is a core principle of sustainable landscaping, driven by a commitment to protect environmental and human health while promoting ecological resilience. Traditional chemical pesticides, herbicides, and fertilizers pose significant risks to ecosystems, wildlife, and water quality, making their reduction and substitution with natural alternatives imperative for sustainable landscaping practices. By adopting organic and eco-friendly approaches to pest and soil management, landscapers can minimize environmental impacts, safeguard biodiversity, and create healthier, more resilient landscapes.

Synthetic pesticides and herbicides are known to have adverse effects on beneficial insects, including pollinators such as bees and butterflies, as well as natural predators that help control pest populations. These chemicals can disrupt ecosystem balance, leading to declines in insect populations, loss of biodiversity, and ecological imbalances. Moreover, runoff from chemical applications can contaminate waterways, posing risks to aquatic organisms and human health. Sustainable landscaping seeks to mitigate these risks by reducing reliance on synthetic chemicals and embracing alternative pest management strategies that minimize harm to non-target organisms.

Instead of chemical pesticides, sustainable landscapers employ natural and organic pest control methods that target specific pests while minimizing impacts on beneficial insects and wildlife. These methods may include introducing beneficial insects, such as ladybugs and lacewings, that prey on pest insects, deploying physical barriers or traps to deter pests, and using plant-based repellents or insecticides derived from botanical extracts, such as neem oil or pyrethrin. These natural alternatives offer effective pest control without the environmental risks associated with synthetic chemicals, supporting ecological balance and biodiversity in the landscape.

Similarly, sustainable landscaping practices emphasize the use of organic fertilizers and soil amendments to promote soil health and plant vitality without relying on synthetic nutrients. Chemical fertilizers can contribute to nutrient runoff, soil degradation, and water pollution, posing risks to aquatic ecosystems and human health. In contrast, organic fertilizers, such as compost, compost tea, and organic mulches, provide a sustainable source of nutrients and organic matter that improve soil structure, fertility, and microbial activity. These natural soil amendments enhance plant growth, increase water retention, and support beneficial soil organisms, resulting in healthier, more resilient landscapes.

Furthermore, sustainable landscaping practices prioritize soil health and ecosystem resilience by fostering a balanced and diverse soil microbiome that promotes plant health and vitality. Chemical fertilizers and pesticides can disrupt soil biology, leading to imbalances in microbial populations and reduced soil fertility over time. By minimizing chemical inputs and promoting natural soil processes, such as composting, cover cropping, and crop rotation, sustainable landscapers create soil environments that are rich in beneficial microorganisms, organic matter, and nutrients, supporting robust plant growth and ecological sustainability.

Ecological design lies at the heart of sustainable landscaping, emphasizing the integration of natural systems and processes into the planning and development of outdoor spaces. This approach recognizes that landscapes are dynamic ecosystems shaped by interactions between living organisms, climate patterns, and geological features. Sustainable landscapers prioritize ecological design principles to create outdoor environments that not only enhance aesthetic appeal but also promote environmental sustainability, biodiversity, and ecosystem health.

A key aspect of ecological design is the consideration of site-specific factors, including sun exposure, wind patterns, soil characteristics, and existing vegetation, in the planning and layout of landscapes. By conducting thorough site assessments and analyses, landscapers can identify opportunities and constraints inherent to the site and develop design solutions that maximize ecological function and resilience. For example, selecting plant species adapted to the local climate and soil conditions reduces the need for supplemental irrigation and fertilizer inputs, while strategic placement of trees and shrubs can provide shade, wind protection, and habitat for wildlife.

Incorporating principles of ecological succession and natural plant communities into landscape design enhances ecological resilience and promotes biodiversity. Rather than relying on monoculture plantings or exotic species, sustainable landscapers emulate natural ecosystems by integrating diverse plant species that form complex ecological relationships and support native wildlife. This approach fosters habitat diversity, food sources, and nesting sites for birds, insects, and other wildlife, contributing to the overall ecological health and resilience of the landscape.

Furthermore, ecological design seeks to minimize environmental impacts and resource consumption through thoughtful site planning, water-efficient design strategies, and sustainable material choices. Sustainable landscapers prioritize the use of locally sourced materials, recycled products, and permeable paving surfaces to minimize carbon footprint and reduce runoff pollution. Incorporating green infrastructure elements, such as rain gardens, bioswales, and vegetated roofs, helps manage stormwater, improve water quality, and enhance biodiversity while reducing reliance on conventional drainage systems.

Another key aspect of ecological design is the promotion of regenerative practices that restore and enhance ecosystem function over time. Sustainable landscapers employ techniques such as soil building, habitat restoration, and carbon sequestration to regenerate degraded landscapes, improve soil health, and mitigate climate change impacts. By nurturing healthy soil ecosystems, conserving water resources, and supporting native biodiversity, ecological design contributes to the resilience and sustainability of landscapes in the face of environmental challenges and uncertainties.

Permeable surfaces play a crucial role in sustainable landscaping by mitigating the adverse impacts of stormwater runoff and promoting groundwater recharge. Unlike traditional impermeable surfaces like asphalt and concrete, which hinder water infiltration and contribute to stormwater pollution, permeable paving materials allow rainwater to pass through, effectively reducing runoff volumes and pollutant loads.

One of the primary benefits of permeable surfaces is their ability to facilitate natural water infiltration into the soil. When rainwater hits impermeable surfaces, such as roads, parking lots, and sidewalks, it is unable to penetrate the ground and instead flows over the surface, picking up pollutants and carrying them into nearby waterways. In contrast, permeable paving materials feature void spaces or pores that enable water to infiltrate into the underlying soil, where it can be naturally filtered and absorbed. This process helps replenish groundwater supplies, maintain soil moisture levels, and support healthy vegetation growth.

By promoting groundwater recharge and reducing stormwater runoff, permeable surfaces help mitigate the risk of flooding and erosion in urban and suburban environments. In areas with high impervious surface coverage, such as densely developed urban centres, stormwater runoff can overwhelm drainage systems, leading to localized flooding and streambank erosion. Permeable paving materials help alleviate these issues by allowing rainwater to infiltrate into the ground, thereby reducing the volume and velocity of runoff reaching downstream areas.

Additionally, permeable surfaces contribute to improved water quality by filtering pollutants and contaminants from stormwater runoff. As rainwater infiltrates through permeable paving materials and into the soil, it undergoes natural filtration processes that remove sediments, nutrients, heavy metals, and other pollutants. This filtration mechanism helps protect surface water bodies, such as rivers, lakes, and streams, from pollution and degradation, preserving aquatic habitats and ecosystem health.

Furthermore, permeable paving materials offer aesthetic and functional benefits in landscaping design. They provide a more natural and visually appealing alternative to traditional impervious surfaces, enhancing the aesthetic appeal of outdoor spaces while supporting sustainable water management practices. Permeable surfaces can be incorporated into various landscape features, including driveways, walkways, patios, and parking areas, allowing for creative and versatile design solutions that prioritize both aesthetics and environmental sustainability.

Integrating water conservation, native plant selection, composting, minimizing chemical use, ecological design, and permeable surfaces into landscape design requires a holistic approach that considers environmental factors, site characteristics, and sustainability goals. Each of these elements can be incorporated into landscape design by:

- **Water Conservation**: Efficient water management techniques can be integrated into landscape design by selecting drought-tolerant plants that require minimal irrigation. Designers can utilize native plants adapted to local climate conditions, which naturally conserve water and reduce the need for supplemental watering. Additionally, implementing efficient irrigation systems, such as drip irrigation or smart irrigation controllers, ensures that water is delivered directly to plant roots, minimizing waste and maximizing efficiency. Mulching techniques can further enhance water retention in the soil by reducing evaporation and regulating soil temperature.

- **Native Plant Selection**: Native plants play a vital role in sustainable landscape design by supporting local ecosystems and promoting biodiversity. Incorporating native plants into landscape designs not only conserves water but also reduces the need for chemical inputs and maintenance. Designers can create habitat corridors and wildlife-friendly gardens by selecting a diverse range of native species that attract birds, insects, and pollinators. By mimicking natural ecosystems, native plant landscapes contribute to ecological resilience and enhance overall ecosystem health.

- **Composting**: Integrating composting into landscape design involves establishing composting systems or bins to recycle organic waste materials generated on-site, such as grass clippings, leaves, and kitchen scraps. Compost produced from these materials can be used as a natural soil amendment and fertilizer to improve soil structure, fertility, and nutrient cycling. Landscape designers can incorporate composting areas or bins into garden layouts, encouraging homeowners to participate in organic waste recycling and soil enrichment practices.

- **Minimizing Chemical Use**: Sustainable landscape design prioritizes the reduction of synthetic pesticides, herbicides, and fertilizers, opting instead for natural and organic alternatives that promote soil and plant health. Designers can recommend integrated pest management (IPM) strategies, such as beneficial insect release, companion planting, and cultural practices, to manage pests and diseases without relying on chemical treatments. By minimizing chemical inputs, landscape designs support biodiversity, protect water quality, and create healthier environments for humans and wildlife alike.

- **Ecological Design**: Designing landscapes in harmony with the surrounding environment involves considering site-specific factors such as sun exposure, wind patterns, soil type, and existing vegetation. Sustainable landscape designers assess ecological conditions and site constraints to create resilient and low-maintenance landscapes that require minimal inputs and interventions. By integrating ecological principles into design decisions, such as selecting appropriate plant species, optimizing microclimates, and preserving natural habitats, designers can enhance ecosystem services, conserve resources, and promote environmental stewardship.

- **Permeable Surfaces**: Incorporating permeable paving materials into landscape design helps manage stormwater runoff, reduce flooding, and replenish groundwater supplies. Designers can specify permeable surfaces, such as gravel pathways, permeable concrete driveways, or porous paver patios, to allow rainwater to infiltrate into the soil and recharge aquifers. By integrating permeable surfaces into hardscape elements, designers mitigate the adverse impacts of urbanization on hydrological systems, improve water quality, and enhance overall landscape sustainability.

Xeriscaping

Xeriscape is a landscaping approach designed to conserve water and promote sustainability in regions prone to drought or limited water resources. The term "xeriscape" originates from the Greek word "xeros," meaning dry, and "scape," which refers to a view or scene. Developed in response to water scarcity and the need for more efficient landscaping practices, xeriscaping emphasizes water conservation, drought-tolerant plants, and low-maintenance design principles.

Figure 304: Xeriscape. Jeremy Levine, CC BY 2.0, via Flickr.

Key principles of xeriscape landscaping include:
- **Water Conservation**: Xeriscaping focuses on reducing water consumption by employing water-efficient techniques and technologies. This includes using native or drought-tolerant plants that require minimal irrigation once established, as well as implementing efficient irrigation systems such as drip irrigation or micro-sprinklers. By optimizing water use, xeriscape landscapes can thrive with significantly less water compared to traditional landscaping approaches.
- **Drought-Tolerant Plants**: Xeriscape gardens feature a diverse selection of plants that are adapted to arid or semi-arid climates and require little supplemental watering. These plants are chosen for their ability to survive and thrive in chal-

lenging environmental conditions, including periods of drought or water scarcity. Common examples of drought-tolerant plants used in xeriscape landscaping include succulents, cacti, ornamental grasses, and native wildflowers.

- **Soil Improvement**: Xeriscaping emphasizes the importance of soil health and quality in promoting plant growth and water retention. Soil amendments such as compost, organic matter, and mulch are incorporated into the soil to improve its structure, fertility, and water-holding capacity. By enhancing soil quality, xeriscape landscapes can better absorb and retain moisture, reducing the need for frequent irrigation and minimizing water runoff.

- **Efficient Irrigation**: Xeriscape designs prioritize efficient irrigation methods that deliver water directly to plant roots while minimizing waste and evaporation. Techniques such as drip irrigation, which delivers water slowly and precisely to individual plants, are preferred over traditional overhead sprinkler systems. Smart irrigation controllers and soil moisture sensors may also be utilized to optimize watering schedules and avoid overwatering.

- **Mulching**: Mulching is an essential component of xeriscape landscaping, serving multiple purposes such as conserving soil moisture, suppressing weed growth, and moderating soil temperature. Organic mulches such as wood chips, bark, or compost help retain soil moisture by reducing evaporation and preventing runoff. Additionally, mulch enhances soil fertility as it breaks down over time, providing nutrients to plants and improving overall soil health.

- **Low-Maintenance Design**: Xeriscape landscapes are designed to be low-maintenance and sustainable, requiring minimal inputs of water, fertilizer, and pesticides. By selecting low-maintenance plant species, minimizing turf areas, and incorporating hardscape features such as pathways, patios, and rock gardens, xeriscape designs reduce the need for ongoing maintenance tasks such as mowing, trimming, and watering. This not only saves time and resources but also promotes environmental stewardship and resilience in the face of changing climate conditions.

Figure 305: Xeriscape landscape. Downtowngal, CC BY-SA 3.0, via Wikimedia Commons.

Xeriscape landscaping offers a practical and environmentally conscious approach to landscaping, allowing homeowners and property managers to create beautiful, sustainable outdoor spaces that conserve water, support biodiversity, and withstand the challenges of water scarcity and climate change.

REFERENCES

1. Swift, J.K., J.L. Callahan, and B.M. Vollmer, *Preferences.* Journal of clinical psychology, 2011. **67**(2): p. 155-165.

2. Swift, J.K. and J.L. Callahan, *The impact of client treatment preferences on outcome: A meta-analysis.* Journal of clinical psychology, 2009. **65**(4): p. 368-381.

3. Swift, J.K., et al., *The impact of accommodating client preference in psychotherapy: A meta-analysis.* Journal of clinical psychology, 2018. **74**(11): p. 1924-1937.

4. Alizadeh, S., M. Sadeghi, and A. Abdullah, *The appraisal model of teenagers' landscape preference based on demographic and personality characteristics.* Journal of Design and Built Environment, 2018. **18**(1): p. 9-18.

5. Chen, Z. and B. Xu, *Enhancing urban landscape configurations by integrating 3D landscape pattern analysis with people's landscape preferences.* Environmental Earth Sciences, 2016. **75**: p. 1-13.

6. Huang, X. and J.T. Sherk, *Evaluation and comparison of sustainability performance and visual preference of residential landscape elements.* HortTechnology, 2014. **24**(3): p. 318-324.

7. Zagroba, M., A. Szczepańska, and A. Senetra, *Analysis and Evaluation of Historical Public Spaces in Small Towns in the Polish Region of Warmia.* Sustainability, 2020. **12**(20): p. 8356.

8. Chen, Z. and B. Xu, *Enhancing Urban Landscape Configurations by Integrating 3D Landscape Pattern Analysis With People's Landscape Preferences.* Environmental Earth Sciences, 2016. **75**(12).

9. Chen, Y., Z. Zhang, and X. Lai, *Based on Artificial Intelligence and Digital Space Technology, Research on Environmental Landscape Design of Jinghe Art and Culture Centre.* 2024.

10. Li, Z., et al., *Landscape Efficiency Assessment of Urban Subway Station Entrance Based on Structural Equation Model: Case Study of Main Urban Area of Nanjing.* Buildings, 2022. **12**(3): p. 294.

11. Qin, J. and L. Pan, *Exploration of Space Art in Modern Landscape Architecture Design.* SHS Web of Conferences, 2023. **162**: p. 01020.

12. Kempenaar, A., *Learning to Design With Stakeholders: Participatory, Collaborative, and Transdisciplinary Design in Postgraduate Landscape Architecture Education in Europe.* Land, 2021. **10**(3): p. 243.

13. Lu, Y., et al., *Simulation Design of Intelligent Garden Based on Climate Adaptability and Nonlinear Random Matrix.* Mathematical Problems in Engineering, 2022. **2022**: p. 1-10.

14. Zhang, X. and D. Zhang, *Teaching of Remote Sensing Technology for Landscape Architecture in the Context of Spatial Information Technology.* International Journal of Emerging Technologies in Learning (Ijet), 2021. **16**(15): p. 125.

15. Xi, J. and X. Wang, *Development of Landscape Architecture Design Students' Pro-Environmental Awareness by Project-Based Learning.* Sustainability, 2022. **14**(4): p. 2164.

16. Vartanian, O., et al., *Impact of Contour on Aesthetic Judgments and Approach-Avoidance Decisions in Architecture.* Proceedings of the National Academy of Sciences, 2013. **110**(supplement_2): p. 10446-10453.

17. Vessel, E.A., et al., *The Default-Mode Network Represents Aesthetic Appeal That Generalizes Across Visual Domains.* Proceedings of the National Academy of Sciences, 2019. **116**(38): p. 19155-19164.

18. Li, C., S. Shen, and L. Ding, *Evaluation of the Winter Landscape of the Plant Community of Urban Park Green Spaces Based on the Scenic Beauty Esitimation Method in Yangzhou, China.* Plos One, 2020. **15**(10): p. e0239849.

19. Ma, Z., et al., *Understanding the Drivers of Woody Plant Diversity in Urban Parks in a Snow Climate City of China.* Journal of Forestry Research, 2022. **34**(4): p. 1021-1032.

20. Ning, Q., et al., *Uniqueness Evaluation Indicators for Woody Plant Communities in Urban Park Green Spaces Based on Importance Value: A Case Study in Qingdao City.* 2023.

21. Gallo, T., et al., *Mammal Diversity and Metacommunity Dynamics in Urban Green Spaces: Implications for Urban Wildlife Conservation.* Ecological Applications, 2017. **27**(8): p. 2330-2341.

22. Lee, Y.-C. and K.-H. Kim, *Attitudes of Citizens Towards Urban Parks and Green Spaces for Urban Sustainability: The Case of Gyeongsan City, Republic of Korea.* Sustainability, 2015. **7**(7): p. 8240-8254.

23. He, S. and T. Dou, *Study on Diversity and Protection Countermeasures of Zhongshan Park in Wuhan City.* E3s Web of Conferences, 2021. **237**: p. 01003.

24. Tikul, N., *Amelioration of Building Microclimates Through Landscape Design Approaching Hot-Humid Climate.* 2019.

25. Dagher, S.F.A., M. Refaat, and R.E. Messeidy, *Landscape Design as a Tool to Meet Children's Needs in Residual Urban Spaces.* Civil Engineering and Architecture, 2022. **10**(5A): p. 271-287.

26. Gupta-Nigam, A., *Plastic Flowers: Overlooking Resource Scarcity in Postwar America.* Theory Culture & Society, 2020. **37**(6): p. 111-133.

27. Andrew, O.C., S.N. Azmy, and Z. Majid, *Evaluating Terrestrial Laser Scanning (Tls) for Hard and Soft Landscape Mapping.* The International Archives of the Photogrammetry Remote Sensing and Spatial Information Sciences, 2023. **XLVI-II-4/W6-2022**: p. 439-444.

28. Hami, A. and B. Abdi, *Students' Landscaping Preferences for Open Spaces for Their Campus Environment.* Indoor and Built Environment, 2019. **30**(1): p. 87-98.

29. Torun, A.Ö., et al., *A Quantitative Investigation of the Factors Affecting Patterns of Occupation in a Suburban Campus: The Case of Ozyegin University in Istanbul.* International Journal of Architectural Research Archnet-Ijar, 2018. **12**(2): p. 98.

30. McIntosh, J., B. Marques, and G. Jenkin, *The Role of Courtyards Within Acute Mental Health Wards: Designing With Recovery in Mind.* International Journal of Environmental Research and Public Health, 2022. **19**(18): p. 11414.

31. Tseung, V., et al., *Hospital Outdoor Spaces: User Experience and Implications for Design.* Herd Health Environments Research & Design Journal, 2021. **15**(1): p. 256-267.

32. Ellis, E.C., et al., *Used Planet: A Global History.* Proceedings of the National Academy of Sciences, 2013. **110**(20): p. 7978-7985.

33. Kabisch, N., et al., *Nature-Based Solutions to Climate Change Mitigation and Adaptation in Urban Areas: Perspectives on Indicators, Knowledge Gaps, Barriers, and Opportunities for Action.* Ecology and Society, 2016. **21**(2).

34. Zhang, X., H. Khachatryan, and M. Knuth, *Relating Knowledge and Perception of Sustainable Landscape Practices to the Adoption Intention of Environmentally Friendly Landscapes.* Sustainability, 2021. **13**(24): p. 14070.

35. Mbanaso, F.U., et al., *State of a Sustainable Drainage System at End-of-Life: Assessment of Potential Water Pollution by Leached Metals From Recycled Pervious Pavement Materials When Used as Secondary Aggregate.* Environmental Science and Pollution Research, 2019. **27**(5): p. 4630-4639.

36. Silva, M.D.F.M.e., et al., *Integration of Technologies and Alternative Sources of Water and Energy to Promote the Sustainability of Urban Landscapes.* Resources Conservation and Recycling, 2014. **91**: p. 71-81.

37. Sambucci, M. and M. Valente, *Ground Waste Tire Rubber as a Total Replacement of Natural Aggregates in Concrete Mixes: Application for Lightweight Paving Blocks.* Materials, 2021. **14**(24): p. 7493.

38. Ryu, B.-H., S. Lee, and I. Chang, *Pervious Pavement Blocks Made From Recycled Polyethylene Terephthalate (PET): Fabrication and Engineering Properties.* Sustainability, 2020. **12**(16): p. 6356.

39. Özkan, U.Y. and İ. Özdemir, *Assessment of Landscape Silhouette Value in Urban Forests Based on Structural Diversity Indices.* International Journal of Environmental Science and Technology, 2015. **12**(12): p. 3971-3980.

40. Junge, X., et al., *Aesthetic Quality of Agricultural Landscape Elements in Different Seasonal Stages in Switzerland.* Landscape and Urban Planning, 2015. **133**: p. 67-77.

41. Schirpke, U., et al., *Cultural Ecosystem Services of Mountain Regions: Modelling the Aesthetic Value.* Ecological Indicators, 2016. **69**: p. 78-90.

42. Ma, B., R.J. Hauer, and C. Xu, *Effects of Design Proportion and Distribution of Color in Urban and Suburban Green Space Planning to Visual Aesthetics Quality.* Forests, 2020. **11**(3): p. 278.

43. Chien, Y.-M.C., S. Carver, and A. Comber, *An Exploratory Analysis of Expert and Nonexpert-Based Land-Scape Aesthetics Evaluations: A Case Study From Wales.* Land, 2021. **10**(2): p. 192.

44. Gao, S. and L. Song-fu, *Exploration and Analysis of the Aesthetic Cognitive Schema of Contemporary Western Urban Landscapes.* International Journal of Environmental Research and Public Health, 2021. **18**(10): p. 5152.

45. University of Florida. *Types of Gardens.* 2024 [cited 2024 28/5/2024]; Available from: https://gardeningsolutions.ifas.ufl.edu/design/types-of-gardens/.

46. Kortright, R. and S. Wakefield, *Edible Backyards: A Qualitative Study of Household Food Growing and Its Contributions to Food Security.* Agriculture and Human Values, 2010. **28**(1): p. 39-53.

47. Junker, B. and M. Buchecker, *Aesthetic Preferences Versus Ecological Objectives in River Restorations.* Landscape and Urban Planning, 2008. **85**(3-4): p. 141-154.

48. Heezik, Y.v., et al., *Factors Affecting the Extent and Quality of Nature Engagement of Older Adults Living in a Range of Home Types.* Environment and Behavior, 2018. **52**(8): p. 799-829.

49. Klepacki, P. and M. Kujawska, *Urban Allotment Gardens in Poland: Implications for Botanical and Landscape Diversity.* Journal of Ethnobiology, 2018. **38**(1): p. 123.

50. Shin, D.W. and L. McCann, *Enhancing Adoption Studies: The Case of Residential Stormwater Management Practices in the Midwest.* Agricultural and Resource Economics Review, 2017. **47**(1): p. 32-65.

51. Li, X., et al., *Characterization of the Soil Bacterial Community From Selected Boxwood Gardens Across the United States.* Microorganisms, 2022. **10**(8): p. 1514.

52. Larson, K.L., et al., *Ecosystem Services in Managing Residential Landscapes: Priorities, Value Dimensions, and Cross-Regional Patterns.* Urban Ecosystems, 2015. **19**(1): p. 95-113.

53. Kelly, D., *Impact of Paved Front Gardens on Current and Future Urban Flooding.* Journal of Flood Risk Management, 2016. **11**(S1).

54. Walsh, C.M., et al., *The Impact of a Household Food Garden Intervention on Food Security in Lesotho.* International Journal of Environmental Research and Public Health, 2020. **17**(22): p. 8625.

55. Beaulieu, D., *Landscape Design for Beginners*, in *The Spruce*. 2023, Dotdash Meredith Publishing.

56. Hansen, G., *Basic Principles of Landscape Design.* 2024, IFAS Extension.

57. Wenjing, L. and N.M. Nasir, *Principles and Practice of Landscape Design: An Application of Traditional Chinese Landscape Painting.* 2023. **1**(1): p. 12-18.

58. Liu, Z., *The Application of Genetic Algorithm in the Optimal Design of Landscape Space Environment.* Mathematical Problems in Engineering, 2022. **2022**: p. 1-12.

59. Lu, M. and C. Wang, *An Explorative Study on Ecological Designs of the Landscape of River Channels.* 2013.

60. Lovell, S.T. and D.M. Johnston, *Creating Multifunctional Landscapes: How Can the Field of Ecology Inform the Design of the Landscape?* Frontiers in Ecology and the Environment, 2008. **7**(4): p. 212-220.

61. Yuslim, S. and E. Indrawati, *Performance Evaluation of City Parks Based on Sustainable Landscape Design in Jakarta.* Jurnal Pembangunan Wilayah Dan Kota, 2022. **18**(2): p. 150-163.

62. Liu, Z., *Research on the Application of Traditional Culture in Landscape Design.* Applied Mathematics and Nonlinear Sciences, 2023. **8**(1): p. 3203-3216.

63. Chen, X., *An Analysis of Climate Impact on Landscape Design.* Atmospheric and Climate Sciences, 2016. **06**(03): p. 475-481.

64. Li, T., Y. Jin, and Y. Huang, *Water Quality Improvement Performance of Two Urban Constructed Water Quality Treatment Wetland Engineering Landscaping in Hangzhou, China.* Water Science & Technology, 2022. **85**(5): p. 1454-1469.

65. McCollough, M., *Design Your Landscape.* 2023.

66. Denny, G. and G. Hansen, *Right Plant, Right Place: The Art and Science of Landscape Design—Plant Selection and Siting.* 2024, IFAS Extension.

67. Australian Plants Society (Victoria). *Garden Design.* 2024 [cited 2024 30/5/2024]; Available from: https://apsvic.org.au/garden-design/.

68. Zacharatos, A., J. Barling, and R.D. Iverson, *High-Performance Work Systems and Occupational Safety.* Journal of Applied Psychology, 2005. **90**(1): p. 77-93.

69. Dobson, A., *Section 37 of the Health and Safety at Work Act 1974 – Re-invigorated.* International Journal of Law and Management, 2013. **55**(2): p. 141-155.

70. Topping, M.D., *Occupational Exposure Limits for Chemicals.* Occupational and Environmental Medicine, 2001. **58**(2): p. 138-144.

71. Takhar, S.S. and K. Liyanage, *Framework for a Chemical Substance Reporting System.* Advances in Science Technology and Engineering Systems Journal, 2018. **3**(5): p. 459-477.

72. Kim, M.U., S. Shin, and S.H. Byeon, *Comparison of Chemical Risk Assessment Methods in South Korea and the United Kingdom.* Journal of Occupational Health, 2015. **57**(4): p. 339-345.

73. Andersen, J.H., et al., *Systematic Literature Review on the Effects of Occupational Safety and Health (OSH) Interventions At the Workplace.* Scandinavian Journal of Work Environment & Health, 2018. **45**(2): p. 103-113.

74. UniPrint,

Why It's Important to Report Hazards in the Workplace. 2023, UniPrint.

75. Chausson, A., et al., *Mapping the Effectiveness of Nature-based Solutions for Climate Change Adaptation.* Global Change Biology, 2020. **26**(11): p. 6134-6155.

76. Gangolells, M., et al., *Mitigating Construction Safety Risks Using Prevention Through Design.* Journal of Safety Research, 2010. **41**(2): p. 107-122.

77. Khan, F. and P. Amyotte, *How to Make Inherent Safety Practice a Reality.* The Canadian Journal of Chemical Engineering, 2003. **81**(1): p. 2-16.

78. Meyer, V., et al., *MY-CO SPACE: An Artistic-Scientific Vision on How to Build With Fungi.* Iop Conference Series Earth and Environmental Science, 2022. **1078**(1): p. 012070.

79. Rodriguez, J., *How to Choose the Right Mortar Mix Type: N, O, S, or M: Understanding the Differences for Your Next Project.* 2024, The Spruce.

80. Minas, A., *How to Lay Natural Stone Pavers? Informative and Technical.* 2017, Armstone.

81. Sole, C. *How to Pour Concrete Steps for a Porch or Outdoor Entryway.* 2022 [cited 2024 6/6/2024]; Available from: https://www.bhg.com/home-improvement/outdoor/walkways/how-to-pour-concrete-steps/.

82. Bezemer, T.M., J.A. Harvey, and J.T. Cronin, *Response of Native Insect Communities to Invasive Plants.* Annual Review of Entomology, 2014. **59**(1): p. 119-141.

83. Paré, P.W. and J.H. Tumlinson, *Plant Volatiles as a Defense Against Insect Herbivores.* Plant Physiology, 1999. **121**(2): p. 325-332.

84. Grandez-Rios, J.M., et al., *The Effect of Host-Plant Phylogenetic Isolation on Species Richness, Composition and Specialization of Insect Herbivores: A Comparison Between Native and Exotic Hosts.* Plos One, 2015. **10**(9): p. e0138031.

85. Hahn, P.G. and J.L. Maron, *Plant Water Stress and Previous Herbivore Damage Affect Insect Performance.* Ecological Entomology, 2017. **43**(1): p. 47-54.

86. Yguel, B., et al., *Insect Herbivores Should Follow Plants Escaping Their Relatives.* Oecologia, 2014. **176**(2): p. 521-532.

87. Silva, R., et al., *How Predictable Are the Behavioral Responses of Insects to Herbivore Induced Changes in Plants? Responses of Two Congeneric Thrips to Induced Cotton Plants.* Plos One, 2013. **8**(5): p. e63611.

88. Dostálek, T., M.B. Rokaya, and Z. Münzbergová, *Altitude, Habitat Type and Herbivore Damage Interact in Their Effects on Plant Population Dynamics.* Plos One, 2018. **13**(12): p. e0209149.

89. Emer, C., et al., *The Interplay Between Defaunation and Phylogenetic Diversity Affects Leaf Damage by Natural Enemies in Tropical Plants.* Journal of Ecology, 2024. **112**(5): p. 971-984.

90. VanGorder, A.E., et al., *Indirect Effects of Deer on Insect Pests and Soybean Plants.* Agricultural and Forest Entomology, 2020. **23**(1): p. 41-48.

91. Murphy, J.M., et al., *Forest Fire Severity Affects Host Plant Quality and Insect Herbivore Damage.* Frontiers in Ecology and Evolution, 2018. **6**.

92. Guo, H., et al., *Grazing Limits Natural Biological Controls of Woody Encroachment in Inner Mongolia Steppe.* Biology Open, 2017.

93. Rose, K., F. Russell, and S.M. Louda, *Integral Projection Model of Insect Herbivore Effects On<i>Cirsium Altissimum</I>populations Along Productivity Gradients.* Ecosphere, 2011. **2**(8): p. art97.

94. Joppa, L., et al., *Biodiversity Hotspots House Most Undiscovered Plant Species.* Proceedings of the National Academy of Sciences, 2011. **108**(32): p. 13171-13176.

95. ACS Garden, *Plant Establishment Methods*. 2024.
96. Dawsons Garden World, *Going Troppo!* 2005.
97. Department of Primary Industries. *Plant nutrients in the soil*. 1992 [cited 2024 9/6/2024]; Available from: https://www.dpi.nsw.gov.au/agriculture/soils/soil-testing-and-analysis/plant-nutrients.
98. Handyman, *How To Build The Ultimate Resort-Style Pergola*. 2024, Handyman.
99. Green Oasis Landscaping, *Elevate Your Outdoor Space with Landscape Lights*. 2022.
100. Salisbury Landscaping, *The Essentials of Maintaining Your Landscape*. 2022.

INDEX

A

adaptation, 18, 290, 397, 405–406, 408–410, 412–413, 419, 427, 612, 614, 623, 626

Arbor, 513–515, 538, 556

B

biology, 616, 626

Block, 154–155, 165, 181, 190, 202, 208, 239–242, 245, 248, 251, 254, 257, 262–263, 266, 349–351, 353–361, 624

Blowers, 597

Bog garden, 27–28

Botany, 402, 410, 422–423

Boulder, 550

breeding, 446

Brick, 88, 119, 205, 210, 214, 239–245, 248–251, 253, 257–259, 262–267, 269, 277, 325, 327, 339, 341, 346–347, 349

Bulbs, 465

Butterfly garden, 38, 40

C

cells, 518, 525, 531

Chainsaws, 99–100, 102–103, 106, 595–596

Coastal garden, 430

Composting, 235, 470, 499, 508, 610, 613, 615–616, 618

conservation, 402, 410, 414, 423, 425–426, 428, 430–431, 443–444, 446, 448, 453, 466, 468–469, 613–614, 618–619, 623–624

Construction, 9–13, 19–21, 70, 75, 103, 111–115, 120, 122–123, 125, 128–129, 132, 134, 138, 141–142, 145, 148, 153–162, 164–170, 172–173, 176, 181–187, 189–194, 196–197, 199–200, 202, 204–205, 208–210, 212–217, 233, 237, 239–245, 247–251, 253, 257, 259–261, 263–267, 270, 273–277, 280–281, 284, 286–288, 296–298, 303–304, 306, 314, 317,

321, 327–338, 341, 343, 346, 350–352, 354–357, 360–361, 411, 420, 434, 450, 456, 503, 513, 516–519, 523–524, 527–529, 531–541, 550–552, 556–558, 560–569, 571, 595, 623, 625–627

Cottage garden, 55

D

Deck, 88, 172, 244, 282, 326
development, 106, 118, 167–170, 197, 210, 261, 403, 408–409, 414, 450, 487, 529, 578, 615–616, 623
diseases, 94–95, 119–120, 130, 137, 366–367, 446, 456, 474, 501, 506, 509, 585, 615, 618
diversity, 242, 399, 406–407, 410, 426, 428–429, 441, 446, 448, 467, 615, 617, 623–624, 626
Drainage systems, 88, 169, 191, 218–220, 224–228, 237–238, 350, 500, 510, 617
Drought-tolerant plants, 613–614, 618–620

E

Ear protection, 98, 350
Earthworks, 172
ecology, 83, 623, 625–626
Edgers, 596–597
Edible garden, 33
evolution, 401, 410, 626
Excavation, 139, 151, 156, 158, 168, 180, 211–216, 262, 550–551

F

Fence, 73–74, 90, 96, 155, 158, 169–171, 180, 232, 258, 297, 439, 458, 512, 514, 538–539, 552, 556, 558–560
Fieldstone, 295
Fire pits, 325
Flagstone, 293, 326
flowers, 416, 418, 420–421, 610, 623
Formal garden, 67
Fountains, 90
fruits, 399, 403, 410, 414, 423–425, 427, 456, 518

G

Garden features, 57, 75, 511–512
Garden layout, 92, 239, 618
Garden lighting, 577
Garden planning, 92
Garden structures, 81, 540
Garden styles, 75, 78, 430–431
Garden walls, 73, 86

Gate, 540

Geogrids, 356

Gloves, 98, 102, 115, 118–120, 123, 140, 251, 259–260, 350, 480, 482

Grading, 13, 19–20, 112, 166–172, 181, 212–213, 218–219, 228, 339, 500, 526–529, 550, 560

Granite, 273–274, 276, 278–280

Grasses, 82, 398, 405, 409–410, 620

growth, 93–97, 172, 327, 399, 405, 407–409, 414, 416–419, 422–424, 428, 431, 433, 436, 439, 443, 453, 457–458, 460–461, 463, 467, 490–495, 498–501, 503, 506–509, 587, 610–611, 613, 615–617, 620

H

Hand tools, 127, 130, 266–267, 335, 597–598

Hard hats, 98, 140, 593, 595

Hardscaping, 173

Hedge trimmers, 99, 597–598

Horticulture, 111, 414, 422–423, 428, 430–431, 441, 459

Hose reels, 145, 147

I

Informal garden, 75

Irrigation systems, 112, 469, 504, 613–614, 618–619

J

Japanese garden, 59–60

L

Landscape architecture, 83, 622–623

Landscape design, 11–19, 21, 70–74, 78–83, 86, 89–93, 155, 167, 171, 173, 286, 295, 357, 360, 448, 476, 512, 577, 610, 617–618, 622–623, 625, 627

Landscaping, 9–12, 18, 71–72, 79, 83, 89, 92–93, 95, 98–103, 105–106, 110, 114, 122–123, 128–129, 155, 166–167, 169–170, 180–181, 192, 196–197, 200, 212, 216, 218–220, 230–231, 237, 239, 249–250, 253, 271–275, 277, 281–282, 287–290, 294–295, 301–304, 307–308, 310, 325–327, 349, 352, 354, 414, 416, 419, 423, 428, 430–431, 443, 458–460, 467–468, 474, 483, 501, 505, 511–512, 514, 550–553, 555–556, 579, 583, 585, 595, 597–598, 613–617, 619–621, 623, 625, 627

Lawn care, 490

Lawn mowers, 587–589

leaves, 257, 338, 368–369, 377, 399, 402–403, 405–409, 411, 413–414, 416, 418–423, 426–432, 436, 439–440, 442, 445, 447–448, 452, 454, 456–459, 461, 463, 465, 485, 518, 613, 618

Limestone, 281

Loppers, 411, 597

Low-voltage lighting, 84

M
Marble, 283
Mediterranean garden, 42
morphology, 405–406, 409, 426
Mulching, 473, 488, 610, 613–614, 620

N
Native plant garden, 448
Native plants, 448, 613–615, 618
nutrition, 460, 500, 506

O
Occupational safety, 99–102, 625
Outdoor kitchens, 172
Outdoor lighting, 577–582
Outdoor living spaces, 172, 239, 325, 575
Outdoor spaces, 10, 12–13, 15, 18, 20–21, 72, 92, 166–167, 171–173, 213, 218, 239–240, 272, 275, 289–291, 294, 313, 325–326, 349, 459, 476, 511, 514–515, 576–579, 585–586, 597, 613–614, 616, 621, 623

P
Pathways, 73, 75, 81, 83, 86, 89–90, 96, 155, 166, 168, 172–173, 180, 212, 239–241, 325, 327, 350, 493, 619–620
Patio, 78, 84, 88, 172, 180, 199, 218, 238–240, 244, 249, 286, 294–295, 302, 325–327, 339, 345, 350, 556–557, 579, 610, 618–620
Perennials, 426, 478
Pergola, 84, 88, 171, 511–516, 538–540, 550, 560–567, 569–570, 574, 627
Personal protective equipment (PPE), 131, 149
pest control, 120, 467, 585–586, 612, 616
pest management, 586, 616, 618
pests, 20, 94–95, 120, 137, 236, 366, 435, 446, 450, 456, 471, 474, 585, 613, 615–616, 618, 626
physiology, 626
Plant selection, 11, 13, 18, 70, 92–94, 289, 468, 474, 613–615, 618, 625
Planting, 9, 17, 19–20, 70–72, 74, 77, 84, 88, 90, 93, 98, 112, 155, 166, 171–173, 180, 239, 289–290, 294–295, 299, 326, 351, 354, 356, 416, 419, 422, 443, 453, 458, 466, 469–470, 472–478, 480–486, 488, 491, 510, 539, 550, 586–587, 610–611, 617–618
Ponds, 88, 90, 292, 475
Power tools, 112, 122, 130, 256, 338, 539–540
propagation, 331, 410, 423, 425–426, 428, 430, 443

Pruning shears, 480, 485, 597

R

Rain gardens, 617

Raised beds, 239–240

reproduction, 402, 409–410, 426, 428–429, 518

Respirators, 130, 598

Retaining walls, 84, 90, 168, 171, 173, 180, 212, 241, 244–246, 248–249, 269, 305, 325, 349–352, 355, 357–358, 360–361, 511, 538

Rock garden, 65, 76, 288–289, 293, 620

Rock retaining wall, 349

Rockery, 75, 300

Rooftop garden, 313

roots, 226, 233, 236, 300, 314, 408–409, 426, 442–443, 482–486, 490, 494, 499–500, 506–507, 509–510, 550, 552–553, 618, 620

S

Safety awareness, 123

Safety boots, 132, 259

Safety culture, 103

Safety glasses, 115, 118, 132, 140, 149, 260, 350

Safety guidelines, 251, 253, 259, 338

Safety hazards, 134, 143

Safety improvements, 116

Safety initiatives, 107–108

Safety inspections, 109, 115

Safety management, 105

Safety measures, 98, 119–120, 129, 131–132, 137, 150–151, 253, 259, 267, 337

Safety performance, 104, 115, 153

Safety practices, 107

Safety precautions, 120, 123, 142

Safety procedures, 149, 259

Safety protocols, 98–99, 105, 107, 112, 115, 120, 129, 133, 136, 139, 145, 251

Safety regulations, 109, 115–116, 154

Safety signage, 109, 112

Safety standards, 101–102, 105–106, 124, 134, 142, 152, 197, 214, 250

Safety training, 116

Sandstone, 273, 276–278, 292, 307

Seeding, 9, 300, 343, 437, 473

seeds, 403, 410, 413, 424–427, 433–434, 437, 441, 443, 449, 452–453, 461, 463–464, 473, 518, 603, 607

Sensory garden, 48, 50

Shade structures, 99

Shovels, 252, 262

Shrubs, 57, 65, 88, 91–92, 96, 172, 398, 406, 409, 411–412, 414–416, 418–419, 421–423, 426–428, 430, 476–478, 480, 486, 488, 610, 617

Site analysis, 12, 14, 88, 166

Site planning, 168, 617

Slate, 240, 284–285, 307, 342

Soil improvement, 469, 490, 506, 620

stems, 79, 111, 408–409, 418–419, 423, 427, 430, 436, 440, 442, 447, 449, 453, 465, 469, 485, 526–529, 550–552, 610

Streams, 75, 230, 232, 617

Sustainable landscaping, 613–617

T

taxonomy, 399, 401

Travertine, 282

Trees, 9, 57, 71, 73, 82, 85–86, 88–92, 95–96, 112, 155, 169, 172, 187, 237, 394, 397–398, 406–407, 409, 411–412, 414–416, 418–423, 426, 428, 430, 433–434, 439, 445–446, 450, 456, 458, 460, 465, 470, 476–478, 480, 483, 486, 488–489, 510, 518, 523, 527–529, 539, 550, 577, 585, 587, 595, 597, 611, 617

Trellises, 513, 538

Trimmers, 99, 102, 572–574, 596–598

Tropical garden, 475

Trowels, 251–252, 254, 335, 338, 340

Turf, 300, 323, 337, 490–491, 495, 501, 503–504, 552, 620

W

Walkways, 89, 127, 133, 141, 169, 244, 249, 350, 618, 626

Water features, 90, 155, 166, 240, 325, 512

Wheelbarrows, 99, 260, 328

Wildlife garden, 417

X

Xeriscaping, 619

www.ingramcontent.com/pod-product-compliance
Lightning Source LLC
Chambersburg PA
CBHW081151020426
42333CB00020B/2477